W9-DCA-990

Microsoft®

# PROGRAMMING MICROSOFT® ASP.NET

Microsoft® .net™

Dino Esposito

PUBLISHED BY
Microsoft Press
A Division of Microsoft Corporation
One Microsoft Way
Redmond, Washington 98052-6399



Library of Congress Cataloging-in-Publication Data
Esposito, Dino, 1965-
Programming Microsoft ASP.NET / Dino Esposito.
p. cm.
ISBN 0-7356-1903-4
1. Active server pages. 2. Web sites--Design. 3. Web site development. I. Internet programming. I. Title.

TK5105.8885.A26E88 2003
005.2'76--dc21 2003046492

Printed and bound in the United States of America.

1 2 3 4 5 6 7 8 9 QWT 8 7 6 5 4 3

Distributed in Canada by H.B. Fenn and Company Ltd.

A CIP catalogue record for this book is available from the British Library.

Microsoft Press books are available through booksellers and distributors worldwide. For further information about international editions, contact your local Microsoft Corporation office or contact Microsoft Press International directly at fax (425) 936-7329. Visit our Web site at www.microsoft.com/mspress. Send comments to *mspinput@microsoft.com*.



**Acquisitions Editor:** Anne Hamilton
**Project Editor:** Devon Musgrave
**Technical Editor:** Robert Lyon
**Copyeditor:** Roger LeBlanc
**Principal Desktop Publisher:** Kerri DeVault
**Interior Artist:** Andrea Houston
**Interior Graphic Designer:** James D. Kramer
**Cover Designer:** Methodologie, Inc.

Body Part No. X09-39053

*To Silvia, Francesco, and Michela*
*To my mom and dad*

*"I know nothing except the fact of my ignorance."*
*—Socrates*

# Contents at a Glance

## Part VI Advanced Topics

# Table of Contents

# Acknowledgments

My name is the only one to appear on the cover, but my two kids, Francesco and Michela, contributed a lot. Instead of watching movies or playing with cars and dolls, many nights they sat close to me (often too close, actually) with the precise intention of helping out. Francesco, five years old, asked for an Internet connection and a shortcut to the FBI's Web site on the desktop of my secondary laptop. The official explanation is that he has a particular interest in the fate of the FBI's ten most-wanted fugitives. A former hot fan of New York firefighters, Francesco is now considering joining the New York Police Department. (Thanks to Josh Trupin who quite timely got him a football with the NYPD logo just the day before Christmas.) Francesco has chosen to work with Word 2000 because he doesn't feel particularly comfortable with Office XP.

Michela, two years old, at first contented herself with a toy laptop that plays music as one clicks buttons—yep, much like real ones! Soon after, though, as expected, she applied for an upgrade, and my working laptop was the dangerously nearest one. Michela is a great fan of Winnie the Pooh and can be still well over 15 minutes watching a movie. She's learning about honey and bees and gets a little bit confused when she hears me speaking about API. In Italian, "bees" and the acronym "API" (application programming interface) are pronounced the same way. It's hard to explain context to a two-year-old child!

So, many nights, after dinner, we started working together, everyone on a separate machine. Sounds like the perfect family, in which all members unite efforts to reach a goal and each one gives his best contribution? Well, it normally lasts five, maybe ten, minutes. Then Francesco wants to try the newest—dad's—laptop, and Michela is fascinated by the colorful screen. After the third cry in the night, Silvia, mom and wife, gets involved and fixes things. The really great news is that a day has 24 hours. (But I wouldn't mind an upgrade to at least 32, like the bits of the operating system!)

Anne Hamilton, acquisitions editor, firmly believed in this project and quickly arranged it. I still remember her first suggested deadline, dreadfully close to the start date! Thanks, Anne, for your confidence in me.

Erik Olson from the ASP.NET team played an important role. I don't even recall how I got in contact with him, but I do remember that I said, "I'm looking for someone to pester with questions at all hours." And his quiet reply was "OK, what's your first one?" Thanks, Erik, you did a great job, in all ways.

Other people also did an excellent job with this book—Devon Musgrave, project editor, coordinated, and Roger LeBlanc, copyeditor, edited text, smoothing humps, and shedding light on twisted and intricate periods (:-)). Robert Lyon, technical editor, worked patiently and effectively on all chapters and the code of the book and provided invaluable help by catching errors and omissions. Laura Barsan, Susan Chory, Joseph Croney, Luca Passani, Chris Riccio, Andres Sanabria, David Sceppa, and Kenn Scribner all shared their hands-on experience and added many insights on various topics. Definitely, they added incalculable value to the book.

Next are the 24x7 people, available at all times, who in a way or the other, directly or indirectly, contributed tips, tricks, suggestions, advice, gotchas, or simply their own work that I used as a resource. They are, in no particular order, Jeff Prosise, Jason Clark, John Lam, Francesco Balena, Jeffrey Richter, Peter Debetta, Berni McCoy, John Robbins, Don Kiely, and Paul Wilson.

A special thanks goes to Jay Freeman, the author of Anakrino, a .NET decompiler that proved to be the perfect tool for me to discover the hidden wonders of ASP.NET and explore its largely untangled underwood.

My final thought is for Silvia, my wife. Without you, the world looks like sand. Maybe warm, maybe rich, maybe concrete, maybe beautiful and palpable, but with no substance to build anything on. You're my essence and my strength.

Thanks you to all.

—Dino

# Introduction

Some years ago, on a rainy Italian morning in November, I was sitting in front of a top manager of a top consulting firm for a job interview. To the developer/consultant/solution builder I was then, the Internet meant very little. I was still making a living with my Win32 and C++ skills. Yes, I had heard about something named HTTP that was widely used to browse Web pages, but I'd never considered writing such applications. At that time, I would have seriously hesitated before associating the words "Web" and "application"! To me, an application was too far serious a thing to reduce to a handful of script and markup code.

To somehow justify my salary request, I came up with a throwaway remark about the growing importance of the Internet to the industry. Much more serious than I was, the manager cast a glance at me and, nodding, pronounced the words that, well, changed my career and even my whole professional life. He said, "The Internet is a real breakthrough; it allows you to achieve outcomes impossible with traditional means." You can easily imagine the rest of the story. I was hired and soon began working on my first Web project. A few weeks later, my project manager came to see me looking rather worried. He asked, "How much C++ do you do?" "C++?" I replied, "I was born—instantiated, actually—in C++." What sort of a question was that? With the Internet, a new world of business opportunities opened up in the industry. Web specialists soon became a valuable resource, but only in a few cases could they solve tough system or network issues. In a certain way, while the Internet was getting more and more popular, its back-end programming model was still a distinct, stand-alone API bolted onto the operating system and following a different API and scheme.

Microsoft first attempted to solve this system issue with COM, and ASP was the perfect tool to use COM over the Web. But it's only with the Microsoft .NET Framework and Microsoft ASP.NET that the circle—which for me opened that rainy November morning—is finally closed. With ASP.NET, you have a rich Web development platform perfectly integrated with the operating system's programming framework. Like icing on the cake, this programming framework—the .NET Framework—is also language-neutral. I quit that consulting firm a few years ago, but I'm sure that with ASP.NET, my work there would have been easier and my productivity much higher.

So, you want to write Web applications by using Microsoft technologies. Welcome, you've come to just the right place! The ultimate goal of this book is to take you to a more advanced level of knowledge of ASP.NET so that you can shave precious hours off your development time. No matter what your starting point is, this book should make you a smarter programmer or simply—and who isn't interested in this?—a more productive developer. Plato used to say that nobody who continually makes progress, no matter how slowly, should be discouraged.

This book contains several layers—much like an onion—and several perspectives, too. You don't need to know ASP to use this book, but if you're a former ASP programmer you'll more fully catch the gist of the new Web platform. Also, you don't need knowledge of ASP.NET 1.0, but if you're an experienced developer you can enjoy the changes in the newest version more deeply, ASP.NET 1.1, and in Microsoft Internet Information Services 6.0 (IIS). Finally, if you're a skilled programmer, this book has several sections where the internals of ASP.NET components are thoroughly discussed, making the book an ideal complement to the public MSDN documentation.

## What Does This Book Cover?

This book is divided into six parts that outline a relatively common learning path. In Part I, "Building an ASP.NET Page," you'll build a page and understand the basics of the ASP.NET model and its controls. In Part II, "Adding Data in an ASP.NET Site," you'll add some data support and meet the ADO.NET object model. After that, in Part III, "ASP.NET Controls," we'll return to server controls—a central element in ASP.NET's architecture—to cover the richest controls, including mobile controls. At this point, you'll have learned enough to work on real-world projects and be reasonably productive. If you want to do more, you'll need to go a level or two deeper and understand other essential aspects of ASP.NET applications, which are covered in Part IV, "ASP.NET Application Essentials." These essentials include configuration, security, and state management, as well as file I/O and Web services—a system component and an application model that are often used within ASP.NET projects. Once you appreciate server controls, can you do without custom controls? Part V, "Custom ASP.NET Controls," is an entire section devoted to custom controls. And Part VI, "Advanced Topics," covers image processing, HTTP handlers and modules, and hosting ASP.NET outside IIS.

In this book, I'll answer, among others, the following common questions:

- How does ASP.NET compile a page?
- Where are dynamic assemblies created and stored?
- What is the HTTP pipeline?
- What is the exact sequence of events in the page life cycle?

- What's the difference between HTML and Web controls?
- Why is a single form always used?
- How can I more effectively work with a *DataSet* object?
- What's the best way to page through a data set?
- Can I achieve *that* effect with the *DataGrid* control? (Yes, you typically can.)
- Are the *DataList* and the *Repeater* controls more flexible than the *DataGrid* control?
- How can I leverage my ASP.NET skills to write applications for mobile devices?
- Web user controls? What are those?
- What's the difference between the various Session modes?
- How can I take advantage of the Cache object?
- Is the ViewState encrypted or encoded? Is it really safe to use?
- What's the most flexible way to authenticate users?
- What's the ASPNET user?
- Can I share session state between Web services and ASP.NET applications?
- How can I configure my custom controls to look great at design time?
- Can I generate images dynamically?
- How can I use HTTP handlers and HTTP modules?
- Is there a way to run ASP.NET without IIS?

Some of the most interesting examples you can find in this book are:

- A *LinkLabel* Web control that uses regular expressions to transforms Web site names and e-mail addresses into hyperlinks
- A *DataGrid* control whose pager bar is rendered as a tab strip
- A *Form* control that allows to set the action URL explicitly
- Data-bound tooltip and subtotals in the *DataGrid* control
- An HTML-based control to generate bar charts
- A demonstration of response output filters
- Multirow *DataGrid* controls

## System Requirements

This book is designed to be used with the following software:

- Microsoft Windows with IIS installed (one of the following)
    - Windows 2000
    - Windows XP Professional
    - Windows Server 2003
- Microsoft Visual Studio .NET 2003 (one of the following)
    - Visual C# .NET Standard 2003
    - Visual Basic .NET Standard 2003
    - Visual Studio .NET Professional 2003
    - Visual Studio .NET Enterprise Developer 2003
    - Visual Studio .NET Enterprise Architect 2003
- Microsoft SQL Server (one of the following)
    - SQL Server 2000
    - SQL Server 2000 Desktop Engine (available for download)

This book is written for the .NET Framework 1.1 and Visual Studio .NET 2003. Most of the code will work with version 1.0 of the .NET Framework, but all the code samples were tested using the .NET Framework 1.1 and Visual Studio .NET 2003. Some code samples require that you have Microsoft SQL Server 2000 or Microsoft SQL Server 2000 Desktop Engine (MSDE 2000) installed. The code samples that use SQL Server assume a blank *sa* password, although the use of a blank password is strongly discouraged in any serious development environment. If you don't use a blank *sa* password in your SQL Server installation, you'll need to add your own password to the connection strings. For example, if your password is "Hello", you should change the connection strings to the following:

```
string nwind = "SERVER=localhost;UID=sa;PWD=Hello;DATABASE=northwind;";
```

## Code Samples

The book doesn't have a companion CD, but all the code samples discussed in the book are available on the Web at the following address. Click the Companion Content link in the More Information box on the right side of the page.

- *http://www.microsoft.com/mspress/books/6667.asp*

The language used in the book is C#, but all the code samples are written in both C# and Visual Basic .NET.

## How to Touch Base

Please feel free to send any question about the book directly to the author. Dino Esposito can be reached via e-mail at one of the following addresses:

- dinoe@wintellect.com
- desposito@vb2themax.com

For additional information and resources, check out the following Web sites: Wintellect at *http://www.wintellect.com* and VB2-The-Max at *http://www.vb2themax.com*.

## Microsoft Press Support

Every effort has been made to ensure the accuracy of the book and the companion content. Microsoft Press provides corrections for books through the World Wide Web at:

*http://www.microsoft.com/mspress/support/*

If you have comments, questions, or ideas regarding the book or the companion content, or questions that are not answered by querying the Knowledge Base, send them to Microsoft Press via e-mail to

*mspinput@microsoft.com*

or via postal mail to

Microsoft Press
Attn: Programming Microsoft ASP.NET Editor
One Microsoft Way
Redmond, WA 98052-6399

Please note that product support is not offered through the above addresses.

# Part I

# Building an ASP.NET Page

1

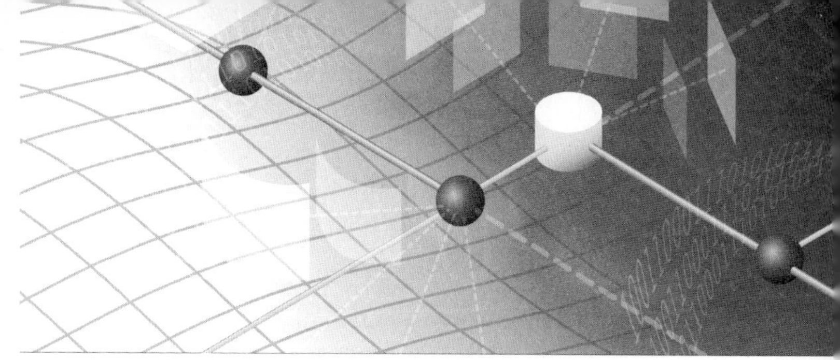

# The Web Forms Model

*A journey of a thousand miles begins with a single step.*

—*Lao Tzu*

ASP.NET is a Web development platform that provides the programming model and software infrastructure necessary to build enterprise-class applications. Although largely syntax compatible with its popular predecessor—Active Server Pages (ASP)—ASP.NET is a revolutionary new programming framework designed to enable the rapid development of Web applications and Web services. As part of the Microsoft .NET platform, ASP.NET provides a component-based, extensible, and easy-to-use way to build, deploy, and run Web applications that target any browser or mobile device.

ASP.NET is supported on a variety of platforms, including Microsoft Windows 2000 with at least Service Pack 2, Windows XP Professional, and Windows Server 2003. To develop ASP.NET server applications, Internet Information Services (IIS) version 5.0 or later is also required. Other software you need—for example, Microsoft Data Access Components (MDAC) 2.7—is automatically installed when you set up the .NET Framework.

ASP.NET fits perfectly in the trend that has shifted the focus of development from client/server applications to Web-based architectures and Internet-deployed applications. It is the next step in the evolution and a giant step indeed. ASP.NET is the summation of Web development technologies that rapidly followed one after another in the past five years—one building over another, and each filling the gaps of its predecessor. As a result, ASP.NET is currently the most technologically advanced, feature-rich, and powerful platform for building distributed applications transported by the HTTP protocol. The

*Web Forms model* is simply a blanket term that figuratively describes the abstraction model ASP.NET constructs atop the evergreen, old, and faithful HTTP protocol.

## What's ASP.NET, Anyway?

Prior to the advent of ASP.NET, three main technologies and platforms were available to develop Web applications: ASP, Java Server Pages (JSP), and the open source Web platform commonly referred to as LAMP (Linux plus Apache plus MySQL plus either Perl, Python, or PHP as the programming language).

> **Note** For completeness, we should also mention a couple of platform-specific, lower-level technologies that ASP and JSP rely on. ASP is actually an Internet Server Application Programming Interface (ISAPI) extension, whereas JSP is implemented as a special *servlet* application. ISAPI extensions on IIS-based platforms and servlets on Java-based systems let you create server-side, Web-deployed applications using a more classic approach. You write a module that builds and renders the page rather than declaratively design the page using a mix of markup text and embedded code.

Although each has language-specific and architecture-specific features, all these Web development platforms are designed to create interactive pages as part of a Web-based application. To some extent, all enable developers to separate programming logic from the page layout through the use of components that the page itself is responsible to call and render. Aside from this common ultimate goal, significant differences exist among those platforms, most of which relate to the programming model and languages they promote and support. For example, JSP exploits the Java framework of classes and, with JavaBeans, provides an effective extensibility model for reusing components. In addition, JSP supports tag customization and lets developers associate code with a custom tag definition. Finally, because it's a key element of the Java 2 Enterprise Edition (J2EE) platform, JSP relies on the Java language, a first-class language as opposed to the scripting languages used by both ASP and LAMP platforms. So how does ASP.NET fit in exactly?

Like ASP and other Web development environments, ASP.NET also works on top of the HTTP protocol and takes advantage of HTTP commands and policies to set up two-way, browser-to-server communication and cooperation.

What really differentiates ASP.NET from the plethora of other Web development technologies—and what makes it especially *revolutionary*—is the abstract programming model it propounds, the Web Forms model. In addition, the whole ASP.NET platform comes as a native part of the Microsoft .NET Framework. To be sure you grasp the importance of this last point, let me explain. ASP.NET applications are now compiled pieces of code, are made of reusable and extensible components, can be authored with first-class languages (including C#, Microsoft Visual Basic .NET, JScript .NET, and J#), and can access the entire hierarchy of classes in the .NET Framework.

In short, ASP.NET combines the best of all worlds. It is syntax compatible (and to a large extent, also language compatible) with ASP. It provides the same object-oriented features as JSP applications (tag customization, first-class compiled languages, components, extensibility, and reusability). And as icing on the cake, ASP.NET delivers a wealth of goodies, tools, and powerful system features that can be effectively grouped within the blanket expression *tools for abstracting the HTTP programming model*. Lots of programmer-friendly classes let you develop pages using typical desktop methods. The Web Forms model promotes an overall event-driven approach, but it's deployed over the Web and has the potential to target any vendor's platform through the support of XML.

> **Note** From a technical point of view, ASP.NET adopts the best of the ASP and JSP programming models. Conversely, it doesn't inherit much from the LAMP platform in terms of technical aspects. The appeal of LAMP is that it excels as a robust and extensible (because it is open-source) platform with flourishing and proactive grassroots community sites and Web boards.

Whichever way you look at ASP.NET, it's a quantum leap beyond any other Web programming style you might have experienced in the past. In this chapter, we'll present an overview of the ASP.NET platform, introducing topics such as the Web Forms model, structure of Web pages, and tasks involved when building ASP.NET applications. In Chapter 2, "Web Forms Internals," we'll drill down into the architectural elements of the Web Forms model, and then bear off into the sea of ASP.NET features and widgets. So get ready, and let the show begin.

## Programming in the Age of Web Forms

A key point I need to explain so that you understand the rationale behind the ASP.NET Web Forms model is that there is a need to provide a better strategy to deal with the strong and growing demand for cheap Web interaction. As a matter of fact, the HTTP protocol, especially its stateless nature, creates a sort of bottleneck for the development of Web applications. On the other hand, the inherent simplicity of HTTP is the key to its worldwide adoption and effectiveness—in short, we probably couldn't have the Internet as we know it without a protocol like HTTP. Yet, as demand increases, programmers have to devise better ways of setting up easy and effective communication from the client to the server and vice versa.

Various techniques have been experimented with over time to smooth the communication across different pages and across multiple invocations of the same page. Programmers are used to thinking in terms of a client-generated action that results in a server-side reaction. Such a basic and fundamental pattern simply cannot be accomplished, at least not literally, over the Web. A certain degree of abstraction and some system-provided services are needed to make smooth communication happen. Although they aren't perfect, JSP and ASP let programmers target any browser while coding against a relatively familiar and understandable model. ASP, much more than JSP, thinks declaratively and has quite a slim and scanty object model. Overall, programmers who become Web programmers are forced to adopt a different mindset and toss the familiar action/reaction paradigm out the door.

## Event-Driven Programming over HTTP

With Web Forms, the event-driven model of interaction finally comes to the Web. Implementing an event model over the Web requires any data related to the client-side user's activity to be forwarded to the server for corresponding and *stateful* processing. For the model to work, the server needs to process the output of client actions and trigger reactions while being aware of the overall state of the application. The state of the application contains two types of information: the state of the client and the state of the session. The state of the client is easily accessible through the syntax and the implementation of the *<form>* HTML element. But what about the overall state of the session?

As mentioned, HTTP is a stateless protocol, which means two successive requests across the same session are resolved by newly instantiated environments in which no session-specific information is maintained, except all the information the application itself might have stored in global objects. In ASP, reentrant forms are a common way to work around such a system limitation. A reentrant form is an HTML *<form>* element that posts to the same page that contains it. Reentrant forms alone do not fully solve the issue. However, by combining them with code blocks and hidden fields storing state information that is critical for the page, many developers elegantly overcame the obstacle.

What was once an ASP best-practice has been standardized and integrated in the ASP.NET runtime to become the key feature that endows ASP.NET applications with automatic state maintenance. The ASP.NET runtime carries the page state back and forth across page requests. When generating HTML code for a given page, ASP.NET encodes and stuffs the state of server-side objects into a few hidden, and transparently created, fields. When the page is requested, the same ASP.NET runtime engine checks for embedded state information—the hidden fields—and utilizes any decoded information to set up newly created instances of server-side objects. The net effect of such a mechanism is not unlike the Windows Forms model on the desktop and is summarized in Figure 1-1.

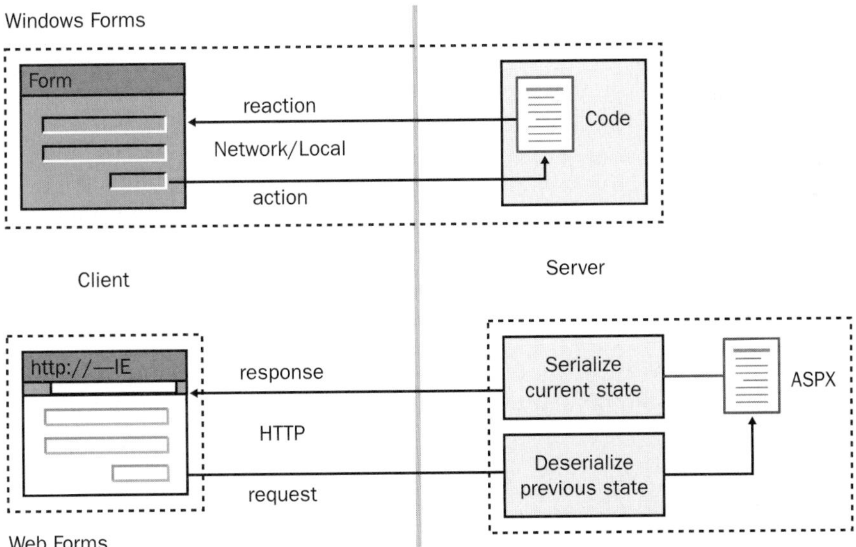


**Figure 1-1** Comparing the Windows Forms and Web Forms models in the .NET Framework.

The Windows Forms model stems from the typical event-driven desktop programming style. No matter what connectivity exists between the client and server components, the server always works in reaction to the client's input. The server is aware of the overall application state and operates in a two-tier, connected manner. The Web Forms model needs some machinery to support the same event-driven programming model. In Figure 1-1, the needed machinery is represented by the state deserialization that occurs when the page is requested and the state serialization performed when the HTML response is being generated.

In charge of this filtering work is the ASP.NET HTTP runtime—a piece of code that extends and specializes the overall capabilities of the hosting Web server. Reentrant forms and hidden fields are the low-level tools used to perform the trick. Such a model wouldn't be as effective without a back-end, rich object model spanning the whole content of the server page. Crucial to the building and effective working of the ASP.NET development platform is the component model. The ASP.NET component model is shared with all other types of .NET applications—Windows Forms, console applications, and Web services.

The ASP.NET object model is a branch of the .NET Framework and is designed to provide a server-side counterpart to virtually any HTML page elements, such as HTML tags like *<form>* and *<input>* and page-wide tags like *<link>* and *<script>*. In addition, the ASP.NET object model includes numerous components (called server controls or Web controls) that represent more complex elements of the user interface (UI). Some of these controls have no direct mapping with individual HTML elements but are implemented by combining multiple HTML tags. Typical examples of complex UI elements are the *Calendar* control and the *DataGrid* control. An ASP.NET page is made of any number of server controls mixed with verbatim text, markup, and images. Sensitive data excerpted from the state of each constituent control is silently stored in hidden fields, and it forms the context of that page request. The association between an instance of the page and its state is unambiguous, not programmatically modifiable, and controlled by the ASP.NET HTTP runtime. We'll delve more deeply into this topic in Chapter 2, which also covers the Web Forms architecture in detail.

In the meantime, let's briefly review the basics of the HTTP protocol—which remains at the foundation of Web interaction. After that, we'll move on to describe the structure of an ASP.NET page and how to write and deploy ASP.NET applications.

## The HTTP Protocol

This section provides a relatively quick overview of the way in which Web applications operate. If you already have a good knowledge of the Web underpinnings, feel free to jump ahead directly to the section "The Structure of ASP.NET Pages."

The acronym HTTP became so familiar to us developers that we sometimes don't remember exactly what it stands for. Actually, HTTP stands for Hypertext Transfer Protocol. HTTP is a text-based protocol and defines how Web browsers and Web servers communicate. The format of HTTP packets is fully described in RFC 2068 and is available for download from *http://www.w3.org/Protocols/rfc2068/rfc2068.txt*. HTTP packets travel over a TCP connection directed toward default port 80 at the target Internet Protocol (IP) address.

## The HTTP Request

When you point the browser to a URL, it utilizes the available Domain Name System (DNS) to translate the server name you provided with the URL into an IP address. Next, the browser opens a socket and connects to port 80 at that address. The packet with the download request for *http://expo-one/page.aspx* can take the following simple form:

```
GET /page.aspx HTTP/1.1
Host: expo-one
```

An HTTP request can contain, and usually does contain, a number of headers. These include: *User-Agent*, to identify the type of browser that originated the request; *Connection*, to close a connection or keep a connection alive; and *If-Modified-Since*, to provide client-side cache validation. An HTTP header is a line of text that provides additional information about the request. The first line of text represents the *start line* of the request. It must contain the name of the HTTP command to execute (GET, in this case), the URL of the resource, plus the version of the HTTP protocol you want to target.

## The HTTP Response

The server's response includes a *status line* made from the message's protocol version and an exit code (indicating success or error). The status line is followed by a bunch of headers—typically the page content type and length—and the body content. A blank line separates the body content from the rest of the message, as shown in the following response:

```
HTTP/1.1 200 OK
Server: Microsoft-IIS/5.0
Content-Type: text/html
Content-Length: 51

<html><body><h1>ASP.NET is cool!</h1></body></html>
```

The preceding code illustrates the simple HTML output returned by the Web server. Requests and responses are strings formatted according to the HTTP schema, and they travel over a TCP connection. The code *200* means that all went OK with the request. The specified Web server processes the request and returns some content expressed in the given Multipurpose Internet Mail Extensions (MIME) type (*text/html*) and of a certain length.

What happens next mostly depends on the MIME type and the browser's capabilities. As long as the MIME type is *text/html*, the browser displays the content as HTML. If the MIME type is, say, *text/xml* some browsers will render the content as plain text, while others (for example, Internet Explorer 6.0) will apply a built-in style sheet.

## Building a Server-Side Abstraction Layer

Every conversation between browsers and Web servers consists of the exchange of packets similar to the ones we have just examined. If the requested URL is an HTML page, the Web server typically reads the contents of the .html file and flushes it into the body of the response packet. If the URL is an ASP.NET page, a special IIS module gets involved. The module is an IIS plug-in known as an ISAPI extension. An ISAPI extension is a dynamic-link library (DLL) registered on a per-file extension basis. An ISAPI extension registered to handle .aspx files will get involved whenever a request comes in for this type of resource.

The ISAPI extension analyzes the request and uses any contained information to configure the server-side environment that will actually process the source of the page.

> **Note** As we'll see in more detail in Chapter 2, the ISAPI extension that processes .aspx pages first deserializes the session state carried back and forth through hidden fields—the call context. The information is used to configure newly instantiated controls that create the page output. The persisted call context is then merged with any fresh information that comes from client-side controls such as text boxes and check boxes. When the state has been restored completely, the page is allowed to run and produce the HTML output.

## Submitting Forms

The HTML *<form>* tag is the only element authorized to transmit client-side data to the server. When the user clicks a button of type *submit*, by design the browser stuffs the current content of all the controls that belong to the form into a string. The string is then passed to the server as part of the GET or POST command.

The following HTML snippet illustrates a simple form containing a text box and submit button. As you can see, the form is associated with the POST command and the page.aspx URL:

```
<form method="post" action="page.aspx">
    <input type="text" name="EmpCode" />
    <input type="submit" value="Send" />
</form>
```

The following request shows the POST command that hits the Web server when the user clicks the submit button:

```
POST /page.aspx HTTP/1.1
Host: expo-one
Content-Type: application/x-www-form-urlencoded
Content-Length: 12

EmpCode=1001
```

While processing the page request, the ISAPI extension parses the body of the request and exposes any information found through a more programmer-friendly object model. For example, instead of remaining a simple name/value string, the *EmpCode* variable is moved within an application-wide collection—the *Request.Form* collection. This represents a first level of abstraction built over the raw HTTP programming model. Objects such as *Request*, *Response*, and *Server* form the HTTP context for the call and, as such, represent the minimum set of objects you find in all Web development platforms, including JSP, ASP and, of course, ASP.NET. In ASP.NET, though, you find much more.

# The Structure of ASP.NET Pages

An ASP.NET page is a server-side text file saved with the .aspx extension. The internal structure of the page is extremely modular and comprises three distinct sections—page directives, code, and page layout:

- **Page directives** Page directives set up the environment in which the page will run, specify how the HTTP runtime should process the page, and determine which assumptions about the page are safe to make. Directives also let you import namespaces to simplify coding, load assemblies not currently in the global assembly cache (GAC), and register new controls with custom tag names and namespace prefixes.
- **Code section** The code section, with the misleading tag name of *<script>*, includes any source code pertinent to the page. (The name *<script>* has been chosen for backward-compatibility reasons.) You

typically place event handlers and helper routines here. Code in this section is always compiled before execution.

- **Page layout** The page layout represents the skeleton of the page. It includes server controls, literal text, and HTML tags. The user interface of the server controls can be fleshed out a bit using either inline or declared code.

For the page to work, you don't need to specify all sections. Although real-world pages include all the sections mentioned, perfectly valid and functional pages can include only the code section or page layout. In some very special cases, you can even have an ASP.NET page made of a single directive.

## A Sample ASP.NET Page

Let's consider our first ASP.NET page. To start off, a simple text editor will suffice; let's open Notepad and let the sleeping giant (Microsoft Visual Studio .NET) lie. The following code implements a simple ASP.NET page that lets you enter a string and then makes it uppercase:

```
<% @Page Language="C#" %>

<script runat="server">
private void MakeUpper(object sender, EventArgs e)
{
    string buf = TheString.Value;
    TheResult.InnerText = buf.ToUpper();
}
</script>

<html>
<title>Pro ASP.NET (Ch 01)</title>
<body>
<h1>String Converter</h1>
<form runat="server">
    <input runat="server" type="text" id="TheString" />
    <input runat="server" type="submit" value="Convert..."
        OnServerClick="MakeUpper" />
    <hr><span runat="server" id="TheResult" />
</form>
</body>
</html>
```

Blank lines in the preceding listing separate the three sections—directives, code, and page layout. Notice the unsparing use of the *runat* attribute—it's one of the most important pieces of the whole ASP.NET jigsaw puzzle. Later in this chapter, we'll discuss *runat* in more detail. For now, it suffices to say that the *runat* attribute promotes an otherwise lifeless server-side tag to the rank of a component instance. Let's quickly review the code.

Thanks to the *runat* attribute, the input text box becomes an instance of the *HtmlInputControl* class when the page is processed on the server. The *Value* property of the class returns the current content of the control. This value is converted to uppercase and then assigned to the *InnerText* property of the server-side control used to render an HTML *<span>* tag. When the user clicks the Submit button, the page automatically posts back to itself. This time, the magic is performed by the *runat* attribute set for the *<form>* tag. Once on the server, the current value of the text box is read and automatically assigned to a newly created instance of the *HtmlInputControl*. Next, the code associated with the *OnServerClick* event runs. The code works on controls whose state has been restored and updated with client information. When the *MakeUpper* event handler completes, the page is ready for rendering. At this point, updated HTML code is sent to the browser.

To test the page, copy the .aspx file to your Web server's root directory. Normally, this is c:\inetpub\wwwroot. If you want, create an ad hoc virtual directory. Next, point the browser to the page. Figure 1-2 shows what you get.

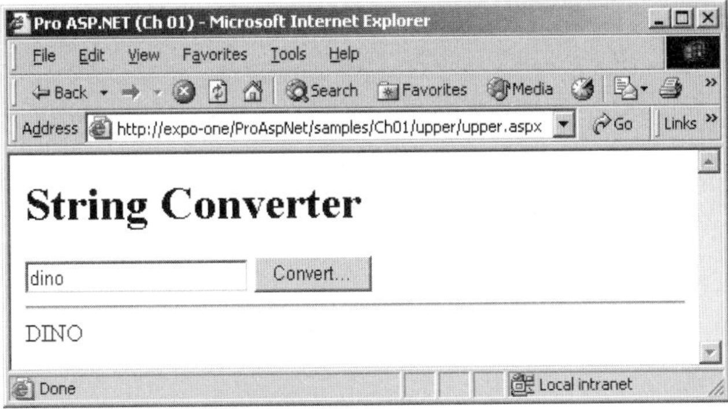


**Figure 1-2** Our first ASP.NET page in action.

No matter how simple you keep a test ASP.NET page, a lot of complex features and techniques are always involved. This page is no exception. In the following chapters, you'll learn more about server-side controls and the difference between HTML and Web controls. You'll also see how to deploy real applications and not just individual pages. Now that we've dirtied our hands with some ASP.NET code, let's step back and review the layers that actually make an ASP.NET page.

## The Processing Directives of a Page

Directives configure the run-time environment that will execute the page. In ASP, only one directive was supported—*@Language*—and you had to place it on the very first line of the page. The following code shows an ASP directive:

```
<% @Language="VBScript" CodePage="1232" %>
```

Several new directives have been added to ASP.NET and, at the same time, their usage has been made easier and dependent on less strict conditions. In ASP.NET, directives can be located anywhere in the page, although it's a good and common practice to place them at the beginning of the file. In addition, the name of a directive is case-insensitive and the values of directive attributes don't need to be quoted.

> **Tip** The ASP *@Language* directive is no longer officially supported in ASP.NET. The same goal is accomplished by the *Language* attribute within the *@Page* directive. However, for migration purposes, ASP.NET treats the old-style *@Language* directive block as an *@Page* directive with the *Language* attribute set. As a result, the ASP-style syntax shown below is still accepted:
>
> ```
> <% @Language="VBScript" CodePage="1232" %>
> ```
>
> It gets silently translated into the following code:
>
> ```
> <% @Page Language="VBScript" CodePage="1232" %>
> ```
>
> The ASP.NET *@Page* directive supports the same set of processing directives as ASP—*CodePage*, *EnableSessionState*, *LCID*, *Transaction*—plus a few more.

The most important and most frequently used directive in ASP.NET is *@Page*. The complete list of ASP.NET directives is shown in Table 1-1.

**Table 1-1 Directives Supported by ASP.NET Pages**

| Directive | Description |
|---|---|
| *@ Assembly* | Links an assembly to the current page or user control |
| *@ Control* | Defines control-specific attributes that guide the behavior of the control compiler |
| *@ Implements* | Indicates that the page, or the user control, implements a specified .NET Framework interface |
| *@ Import* | Indicates a namespace to import into a page or user control |
| *@ OutputCache* | Controls the output caching policies of a page or user control |
| *@ Page* | Defines page-specific attributes that guide the behavior of the page compiler and the language parser that will preprocess the page |

**Table 1-1 Directives Supported by ASP.NET Pages**

| Directive | Description |
|---|---|
| *@ Reference* | Links a page or user control to the current page or user control |
| *@ Register* | Creates a custom tag in the page or the control. The new tag (prefix and name) is associated with the namespace and the code of a user-defined control |

With the exception of *@Page* and *@Control*, all directives can be used both within a page and a control declaration. *@Page* and *@Control* are mutually exclusive. *@Page* can be used only in .aspx files, while the *@Control* directive can be used only in .ascx files.

> **Note** As we'll see in more detail in Chapter 10 and Chapter 18, ASP.NET features two types of user-defined controls. Custom controls are controls that derive from existing .NET Framework classes. User controls (also known as pagelets) are smaller and simpler ASP.NET pages that can be embedded in host pages and programmatically driven through methods and properties. Custom controls are created as assemblies and have a .dll extension. User controls are source files, similar to ASP.NET pages, but they have the .ascx extension.

We'll cover the *@Control*, *@OutputCache*, and *@Register* directives in detail in Chapter 10. In the meantime, let's learn more about the other, more page-specific, directives.

The syntax of a processing directive is unique and common to all supported types of directives. Multiple attributes must be separated with blanks, and no blank can be placed around the equals sign (=) that assigns a value to an attribute, as the following line of code demonstrates:

```
<%@ Directive_Name attribute="value" [attribute="value"...] %>
```

Each directive has its own closed set of typed attributes. Assigning a value of the wrong type to an attribute, or using a wrong attribute with a directive, results in a compilation error.

> **Important** The content of directive attributes is always rendered as plain text. However, attributes are expected to contain values that can be rendered to a particular type. When the ASP.NET page is parsed, all the directive attributes are extracted and stored in a dictionary. The names and number of attributes must match the expected schema for the directive. The string that express the value of an attribute is valid as long as it can be converted into the expected type. For example, if the attribute is designed to take a Boolean value, "*true*" or "*false*" are its only acceptable values.

## The *@Page* Directive

The *@Page* directive can be used only in .aspx pages and generates a compile error if used with other types of ASP.NET pages such as controls and Web services. Each .aspx file is allowed to include at most one *@Page* directive. Although not strictly necessary from the syntax point of view, the directive is realistically required by all pages of some complexity.

*@Page* features about 30 attributes that can be logically grouped in three categories: compilation (Table 1-2), overall page behavior (Table 1-3), and page output (Table 1-4). Each ASP.NET page is compiled upon first request, and the HTML actually served to the browser is generated by the methods of the dynamically generated class. Attributes in Table 1-2 let you fine-tune parameters for the compiler and choose the language to use.

**Table 1-2 *@Page* Attributes for Page Compilation**

| Attribute | Description |
|---|---|
| *ClassName* | Specifies the name of the class that will be dynamically compiled when the page is requested. Must be a class name without namespace information. |
| *CompilerOptions* | A sequence of compiler command-line switches used to compile the page. |
| *Debug* | A Boolean value that indicates whether the page should be compiled with debug symbols. |
| *Explicit* | A Boolean value that determines whether the page is compiled with the Visual Basic *Option Explicit* mode set to *On*. *Option Explicit* forces the programmer to explicitly declare all variables. The attribute is ignored if the page language is not Visual Basic .NET. |

**Table 1-2 *@Page* Attributes for Page Compilation**

| Attribute | Description |
|---|---|
| *Inherits* | Defines the base class for the page to inherit. It can be any class derived from the *Page* class. (I'll cover this in Chapter 2.) |
| *Language* | Indicates the language to use when compiling inline code blocks (<% … %>) and all the code that appears in the page *<script>* section. Supported languages include Visual Basic .NET, C#, JScript .NET, and J#. *(J# is not allowed with version 1.0 of the .NET Framework and Visual Studio .NET 2002.)* If not otherwise specified, the language defaults to Visual Basic .NET. |
| *Src* | Indicates the source file that contains the implementation of the base class specified with *Inherits*. The attribute is not used by Visual Studio .NET and other RAD designers. They, in fact, precompile the class and make the assembly available in the application's virtual directory. |
| *Strict* | A Boolean value that determines whether the page is compiled with the Visual Basic *Option Strict* mode set to *On*. When enabled, *Option Strict* permits only type-safe conversions and prohibits implicit conversions in which loss of data is possible. (In this case, the behavior is identical to that of C#.) The attribute is ignored if the page language is not Visual Basic .NET. |
| *Trace* | A Boolean value that indicates whether tracing is enabled. If tracing is enabled, extra information is appended to the page's output. The default is *false*. |
| *TraceMode* | Indicates how trace messages are to be displayed for the page when tracing is enabled. Acceptable values are *SortByTime* and *SortByCategory*. The default, when tracing is enabled, is *SortByTime*. |
| *WarningLevel* | Indicates the compiler warning level at which you want the compiler to abort compilation for the page. Possible values are 0 through 4. |

Notice that the default values of the *Explicit* and *Strict* attributes are read from the application's configuration settings. As we'll see in greater detail in Chapter 12, the configuration settings of an ASP.NET application are obtained by merging all machine-wide settings with application-wide and even folder-wide settings. This means you can also control what the default values for the *Explicit* and *Strict* attributes are. Unless you change the default configuration settings—the .config files are created when the .NET Framework is installed—both *Explicit* and *Strict* default to *True*. Should the related settings be removed from the configuration files, both attributes would default to *False* instead.

## ASP.NET Languages

As of version 1.0 of the .NET Framework, ASP.NET supports three programming languages—Visual Basic .NET, C#, and JScript .NET. To choose Visual Basic .NET, set the *Language* attribute to any of the following strings: *VB*, *VBS*, *VisualBasic*, or *VBScript*. Valid shortcuts to select C# are *C#*, *CS*, or *CSharp*. Finally, if your language of choice is JScript .NET, use *JS*, *JScript*, or *JavaScript*.

Support for a fourth language—J#—has been added in version 1.1 of the .NET Framework. To choose J#, set the *Language* attribute to *VJ#*. Generally, though, you can make ASP.NET support any language for which you hold a .NET-compatible compiler and a companion class implementing the compiler's object model. To extend ASP.NET with new languages, add a new row to the machine.config file (or the application's web.config file) that looks like the following:

```
<compiler language="Pascal;Delphi" extension=".pas;"
   type="MyCompany.PascalCodeProvider,MyAssembly" />
```

The new line would add support for the Pascal language, whose files are expected to have a .pas extension. Pascal and Delphi are both valid words to use with the *@Page Language* attribute. In the *type* attribute, *MyCompany.PascalCodeProvider* identifies the class that implements the compiler's object model. *MyAssembly* is the name of the assembly in which the class is contained.

Attributes listed in Table 1-3 allow you to control to some extent the overall behavior of the page and the supported range of features. For example, you can set a custom error page, disable session state, and control the transactional behavior of the page.

**Table 1-3 *@Page* Attributes for Page Behavior**

| Attribute | Description |
|---|---|
| AspCompat | A Boolean attribute that, when set to *true*, allows the page to be executed on a single-threaded apartment (STA) thread. The setting allows the page to call COM+ 1.0 components and components developed with Microsoft Visual Basic 6.0 that require access to the unmanaged ASP built-in objects. (I'll cover this in Chapter 13.) |

**Table 1-3 *@Page* Attributes for Page Behavior**

| Attribute | Description |
|---|---|
| *AutoEventWireup* | A Boolean attribute that indicates whether or not page events are automatically enabled. Set to *true* by default. Pages developed with Visual Studio .NET have this attribute set to *false*, and page events are individually tied to handlers. (I'll cover this in Chapter 2.) |
| *Buffer* | A Boolean attribute that determines whether HTTP response buffering is enabled. Set to *true* by default. |
| *Description* | Provides a text description of the page. The ASP.NET page parser ignores the attribute, which subsequently has only a documentation purpose. |
| *EnableSessionState* | Defines how the page should treat session data. If set to *true*, the session state can read and be written. If set to *false*, session data is not available to the application. Finally, if set to *ReadOnly*, the session state can be read but not changed. |
| *EnableViewState* | A Boolean value that indicates whether the page *view state* is maintained across page requests. The view state is the page call context—a collection of values that retain the state of the page and are carried back and forth. View state is enabled by default. (I'll cover this in Chapter 14.) |
| *EnableViewStateMac* | A Boolean value that indicates ASP.NET should calculate a machine-specific authentication code and append it to the view state of the page (in addition to Base64 encoding). The Mac in the attribute name stands for *machine authentication check*. When the attribute is *true*, upon postbacks ASP.NET will check the authentication code of the view state to make sure that it hasn't been tampered with on the client. |
| *ErrorPage* | Defines the target URL to which users will be automatically redirected in case of unhandled page exceptions. |
| *SmartNavigation* | A Boolean value that indicates whether the page supports the Internet Explorer 5 or later smart navigation feature. Smart navigation allows a page to be refreshed without losing scroll position and element focus. |
| *Transaction* | Indicates whether the page supports or requires transactions. Acceptable values are: *Disabled*, *NotSupported*, *Supported*, *Required*, and *RequiresNew*. Transaction support is disabled by default. |
| *ValidateRequest* | A Boolean value that indicates whether request validation should occur. If *true*, ASP.NET checks all input data against a hard-coded list of potentially dangerous values. This functionality helps reduce the risk of cross-site scripting attacks for pages. *True* by default. (This feature is not supported in ASP.NET 1.0.) |

Attributes listed in Table 1-4 allow you to control the format of the output being generated for the page. For example, you can set the content type of the page or localize the output to the extent possible.

**Table 1-4 *@Page* Directives for Page Output**

| Attribute | Description |
|---|---|
| *ClientTarget* | Indicates the target browser for which ASP.NET server controls should render content. |
| *CodePage* | Indicates the code page value for the response. Set this attribute only if you created the page using a code page other than the default code page of the Web server on which the page will run. In this case, set the attribute to the code page of your development machine. A code page is a character set that includes numbers, punctuation marks, and other glyphs. Code pages differ on a per-language basis. |
| *ContentType* | Defines the content type of the response as a standard MIME type. Supports any valid HTTP content type string. |
| *Culture* | Indicates the culture setting for the page. Culture information includes the writing and sorting system, calendar, and date and currency formats. The attribute must be set to a non-neutral culture name, which means it must contain both language and country information. For example, *en-US* is a valid value unlike *en* alone, which is considered country neutral. |
| *LCID* | A 32-bit value that defines the locale identifier for the page. By default, ASP.NET uses the locale of the Web server. |
| *ResponseEncoding* | Indicates the character encoding of the page. The value is used to set the *CharSet* attribute on the content type HTTP header. Internally, ASP.NET handles all strings as Unicode. |
| *UICulture* | Specifies the default culture name used by the Resource Manager to look up culture-specific resources at run time. |

As you can see, many attributes discussed in Table 1-4 concern the issue of page localization. Building multilanguage and international applications is a task that ASP.NET, and the .NET Framework in general, greatly simplify. In Chapter 5, we'll delve into the topic.

### The *@Assembly* Directive

The *@Assembly* directive links an assembly to the current page so that its classes and interfaces are available for use on the page. When ASP.NET compiles the page, a few assemblies are linked by default. So you should resort to the directive only if you need linkage to a nondefault assembly. Table 1-5 lists the .NET assemblies that are automatically provided to the compiler.

**Table 1-5 Assemblies Linked by Default**

| Assembly File Name | Description |
|---|---|
| Mscorlib.dll | Provides the core functionality of the .NET Framework, including types, *AppDomains*, and run-time services. |
| System.dll | Provides another bunch of system services, including regular expressions, compilation, native methods, file I/O, and networking. |
| System.Data.dll | Defines data-container and data-access classes, including the whole ADO.NET framework. |
| System.Drawing.dll | Implements the GDI+ features. |
| System.EnterpriseServices.dll | Provides the classes that allow for serviced components and COM+ interaction. |
| System.Web.dll | The assembly implements the core ASP.NET services, controls, and classes. |
| System.Web.Mobile.dll | The assembly implements the core ASP.NET mobile services, controls, and classes. *Not included if version 1.0 of the .NET Framework is installed.* |
| System.Web.Services.dll | Contains the core code that makes Web services run. |
| System.Xml.dll | Implements the .NET Framework XML features. |

In addition to these assemblies, the ASP.NET runtime automatically links to the page all the assemblies that reside in the Web application *Bin* subdirectory. Note that you can modify, extend, or restrict the list of default assemblies by editing the machinewide configuration settings set in the machine.config file. In this case, changes apply to all ASP.NET applications run on that Web server. Alternately, you can modify the assembly list on a per-application basis by editing the application's specific web.config file. (I'll cover configuration settings in Chapter 12.) To prevent all assemblies found in the *Bin* directory from being linked to the page, remove the following line from the machine.config file:

```
<add assembly="*" />
```

To link a needed assembly to the page, use the following syntax:

```
<%@ Assembly Name="AssemblyName" %>
<%@ Assembly Src="assembly_code.cs" %>
```

The *@Assembly* directive supports two mutually exclusive attributes: *Name* and *Src*. *Name* indicates the name of the assembly to link to the page. The name cannot include the path or the extension. *Src* indicates the path to a source file to dynamically compile and link against the page. The *@Assembly* directive can appear multiple times in the body of the page. In fact, you need a new directive for each assembly to link. *Name* and *Src* cannot be used in the same *@Assembly* directive, but multiple directives defined in the same page can use either.

> **Note** In terms of performance, the difference between *Name* and *Src* is minimal, although *Name* points to an existing and ready-to-load assembly. The source file referenced by *Src* is compiled only the first time it is requested. As we'll see in more detail in Chapter 2, the ASP.NET runtime maps a source file with a dynamically compiled assembly and keeps using the compiled code until the original file undergoes changes. This means that after the first application-level call, the impact on the page performance is identical whether you use *Name* or *Src*.

### The *@Import* Directive

The *@Import* directive links the specified namespace to the page so that all the types defined can be accessed from the page without specifying the fully qualified name. For example, to create a new instance of the ADO.NET *DataSet* class, you either import the *System.Data* namespace or resort to the following code:

```
System.Data.DataSet ds = new System.Data.DataSet();
```

Once you've imported the *System.Data* namespace into the page, you can use more natural coding, as shown here:

```
DataSet ds = new DataSet();
```

The syntax of the *@Import* directive is rather self-explanatory:

```
<%@ Import namespace="value" %>
```

As with *@Assembly*, *@Import* can be used as many times as needed in the body of the page. The *@Import* directive is the ASP.NET counterpart of the C#

*using* statement and the Visual Basic .NET *Imports* statement. Looking back at unmanaged C/C++, we could say the directive plays a role nearly identical to the *#include* directive.

For example, to be able to connect to a Microsoft SQL Server database and grab some disconnected data, you need to import the following two namespaces:

```
<%@ Import namespace="System.Data" %>
<%@ Import namespace=" System.Data.SqlClient" %>
```

> **Caution** *@Import* helps the compiler only to resolve class names; it doesn't automatically link required assemblies. Using the *@Import* directive allows you to use shorter class names, but as long as the assembly that contains the class code is not properly linked, you have a type error. In this case, using the fully qualified class name is of no help because the compiler lacks the type definition.
>
> You might have noticed that, more often than not, assembly and namespace names coincide. Bear in mind this happens only by chance and assemblies and namespaces are radically different entities, each requiring the proper directive.

You need the *System.Data* namespace to work with the *DataSet* and *DataTable* classes, and you need the *System.Data.SqlClient* namespace to prepare and issue the command. In this case, you don't need to link against additional assemblies because the System.Data.dll assembly is linked by default. The namespaces listed in Table 1-6 are automatically imported into all pages.

**Table 1-6 Namespaces Imported by Default**

| Namespace | Description |
|---|---|
| *System* | Contains the definition of the basic types. |
| *System.Collections* | Contains base collections classes, arrays, and lists. |
| *System.Collections.Specialized* | Contains more advanced collection classes, including strings and name/values collection. |
| *System.Configuration* | Contains classes to read configuration settings. |
| *System.IO* | Contains classes to perform file I/O. |
| *System.Text* | Contains classes to manage string builders and character sets. |
| *System.Text.RegularExpressions* | Contains classes to process regular expressions. |

**Table 1-6 Namespaces Imported by Default** *(continued)*

| Namespace | Description |
|---|---|
| *System.Web* | Contains classes that implement the ASP.NET runtime underpinnings. |
| *System.Web.Caching* | Contains classes to implement caching. |
| *System.Web.Security* | Provides the definition of classes for ASP.NET security. |
| *System.Web.SessionState* | Provides the definition of classes for ASP.NET session state. |
| *System.Web.UI* | Contains classes for ASP.NET data-binding, page compilation, and user controls. |
| *System.Web.UI.HtmlControls* | Contains HTML control classes. |
| *System.Web.UI.WebControls* | Contains Web control classes. |

### The *@Implements* Directive

The directive indicates that the current page implements the specified .NET Framework interface. An interface is a set of signatures for a logically related group of functions. An interface is a sort of contract that shows the component's commitment to expose that group of functions. Unlike abstract classes, an interface doesn't provide code or executable functionality. When you implement an interface in an ASP.NET page, you declare any required methods and properties within the *<script>* section. The syntax of the *@Implements* directive is as follows:

```
<%@ Implements interface="InterfaceName" %>
```

The *@Implements* directive can appear multiple times in the page if the page has to implement multiple interfaces. Note that if you decide to put all the page logic in a separate class file (code-behind), you can't use the directive to implement interfaces. Instead, you implement the interface in the code-behind class. We'll cover code-behind in Chapter 2.

### The *@Reference* Directive

The *@Reference* directive is used to establish a dynamic link between the current page and the specified page or user control. This feature has significant relapses in the way in which you set up cross-page communication. It also lets you create strongly typed instances of user controls. Let's review the syntax.

The directive can appear multiple times in the page, and it features two mutually exclusive attributes—*Page* and *Control*. Both attributes are expected to contain a path to a source file:

```
<%@ Reference page="source_page" %>
<%@ Reference control="source_user_control" %>
```

The *Page* attribute points to a .aspx source file, whereas the *Control* attribute contains the path of a .ascx user control. In both cases, the referenced source file will be dynamically compiled into an assembly, thus making the classes defined in the source programmatically available to the referencing page. When running, an ASP.NET page is an instance of a .NET Framework class with a specific interface made of methods and properties. When the referencing page executes, a referenced page becomes a class that represents the .aspx source file and can be instantiated and programmed at will. Note that for the directive to work the referenced page must belong to the same domain as the calling page. Cross-site calls are not allowed, and both the *Page* and *Control* attributes expect to receive a relative virtual path. We'll return to this topic, with practical examples, in Chapter 4, "Working with the Page."

## The *<script>* Section

The *<script>* section of an ASP.NET page contains all the declared code that makes up the page. If the page implements an interface, the code for the interface methods is placed here. If the page handles some system events, the needed code belongs here. Likewise, the *<script>* section contains all the code to execute when the controls in the page are clicked or change their state. The *<script>* tag supports the following syntax:

```
<script runat="server" language="..." src="...">
   Code goes here...
</script>
```

When the *runat* attribute is set to *server*, all the code comprised between the opening and closing tags is given special meaning. In this case, the code is extracted from the .aspx source file, compiled into an assembly, and then executed when the page runs. No line of this code will ever be output to the client.

When the *runat* attribute is not included, the content of the *<script>* block is considered as client-side script code and emitted verbatim in the resulting HTML page. ASP.NET pages can have both server-side and client-side *<script>* blocks.

> **Note** The .NET Framework documentation uses the name *code declaration block* to refer to the content of a *<script>* block in which the *runat* attribute equals *server*. The name code render block refers to an ASP-style code block, which is defined as inline code (*<%...%>*) or inline expression (*<%=...%>*). Declared code becomes part of the page's programming interface once the page is compiled into an assembly. Rendered code is embedded in the class logic and executes only when the page is rendered.

### The *Language* Attribute

The *Language* attribute defines the language used within the block. Of course, the range of acceptable values is slightly different according to the value of the *runat* attribute. If the *runat* attribute is set to *server*, you can use C#, Visual Basic .NET, JScript .NET, or maybe J# (if version 1.1 of the .NET Framework is used). If the *runat* attribute is not included, the code will run on the client, which allows you to use JavaScript or maybe VBScript (if the Web browser supports VBScript).

Generally, valid languages for the server-side script block are those for which you have a .NET assembly that implements the interfaces defined in the .NET compilers object model. Similarly, valid languages for the client-side script block are those languages that are supported by the client Web browser. For example, Netscape browsers support JavaScript and Internet Explorer supports JavaScript and VBScript.

The behavior of the *<script>* tag changes considerably according to the value of the *runat* attribute. The presence of the *runat* attribute marks an important difference regarding the use of the *Language* attribute. While you can have multiple client-side scripts each using a different language, you can't have more than one language in use within an ASP.NET page. If you have multiple server-side *<script>* blocks, make sure all of them use the same language. Although this seems to violate the much-hyped language neutrality of .NET, the reason will be made clear in Chapter 2.

If the *<script>* block doesn't contain a *Language* attribute, the language set in the *@Page* directive is used. You could also set the language both in the directive and script block, but in this case the settings must match. In no way, in fact, does ASP.NET make one of them win. When settings conflict, you simply get a compile error on the *<script>* line stating that another language has been specified earlier in the page.

### The *Src* Attribute

The *Src* attribute denotes the URL of the source file to load. When this attribute is used, any other code specified in the *<script>* block is ignored:

```
<script runat="server" language="c#" src="content.cs" />
```

If you plan to use the *Src* attribute, you might want to be more elegant and use an empty *<script>* tag, as in the code just shown.

## ASP-Style Code Blocks in ASP.NET

As mentioned earlier, ASP.NET supports two types of code blocks—those declared in a server-side *<script>* block, and those defined as inline code or inline expressions in the body of the page. Obviously, there's nothing you can do with inline code that can't be done even more elegantly and more effectively with declared code. ASP.NET supports inline code blocks simply to ease the migration of ASP applications.

ASP.NET inline code and inline expressions follow this quite familiar syntax:

```
<% inline code %>
<%=inline expression %>
```

Just as in ASP, inline expressions are simply shortcuts for the *Response.Write* method. Inline code, on the other hand, is a sequence of statements and variable declarations that are executed in a top-down fashion, as in ASP. However, unlike ASP, ASP.NET won't allow you to declare a function between <% and %> tags. The following ASP-style code is no longer supported and, if used, generates a compile error:

```
<% Sub DeclareLove() %>
    <h1>ASP.NET Is Love!</h1>
<% End Sub %>
```

The code can be rewritten as follows:

```
<script language="VB" runat="server">
    Sub DeclareLove()
        Response.Write("<h1>ASP.NET Is Love!</h1>")
    End Sub
</script>
```

You can use the method *DeclareLove* from within a <% … %> block. Another difference with ASP concerns variable declarations. In ASP.NET, the variables declared in <% … %> blocks are no longer globally available to other functions and methods in the page; they can be accessed only by code defined in other render blocks on the page.

In ASP, you were used to putting all initialization code at the beginning of the first code block. In ASP.NET, initialization code must be included within the *Page_Load* method. You can still use ASP-style programming, but keep in mind that all the code in <% … %> blocks will be executed only when the page is rendered, and therefore, after the page is loaded.

Aside from the few but important differences we just mentioned, ASP.NET can run a significant portion of the existing old-style ASP code. For example, the following typical loop produces the same results as in ASP:

```
<% for (int i=0; i<8; i++) { %>
    <font size="<%=i %>"> ASP.NET is Love! </font><br>
<% } %>
```

Figure 1-3 shows the output when you run this code.

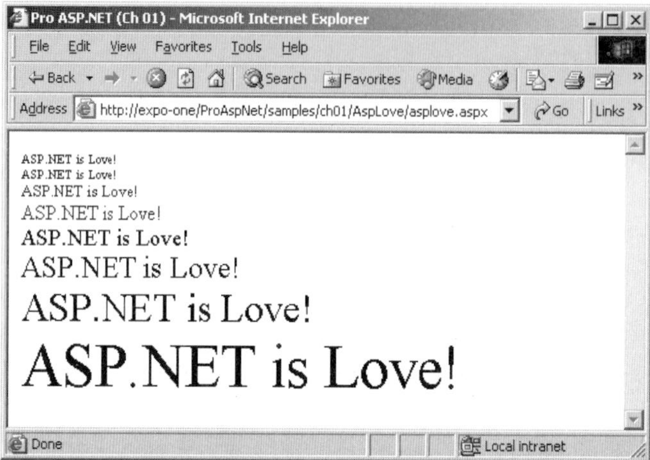


**Figure 1-3** Programmers' love for ASP.NET grows constantly.

> **Note** Some ASP.NET pages can lack the *<script>* section completely. These pages exploit a unique ASP.NET feature called *code-behind*. With code-behind, you isolate the code for the page in a distinct class, thus obtaining a physical separation between code and page layout. We'll learn more about code-behind in Chapter 2.

## The Layout Section

The layout section of an ASP.NET page contains the literals and markup text that provides the graphical infrastructure of the page. The layout can also contain ASP-style code blocks, although their use is discouraged. Simply put, the layout is an HTML page with some *placeholders* that are expanded on the server and generate the HTML that is sent to the browser.

All the literal text in the layout section is emitted verbatim in the target HTML page. What will become of markup text depends on the *runat* attribute. If the *runat* attribute is present, the ASP.NET runtime attempts to map that tag with an instance of a server control. If a match is found, an instance of that control is created. Otherwise, a type-not-defined exception is thrown. Markup text without the *runat* attribute is treated like literal text and emitted verbatim.

ASP.NET comes with a full complement of server-side controls—that is, .NET classes that implement ad hoc interfaces and render their content as HTML. Classic HTML tags automatically map to a particular family of ASP.NET server controls known as *HTML server controls*. Their programming interface mirrors the set of attributes of the native HTML tag. Another family of ASP.NET server controls are known as *Web server controls*. Web server controls are prefixed by the *<asp>* namespace and represent more complex user-interface elements. Custom controls can be mapped to custom tags using the *@Register* directive.

User controls are an effective way to simplify and componentize the page layout. HTML is quite verbose as a language. Especially in cases where you need to structure the contents with tables, the final markup can be quite complex and hard to read and maintain. User controls are to Web pages as classes or subroutines are to applications. They provide a way to encapsulate logical blocks of the user interface (such as the toolbar, menu, grids, and headers) into more manageable and object-oriented components.

Finally, the layout of an ASP.NET page must group all interactive controls under a single *<form>* tag marked with the *runat* attribute. Only the controls that belong to this server-side form can persist their state across page requests and actually be an active part of the page. Place only decorative controls and static user-interface elements such as images, headers, and footers outside of the *<form>* tag. We'll return to this point in Chapter 2 and in Chapter 4.

## The ASP.NET Component Model

A key aspect of ASP.NET is that it represents the Web branch of the .NET Framework. The .NET Framework is made entirely of an object-oriented hierarchy of classes (about 9,000 classes) that span all programming topics for Windows operating systems. A Web application is made of pages the user requests from a server and that the server processes and returns as HTML code. How the requested resource is processed is server-specific. In particular, when the resource happens to have a .aspx extension, IIS delegates any elaboration to the ASP.NET runtime system.

The ASP.NET runtime transforms the source code of the requested .aspx page into the living instance of a .NET Framework class that inherits from the base *Page* class. (How such a transformation takes place is the subject of Chapter 2.) At the end of the day, a running ASP.NET page is an object, and so it is for some of its components—the server-side controls.

A large number of new ASP.NET features are just a direct or an indirect propagation of the .NET infrastructure. ASP.NET benefits from cross-language integration and exception handling, garbage collection and code access security, deployment and configuration, and an incredibly rich class library. All these features aren't the products of a self-contained engine, they are available to you because ASP.NET applications are a special breed of a .NET application.

## A Model for Component Interaction

A close metaphor for client-side scripting is found in ASP.NET—the Dynamic HTML object model (DHTML). Any element can be identified through an ID, and you can write code against it. While this is a natural approach on the client, it represents a brand new scheme for server applications. Two factors make this revolutionary approach possible:

- The component-based architecture of the .NET platform and the fact that ASP.NET is a constituent part of it
- The ASP.NET built-in mechanism for the application's state management

The component-based design of .NET makes component interaction easy and effective in all environments including ASP.NET applications. On the other hand, the availability of an automatic mechanism for state persistence overcomes all the hurdles represented by the stateless nature of the HTTP protocol. ASP.NET components access page features and interact by calling one another's methods and setting properties.

The fact that all elements in the page are true components, and not simply parsable text, provides a flexible and powerful extensibility model. Creating new controls is as easy as deriving a new class; creating master pages is as easy as specifying a code-behind page more complex than the base *Page* class.

## The *runat* Attribute

The *runat* attribute is what determines whether a piece of markup text is to be emitted verbatim at render time or transformed into a stateful instance of a particular .NET class. In an ASP.NET page, all markup elements that have the *runat* attribute set to *server* are considered server-side controls. The control class exposes methods and properties that let you configure the state of the component. The control is responsible for emitting HTML code when the page is rendered to the browser. Let's consider the following simple code that creates an anchor element in the page:

```
Response.Write("<A id=myAnchor href=www.asp.net>Click me</A>")
```

The anchor element is created programmatically and is not defined in the page layout. In ASP, code blocks and the *Response.Write* method are the only ways you have to create or configure controls dynamically. In some development environments, such as Microsoft Visual InterDev, *design-time controls* provided an object-based way to output dynamically generated HTML. Design-time controls, though, are just what the name indicates—that is, controls you can use at design time to generate markup and script code. In ASP.NET, you have a new breed of controls that we could call *run-time controls* to mark the contrast with design-time controls.

### Working with Server-Side Controls

Within an ASP page, there's no way for you to code against the *myAnchor* element. It's just frozen, lifeless text, only good for sending to the browser. Once on a client, the *myAnchor* element gets back to life and can accept script instructions. Suppose now that you need to set the *href* attribute of the anchor based on run-time conditions. In ASP, you could first obtain the value for the *href* attribute and then call *Response.Write*:

```
strHref = "www.asp.net"
strHtml = "<A id=myAnchor "
strHtml = strHtml + "href=" + strHref
strHtml = strHtml + ">Click me</A>"
Response.Write(strHtml)
```

This code will work unchanged in an ASP.NET page, but it's certainly not the best you can do. By declaring the *<A>* tag with the *runat* attribute, you can give life to the anchor element on the server too:

```
<A runat="server" id="myAnchor">Click me</A>
```

When the page is loaded, the ASP.NET runtime parses the source code and creates instances of all controls marked with the *runat* attribute. Throughout the page, the *myAnchor* ID identifies an instance of the server-side control mapped to the *<A>* tag. The following code can be used to set the *href* attribute programmatically:

```
<script runat="server" language="C#">
void Page_Load(object sender, EventArgs e)
{
    myAnchor.HRef = "http://www.asp.net";
}
</script>
```

The markup elements found in the body of the page whose name matches an HTML element are mapped to the corresponding HTML server control. Elements that belong to the *<asp>* namespace are mapped to Web server controls. Other markup elements are mapped to the assembly and class name declared by using an *@Register* directive.

### Pagewide Tags

The *runat* attribute can be used also with pagewide tags such as *<title>*, *<link>*, and *<body>*. These tags are represented through an instance of the *HtmlGenericControl* class. *HtmlGenericControl* is the .NET class used to represent an HTML server-side tag not directly represented by a .NET Framework class. The list of such tags also includes *<span>*, *<div>*, *<font>*, and *<iframe>*.

In the following page, the page title and page background are set programmatically using a server-side object instance:

```
<%@ Page Language="C#" %>
<script runat="server">
void Page_Load(object sender, EventArgs e) {
    TheTitle.InnerText = "Pro ASP.NET (Ch 01)";
    TheBody.Attributes["bgcolor"] = "yellow";
}
</script>
<html>
<title id="TheTitle" runat="server" />
<body id="TheBody" runat="server" >
Click the <b>View|Source</b> menu item...
</body>
</html>
```

The resulting HTML code is as follows:

```
<html>
<title id="TheTitle">Pro ASP.NET (Ch 01)</title>
<body id="TheBody" bgcolor="yellow">
Click the <b>View|Source</b> menu item...
</body>
</html>
```

Likewise, you can set any of the properties of the *<link>* tag, thus deciding programmatically, say, which style sheet to use for the page. You use the *HtmlGenericControl*'s *Attributes* collection to create attributes on the tag and the *InnerText* property to set the text. We'll discuss the programming interface of the *HtmlGenericControl* class in Chapter 3.

## Meta Tags

The *runat* attribute can be applied also to the *<meta>* tag, but a little trick is needed this time. In HTML, you normally add the *<meta>* tag without a closing tag. This is not permitted by ASP.NET when the *runat* attribute is added. The ASP.NET parser scans the whole file looking for *</meta>* tag; if the tag is not found, a compile error is generated.

The following code shows how to programmatically set meta content that instructs the browser to wait four seconds and then to go to the specified URL:

```
<%@ Page Language="C#" %>
<script runat="server">
void Page_Load(object sender, EventArgs e) {
    meta1.Attributes["content"] = "4;URL=http://www.asp.net";
}
</script>
<html>
<meta id="meta1" runat="server" http-equiv="refresh" />
<title>Pro ASP.NET (Ch 01)</title>
<body>
```

```
Click the <b>View|Source</b> menu item in the next few seconds...
</body>
</html>
```

The resulting HTML meta tag is shown below. Notice the fundamental presence of the closing tag:

```
<meta id="meta1" http-equiv="refresh"
content="4;URL=http://www.asp.net"></meta>
```

> **Note** You can also use the *Response.AppendHeader* method to add an HTTP header to the output stream. The programming interface of the *Response* object also features an *AddHeader* method. *AddHeader* is the same as *AppendHeader* and is provided only for compatibility with previous versions of ASP. With ASP.NET, you should always use *AppendHeader.*

## Unknown Tags

In case of unknown tags, namely tags that are neither predefined nor user-defined, the ASP.NET runtime can behave in two different ways. If the tag doesn't contain namespace information, ASP.NET treats it like a generic HTML control. The empty namespace, in fact, evaluates to the HTML namespace, thereby leading the ASP.NET runtime to believe the tag is really an HTML element. No exception is raised, and markup text is generated on the server. For example, let's consider the following ASP.NET page:

```
<%@ Page Language="C#" %>
<script runat="server">
void Page_Load(object sender, EventArgs e) {
    dinoe.Attributes["FavoriteFood"] = "T-bone steak";
}
</script>
<html><body>
<Person id="dinoe" runat="server" />
Click the <b>View|Source</b> menu item...
</body></html>
```

The *<Person>* tag is still processed as if it was a regular HTML tag, and the *FavoriteFood* attribute is added. Figure 1-4 shows what the HTML code for this page actually is. In the preceding sample, the type of the *dinoe* object is *HtmlGenericControl.*

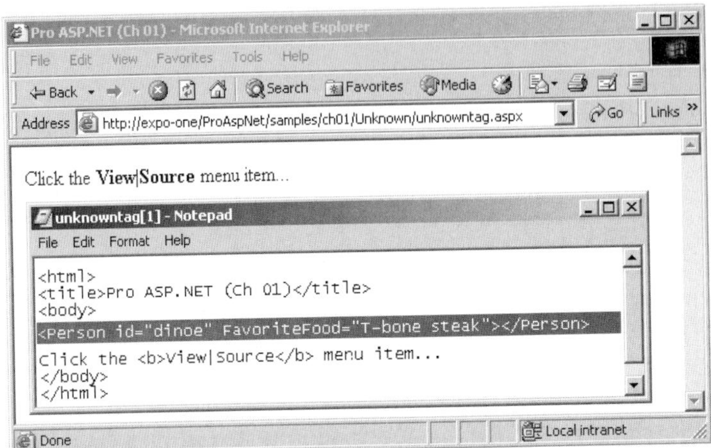


**Figure 1-4** ASP.NET also processes namespace-less custom tags, mapping them to the *HtmlGenericControl* class.

If the tag does contain namespace information, it is acceptable as long as the namespace is *<asp>* or a namespace explicitly associated with the tag name using an *@Register* directive. If the namespace is unknown, a compile error occurs.

## ASP.NET Server Controls

There are basically two families of ASP.NET server controls. They are HTML server controls and Web server controls. *System.Web.UI.HtmlControls* is the namespace of HTML server controls. *System.Web.UI.WebControls* groups all the Web server controls.

HTML server controls are classes that represent a standard HTML tag supported by most browsers. The set of properties of an HTML server control matches exactly the set of attributes of the corresponding tag. The control features properties such as *InnerText*, *InnerHtml*, *Style*, and *Value* and collections such as *Attributes*. Instances of HTML server controls are automatically created by the ASP.NET runtime each time the corresponding HTML tag marked with *runat="server"* is found in the page source.

Web server controls are controls with more features than HTML server controls. Web server controls include not only input controls such as buttons and textboxes, but also special-purpose controls such as a calendar, an ad-rotator, a drop-down list, and a data grid. Web server controls also include components that closely resemble some HTML server controls. Web server controls, though, are more abstract than the corresponding HTML server controls in that their object model doesn't necessarily reflect the HTML syntax. For example, let's compare the HTML server text control and the Web server *TextBox* control. The HTML server text control has the following markup:

```
<input runat="server" id="FirstName" type="text" value="Dino" />
```

The Web server *TextBox* control has the following markup:

```
<asp:textbox runat="server" id="FirstName" text="Dino" />
```

Both controls generate the same HTML code. However, the programming interface of the HTML server text control matches closely that of the HTML *<input>* tag, while methods and properties of the Web server *TextBox* control are named in a more abstract way. For example, to set the content of an HTML server text control, you must use the *Value* property because *Value* is the corresponding HTML attribute name. If you work with the Web server *TextBox* control, you must resort to *Text*. With very few exceptions (which I'll discuss in Chapter 3), using HTML server controls or Web server controls to represent HTML elements is only a matter of preference.

# Migrating from ASP to ASP.NET

In the past five years, one million developers all over the world have chosen ASP as the development platform of choice to build Web applications. You can bet that with such a huge base of installed applications, the problem of ensuring backward compatibility between ASP and ASP.NET has been taken very seriously. The result is that ASP and ASP.NET applications can run side by side on an IIS Web server without any form of interference occurring. In addition, and in spite of the radical changes in the underlying architecture and implementation, a significant portion of existing ASP pages can just be renamed as .aspx files and will continue working (even a bit faster) and be managed by a different IIS module. Does this really mean you can migrate ASP applications to ASP.NET simply by renaming files? Well, not exactly. As always, code migration is a delicate art that becomes impracticable when huge architectural differences exist between the starting and ending points. ASP.NET is designed to make migration easier, but a migration plan is still needed and a 100 percent pure ASP.NET solution is needed to be really effective.

## Side-by-Side Execution

IIS makes use of the file extension to determine which module has to process a requested resource. As a result, only files with a .aspx extension are served by ASP.NET. All the files with a .asp extension will continue to be served by the existing (and unchanged) ASP engine. Because completely different and independent modules serve ASP and ASP.NET requests, existing ASP applications cannot be corrupted simply by installing and running ASP.NET applications on the same Web server.

Not only can you make ASP and ASP.NET applications live side by side on the same Web server, but—more importantly—you can also manage to create applications that use both ASP and ASP.NET pages. After all, from the perspective of an ASP application, what's a .aspx resource if not a simple URL on the same domain?

> **Important** Obviously, mixed applications—applications in which ASP and ASP.NET pages run side-by-side—are recommended only if you take an existing, complex ASP application and enhance it with new ASP.NET pages. The opposite approach, although possible, doesn't make sense. If you're engaged on a new ASP.NET project, by all means forget about ASP.

Note, though, that when ASP and ASP.NET pages live within the context of the same application, some restrictions apply. For example, session state and application state are not shared between ASP and ASP.NET pages. In particular, the problem of sharing session state between ASP and ASP.NET applications is fully dissected in an article available at *http://msdn.microsoft.com/library/en-us/dnaspp/html/converttoaspnet.asp*.

## Rewriting ASP Pages as ASP.NET Pages

Although far richer and created with different design centers, the new ASP.NET programming model has been kept as close as possible to the old ASP model. As a result, ASP.NET programming might seem familiar to developers with good ASP skills. However, although still available in ASP.NET, the ASP-intrinsic objects have been redesigned to make them more structured and object-oriented, and new objects have been provided.

The net effect is that existing ASP code, albeit accepted and functional, is not necessarily the best way of accomplishing a given task. For example, you can still build a list of check-box items by merging plain HTML text and data-bound information in a string buffer. Nevertheless, using the new *CheckBoxList* control would result in more compact, safe, readable, and maintainable code. Likewise, using ActiveX Data Objects (ADO) to access a back-end database server is supported, but it might require some changes to the code and would penalize the performance because data destined to COM objects must be marshaled in and out of the .NET Common Language Runtime (CLR). Global data that you stored in the *Application* object sometimes can be more efficiently stored in the new *Cache* object, which manages perishable data and automatically garbage-collects it when needed.

These are a few examples of the performance hitches you can unwittingly generate in your ASP.NET pages if you create them to resemble existing ASP pages. But there's another key issue to consider when you plan to rewrite ASP pages as ASP.NET pages—the language. Many existing ASP pages are written with VBScript, but only a small portion of the VBScript syntax is acceptable to the Visual Basic .NET compiler. Those pages will not port directly to ASP.NET and will require changes. The necessary changes will probably be limited to only a few lines of code, but those changes must be applied to all pages in the application.

All in all, adapting existing pages as ASP.NET pages is possible but comes at a cost; and such adaptations will not give you highly optimized code. So what should you do with existing ASP applications?

## Suggested Migration Plans

Before continuing with this topic, I need to issue a disclaimer of sorts and mention situations in which migrating to ASP.NET might not be ideal. Understand that ASP.NET—and the subsequent installation of the ASP.NET runtime and the .NET Framework on the Web server—does not affect or compromise existing ASP applications. Existing applications will continue working in the same way and with the same performance as before. Additionally, new and ad hoc designed ASP.NET applications feature far better performance and an improved scalability and programming model. If I had to choose a single word to explain what ASP.NET is all about, that word would be productivity.

ASP.NET-enhanced productivity applies at all levels. You have less code to write (and that code is easier to understand and maintain); a relatively flat learning curve; significant cuts in the cost of the deployment; and a greatly simplified model for localization and customization. ASP.NET is also language-independent and performs much better than ASP. And in my humble opinion, even all that pales in comparison to the gains you experience in productivity.

With that said, I can issue my disclaimer. You probably know better than I do that in this little imperfect world, new projects require new budgets. Upgrading a huge and complex Web site, such as a portal, can be expensive even with the productivity advantages of ASP.NET. If budget is not a concern, then by all means redesign and rewrite the application from scratch. Period. If the budget is a severe concern, you should seriously consider holding off and waiting for better times—the old ASP application will still work. At the very least, the current version of ASP.NET increases your productivity and the application's overall performance, but as of now it can't fit more cheaply into a project's budget! For that to happen, we have to wait for the next version at the earliest.

In between upgrading and not upgrading, I see a few options to move ASP applications towards ASP.NET even when working with relatively small budgets.

## Same Application, New Pages

My first suggestion is that you keep the existing ASP application as is and use ASP.NET only if you're required to add new features and new pages. While extremely cost-effective, the plan poses a few development issues because ASP and ASP.NET pages running together can't share the internal state. Aside from this, no other interoperability issues or interference exist between old and new pages.

## New Application, Same Framework, New Pages

In this case, you develop a new ASP.NET application but without revisiting and redesigning the application's framework. The skeleton and the functions of the application remain the same. The migration roughly consists of translating the constituent pages from ASP to ASP.NET. Basically, you rename each .asp page to .aspx and adapt it to work.

We already discussed the nature of this approach in the "Rewriting ASP Pages as ASP.NET Pages" section. Here, we provide a more detailed list of the issues you must be ready to face:

- **Page directives** ASP has a rough model for setting up the environment in which the page will run. ASP.NET directives have been designed to be fully compatible with ASP directives. However, in an ASP.NET page you might want to exploit some extra *@Page* attributes for a more effective compilation (for example, *AspCompat*, *Explicit*, and *Strict*) and certainly for tracing or debugging purposes. Finally, bear in mind that you also need to link extra assemblies if you import .NET wrappers of COM components.

- **Programming languages** ASP pages are normally written with VBScript, but VBScript is scarcely compatible with Visual Basic .NET. You must carefully review the code of all pages and probably replace *On Error* statements with the more effective .NET exception handling. You must replace the VBScript *CreateObject* with *Server.CreateObject* to preserve the syntax to some extent, or choose a different approach and import the COM object through a .NET wrapper class. Pay attention to turn the *@Page*'s *AspCompat* attribute on if you're using COM and COM+ objects within an ASP.NET page. If the page was written with JScript, things are a bit simpler, as JScript is highly compatible with JScript .NET. However, a careful code review is nevertheless in order.

- **Code blocks** ASP.NET pages support ASP-style code blocks but with some limitation, as explained previously in the "The *<script>* Section" section. The suggestion is to remove all ASP code blocks and rewrite the page, taking advantage of ASP.NET declared code.
- **Security** In ASP.NET, impersonation is disabled by default and you must explicitly enable it to preserve ASP compatibility. A simple line of text in the web.config file would do the job. (I'll cover this in Chapter 12.) Unlike ASP, ASP.NET does not run applications within the context of the System account. ASP.NET applications execute under the ASPNET account and by default have no writing permissions. Subsequently, pages accessing the Web server's file system will explicitly need to be granted write permissions on files and folders to operate successfully.
- **Data Access and XML** ASP pages normally use ADO for any data access need and Microsoft XML Core Services (MSXML) to parse XML documents. Both are COM components and can be used in ASP.NET pages, although you'll pay a bit in performance. The .NET Framework provides an effective data access model (ADO.NET) and a bunch of powerful XML classes you might want to use instead. However, consider that ADO.NET does not support server cursors (a feature that will come with a future version) and the XML API does not support the Simple API for XML (SAX) parsing model. For server cursors, you can only stick to ADO or redesign the feature; for SAX parsing, you can even more effectively use the XML reader component to obtain the same feature.
- **COM compatibility** ASP.NET pages can use COM objects in two ways: directly as a COM object or through a .NET wrapper class. In the former case, the object is referenced in the page using the *<object runat=server …>* tag or dynamically created using the *Server.CreateObject* method. Alternatively, you can create a .NET wrapper for the COM object and use it as you would any other assembly. In both cases, remember to set the *AspCompat* attribute of the *@Page* directive to *true* to prevent excessive overhead, if not deadlock.

### Same Application, New Presentation Layer

The idea behind this approach is that you completely rewrite the presentation layer of the application—that is, the server pages–based front end of the system. On the other hand, you leave intact any business objects you might have and, to the extent possible, you don't touch the entire middle and data tiers. In the new, ASP.NET-driven presentation layer, you make use of Web server controls, data-binding, configuration, and all the features that make ASP.NET so cool and effective.

The connection between the COM-based middle tier and the managed presentation tier is ensured by the ADO.NET OLE DB data adapter class. (I'll cover ADO.NET in Chapter 5.) Methods on the OLE DB data adapter class are able to import an ADO *Recordset* into ADO.NET objects. In this way, you call your middle-tier objects from ASP.NET pages, get their output in the form of ADO *Recordset* objects, transform them into managed data containers, and link to the page's data-bound controls. Of course, this approach is recommended (and works) only if your middle-tier objects communicate with the rest of the system by exchanging ADO *Recordset* objects. You should also note that the OLE DB data adapter component provides a one-way data-binding mechanism. You should figure out a way to send an updated ADO *Recordset* back to the middle tier.

So much for ASP compatibility and migration. Let's see how to create full-blown ASP.NET applications using the king of all .NET programming tools—Visual Studio .NET.

## Setting Up ASP.NET Applications

To create an ASP.NET application, you need very few ingredients—pages, assemblies, a virtual directory, and maybe some ancillary files to provide for initialization and configuration. Once everything is in place and the virtual directory is properly set up, to test the application you simply point the browser to the URL of the application's main page. What you need to do to build a Web application is quite different from what you need to do to build, say, a Windows Forms application. In spite of these structural differences, Visual Studio .NET manages to unify the working model and successfully brings the familiar rapid application development (RAD) approach to the Web.

Much better than its Web predecessor—Visual InterDev—Visual Studio .NET lets you create ASP.NET pages as Web-based visual forms. You work on an empty surface that mimics the body of an HTML page and populate it with server controls picked from a palette of components. Once dropped on the Web form, the control can be configured using the Properties browser and moved around as appropriate. To handle the events fired by the control, you just select the event from a list or double-click the control in the designer area. If you find that all this eerily resembles the Visual Basic way of working, well, it's not coincidental!

## Creating a Visual Studio Project

When you create a new ASP.NET application with Visual Studio .NET, you specify a virtual path, not a physical directory. You pass Visual Studio .NET the URL of the virtual directory in which the project files are to be created. As shown in Figure 1-5, you also select the language for the project. Visual Studio .NET lets you create ASP.NET applications only in Visual Basic .NET and C#. (You can use J# only if you have installed the version 1.1 of the .NET Framework along with Visual Studio .NET 2003.)

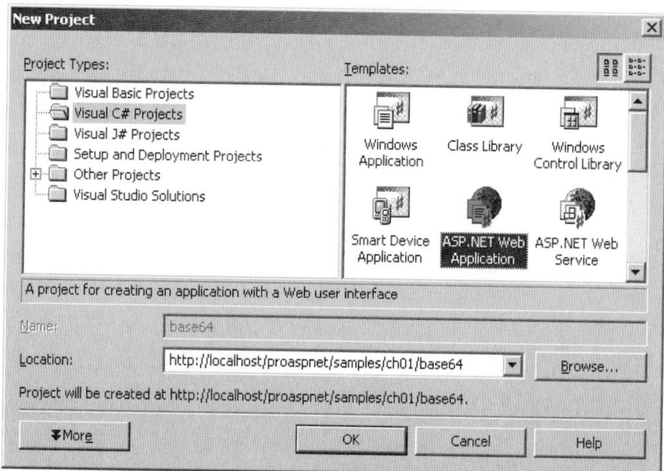


**Figure 1-5** Starting a new ASP.NET project with Visual Studio .NET 2003.

All the classes that the Visual Studio .NET wizard generates belong to a namespace named after the project. The classes will be compiled into an assembly that will be given the same name as the project. The assembly is created when you build the solution and put it in the *Bin* subdirectory of the virtual directory. The namespace name, as well as the name of the project's assembly, can be changed by right-clicking the project node in Solution Explorer, and choosing Properties. Figure 1-6 shows the project Property Pages dialog box for a project in Visual Studio .NET 2003.

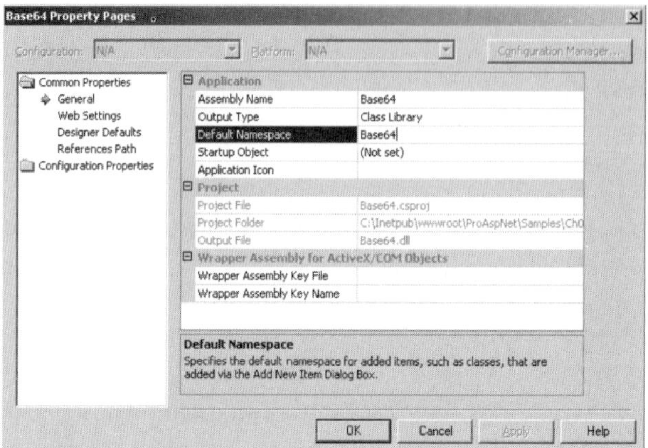


**Figure 1-6** Renaming assembly and default namespaces in Visual Studio .NET 2003.

Upon creation, the project includes an empty page named WebForm1.aspx. The page supports code-behind, meaning that all the code for the page resides in a separate class—the code-behind class. The name of the code-behind class matches the name of the .aspx file. (In Chapter 2, you'll learn more about code-behind classes.) As shown in the References node of Solution Explorer, an ASP.NET project references a few assemblies by default. They are: *System*, *System.Data*, *System.Drawing*, *System.Web*, and *System.Xml*.

> **Caution** The Visual Studio default procedure for naming newly created pages and related code-behind classes causes a little hassle when you have multiple pages with the same name, even though they might be located in different folders. Visual Studio .NET doesn't consider that, say, the new default.aspx page you're adding to the project actually resides in a different folder and indeed has a unique path. Visual Studio .NET correctly detects that a *Default* class already exists in the namespace and automatically renames the class adding a trailing index (for example, *Default1*). If you don't like this approach—and you'd be wise not to—either give the class a new name or, better yet, call it *Default*, but define the class in a child namespace to reflect the fact that the file belongs to a different directory.

## The Project Files

Aside from the pages, classes, and resources that actually comprise the application, a number of additional files form a Visual Studio .NET ASP.NET project. In a C# project named MyProject, they would be:

- **MyProject.csproj** This XML file contains build and file information for the project. The *<Build>* section contains the application settings (root namespace, output type, and default client script) and the assemblies to link. The *<Files>* section contains the list of the files in the project. A file is identified by a relative path, a build action, a type, and optionally a dependency. To view the content of this file, use a text editor or make a copy and change the extension to .xml.
- **MyProject.csproj.webinfo** This XML file contains the path of the .csproj file expressed as a URL. The information in this file complements the content of the previous file in that the .csproj file doesn't contain absolute path information.
- **MyProject.vsdisco** This Web service dynamic discovery file is used to track the project's Web references—that is, project references that point to Web services.
- **AssemblyInfo.cs** This codeless C# file is filled only with attributes. It contains information to sign the assembly being generated as well as general assembly information such as the build number, copyright text, and the company and product name.
- **Global.asax** This optional file contains code for responding to application-level events raised by ASP.NET. Visual Studio .NET always adds such a file to its ASP.NET projects. Just as with Web pages, the global.asax file can be constructed using code-behind, thus delegating a background class to implement all needed event handlers. All global.asax files created by Visual Studio .NET are code-behind.
- **Global.asax.cs** This is the code-behind class for global.asax. The class is named *Global* by default and inherits from *HttpApplication*. We'll cover global.asax in Chapter 13.
- **Global.asax.resx** This is the XML resource file for the global.asax.cs file, and it's marked as being dependent on the global.asax.cs file. By default, the file contains a standard block of information that specifies the schema of the contained resources. You can fill a .resx file with name/value pairs of application-specific data.

- **Web.config** This XML file contains configuration information for the Web application. Multiple configuration files, all named web.config, can appear in multiple directories on an ASP.NET Web application. We'll discuss the web.config file in detail in Chapter 12.

Each ASP.NET page included in the project features three files: .aspx, .cs, and .resx. The .aspx file contains the layout of the page; the .cs contains the code-behind class; the .resx file contains resources associated with the page. You should note, however, that having three files per page is simply the Visual Studio way of working. In no way is this a strict syntactical or architectural requirement.

> **Note** A Visual Basic .NET ASP.NET project contains an extra file—styles.css. This file contains the default cascading style sheet (CSS) definitions for the HTML tags you can use throughout the project.

## Creating the Web Forms Page

Creating a Web Forms page is as easy as picking controls from the Visual Studio toolbox and dropping them onto the surface that represents the page. If you're like me and feel more comfortable when you can see some HTML code every now and then, you'll consider it good news that you can switch between HTML and design view at any time with a simple click. The following code snippet is the HTML code being generated for an empty ASP.NET page belonging to a project named Base64:

```
<%@ Page language="c#" Codebehind="WebForm1.aspx.cs"
    AutoEventWireup="false" Inherits="Base64.WebForm1" %>
<!DOCTYPE HTML PUBLIC "-//W3C//DTD HTML 4.0 Transitional//EN" >
<HTML>
    <HEAD>
        <title>WebForm</title>
        <meta name="GENERATOR" Content="Microsoft Visual Studio 7.1">
        <meta name="CODE_LANGUAGE" Content="C#">
        <meta name="vs_defaultClientScript" content="JavaScript">
        <meta name="vs_targetSchema"
            content="http://schemas.microsoft.com/intellisense/ie5">
    </HEAD>
    <body MS_POSITIONING="GridLayout">
        <form id="Form1" method="post" runat="server">
             
        </form>
    </body>
</HTML>
```

The page has a code-behind class in the file webform1.aspx.cs that explicitly wires up to all the page events it needs to handle. (*AutoEventWireup* is purposefully set to *false*.) The name of the class that implements the page behavior is *Base64.WebForm1*.

The *vs_defaultClientScript* meta tag indicates that the page will use JavaScript for client-side scripting. More interesting is the role of the *vs_targetSchema* tag. It contains a Uniform Resource Identifier (URI) that uniquely identifies the HTML schema being supported. By default, Visual Studio .NET generates HTML code targeted to Internet Explorer 5.0. You can change meta tag settings using the project Property Pages dialog box shown in Figure 1-7. You display the dialog box by right-clicking the project in Solution Explorer and choosing Properties.

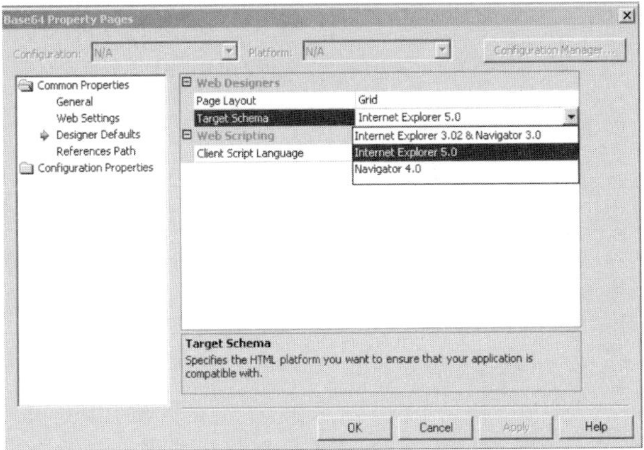


**Figure 1-7** Choosing a target HTML schema for the application.

In the HTML code examined a moment ago, you might have noticed the MS_POSITIONING attribute within the *<body>* tag. The *GridLayout* value lets you place HTML controls on the form at absolute positions, similar to the procedure you'd follow with a Windows Forms application. The *GridLayout* mode leverages the underlying browser support for CSS absolute positioning. However, not all browsers support this feature, so this will probably be a setting you want to change to safely reach a wider audience. From the project Property Pages dialog box shown in Figure 1-7, set the page layout attribute of the Web designer to *Flow*.

> **Tip** You can also set the page layout attribute from the Properties browser window. Select the DOCUMENT view from the top drop-down list in the Properties window, and scroll the list to the *pageLayout* property. The property list also lets you declaratively set graphical settings for the page, including margins, colors, and styles.

After you change the page layout from *Grid* to *Flow*, the *<body>* tag is rendered without the MS_POSITIONING attribute. Note, though, that if you change the page layout attribute on a nonempty page, existing controls maintain their absolute positions and the new settings are applied only to new controls. Let's rename the page and add a label and a text box (both Web server controls) to the page as shown in Figure 1-8.

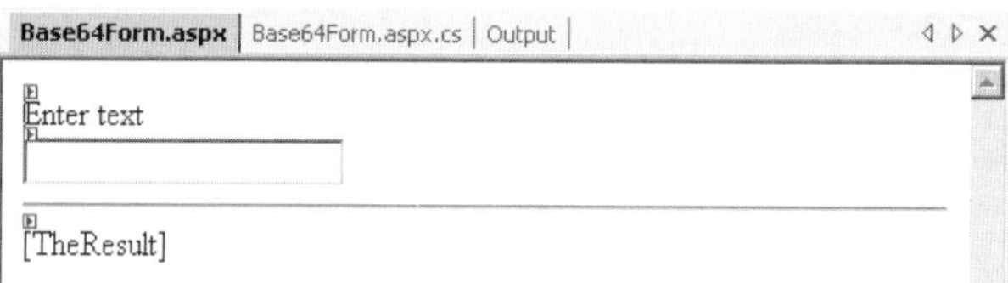


**Figure 1-8** The visual designer completed with a few server controls.

On the Web Forms tab of the Toolbox, add a *Label* control and a *TextBox* control. Set the *Text* property of the *Label* control to "Enter text", and the *ID* property of the *TextBox* control to "TheText". Here's the HTML code that's added:

```
<form id="Form1" method="post" runat="server">
    <asp:Label id="Label1" runat="server">Enter text</asp:Label>
    <br>
    <asp:TextBox id="TheText" runat="server"></asp:TextBox>
</form>
```

Only a few HTML elements such as the inline frame (*<iframe>*) and page-break (*<br>*) can't be added visually. However, as shown in Figure 1-9, the Visual Studio IntelliSense feature intercepts your typing and prompts suggestions.

**Figure 1-9** IntelliSense at work trying to make your programming life easier.

To top off the Web Forms, let's add a button and connect it to some concrete code. The *ID* property is set to "DoIt" and the *Text* property is set to "Encode…". The output generated by the code behind the button will be displayed through a new *Label* control named "TheResult". Figure 1-10 shows the form.

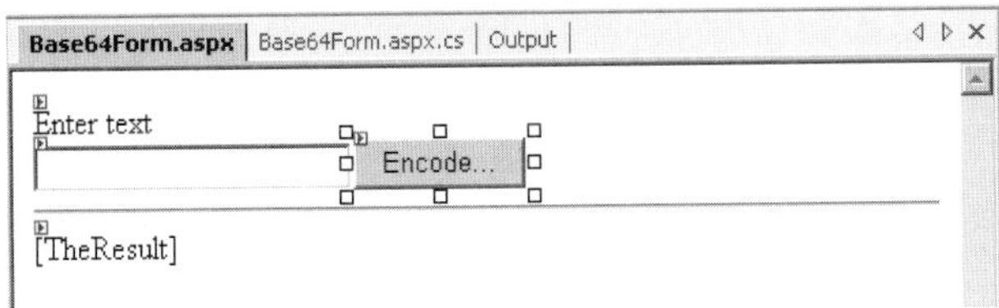


**Figure 1-10** A submit button has been added to the page.

```
<form id="Form1" method="post" runat="server">
    <asp:Label id="Label1" runat="server">Enter text</asp:Label><br>
    <asp:TextBox id="TheText" runat="server"></asp:TextBox>
    <asp:Button id="DoIt" runat="server" Text="Encode..." />
    <hr>
    <asp:Label id="TheResult" runat="server" />
</form>
```

The simplest way to add some code to the button's click event is by double-clicking the button in the Web Forms editor. Visual Studio changes the view and then prompts you with some C# code—the code-behind class:

```
public class WebForm1 : System.Web.UI.Page
{
    protected System.Web.UI.WebControls.Label Label1;
    protected System.Web.UI.WebControls.Button DoIt;
    protected System.Web.UI.WebControls.Label TheResult;
    protected System.Web.UI.WebControls.TextBox TheText;

    private void Page_Load(object sender, EventArgs e)
    {
        // Put user code to initialize the page here
```

```
        }

        override protected void OnInit(EventArgs e)
        {
            InitializeComponent();
            base.OnInit(e);
        }

        private void InitializeComponent()
        {
            this.DoIt.Click += new System.EventHandler(this.DoIt_Click);
            this.Load += new System.EventHandler(this.Page_Load);
        }
        private void DoIt_Click(object sender, System.EventArgs e)
        {
            // Execute when the button is clicked...
        }
}
```

Interestingly, the link between the button-click event and the code is established directly in the code-behind class. The class method *DoIt_Click* runs when the user clicks the button. The same link can be established in the .aspx code through the *OnClick* attribute of the *<asp:Button>* element.

```
<asp:Button id="DoIt" runat="server" Text="Encode..."
    onclick="DoIt_Click" />
```

As you can see, though, this approach is much less neat and elegant because it violates the principle of separation between the code and the layout of the page.

At this point, let's complete the example by adding some significant code to the button handler. The idea is to take the text written in the text box, encode it as a Base64 string, and display it. The following code shows how we fill the *DoIt_Click* method:

```
private void DoIt_Click(object sender, EventArgs e)
{
    string buf = TheText.Text;
    TheResult.Text = ConvertToBase64String(buf);
}

private string ConvertToBase64String(string input)
{
    byte[] info = Encoding.Unicode.GetBytes(input);

    // Convert the binary input into Base64 UUEncoded output.
    // Each 3 byte sequence in the source data becomes a 4 byte
    // sequence in the character array.
    long dataLength = (long) ((4.0d/3.0d) * info.Length);

    // If length is not divisible by 4, go up to the next multiple of 4.
```

```
    if(dataLength % 4 != 0)
        dataLength += 4 - dataLength % 4;

    // Allocate the output buffer
    char[] base64CharArray = new char[dataLength];

    // Converting...
    Convert.ToBase64CharArray(info, 0, info.Length, base64CharArray, 0);

    // Display the converted data
    return new string(base64CharArray);
}
```

The core code of the *ConvertToBase64String* method has been borrowed from the MSDN documentation. To use the *Encoding* class, you must import the *System.Text* namespace. Figure 1-11 shows the page in action.

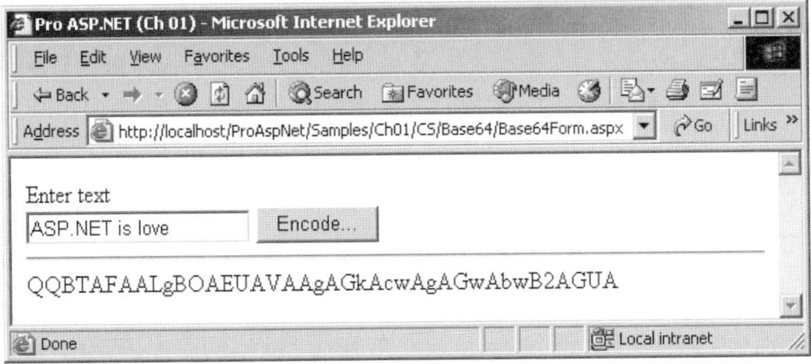


**Figure 1-11** ASP.NET is love…even if encoded as Base64.

## Building and Debugging

To build and run the ASP.NET application, you simply click the Start button and wait for something—typically an Internet Explorer window—to pop up. Visual Studio .NET compiles all the classes in the project into an assembly and gives it the name of the project. The assembly is created in the Bin subdirectory of the source virtual directory. The Bin subdirectory is specifically created during the setup of the project. The Bin directory of a virtual directory is the principal location in which ASP.NET attempts to locate the assemblies needed to run a page.

> **Note** If you run a manually created page from within the root of your Web server—typically the \inetpub\wwwroot directory—you should put any needed assemblies in the \inetpub\wwwroot\bin subdirectory. In most cases, this directory does not exist and will have to be created manually.

Once the project assembly has been successfully built, Visual Studio .NET auto-attaches to the ASP.NET run-time process—aspnet_wp.exe—for debugging purposes. Next, it opens the start page of the application, causing the browser to issue a page request to the ASP.NET runtime. Once the runtime has loaded all the assemblies and processed the page source, the browser appears with the final HTML output. As long as you compiled the project in debug mode (the default), you can set a few breakpoints in the page class source and step into the code, as shown in Figure 1-12.

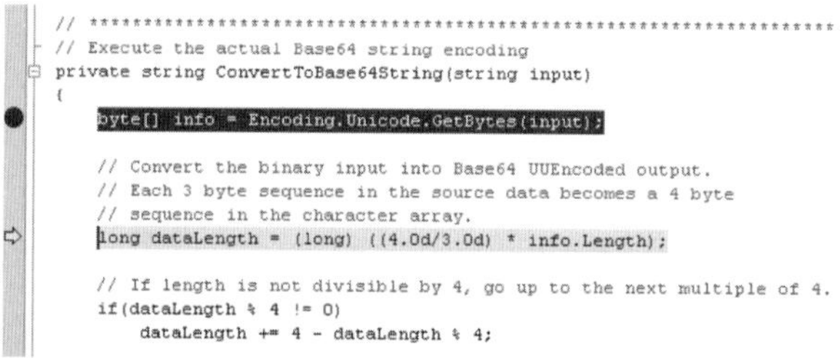

```
// ****************************************************************
// Execute the actual Base64 string encoding
private string ConvertToBase64String(string input)
{
    byte[] info = Encoding.Unicode.GetBytes(input);

    // Convert the binary input into Base64 UUEncoded output.
    // Each 3 byte sequence in the source data becomes a 4 byte
    // sequence in the character array.
    long dataLength = (long) ((4.0d/3.0d) * info.Length);

    // If length is not divisible by 4, go up to the next multiple of 4.
    if(dataLength % 4 != 0)
        dataLength += 4 - dataLength % 4;
```

**Figure 1-12** Stepping into the code of the page using the Visual Studio .NET integrated debugger.

> **Note** Many practical reasons justify the Visual Studio .NET choice of implementing a full object-oriented approach to Web Forms application development. Even more than design considerations about code and layout separation was the need to support step-by-step debugging, syntax-coloring, and RAD features while maintaining a uniform, consistent, and cross-project approach to development. In this context, having a class behind each page is a wise and timely choice.
>
> This said, if you've been a former brave-heart Win32 SDK programmer, bear in mind that a Visual Studio–generated ASP.NET page is to an ordinary ASP.NET page roughly what an MFC application is to an SDK-based Win32 application.

## Deploying the Application

Of all the files that form a Visual Studio .NET project, only a few are actually needed to run the application on a production server. For example, you don't need any of the .cs files. For the sample project, only the following files need to be deployed: base64form.aspx, global.asax, web.config, and base64.vsdisco, as well as the project's assembly. Consider also that global.asax, web.config, and base64.vsdisco are optional files, which means that by using them you can better configure the application. However, choosing not to use them does not affect the functionality of the application.

Deploying a Web application is a two-step operation: create and configure the virtual directory, and copy the needed files. Visual Studio .NET makes creating a Web setup application a snap. You just create a new type of project—Web Setup Project—select the files to copy, and build the project. Figure 1-13 shows the user interface of the setup project.

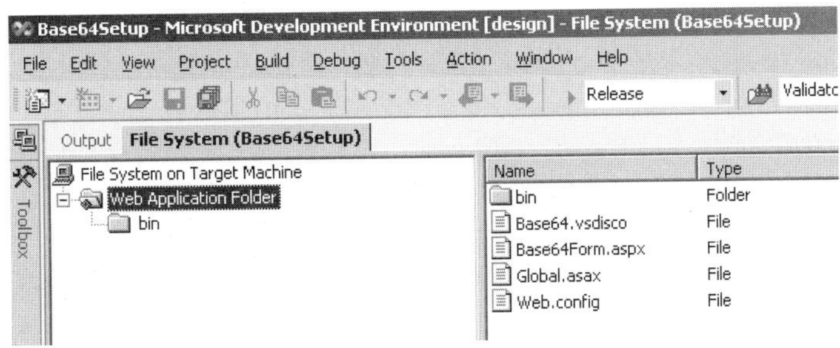


**Figure 1-13** Creating a Web setup project.

The Web Application Folder node represents the virtual directory of the new application on the target machine. The property box lets you configure the settings of the new virtual directory. For example, the *AllowDirectoryBrowsing* property lets you assign browsing permission to the IIS virtual directory you will create. You can also control the virtual directory name, application execute permissions, level of isolation, and default page. The Bin subfolder is automatically created, but you can ask the setup to create and populate as many subfolders as you need.

When you build the project, you obtain a Windows Installer .msi file that constitutes the setup to ship to your clients. The default installer supports repairing and uninstalling the application. The setup you obtain in this way—which is the simplest you can get—does not contain the .NET Framework, which must be installed on the target machine or explicitly included in the setup project itself. I'll make more real-world considerations about deployment of ASP.NET applications in Chapter 12.

## Multilanguage Projects with Visual Studio .NET

ASP.NET projects created with Visual Studio .NET don't allow you to use multiple languages. In other words, you can't have in the same application .aspx pages that use Visual Basic .NET and .aspx pages that use C#. Note, though, that this is a Visual Studio .NET limitation, not an ASP.NET limitation. To work around the issue, you can write your pages (in any language) without the code-behind feature and import them in the project using the Add Existing Item menu. In this case, though, you have all the page-specific code concentrated in the *<script>* section. In addition, no IntelliSense and syntax-coloring facilities will be provided to edit the *<script>* section.

## The *CodeBehind* Attribute in Visual Studio .NET

When you try to add an existing page to a project, Visual Studio .NET proves a bit choosy: it first complains, asks for confirmation, and then looks for a code-behind class for the page. The code-behind class, though, cannot be any source or compiled class that inherits from *Page*. To meet the requirements of Visual Studio .NET, a code-behind class must fulfill a special naming convention and be written in the same language used throughout the project. For example, a page named MyPage.aspx can only have a code-behind class named MyPage.aspx.cs if C# is the project language.

Visual Studio .NET tracks the relationship between the page and the code-behind class through an undocumented *CodeBehind* attribute in the *@Page* directive. The content of the *CodeBehind* attribute cannot be edited from within Visual Studio .NET and, if you edit it with another text editor, you get an error as soon as you reload the page within Visual Studio .NET.

## Visual Studio *CodeBehind* vs. ASP.NET *Src*

Visual Studio utilizes the *CodeBehind* attribute only for internal editing purposes. This probably explains why the attribute is not even mentioned in the MSDN documentation. *CodeBehind* is not intended to be used at the application level and, in fact, the ASP.NET runtime just ignores it. Let's consider the following header, typical of an ASP.NET page developed with Visual Studio .NET:

```
<%@ Page Language="c#" Inherits="ProAspNet.MyBasePage"
    CodeBehind="MyBasePage.cs" %>
```

The ASP.NET runtime expects to find the code for the page in a class named *ProAspNet.MyBasePage* located in one of the reachable assemblies. There's no need to have in the page folder the C# file referenced in the *CodeBehind* attribute—that piece of information is used only by the Visual Studio .NET project.

If you want the .aspx page to inherit from a local .cs or .vb file, use the *Src* attribute of the *@Page* directive instead. You should note that, in turn, Visual Studio .NET ignores the *Src* attribute. Using both *Src* and *CodeBehind* in a page does not result in an error, but it's a programming practice I strongly discourage because of the side-effects and confusion it could generate.

> **Tip** If you need to develop the ASP.NET application using different languages, group the various pages in multiple language-homogeneous projects. Next, make all projects share the same virtual directory. To keep all projects within reach all the time, group them in the same Visual Studio .NET solution.

## The Web Matrix Editor

Developing code for ASP applications has never been particularly easy in spite of the availability of third-party products and Visual InterDev. A much better lot is reserved for ASP.NET applications, which have a comprehensive and easily usable integrated development environment (IDE) in Visual Studio .NET. Visual Studio .NET, though, is certainly not the only tool available for quickly and effectively building ASP.NET applications. Furthermore, Visual Studio .NET is a full-blown IDE designed to build multiple types of applications, including Windows applications, console applications, Web services, and setup programs. Other commercial products focus more on the building of ASP.NET-specific solutions. One of the most complete products is Macromedia Dreamweaver MX.

ASP.NET Web Matrix is another story. Web Matrix is a community-supported, totally free tool and has been specifically designed for ASP.NET applications. To get it, you simply need a 1.2 MB download from the ASP.NET community Web site. The URL is *http://www.asp.net/webmatrix/download.aspx*. Web Matrix provides most of the features of cutting-edge code editors (such as syntax-coloring, WYSIWYG designers, and different views of the code), and although it has different goals than Visual Studio .NET, in some ways Web Matrix complements it.

### Visual Studio .NET vs. Web Matrix

Let's say it up front: Visual Studio .NET is much more powerful than Web Matrix. While Visual Studio .NET is the must-have tool for building complex, professional ASP.NET Web applications, Web Matrix is a more compact, efficient, and made-to-measure tool for those frequent situations in which Visual Studio .NET would be overkill. For example, in a previous comment, I noted that Visual Studio .NET forces you to always use the code-behind approach to develop ASP.NET pages. Visual Studio .NET insists on a project-based approach, which certainly makes a lot of sense for many real-world projects. In contrast, Web Matrix is designed around the standalone ASP.NET page. It supports only pages with inline code and lets you develop applications as a set of standalone pages and resources.

> **Note** Web Matrix was created entirely using .NET technologies! In particular, the team used Windows Forms to set up the user interface and Web services to communicate with the back-end system on *http://www.asp.net*. The code was written in C# and spans about 150,000 lines of code, resulting in an installed base of about 2.5 MB.

### What Web Matrix Doesn't Provide

By design, Web Matrix lacks a number of user-interface features that are available in Visual Studio .NET. A short list includes primarily IntelliSense support, statement completion and code tips, debugging support, version source control for multideveloper projects, and almost all class and code designers you find in Visual Studio .NET.

Note also that Web Matrix can be used only to create ASP.NET and mobile applications and Web services. No support is provided for building Windows Forms and Windows NT services and languages other than Visual Basic .NET and C#.

> **Caution** If you make use of classes in your Web Matrix project, bear in mind that, unlike Visual Studio .NET, Web Matrix does not compile your classes in assemblies. To accomplish this, you must resort to the command-line compiler. The following code shows a typical command line for compiling a C# and Visual Basic .NET class:
>
> ```
> csc.exe /r:system.dll myclass.c
> vbc.exe /r:system.dll myclass.vb
> ```
>
> The */r* switch is used to link a needed assembly. You get the above compilers with the .NET Framework installation. They are located in the \Microsoft.NET\Framework\v1.1.4322 directory under the Windows folder. Note that for ASP.NET 1.0, the final directory of the path changes to v1.0.3705.

### What Web Matrix Does Provide

As a community-supported product, Web Matrix is rigorously built around the feedback users provide through the *http://www.asp.net/webmatrix* Web site. Given this, it comes as no surprise that the overall user interface presents handy features and facilities you won't find even in Visual Studio .NET.

The page you're editing provides four views—a graphical view of the page, HTML markup, code (the *<script>* section), and the full .aspx file. The

Web Matrix toolbox (shown in Figure 1-14) separates custom controls from standard HTML and Web server controls and provides a couple of extra tabs for code snippets and code builders.

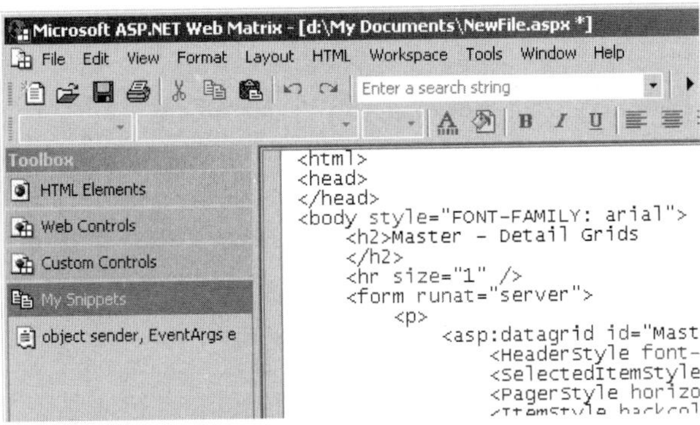


**Figure 1-14** The My Snippets tab shows off the toolbox of Web Matrix.

My Snippets is a tab similar to the Visual Studio Clipboard Ring but with a couple of key differences: you can drag and drop text onto it and the snippets are persisted to disk, allowing you to retrieve them the next time Web Matrix starts up. The Code Builders tab appears only when you're in code view mode and provides a list of wizards to build commonplace pieces of code such as database commands or code to send an e-mail.

Another interesting aspect of the Web Matrix user interface is that it provides a lot of predefined templates for commonly used types of pages. Figure 1-15 shows some of them.

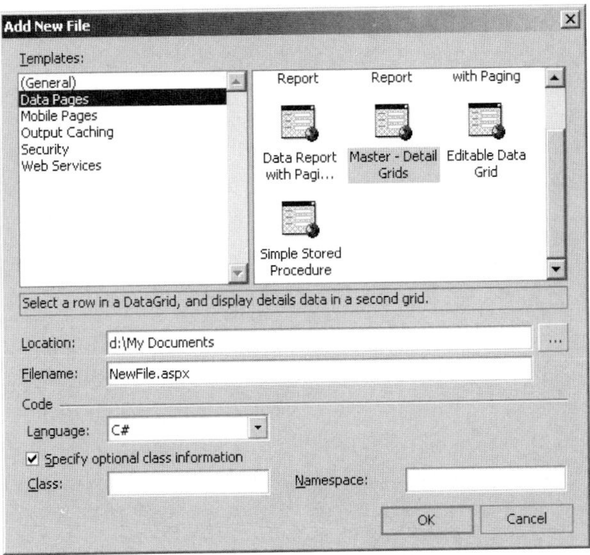


**Figure 1-15** Some of the Web Matrix page templates.

As you can see, Web Matrix provides standard pieces of code to implement editable grids, master/detail views, and pageable reports. Other templates provide for login and logout pages, cacheable pages, Web services, SOAP headers, and pages for mobile controls.

As a final note, consider that Web Matrix ships with FTP client support, which means you can develop ASP.NET applications remotely and host them at any provider that offers both ASP.NET and FTP support.

> **Note** Web Matrix does not require IIS on a machine used for development purposes. Web Matrix, in fact, includes its own mini-Web server capable of hosting the ASP.NET runtime locally. (I'll cover this ASP.NET feature in Chapter 24.) This mini-Web server—codenamed Cassini—handles only local requests and does not allow remote connections. Of course, you need IIS running on the production server to deploy ASP.NET applications developed using Web Matrix or any other product.

## Help and Community

Web Matrix comes with no compiled help files. All the support you get from the Help menu and Community page comes from the ASP.NET Web site and is gathered through Web services calls. Figure 1-16 shows the page with all the links to documentation, Web sites, forums, and other online resources.

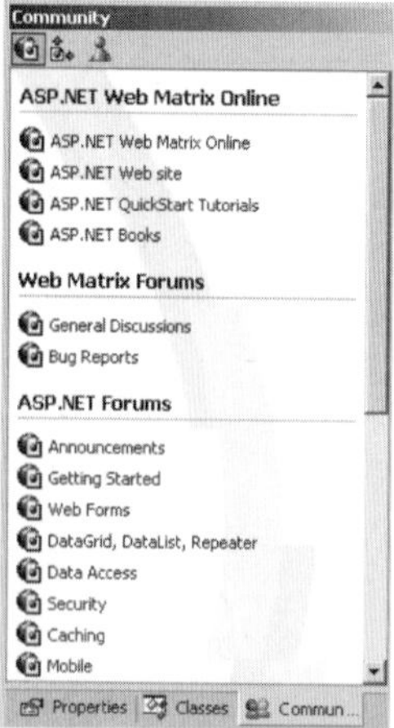


**Figure 1-16** The Community tab with links to online resources.

Web Matrix also distributes a class browser with direct links to the Web or local documentation. In terms of information retrieval, the class browser can be as useful as the official .NET Framework documentation, but it provides a class-based view of the information. To display the class browser, double-click a class in the Classes window. Figure 1-17 shows the class browser.

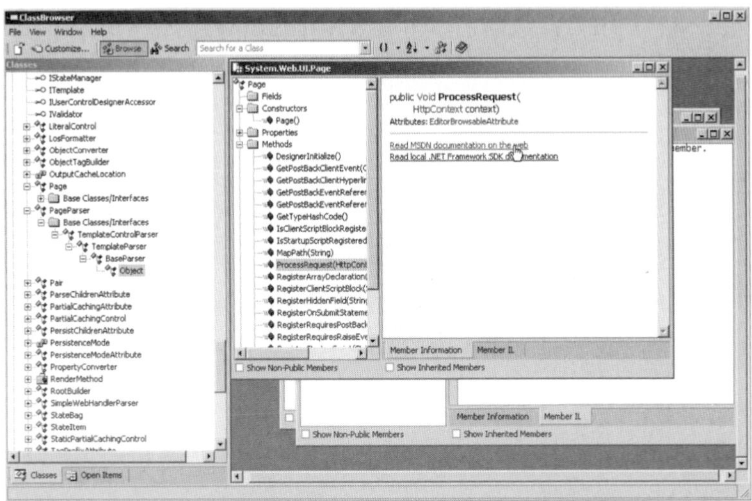

**Figure 1-17** The Web Matrix class browser in action.

# Conclusion

In this chapter, we discussed the Web Forms model of ASP.NET as a new and, in many aspects, revolutionary approach to Web programming. As part of the .NET Framework and therefore designed completely from scratch, ASP.NET is perceived as the inevitable successor to ASP. It is a Web development platform that more than one million developers have chosen over the past few years.

The programmer affinity for ASP and ASP.NET and compatibility between the two platforms is only part of the success of the approach. The key aspect of ASP.NET is that it is part of the .NET Framework. As such, it allows you to take full advantage of features of the common-language runtime, such as type safety, inheritance, language interoperability, and versioning. We analyzed the component model of ASP.NET and reviewed the main differences between ASP and ASP.NET you should take into account if you have an existing ASP application to upgrade or maintain. Visual Studio .NET is probably the most feature-rich and professional tool to employ for building ASP.NET applications. Web Matrix is a free ASP.NET-specific development tool with unique and handy features.

ASP.NET promotes a programming model that, although built on top of the stateless HTTP protocol, appears to be stateful and event-driven to programmers. The abstraction layer that performs the magic is the Web Forms model, whose underpinnings will be tackled and unveiled in the next chapter.

## Resources

- ASP.NET: Web Forms Let You Drag and Drop Your Way to Powerful Web Apps (*http://msdn.microsoft.com/msdnmag/issues/01/05/webforms*)
- How to Share Session State Between Classic ASP and ASP.NET (*http://msdn.microsoft.com/library/en-us/dnaspp/html/converttoaspnet.asp*)
- NET Migration Case Study: Using ASP.NET to Build the beta.visualstudio.net Web Site (*http://msdn.microsoft.com/msdnmag/issues/01/09/migration*)
- Migrating to ASP.NET: Key Considerations (*http://msdn.microsoft.com/library/en-us/dnaspp/html/aspnetmigrissues.asp*)
- *Debugging Applications for Microsoft .NET and Microsoft Windows*, by John Robbins (Microsoft Press, 2003)

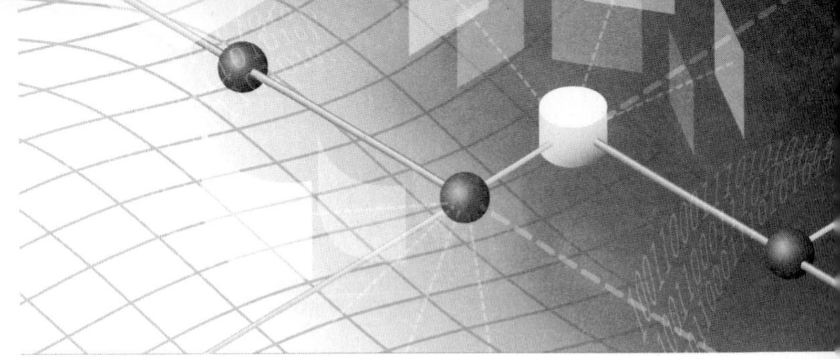

# 2

# Web Forms Internals

*Few things are harder to put up with than the annoyance of a good example.*
—*Mark Twain*

ASP.NET pages are dynamically compiled on demand when first required in the context of a Web application. Dynamic compilation is not specific to ASP.NET pages (.aspx files); it also occurs with Web Services (.asmx files), Web user controls (.ascx files), HTTP handlers (.ashx files), and ASP.NET application files such as the global.asax file. But what does it mean exactly that an ASP.NET page is compiled? How does the ASP.NET runtime turn the source code of an .aspx file into a .NET Framework compilable class? And what becomes of the dynamically created assembly when the associated source file gets updated? And finally, what happens once a compiled assembly has been associated with the requested .aspx URL?

Don't be too surprised to find all these questions crowding your mind at this time. Their presence indicates you're on the right track and ready to learn more about the underpinnings of the Web Forms programming model.

## Executing ASP.NET Pages

The expression *compiled page* is at once precise as well as vague and generic. It is *precise* because it tells you exactly what happens when a URL with an .aspx extension is requested. It is *vague* because it doesn't specify which module launches and controls the compiler and what actual input the compiler receives on the command line. Finally, it is *generic* because it omits a fair number of details.

In this chapter, we simply aim to unveil all the mysteries fluttering around the dynamic compilation of ASP.NET pages. We'll do this by considering the actions performed on the Web server, and which modules perform them, when a request arrives for an .aspx page.

> **Note** Much of the content of this chapter is based on the behavior of the ASP.NET runtime version 1.0 and version 1.1 with Internet Information Services (IIS) 5.0 serving as the Web server. Some key differences apply when using Windows Server 2003 and IIS 6.0. Any significant differences that affect the ASP.NET way of working are noted. Throughout this chapter, IIS is always IIS 5.0 unless another version is explicitly mentioned.
>
> The first part of this chapter discusses under-the-hood details that might not interest you, as they aren't strictly concerned with the development of ASP.NET applications. Reading this chapter in its entirety is not essential to understanding fundamental techniques of ASP.NET programming. So, if you want, you can jump directly to the "The Event Model" section, which is the section in which we discuss what happens once an ASP.NET page has been requested and starts being processed.

## The IIS Resource Mappings

All resources you can access on an IIS-based Web server are grouped by their file extension. Any incoming request is then assigned to a particular run-time module for actual processing. Modules that can handle Web resources within the context of IIS are ISAPI extensions—that is, plain-old Win32 DLLs that expose, much like an interface, a bunch of API functions with predefined names and prototypes. IIS and ISAPI extensions use these DLL entries as a sort of private communication protocol. When IIS needs an ISAPI extension to accomplish a certain task, it simply loads the DLL and calls the appropriate function with valid arguments. Although the ISAPI documentation doesn't mention an ISAPI extension as an interface, it is just that—a module that implements a well-known programming interface.

When the request for a resource arrives, IIS first verifies the type of the resource. Static resources such as images, text files, HTML pages, and scriptless ASP pages are resolved directly by IIS without the involvement of external modules. IIS accesses the file on the local Web server and flushes its contents to the output console so that the requesting browser can get it. Resources that require server-side elaboration are passed on to the registered module. For example, ASP pages are processed by an ISAPI extension named asp.dll. In general, when the resource is associated with executable code, IIS hands the request to that executable for further processing. Files with an .aspx extension are assigned to an ISAPI extension named aspnet_isapi.dll, as shown in Figure 2-1.

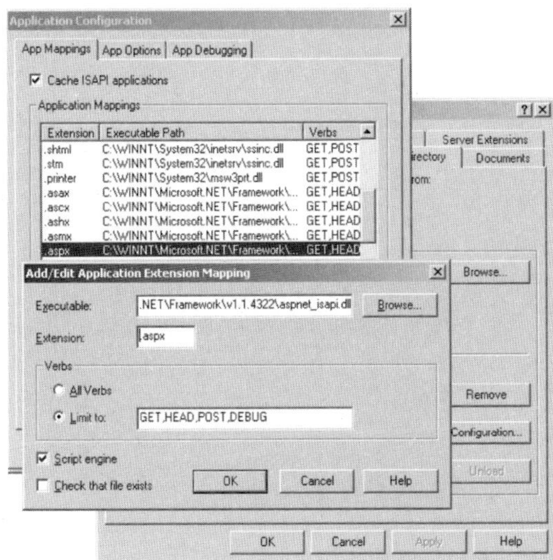

**Figure 2-1** The IIS application mappings for resources with an .aspx extension.

Just like any other ISAPI extension, aspnet_isapi.dll is hosted by the IIS 5.0 process—the executable named inetinfo.exe. Resource mappings are stored in the IIS metabase. Upon installation, ASP.NET modifies the IIS metabase to make sure that aspnet_isapi.dll can handle all the resources identified by the extensions listed in Table 2-1.

**Table 2-1 IIS Application Mappings for aspnet_isapi.dll**

| Extension | Resource Type |
|---|---|
| .asax | ASP.NET application files. The typical example is global.asax. |
| .ascx | Web user control files used to embed pagelets in ASP.NET pages. |
| .ashx | HTTP handlers, namely managed modules that interact with the low-level request and response services of IIS. (See Chapter 23.) |
| .asmx | Files that implement XML Web services. |
| .aspx | Files that represent ASP.NET pages. |

*(continued)*

**Table 2-1 IIS Application Mappings for aspnet_isapi.dll** *(continued)*

| Extension | Resource Type |
|---|---|
| .axd | Extension that identifies the ASP.NET trace-viewer application (trace.axd). When invoked in a virtual folder, the trace viewer displays trace information for every page in the application. (See Chapter 4.) |
| .rem | Fake resource used to qualify the Uniform Resource Identifier (URI) of a .NET Remoting object hosted by IIS. |
| .soap | Same as .rem. |

In addition, the aspnet_isapi.dll extension handles other typical Microsoft Visual Studio .NET extensions such as .cs, .csproj, .vb, .vbproj, .licx, .config, .resx, .webinfo, and .vsdisco. Other extensions added with Visual Studio .NET 2003 for J# projects are .java, .jsl, .resources, .vjsproj.

The ASP.NET ISAPI extension doesn't process the .aspx file but acts as a dispatcher. It collects all the information available about the invoked URL and the underlying resource, and it routes the request toward another distinct process—the ASP.NET worker process.

## The ASP.NET Worker Process

The ASP.NET worker process represents the ASP.NET runtime environment. It consists of a Win32 unmanaged executable named aspnet_wp.exe, which hosts the .NET common language runtime (CLR). This process is the executable you need to attach to in order to debug ASP.NET applications. The ASP.NET worker process activates the HTTP pipeline that will actually process the page request. The HTTP pipeline is a collection of .NET Framework classes that take care of compiling the page assembly and instantiating the related page class.

The connection between aspnet_isapi.dll and aspnet_wp.exe is established through a *named pipe*—a Win32 mechanism for transferring data over process boundaries. As the name suggests, a named pipe works like a pipe: you enter data in one end, and the same data comes out the other end. Pipes can be established both to connect local processes and processes running on remote machines. Figure 2-2 illustrates the ASP.NET layer built on top of IIS.

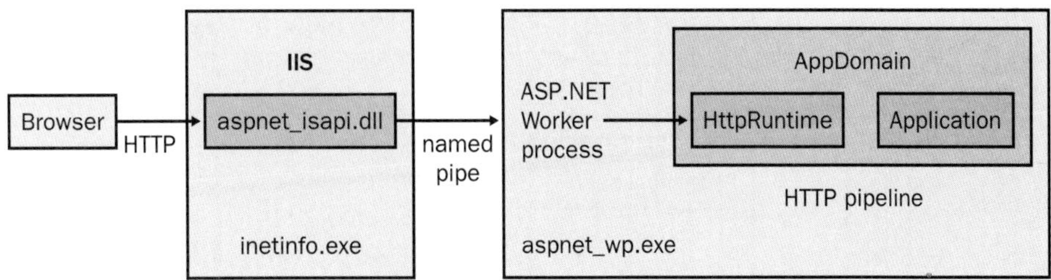


**Figure 2-2** IIS receives page requests and forwards them to the ASP.NET runtime.

## How the ASP.NET Runtime Works

A single copy of the worker process runs all the time and hosts all the active Web applications. The only exception to this situation is when you have a Web server with multiple CPUs. In this case, you can configure the ASP.NET runtime so that multiple worker processes run, one for each available CPU. A model in which multiple processes run on multiple CPUs in a single server machine is known as a *Web garden* and is controlled by attributes on the *<processModel>* section in the machine.config file. (I'll cover ASP.NET configuration files in Chapter 12.)

When a single worker process is used by all CPUs and controls all Web applications, it doesn't necessarily mean that no process isolation is achieved. Each Web application is, in fact, identified with its virtual directory and belongs to a distinct application domain, commonly referred to as an AppDomain. A new AppDomain is created within the ASP.NET worker process whenever a client addresses a virtual directory for the first time. After creating the new AppDomain, the ASP.NET runtime loads all the needed assemblies and passes control to the HTTP pipeline to actually service the request.

If a client requests a page from an already running Web application, the ASP.NET runtime simply forwards the request to the existing AppDomain associated with that virtual directory. All the assemblies needed to process the page are now ready to use because they were compiled upon the first call. Figure 2-3 provides a more general view of the ASP.NET runtime.

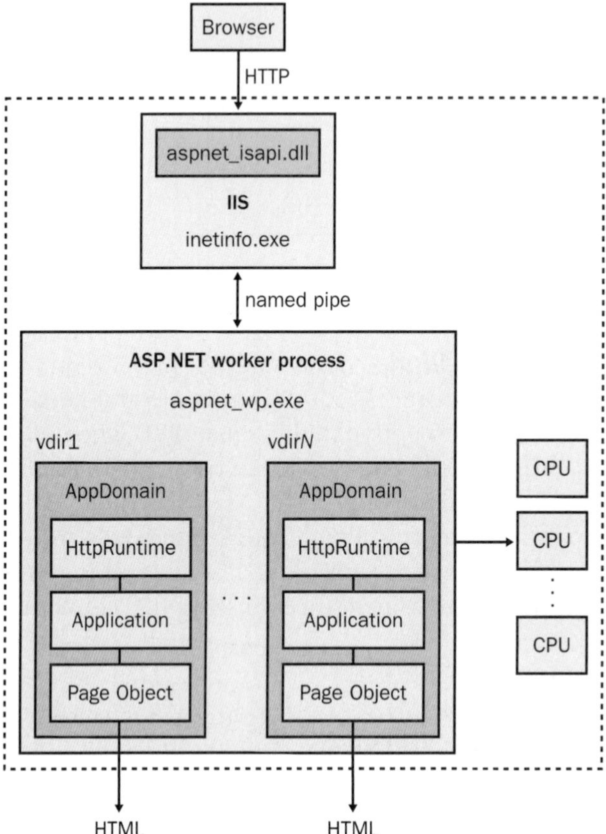


**Figure 2-3** The ASP.NET runtime and the various AppDomains.

> **Tip** To configure the ASP.NET runtime to work as a Web garden—that is, to have more worker processes running on multiple CPUs in the same physical server—open the machine.config file and locate the *<processModel>* section. Next, you set the *webGarden* attribute to *true* (because it is *false* by default) and the *cpuMask* attribute to a bit mask in which each 1 identifies an available and affined CPU. If ASP.NET is running with IIS 6.0, you must use the IIS Manager to configure Web gardens. In this case, the settings in machine.config are ignored. If *webGarden* is *false*, the *cpuMask* setting is ignored and only one process is scheduled regardless of how many CPUs you have.
>
> *Note that the documentation available with version 1.0 of the .NET Framework is a bit confusing on this point. Documentation in version 1.1 is clear and correct.*

## Processes, AppDomains, and Threads

In .NET, executable code must be loaded into the CLR to be *managed* while running. To manage the application's code, the CLR must first obtain a pointer to an AppDomain. AppDomains are separate units of processing that the CLR recognizes in a running process. All .NET processes run at least one AppDomain—known as the default AppDomain—that gets created during the CLR initialization. An application can have additional AppDomains. Each AppDomain is independently configured and given personal settings, such as security settings, reference paths, and configuration files.

AppDomains are separated and isolated from one another in a way that resembles process separation in Win32. The CLR enforces isolation by preventing direct calls between objects living in different AppDomains. From the CPU perspective, AppDomains are much more lightweight than Win32 processes. The certainty that AppDomains run type-safe code allows the CLR to provide a level of isolation that's as strong as the process boundaries but more cost effective. Type-safe code cannot cause memory faults, which in Win32 were one of the reasons to have a physical separation between process-memory contexts. An AppDomain is a logical process and, as such, is more lightweight than a true process.

Managed code running in an AppDomain is carried out by a particular thread. However, threads and AppDomains are orthogonal entities in the sense that you can have several threads active during the execution of the AppDomain code, but a single thread is in no way tied to run only within the context of a given AppDomain.

The .NET Remoting API is as a tailor-made set of system services for accessing an object in an external AppDomain.

### Process Recycling

The behavior and performance of the ASP.NET worker process is constantly monitored to catch any form of decay as soon as possible. Parameters used to evaluate the performance include the number of requests served and queued, the total life of the process, and the percentage of physical memory (60% by default) it can use.

The *<processModel>* element of the machine.config file defines threshold values for all these parameters. The aspnet_isapi.dll checks the overall state of the current worker process before forwarding any request to it. If the process breaks one of these measures of good performance, a new worker process is started to serve the next request. The old process continues running as long as there are requests pending in its own queue. After that, when it ceases to be invoked, it goes into idle mode and is then shut down.

This automatic scavenging mechanism is known as *process recycling* and is one of the aspects that improve the overall robustness and efficiency of the ASP.NET platform. In this way, in fact, memory leaks and run-time anomalies are promptly detected and overcome.

### Process Recycling in IIS 6.0

Process recycling is also a built-in feature of IIS 6.0 that all types of Web applications, including ASP.NET and ASP applications, automatically take advantage of. More often than not and in spite of the best efforts to properly build them, Web applications leak memory, are poorly coded, or have other run-time problems. For this reason, administrators will periodically encounter situations that necessitate rebooting or restarting a Web server.

Up to the release of IIS 6.0, restarting a Web site required interrupting the entire Web server. In IIS 6.0, all user code is handled by worker processes, which are completely isolated from the core Web server. Worker processes are periodically recycled according to the number of requests they served, the memory occupied, and the time elapsed since activation. Worker processes are also automatically shut down if they appear to hang or respond too slowly. An ad hoc module in IIS 6.0 takes care of replacing faulty processes with fresh new ones.

> **Note** In IIS 6.0, you'll find many design and implementation features of ASP.NET that are enhanced and extended to all resources. Historically, Microsoft was originally developing IIS 6.0 and ASP.NET together. Microsoft split them into separate projects when a decision was made to ship an initial version of ASP.NET prior to shipping IIS with a new version of Windows. ASP.NET clearly needed to support older versions of IIS, so a parallel IIS 5.0 model for ASP.NET was also built. In that sense, the ASP.NET model for IIS 5.0 matured much more quickly and inspired a lot of features in the newest IIS 6.0 model. As a significantly different product, IIS 6.0 takes the essence of the ASP.NET innovations and re-architects them in a wider and more general context. As a result, specific features of ASP.NET (for example, output caching and process recycling) become features of the whole Web server infrastructure with IIS 6.0. Those features are available to all Web applications hosted by IIS 6.0, including ASP.NET applications. ASP.NET is designed to detect the version of IIS and adjust its way of working.

## Configuring the ASP.NET Worker Process

The aspnet_isapi module controls the behavior of the ASP.NET worker process through a few parameters. Table 2-2 details the information that gets passed between the ASP.NET ISAPI extension and the ASP.NET worker process.

**Table 2-2 Parameters of the ASP.NET Process**

| Parameter | Description |
|---|---|
| *IIS-Process-ID* | The process ID number of the parent IIS process. |
| *This-Process-Unique-ID* | A unique process ID used to identify the worker process in a Web garden configuration. |
| *Number-of-Sync-Pipes* | Number of pipes to listen to for information. |
| *RPC_C_AUTHN_LEVEL_XXX* | Indicates the required level of authentication for DCOM security. Default is *Connect*. |
| *RPC_C_IMP_LEVEL_XXX* | Indicates the authentication level required for COM security. Default is *Impersonate*. |
| *CPU-Mask* | Bit mask indicating which CPUs are available for ASP.NET processes if the run time is configured to work as a Web garden. |
| *Max-Worker-Threads* | Maximum number of worker threads per CPU in the thread pool. |
| *Max-IO-Threads* | Maximum number of IO threads per CPU in the thread pool. |

Default values for the arguments in Table 2-2 can be set by editing the attributes of the *<processModel>* section in the machine.config file. (I'll cover the machine.config file in more detail in Chapter 12.)

These parameters instruct the process how to perform tasks that need to happen before the CLR is loaded. Setting COM security is just one such task, and that's why authentication-level values need to be passed to the ASP.NET worker process. What does ASP.NET have to do with COM security? Well, the CLR is actually exposed as a COM object. (Note that the CLR itself is not made of COM code, but the interface to the CLR is a COM object.)

Other parameters are the information needed to hook up the named pipes between the ISAPI extension and the worker process. The names for the pipes are generated randomly and have to be communicated. The worker process retrieves the names of the pipes by using the parent process ID (that is, the IIS process) and the number of pipes created.

**Note** All the system information needed to set up the ASP.NET worker process (that is, the contents of the machine.config file) is read by the aspnet_isapi.dll unmanaged code prior to spawning any instance of the worker process.

## About the Web Garden Model

The *This-Process-Unique-ID* parameter is associated with Web garden support. When multiple worker processes are used in a Web garden scenario, the aspnet_isapi.dll needs to know which process it's dealing with. Any HTTP request posted to the pipe must address a precise target process, and this information must be written into the packet sent through the pipe. The typical way of identifying a process is by means of its process ID.

Unfortunately, though, aspnet_isapi.dll can't know the actual ID of the worker process being spawned because the ID won't be determined until the kernel is done with the *CreateProcess* API function. The following pseudocode demonstrates that the *[process_id]* argument of aspnet_wp.exe can't be the process ID of the same process being created!

```
// aspnet_isapi.dll uses this code to create a worker process
CreateProcess("aspnet_wp.exe", "[iis_id] [process_id] ...", ...);
```

For this reason, aspnet_isapi.dll generates a unique but fake process ID and uses that ID to uniquely identify each worker process running on a multiprocessor machine configured as a Web garden. In this way, the call we just saw is rewritten as follows:

```
// [This-Process-Unique-ID] is a unique GUID
// generated by aspnet_isapi.dll
CreateProcess("aspnet_wp.exe", "[iis_id] [This-Process-Unique-ID] ...", ...);
```

The worker process caches the *This-Process-Unique-ID* argument and uses it to recognize which named-pipe messages it has to serve.

## ASP.NET and the IIS 6.0 Process Model

IIS 6.0, which ships as a part of Windows Server 2003, implements its HTTP listener as a kernel-level module. As a result, all incoming requests are first managed by such a driver—http.sys—and in kernel mode. No third-party code ever interacts with the listener, and no user-mode crashes will ever affect the stability of IIS. The http.sys driver listens for requests and posts them to the request queue of the appropriate *application pool*. An application pool is a blanket term that identifies a worker process and a virtual directory. A module, known as the Web Administration Service (WAS), reads from the IIS metabase and instructs the http.sys driver to create as many request queues as there are application pools registered in the metabase.

So when a request arrives, the driver looks at the URL and queues the request to the corresponding application pool. The WAS is responsible for creating and administering the worker processes for the various pools. The IIS worker process is an executable named w3wp.exe, whose main purpose is extracting HTTP requests from the kernel-mode queue. The worker process hosts a core application handler DLL to actually process the request and load ISAPI extensions and filters as appropriate.

Looking at the diagram of ASP.NET applications in Figure 2-4, you can see the IIS 6.0 process model eliminates the need for aspnet_wp.exe. The w3wp.exe loads the aspnet_isapi.dll, and in turn, the ISAPI extension loads the CLR in the worker process and launches the pipeline. With IIS 6.0, ASP.NET is managed by IIS and no longer concerns itself with things like process recycling, Web gardening, and isolation from the Web server.

*(continued)*

## ASP.NET and the IIS 6.0 Process Model (continued)

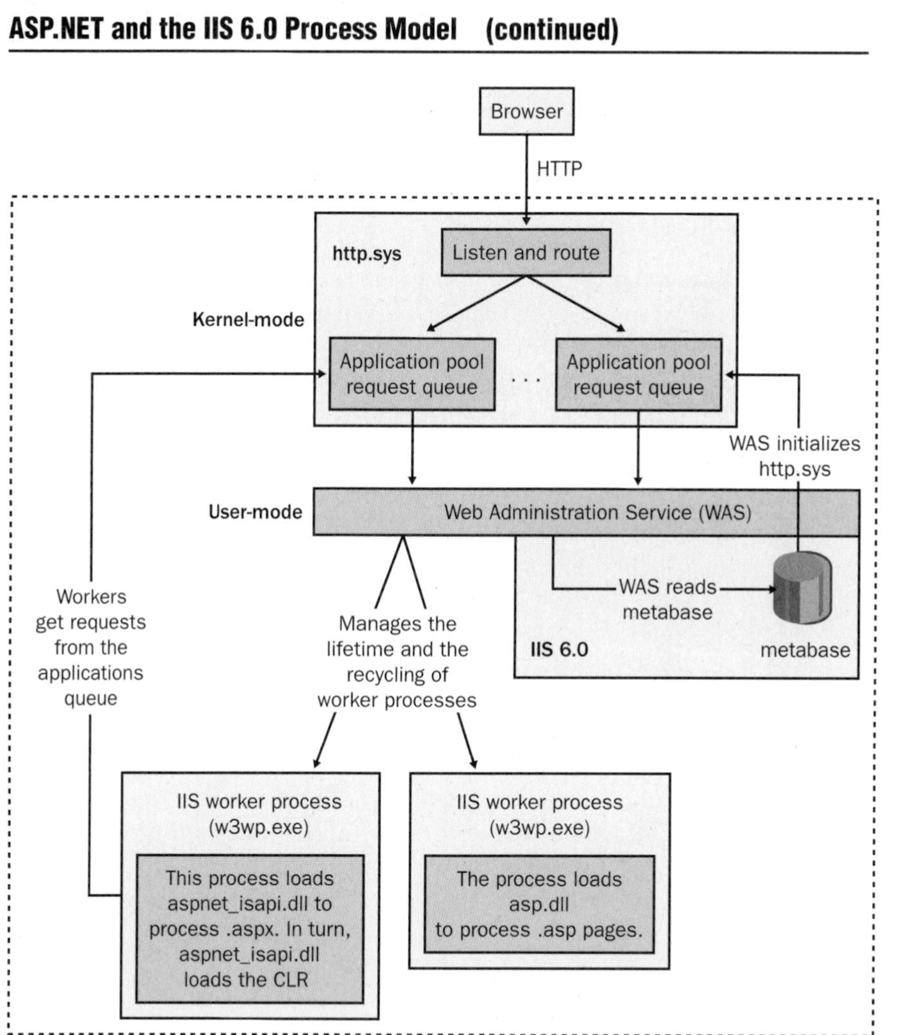


**Figure 2-4** How Web applications are processed in IIS 6.0.

In summary, in the IIS 6.0 process model, ASP.NET runs even faster because no interprocess communication between inetinfo.exe (the IIS executable) and aspnet_wp.exe is required. The HTTP request arrives directly at the worker process that hosts the CLR. Furthermore, the ASP.NET worker process is not a special process but simply a copy of the IIS worker process. This fact shifts to IIS the burden of process recycling and health checks.

**ASP.NET and the IIS 6.0 Process Model**

In IIS 6.0, ASP.NET ignores the contents of the *<processModel>* section from the machine.config file. Only thread and deadlock settings are read from that section of the machine.config. Everything else goes through the metabase and can be configured only by using the IIS Manager. (Other configuration information continues being read from .config files.)

## The ASP.NET HTTP Pipeline

The ASP.NET worker process is responsible for running the Web application that lives behind the requested URL. It passes any incoming HTTP requests to the so-called HTTP pipeline—that is, the fully extensible chain of managed objects that works according to the classic concept of a pipeline. Unlike ASP pages, ASP.NET pages are not simply parsed and served to the user. While serving pages is the ultimate goal of ASP.NET, the way in which the resultant HTML code is generated is much more sophisticated than in ASP and involves many more objects.

A page request passes through a pipeline of objects that process the HTTP content and, at the end of the chain, produce some HTML code for the browser. The entry point in this pipeline is the *HttpRuntime* class. The ASP.NET runtime activates the HTTP pipeline by creating a new instance of the *HttpRuntime* class and then calling the method *ProcessRequest*.

### The *HttpRuntime* Object

Upon creation, the *HttpRuntime* object initializes a number of internal objects that will help carry out the page request. Helper objects include the cache manager and the file system monitor used to detect changes in the files that form the application.

When the *ProcessRequest* method is called, the *HttpRuntime* object starts working to serve a page to the browser. It creates a new context for the request and initializes a specialized text writer object in which the HTML code will be accumulated. A context is given by an instance of the *HttpContext* class, which encapsulates all HTTP-specific information about the request. The text writer is an instance of the *HttpWriter* class and is the object that actually buffers text sent out through the *Response* object.

After that, the *HttpRuntime* object uses the context information to either locate or create a Web application object capable of handling the request. A Web application is searched using the virtual directory information contained in the URL. The object used to find or create a new Web application is *HttpApplicationFactory*—an internal-use object responsible for returning a valid object capable of handling the request.

### The Application Factory

During the lifetime of the application, the *HttpApplicationFactory* object maintains a pool of *HttpApplication* objects to serve incoming HTTP requests. When invoked, the application factory object verifies that an AppDomain exists for the virtual folder the request targets. If the application is already running, the factory picks an *HttpApplication* out of the pool of available objects and passes it the request. A new *HttpApplication* object is created if an existing object is not available.

If the virtual folder has not yet been called, a new *HttpApplication* object for the virtual folder is created in a new AppDomain. In this case, the creation of an *HttpApplication* object entails the compilation of the global.asax application file, if any is present, and the creation of the assembly that represents the actual page requested. An *HttpApplication* object is used to process a single page request at a time; multiple objects are used to serve simultaneous requests for the same page.

> **Note** ASP.NET global.asax files are dynamically compiled the first time any page or Web service is requested in the virtual directory. This happens even before the target page or Web service is compiled. ASP.NET pages and Web services within that Web application are subsequently linked to the resulting global.asax compiled class when they are in turn compiled.

### The *HttpApplication* Object

*HttpApplication* is a global.asax-derived object that the ASP.NET worker process uses to handle HTTP requests that hit a particular virtual directory. A particular *HttpApplication* instance is responsible for managing the entire lifetime of the request it is assigned to, and the instance of *HttpApplication* can be reused only after the request has been completed. The *HttpApplication* class defines the methods, properties, and events common to all application objects—.aspx pages, user controls, Web services, and HTTP handlers—within an ASP.NET application.

The *HttpApplication* maintains a list of HTTP module objects that can filter and even modify the content of the request. Registered modules are called during various moments of the elaboration as the request passes through the pipeline.

HTTP modules represent the managed counterpart of ISAPI filters and will be covered in greater detail in Chapter 23.

The *HttpApplication* object determines the type of object that represents the resource being requested—typically, an ASP.NET page. It then uses a handler factory object to either instantiate the type from an existing assembly or dynamically create the assembly and then an instance of the type. A handler factory object is a class that implements the *IHttpHandlerFactory* interface and is responsible for returning an instance of a managed class that can handle the HTTP request—an HTTP handler. An ASP.NET page is simply a handler object—that is, an instance of a class that implements the *IHttpHandler* interface.

> **Caution** Although the name sounds vaguely evocative of the intrinsic ASP *Application* object, the ASP.NET *HttpApplication* has nothing to do with it. The ASP *Application* object is fully supported in ASP.NET, but it maps to an object of type *HttpApplicationState*. However, the *HttpApplication* object has a property named *Application*, which returns just the ASP.NET counterpart of the ASP intrinsic application-state object.

### The Handler Factory

The *HttpApplication* determines the type of object that must handle the request, and it delegates the type-specific handler factory to create an instance of that type. Let's see what happens when the resource requested is a page.

Once the *HttpApplication* object in charge of the request has figured out the proper handler, it creates an instance of the handler factory object. For a request that targets a page, the factory is an undocumented class named *PageHandlerFactory*.

> **Note** The *HttpApplication* object determines the proper handler for the request and creates an instance of that class. To find the appropriate handler, it uses the information in the *<httpHandlers>* section of the machine.config file. The section lists all the currently registered handlers for the application.

The page handler factory is responsible for either finding the assembly that contains the page class or dynamically creating an ad hoc assembly. The *System.Web* namespace defines a few handler factory classes. These are listed in Table 2-3.

**Table 2-3 Handler Factory Classes in the .NET Framework**

| Handler Factory | Type | Description |
|---|---|---|
| *HttpRemotingHandlerFactory* | *.rem; *.soap | Instantiates the object that will take care of a .NET Remoting request routed through IIS. Instantiates an object of type *HttpRemotingHandler*. |
| *PageHandlerFactory* | *.aspx | Compiles and instantiates the type that represents the page. The source code for the class is built while parsing the source code of the .aspx file. Instantiates an object of a type that derives from *Page*. |
| *SimpleHandlerFactory* | *.ashx | Compiles and instantiates the specified HTTP handler from the source code of the .ashx file. Instantiates an object that implements the *IHttpHandler* interface. |
| *WebServiceHandlerFactory* | *.asmx | Compiles the source code of a Web service, and translates the SOAP payload into a method invocation. Instantiates an object of the type specified in the Web service file. |

Bear in mind that handler factory objects do not compile the requested resource each time it is invoked. The compiled code is stored in a directory on the Web server and used until the corresponding resource file is modified.

So the page handler factory creates an instance of an object that represents the particular page requested. This object inherits from the *System.Web.UI.Page* class, which in turn implements the *IHttpHandler* interface. The page object is built as an instance of a dynamically generated class based on the source code embedded in the .aspx file. The page object is returned to the application factory, which passes that back to the *HttpRuntime* object. The final step accomplished by the ASP.NET runtime is calling the *ProcessRequest* method on the page object. This call causes the page to execute the user-defined code and generate the HTML text for the browser.

Figure 2-5 illustrates the overall HTTP pipeline architecture.

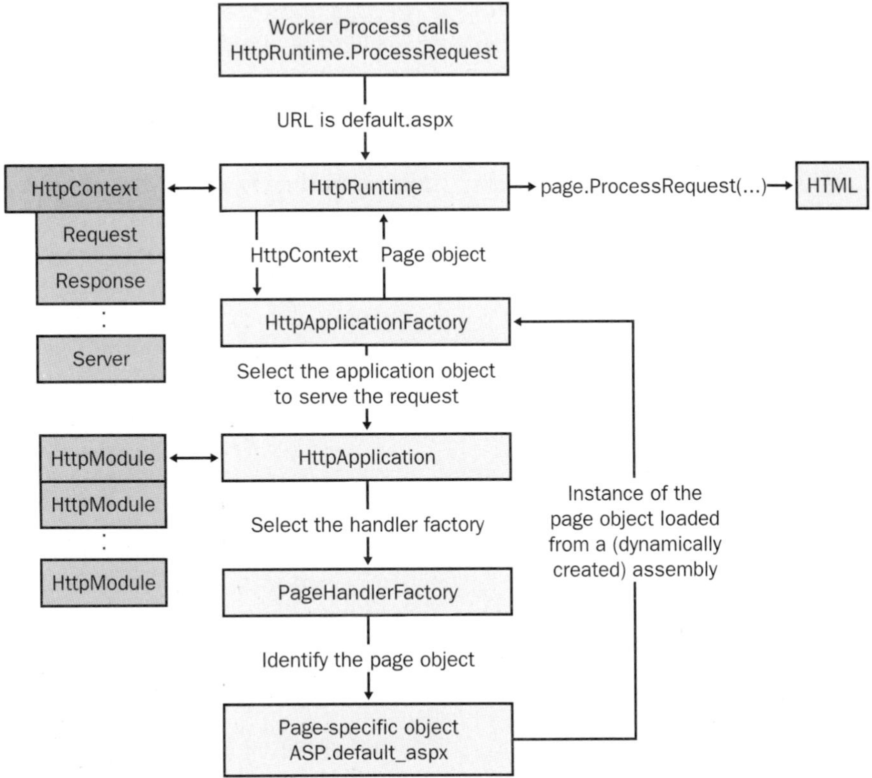


**Figure 2-5** The HTTP pipeline processing for a page.

# The ASP.NET Page Factory Object

Let's examine in detail how the .aspx page is converted into a class and compiled into an assembly. Generating an assembly for a particular .aspx resource is a two-step process. First, the source code for the class is created by merging the content of the *<script>* section with the code-behind file, if any. Second, the dynamically generated class is compiled into an assembly and cached in a well-known directory.

## Locating the Assembly for the Page

Assemblies generated for ASP.NET pages are cached in the Temporary ASP.NET Files folder. The path for version 1.1 of the .NET Framework is as follows.

```
%SystemRoot%\Microsoft.NET\Framework\v1.1.4322\Temporary ASP.NET Files
```

Of course, the directory depends on the version of the .NET Framework you installed. The directory path for version 1.0 of the .NET Framework includes a subdirectory named v1.0.3705. The Temporary ASP.NET Files folder has one child directory for each application ever executed. The name of the subfolder matches the name of the virtual directory of the application. Pages that run from the Web server's root folder are grouped under the Root subfolder.

Page-specific assemblies are cached in a subdirectory placed a couple levels down the virtual directory folder. The names of these child directories are fairly hard to make sense of. Names are the result of a hash algorithm based on some randomized factor along with the application name. A typical path is shown in the following listing. The last two directories (in boldface) have fake but realistic names.

```
\Framework
    \v1.1.4322
        \Temporary ASP.NET Files
            \MyWebApp
                \3678b103
                    \e60405c7
```

Regardless of the actual algorithm implemented to determine the folder names, from within an ASP.NET application the full folder path is retrieved using the following, pretty simple, code:

```
string tempAspNetDir = HttpRuntime.CodegenDir;
```

So much for the location of the dynamic assembly. So how does the ASP.NET runtime determine the assembly name for a particular .aspx page? The assembly folder contains a few XML files with a particular naming convention:

```
[filename].[hashcode].xml
```

If the page is named, say, default.aspx, the corresponding XML file can be named like this:

```
default.aspx.2cf84ad4.xml
```

The XML file is created when the page is compiled. This is the typical content of this XML file:

```
<preserve assem="c5gaxkyh" type="ASP.Default_aspx"
    hash="fffffeda266fd5f7">
    <filedep name="C:\Inetpub\wwwroot\MyWebApp\Default.aspx" />
</preserve>
```

I'll say more about the schema of the file in a moment. For now, it will suffice to look at the *assem* attribute. The attribute value is just the name of the assembly (without extension) created to execute the default.aspx page. Figure 2-6 provides a view of the folder.

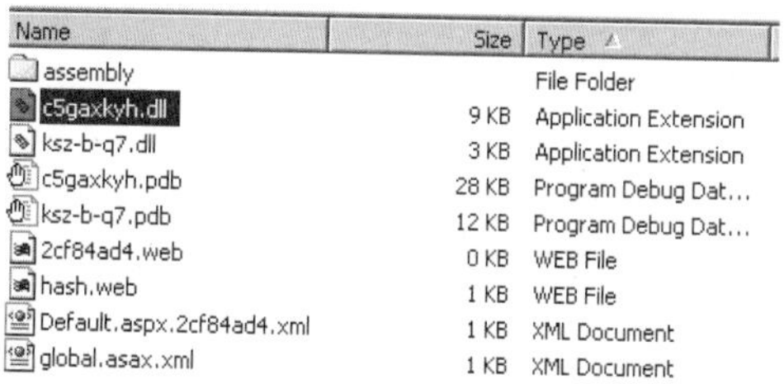

| Name | Size | Type |
|---|---|---|
| assembly | | File Folder |
| c5gaxkyh.dll | 9 KB | Application Extension |
| ksz-b-q7.dll | 3 KB | Application Extension |
| c5gaxkyh.pdb | 28 KB | Program Debug Dat... |
| ksz-b-q7.pdb | 12 KB | Program Debug Dat... |
| 2cf84ad4.web | 0 KB | WEB File |
| hash.web | 1 KB | WEB File |
| Default.aspx.2cf84ad4.xml | 1 KB | XML Document |
| global.asax.xml | 1 KB | XML Document |

**Figure 2-6** Temporary ASP.NET Files: a view of interiors.

The file c5gaxkyh.dll is the assembly that represents the default.aspx page. The other assembly is the compiled version of the global.asax file. (If not specified, a standard global.asax file is used.) The objects defined in these assemblies can be viewed with any class browser tool, including Microsoft IL Disassembler, ILDASM.exe.

> **Important** If the *Debug* attribute of the *@Page* directive is set to *true*, in the same folder as the assembly, you'll also find the source code of the page class. The source code is a Microsoft Visual Basic .NET or C# file according to the value of the *Language* attribute. The name of the source file is *assembly_name.0.ext*, where *assembly_name* denotes the name (without extension) of the assembly and *ext* denotes the language extension. For example, c5gaxkyh.0.cs is the C# source file for default.aspx.

## Detecting Page Changes

As mentioned earlier, the dynamically compiled assembly is cached and used to serve any future request for the page. However, changes made to an .aspx file will automatically invalidate the assembly, which will be recompiled to serve the next request. The link between the assembly and the source .aspx file is kept in the XML file we mentioned a bit earlier. Let's recall it:

```
<preserve assem="c5gaxkyh" type="ASP.Default_aspx" hash="fffffeda266fd5f7">
    <filedep name="C:\Inetpub\wwwroot\MyWebApp\Default.aspx" />
</preserve>
```

The *name* attribute of the *<filedep>* node contains just the full path of the file associated with the assembly whose name is stored in the *assem* attribute of the *<preserve>* node. The *type* attribute, on the other hand, contains the name of the class that renders the .aspx file in the assembly. The actual object running when, say, default.aspx is served is an instance of a class named *ASP.Default_aspx*.

Based on the Win32 file notification change system, this ASP.NET feature enables developers to quickly build applications with a minimum of process overhead. Users, in fact, can "just hit Save" to cause code changes to immediately take effect within the application. In addition to this development-oriented benefit, deployment of applications is greatly enhanced by this feature, as you can simply deploy a new version of the page that overwrites the old one.

When a page is changed, it's recompiled as a single assembly, or as part of an existing assembly, and reloaded. ASP.NET ensures that the next user will be served the new page outfit by the new assembly. Current users, on the other hand, will continue viewing the old page served by the old assembly. The two assemblies are given different (because they are randomly generated) names and therefore can happily live side by side in the same folder as well as be loaded in the same AppDomain. Because that was so much fun, let's drill down a little more into this topic.

## How ASP.NET Replaces Page Assemblies

When a new assembly is created for a page as the effect of an update, ASP.NET verifies whether the old assembly can be deleted. If the assembly contains only that page class, ASP.NET attempts to delete the assembly. Often, though, it finds the file loaded and locked, and the deletion fails. In this case, the old assembly is renamed by adding a .DELETE extension. (All executables loaded in Windows can be renamed at any time, but they cannot be deleted until they are released.) Renaming an assembly in use is no big deal in this case because the image of the executable is already loaded in memory and there will be no need to reload it later. The file, in fact, is destined for deletion. Note that .DELETE files are cleaned up when the directory is next accessed in *sweep* mode, so to speak. The directory, in fact, is not scavenged each time it is accessed but only when the application is restarted or an application file (global.asax or web.config) changes.

Each ASP.NET application is allowed a maximum number of recompiles (with 15 as the default) before the whole application is restarted. The threshold value is set in the machine.config file. If the latest compilation exceeds the threshold, the AppDomain is unloaded and the application is restarted. Bear in mind that the atomic unit of code you can unload in the CLR is the AppDomain, not the assembly. Put another way, you can't unload a single assembly without unloading the whole AppDomain. As a result, when a page is recompiled, the old version stays in memory until the AppDomain is unloaded because either the Web application exceeded its limit of recompiles or the ASP.NET worker process is taking up too much memory.

## Getting ASP.NET Runtime Information

The page runtimeinfo.aspx in the book samples displays some run-time information about the running application and AppDomains. Obtained from properties of the *HttpRuntime* class, the information includes the ID, path, and virtual path of the current AppDomain, plus useful paths such as the directory in which ASP.NET generates dynamic assemblies (*CodegenDir*), the machine.config path, and the Bin directory of the application (*BinDirectory*).

The runtimeinfo.aspx page also lists all the assemblies currently loaded in the AppDomain. The sample page needs 12 system assemblies, including those specific to the application—global.asax and the page class. This number increases each time you save the .aspx file because after a page update, a new assembly is loaded but the old one is not unloaded until the whole AppDomain is unloaded. If you save the .aspx file several times (by just opening the file and hitting Ctrl+S), you see that after 15 recompiles the AppDomain ID changes and the number of loaded assemblies reverts back to 12 (or whatever it was). Figure 2-7 shows the result of this exercise.

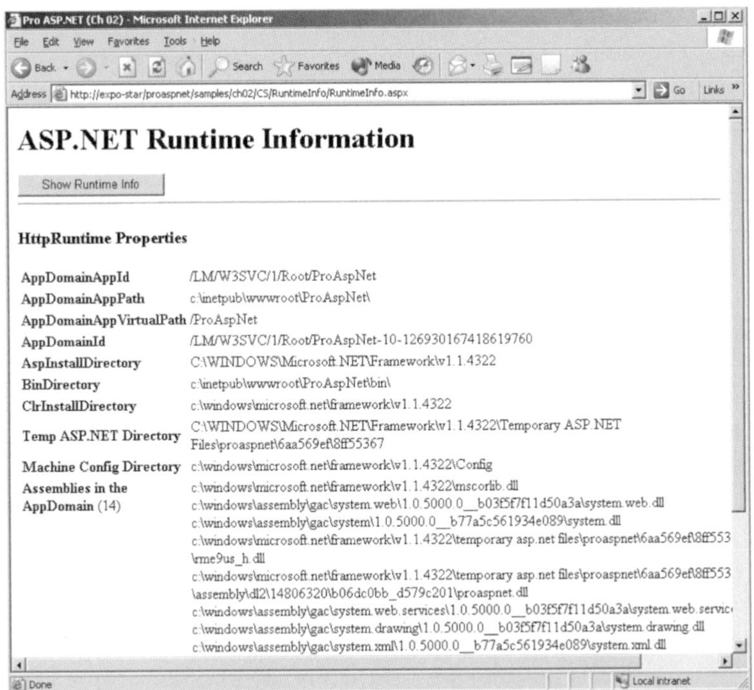


**Figure 2-7** Runtimeinfo.aspx shows ASP.NET runtime information.

## Batch Compilation

Compiling an ASP.NET page takes a while. So even though you pay this price only once, you might encounter situations in which you decide it's best to happily avoid that. Unfortunately, as of version 1.1, ASP.NET lacks a tool (or a built-in mechanism) to scan the entire tree of a Web application and do a precompilation of all pages. However, you can always request each page of a site before the site goes live or, better yet, have an ad hoc application do it.

In effect, since version 1.0, ASP.NET has supported batch compilation, but this support takes place only at run time. ASP.NET attempts to batch into a single compiled assembly as many pages as possible without exceeding the configured maximum batch size. Furthermore, batch compilation groups pages by language, and it doesn't group in the same assembly pages that reside in different directories.

Just as with many other aspects of ASP.NET, batch compilation is highly configurable and is a critical factor for overall site performance. Fine-tuning the related parameters in the *<compilation>* section of the machine.config file is important and should save you from having and loading 1000 different assemblies for as many pages or from having a single huge assembly with 1000 classes inside. Notice, though, that the problem here is not only with the size and the number of the assemblies but also with the time needed to recompile the assemblies in case of updates.

> **Note** The next version of ASP.NET should fully support precompilation of Web sites and provide an offline tool to precompile an entire Web site as well as build manager classes to programmatically control the process. In addition, ASP.NET 2.0 will extend dynamic compilation to class files (typically, code-behind .cs or .vb files) that currently must be compiled either manually or through Visual Studio.

## How ASP.NET Creates a Class for the Page

An ASP.NET page executes as an instance of a type that, by default, inherits from *System.Web.UI.Page*. The page handler factory creates the source code for this class by putting a parser to work on the content of the physical .aspx file. The parser produces a class written with the language the developer specified. The class belongs to the *ASP* namespace and is given a file-specific name. Typically, it is the name and the extension of the file with the dot (.) replaced by an underscore (_). If the page is default.aspx, the class name will be *ASP.Default_aspx*. You can check the truthfulness of this statement with the following simple code:

```
void Page_Load(object sender, EventArgs e)
{
    Response.Write(sender.ToString());
}
```

As mentioned earlier, when the page runs with the *Debug* attribute set to *true*, the ASP.NET runtime does not delete the source code used to create the assembly. Let's have a quick look at the key parts of the source code generated. (Complete sources are included in this book's sample code.)

> **Important** As hinted earlier, the base page class is *System.Web.UI.Page* only by default. In either machine.config or web.config, you can change the base class by using the *pageBaseType* attribute of the *<pages>* element. The same thing can be done for user controls. We'll return to this point later in this chapter and in Chapter 12.

### Reviewing the Class Source Code

For a better understanding of the code generated by ASP.NET, let's first quickly review the starting point—the .aspx source code:

```
<%@ Page Language="C#" Debug="true" %>
<%@ Import Namespace="System.IO" %>

<script runat="server">
private void Page_Load(object sender, EventArgs e)  {
    TheSourceFile.Text = HttpRuntime.CodegenDir;
}
private void MakeUpper(object sender, EventArgs e)  {
        string buf = TheString.Value;
        TheResult.InnerText = buf.ToUpper();
}
</script>

<html>
<head><title>Pro ASP.NET (Ch 02)</title></head>
<body>
    <h1>Sample Page</h1>
    <form runat="server">
        <asp:Label runat="server" id="TheSourceFile" /><hr>
        <input runat="server" type="text" id="TheString" />
        <input runat="server" type="submit" id="TheButton"
            value="Uppercase..." onserverclick="MakeUpper" /><br>
        <span id="TheResult" runat="server"></span>
    </form>
</body>
</html>
```

The following listing shows the source code that ASP.NET generates to process the preceding page. The text in boldface type indicates code extracted from the .aspx file:

```
namespace ASP
{
    using System;
    ⋮
    using ASP;
    using System.IO;

    public class Default_aspx : Page, IRequiresSessionState
    {
        private static int __autoHandlers;
        protected Label TheSourceFile;
        protected HtmlInputText TheString;
        protected HtmlInputButton TheButton;
        protected HtmlGenericControl TheResult;
        protected HtmlForm TheAppForm;
        private static bool __initialized = false;
        private static ArrayList __fileDependencies;

        private void Page_Load(object sender, EventArgs e)
        {
            TheSourceFile.Text = HttpRuntime.CodegenDir;
        }
        private void MakeUpper(object sender, EventArgs e)
        {
            string buf = TheString.Value;
            TheResult.InnerText = buf.ToUpper();
        }

        public Default_aspx()
        {
            ArrayList dependencies;
            if (__initialized == false)
            {
                dependencies = new ArrayList();
                dependencies.Add(
                  "c:\\inetpub\\wwwroot\\vdir\\Default.aspx");
                __fileDependencies = dependencies;
                __initialized = true;
            }
            this.Server.ScriptTimeout = 30000000;
        }

        protected override int AutoHandlers {
            get {return __autoHandlers;}
            set {__autoHandlers = value;}
        }

        protected Global_asax ApplicationInstance {
```

```
    get {return (Global_asax)(this.Context.ApplicationInstance));}
}

public override string TemplateSourceDirectory {
    get {return "/vdir";}
}

private Control __BuildControlTheSourceFile() {
    Label __ctrl = new Label();
    this.TheSourceFile = __ctrl;
    __ctrl.ID = "TheSourceFile";
    return __ctrl;
}

private Control __BuildControlTheString() {
    // initialize the TheString control
}

private Control __BuildControlTheButton() {
    // initialize the TheButton control
}

private Control __BuildControlTheResult() {
    // initialize the TheResult control
}

private Control __BuildControlTheAppForm() {
    HtmlForm __ctrl = new HtmlForm();
    this.TheAppForm = __ctrl;
    __ctrl.ID = "TheAppForm";
    IParserAccessor __parser = (IParserAccessor) __ctrl;
    this.__BuildControlTheSourceFile();
    __parser.AddParsedSubObject(this.TheSourceFile);
    __parser.AddParsedSubObject(new LiteralControl("<hr>"));
    this.__BuildControlTheString();
    __parser.AddParsedSubObject(this.TheString);
    this.__BuildControlTheButton();
    __parser.AddParsedSubObject(this.TheButton);
    __parser.AddParsedSubObject(new LiteralControl("<br>"));
    this.__BuildControlTheResult();
    __parser.AddParsedSubObject(this.TheResult);
    return __ctrl;
}

private void __BuildControlTree(Control __ctrl)
{
    IParserAccessor __parser = (IParserAccessor)__ctrl;
    __parser.AddParsedSubObject(
        new LiteralControl("<html>…</h1>"));
    this.__BuildControlTheAppForm();
    __parser.AddParsedSubObject(this.TheAppForm);
    __parser.AddParsedSubObject(new LiteralControl("…</html>"));
}
```

```
        protected override void FrameworkInitialize() {
            this.__BuildControlTree(this);
            this.FileDependencies = __fileDependencies;
            this.EnableViewStateMac = true;
this.Request.ValidateInput();
        }

        public override int GetTypeHashCode() {
            return 2003216705;
        }
    }
}
```

**Important** As you can see, portions of the source code in the .aspx file are used to generate a new class in the specified language. Just because the inline code in a page will be glued together in a class doesn't mean you can use multiple languages to develop an ASP.NET page. The .NET platform is language-neutral but, unfortunately, .NET compilers are not capable of cross-language compilation!

In addition, for ASP.NET pages, the language declared in the *@Page* directive must match the language of the inline code. The *Language* attribute, in fact, is used to determine the language in which the class is to be created. Finally, the source code is generated using the classes of the language's Code Document Object Model (CodeDOM). CodeDOM can be used to create and retrieve instances of code generators and code compilers. Code generators can be used to generate code in a particular language, and code compilers can be used to compile code into assemblies. Not all .NET languages provide such classes, and this is why not all languages can be used to develop ASP.NET applications. For example, the CodeDOM for J# has been added only in version 1.1 of the .NET Framework, but there is a J# redistributable that adds this functionality to version 1.0.

All the controls in the page marked with the *runat* attribute are rendered as protected properties of the type that corresponds to the tag. Those controls are instantiated and initialized in the various *__BuildControlXXX* methods. The initialization is done using the attributes specified in the .aspx page. The build method for the form adds child-parsed objects to the *HtmlForm* instance. This means that all the parent-child relationships between the controls within the form are registered. The *__BuildControlTree* method ensures that all controls in the whole page are correctly registered with the page object.

All the members defined in the *<script>* block are copied verbatim as members of the new class with the same level of visibility you declared. The base class for the dynamically generated source is *Page* unless the code-behind approach is used. In that case, the base class is just the code-behind class. We'll return to this later in "The Code-Behind Technique" section.

## Processing the Page Request

The *HttpRuntime* object governs the HTTP pipeline in which a page request is transformed into a living instance of a *Page*-derived class. The *HttpRuntime* object causes the page to generate its HTML output by calling the *ProcessRequest* method on the *Page*-derived class that comes out of the pipeline. *ProcessRequest* is a method defined on the *IHttpHandler* interface that the *Page* class implements.

### The Page Life Cycle

Within the base implementation of *ProcessRequest*, the *Page* class first calls the *FrameworkInitialize* method, which, as seen in the source code examined a moment ago, builds the controls tree for the page. Next, *ProcessRequest* makes the page go through various phases: initialization, loading of view-state information and postback data, loading of the page's user code, and execution of postback server-side events. After that, the page enters rendering mode: the updated view state is collected, and the HTML code is generated and sent to the output console. Finally, the page is unloaded and the request is considered completely served.

During the various phases, the page fires a few events that Web controls and user-defined code can intercept and handle. Some of these events are specific to controls and can't be handled at the level of the .aspx code. In theory, a page that wants to handle a certain event should explicitly register an appropriate handler. However, for backward compatibility with the Visual Basic programming style, ASP.NET also supports a form of implicit event hooking. By default, the page tries to match method names and events and considers the method a handler for the event. For example, a method named *Page_Load* is the handler for the page's *Load* event. This behavior is controlled by the *AutoEventWireup* attribute on the *@Page* directive. If the attribute is set to *false*, any applications that want to handle an event need to connect explicitly to the page event. The following code shows how to proceed from within a page class:

```
// C# code
this.Load += new EventHandler(this.MyPageLoad);
' VB code
AddHandler Load, AddressOf Me.MyPageLoad
```

By proceeding this way, you will enable the page to get a slight performance boost by not having to do the extra work of matching names and events. Visual Studio .NET disables the *AutoEventWireup* attribute.

## Page-Related Events

To handle a page-related event, an ASP.NET page can either hook up the event (for example, *Load*) or, in a derived class, override the corresponding method—for example, *OnLoad*. The second approach provides for greater flexibility because you can decide whether and when to call the base method, which, in the end, fires the event to the user-code. Let's review in detail the various phases in the page life cycle:

- **Page initialization** At this stage, the page is called to initialize all the settings needed during the lifetime of the incoming page request. The event you need to hook up from an ASP.NET page is *Init*. The method to use to override in a derived class (for example, code-behind) is *OnInit*.

- **Loading the view state** During this phase, the previously saved state of the page—the *ViewState* property—is restored. The restored value for *ViewState* comes from a hidden field that ASP.NET spookily inserts in the HTML code (more on this later). There is no event associated with this phase. You can override the default implementation of the *LoadViewState* method of the *Page* only by deriving a new class.

- **Loading postback data** The page loads all incoming *<form>* data cached in *Request* and updates page and control properties accordingly. For example, suppose a page contained a list of check boxes. In *ViewState*, the page stores the selected items when the page is generated. Next, the user works with check boxes on the client, selects a different set of items, and posts back. In the previous phase, the server-side list of check boxes has been restored to the state it was in the last time it was processed on the server. In this stage, the list of check boxes is updated to reflect client-side changes. No user event is associated with this stage.

- **Loading the user code** At this point, server controls in the page tree are created and initialized, the state is restored, and form controls reflect client-side data. The page is ready to execute any initialization code that has to do with the logic and behavior of the page. The event you need to hook up from an ASP.NET page is *Load*. The method to use to override in a derived class (for example, code-behind) is *OnLoad*.

- **Send postback change notifications** Raise change events in response to state changes between the current and previous postbacks. Any further change entered by the *Load* event handler is also taken into account to determine any difference. This notification is sent if, for example, the aforementioned list of check boxes is changed on the client.
- **Handle postback events** Execute the .aspx code associated with the client-side event that caused the postback. For example, if you click a Submit button, the page posts back and, at this stage, executes the code bound to the *onclick* event of the button. This phase represents the core of the event model of ASP.NET.
- **Prerendering** Perform any updates before the output is rendered. Any changes made to the state of the control in the prerender phase can be saved, while changes made in the rendering phase are lost. The event you need to hook up from an ASP.NET page is *PreRender*. The method to use to override in a derived class (for example, code-behind) is *OnPreRender*.
- **Saving the view state** During this phase, the page serializes the content of the *ViewState* property to a string, which will then be appended to the HTML page as a hidden field. No user event is associated with this phase. You can override the default implementation of the *SaveViewState* method of the *Page* only by deriving a new class.
- **Page rendering** Generate the HTML output to be rendered to the client. The default implementation can be customized by overriding the *Render* method. No user event is associated with this phase.
- **Page unload** Perform any final cleanup before the *Page* object is released. Typical operations are closing files and database connections. The event you need to hook up from an ASP.NET page is *Unload*. The method to use to override in a derived class (for example, code-behind) is *OnUnload*. The page unload notification arrives when the page is unloaded. The *Dispose* method of the *Page* provides the last possibility for the page to perform final clean up before it is released from memory. To customize the behavior of *Dispose*, you need to derive a new class. *Dispose* is called immediately after the *OnUnload* method returns.

# The Event Model

When a page is requested, its class and the server controls it contains are responsible for executing the request and rendering HTML back to the client. The communication between the client and the server is stateless and disconnected because of the HTTP protocol. Real-world applications, though, need some state to be maintained between successive calls made to the same page. With ASP, and with other server-side development platforms such as Java Server Pages (JSP) and LAMP (Linux plus Apache plus MySQL plus either Perl, Python, or PHP as the programming language), the programmer is entirely responsible for persisting the state. In contrast, ASP.NET provides a built-in infrastructure that saves and restores the state of a page in a transparent manner. In this way, and in spite of the underlying stateless protocol, the client experience appears to be that of a continuously executing process. It's just an illusion, though.

The illusion of continuity is created by the view-state feature of ASP.NET pages and is based on some assumptions on how the page is designed and works. Also server-side Web controls play a remarkable role. In brief, before rendering its contents to HTML, the page encodes and stuffs into a hidden field all the state information that the page itself and its constituent controls want to save. When the page posts back, the state information is deserialized from the hidden field and used to initialize instances of the server controls declared in the page layout.

The view state is specific to each instance of the page because it is embedded in the HTML. The net effect of this is that controls are initialized with the same values they had the last time the view state was created—that is, the last time the page was rendered to the client. Furthermore, an additional step in the page life cycle merges the persisted state with any updates introduced by client-side actions. When the page executes after a postback, it finds a stateful and up-to-date context just as it is working over a continuous point-to-point connection.

Two basic assumptions are made. The first assumption is that the page always posts to itself and carries its state back and forth. The second assumption is that the server-side controls have to be declared with the *runat* attribute.

## The Single Form Model

Admittedly, for programmers whose experience is with ASP, the single form model of ASP.NET can be difficult to understand. Where's the *Action* property of the form? Why can't I redirect to a particular page when a form is submitted? These are common questions, frequently asked on forums and newsgroups.

ASP.NET pages are built to support exactly one server-side *<form>* tag. The form must include all the controls you want to interact with on the server.

Both the form and the controls must be marked with the *runat* attribute; otherwise, they will be considered as plain text to be output verbatim. A server-side form is an instance of the *HtmlForm* class. The *HtmlForm* class does not expose any property equivalent to the *Action* property of the HTML *<form>* tag. The reason is that an ASP.NET page always posts to itself. Unlike the *Action* property, other common form properties such as *Method* and *Target* are fully supported.

> **Note** Valid ASP.NET pages are also those that have no server-side forms and those that run HTML forms—a *<form>* tag without the *runat* attribute. In an ASP.NET page, you can also have both HTML and server forms. In no case, though, can you have more than one *<form>* tag with the *runat* attribute set to *server*. HTML forms work as usual and let you post to any page in the application. The drawback is that in this case, no state will be automatically restored. In other words, the ASP.NET Web Forms model works only if you use exactly one server *<form>* element.

## Auto-Reentrant Web Pages

Let's consider a simple ASP.NET page and see the HTML code that ASP.NET generates for it:

```
<% @Page Language="C#" %>
<script runat="server">
private void MakeUpper(object sender, EventArgs e)
{
    string buf = TheString.Text;
    TheResult.Text = buf.ToUpper();
}
</script>

<html>
<body>
<form runat="server" id="TheForm">
    <asp:textbox runat="server" id="TheString" />
    <asp:button runat="server" text="Convert..." onclick="MakeUpper" /><hr>
    <asp:label runat="server" id="TheResult" />
</form>
</body>
</html>
```

As shown in Figure 2-8, the page lets the user type some text in an input field and then posts all the data to the server for further processing. If you point your browser to this page, the actual HTML code being displayed is the following. The text in boldface is the page's view state:

```
<html>
<body>
<form name="TheForm" method="post" action="MyForm.aspx" id="TheForm">
    <input type="hidden"
        name="__VIEWSTATE"
        value="dDwtMTM3NjQ2NjY2NTs7PrH3U/xuqPTNI63I1Lw5THHvPFUf" />
    <input name="TheString" type="text" id="TheString" />
    <input type="submit" name="_ctl0" value="Convert..." /><hr>
    <span id="TheResult"></span>
</form>
</body>
</html>
```

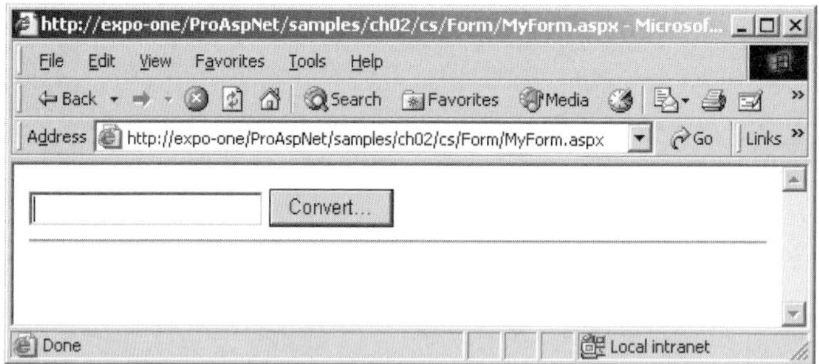

**Figure 2-8** The sample ASP.NET page in action.

> **Note** A question I often get at conferences and classes (but rarely a publicly asked question) concerns the use of hidden fields in ASP.NET. The question is typically, "Should I really use hidden fields also in ASP.NET?" Hidden fields have a bad reputation among ASP developers because they appear to be a quick fix and a sort of dirty trick. In some way, developers tend to think that they use hidden fields because they're unable to find a better solution. A similar feeling was common among Windows SDK programmers regarding the use of global variables or temporary files.
>
> Developers seem to fear using hidden fields in the dazzling new object-oriented world of ASP.NET. Well, nothing really prohibits the use of hidden fields in ASP.NET applications and using them is in no way shameful, as long as HTTP remains the underlying protocol. The real point is even more positive.
>
> Using hidden fields in ASP.NET allows you to create more useful Web pages—for example, the view-state mechanism. In light of this, hidden fields are especially recommended when you need to pass information to be consumed through client-side scripts.

The server-side *<form>* tag is rendered as a plain old HTML form in which the *Name* attribute matches the ID property of the *HtmlForm* control, the *Method* attribute defaults to POST and *Action* is automatically set with the URL of the same page. The form contains as many HTML elements as there are server controls in the .aspx source. The form also includes any static text or HTML tags declared in the page layout. The view state is rendered as a hidden field named __VIEWSTATE and filled with Base64-encoded text.

### The View State of the Page

The contents of the view state are determined by the contents of the *ViewState* property of the page and its controls. The *ViewState* property is a collection of name/value pairs that both pages and controls fill with data they determine should be preserved across page requests. The various collections are merged together to form a unique object graph, which is then encoded as a Base64 string. Seen from the client side, the __VIEWSTATE hidden field is just a more or less overwhelming sequence of characters. The more state information you save in the *ViewState* property, the bigger your page becomes. Other security and performance concerns apply to the page view state, but we'll cover them in greater detail in Chapter 14. Note that for a real-world page, the size of the view state can easily be more than 10 KB of data, which is an extra burden of 10 KB transmitted over the network and simply ignored on the client.

> **Note** The implementation of the view state in ASP.NET raises hidden fields from the rank of a dirty trick to the higher and more noble role of an internal system feature. Today, lots of ASP developers use hidden fields to persist small pieces of page-specific information. This information is, in most cases, written as plain text and serialized with home-made schemes. The view state implementation revamps that old trick and, more, exposes persisted information in an extremely handy, object-based fashion.
>
> Some developers are afraid of having their own state information at the mercy of the client. That this is the actual situation cannot be denied; but that this automatically qualifies as a security hole has yet to be proven. However, if you were among the many who used to cache plain text in hidden fields, the ASP.NET view state represents a quantum leap! In addition, there are some extra security enforcements that can be applied to the view state. We'll review those in Chapter 14.

## Postback Events

A postback event is a page request that results from a client action. Typically, when the user clicks on a submit button, like the Convert button in Figure 2-8, a postback event occurs. In this case, the HTML form posts to the same .aspx page and, as normally happens with HTTP POST commands, the contents of the various input fields in the form are packed in the body of the request.

On the server, the code in charge of processing the request first gets an instance of the class that represents the .aspx page and then goes through the steps described earlier in the "Page-Related Events" section.

### State Restoration

As the first step of the page processing, the HTTP runtime builds the tree of controls for the page and sets the *IsPostBack* property. *IsPostBack* is a Boolean property that equals *true* if the page is being processed after a post from the same page—a postback event.

After initialization, the HTTP runtime instructs the page to deserialize the view-state string and transform it into an instance of the *StateBag* class. *StateBag* implements a dictionary that is populated with the name/value pairs stored and encoded in the view-state string. Once the *StateBag* object has been completely set up, user code can start playing with its contents. From a user-code perspective, however, this timing means it can't do anything before the *OnLoad* event fires. Before *OnLoad* is fired, though, another step needs to be accomplished.

At this point, the various controls active on the page have been restored to the state stored in the view state. Unless the view state has been sapiently and maliciously corrupted on the client (an extremely remote possibility, if not completely impossible), the state of the objects is the state that existed when that page was rendered to the client. It is not yet the state the user set with client-side input actions such as checking radio buttons or typing text. The next step updates the state of the various controls to reflect any client action. This final step ends the state restoration phase, and the page is now ready to process user code. Fire the *OnLoad* event.

### Handling the Server-Side Event

The goal of a postback event is executing some server-side code to respond to user input. How can the page know what method it has to execute? The post is always the result of a form submission. However, the submit action can be accomplished in two ways: if the user clicks a control or if the user takes some action that causes some script to run. Let's examine the first case.

The HTML syntax dictates that the ID of the button clicked be inserted in the post data. On the server, the ASP.NET page digs out this information in its attempt to locate an element whose name matches one of its server controls. If a match is found, ASP.NET verifies that the control implements *IPostBackEventHandler*. This is enough to guarantee that the button clicked on the server was a submit button. Generally, it means the control has some code to execute upon postback. At this point, the page raises the postback event on the control and has the control execute some code. To raise the postback event on the control, the ASP.NET page invokes the control's *RaisePostBackEvent* method—one of the members of the *IPostBackEventHandler* interface. For a submit button, this causes the invocation of the method associated with the *onclick* property.

If some script code can post the page back to the server, the author of the script is responsible for letting ASP.NET know about the sender of the event. To understand how to accomplish this, let's see what happens when you use a Web control such as the *LinkButton*—a button rendered as a hyperlink:

```
<asp:linkbutton runat="server" id="TheLink"
    text="Convert..." onclick="MakeUpper" />
```

The HTML code for the page changes slightly. A JavaScript function and a couple of extra hidden fields are added. The two hidden fields are __EVENTTARGET and __EVENTARGUMENT. They are empty when the page is rendered to the browser and contain event data when the page is posted back. In particular, __EVENTTARGET contains the name of the control that caused the postback. The __EVENTARGUMENT field contains any argument that might be useful to carry out the call. A short piece of JavaScript code sets the two fields and submits the form:

```
<!--
<script language="javascript">
function __doPostBack(eventTarget, eventArgument) {
var theform;
if (window.navigator.appName.toLowerCase().indexOf("netscape") > -1) {
theform = document.forms["TheForm"];
}
else {
theform = document.TheForm;
}
theform.__EVENTTARGET.value = eventTarget.split("$").join(":");
theform.__EVENTARGUMENT.value = eventArgument;
theform.submit();
}
// -->
</script>
```

But what's the link between the *__doPostBack* function and the *LinkButton* object? Let's look at the HTML generated for the *LinkButton*:

```
<a href="javascript:__doPostBack('TheLink','')">Convert...</a>
```

Quite simply, any click on the anchor is resolved by executing the *__doPostBack* function.

If you want to provide a completely custom mechanism to post the page back, just borrow the preceding code and make sure the form is submitted with the __EVENTTARGET field set to the name of the sender of the event. (For example, you could have the page post back when the mouse hovers over a certain image.)

To find the sender control that will handle the server-side event, ASP.NET looks at the __EVENTTARGET hidden field if no match is found between its controls and the content of the *Request.Form* collection—that is, if the previous case (the submit button) does not apply.

### Rendering Back the Page

After executing the server-side code, the page begins its rendering phase. At first, the page fires the *PreRender* event; it then serializes the content of the *ViewState* object—that is, the current state of the various controls active on the page—to a Base64 string. Next, the HTML code is generated and that Base64 string becomes the value of the __VIEWSTATE hidden field. And so on for the next round-trip.

## The *Page* Class

In the .NET Framework, the *Page* class provides the basic behavior for all objects that an ASP.NET application builds starting from .aspx files. Defined in the *System.Web.UI* namespace, the class derives from *TemplateControl* and implements the *IHttpHandler* interface:

```
public class Page : TemplateControl, IHttpHandler
```

In particular, *TemplateControl* is the abstract class that provides both ASP.NET pages and user controls with a base set of functionality. At the upper level of the hierarchy, we find the *Control* class. It defines the properties, methods, and events shared by all ASP.NET server-side elements—pages, controls, and user controls. It's useful to also look at the functionalities of the *Page* class from an interface perspective, as in Figure 2-9.

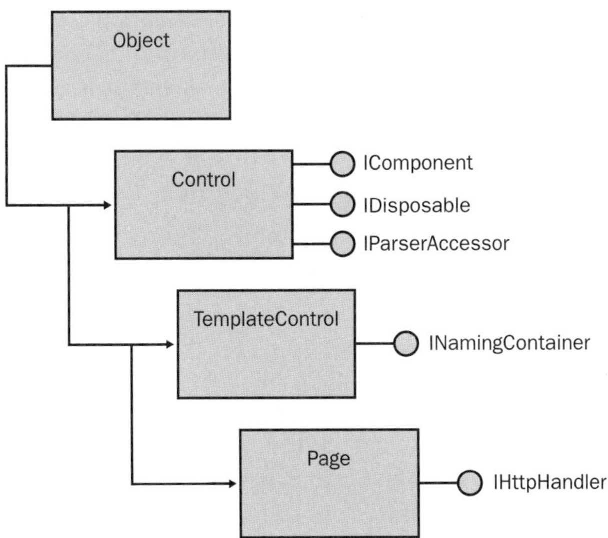


**Figure 2-9** The hierarchy of classes from which *Page* inherits.

From the parent *Control* class, *Page* inherits the base behavior for interacting with all other components in the CLR—the *IComponent* interface—and for releasing unmanaged resources (the *IDisposable* interface). In addition, the *IParserAccessor* interface groups the methods that ASP.NET controls must implement to recognize parsed child elements. The *IParserAccessor* interface plays a key role in the implementation of the control tree in the dynamically generated source code for requested ASP.NET pages. (Actually, the *IParserAccessor* interface consists of the single *AddParsedSubObject* method we saw largely used in the code shown in "Reviewing the Class Source Code" section.)

> **Note** The *Control* class also implements the *IDataBindingsAccessor* interface. This interface, though, is not involved with the run-time behavior of server controls. The interface allows access to the collection of data-binding expressions on a control at design time.

Derived from a class—*TemplateControl*—that implements *INamingContainer*, *Page* also serves as the naming container for all its constituent controls. In the .NET Framework, the naming container for a control is the first parent control that implements the *INamingContainer* interface. For any class that implements the naming container interface, ASP.NET creates a new virtual namespace in which all child controls are guaranteed to have unique names in the overall tree of controls. (This is also a very important feature for iterative data-bound controls, such as *DataGrid*, and for user controls.)

The *Page* class also implements the methods of the *IHttpHandler* interface, thus qualifying as the handler of a particular type of HTTP requests—those for .aspx files. The key element of the *IHttpHandler* interface is the *ProcessRequest* method, which is the method the ASP.NET runtime calls to start the page processing that will actually serve the request.

> **Note** *INamingContainer* is a marker interface that has no methods. Its presence alone, though, forces the ASP.NET runtime to create an additional namespace for naming the child controls of the page (or the control) that implements it. The *Page* class is the naming container of all the page's controls, with the clear exception of those controls that implement the *INamingContainer* interface themselves or are children of controls that implement the interface.

## Properties of the *Page* Object

The properties of the *Page* object can be classified in three distinct groups: intrinsic objects, worker properties, and page-specific properties. Tables 2-4, 2-5, and 2-6 enumerate and describe them.

**Table 2-4 ASP.NET Intrinsic Objects in the *Page* Class**

| Property | Description |
| --- | --- |
| *Application* | Instance of the *HttpApplicationState* class, represents the state of the application. Functionally equivalent to the ASP intrinsic *Application* object. |
| *Cache* | Instance of the *Cache* class, implements the cache for an ASP.NET application. More efficient and powerful than *Application*, it supports item decay and expiration. |
| *Request* | Instance of the *HttpRequest* class, represents the current HTTP request. Functionally equivalent to the ASP intrinsic *Request* object. |
| *Response* | Instance of the *HttpResponse* class, sends HTTP response data to the client. Functionally equivalent to the ASP intrinsic *Response* object. |

**Table 2-4 ASP.NET Intrinsic Objects in the *Page* Class**

| Property | Description |
|---|---|
| *Server* | Instance of the *HttpServerUtility* class, provides helper methods for processing Web requests. Functionally equivalent to the ASP intrinsic *Server* object. |
| *Session* | Instance of the *HttpSessionState* class, manages user-specific data. Functionally equivalent to the ASP intrinsic *Session* object. |
| *Trace* | Instance of the *TraceContext* class, performs tracing on the page. |
| *User* | An *IPrincipal* object that represents the user making the request. |

We'll cover *Request*, *Response*, and *Server* in Chapter 13; *Application*, *Cache*, and *Session* in Chapter 14; and *User* and security will be the subject of Chapter 15.

**Table 2-5 Worker Properties of the *Page* Class**

| Property | Description |
|---|---|
| *Controls* | Returns the collection of all the child controls contained in the current page |
| *ErrorPage* | Gets or sets the error page to which the requesting browser is redirected in case of an unhandled page exception |
| *IsPostBack* | Indicates whether the page is being loaded in response to a client postback or whether it is being loaded for the first time |
| *IsValid* | Indicates whether page validation succeeded |
| *NamingContainer* | Returns *null* |
| *Page* | Returns the current *Page* object |
| *Parent* | Returns *null* |
| *TemplateSourceDirectory* | Gets the virtual directory of the page |
| *Validators* | Returns the collection of all validation controls contained in the page |
| *ViewStateUserKey* | String property used to assign an identifier to the view state variable for individual users. This trick is a line of defense against one-click attacks. *The property is not available with ASP.NET 1.0.* |

In the context of an ASP.NET application, the *Page* object is the root of the hierarchy. For this reason, inherited properties such as *NamingContainer* and *Parent* always return *null*. The *Page* property, on the other hand, returns an instance of the same object (*this* in C# and *Me* in Visual Basic .NET).

A special note deserves the *ViewStateUserKey* property that has been added with version 1.1 of the .NET Framework. A common use for the user key would be to stuff user-specific information that will then be used to hash the contents of the view state along with other information. (See Chapter 14.) A typical value for the *ViewStateUserKey* property is the name of the authenticated user or the user's session ID. This contrivance reinforces the security level for the view-state information and further lowers the likelihood of attacks. If you employ a user-specific key, an attacker couldn't construct a valid view state for your user account unless he could also authenticate as you. That way, you have another barrier against on-click attacks. This technique, though, might not be really effective for Web sites that allow anonymous access unless you have some other unique tracking device running.

Note that if you plan to set the *ViewStateUserKey* property, you must do that during the *Page_Init* event. If you attempt to do it later (for example, when *Page_Load* fires), an exception will be thrown.

**Table 2-6 Page-Specific Properties of the *Page* Class**

| Property | Description |
|---|---|
| *ClientID* | Always returns the empty string. |
| *ClientTarget* | Set to the empty string by default, allows you to specify the type of browser the HTML should comply with. Setting this property disables automatic detection of browser capabilities. |
| *EnableViewState* | Gets or sets whether the page has to manage view-state data. You can also enable or disable the view-state feature through the *EnableViewState* attribute of the *@Page* directive. |
| *ID* | Always returns the empty string. |
| *SmartNavigation* | Gets or sets a value indicating whether smart navigation is enabled. Smart navigation exploits a bunch of browser-specific capabilities to enhance the user's experience with the page. The feature works only with Internet Explorer 5.5 and newer versions. You can also enable or disable this feature through the *SmartNavigation* attribute of the *@Page* directive. |
| *UniqueID* | Always returns the empty string. |
| *Visible* | Indicates whether ASP.NET has to render the page. If you set *Visible* to *false*, ASP.NET doesn't generate any HTML code for the page. When *Visible* is *false*, only the text explicitly written using *Response.Write* hits the client. |

The three ID properties (*ID*, *ClientID*, and *UniqueID*) always return the empty string from a *Page* object. They make sense only for server controls.

## Methods of the *Page* Object

The whole range of *Page* methods can be classified in a few categories based on the tasks each method accomplishes. A few methods are involved with the generation of the HTML for the page (as shown in Table 2-7); others are helper methods to build the page and manage the constituent controls (as shown in Table 2-8). Finally, a third group collects all the methods that have to do with client-side scripting (as shown in Table 2-9).

**Table 2-7 Methods for HTML Generation**

| Method | Description |
|---|---|
| *DataBind* | Binds all the data-bound controls contained in the page to their data sources. The *DataBind* method doesn't generate code itself but prepares the ground for the forthcoming rendering. |
| *RegisterRequiresPostBack* | Registers the specified control with the page so that the control will receive a post-back handling notice. In other words, the page will call the *LoadPostData* method of registered controls. *LoadPostData* requires the implementation of the *IPostBackDataHandler* interface. |
| *RegisterRequiresRaiseEvent* | Registers the specified control to handle an incoming postback event. The control must implement the *IPostBackEventHandler* interface. |
| *RenderControl* | Outputs the HTML text for the page, including tracing information if tracing is enabled. |
| *VerifyRenderingInServerForm* | Controls call this method when they render to ensure they are included in the body of a server form. The method does not return a value, but it throws an exception in case of error. |

In an ASP.NET page, no control can be placed outside a *<form>* tag with the *runat* attribute set to *server*. The *VerifyRenderingInServerForm* method is used by Web and HTML controls to ensure they are rendered correctly. In theory, custom controls should call this method during the rendering phase. In many situations, the custom control embeds or derives an existing Web or HTML control that will make the check itself.

**Table 2-8 Worker Methods of the *Page* Object**

| Method | Description |
|---|---|
| *DesignerInitialize* | Initializes the instance of the *Page* class at design time, when the page is being hosted by RAD designers like Visual Studio. |
| *FindControl* | Takes a control's ID and searches for it in the page's naming container. The search doesn't dig out child controls that are naming containers themselves. |
| *GetTypeHashCode* | Retrieves the hash code generated by *ASP.xxx_aspx* page objects at run time. (See the source code of the sample page class we discussed earlier in the "Reviewing the Class Source Code" section.) In the base *Page* class, the method implementation simply returns 0; significant numbers are returned by classes used for actual pages. |
| *HasControls* | Determines whether the page contains any child controls. |
| *LoadControl* | Compiles and loads a user control from a .ascx file, and returns a *Control* object. If the user control supports caching, the object returned is *PartialCachingControl*. |
| *LoadTemplate* | Compiles and loads a user control from a .ascx file, and returns it wrapped in an instance of an internal class that implements the *ITemplate* interface. The internal class is named *SimpleTemplate*. |
| *MapPath* | Retrieves the physical, fully qualified path that an absolute or relative virtual path maps to. |
| *ParseControl* | Parses a well-formed input string, and returns an instance of the control that corresponds to the specified markup text. If the string contains more controls, only the first is taken into account. The *runat* attribute can be omitted. The method returns an object of type *Control* and must be cast to a more specific type. |
| *RegisterViewStateHandler* | Mostly for internal use, the method sets an internal flag causing the page view state to be persisted. If this method is not called in the prerendering phase, no view state will ever be written. Typically, only the *HtmlForm* server control for the page calls this method. There's no need to call it from within user applications. |
| *ResolveUrl* | Resolves a relative URL into an absolute URL based on the value of the *TemplateSourceDirectory* property. |
| *Validate* | Instructs any validation controls included on the page to validate their assigned information. |

The methods *LoadControl* and *LoadTemplate* share a common code infrastructure but return different objects, as the following pseudocode shows:

```
public Control LoadControl(string virtualPath) {
    Control ascx = GetCompiledUserControlType(virtualPath);
    ascx.InitializeAsUserControl();
    return ascx;
}
public ITemplate LoadTemplate(string virtualPath) {
    Control ascx = GetCompiledUserControlType(virtualPath);
    return new SimpleTemplate(ascx);
}
```

Both methods differ from *ParseControl* in that the latter never causes compilation but simply parses the string and infers control information. The information is then used to create and initialize a new instance of the control class. As mentioned, the *runat* attribute is unnecessary in this context. In ASP.NET, the *runat* attribute is key, but in practice, it has no other role than marking the surrounding markup text for parsing and instantiation. It does not contain information useful to instantiate a control, and for this reason can be omitted from the strings you pass directly to *ParseControl.*

Table 2-9 enumerates all the methods in the *Page* class that have to do with HTML and script code to be inserted in the client page.

**Table 2-9 Script-Related Methods**

| Method | Description |
|---|---|
| *GetPostBackClientEvent* | Calls into *GetPostBackEventReference.* |
| *GetPostBackClientHyperlink* | Appends *javascript:* to the beginning of the return string received from *GetPostBackEventReference.*<br>`javascript:__doPostBack('CtlID','')` |
| *GetPostBackEventReference* | Returns the prototype of the client-side script function that causes, when invoked, a postback. It takes a *Control* and an argument, and it returns a string like this:<br>`__doPostBack('CtlID','')` |
| *IsClientScriptBlockRegistered* | Determines whether the specified client script is registered with the page. |
| *IsStartupScriptRegistered* | Determines whether the specified client startup script is registered with the page. |
| *RegisterArrayDeclaration* | Use this method to add an *ECMAScript* array to the client page. This method accepts the name of the array and a string that will be used verbatim as the body of the array. For example, if you call the method with arguments such as "*theArray*" and "*'a', 'b'*", you get the following JavaScript code:<br>`var theArray = new Array('a', 'b');` |

*(continued)*

**Table 2-9 Script-Related Methods** *(continued)*

| Method | Description |
|---|---|
| *RegisterClientScriptBlock* | An ASP.NET page uses this method to emit client-side script blocks in the client page just after the opening tag of the HTML *<form>* element. |
| *RegisterHiddenField* | Use this method to automatically register a hidden field on the page. |
| *RegisterOnSubmitStatement* | Use this method to emit client script code that handles the client *OnSubmit* event. The script should be a JavaScript function call to client code registered elsewhere. |
| *RegisterStartupScript* | An ASP.NET page uses this method to emit client-side script blocks in the client page just before closing the HTML *<form>* element. |

Many methods listed in Table 2-9 let you emit script in the client page—either JavaScript or VBScript. When you use any of these methods, you actually tell the page to insert that script code when the page is rendered. So when any of these methods execute, the script-related information is simply cached in internal structures and used later when the page object generates its HTML text. The same pattern applies to hidden fields and *ECMAScript* arrays.

> **Note** JavaScript is the script language that virtually any available browser supports. For this reason, some of the methods in Table 2-9 default to JavaScript. However, when you register a script block, nothing really prevents you from using VBScript as long as you set the language attribute of the *<script>* tag accordingly. On the other hand, methods such as *RegisterOnSubmitStatement* and *RegisterArrayDeclaration* can be used only with JavaScript code.

## Events of the *Page* Object

In addition to the events we mentioned earlier, the *Page* class fires a few extra events that are notified during the page life cycle. As Table 2-10 shows, some events are orthogonal to the typical life cycle of a page and are fired as extra-page situations evolve.

**Table 2-10 Events That a Page Can Fire**

| Event | Description |
|---|---|
| *AbortTransaction* | Occurs for ASP.NET pages marked to participate in an automatic transaction when a transaction aborts. |
| *CommitTransaction* | Occurs for ASP.NET pages marked to participate in an automatic transaction when a transaction commits. |
| *DataBinding* | Occurs when the *DataBind* method is called on the page to bind all the child controls to their respective data sources. |
| *Disposed* | Occurs when the page is released from memory, which is the last stage of the page life cycle. |
| *Error* | Occurs when an unhandled exception is thrown. |
| *Init* | Occurs when the page is initialized, which is the first step in the page life cycle. |
| *Load* | Occurs when the page loads up. |
| *PreRender* | Occurs when the page is about to render. |
| *Unload* | Occurs when the page is unloaded from memory but not yet disposed. |

## The Code-Behind Technique

At the highest level of abstraction, an ASP.NET page is made of page layout information and code. The code for the page can be developed in two ways: inline through the *<script>* tag or by using a code-behind class. All inline code must be written in the same language declared for the page and will be copied verbatim in the source code of the dynamically generated class that represents the .aspx resource in execution.

A code-behind class inherits from *Page*, either directly or indirectly. As such, the code-behind class encapsulates in an object-oriented fashion all the functionalities you're building in the page—event handlers, method and property overrides, and new members. Visual Studio .NET takes advantage of code-behind classes to implement an efficient and effective code editor. As mentioned in Chapter 1, though, the code-behind syntax used by Visual Studio .NET is a bit unusual and to some extent undocumented. As a matter of fact, though, the resultant page architecture is even more efficient in practice.

In this section, we'll start with a review of the code-behind scheme of Visual Studio .NET, and then we'll move on to more general considerations of code-behind.

## Code and Layout Separation

Code-behind is an architectural feature designed to clearly separate code and layout in an ASP.NET page. To achieve this, though, it exploits one of the cornerstones of object-oriented programming (OOP)—class inheritance. Just the capability to inherit pages from existing pages leads to even more attractive and compelling uses of the code-behind feature, such as visual inheritance and Web site master pages.

### Code-Behind in Visual Studio .NET

When you create a new page in an ASP.NET project, Visual Studio .NET creates an .aspx file and a ghost file with the same name as the .aspx plus a .cs or .vb extension, depending on the project language. The .aspx file contains control declarations and other layout information. The .cs (or .vb) file contains all the code for the page. The page is seen as a class derived from *Page* with overrides and new members as appropriate.

When you build the Visual Studio .NET project, the page class is compiled into the project's assembly and the run-time link between the .aspx file and its base class is given by the value of the *Inherits* attribute in the *@Page* directive. The design-time link between the .aspx file and its code-behind class is given by the value of the *CodeBehind* attribute in the *@Page* directive. The *CodeBehind* attribute is blissfully ignored by the ASP.NET runtime and makes sense only to Visual Studio .NET.

The separation between code and layout is achieved by using two distinct files—the .aspx for the layout and the .cs (or whatever language you use) for the code—that the IDE manages transparently.

### Code-Behind in Action at Run Time

For example, if the ASP.NET runtime receives a request for a page.aspx resource, the runtime creates an instance of a dynamically generated class named *ASP.Page_aspx*. By default, this class inherits from *Page* or from the class you specify in the configuration. The base class can be changed on a per-page basis also through the *Inherits* attribute in the *@Page* directive. The *Inherits* attribute contains only the fully qualified name of the class from which *ASP.Page_aspx* must derive. It doesn't say anything about the actual location of the class.

The ASP.NET runtime locates the base class assembly using the usual probing algorithm for missing assemblies. One of the directories scanned is the virtual folder's Bin directory, which is the location in which Visual Studio .NET places the project assemblies at development time.

For the code-behind feature to work, the *Inherits* attribute is always necessary, as it is the only supported way to inform the ASP.NET runtime to derive *ASP.Page_aspx* from a different and more specific page class. (The code-behind class itself must necessarily derive from *Page* or from a class that, in turn, inherits from *Page*.)

You can also deploy a code-behind class as plain source code. In this case, you use *Inherits* to indicate the name of the class and the *Src* attribute to specify the URL from which the class can be loaded and compiled, as shown in the following line of code:

```
<%@ Page Language="C#" Inherits="MyBasePageClass" Src="MyBasePage.cs" %>
```

The file pointed to by the *Src* attribute is automatically compiled on demand and recompiled in case of updates. It goes without saying that the class file used must match the language of the page.

> **Tip** Code-behind classes and inline code can happily cohabit within the same Web Forms page. Interestingly, this fact alone opens up the possibility of using multiple languages to develop the page. In fact, you could use one language to develop the code-behind class and then link it to the page using the *Inherits* attribute. You're responsible for compiling the class and deploying the class through an assembly. Next, you'd use the other language to set the *Language* attribute and develop inline code for the page. Finally, you should note that this programming style is not supported by Visual Studio .NET. If you like it, use Web Matrix or other third-party commercial products.

If you decide to use the *Src* attribute, you have to deploy the source code of the class, thus making the logic of your solution available on the Web server. On the other hand, this approach simplifies the maintenance of the Web site because you could modify the file (or better yet, a copy of it) on the Web server. Otherwise, you have to modify the source, rebuild the project yourself, and then deploy it again to the Web server.

> **Note** Visual Studio .NET does not support code-behind if it is implemented through the *Src* attribute. In this case, you can either resort to your own code editor or, better yet, download and install the free Web Matrix editor.

## Moving to Code-Behind

A practical advantage of the code-behind approach is that it allows two programmers or programming teams to simultaneously work on the development of a Web page. After the structure of a page is defined in terms of the number, names, and types of constituent controls, HTML designers can work on the appearance of the page, determining the position, colors, and fonts of the controls; they can even determine the necessity for client-side scripting. At the same time, programmers can develop the code and event handlers required for the page to work properly and fulfill users' expectations.

Any existing ASP.NET page can migrate to code-behind with very few changes. The first step is writing a class that inherits, either directly or indirectly, from *Page*. Next, you add to the class, as a protected or public member, any control declared in the page layout that has the *runat* attribute set to *server*. Also, convert any global variable or procedure in the *<script>* section of the original ASP.NET page into a new member of the class with the scope and visibility you want.

Be sure to choose the right control type that will lie behind an ASP.NET or HTML tag. For example, an *<asp:textbox runat="server">* tag maps to a *TextBox* control, whereas an equivalent *<input type=text runat="server">* tag maps to *HtmlInputText*.

> **Caution** Because the actual page class being processed will inherit from the code-behind class, make sure you don't declare any control members as *private*. In this case, in fact, the actual derived class won't be able to access the control because of the protection level. Use the *public* modifier—or better yet, the *protected* modifier—instead.

Once you've accomplished this, you're almost done. A subtle design issue you might want to consider is the following. Typically, your Web page will have controls that fire server-side events—for example, a submit button:

```
<asp:button runat="server" id="TheButton" text="Submit" />
```

To make the control usable, you need to bind it to some code. You can do this in two ways. You could either add an *onclick* attribute to the tag or programmatically define an event handler in the code-behind class. In the former case, you end up having the following code:

```
<asp:button runat="server" id="TheButton" text="Submit"
    onclick="OnSubmitDocument" />
```

There's nothing bad about this code, at least in terms of overall functionality. However, it makes the ideal of neat separation between code and layout a bit less neat. The page layout, in fact, contains a reference to a piece of code. Among other things, this means HTML designers must remember to change the attribute should they decide to rename the handler.

From a design standpoint, a much better approach is to go the programmatic route and register the event handler with code. In C#, you would accomplish this with the following code:

```
override protected void OnInit(EventArgs e)
{
    this.TheButton.Click += new System.EventHandler(this.OnSubmitDocument);
}
```

In both cases, the *OnSubmitDocument* method should be defined in the code-behind class.

## Page Inheritance

It's hard to say whether code-behind inspired the separation between code and layout or whether things happened the other way around—that is, code-behind was invented as a way to implement code and layout separation. Rather than concern ourselves with how it all developed, let's look at code-behind from another, more architectural, perspective.

At the end of the day, code-behind is just a fancy name for the ASP.NET feature that lets you explicitly set the base class for the dynamically created page class. And I think this feature alone is much more important to developers than the separation between code and layout. To achieve code separation, you don't need to know about the architecture of code-behind—just use Visual Studio .NET and you're done.

The capability of changing the base class of dynamic pages opens a new world of possibilities that can be described as the Web counterpart of the visual form inheritance we have in Windows Forms applications. For Windows Forms, visual inheritance indicates the .NET Framework ability to let you create new forms by inheriting from previously created forms. The .NET Framework provides you with a base *Form* class that you extend in user projects by adding child controls. Each application form is definitely an instance of some user-defined, *Form*-based class.

You normally inherit your custom forms always from the base class *Form*, but a smarter approach is possible. For example, to make all your applications share the same look and feel, you could create a form class inheriting from *Form*, add some features and controls, and compile the resultant class into a new assembly. Suppose you call this form class *AcmeForm*. Next, whenever you need to create a new Windows Forms application with the same characteristics, you simply derive the main window from *AcmeForm* and get a ready-to-use and feature-rich form window. Although it's impressive to show, this feature involves nothing that qualifies as rocket science; it's just the offspring of class inheritance. As such, it can be applied to ASP.NET pages as well. Code-behind and the *Inherits* attribute of the *@Page* directive are the underpinnings of this important feature.

### A Server-Side Abstraction for Client-Side Events

To demonstrate a real-world application of the code-behind technique, let's consider the level of server-side abstraction that ASP.NET provides for client-side events such as setting the input focus. ASP.NET doesn't provide, and it is not supposed to provide, a rich object model for client-side scripting and page decoration. In other words, you have to write any JavaScript code you might need and attach it to the page using the *RegisterXXX* methods of the *Page* class.

That said, though, consider that almost every Web page displays some HTML control that would work much better if you could set the input focus. For example, a page that contains a list of text boxes for data entry would look much more user-friendly if the input focus was automatically placed on the first field. After all, it's not such a hard task; a few lines of JavaScript code would do the job quickly and effectively. You need to write a small script to set the focus and call it from the body's *onload* method. The following HTML page shows just that:

```
<html>
<script language="javascript">
function SetInputFocus() {
    if(document.__theForm["fname"] != null)
        document.__theForm["fname"].focus();
}
</script>

<body onload="SetInputFocus()">
<form name="__theForm">
    <input type="text" value="Joe" name="fname">
    <input type="text" value="Users" name="lname">
</form>
</body>
</html>
```

Although it's easy to understand and implement, the solution is still boring to code (or even to cut and paste) for each page of the application. The code-behind technique comes to the rescue. The idea is that you derive a new class from *Page* and make sure it contains the needed script code and runs it upon startup.

### A Better Page Class

The following listing demonstrates an alternative *Page* class. It inherits from the *System.Web.UI.Page* class and exposes a *Focus* property that clients can set with the name of the HTML control with the input focus:

```
using System;
using System.Web.UI;
using System.Text;

namespace ProAspNet.CS.Ch02
{
    public class Page : System.Web.UI.Page
    {
        public Page()
        {
        }

        // Internals
        private const string FUNCTION_NAME = "__setFocus";
        private const string SCRIPT_NAME = "__inputFocusHandler";

        // Gets/Sets the name of the HTML control with the input focus
        public string Focus;

        // Registers client-side script
        protected override void OnPreRender(EventArgs e)
        {
            base.OnPreRender(e);
            AddStartupScript();
        }

        // Create the script strings
        private void AddStartupScript()
        {
            // Find the ID of the ASP.NET form
            string formName = "";
            foreach(Control ctl in this.Controls)
                if (ctl is HtmlForm)  {
                    formName = "\"" + ctl.UniqueID + "\"";
                    break;
                }

            // Add the script to declare the function
            StringBuilder sb = new StringBuilder("");
            sb.Append("\n<script language=javascript>\n");
            sb.Append("function ");
            sb.Append(FUNCTION_NAME);
            sb.Append("(ctl) {");
            sb.Append("\n  if (document.forms[");
            sb.Append(formName);
            sb.Append("][ctl] != null)  {");
            sb.Append("\n      document.forms[");
```

```
                sb.Append(formName);
                sb.Append("][ctl].focus();");
                sb.Append("\n  }");
                sb.Append("\n}\n");

                // Add the script to call the function
                sb.Append(FUNCTION_NAME);
                sb.Append("('");
                sb.Append(Focus);
                sb.Append("');\n<");
                sb.Append("/");
                sb.Append("script>");

                // Register the script (names are CASE-SENSITIVE)
                if (!IsStartupScriptRegistered(SCRIPT_NAME))
                    RegisterStartupScript(SCRIPT_NAME, sb.ToString());
            }
        }
}
```

In the *PreRender* event, the page registers a startup script. If the server form is named *theForm* and the *Focus* property is set to *user*, the following script will be generated:

```
<script language=javascript>
function __setFocus(ctl) {
    if (document.forms["theForm"][ctl] != null)  {
        document.forms["theForm"][ctl].focus();
    }
}
__setFocus('user');
</script>
```

The *__setFocus* JavaScript function is first declared and then invoked with a particular argument. The script is registered using the *RegisterStartupScript* method. A startup script is placed exactly before closing the *<form>* tag and executed when the browser has finished with the rest of the form—in this sense, it is called a startup script and is functionally equivalent to setting the *onload* attribute of the page body.

### Programmatically Set the Input Focus

Because the *ProAspNet.CS.Ch02.Page* class inherits from *Page*, you can use it wherever a page class is acceptable. To make sure that ASP.NET builds an .aspx page just from the *ProAspNet.CS.Ch02.Page* class, use this type with the *Inherits* attribute of the page directive. Of course, you need to have an assembly for the class in one of the paths the ASP.NET runtime can reach—typically the virtual folder's Bin directory. The following page automatically sets the input focus to the field named *user*. The code in boldface type is all you have to add to an existing page to support the feature, which sets a new base class and the input focus:

```
<%@ Page Language="C#" Inherits="ProAspNet.CS.Ch02.Page" %>

<script runat="server">
    public void Page_Load(object sender, EventArgs e)
    {
        if (!IsPostBack)
            this.Focus = "user";
    }
</script>

<html>
<head><title>Pro ASP.NET (Ch 02)</title></head>
<body>
    <h2>Log on to the System</h2>
    <form runat="server">
        <b>UserName</b><br>
        <asp:textbox runat="server" id="user" /><br>
        <b>Password</b><br>
        <asp:textbox runat="server" id="pswd" /><br>
        <asp:button id="go" runat="server" text="Connect" />
    </form>
</body>
</html>
```

The *IsPostBack* property is set to *true* if the page is being displayed after a postback. If you don't check against *IsPostBack*, the input focus will be set to the control named *user* each time the page is accessed; otherwise, it will be set only the first time the page is accessed in the session.

## Changing the Default Page Base Type

As mentioned earlier, by default a page inherits from the *Page* class or from any other code-behind class specified in the *@Page* directive. If you need all pages in an application (or in a certain folder) to inherit from a common and user-defined class, you can override the base page type from the *System.Web.UI.Page* class to whatever class you want. Obviously, the new page class must in turn inherit from *System.Web.UI.Page*.

For example, to make all the pages in a Web application inherit the focus feature we discussed earlier, create a web.config file in the application's root folder and give it the following content:

```
<configuration>
    <system.web>
        <pages pageBaseType="ProAspNet.CS.Ch02.Page, Page" />
    </system.web>
</configuration>
```

The *pageBaseType* attribute must be set to a valid type name—that is, a comma-separated string formed by a type name and the assembly name. In the preceding code, the specified class is implemented in the page.dll assembly.

Note that the base page could also be changed for all the applications running on a server machine. In this case, you must edit the machine.config file, locate the *<pages>* section, and add the *pageBaseType* attribute. By default, the attribute is initialized implicitly and is not listed in the configuration file. To edit both web.config and machine.config, you need administrator privileges.

> **Note** In the next version of ASP.NET, the *WebControl* class and the *Page* class will provide a nearly identical feature through a method named *SetFocus*. The method takes the ID of a control and caches it internally. When the page is rendered to HTML, ad hoc script code will be generated to set the focus to the control.

## Master Pages in ASP.NET

A large number of Web sites these days contain similar-looking pages that share the same header, footer, and perhaps some navigational menus or search forms. What's the recommended approach for reusing code across pages? One possibility is wrapping these user-interface elements in user controls and referencing them in each page. Although the model is extremely powerful and produces highly modular code, when you have hundreds of pages to work with, it soon becomes unmanageable.

An alternative approach entails using code-behind to aim at a kind of visual inheritance akin to that of Windows Forms. In this case, the custom base class programmatically generates user-interface elements such as the page header. In addition, the page class could expose custom objects as programmable entities—for example, a collection for the links to display on the header. To build a new page, you simply set the *Inherits* attribute with the class name. When part of the user interface (UI) is programmatically generated, merging the base elements and the actual content of the content page can be problematic unless absolute positioning is used. In the sample code of this chapter (located at ch02\Inherit), you find an application that solves this issue by forcing the client page to include an *<asp:placeholder>* control with a particular ID just where a particular parent UI element should appear.

In the next version of ASP.NET, the concept of the *master page* will be introduced. A master page is a distinct file referenced at the application level, as well as at the page level, that contains the static layout of the page. Regions that each *derived* page can customize are referenced in the master page with a special placeholder control. A derived page is simply a collection of blocks the run time will use to fill the holes in the master. Master pages in the next version of

ASP.NET are orthogonal to true visual inheritance. The contents of the master, in fact, are merged into the derived page rather than serving as a base class for the derived page.

## Conclusion

ASP.NET is a complex technology built on top of a simple and, fortunately, solid and stable Web infrastructure. To provide highly improved performance and a richer programming tool set, ASP.NET builds a desktop-like abstraction model, but it still has to rely on HTTP and HTML to hit the target and meet end-user expectations.

There are two relevant aspects in the ASP.NET Web Forms model: the process model, including the Web server process model, and the page object model. ASP.NET anticipates some of the features of IIS 6.0—the new and revolutionary version of the Microsoft Web information services. ASP.NET applications run in a separate worker process (as all applications will do in IIS 6.0); ASP.NET applications support output caching (as IIS 6.0 will do on behalf of all types of Web applications); and finally, the ASP.NET runtime automatically recycles processes to guarantee excellent performance in spite of run-time anomalies, memory leaks, and programming errors. The same feature becomes a system feature in IIS 6.0.

Each request of a URL that ends with .aspx is assigned to an application object working within the CLR hosted by the worker process. The request results in a dynamically compiled class that is then instantiated and put to work. The *Page* class is the base class for all ASP.NET pages. An instance of this class runs behind any URL that ends with .aspx. The code-behind technique allows you to programmatically change the base class for a given .aspx resource. The net effect of code-behind is the possibility to implement very cool features such as code and layout separation and page inheritance.

In this chapter, we mentioned controls several times. Server controls are components that get input from the user, process the input, and output a response as HTML. In the next chapter, we'll explore various server controls, which include Web controls, HTML controls, validation controls, and data-bound controls.

## Resources

- HTTP Architecture (*http://www.develop.com/conferences/conferencedotnet/materials/A4.pdf*)
- HTTP Pipeline (*http://www.develop.com/summercamp/conferencedotnet/materials/W2.pdf*)
- Securely Implement Request Processing, Filtering, and Content Redirection with HTTP Pipelines in ASP.NET (*http://msdn.microsoft.com/msdnmag/issues/02/09/HTTPPipelines*)
- Viewstate Optimization Strategies in ASP.NET (*http://www.webreference.com/programming/asp/viewstate*)
- KB306005 Repair IIS Mapping After You Remove and Reinstall IIS
- KB315158 ASP.NET Does Not Work with the Default ASPNET Account on a Domain Controller

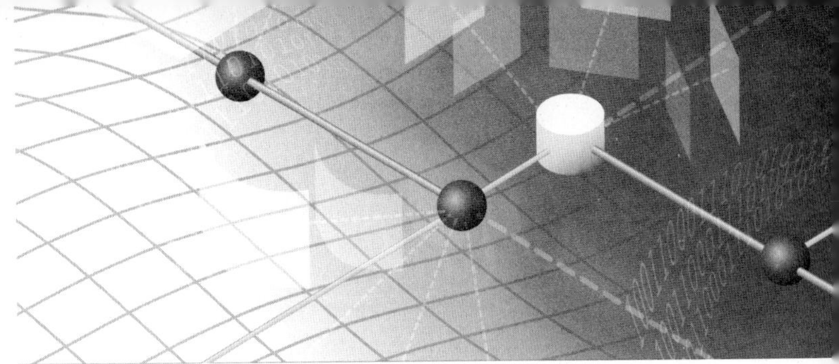

# 3

# ASP.NET Core Server Controls

*It does not matter how slowly you go so long as you do not stop.*
—*Confucius*

ASP.NET pages are made of code, markup tags, literal text, and server controls. Based on the request, the server controls generate the right markup language. The ASP.NET runtime combines the output of all controls and serves the client a page to display in a browser.

The programming richness of ASP.NET springs from the wide library of server controls that covers the basic tasks of HTML interaction—for example, collecting text through input tags—as well as more advanced functionalities such as grid-based data display. In the ASP.NET world, more advanced and very specific controls ensure all basic tasks and common functionalities are available. The *AdRotator* and *Calendar* controls are two illustrious examples.

Key to ASP.NET control programming is the *runat* attribute. If a control is declared without the *runat* attribute, it is considered plain text and is output verbatim. If a control contains the *runat* attribute set to the value of "*server*", ASP.NET creates and handles an instance of the control while processing the page on the server. All this happens transparently to the user and the programmer as part of the ASP.NET runtime infrastructure.

In Chapter 1, we identified two main families of server controls—HTML server controls and Web server controls. In ASP.NET, these controls are typically referred to as HTML controls and Web controls. HTML controls map to HTML tags and are implemented through server-side classes whose programming interface faithfully represents the standard set of attributes for the corresponding HTML tag. Web controls, in turn, are a more abstract library of controls in which adherence to HTML syntax is much less strict. As a result, Web and HTML controls share a large common subset of functionalities and, in spite of a few exceptions, we could say that Web controls, functionally speaking, are a superset of HTML controls. Web controls also feature a richer development environment with a larger set of methods, properties and events.

As we'll see in more detail in the following pages, a second and more thoughtful look at the characteristics of the server controls in ASP.NET reveals the existence of more than just two families of controls. In real-world ASP.NET applications, you'll end up using controls from at least the following categories: HTML controls, Web controls, validation controls, data-bound controls, user controls, mobile controls, and custom controls. Validation controls are a special subset of Web controls and deserve to be treated in a separate section. Data-bound controls are not a category per se, with features that make them different from HTML or Web controls. Data-binding, instead, refers to the control's capability of connecting some of its properties to particular data sources. Hence, data-bound controls fall into any of the previously listed groups of server controls, but deserve a section of their own because of their importance and frequent use. User controls—also referred to as *pagelets* in relatively outdated literature—are visual aggregates of existing Web and HTML controls that appear as individual, encapsulated, programmable controls to external callers. Mobile controls are used when creating Web applications that target mobile devices. Custom controls refer to server controls you create that derive from a base control class.

In this chapter, we'll cover HTML controls, Web controls, validation controls, and data-bound controls. We'll cover user controls in Chapter 10, mobile controls in Chapter 11, and custom controls in Chapter 18 through Chapter 20.

## Generalities of ASP.NET Server Controls

All ASP.NET server controls, including HTML and Web controls plus any custom controls you create or download, descend from the *Control* class. The class is defined in the *System.Web.UI* namespace and, as we discussed in Chapter 2, also represents the foundation of all ASP.NET pages. The *Control* class is declared as follows:

```
public class Control : IComponent, IDisposable, IParserAccessor,
    IDataBindingsAccessor
```

The *IComponent* interface defines the way in which the control interacts with the other components running in the common language runtime (CLR), whereas *IDisposable* implements the common pattern for releasing unmanaged resources. The *IParserAccessor* interface enables the control to work as the container of child controls. Finally, the *IDataBindingsAccessor* interface makes the control capable of supporting data-binding expressions at design time. The *IDataBindingsAccessor* interface defines a read-only collection—the *DataBindings* property—that contains all the data bindings for the controls available to rapid application development (RAD) designers such as Microsoft Visual Studio .NET. Note that the collection of data bindings exist only at design time and, as such, is useful only if you write a RAD designer for the control. (Design-time features are discussed further in Chapter 21.)

## Properties of the *Control* Class

The properties of the *Control* class have no user interface–specific features. The class, in fact, represents the minimum set of functionalities expected from a server control. The list of properties for the *Control* class is shown in Table 3-1.

**Table 3-1 Properties of a Server Control**

| Property | Description |
|---|---|
| *ClientID* | Gets the ID assigned to the control in the HTML page. The string is a slightly different version of the *UniqueID* property. *UniqueID* can contain the colon symbol (:), but this symbol is not allowed in *ClientID* and is replaced with the underscore (_). |
| *Controls* | Gets a collection filled with references to all the child controls. |
| *EnableViewState* | Gets or sets whether the control should persist its view state—and the view state of any child controls across multiple requests—to the configured location (for example, HTML hidden field, Web server memory, server-side databases or files). |
| *ID* | Gets or sets the name that will be used to programmatically identify the control in the ASP.NET page. |
| *NamingContainer* | Gets a reference to the control's naming container. A naming container is the namespace to which the control belongs. If the control doesn't define its own naming space, a reference to the parent control (or the page) is returned. |

*(continued)*

**Table 3-1 Properties of a Server Control** *(continued)*

| Property | Description |
|---|---|
| *Page* | Gets a reference to the *Page* instance that contains the control. |
| *Parent* | Gets a reference to the parent of the control in the page hierarchy. |
| *TemplateSourceDirectory* | Gets the virtual directory of the host page. |
| *UniqueID* | Gets a hierarchically qualified ID for the control. |
| *Visible* | Gets or sets whether ASP.NET has to render the control. |

The *Control* class is the ideal base class for new controls that have no user interface and don't require style information.

## Identifying a Server Control

The client ID of a control is generated from the value of the *UniqueID* property—the truly server-side identifier that ASP.NET generates for each control. The contents of the *ClientID* property differ from *UniqueID* simply in that all occurrences of the colon symbol (:) are replaced with the underscore (_). Colons in the *UniqueID* string are possible only if the control belongs to a naming container different than the current one—typically, the page.

ASP.NET generates the value for the *UniqueID* property based on the value of the *ID* property that the programmer indicates. If no ID has been specified, ASP.NET autogenerates a name such as *_ctlX*, where *X* is a progressive 0-based index. If the control's naming container is the host page, *UniqueID* simply takes the value of *ID*. Otherwise, the value of *ID* is prefixed with the string representing the naming container and the result is assigned to *UniqueID*.

> **Note** For performance reasons, ASP.NET caches into a static array defined on the *Control* class the strings ranging from *_ctl0* to *_ctl127*. These autogenerated and cached IDs will be used for the first 128 controls in the page defined with an empty ID string. If you have more than 128 controls with an empty ID, the ID string is generated on the fly for each control instance.

### Visibility of a Server Control

If you set *Visible* to *false*, ASP.NET doesn't generate any HTML code for the control. However, having *Visible* set to *false* doesn't really mean the control's code can't output text. The control is still an active object that exposes methods and handles events. If a method, or an event handler, sends text directly to the output console through *Response.Write*, this text will be displayed to the user anyway. A control with the *Visible* attribute set to *false* is still part of the page and maintains its position in the control tree.

## Methods of the *Control* Class

The methods of the *Control* class are listed and described in Table 3-2.

**Table 3-2 Methods of a Server Control**

| Method | Description |
|---|---|
| *DataBind* | Fires the *OnDataBinding* event and then invokes the *DataBind* method on all child controls |
| *Dispose* | Gives the control a chance to perform clean-up tasks before it gets released from memory |
| *FindControl* | Looks for the specified control in the collection of child controls. Child controls belonging to a different naming container are not sought. |
| *HasControls* | Indicates whether the control contains any child controls |
| *RenderControl* | Generates the HTML output for the control |
| *ResolveUrl* | Resolves a relative URL to an absolute URL based on the value passed to the *TemplateSourceDirectory* property |

At the *Control* class level, the *DataBind* method works recursively and simply loops through all the child controls and calls *DataBind* on each of them. On derived data-bound controls, the method resolves all data-binding expressions and updates the status of the control itself.

## Events of the *Control* Class

The *Control* class also defines a set of base events that all server controls in the .NET Framework support, as described in Table 3-3.

**Table 3-3 Events of a Server Control**

| Event | Description |
|---|---|
| *DataBinding* | Occurs when the *DataBind* method is called on a control and the control is binding to a data source |
| *Disposed* | Occurs when a control is released from memory—the last stage in the control life cycle |
| *Init* | Occurs when the control is initialized—the first step in the life cycle |
| *Load* | Occurs when the control is loaded into the page. Occurs after *Init*. |
| *PreRender* | Occurs when the control is about to render its content |
| *Unload* | Occurs when the control is unloaded from memory |

All server controls are rendered to HTML using the *RenderControl* method and, when this happens, the *PreRender* event is fired.

## HTML Controls

In ASP, HTML tags inserted in the layout of the server page were treated as opaque text and output to the client verbatim. This behavior has been entirely maintained in ASP.NET. A big difference, though, is that in ASP.NET, by simply adding the *runat* attribute with a value of *"server"*, you can bring to life otherwise-dead HTML text. Once transformed into a living instance of a server-side component, the original tag can be configured programmatically using an object-oriented approach. By design, HTML controls expose a set of methods and properties that carefully reflect the HTML syntax. For example, to set the default text of an input form field, you use a property named *Value*—case does matter in C# but not in Microsoft Visual Basic .NET—instead of the more expressive *Text*. The name of the server control is determined by the value of the *id* attribute. The following code snippet shows how to define a server-side input tag named *lastName*:

```
<input runat="server" id="lastName" type="text" />
```

The tag declaration does not include an explicit and static value for the *Value* attribute, which can be configured programmatically as follows:

```
void Page_Load(object sender, EventArgs e)
{
    lastName.Value = "Esposito";
}
```

After being processed by the ASP.NET runtime, the preceding declaration generates the following HTML code:

```
<input name="myName" id="myName" type="text" value="Esposito" />
```

Notice that a server-side *id* attribute expands to a pair of HTML attributes—*name* and *id*. Be aware that this happens for browser compatibility. In no way, does this mean that on the server *name* and *id* can be interchangeably used to name the server instance of the control. The name of the server control instance is given by *id*. If you specify both *name* and *id* on a server-side tag, the value assigned to *name* will be silently overridden.

## Generalities of HTML Controls

The .NET Framework provides predefined server controls for commonly used HTML elements such as *<form>*, *<input>*, and *<select>*, as well as for tables, images, and hyperlinks. All the predefined HTML server controls inherit from the same base class—the *HtmlControl* class. In addition, each control then provides its own set of specific properties and its own events.

Controls typically supply properties that allow you to manipulate the HTML attributes programmatically from within server code. HTML controls integrate well with data-binding and the ASP.NET state maintenance, and they also provide full support for postback events and client scripting. For example, for a button that gets clicked, you can have some JavaScript code running on the client responding to the *onclick* event as well as some code that handles the event on the server if the page posts back as the result of that event.

HTML controls are defined in the *System.Web.UI.HtmlControls* namespace. As mentioned, most HTML tags have a direct class counterpart in the .NET Framework, but not all do. HTML elements that don't map to a made-to-measure class are rendered through the *HtmlGenericControl* class and have attributes set using generic collections rather than direct properties. Generic controls include *<div>*, *<iframe>*, *<span>*, *<hr>*, *<font>*, and *<body>*. In general, you should bear in mind that every element that can appear in an HTML page can be marked as *runat="server"* and programmed and styled on the server.

### The *HtmlControl* Base Class

The *HtmlControl* class inherits from *Control* and defines the methods, properties, and events common to all HTML controls. Actually, many properties and all methods and events are simply inherited from the base class. Table 3-4 shows the list of properties specific to HTML controls.

**Table 3-4 Specific Properties of an HTML Control**

| Property | Description |
|---|---|
| *Attributes* | Gets a collection object representing all the attributes set on the control with the corresponding value |
| *Disabled* | Gets or sets a Boolean value, which indicates whether the HTML control is disabled |
| *Style* | Gets a collection object representing all CSS properties applied to the control |
| *TagName* | Gets the name of the HTML tag behind the control |

A disabled HTML server control is visible and always gets generated as HTML code. If the *Disabled* property is set to *true*, the *disabled* HTML attribute is inserted in the HTML output for the control. As mentioned earlier, if the *Visible* property is set to *false*, HTML is not generated for the control.

## Working with HTML Attributes

Each HTML control features more properties than those listed in Table 3-4. Properties of HTML server controls map to HTML attributes, and the values assigned to the properties are replicated in the HTML output. For controls that don't have an HTML direct counterpart, the *Attributes* collection is used to set attributes on the resulting HTML tag. This collection can also be used to set properties not mapped by the control's interface and, if needed, to define custom HTML attributes. Any content of the *Attributes* collection is managed as a string.

Given the following HTML code snippet, let's see how to programmatically set some attributes on the *<body>* tag:

```
<script>
function Init() {
    alert("Hello");
}
</script>

<script runat=server language="C#">
    void Page_Load(object sender, EventArgs e) {
        theBody.Attributes["onload"] = "Init()";
    }
</script>

<html>
    <body runat="server" id="theBody">
    </body>
</html>
```

You bind a JavaScript script to the *onload* attribute of the *<body>* tag. The resulting HTML code that the browser displays is as follows:

```
<script>
function Init() {
    alert("Hello");
}
</script>

<html>
    <body id="theBody" onload="Init()">
    </body>
</html>
```

The *Attributes* property is rendered through a special type of class named *AttributeCollection*. In spite of the name, the content of the class is not enumerable using the *for...each* statement because the *IEnumerable* interface is not supported. The content is instead stored in a *StateBag* object—the same class used for the ASP.NET view state—which is enumerable. However, the enumerability of the internal data container is exposed to the world. The *AttributeCollection* class provides ad hoc methods to render attributes of a text writer object and to add and remove elements. Interestingly, if you add an attribute named *Style*, the class is smart enough to reroute the assigned content to the *Style* collection.

### Hierarchy of HTML Controls

HTML controls can be grouped into two main categories—container and input controls. One control, though, cannot be easily catalogued in either of the two groups—the *HtmlImage* control, which is the ASP.NET counterpart of the *<img>* tag. Figure 3-1 shows the tree of HTML controls.

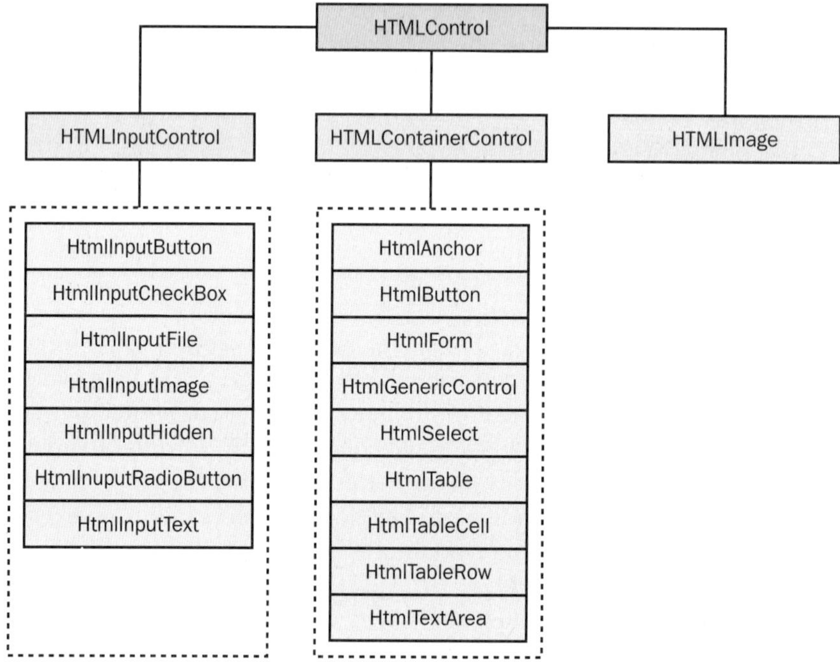


**Figure 3-1** A diagram that groups all HTML controls.

Notice that the controls in the figure are not grouped based on discretionary and perhaps arguable rules; instead they are grouped simply by looking at the base class of each control. The *HtmlImage* control forms a group of its own because it inherits directly from *HTMLControl* without any other intermediary class.

The input controls category includes all possible variations of the *<input>* tag, from submit buttons to check boxes and from text fields to radio buttons. The container controls category lists anchors, tables, forms, and in general, all HTML tags that might contain child elements.

## HTML Container Controls

The base class for container controls is the *HtmlContainerControl* class, which descends directly from *HtmlControl*. The HTML elements addressed by this tag are elements that must have a closing tag—that is, forms, selection boxes, and tables, as well as anchors and text areas. Compared to the *HtmlControl* class, a container control features a couple of additional string properties—*InnerHtml* and *InnerText*.

Both properties manipulate the reading and writing of literal content found between the opening and closing tags of the tag. Note that you cannot get the inner content of a control if the content includes server controls. *InnerHtml* and *InnerText* work only in the presence of all literal content. The tag itself is not considered for the output. Unlike *InnerText*, though, *InnerHtml* lets you work with HTML rich text and doesn't automatically encode and decode text. In other words, *InnerText* retrieves and sets the content of the tag as plain text, whereas *InnerHtml* retrieves and sets the same content but in HTML format.

Table 3-5 lists the HTML container controls defined in ASP.NET 1.1.

**Table 3-5 HTML Container Controls**

| Class | Description |
|---|---|
| *HtmlAnchor* | Represents an HTML anchor—specifically, the <*a*> tag. |
| *HtmlButton* | Represents the HTML <*button*> tag. The <*button*> element is defined in the HTML 4.0 specification and supported only in Internet Explorer version 4.0 and later. |
| *HtmlForm* | Represents the <*form*> tag, but can be used only as a container of interactive server controls on a Web page. Cannot really be used to create HTML forms programmable on the server. |
| *HtmlGenericControl* | Represents an HTML tag for which the .NET Framework does not provide a direct class. Sample tags include <*span*>, <*font*>, <*div*>, <*hr*>, <*link*>, and <*iframe*>. You program these controls using the *Attributes* collection and set attributes indirectly. |
| *HtmlSelect* | Represents the <*select*> tag—that is, an HTML selection box. |
| *HtmlTable* | Represents an HTML table—specifically, the <*table*> tag. |
| *HtmlTableCell* | Represents the <*td*> HTML tag—that is, a cell in a table. |
| *HtmlTableRow* | Represents the <*tr*> HTML tag—that is, a row in a table. |
| *HtmlTextArea* | Represents a multiline text box, and maps the <*textarea*> HTML tag. |

Note that the *HtmlButton* control is different than *HtmlInputButton*, which represents the button variation of the <*input*> tag. We'll say more about buttons in the next section while discussing the Web controls. Server-side forms play a key role in the economy of ASP.NET applications, as they are the means for implementing postbacks and guaranteeing state maintenance. For this reason, the *HtmlForm* control is not simply a form element you can program on the server. In particular, the *HtmlForm* hides the *Action* property and cannot be used to post content to a page different than the content that generated the HTML for the browser. We will cover HTML forms in great detail in Chapter 4.

### Navigating to a URL

The *HtmlAnchor* class is the programmatic way of accessing and configuring the *<a>* tag. With respect to the other container controls, the *HtmlAnchor* class provides a few extra properties, such as *HRef*, *Name*, *Target*, and *Title*. The *HRef* property sets the target of the hyperlink and can be used to navigate to the specified location. The *Name* property names a section in the ASP.NET page that can be reached from anywhere on the same page through #-prefixed *HRefs*. The following code demonstrates a bookmarked anchor named *MoreInfo*:

```
<a name="MoreInfo" />
```

This anchor can be reached using the following hyperlink:

```
<a href="#MoreInfo">Get More Info</a>
```

The *Target* property identifies the target window or the frame where the linked URL will be loaded. Common values for *Target* are *_self*, *_top*, *_blank*, and *_parent*, as well as any other name that refers to a page-specific frame. Although the feature is mostly browser dependent, you should always consider these special names as lowercase. Finally, the *Title* property contains the text that is displayed as a ToolTip when the mouse hovers over the anchor's area.

### Handling Events on the Server

In addition to being used for navigating to a different page, the anchor control—as well as the *HtmlButton* control—can be used to post back the page. Key to this behavior is the *ServerClick* event, which lets you define the name of the method that will handle, on the server, the event generated when the user clicks the control. The following code demonstrates an anchor in which the click event is handled on both the client and server:

```
<a runat=server onclick="Run()" onserverclick="DoSomething">Click</a>
```

The *onclick* attribute defines the client-side event handler written using JavaScript; the *onserverclick* attribute refers to the server-side code that will run after the page posts back. Of course, if both event handlers are specified, the client-side handler executes first before the post back occurs.

### The *HtmlSelect* Control

The *HtmlSelect* control represents a list of options from which you choose one or more. You control the appearance and behavior of the control by setting the *Size* and *Multiple* properties. The *Size* property specifies the number of rows to be displayed by the control, whereas the *Multiple* property indicates whether more than one item can be selected in the control. Internal items are grouped in the *Items* collection, and each element is represented by a *ListItem* object. Interestingly, the *ListItem* class is not defined in the *HtmlControls* namespace but lives instead in the *WebControls* namespace. To specify the text for each selectable item, you can either set the *Text* property of the *ListItem* or simply define a series of *<option>* tags within the opening and closing tags of the *<select>* element.

By default, the *HtmlSelect* control shows up as a drop-down list. However, if multiple selections are allowed or the height is set to more than one row, the control is displayed as a list box. The index of the selected item in a single-selection control is returned through the *SelectedIndex* property. If the multiple selection is enabled, you just loop through the *Items* collection and check the *Selected* property on individual list items.

The *HtmlSelect* control supports data binding through additional properties. The *DataSource* property lets you set the data source, which can be any .NET object that implements the *ICollection* interface. If the data source contains multiple bindable tables (for example, a *DataSet* object), by using the *DataMember* property you can choose a particular one. Finally, the *DataTextField* and *DataValueField* properties are used to bind the list item's *Text* and *Value* properties to columns in the data source.

## HTML Tables

In ASP.NET, HTML tables provide a minimum set of functions when rendered using the *HtmlTable* control. In most cases, you don't need to use server-side tables because you typically rely on richer list and grid controls to do the job of displaying tables or records. So you resort to tables when you need to define a fixed layout for graphical elements of the page, but this is not a feature that requires a server-side table.

However, server-side tables are not as powerful as pure HTML tables—which are created by using the *<table>* tag. The main limitation is that rich and complex tables are not supported. The *HtmlTable* class does not support HTML elements such as *<caption>*, *<col>*, *<colgroup>*, *<tbody>*, *<thead>*, and *<tfoot>*. If you use these elements in your ASP.NET code, no run-time exception or compile error is ever thrown. Nevertheless, those elements are silently removed from the HTML code being generated. For example, let's consider the following code:

```
<table runat="server">
    <thead><th>Name</th><th>Last Name</th></thead>
    <tr><td>Joe</td><td>Users</td></tr>
    <tr><td>Bob</td><td>Whosthisguy</td></tr>
</table>
```

As you can see in the following code, the HTML output that is generated by the preceding example does not include the *<thead>* element:

```
<table>
    <tr><td>Joe</td><td>Users</td></tr>
    <tr><td>Bob</td><td>Whosthisguy</td></tr>
</table>
```

By design, an *HtmlTable* control can have only children of the *HtmlTableRow* class. Any attempt to programmatically add other table elements, such as a *<thead>* or a *<tfoot>*, will generate an exception.

## The *HtmlTextArea* Control

The *HtmlTextArea* control corresponds to the *<textarea>* HTML element and allows you to programmatically create and configure a multiline text box. The *HtmlTextArea* class provides the *Rows* and *Cols* properties to control the number of rows and columns of the text box. The *Value* property can be used to assign some text to display in the control area.

The *HtmlTextArea* class also provides a *ServerChange* event that fires during a postback and allows you to validate on the server the data contained in the control. Note that the *HtmlTextArea* control does not fire the event itself and does not directly cause the page to post back. Rather, when the page posts back in response to a click on a link or submit button, the *HtmlTextArea* control intervenes in the server-side chain of events and gives the programmer a chance to run some code if the internal content of the control is changed between two successive postbacks.

All ASP.NET controls that, like *HtmlTextArea*, implement the *IPostBackDataHandler* interface can invoke user-defined code when the control's internal state changes. In particular, controls can fire custom events by overriding the *RaisePostDataChangedEvent* method on the aforementioned interface. The following pseudocode shows what happens in the method's implementation of *HtmlTextArea*:

```
void System.Web.UI.IPostBackDataHandler.RaisePostDataChangedEvent() {
    this.OnServerChange(EventArgs.Empty);
}
```

Finally, note that the control raises the event only if the state has changed between two successive posts. To determine whether that has happened, the control needs to track the content it had the time before. This value can be stored only in the view state. Of course, the *ServerChange* won't even fire if you disable the view state for the host page or the control.

## HTML Input Controls

In HTML, the *<input>* element has several variations and can be used to provide a submit button as well as a check box or text box. In ASP.NET, each possible instance of the *<input>* element is mapped to a specific class. All input classes derive from the *HtmlInputControl* class. *HtmlInputControl* is the abstract class that defines the common programming interface for all input controls. The class inherits from *HtmlControl* and simply adds three custom properties to the inherited interface: *Name*, *Type*, and *Value*.

The *Name* property returns the name assigned to the control. In ASP.NET, this property is peculiar because, although marked as read/write, it actually works as a read-only property. The *get* accessor returns the control's *UniqueID* property, while the *set* accessor is just void. As a result, whatever value you assign to the property, either programmatically or declaratively, is just ignored and no exception or compile error is ever thrown.

The *Type* property mirrors the *type* attribute of the HTML input elements. The property is read-only. Finally, the *Value* property is read/write and represents the content of the input field.

Table 3-6 lists the HTML input controls defined in ASP.NET 1.1.

**Table 3-6 HTML Input Controls**

| Class | Description |
|---|---|
| *HtmlInputButton* | Represents the various flavors of a command button supported by HTML. Feasible values for the *Type* attribute are *button*, *submit*, and *reset*. |
| *HtmlInputCheckBox* | Represents an HTML check box—that is, the *<input>* tag with a type equal to *checkbox*. |
| *HtmlInputFile* | Represents the file uploader—that is, the *<input>* tag with a type equal to *file*. |
| *HtmlInputHidden* | Represents a hidden buffer of text data—that is, the *<input>* tag with a type equal to *hidden*. |
| *HtmlInputImage* | Represents a graphic button—that is, the *<input>* tag with a type equal to *image*. Note that this tag is supported by all browsers. |
| *HtmlInputRadioButton* | Represents a radio button—that is, the *<input>* tag with a type equal to *radio*. |
| *HtmlInputText* | Represents a text field—that is, the *<input>* tag with a type of either *password* or *text*. |

The hidden and text-input controls are nearly identical, and the contents of both are posted back. They basically differ only in that hidden fields are not displayed and, subsequently, don't provide some UI-related properties such as *MaxLength* and *Size*.

## Command Buttons

The *HtmlInputButton* class is the most flexible button class in the .NET Framework. It differs from the *HtmlButton* class we encountered earlier in that it renders through the *<input>* tag rather than the Internet Explorer–specific *<button>* tag. This fact ensures for the control much wider support from browsers.

The HTML input button controls support the *ServerClick* event, which allows you to set the code to run on the server after the button is clicked. Note that if you set the button type to *Button* and the *ServerClick* event handler is specified, the control automatically adds the postback script code to the *onclick* HTML attribute. In this way, any click causes the page to post back and the code to execute. Let's consider the following ASP.NET code:

```
<input runat="server" type="button" id="btn" value="Click"
    onserverclick="buttonClicked" />
```

The corresponding HTML code is as follows:

```
<input language="javascript" onclick="__doPostBack('btn','')" name="btn"
    type="button" value="Click" />
```

The client-side *__doPostBack* script function is the standard piece of code generated by ASP.NET to implement the postback. The code is actually emitted through a call to the *RegisterPostBackScript* method of the *Page* class. If the button type is set to *Submit*—that is, a value that would always cause a postback—no client-side script code is generated and the *onclick* attribute is not set.

> **Note** The *HtmlInputImage* control supports a nearly identical pattern for handling server-side events and validation. The *HtmlInputImage* control features a few more properties specific to the image it shows. In particular, you can set the alternate text for the image, the border, and the alignment with respect to the rest of the page. The *ServerClick* event handler has a slightly different form and looks like the following:
>
> ```
> void ImageClickEventHandler(object sender,
>     ImageClickEventArgs e);
> ```
>
> When an image button is clicked, the coordinates of the click are determined by using the *X* and *Y* properties of the *ImageClickEventArgs* data structure.

## Controlling Validation

The *HtmlInputButton* class, as well as the *HtmlButton* class, support a Boolean property named *CausesValidation*. The property indicates whether the content of the input fields should be validated when the button is clicked. By default, the property is set to *true*, meaning the validation always takes place. We'll examine data validation later in the chapter. For now, it suffices to say, you can programmatically enable or disable the validation step by using the *CausesValidation* property.

Typically, you might want to disable validation if the button that has been clicked doesn't perform a concrete operation but simply clears the user interface or cancels an ongoing operation. By design, in fact, server-side page validation takes place just before the *ServerClick* event handler is executed. Setting the *CausesValidation* property to *false* is the only means you have to prevent an unnecessary validation.

## Detecting State Changes of Controls

Earlier in this chapter, while discussing the features of the *HtmlTextArea* control, we ran into the *ServerChange* event and described it as the mechanism to detect and validate changes in the control's state between two successive postbacks. The *ServerChange* event is not an exclusive feature of the *HtmlTextArea* control but is also supported by other input controls such as *HtmlInputCheckBox*, *HtmlInputRadioButton*, *HtmlInputHidden*, and *HtmlInputText*. Let's look at an example in which we use the *ServerChange* event to detect which elements have been checked since last time the control was processed on the server.

We build a page with a list of check boxes and a button to let the user post back to the server when finished. Notice, in fact, that neither the *HtmlInputCheckBox* control nor any other input control except buttons, post back to the server when clicked. For this reason, you must provide another control on the Web page that supports posting to the server—for example, an *HtmlButton* or an *HtmlInputButton* control. The following code implements the page shown in Figure 3-2:

```
<%@ Page Language="C#" %>
<html>
<script runat="server">
public void DetectChange(object sender, EventArgs e) {
    HtmlInputCheckBox cb = (HtmlInputCheckBox) sender;
    Response.Write("Control <b>" + cb.UniqueID + "</b> changed<br>");
}
</script>

<body>
<form runat="server">
```

```
    <input runat="server" type="checkbox" id="one"
        OnServerChange="DetectChange">One<br>
    <input runat="server" type="checkbox" id="two"
        OnServerChange="DetectChange">Two<br>
    <input runat="server" type="checkbox" id="three"
        OnServerChange="DetectChange">Three<br>
    <input runat="server" type="submit" value="Submit" />
</form>
</body>
</html>
```

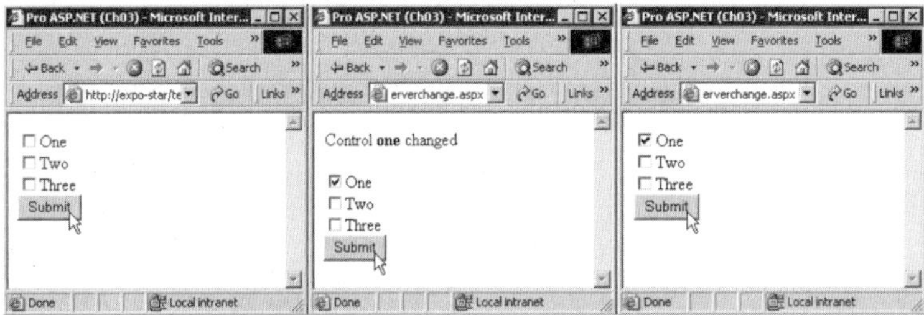

**Figure 3-2** The *ServerChange* event fires only if the status of the control has changed since the last time the control was processed on the server.

The *ServerChange* event is fired only if the state of the control results changed after two postbacks.

By implementing the *IPostBackDataHandler* interface, each server control takes a chance to update its current state with data posted by the client. The ASP.NET runtime invokes *LoadPostData* on each control that implements the interface.

```
public bool LoadPostData(string postDataKey,
    NameValueCollection postCollection);
```

The first argument of *LoadPostData* is the client ID of the control; the second argument is a name-value collection that contains the posted data. Posted data can either be *Request.Form* or *Request.QueryString* depending on the form's method. Each control compares the value posted by an HTML element with the same ID with the contents of a particular property. It is *Value* for text boxes and *Checked* for check boxes. The posted value is obtained using the *postDataKey* string as a key to access the values stored in the collection.

Controls that implement the *IPostBackDataHandler* interface use a boilerplate piece of code to implement the *LoadPostData* method. Basically, the method updates the key property of the control with the posted value. The following code shows how *LoadPostData* works for the *HtmlInputText* control:

```
bool LoadPostData(string postDataKey, NameValueCollection postColl) {
    string oldValue;
```

```
    string postedValue;

    // At this point, the view state has been restored
    oldValue = this.Value;

    // Get the posted value for the HTML element with the same
    // ID as the control
    postedValue = postColl[postDataKey];

    // Compare the posted value with Text and updates if needed
    if (oldValue != postedValue) {
        this.Value = postedValue;
        return true;
    }

    // Return a Boolean value denoting whether the state has changed
    return false;
}
```

*LoadPostData* returns true if the state of the control changes as a result of the post back—that is, if the user generated a new state for the control. For this infrastructure to work, it is key that the value of the server control's *UniqueID* property be assigned to the name attribute of the HTML element. Otherwise, the ASP.NET runtime will not be able to handle postback data for that control.

The ASP.NET runtime tracks all the controls that return true to *LoadPostData* and then invokes the *RaisePostDataChangedEvent* method for each of them—the second method on the *IPostBackDataHandler* interface. The following code snippet reports what that method does for the *HtmlInputText* control:

```
// System.Web.UI.IPostBackDataHandler
void RaisePostDataChangedEvent() {
    this.OnServerChange(EventArgs.Empty);
}
```

For the *HtmlInputCheckBox* control in the preceding sample, a change of state occurs whenever the *Checked* property changes. Note that a nearly identical mechanism exists for Web controls.

## Uploading Files

The *HtmlInputFile* control is the HTML tool for uploading files from a browser to the Web server. Note that file upload requires Internet Explorer version 3.0 or newer. To exploit the *HtmlInputFile* control in a form, you should first set the server form's *Enctype* property to *multipart/form-data*.

```
<form runat="server" enctype="multipart/form-data">
    <input runat="server" type="file" id="upLoader" >
    <input runat="server" type="submit" value="Upload..." />
</form>
```

The way in which the *HtmlInputFile* control is rendered to HTML is browser-specific, but it normally consists of a text box and a Browse button. The user selects a file from the local machine and then clicks the button to submit the page to the server. When this occurs, the browser uploads the selected file to the server. Prior to ASP.NET, a server-side process—the posting acceptor—was required to run in the background to handle multipart/form-data submissions. In ASP.NET the role of the posting acceptor is no longer necessary as it is carried out by the ASP.NET runtime itself.

On the server, the file is parked into an object of type *HttpPostedFile* and stays there until explicitly saved to disk. The *HttpPostedFile* object provides properties and methods to get information on an individual file and to read and save the file. The following code shows how to save a posted file to disk:

```
upLoader.PostedFile.SaveAs(serverFile);
```

You can also use the *InputStream* property of the *HttpPostedFile* object to read the posted data without creating a disk file. The *HtmlInputFile* control also allows you to restrict the file types that can be uploaded to the server. You do this by setting the *Accept* property with a comma-separated list of MIME types.

> **Caution** When you use the *SaveAs* method, you should pay attention to specify the full path to the output file. If a relative path is provided, ASP.NET attempts to place the file in the system directory. This practice might result in an access-denied error. Furthermore, make sure to provide write permission for the account used by ASP.NET for the directory where you want to store the file.

ASP.NET exercises some control on the amount of data being uploaded. The *maxRequestLength* attribute in the *<httpRuntime>* section of the configuration file sets the maximum allowable file size. An error is generated in the browser when the file exceeds the specified size—4 MB by default. Uploading large files might also generate another runtime error due to an excessive consumption of system memory. As we've seen in Chapter 2, when more than 60% of the available RAM is consumed the ASP.NET runtime recycles the worker process (aspnet_wp.exe). Of course, this fact breaks the upload process. To avoid this error, you should increase the value of the *memoryLimit* attribute in the *<processModel>* element of the configuration file for the application.

## The *HtmlImage* Control

The *HtmlImage* class is the ASP.NET counterpart of the <*img*> tag. You can use it to configure on the server the display of an image. Possible parameters you can set are the size of the image, the border, and the alternate text. An instance of the *HtmlImage* is created only when the *runat* attribute is added to the <*img*> tag. If you simply need to display an image within a page, and the image is not dynamically determined or configured, there is no need to resort to the *HtmlImage* control, which would add unnecessary overhead to the page. The following code snippet shows how to configure a server-side <*img*> tag called to display an image whose name is determined based on run-time conditions.

```
theImg.Width = 100;
theImg.Height = 100;
theImg.Src = GetImageUrl(Request);
```

The *HtmlImage* control should be used to programmatically manipulate the image to change the source file, the width and height, or the alignment of the image relative to other page elements. The majority of properties of the *HtmlImage* control are implemented as strings, including *Src*—the URL of the image—and *Align*. Feasible values of *Align* are only a small set of words such as *left*, *right*, *top*, and so forth. These words would have been more appropriately grouped in a custom-enumerated type, thus providing for a strongly typed programming model. If you think so, too, you just grabbed the gist of the difference between HTML and Web server controls! HTML controls just mirror HTML tags; Web controls attempt to provide a more consistent and effective programming interface by exploiting the characteristics of the .NET Framework.

### Literal Controls

Literal controls are a special type of server control that ASP.NET creates and uses whenever it encounters plain text that doesn't require server-side processing. In general, everything that appears in the context of an ASP.NET page is treated like a control. If a tag includes the *runat="server"* attribute, ASP.NET creates an instance of a specific class; otherwise, if no *runat* attribute has been specified, the text is compiled into a *LiteralControl* object. Literal controls are simple text holders that are added to and removed from pages using the same programming interface defined for other server controls.

# Web Controls

Web controls are defined in the *System.Web.UI.WebControls* namespace and represent an alternative approach to HTML server controls. Like HTML controls, Web controls are server-side components that spring to life thanks to the *runat="server"* attribute. Unlike HTML controls, Web controls are designed from scratch without needing to be compliant with the HTML syntax, but generate valid HTML. For this reason, they sometimes appear to be more consistent and abstract in the API design and richer in functionality. When hosted in .aspx pages, Web controls are characterized by the *asp* namespace prefix.

To a large degree, Web controls and HTML controls overlap and generate almost the same client code, although they do it through different programming interfaces. For example, the Web controls namespace defines the *TextBox* control and makes it available through the *<asp:textbox>* tag; similarly, the HTML controls namespace provides the *HtmlInputText* control and declares it using the *<input>* tag. The output that both produce is nearly identical. Using either is mostly a matter of preference; only in a few cases will you run into slight functionality differences. Using Web controls gives you a far richer development model and exception management.

## Generalities of Web Controls

The *WebControl* class is the base class from which all Web controls inherit. The class defines several properties and methods that are shared, but not necessarily implemented, by derived controls. Many of the properties have the look and feel of the controls and are subject to browser and HTML version. For example, although all Web controls provide the ability to define a border, not all underlying HTML tags actually support a border.

### Properties of Web Controls

Table 3-7 lists the properties available on the *WebControl* class.

**Table 3-7 Specific Properties of Web Controls**

| Property | Description |
|---|---|
| *AccessKey* | Gets or sets the letter to press (together with ALT) to quickly set focus to the control in a Web form. Supported on Internet Explorer 4.0 and newer. |
| *Attributes* | Gets the collection of attributes that do not correspond to properties on the control. Attributes set in this way will be rendered as HTML attributes in the resulting page. |

**Table 3-7 Specific Properties of Web Controls**

| Property | Description |
|---|---|
| *BackColor* | Gets or sets the background color of the Web control. |
| *BorderColor* | Gets or sets the border color of the Web control. |
| *BorderStyle* | Gets or sets the border style of the Web control. |
| *BorderWidth* | Gets or sets the border width of the Web control. |
| *ControlStyle* | Gets the style of the Web server control. The style is an object of type *Style*. |
| *ControlStyleCreated* | Gets a value that indicates whether a *Style* object has been created for the *ControlStyle* property. |
| *CssClass* | Get or sets the cascading style sheet (CSS) class associated with the client. |
| *Enabled* | Gets or sets whether the control is enabled. |
| *Font* | Gets the font properties associated with the Web control. |
| *ForeColor* | Gets or sets the foreground color of the Web control mostly used to draw text. |
| *Height* | Gets or sets the height of the control. The height is expressed as a member of type *Unit*. |
| *Style* | Gets a *CssStyleCollection* collection object made of all the attributes assigned to the outer tag of the Web control. |
| *TabIndex* | Gets or sets the tab index of the control. |
| *ToolTip* | Gets or sets the text displayed when the mouse pointer hovers over the control. |
| *Width* | Gets or sets the width of the control. The width is expressed as a member of type *Unit*. |

The *ControlStyle* and *ControlStyleCreated* properties are used primarily by control developers, while the *Style* property is what application developers would typically use to set CSS attributes on the outer tag of the control. The *Style* property is implemented using an instance of the class *CssStyleCollection*. The class is a simple collection of string values—the values you set either declaratively or programmatically through the *Style* property. The *ControlStyle* property, on the other hand, evaluates to an object of type *Style*—a class that encapsulates the appearance properties of the control. In other words, the *Style* class works as the repository of the graphical and cosmetic attributes that characterize all Web controls. All properties are strongly typed. In contrast, the *CssStyleCollection* class is just the collection of CSS styles defined in the tags. The *Style* class groups together some of the properties that were shown in Table 3-7. The grouped properties are: *BackColor*, *BorderColor*, *BorderStyle*, *BorderWidth*, *CssClass*, *Font*, *ForeColor*,

*Height*, and *Width*. Note that style values set through the *CssStyleCollection* class are not automatically reflected by the (strongly typed) values in the *Style* object.

## Styling a Web Control

The style properties of a Web control can be programmatically manipulated to some extent. For example, in the *Style* class, you can count on a *CopyFrom* method to duplicate the object and you can take advantage of the *MergeWith* method to combine two style objects.

```
currentStyle.MergeStyle(newStyle);
```

The *MergeWith* method joins the properties of both objects. In doing so, it does not replace any property that is already set in the base object but limits itself to defining uninitialized properties. Finally, the *Reset* method clears all current attributes in the various properties of the style object.

## Methods of Web Controls

The *WebControl* class supports a few particular methods that are not part of the *Control* interface. These methods are listed in Table 3-8.

**Table 3-8 Specific Methods of Web Controls**

| Method | Description |
|---|---|
| *ApplyStyle* | Copies any nonempty elements of the specified style to the control. Existing style properties are overwritten. |
| *CopyBaseAttributes* | Imports from the specified Web control the properties *AccessKey*, *Enabled*, *ToolTip*, *TabIndex*, and *Attributes*. Basically, it copies all the properties not encapsulated in the *Style* object. |
| *MergeStyle* | Like *ApplyStyle*, copies any nonempty elements of the specified style to the control. Existing style properties are *not* overwritten, though. |
| *RenderBeginTag* | Renders the HTML opening tag of the control into the specified writer. The method is called right before the control's *RenderControl* method. |
| *RenderEndTag* | Renders the HTML closing tag of the control into the specified writer. The method is called right after the control's *RenderControl* method. |

All these methods are rarely of interest to application developers. They are mostly designed to help control developers.

## Core Web Controls

The set of Web controls can be divided in four main categories: core controls, validators, data-bound controls, and list controls. A fifth category of Web controls—iterative data-bound controls—will be examined separately in future chapters. In addition, the .NET Framework also provides a few miscellaneous controls that provide ad hoc functionalities and are as common on the Web as they are hard to catalogue. We'll cover these controls in the section "Miscellaneous Web Controls." Let's start off with a look at the core Web controls, which are described in Table 3-9.

**Table 3-9 Core Web Controls**

| Control | Description |
|---|---|
| *Button* | Implements a submit push button through the *<input>* tag. |
| *CheckBox* | Implements a check box through the *<input>* tag. |
| *HyperLink* | Implements an anchor *<a>* tag, and lets you specify either the location to jump to or the script code to execute. |
| *Image* | Implements a picture box through the *<img>* tag. |
| *Label* | Represents a static, nonclickable piece of text. Implemented through the *<span>* tag. |
| *Panel* | Implements an HTML container using the *<div>* block element. Note that in down-level browsers it is rendered as a *<table>*. |
| *RadioButton* | Implements a single radio button through the *<input>* tag. |
| *Table* | Implements the outer table container. Equivalent to the HTML *<table>* element. |
| *TableCell* | A table cell; is equivalent to the HTML *<td>* element. |
| *TableRow* | A table row; is equivalent to the HTML *<tr>* element. |
| *TextBox* | Implements a text box using the *<input>* or *<textarea>* tag as appropriate and according to the requested text mode. Can work in single-line, multiline, or password mode. |

The *Table* class and its related classes allow you to build and configure an HTML table using the same abstract object model used for building other Web controls. The power of the *Table* class, though, is particularly evident when it comes to building tables programmatically with dynamic contents. No matter how complex the programming model is, all Web controls produce HTML for both up-level and down-level browsers.

## Images and Image Buttons

The *Image* control displays an image on the Web page. The path to the image is set through the *ImageUrl* property. Image URLs can be either relative or absolute, with most programmers showing a clear preference for relative URLs, which make a Web site inherently easier to move. You can also specify alternate text to display when the image is not available. The property to use in this case is *AlternateText*. The image alignment with respect to other elements on the page is set by using the *ImageAlign* property. Feasible values are taken from the homonymous *enum* type.

The *Image* control is not a clickable component and is simply limited to displaying an image. If you need to capture mouse clicks on the image, use the *ImageButton* control instead. The *ImageButton* class descends from *Image* and extends it with a couple of events—*Click* and *Command*—that are raised when the control is clicked. The *OnClick* event handler provides you with an *ImageClickEventArgs* data structure that contains information about the coordinates for the location at which the image is clicked.

The *OnCommand* event handler makes the *ImageButton* control behave like a command button. A command button has an associated name that you can control through the *CommandName* property. If you have multiple *ImageButton* controls on the same page, the command name allows you to distinguish which one is actually clicked. The *CommandArgument* property can be used to pass additional information about the command and the control.

## Check Boxes and Radio Buttons

Check boxes and radio buttons are implemented through the *<input>* tag and the *type* attribute set to *checkbox* or *radio*. Unlike using the HTML control versions, the Web control versions of check boxes and radio buttons let you specify the associated text as a property. The HTML elements and the corresponding HTML controls lack an attribute whose content becomes the text near the check box or radio button. In HTML, to make the text near the check box or radio button clickable, you have to resort to the *<label>* tag with the *for* attribute.

```
<input type="checkbox" id="ctl" />
<label for="ctl">Check me</label>
```

Neither the *HtmlInputCheckBox* nor the *HtmlInputRadioButton* control add a label, which leaves you responsible for doing that. These Web controls counterpart, on the other hand, are not bound to the HTML syntax and do precisely that—they automatically add a *Text* property, which results in an appropriate *<label>* tag. For example, consider the following ASP.NET code:

```
<asp:checkbox runat="server" id="ctl" text="Check me" />
```

It results in the following HTML code:

```
<input type="checkbox" id="ctl" />
<label for="ctl">Check me</label>
```

### HyperLinks

The *HyperLink* control creates a link to another Web page and is typically displayed through the text stored in the *Text* property. Alternatively, the hyperlink can be displayed as an image; in this case, the URL of the image is stored in the *ImageUrl* property. Note that if both the *Text* and *ImageUrl* properties are set, the *ImageUrl* property takes precedence. In this case, the content of the *Text* property is displayed as a ToolTip when the mouse hovers over the control's area.

The *NavigateUrl* property indicates the URL the hyperlink is pointing to. The *Target* property is the name of the window or frame that will contain the output of the target URL.

## Miscellaneous Web Controls

The *WebControls* namespace also includes a few controls that provide useful functionality that is common in Web applications. In particular, we'll examine the *AdRotator* control, which works like an advertisement banner, and the *Calendar* control, which is a flexible and highly interactive control used to specify a date.

### The *AdRotator* Control

Abstractly speaking, the *AdRotator* control displays an automatically sized image button and updates both the image and the URL each time the page refreshes. The image to display and other information is read from an XML file written according to a specific schema. More concretely, you use the *AdRotator* control to create an advertisement banner on a Web Forms page. The control actually inserts an image and hyperlink in the page and makes them point to the advertisement page selected. The image is sized by the browser to the dimensions of the *AdRotator* control, regardless of its actual size. The following code shows a typical XML advertisement file:

```
<Advertisements>
<Ad>
    <ImageUrl>6235.gif</ImageUrl>
    <NavigateUrl>www.microsoft.com/MSPress/books/6235.asp</NavigateUrl>
    <AlternateText>Applied XML Programming with .NET</AlternateText>
    <Impressions>50</Impressions>
</Ad>
<Ad>
    <ImageUrl>5727.gif</ImageUrl>
```

```
        <NavigateUrl>www.microsoft.com/MSPress/books/5727.asp</NavigateUrl>
        <AlternateText>Building Web Solutions with ASP.NET</AlternateText>
        <Impressions>50</Impressions>
    </Ad>
</Advertisements>
```

The *<Advertisement>* root node contains multiple *<Ad>* elements, one per each image to show. The syntax of the *AdRotator* control is as follows:

```
<%@ Page Language="C#" %>
<html>
<head><title>Pro ASP.NET (Ch03)</title></head>
<body>
    <form runat="server">
        <h1>Dino Esposito's Books</h1>
        <asp:AdRotator runat="server" id="bookRotator"
            AdvertisementFile="MyBooks.xml" />
    </form>
</body>
</html>
```

In the XML advertisement file, you use the *<ImageUrl>* node to indicate the image to load and the *<NavigateUrl>* node to specify where to go in case of a click. The *<AlternateText>* node indicates the alternate text to use if the image is unavailable. Finally, *<Impressions>* indicates how often an image should be displayed in relation to other images in the advertisement file.

Once per roundtrip, the *AdRotator* control fires the server-side *AdCreated* event. The event occurs before the page is rendered. The event handler receives an argument of type *AdCreatedEventArgs*, which contains information about the image, the navigation URL, and the alternate text. The *AdRotator* control exposes a few custom properties, including *Target* to set the target of the hyperlink and *AdvertisementFile* to set the file with image names.

## The *Calendar* Control

The *Calendar* control displays a one-month calendar and allows you to choose dates and navigate backward and forward through the months of the year. The control is highly customizable both for appearance and functionality. For example, by setting the *SelectionMode* property, you can decide what the user can select—that is, whether a single date, week, or month can be selected. Figure 3-3 provides a view of the *Calender* control.

```
<asp:calendar runat="server" id="hireDate"
    BackColor="white" ForeColor="black" Font-Size="9px"
    SelectionMode="" DayHeaderStyle-Font-Bold="True" />
```

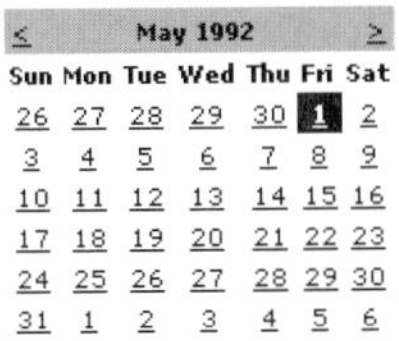

| < | | | May 1992 | | | > |
|---|---|---|---|---|---|---|
| Sun | Mon | Tue | Wed | Thu | Fri | Sat |
| 26 | 27 | 28 | 29 | 30 | 1 | 2 |
| 3 | 4 | 5 | 6 | 7 | 8 | 9 |
| 10 | 11 | 12 | 13 | 14 | 15 | 16 |
| 17 | 18 | 19 | 20 | 21 | 22 | 23 |
| 24 | 25 | 26 | 27 | 28 | 29 | 30 |
| 31 | 1 | 2 | 3 | 4 | 5 | 6 |

**Figure 3-3** The *Calendar* control in action.

The *VisibleDate* property sets a date that must be visible in the calendar, while *SelectedDate* sets with a different style the date that is rendered as selected. The control also fires three ad hoc events: *DayRender*, *SelectionChanged*, and *VisibleMonthChanged*. The *DayRender* event signals that the control has just created a new day cell. You can hook the event if you think you need to customize the cell output. The *SelectionChanged* event fires when the selected date changes, while *VisibleMonthChanged* is raised whenever the user moves to another month using the control's selector buttons.

The *Calendar* control originates a roundtrip for each selection you make. Although it is cool and powerful on its own, for better performance you might also want to provide a plain text box for manually typing dates.

## The *Xml* Control

The *Xml* control, defined by the *<asp:xml>* tag, is used to output the content of an XML document directly into an ASP.NET page. The control can display the source XML as-is or as the results of an XSL transformation (XSLT). The *Xml* control is a sort of declarative counterpart for the *XslTransform* class and can make use of the .NET Framework XSLT transform class internally.

You use the *Xml* control when you need to embed XML documents in a Web page. For example, the control is extremely handy when you need to create XML data islands for the client to consume. The control lets you specify a document to work with and, optionally, a transformation to apply. The XML document can be specified in a variety of formats—an XML document object model, string, or file name. The XSLT transformation can be defined through either an already configured instance of the .NET Framework *XslTransform* class or a file name.

```
<asp:xml runat="server"
    documentsource="document.xml"
    transformsource="transform.xsl" />
```

If you're going to apply some transformation to the XML data, you could also embed it inline between the opening and closing tags of the control. The control also makes it easier to accomplish a common ASP task: apply browser-dependent transformations to portions of the page expressed in an XML meta language. In this case, you exploit the programming interface of the control as follows:

```
<asp:xml runat="server" id="theXml" documentsource="document.xml" />
```

In the *Page_Load* event, you just check the browser capabilities and decide which transformation should be applied.

```
void Page_Load(object sender, EventArgs e) {
    if (IsInternetExplorer(Request.Browser))
        theXml.TransformSource = "ie5.xsl";
    else
        theXml.TransformSource = "downlevel.xsl";
}
```

### The *PlaceHolder* Control

The *PlaceHolder* control is one of the few controls in the *WebControls* namespace that isn't derived from the *WebControl* class. It inherits from *Control* and is used only as a container for other controls in the page. The *PlaceHolder* control does not produce visible output of its own and is limited to containing child controls dynamically added through the *Controls* collection. The following code shows how to embed the *PlaceHolder* control in a Web page:

```
<asp:placeholder runat="server" id="theToolbar" />
```

Once you have a placeholder, you can add controls to it. As mentioned, the placeholder does not add extra functionality, but it provides for grouping and easy and direct identification of a group of related controls. The following code demonstrates how to create a new button and add it to an existing placeholder:

```
btn = new Button();
btn.Text = "Click me";
theToolbar.Controls.Add(btn);
```

The *PlaceHolder* control reserves a location in the control tree and can be extremely helpful in identifying specific areas of the page to customize and extend by adding controls programmatically.

## Validation Controls

A key rule for writing more secure applications is to get the data right before you use it. Getting the data right requires you to apply a validation step to any external input. In ASP.NET, validator controls are used to verify the input of the form fields within a Web page. Validation controls provide an easy-to-use mechanism to perform a variety of validation tasks, including testing for valid types, values within a given range, or required fields.

The validator controls are Web server controls and inherit from the *BaseValidator* class which, in turn, descends from *Label*. All validator controls defined on a page are automatically grouped in the *Validators* collection of the *Page* class. You can validate them all in a single shot using the *Validate* method in the *Page* class or individually by calling the *Validate* method on each validator. The *Validate* method sets the *IsValid* property both on the page and on the individual validator. The *IsValid* property indicates whether the user's entries match the requirements of the validators.

> **Note** The *Validate* method on the validator control performs any needed checks on the associated control and, as a result, updates the control's *IsValid* property. The *Validate* method, when called on the page, cumulatively validates all validation controls defined within the page. The page's *IsValid* property is the logical AND of the values of *IsValid* on all embedded validation controls.

Other than explicitly using the *Validate* method, the user's entry is also automatically validated whenever the page posts back. In this case, validation is performed when a button control is clicked. The button controls that can automatically apply validation are *Button*, *HtmlButton*, *HtmlInputButton*, *HtmlInputImage*, *ImageButton*, and *LinkButton*. You can enable or disable a button's validation capability by using the *CausesValidation* Boolean property.

The .NET Framework also provides complete client-side implementation for validation controls. This allows Dynamic HTML–enabled browsers (such as Internet Explorer version 4.0 and later) to perform validation on the client as soon as the user tabs out of a monitored input field.

## Types of Validation Controls

Each validation control references an input control located elsewhere on the page. When the page is going to be submitted, the contents of the monitored server control is passed to the validator for further processing. Each validator would perform a different type of verification. Table 3-10 shows the types of validation supported by the .NET Framework.

**Table 3-10 Validator Controls in the .NET Framework**

| Validator | Description |
|---|---|
| *CompareValidator* | Compares the user's entry against a fixed value by using a comparison operator such as *LessThan*, *Equal*, or *GreaterThan*. Can also compare against the value of a property in another control on the same page. |
| *CustomValidator* | Employs a programmatically defined validation logic to check the validity of the user's entry. You use this validator when the other validators cannot perform the necessary validation and you want to provide custom code that validates the input. |
| *RangeValidator* | Ensures that the user's entry falls within a specified range. Lower and upper boundaries can be expressed as numbers, strings or dates. |
| *RegularExpressionValidator* | Validates the user's entry only if it matches a pattern defined by a regular expression. |
| *RequiredFieldValidator* | Ensures that the user specifies a value for the field. |

Multiple validation controls can be used with an individual input control to validate according to different criteria. For example, you can apply multiple validation controls on a text box that is expected to contain an e-mail address. In particular, you can impose that the field is not skipped (*RequiredFieldValidator*) and that its content matches the typical format of e-mail addresses (*RegularExpressionValidator*).

Table 3-10 lacks a reference to the *ValidationSummary* control. The control does not perform validation tasks itself. It displays a label to summarize all the validation error messages found on a Web page as the effect of other validators. We'll cover the *ValidationSummary* control later in the chapter.

## The *BaseValidator* Class

Figure 3-4 shows the relationship between the various validation controls and their parent classes.

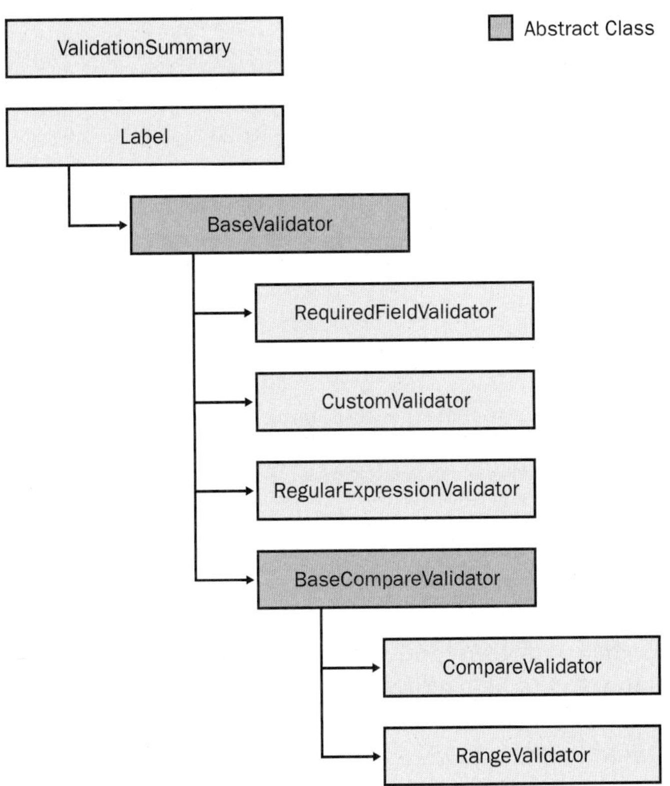


**Figure 3-4** Diagram of validation controls in ASP.NET. Gray boxes represent abstract classes.

Table 3-11 details the specific properties of validation controls. Some properties, such as *ForeColor*, *Enabled*, and *Text*, are overridden versions of base properties on base classes.

**Table 3-11 Basic Properties of Validators**

| Property | Description |
|---|---|
| *ControlToValidate* | Gets or sets the input control to validate. The control is identified by name—that is, by using the value of the *ID* attribute. |
| *Display* | If client-side validation is supported and enabled, gets or sets how the space for the error message should be allocated—either statically or dynamically. In case of server-side validation, this property is ignored. A *Static* display is possible only if the browser supports the *display* CSS style. The default is *Dynamic*. |

*(continued)*

**Table 3-11 Basic Properties of Validators** *(continued)*

| Property | Description |
|---|---|
| *EnableClientScript* | *True* by default; gets or sets whether client-side validation is enabled. |
| *Enabled* | Gets or sets whether the validation control is enabled. |
| *ErrorMessage* | Gets or sets the text for the error message. |
| *ForeColor* | Gets or sets the color of the message displayed when validation fails. |
| *IsValid* | Gets or sets whether the associated input control passes validation. |
| *Text* | Gets or sets the description displayed for the validator in lieu of the error message. Note, though, this text does not replace the contents of *ErrorMessage* in the summary text. |

All validation controls inherit from the *BaseValidator* class except for compare validators, for which a further intermediate class—the *BaseCompareValidator* class—exists. The *BaseCompareValidator* class serves as the foundation for validators that perform typed comparisons. An ad hoc property, named *Type*, is used to specify the data type the values are converted to before being compared. The *CanConvert* static method determines whether the user's entry can be converted to the specified data type. Supported types includes string, integer, double, date, and currency. As shown in Figure 3-4, the classes acting as compare validators are *RangeValidator* and *CompareValidator*.

## Associating Validators with Input Controls

The link between each validator and its associated input control is established through the *ControlToValidate* property. The property must be set to the ID of the input control. If you do not specify a valid input control, an exception will be thrown when the page is rendered. The association validator/control is between two controls within the same container—be it a page, user control, or template.

Not all server controls can be validated. Those which can be validated specify their validation property through an attribute named *[ValidationPropertyAttribute]*. The attribute takes the name of the property that contains the user's entry. For example, the validation property for a *TextBox* is *Text* and is indicated as follows:

```
[ValidationPropertyAttribute("Text")]
public class TextBox : WebControl {
    ⋮
}
```

The standard list of validating controls include *TextBox*, *DropDownList*, *HtmlInputFile*, *HtmlInputText*, *HtmlSelect*, *HtmlTextArea*, *ListBox*, and *RadioButtonList*. Custom controls can be validated too, as long as they are marked with the aforementioned *ValidationPropertyAttribute* attribute.

> **Note** If the validation property of the associated input control is left empty, all validators accept the value and pass the test. The *RequiredFieldValidator* control represents a rather natural exception to this rule, as it has been specifically designed to detect fields the user skipped and left blank.

## The *CompareValidator* Control

The *CompareValidator* control lets you compare the value entered by the user with a constant value or the value specified in another control in the same naming container. The behavior of the control is characterized by the following additional properties:

- ***ControlToCompare*** Represents the ID of the control to compare with the current user's entry. You should avoid setting the *ControlToCompare* and *ValueToCompare* properties at the same time. They are considered mutually exclusive; if you set both, the *ControlToCompare* property takes precedence.
- ***Operator*** Specifies the comparison operation to perform. The list of feasible operations is defined in the *ValidationCompareOperator* enumeration. The default operator is *Equal*. Other operators are *NotEqual*, *LessThan*, *GreaterThan*, *GreaterThanEqual*, *LessThanEqual*, and *DataTypeCheck*. The last operator in particular is useful when you want to make sure certain input data can be converted to a certain type. When the *DataTypeCheck* operator is specified, both *ValueToCompare* and *ControlToCompare* are ignored. In this case, the test is made on the type of the input data and returns *true* if the specified data can be converted to the expected type. Supported types are expressed through the following keywords: *String*, *Integer*, *Double*, *Date*, and *Currency* (decimal).
- ***ValueToCompare*** Indicates the value to compare the user's input against. If the *Type* property is set, the *ValueToCompare* attribute must comply with it.

The following code demonstrates the typical markup of the *CompareValidator* control when the control is called to validate an integer input from a text box representing someone's age:

```
<asp:CompareValidator runat="server" id="ageValidator"
    ControlToValidate="ageTextBox"
    ValueToCompare="18"
    Operator="GreaterThanEqual"
    Type="Integer"
    ErrorMessage="Must specify an age greater than 17." />
```

### The *CustomValidator* Control

The *CustomValidator* control is a generic and totally user-defined validator that uses custom validation logic to accomplish its task. You typically resort to this control when none of the other validators seems appropriate or, more simply, when you need to execute your own code in addition to that of the standard validators.

To set up a custom validator, you need to indicate a client-side function through the *ClientValidationFunction* property. If client-side validation is disabled or not supported, simply omit this setting. Alternatively, or in addition to client validation, you can define some managed code to execute on the server. You do this by defining a handler for the *ServerValidate* event. The code will be executed when the page is posted back in response to a click on a button control. The following code snippet shows how to configure a custom validator to check the value of a text box against an array of feasible values.

```
<asp:CustomValidator runat="server" id="membershipValidator"
    ControlToValidate="membership"
    ClientValidationFunction="CheckMembership"
    OnServerValidate="ServerValidation"
    ErrorMessage="Membership can be Normal, Silver, Gold, or Platinum." />
```

If specified, the client validation function takes a mandatory signature and looks like this:

```
function CheckMembership(source, arguments)
{ ... }
```

The *source* argument references the HTML tag that represents the validator control—usually, a *<span>* tag. The *arguments* parameter references an object with two properties, *IsValid* and *Value*. The *Value* property is the value stored in the input control to be validated. The *IsValid* property must be set to *false* or *true* according to the result of the validation. The *CustomValidator* control is not associated in all cases with a single input control in the current naming container. For this type of validator, setting the *ControlToValidate* property is not mandatory. For example, if the control has to validate the contents of multiple input fields, you just don't set the *ControlToValidate* property and the *arguments.Value* variable evaluates to the empty string. In this case, you write the validation logic so that any needed values are dynamically retrieved. With client-side script code, this can be done by accessing the members of the document's form, as shown in the following code:

```
function CheckMembership(source, arguments) {
    // Retrieve the current value of the element
    // with the specified ID
    var membership = document.forms[0]["membership"].value;
    ⋮
}
```

Setting only a client-side validation code opens a security hole because an attacker could work around the validation logic and manage to have invalid or malicious data sent to the server. By defining a server event handler, you have one more chance to validate data before applying changes to the back-end system. To define a server-side handler for a custom validator, use the *ServerValidate* event.

```
void ServerValidation(object source, ServerValidateEventArgs e) {
    <$VE;>
}
```

The *ServerValidateEventArgs* structure contains two properties—*IsValid* and *Value*—with the same meaning and goal as in the client validation function. If the control is not bound to a particular input field, the *Value* property is empty and you retrieve any needed value using the ASP.NET object model. For example, the following code shows how to check the status of a check box on the server:

```
void ServerValidation (object source, ServerValidateEventArgs e) {
    e.IsValid = (CheckBox1.Checked == true);
}
```

Note that the *CheckBox* control (as well as *HtmlInputCheckBox*) cannot be validated using the standard validators and the *CustomValidator* control is the only option.

### The *RegularExpressionValidator* Control

Regular expressions are an effective way to ensure that a predictable and well-known sequence of characters form the user's entry. For example, using regular expressions you can validate the format of zip codes, Social Security numbers, client codes, e-mail addresses, telephone numbers, and so on. When using the *RegularExpressionValidator* control, you set the *ValidationExpression* property with the regular expression, which will be used to validate the input. (For more information about regular expressions, see the Visual Studio .NET documentation or the MSDN online documentation.)

The following code snippet shows a regular expression validator that ensures the user's entry is an e-mail address:

```
<asp:RegularExpressionValidator runat="server" id="emailValidator"
    ControlToValidate="email"
    ValidationExpression="[a-zA-Z_0-9.-]+\@[a-zA-Z_0-9.-]+\.\w+"
    ErrorMessage="Must be a valid email address." />
```

The regular expression just shown specifies that valid e-mail addresses are formed by two nonzero sequences of letters, digits, dashes, and dots separated by an @ symbol and followed by a dot (.) and an alphabetic string. (This might not be the perfect regular expression for e-mail addresses, but it certainly incorporates the majority of e-mail address formats.)

> **Note** The regular expression validation syntax is slightly different on the client than on the server. The *RegularExpressionValidator* control uses JScript regular expressions on the client and the .NET Framework *Regex* object on the server. Be aware that the JScript regular expression syntax is a subset of the *Regex* model. Whenever possible, try to use the regular expression syntax supported by JScript so that the same result is obtained for both the client and server.

## The *RangeValidator* Control

The *RangeValidator* control lets you verify that a given value falls within a specified range. The type of the values involved in the check is specified dynamically and picked from a short list that includes strings, numbers, and dates. The following code shows how to use a range validator control. The key properties are *MinimumValue* and *MaximumValue*, which together clearly denote the lower and upper boundaries of the interval.

```
<asp:RangeValidator runat="server" id="hiredDateValidator"
    ControlToValidate="hired"
    MinimumValue="1999-1-1"
    MaximumValue="9999-12-31"
    Type="Date"
    ErrorMessage="Must be a date after <b>Jan 1, 1999</b>." />
```

Note that an exception is thrown if the strings assigned *MinimumValue* or *MaximumValue* cannot be converted to the numbers or dates according to the value of the *Type* property.

If the type is set to *Date*, but no specific culture is set for the application, you should specify dates using a culture-neutral format, such as *yyyy/MM/dd*. If you don't do so, the chances are good that the values will not be interpreted correctly. Also bear in mind that the *RangeValidator* control just extends the capabilities of the more basic *CompareValidator* control by checking for a value in a fixed interval. In light of this, the *RangeValidator* control might raise an exception if either *MinimumValue* or *MaximumValue* is omitted. Whether the exception is thrown or not depends on the type chosen and its inherent ability to interpret the empty string. For example, an empty string on a *Date* type causes an exception.

If you want to operate on an unbound interval—whether lower or upper unbound—either you resort to the *GreaterThan* (or *LessThan*) operator on the *CompareValidator* control or simply use a virtually infinite value such as the *9999-12-31* date.

> **Note** Properties on the validation controls can be configured programmatically—for example, in the *Page_Load* event. In particular, if you're going to define the boundaries of a *RangeValidator* control at run time, be aware that both *MinimumValue* and *MaximumValue* are string properties.

### The *RequiredFieldValidator* Control

To catch when a user skips a mandatory field in an input form, you use the *RequiredFieldValidator* control to show an appropriate error message.

```
<asp:RequiredFieldValidator runat="server" id="lnameValidator"
    ControlToValidate="lname"
    ErrorMessage="Last name is mandatory" />
```

As long as you're using an up-level browser and client-side scripting is enabled for each validator, which is the default, invalid input will display error messages without performing a postback. Note that just tabbing through the controls is not a condition that raises an error; the validator gets involved only if you type blanks or if the field is blank when the page is posted back.

The control that requires input does not automatically display an asterisk or other character near the control to emphasize that it's required. Marking the field so that it stands out from the others is a good programming practice, but it is left up to the programmer to make controls that require input to stand out from the others.

How can you determine whether a certain field is really empty? In many cases, the empty string just pays the bill, but this is not a rule. The *InitialValue* property specifies the initial value of the input control. The validation fails only if the value of the control equals *InitialValue* upon losing focus. By default, *InitialValue* is initialized with the empty string.

## Setting Up a Data Entry Page

Let's see how to build a form that makes intensive use of validators to ensure that the input is always well-formed. The following page contains a couple of mandatory text fields to specify first and last name. Both are associated with an instance of the *RequiredFieldValidator* control. Other controls are expected to accept a minimum age and a date. For them, we'll use *CompareValidator* and *RangeValidator*. An e-mail address is entered and validated using a *RegularExpressionValidator*. Finally, a membership level is validated using a *CustomValidator*.

```
<form runat="server">
    <h3>Fill the form out</h3>

    <table>
        <tr><td>Name</td><td>*</td>
            <td><asp:textbox runat="server" id="fname" />
                <asp:RequiredFieldValidator runat="server"
                    id="fnameValidator"
                    ControlToValidate="fname"
                    ErrorMessage="Name is mandatory" /></td></tr>
        <tr><td>Last Name</td><td>*</td>
            <td><asp:textbox runat="server" id="lname" />
                <asp:RequiredFieldValidator runat="server"
                    id="lnameValidator"
                    ControlToValidate="lname"
                    ErrorMessage="Last name is mandatory" /></td></tr>
        <tr><td>Age</td><td></td>
            <td><asp:textbox runat="server" id="age" />
                <asp:CompareValidator runat="server"
                    id="ageValidator"
                    ControlToValidate="age"
                    Operator="GreaterThanEqual"
                    ValueToCompare="18"
                    Type="integer"
                    ErrorMessage="Age must be at least 18." /></td></tr>
        <tr><td>Email</td><td></td>
            <td><asp:textbox runat="server" id="email" />
                <asp:RegularExpressionValidator runat="server"
                    id="emailValidator"
                    ControlToValidate="email"
                    ValidationExpression=
                        "[a-zA-Z_0-9.-]+\@[a-zA-Z_0-9.-]+\.\w+"
                    ErrorMessage="Must be an email address." /></td></tr>
        <tr><td>Hire Date</td><td></td>
            <td><asp:textbox runat="server" id="hired" />
                <asp:CompareValidator runat="server"
                    id="hiredValidator"
                    ControlToValidate="hired"
                    Display="Dynamic"
```

```
                    Operator="DataTypeCheck"
                    Type="date"
                    ErrorMessage="Must enter a date." />
                <asp:RangeValidator runat="server"
                    id="hiredDateValidator"
                    ControlToValidate="hired"
                    Display="Dynamic"
                    MinimumValue="1999-1-1"
                    MaximumValue="9999-12-31"
                    Type="Date"
                    ErrorMessage="Date after 1-1-99." /></td></tr>
        <tr><td>Membership Level</td><td></td>
            <td><asp:textbox runat="server" id="membership" />
                <asp:CustomValidator runat="server"
                    id="membershipValidator"
                    ControlToValidate="membership"
                    ClientValidationFunction="CheckMembership"
                    ErrorMessage="Must be Gold or Platinum." /></td></tr>
    </table>
</form>
```

By default, if the page runs on an up-level browser such as Internet Explorer 6.0, the validation is automatically enabled on the client as well. As you tab out of each form field, some automatically created Javascript code runs and checks the user input before it is sent to the server.

In the page just listed, each validator control is rendered to the right of the input field so that in case of an error, the error message is displayed to the right of the input field, as shown in Figure 3-5.

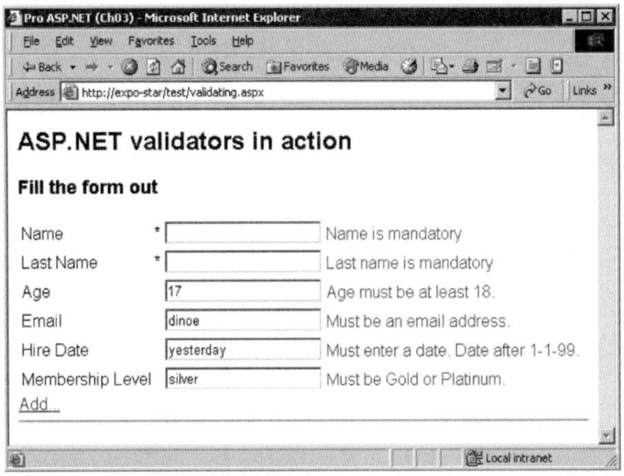

**Figure 3-5** The input form with error messages signaled by validation controls.

If the client script support is disabled or the browser doesn't provide for it, no validation takes place until the page is posted back. In this case, nothing happens as you tab in and out of input fields, but after a postback the page is served with the proper error messages.

## Displaying Error Information

The *ErrorMessage* property determines the static message that each validation control will display in case of error. Note that if the *Text* property is also set, it would take precedence over *ErrorMessage*. *Text* is designed to display inline where the validation control is located; *ErrorMessage* is designed to display in the validation summary. (Strategies for using *Text* and *ErrorMessage* will be discussed more in the next section, "The *ValidationSummary* Control.") Because all validation controls are labels, no other support or helper controls are needed to display any message. The message will be displayed in the body of the validation controls and, subsequently, wherever the validation control is actually placed. The error message is displayed as HTML, so it can contain any HTML formatting attribute.

Validators that work in client mode can create the *<span>* tag for the message either statically or dynamically. You can control this setting by using the *Display* property. When the display mode is set to *Static* (the default), the *<span>* element is given the following style:

```
style="color:Red;visibility:hidden;"
```

The CSS *visibility* style attribute, when set to *Hidden*, causes the browser not to display the element but reserves space for it. If the *Display* property contains *Dynamic*, the style string changes as follows:

```
style="color:Red;display:none;"
```

The CSS *display* attribute, when set to *none*, simply hides the element, which will take up space on the page only if displayed. The value of the *Display* property becomes critical when you have multiple validators associated with the same input control. For example, consider the following code excerpted from the previously considered page:

```
<asp:textbox runat="server" id="hired" />
    <asp:CompareValidator runat="server"
        id="hiredValidator"
        ControlToValidate="hired"
        Display="Dynamic"
        Operator="DataTypeCheck"
        Type="date"
        ErrorMessage="Must enter a date." />
    <asp:RangeValidator runat="server"
        id="hiredDateValidator"
```

```
ControlToValidate="hired"
Display="Dynamic"
MinimumValue="1999-1-1"
MaximumValue="9999-12-31"
Type="Date"
ErrorMessage="Date after 1-1-99." />
```

The value of the *hired* text box is first validated to ensure it contains a valid date and then to verify the specified date is later than 1-1-1999. If the *Display* property is set to *Static* and the date is outside the specified range, you get a page like the one shown in Figure 3-6.

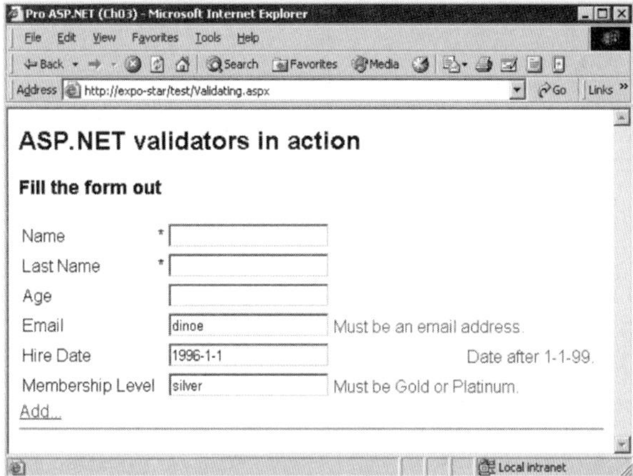


**Figure 3-6** The first error message is not displayed, but it takes up space.

## The *ValidationSummary* Control

The *ValidationSummary* control is a label that summarizes and displays all the validation error messages found on a Web page. The summary is displayed in a single location formatted in a variety of ways. The *DisplayMode* property sets the output format, which can be a list, a bulleted list, or a plain text paragraph. By default, it is a bulleted list. The feasible values are grouped in the *ValidationSummaryDisplayMode* enumeration.

Whatever the format is, the summary can be displayed as text in the page, in a message box, or in both. The Boolean properties *ShowSummary* and *ShowMessageBox* let you decide. The output of the *ValidationSummary* control is not displayed until the page posts back no matter what the value of the *EnableClientScript* property is. The *HeaderText* property defines the text that is displayed atop the summary.

```
<asp:ValidationSummary runat="server"
    ShowMessageBox="true"
```

```
ShowSummary="true"
HeaderText="The following errors occurred:"
DisplayMode="BulletList" />
```

This code snippet originates the screen shown in Figure 3-7.

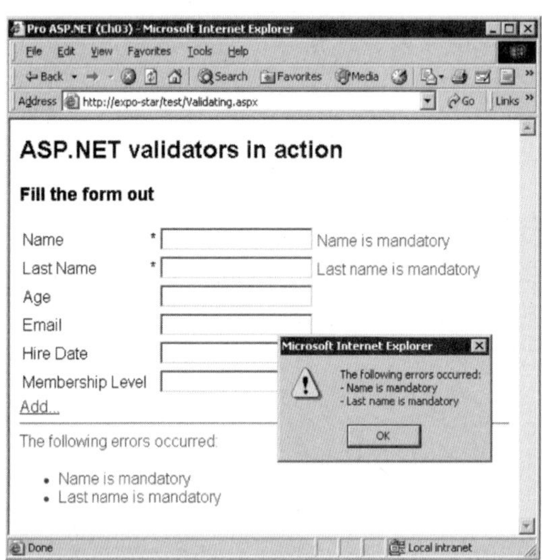


**Figure 3-7** After the page posts back, the validation summary is updated and a message box pops up to inform the user.

The validation summary is displayed only if there's at least one pending error. Note that, in the default case, the labels near the input controls are updated anyway, along with the summary text. You can control the error information in the following ways:

- **Both in-place and summary information** This is the default scenario. Use the *ValidationSummary* control and accept all default settings on the validator controls. If you want to leverage both places to display information, a recommended approach consists of minimizing the in-place information by using the *Text* property rather than *ErrorMessage*. If you set both, *Text* is displayed in-place while *ErrorMessage* shows up in the validation summary. For example, you can set *Text* with a glyph or an asterisk and assign *ErrorMessage* with more detailed text. (This case is illustrated in Figure 3-8.)
- **Only in-place information** Do not use the *ValidationSummary* control, and set the *ErrorMessage* property in each validation control you use.

- **Only summary information** Use the *ValidationSummary* control, and set the *ErrorMessage* property on individual validation controls. Set the *Display* property of validators to *None* so that no in-place error message will ever be displayed.
- **Custom error information** You don't use the *ValidationSummary* control, and you set the *Display* property of the individual validators to *None*. In addition, you collect the various error messages through the *ErrorMessage* property on the validation controls and arrange your own feedback for the user.

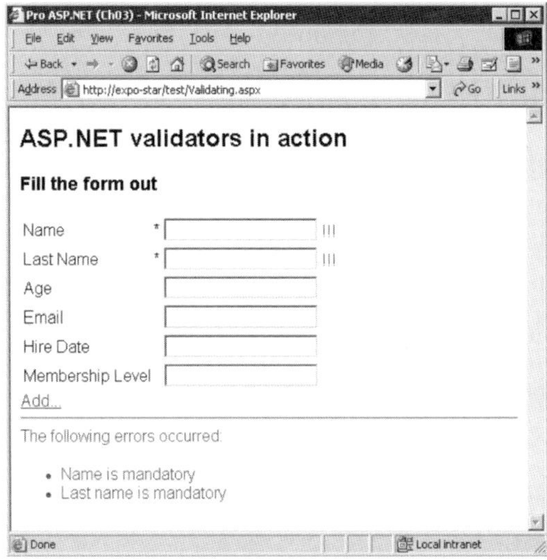


**Figure 3-8** A glyph marks the input data as wrong, and the summary text details the errors.

## Validating for Multiple Conditions

As mentioned earlier, you can associate multiple validators with a single input control. The validation takes place in order, and each validation control generates and displays its own error message. The content of the input control is considered valid if all the validators return *true*.

If an input control has multiple valid patterns—for example, an ID field can take the form of a Social Security number or a VAT number—you can either validate by using custom code or regular expressions.

## Client-Side Validation

As mentioned earlier, the verification normally takes place on the server either after the *Validate* method is called or as the result of a postback event. If the browser supports Dynamic HTML, though, you can also activate the validation process on the client, with a significant gain in responsiveness. To be precise, ASP.NET automatically enables client-side validation if it detects a browser with enough capabilities.

If client-side validation is turned on, the page won't post back until all the input fields contain valid data. To run secure code and prevent malicious and underhanded attacks, you might want to validate data on the server too. Consider also that not all types of validation can be accomplished on the client. In fact, if you need to validate against a database, there's no other option than posting back to the server.

### Enabling Client Validation

Client validation can be controlled on a per-validation control basis by using the *EnableClientScript* Boolean property. By default, the property is set to *true*, meaning client validation is enabled as long as the browser supports it. If you want to control the client validation at the page level, resort to the *ClientTarget* attribute on the *@Page* directive. The following code disables client validation by specifying that any code in the page should target a down-level browser:

```
<% @Page ClientTarget="DownLevel" %>
```

The *ClientTarget* attribute—also available as a property on the *Page* class—overrides the type of browser that ASP.NET should target when generating the page. If the *ClientTarget* attribute is set, ASP.NET doesn't detect the actual browser's capabilities but loads the capabilities for the specified browser from the machine.config file. Feasible values for the *ClientTarget* attribute include any value defined in the configuration *<clientTarget>* section. The standard content is as follows:

```
<clientTarget>
    <add alias="ie5" userAgent="Mozilla/4.0 (compatible; MSIE 5.5; ...)"/>
    <add alias="ie4" userAgent="Mozilla/4.0 (compatible; MSIE 4.0; ...)"/>
    <add alias="uplevel" userAgent="Mozilla/4.0 (compatible; MSIE 4.0;…)"/>
    <add alias="downlevel" userAgent="Unknown" />
</clientTarget>
```

If *ClientTarget* is not set, the browser's capabilities are detected through *Request.Browser* property. The *BaseValidator* class determines whether the browser is up-level or not. Only if the browser is considered up-level, will the client validation be implemented. Browsers and client devices that are considered up-level support at least the following:

- ECMAScript (including JScript and JavaScript) version 1.2
- HTML version 4.0
- The Microsoft Document Object Model
- Cascading style sheets

For down-level browsers, the only requirement is HTML version 3.2.

### Implementing Client Validation

For situations in which validation can be applied on the client, a lot of JavaScript code is silently injected in the page. Let's consider a simple page like the following one:

```
<% @Page language="c#" %>
<script runat="server">
void DoClick(object sender, EventArgs e) {}
</script>

<html>
<body>
<form runat="server" id="theForm">
<asp:textbox runat="server" id="fname" />
<asp:RequiredFieldValidator runat="server" id="fnameValidator"
    ControlToValidate="fname"
    Text="*"
    ErrorMessage="Name is mandatory" />
<br>
<asp:linkbutton runat="server" Text="Click..." OnClick="DoClick" />
</form>
</body>
</html>
```

This page contains a single text box with a required field validator. When viewed through an up-level browser, the HTML output looks like the following code. The code in bold represents specific extensions due to the client validation.

```
<form name="theForm" method="post" action="Simple.aspx" id="theForm"
    language="javascript" onsubmit="ValidatorOnSubmit();">
<input type="hidden" name="__EVENTTARGET" value="" />
<input type="hidden" name="__EVENTARGUMENT" value="" />
<input type="hidden" name="__VIEWSTATE" value="..." />

<script language="javascript">
<!--
    function __doPostBack(eventTarget, eventArgument) {
        var theform = document.theForm;
        theform.__EVENTTARGET.value = eventTarget;
        theform.__EVENTARGUMENT.value = eventArgument;
        theform.submit();
    }
// -->
```

```
</script>

<script language="javascript"
    src="/aspnet_client/system_web/1_x_xxxx_0/WebUIValidation.js" />

<input name="fname" type="text" id="fname" />
<span id="fnameValidator"
    controltovalidate="fname"
    errormessage="Name is mandatory"
    evaluationfunction="RequiredFieldValidatorEvaluateIsValid"
    initialvalue=""
    style="color:Red;visibility:hidden;">*</span>
<br>
<a href="javascript:{if (typeof(Page_ClientValidate) != 'function' ||
    Page_ClientValidate()) __doPostBack('_ctl0','')} ">Click...</a>

<script language="javascript">
<!--
    var Page_Validators =
        new Array(document.all["fnameValidator"]);
// -->
</script>

<script language="javascript">
<!--
var Page_ValidationActive = false;
if (typeof(clientInformation) != "undefined" &&
clientInformation.appName.indexOf("Explorer") != -1) {
    if (typeof(Page_ValidationVer) == "undefined")
        alert("Unable to find script library ....");
    else if (Page_ValidationVer != "125")
        alert("This page uses an incorrect version ...");
    else
        ValidatorOnLoad();
}

function ValidatorOnSubmit() {
    if (Page_ValidationActive) {
        ValidatorCommonOnSubmit();
    }
}
// -->
</script>
</form>
</body>
</html>
```

When the page loads up, the *ValidatorOnLoad* JavaScript function executes and populates the *Page_Validators* array with instances of the JavaScript objects that represent the active validators. Another change to notice is the *onsubmit* client event handler that has been added to the *<form>* element. When the HTML form is going to be submitted, a piece of script code runs and checks the validity of all input fields. The *onsubmit* handler allows the actual post only when all the validators agree to commit.

All the client script functions are imported in the page from a well-known JavaScript file located under the Web server's root:

```
/aspnet_client/system_web/1_x_xxxx_0/WebUIValidation.js
```

The path of this file is controlled by the *<webControls>* section of the machine.config file.

Another interesting change to observe in the ASP.NET code when client validation is enabled is the insertion of extra attributes in the *<span>* tag that represents the validator. The preceding code reveals a couple of custom attributes named *evaluationfunction* and *initialvalue*. The former refers to the JavaScript function that performs the client-side validation. The function is defined in the WebUIValidation.js file. The other attribute, specific to the required field validator, refers to the value to check against—the empty string in this case. The script validator functions receive one argument, that being the JavaScript object representing the validator. Custom attributes are an effective way to pass external data to script objects based on HTML tags. The following code snippet from WebUIValidation.js shows the script implementation of the required field validator:

```
function ValidatorTrim(s) {
    var m = s.match(/^\s*(\S+(\s+\S+)*)\s*$/);
    return (m == null) ? "" : m[1];
}
function RequiredFieldValidatorEvaluateIsValid(val) {
    var t = ValidatorTrim(ValidatorGetValue(val.controltovalidate);
    return (t != ValidatorTrim(val.initialvalue))
}
```

## Internet Explorer WebControls

Although they're not officially part of the .NET Framework and aren't included in the Web controls namespace, other Web controls have been around for some time to address the needs of developers who do a lot of client-side, Internet Explorer–specific Web programming. Unlike controls in the ASP.NET namespace, these controls extensively exploit the Dynamic HTML object model of Internet Explorer 5.x and newer versions. They perform a lot of tasks on the client and make provisions for Web versions of typical desktop controls such as the *TreeView* or *TabStrip*. You can download some of these controls from the control gallery at *http://www.asp.net*. Microsoft has released the following controls:

*(continued)*

## Internet Explorer WebControls *(continued)*

- **IE TreeView** Facilitates rendering of hierarchical data, folder views, and other similar data structures. The control includes support for data binding and rich DHTML behaviors in Internet Explorer 5.5 and newer.

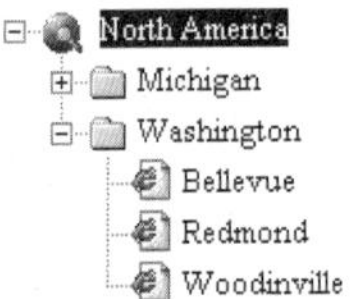


- **IE Toolbar** Web counterpart of the toolbar control commonly used in Microsoft Windows desktop applications.

- **IE TabStrip** Simplifies the authoring of tabbed menus, and is particularly useful for authoring user-interface elements that navigate site content.

- **IE MultiPage** Enables the definition of collections of child page elements. As in a desktop Windows tab control, the control lets you define the content of pages that are navigated.

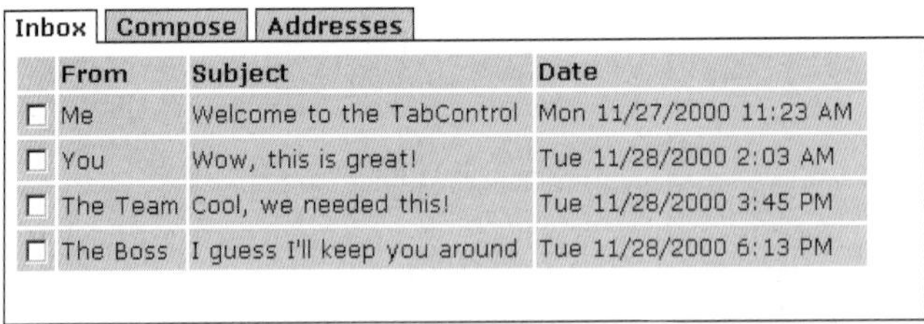


All Internet Explorer WebControls are tailored for both down-level browsers and up-level browsers and renders their advanced functionalities using client-side behaviors when the browser allows for that. In the same gallery of controls on the *http://www.asp.net* portal, you'll also find links to similar third-party products.

# Data-Bound Controls

Web applications are, for the most part, just data-driven applications. For this reason, the ability to bind HTML elements like drop-down lists or tables to structured data represents a key feature for a development platform. Data-bound controls are the ASP.NET answer to the growing demand for automatic binding between data sources and graphical elements. Data binding is the process that retrieves data from a fixed source and dynamically associates this data to properties on server controls. Valid target controls are those that have been specifically designed to support data binding. Data-bound controls are not yet another family of controls. Data-bound controls are simply server controls that feature a few well-known data-related properties, including *Text*, *DataSource*, *DataTextField*, and *DataValueField*.

The *DataSource* property, in particular, lets you specify the data source object the control is linked to. Note that this link is logical and does not result in any overhead or underlying operation until you explicitly order to bind the data to the control. Not all properties in the Web control programming interface are data bindable. You activate data binding on a control by calling the *DataBind* method. When this method executes, the control actually loads data from the associated data source, evaluates the data-bound properties, and redraws its user interface to reflect changes.

## Feasible Data-Binding Sources

Many .NET classes can be used as data sources—and not just those that have to do with database contents. In general, any object that exposes the *ICollection* interface is a valid bindable data source. The *ICollection* interface defines size, enumerators, and synchronization methods for all .NET collections. In particular, you can bind a Web control to the following classes:

- *DataTable*, *DataView*, and *DataSet*
- Data readers
- Dictionaries and arrays

In ASP.NET 1.1, XML documents are not directly bindable unless you load their content in one of the previously mentioned classes. You can do this by loading the XML document into a *DataSet* and then binding to the *DataSet*.

To be honest, I should note that the *DataSet* and *DataTable* classes don't implement *ICollection* or any other interface that inherit from it (for example, *IList*). However, both classes do store collections of data internally. These collections are accessed using the methods of an intermediate interface—*IListSource*—which performs the trick of making the *DataSet* and *DataTable* classes look like they implement a collection. In Chapter 20, we'll discuss in detail the mechanism that makes such ADO.NET objects bindable.

### ADO.NET Classes

As we'll see in greater detail in Chapter 5, ADO.NET—and in particular the *System.Data* namespace—provides a bunch of data container classes that can be filled with any sort of data, including database information. Classes in the *System.Data* namespace are just in-memory caches of data and work disconnected from any database server. The data reader class, on the other hand, is specific to a managed provider and, as such, is tightly bound to a particular data source such as Oracle or Microsoft SQL Server.

Note that the *DataSet* class can contain more than one table; however, only one table can be associated with a data-bound control. In this case, you should assign the *DataSet* object to the *DataSource* property and the selected *DataTable* object to another property acting as a selector—the *DataMember* property.

### Collection-Based Classes

At the highest level of abstraction, a collection serves as a container for instances of other classes. All collection classes implement the *ICollection* interface, which in turn implements the *IEnumerable* interface. As a result, all collection classes provide a basic set of functionalities.

All collection classes have a *Count* property to return the number of cached items; they have a *CopyTo* method to copy their items, in their entirety or in part, to an external array; they have a *GetEnumerator* method that instantiates an enumerator object to loop through the child items. *GetEnumerator* is the method behind the curtain whenever you call the *foreach* statement in C# and the *For...Each* statement in Visual Basic .NET.

*IList* and *IDictionary* are two interfaces that extend *ICollection*, giving a more precise characterization to the resultant collection class. *ICollection* provides only basic and minimal functionality for a collection. For example, *ICollection* does not have any methods to add or remove items. Add and remove functions are exactly what the *IList* interface provides. In the *IList* interface, the *Add* and *Insert* methods place new items at the bottom of the collection or at the specified index. The *Remove* and *RemoveAt* methods remove items, while *Clear* empties the collection. Finally, *Contains* verifies whether an item with a given value belongs to the collection, and *IndexOf* returns the index of the specified item. Commonly used container classes that implement both *ICollection* and *IList* are *Array*, *ArrayList*, and *StringCollection*. Previously mentioned ADO.NET classes—such as the *DataView* class—support data binding via the *ICollection* interface.

The *IDictionary* interface defines the API that represents a collection of key/value pairs. The interface exposes methods similar to *IList*, but with different signatures. Dictionary classes also feature two extra properties, *Keys* and *Values*. They return collections of keys and values, respectively, found in the dictionary. Typical dictionary classes are *ListDictionary*, *Hashtable*, and *SortedList*.

## Simple Data Binding

In ASP.NET, there are two types of data binding—simple and complex. A simple binding is a connection between one piece of data and a server control property. It is established through a special expression and is evaluated when the code in the page calls the *DataBind* method either on the *Page* object or the control.

A data binding expression is any text wrapped by <% ... %> and prefixed by the symbol #. You can use data-binding expressions to set the value of an attribute in the opening tag of a server control. A data-binding expression is programmatically managed via an instance of the *DataBoundLiteralControl* class. The following code snippet shows how to set the text of a label with the current time:

```
<asp:label runat="server" Text='<%# DateTime.Now.ToString() %>' />
```

Within the delimiters, you can invoke user-defined page methods, static methods, and properties and methods of any other page components. The following code demonstrates a label bound to the name of the currently selected element in a drop-down list control:

```
<asp:label runat="server" Text='<%# dropdown.SelectedItem.Text %>' />
```

Note that if you're going to use quotes within the expression, you should wrap the expression itself with single quotes. The data-binding expression can accept a minimal set of operators, mostly for concatenating subexpressions. If you need more advanced processing and use external arguments, resort to a user-defined method. The only requirement is that the method must be callable within the page. If the code of the page is not resident in the .aspx page (for example, you're using code-behind), make sure the method is declared public or protected.

### Simple Data Binding in Action

In the following example, you'll see how to use simple data binding with text boxes to arrange a form-based record viewer. The user interface of the page supplies three text boxes, one for each of the retrieved fields. The data source is the Employees table of the Northwind database in Microsoft SQL Server 2000.

The query that is run against the database selects three fields: employeeid, firstname, and lastname. The binding takes place between the text boxes and the fields. Only one record at a time is displayed, and Previous and Next buttons let you move through the data. You can see what the application looks like in Figure 3-9.

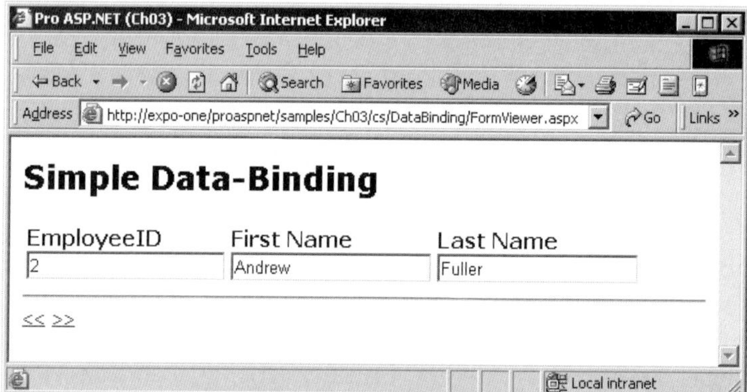


**Figure 3-9** The text boxes in the figure are bound to fields in the Employees table from the SQL Server 2000 Northwind sample database.

The binding expression makes use of a user-defined method named *GetBoundData*.

```
<asp:textbox runat="server" id="txtID"
    Text = '<%# GetBoundData("employeeid") %>' />
```

The method takes the name of the field to display and retrieves the position of the current record from the ASP.NET *Session* object. It then reads the corresponding value and passes it to the ASP.NET runtime for actual rendering.

```
public string GetBoundData(String fieldName)
{
    DataSet ds = (DataSet) Session["MyData"];
    DataTable dt = ds.Tables["EmpTable"];
    int nRowPos = (int) Session["CurrentRecord"];

    String buf = dt.Rows[nRowPos][fieldName].ToString();
    return buf;
}
```

## Implementation of Data-Bound Expressions

What really happens when a data-bound expression is found in a Web page? How does the ASP.NET runtime process it? Let's consider the following base code:

```
<asp:label runat="server" id="today"
    text='<%# DateTime.Now.ToString() %>' />
```

While compiling the source code for the page, the ASP.NET runtime writes a handler for the *DataBinding* event of the control—a *Label* in this case. The following pseudocode shown illustrates the generation of the label in the underlying class. (See Chapter 2 for more details on the compilation of the page.)

```
private Control __BuildControltoday() {
    Label __ctrl = new Label();
    this.today = __ctrl;
    __ctrl.ID = "today";


    __ctrl.DataBinding += new EventHandler(this.__DataBindtoday);
    return __ctrl;
}
```

Basically, the data-binding handler assigns the verbatim expression to the control's property.

```
public void __DataBindtoday(object sender, EventArgs e) {
    Label target;
    target = (Label) sender;
    target.Text = Convert.ToString(DateTime.Now.ToString());
}
```

The value returned by the data-binding expression must be convertible to a string. The code in the event handler does not change if the expression points to another control. The ASP.NET runtime assumes the control exists and is instantiated—which is *true* by design.

## Complex Data Binding

Complex data binding occurs when you bind a list control or an iterative control to one or more columns of data. List controls include the *DropDownList*, *CheckBoxList*, *RadioButtonList*, and *ListBox*. Iterative controls are the *Repeater*, *DataList*, and *DataGrid* controls.

List controls have a more complex and richer user interface than labels and text boxes. They display (or at least need to have in memory) more items at the same time. That's the reason you should associate them explicitly with a collection of data—the data source. Depending on its expected behavior, the control will pick the needed items from memory and properly format and display them.

Iterative controls take a data source, loop through the items, and iteratively apply HTML templates to each row. This basic behavior is common to all three ASP.NET iterators. Beyond that, they differ in terms of layout capabilities and functionality they support. We'll cover iterative controls from various perspectives in Chapter 6 and Chapter 9.

Let's see how complex forms of data binding apply to key list controls. All list controls inherit from the base *ListControl* class.

## The *DropDownList* Control

The *DropDownList* control enables users to select one item from a single-selection drop-down list. You can specify the size of the control by setting its height and width in pixels, but you can't control the number of items displayed when the list drops down. The *DropDownList* control can be filled through data binding. The following code provides an example:

```
<asp:DropDownList runat="server" id="theList"
    DataSource="<%# getData() %>"
    DataTextField="lastname"
    DataValueField="employeeid">
```

You can assign a data binding expression to the *DataSource* property but not to the *DataTextField* and *DataValueField* properties. Their value must match exactly the name of one of the columns in the data source. The properties specific to the *DropDownList* control are shown in Table 3-12.

**Table 3-12 Properties of the *DropDownList* Control**

| Property | Description |
|---|---|
| *AutoPostBack* | Gets or sets whether the control should automatically post back to the server when the user changes the selection |
| *DataMember* | Gets or sets the name of the table in the *DataSource* to bind |
| *DataSource* | Gets or sets the data source that populates the items of the list |
| *DataTextField* | Gets or sets the name of the column in the data source that provides the text content of the list items |
| *DataTextFormatString* | Gets or sets the formatting string used to control how data bound to the list is displayed |
| *DataValueField* | Gets or sets the field of the data source that provides the value of each list item |
| *Items* | Gets the collection of items in the list control |
| *SelectedIndex* | Gets or sets the index of the selected item in the list |
| *SelectedItem* | Gets the selected item in the list |

The programming interface of the *DropDownList* also features three properties to configure the border of the drop-down list—the *BorderColor*, *BorderStyle*, and *BorderWidth* properties. Although the properties are correctly transformed by style properties, most browsers won't use them to change the appearance of the drop-down list.

The *DataTextField* and *DataValueField* properties don't accept expressions, only plain column names. To combine two or more fields of the data source, you can use a calculated column. You can either use a column computed by the database or exploit the power of the ADO.NET object model (as explained in Chapter 5) and add an in-memory column. The following SQL query returns a column obtained by concatenating *lastname* and *firstname.*

```
SELECT lastname + ', ' + firstname AS 'EmployeeName'
FROM Employees
```

The same result can also be obtained, more efficiently, without the involvement of the database. Once you've filled a *DataTable* object with the result of the query, you add a new column to its *Columns* collection. The content of the column is based on an expression. The following code adds an *EmployeeName* column to the data source that concatenates the last name and first name:

```
dataTable.Columns.Add("EmployeeName",
    typeof(string),
    "lastname + ', ' + firstname");
```

An expression-based column does not need to be filled explicitly. The values for all the cells in the column are calculated and cached when the column is added to the table. The table tracks any dependencies and updates the calculated column whenever any of the constituent columns are updated.

## The *CheckBoxList* Control

The *CheckBoxList* control is a single monolithic control that groups a collection of checkable list items, each of which is rendered through an individual *CheckBox* control. The properties of the child check boxes are set by reading the associated data source. You insert a check box list in a page as follows:

```
<asp:CheckBoxList runat="server" id="employeesList">
```

Table 3-13 lists the specific properties of the *CheckBoxList* control.

**Table 3-13 Properties of the *CheckBoxList* Control**

| Property | Description |
|---|---|
| *AutoPostBack* | Gets or sets whether the control should automatically post back to the server when the user changes the selection |
| *CellPadding* | Gets or sets the pixels between the border and contents of the cell |
| *CellSpacing* | Gets or sets the pixels between cells |
| *DataMember* | Gets or sets the name of the table in the *DataSource* to bind |

*(continued)*

**Table 3-13 Properties of the *CheckBoxList* Control** *(continued)*

| Property | Description |
|---|---|
| *DataSource* | Gets or sets the data source that populates the items of the list |
| *DataTextField* | Gets or sets the name of the column in the data source that provides the text content of the list items |
| *DataTextFormatString* | Gets or sets the formatting string used to control how data bound to the list is displayed |
| *DataValueField* | Gets or sets the field of the data source that provides the value of each list item |
| *Items* | Gets the collection of items in the list control |
| *RepeatColumns* | Gets or sets the number of columns to display in the control |
| *RepeatDirection* | Gets or sets a value that indicates whether the control displays vertically or horizontally |
| *RepeatLayout* | Gets or sets the layout of the check boxes (table or flow) |
| *SelectedIndex* | Gets or sets the index of the selected item in the list |
| *SelectedItem* | Gets the selected item in the list |
| *TextAlign* | Gets or sets the text alignment for the check boxes |

Unlike the *DropDownList* control, the *CheckBoxList* does not supply any properties that know which items have been selected. But this aspect is vital for any Web application that utilizes checkable elements. The *CheckBoxList* can have any number of items selected, but how can you retrieve them?

Any list control has an *Items* property that contains the collection of the child items. The *Items* property is implemented through the *ListItemCollection* class and makes each contained item accessible via a *ListItem* object. The following code loops through the items stored in a *CheckBoxList* control and checks the *Selected* property of each of them:

```
foreach(ListItem item in chkList.Items)
{
    if (item.Selected) {
        // this item is selected
    }
}
```

## The *RadioButtonList* Control

The *RadioButtonList* control acts as the parent control for a collection of radio buttons. Each of the child items is rendered through a *RadioButton* control. By design, a *RadioButtonList* can have zero or one item selected. The *SelectedItem* property returns the selected element as a *ListItem* object. Note, though, that there is nothing to guarantee that only one item is selected at any time. For this reason, be extremely careful when you access the *SelectedItem* of a *RadioButtonList* control—it could be null.

The contents of the control can be fetched from a data source as follows:

```
<asp:RadioButtonList runat="server" id="employeesList"
    DataSource="<%# getData() %"
    DataValueField="EmployeeID"
    DataTextField="EmployeeName" />
```

The control supports the same set of properties as the *CheckBoxList* control and, just like it, accepts some layout directives. In particular, you can control the rendering process of the list with the *RepeatLayout* and *RepeatDirection* properties. By default, the list items are rendered within a table, which ensures the vertical alignment of the companion text. The property that governs the layout is *RepeatLayout*. The alternative is displaying the items as free HTML text, using blanks and breaks to guarantee some sort of minimal structure. *RepeatDirection* is the property that controls the direction in which, with or without a tabular structure, the items flow. Feasible values are *Vertical* (the default) and *Horizontal*. *RepeatColumns* is the property that determines how many columns the list should have. By default the value is *0*, which means all the items will be displayed in a single row, vertical or horizontal according to the value of *RepeatDirection*.

## The *ListBox* Control

The *ListBox* control represents a vertical sequence of items displayed in a scrollable window. The *ListBox* control allows single-item or multiple-item selection and exposes its contents through the usual *Items* collection, as shown in the following code:

```
<asp:listbox runat="server" id="theListBox"
    rows="5" selectionmode="Multiple" />
```

You can decide the height of the control through the *Rows* property. The height is measured in number of rows rather than pixels or percentages. When it comes to data binding, the *ListBox* control behaves like the controls discussed earlier in the chapter. It supports properties such as *DataSource* and *DataMember*, and it can be bound to a data source and show its contents.

Two properties make this control slightly different than other list controls—the *Rows* property, which represents the number of visible rows in the control, and the *SelectionMode* property, which determines whether one or multiple items can be selected. The following code demonstrates how to write a comma-separated string with the values of the selected items:

```
public void ShowSelectedItems(object sender, EventArgs e)
{
    StringBuilder sb = new StringBuilder("");
    for (int i=0; i < theList.Items.Count; i++)
```

```
    {
        if (theList.Items[i].Selected)
        {
            sb.Append(theList.Items[i].Text);
            sb.Append(", ");
        }
    }
    Response.Write(sb.ToString());
}
```

This code is nearly identical to the one you would write to accomplish the same operation on a *CheckBoxList* control. The programming interface of the list box also contains a *SelectedItem* property that makes little sense when you work with a multiselection control. In this case, the *SelectedItem* property returns the selected item with the lowest index.

> **Note** All list controls support the *SelectedIndexChanged* event, which is raised when the selection from the list changes and the page posts back to the server. You can use this event to execute server-side code whenever a control is checked or unchecked.

## Conclusion

In ASP.NET pages, server controls are vital components. Server-side controls alone—no matter their capabilities and flavors—constitute a huge difference between ASP and ASP.NET. Server-side controls transform the programming model of ASP.NET from a mere factory of HTML strings to a more modern and effective component-based model.

ASP.NET features a long list of control classes. Looking at the namespaces involved, we should conclude that only two families of controls exist—HTML and Web controls. Controls in the former group simply mirror the set of elements in the HTML syntax. Each constituent control has as many properties as there are attributes in the corresponding HTML tag. Names and behavior have been kept as faithful to the originals as possible. The ultimate goal of the designers of HTML controls is to make the transition from ASP to ASP.NET as seamless as possible—just add *runat="server"* and refresh the page.

The overall design of Web controls is more abstract and much less tied to HTML. In general Web controls do not provide a strict one-to-one correspondence between controls and HTML tags. However, the capabilities of Web and HTML controls overlap. All ASP.NET server controls render in HTML, but Web controls render to more complex HTML representation than HTML controls.

In the family of Web controls, we can identify interesting and powerful subsets of controls—for example, validators, list controls, and iterative controls. Data-bound controls, including list and iterative controls, represent a key enhancement in the ASP.NET programming model. The ability to bind data sources to controls—especially to disconnected and in-memory sources—adds spice to an already powerful model and significantly increases speed and productivity. Just consider the following example. Do you remember the typical check box and radio button code that countless ASP pages implemented? The code walks its way through all the records in a result set and generates a check box or radio button at each step. With this old model, state maintenance is in the care of the programmer, code has to be written over and over again, and extensibility and reusability is a mere dream. In ASP.NET—thanks to server controls—control list generation is as easy as using ad hoc data-bound list controls.

## Resources

- Internet Explorer WebControls (*http://msdn.microsoft.com/workshop/webcontrols/overview/overview.asp*)
- Detect Control Changes (*http://www.aspnetpro.com/features/2003/03/asp200303de_f/asp200303de_f.asp*)
- ASP.NET Validation in Depth (*http://msdn.microsoft.com/library/en-us/dnaspp/html/aspplusvalid.asp*)
- Using the Internet Explorer WebControls (*http://msdn.microsoft.com/msdnmag/issues/03/02/ASPColumn*)

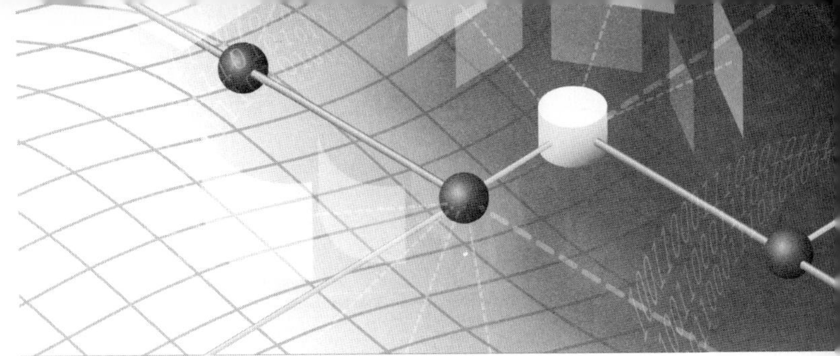

# 4

# Working with the Page

*Whatever you do will be insignificant, but it is very important that you do it.*
*—Mahatma Gandhi*

Although formless pages are still accepted and correctly handled, the typical ASP.NET page is a single form page. The *HtmlForm* class defines the behavior of the server-side form when the *runat* attribute is set to *server*. The *HtmlForm* class acts as a container of server controls and wraps them in an HTML *<form>* element when the page is rendered. The obtained HTML form always posts to the same page and for this reason is said to be *reentrant*. The default method used to submit form data is POST but GET can be used as well.

In most cases, the server form is the outermost tag and is contained directly in *<body>*. In general, though, the server *<form>* tag can be the child of any other server container control such as *<table>*, *<div>*, *<body>*, and any other HTML generic control. (We covered HTML controls and Web controls in Chapter 3.) If any noncontainer controls (for example, a *TextBox*) are placed outside the form tag, an exception is thrown. Note, though, that no check is made at compile time. The exception is raised by the control itself when the host page asks to render. Noncontainer Web controls, in fact, check whether they are being rendered within the boundaries of a server form and throw an *HttpException* if they are not. A call to the *Page*'s *VerifyRenderingInServerForm* method does the job.

In this chapter, we'll examine some aspects of form-based programming in ASP.NET, including how to use multiple forms in the same page. We consider the use of pop-up windows and show how to inject script code in the body of the client page. We'll also consider the styling of the page and how a made-to-measure API, such as the ASP.NET globalization and localization classes, can in some situations help to easily and effectively change the look and feel of the page. When designing a Web site or any application to be consumed over the Web, you can't realistically pretend to keep it error-free! For this reason, debugging, tracing, and effective and user-friendly error handling are key aspects for top-notch ASP.NET developers.

## Programming with Forms

One of the most common snags ASP developers face when they first approach the ASP.NET lifestyle is the fact that managed Web applications support the single-form interface (SFI) model.

> **Note** If you've never heard anyone use the SFI acronym, there's no reason for you to panic. It's an acronym I've created to mimic other more popular acronyms that, although used in different contexts, describe similar programming models—the single-document interface (SDI) and its opposite, the multiple-document interface (MDI).

In the SFI model, each page always posts to itself and does so through the POST or GET HTTP method. The HTTP method and the target frame of the post can be programmatically adjusted using ad hoc *HtmlForm* properties—*Method* and *Target*. The final destination of the postback can't be set in any way. What in HTML and ASP programming was the *Action* property of the form is simply not defined on the ASP.NET *HtmlForm* class. As a result, the SFI model is a built-in feature so much integrated with the ASP.NET platform that you can only take it or code the old ASP way without server forms.

Technically speaking, a kind of multiform interface (MFI) is still possible. Hold on, though. By MFI here, I simply mean the possibility of having multiple forms on the final HTML page. In no way does this mean you can have multiple *server-side* forms in an ASP.NET page. An ASP.NET page can host exactly one server form and as many HTML forms as needed. If you place two or more server forms in a page, you won't get any error at compile time. When processing the request, the *Page*-derived object examines markup blocks one at a time. The first *<form>* block is processed and rendered. After that, the page object sets an internal flag to remember that one form object has been processed for the page. Guess what happens next? When the second *<form runat="server">*

block is found, the page verifies that no other similar block has been processed earlier. If the flag is set, an *HttpException* is thrown. Later in this chapter, we'll discuss an example in which multiple forms—one server and one client—work together.

Multiple forms, though, are sometimes needed—although probably not frequently. You would need them, for example, for functionality hosted by the application pages, such as search or login capabilities.

## The *HtmlForm* Class

The *HtmlForm* class inherits from *HtmlContainerControl* and implements the *IAttributeAccessor* interface. The base class provides *HtmlForm* with the capability of containing child controls. This capability is shared with other HTML control classes, such as *HtmlTable*, characterized by child elements and a closing tag. The *IAttributeAccessor* interface defines two methods—*GetAttribute* and *SetAttribute*—used to read attribute values out of the opening tag.

### Properties of the *HtmlForm* Class

The *HtmlForm* class provides programmatic access to the HTML *<form>* element on the server through the set of properties shown in Table 4-1.

**Table 4-1 Form Properties**

| Property | Description |
|---|---|
| *Attributes* | Gets a name/value collection with all the attributes declared on the tag. |
| *ClientID* | Gets the value of *UniqueID*. |
| *Controls* | Gets a collection object that represents the child controls of the form. |
| *Disabled* | Gets or sets a value indicating whether the form is disabled. Matches the *disabled* HTML attribute. |
| *EnableViewState* | Rarely used at this level, gets or sets a value indicating whether the state of child controls should be persisted. |
| *Enctype* | Gets or sets the encoding type. Matches the *enctype* HTML attribute. |
| *ID* | Gets or sets the programmatic identifier of the form. |
| *InnerHtml* | Gets or sets the markup content found between the opening and closing tags of the form. |
| *InnerText* | Gets or sets the text between the opening and closing tags of the form. |

*(continued)*

**Table 4-1 Form Properties** *(continued)*

| Property | Description |
|---|---|
| *Method* | Gets or sets a value that indicates how a browser posts form data to the server. The default value is POST. Can be set to GET if needed. |
| *Name* | Gets the value of *UniqueID*. |
| *NamingContainer* | Gets a reference to the form's naming container; typically the host page. |
| *Page* | Gets a reference to the host page. |
| *Parent* | Gets a reference to the parent object. The parent object is typically, but not necessarily, the page. Note that if the form is contained in a *<table>* or *<div>* element not marked *"runat=server"*, the parent object is still the page. |
| *Site* | Returns *null*. |
| *Style* | Gets a collection of all cascading style sheet (CSS) properties applied to the form. |
| *TagName* | Returns "form". |
| *Target* | Gets or sets the name of the frame or window to render the HTML generated for the page. |
| *TemplateSource-Directory* | Gets the virtual directory of the page that contains the form. |
| *UniqueID* | Gets the unique, fully qualified name of the form. |
| *Visible* | Gets or sets a value that indicates whether the form is rendered. If *false*, the form is not rendered to HTML. |

The form must have a unique name. If the programmer doesn't assign the name, ASP.NET generates one using a built-in algorithm. The default name follows the pattern *_ctlX*, in which *X* is a unique integer—typically the index of the control in the page. The programmer can set the form's identifier by using either the *ID* or *Name* property. If both are set, the *ID* attribute takes precedence. Based on the value of *ID*, ASP.NET determines the values of *UniqueID* and *ClientID*. *UniqueID* is a fully qualified string based on the naming container of the form. *ClientID*, on the other hand, is used to identify a control for client-side operations, such as JavaScript functions.

The parent object of the form is the outer container control with the *runat* attribute. If such a control exists, the page object is set as the parent. Typical containers for the server form are *<table>* and *<div>* if they are marked as server-side objects.

By default, the *Method* property is set to POST. The value of the property can be modified programmatically. If the form is posted through the GET method, all form data is passed on the URL's query string. However, if you choose the GET method, make sure the limited size of a GET request does not affect the integrity of your application.

### Methods of the *HtmlForm* Class

Table 4-2 lists the methods available on the *HtmlForm* class. All the methods listed in the table are inherited from the base *System.Web.UI.Control* class.

**Table 4-2 Form Methods**

| Method | Description |
|---|---|
| *DataBind* | Calls the *DataBind* method on all child controls. |
| *Dispose* | Performs the final clean up before the object is freed. |
| *FindControl* | Retrieves and returns the control that matches the specified ID. |
| *HasControls* | Indicates whether the form contains any child controls. |
| *RenderControl* | Outputs the HTML code for the form. If tracing is enabled, caches tracing information to be rendered later, at the end of the page. |
| *ResolveUrl* | Ensures that the specified URL is absolute. Reads the base URL from the *TemplateSourceDirectory* property. |

The *FindControl* method searches only in the form's naming container. Controls belonging to an inner or outer naming container are not found.

## Multiple Forms

As mentioned, the SFI model is the default in ASP.NET and plays a key role in the automatic state management mechanism we described in Chapter 2. Some pages, though, would have a more consistent and natural design if they could define multiple *logical* forms. In this context, a *logical* form is a logically related group of input controls. For example, think of a login page for restricted areas of a Web site. Registered users just type in their user name and password and connect. Unregistered users need to fill out a form before they're given the parameters to connect. How do you code this? Let's review a few options.

In ASP, you can use two forms, each posting to a different page. The schema is outlined in Figure 4-1.

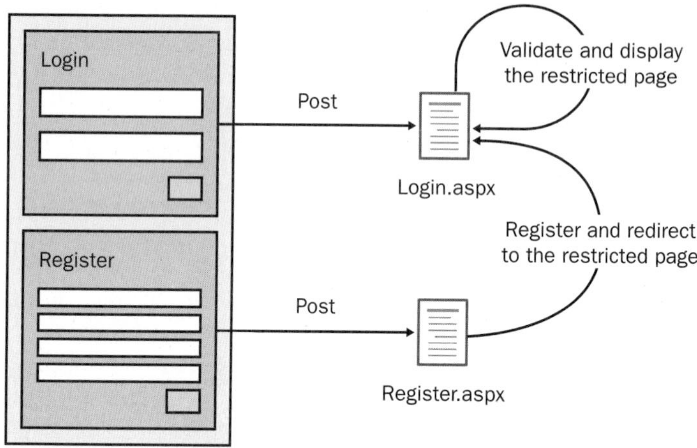


**Figure 4-1** Each form posts to a different page.

This solution is impracticable in ASP.NET unless you resort to a kind of pseudo-trick that basically consists of not using ASP.NET server controls. (More on this in a moment.) More apt to the ASP.NET programming style is the solution depicted in Figure 4-2.

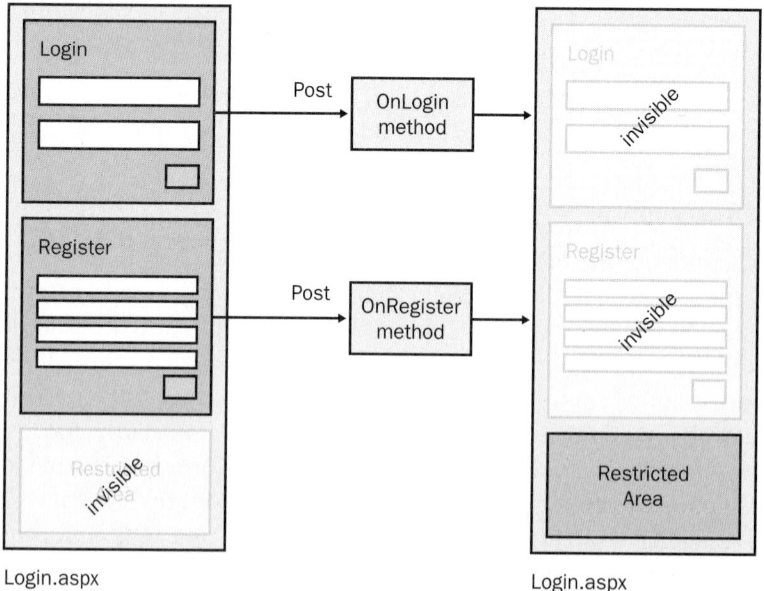


**Figure 4-2** One physical *<form>* tag contains multiple logical forms. All logical forms post to the same page and hide any unneeded user interface element.

A unique page is involved and contains a single *<form>* tag. Within the opening and closing tags of the form, two or more groups of logically related controls find their place. Each group can post back using either a classic submit button or a hyperlink bound to some script code—the entity that ASP.NET renders as a link button. Although the various groups are not forms in the technical sense of the word, they do behave like forms. All groups post to the same page, but the ASP.NET infrastructure guarantees both state maintenance and the execution of a piece of code specific to the group that caused the post. Each link button is associated with a server-side method that runs when the page posts back as the result of a click. Functionally speaking, the mechanism is in no way different than the ASP implementation. Furthermore, the programming model enjoys a higher abstraction layer and handy features such as view state and server-side control programming.

### Toggling the Control's Visibility

How can you update the user interface of the HTML being generated? You should know the answer immediately if you're somewhat familiar with Dynamic HTML (DHTML) and client-side programming. Otherwise, just read on.

ASP.NET server controls can programmatically be hidden from and restored to view. Controls with the *Visible* property set to *false* are ignored by the ASP.NET parser, and no HTML code will ever be generated for them. It turns out that this feature is key to dynamically creating the user interface of a page, piece by piece. So with reference to Figure 4-2, you design your login page to contain three blocks of HTML code: the login form, registration form, and restricted area. The first time you show the page—that is, when *IsPostBack* is set to *false*—the former two blocks are displayed while the restricted area remains invisible. Next, the user clicks to either log in or register. The page posts back to execute ad hoc code. Once you have registered the new user or checked the credentials of a known user, you simply toggle off the visibility of the forms and toggle on that of the restricted area. Et voilà!

> **Note** Playing with the visibility of controls is a key technique in Dynamic HTML and is the underpinning to many animation effects you see on Web sites when you navigate with Internet Explorer. Typically, cascading menus and collapsible views are obtained by putting a hidden *<div>* tag below the clickable text. When you click on the text, some script code simply toggles the display attribute of the *<div>* tag and the browser does the rest, refreshing the page.

### Multiple *<form>* Tags on a Page

For completeness, let's see how to create an ASP.NET page that really contains multiple *<form>* tags. Of course, only one of these tags can have the *runat* attribute set to *server*, and only for the controls contained therein can ASP.NET provide view state management and postback events. Let's consider the following ASP.NET page:

```
<html>
<body>
    <form runat="server">
        <asp:textbox runat="server" id="theTextBox" />
        <asp:button runat="server" text="Post back" />
    </form>

    <form method="post" action="another.aspx">
        <input type="text" name="SecondField " />
        <input type="submit" id="submit1" value="another.aspx" />
    </form>

    <form method="post" action="multiforms.aspx">
        <input type="text" name="ThirdField" />
        <input type="submit" id="submit2" value="This page" />
    </form>
</body>
</html>
```

As you can see, the second and third *<form>* tags are not marked *runat*, meaning that ASP.NET will treat them as plain text to output verbatim. When you click on the *submit1* button, the browser navigates to another.aspx—a different ASP.NET page that knows nothing about the main page's controls. You can still retrieve values from the referrer page by using the old ASP programming style.

```
<% @Page Language="C#" %>
<script runat="server">
void Page_Load(object sender, EventArgs e)
{
    Response.Write(Request.Form["SecondField"]);
}
</script>
```

Note also that when you use the ASP.NET form to post back, the content of the other text boxes is cleared. The same thing happens when you submit form data using the third button—the submit button of an HTML form that posts to the same page. Why doesn't ASP.NET work as usual? It's simple: there's no view-state information for the controls in the third form. That's the importance of working the ASP.NET way.

> **Important** You can have multiple server-side forms in your ASP.NET page as long as only one at a time is visible. For example, a page with, say, three *<form>* tags marked to run at the server is allowed, but only one of them can be actually rendered. Given the dynamics of page rendering, an exception is thrown if more than one *HtmlForm* control attempts to render. By playing with the *Visible* property of the form controls, you can change the active server form during the page lifetime. This approach mimics that of ASP.NET mobile controls. (See Chapter 11.) This trick doesn't really solve the problem of having multiple active forms, but it can be helpful sometimes.

## Passing Variables Across Pages

All in all, the HTML form mechanism is a way to invoke an external page to accomplish some specific tasks. When the form is posted, the browser packs the contents of the form fields in the body of the request. On the server, the target page retrieves those values and processes the request. In other words, you use the HTML *<form>* element when you need to execute some code on the server passing parameters.

Accomplishing this task with ASP.NET is straightforward if you use postback events and the SFI programming model. In this case, you implicitly assume that all the server-side code resides within the same reentrant page. Let's consider, though, the more general case in which you just want to spawn any external page and make sure it can get some parameters from the caller. Figure 4-3 explains a possible ASP.NET architecture to transfer the control from the caller page to external pages passing some context information. This multiple-form model is implemented within the default SFI model.

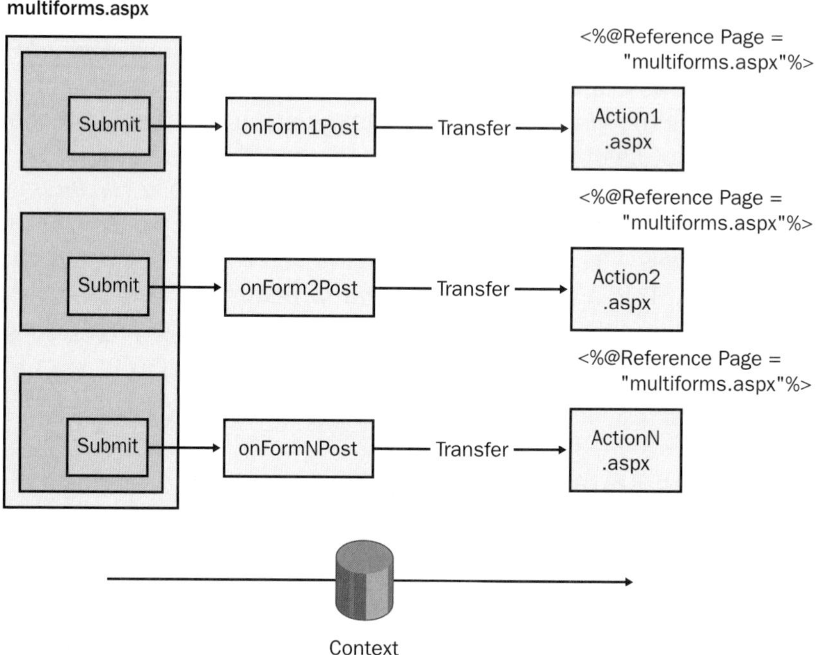


**Figure 4-3** Passing values between Web Forms pages.

The base page contains multiple logical forms—that is, not real *<form>* tags but groups of input fields with each one having a submit button. Each group posts back to the same page, but then in the server-side event handler the page transfers the execution to another page—the actual action page. Should the action page access the context of the referrer by using the *Session* or *Application* objects?

## Referencing Referrer Pages

In this model, the action page is activated through the *Server.Transfer* method. As will be discussed in Chapter 13, a page spawned through *Transfer* is processed in the same AppDomain and by the same *HttpApplication* object that was processing the referrer. The spawned page also inherits the original context of the request—the *HttpContext* object created upon startup.

In Chapter 13, we will learn that the *HttpContext* object has a property named *Handler* that returns the *IHttpHandler* object that is managing the request. When *Transfer* executes, the context of the original request is preserved and made available to the newly running page. Within the context, the *Handler* property in particular is not replaced and continues pointing to the handler that first received the HTTP request from the client. The spawned page can access the page object representing its referrer by using the *Handler* property as follows:

```
Page referrerPage = (Page) Context.Handler;
```

Because *Handler* returns a valid instance of the page object, the spawned page can access all its properties and methods. It cannot directly access the controls because of the protection level. In fact, if you look back at the source code for compiled pages in Chapter 2, you'll see that all page controls are mapped as protected members on the *ASP.Xxx_aspx* class. However, you could define ad hoc public properties on the caller page and expose to spawned pages all the data you want. For example, the following code exposes the content of the *RegUserName* text box through the *RegistrationUserName* public property:

```
<% @Page ClassName="MultiFormPage" %>
<script language="C#" runat="server">
public string RegistrationUserName
{
    get {return RegUserName.Text;}
}
⋮
</script>
```

Notice the *ClassName* attribute in the *@Page* directive. It lets you assign a user-defined alias to the page class. In practice, any spawned pages can access the referrer page as an instance of the class *MultiFormPage* rather than as an instance of the *ASP.Xxx_aspx* class.

## Retrieving Values

As mentioned, the spawned page can access the instance of the parent page using the *Handler* property. However, this fact alone is not sufficient to enable access to additional properties. The value returned by *Handler* must be cast to the actual page type—*ASP.Xxx_aspx* or whatever the *ClassName* attribute specifies. But how can the page add a reference to the type? That's just what the *@Reference* directive is all about. Figure 4-4 shows a page with a couple of logical forms—each of which transfers execution to a different page.

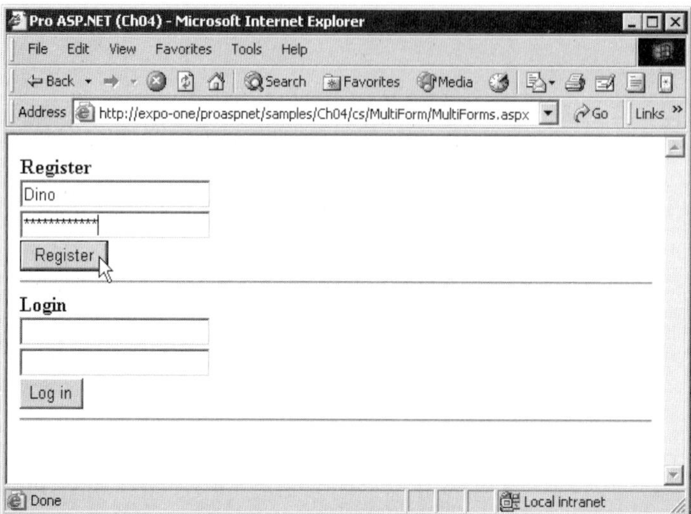


**Figure 4-4** An ASP.NET page that contains multiple groups of logically related controls acting as independent forms.

When the user clicks the Register button, the page posts back and transfers to register.aspx. This page, in turn, retrieves the handler of the original request and casts it to an instance of the *MultiFormPage* class. After that, the register.aspx page can use any of the ad hoc properties defined by the caller page to expose its public data.

```
<!-- multiforms.aspx -->
<% @Page ClassName="MultiFormPage" %>

<script language="C#" runat="server">
    public string RegistrationUserName {
        get {return RegUserName.Text;}
    }
    public string RegistrationPassword {
        get {return RegPassword.Text;}
    }
    public string UserName {
        get {return LogUserName.Text;}
    }
    public string Password {
        get {return LogPassword.Text;}
    }
    void OnRegister(object sender, EventArgs e) {
        Server.Transfer("register.aspx");
    }
    void OnLogIn(object sender, EventArgs e) {
        Server.Transfer("login.aspx");
    }
</script>
```

```
<html>
<body>
<form runat="server">
    <b>Register</b><br>
    <asp:textbox runat="server" id="RegUserName" /><br>
    <asp:textbox runat="server" id="RegPassword" textmode="password" /><br>
    <asp:button runat="server" text="Register" onclick="OnRegister" />
    <hr>

    <b>Login</b><br>
    <asp:textbox runat="server" id="LogUserName" /><br>
    <asp:textbox runat="server" id="LogPassword" textmode="password" /><br>
    <asp:button runat="server" text="Log in" onclick="OnLogIn" />
    <hr>
</form>
</body>
</html>
```

The structure of register.aspx and login.aspx is nearly identical, although the two pages will do quite different things. Both pages access input data from the referrer using the *@Reference* directive and the *Context.Handler* property.

```
<% @Page Language="C#" %>
<% @Reference Page="MultiForms.aspx" %>

<script runat="server">
MultiFormPage refPage;
void Page_Load(object sender, EventArgs e) {
    refPage = (MultiFormPage) Context.Handler;
}
</script>

<html>
<body>
User <b><%= refPage.RegistrationUserName %></b> has been registered.
Password is <b><%= refPage.RegistrationPassword%></b>.
</body>
</html>
```

The model we discussed here has a couple of drawbacks that should be mentioned. First, it makes use of *Server.Transfer*, which is a server-to-server mechanism to transfer control. Although highly efficient in terms of performance, it does not notify the browser of the URL change. Second, the *Server.Transfer* method does not work across domains. In other words, you can't post to a page resident on another server. An alternative is using *Response.Redirect*, but in this case you must take care yourself of posting any relevant data to the target page. For more information and further references, see the "Resources" section at the end of the chapter.

> **Note** From this example, it should be clear that having multiple server forms is not really impossible. The *<form runat="server">* tag will remain unique, but one could create custom, *form*-like container controls and use them within the single server form. The new control will have an *Action* property and manage to handle the submit post-back event on any of its buttons. The onclick handler would simply transfer the control to the page specified in *Action*. To establish uniformity in the way in which spawned pages retrieve input parameters, you could force the host page to implement a particular interface or take greater advantage of hidden fields. We'll return to this in Chapter 18 when discussing custom Web controls.

> **Caution** Note that the approach previously described to pass values to other pages requires the callee to know about the type and the programming interface of the caller. When assuming this is not safe, you might want to consider an alternative scheme for passing values. You can copy relevant information to the *Context.Items* collection and use *Server.Transfer* to pass the control. Because the context for the request is the same, caller and callee share the same HTTP context. In this way, the callee reads input data from a common cargo collection rather than referencing a particular page class. In terms of programming, using the *Context.Items* collection is nearly identical to using *Request.Form* or *Request.QueryString*.

## Pop-Up Forms

The HTML 4.0 object model allows you to use the *window.showModalDialog* method to show a modal window with a Web page inside. In some situations, this is a very viable approach for retrieving information from the user. ASP.NET pages can be used with pop-up windows. If the page has read-only contents, no particular care should be taken—just open the window with some client-side script code and let it go. On the other hand, if the page shown through a modal window is interactive and posts back, some measures should be taken to ensure that all the output goes through the modal dialog until the user closes it.

To show logically modal forms without using client-side modal dialogs, you could resort to the trick we discussed earlier and build multiple forms with 100 percent ASP.NET code. (See Figure 4-2.) Let's drill down a bit into creating modal windows.

## Client Modal Dialogs

To perform a modal operation—that is, a blocking operation that prevents interaction with the main page until terminated—a Web page can resort to the following JavaScript code:

```
<script language="Javascript">
function ShowPopup() {
    window.showModalDialog("dialog.aspx", "Dialog",
        "dialogWidth:200px;dialogHeight:300px;");
}
</script>

<html>
<head><title>Pro ASP.NET (Ch04)</title></head>
<body>
    <input type="button" onclick="ShowPopup()" value="Popup" />
</body>
</html>
```

The *showModalDialog* method on the *window* object opens the specified page in a Windows dialog box with the given title and styles. (For more information about the styling options of the dialog, see the MSDN documentation.) The preceding code pops up a 200-by-300-pixel modal window filled with the HTML content generated by dialog.aspx. So far so good.

Suppose now that the dialog.aspx page contains some links and buttons you can click. Again, think of a modal page you want to pop up for users' registration and logging. The user enters some data and then clicks; the page posts back, but the new output is displayed in a new browser window. Any value you can assign to the form's *target* value seems to be ineffective. The behavior is by design, but is there a workaround? Yes, for the browsers that support it, you can use a wrapper inline frame. (The *<iframe>* tag is part of the HTML 4.0 specification.)

Instead of containing the code to display the window contents, dialog.aspx contains a properly sized *<iframe>* tag.

```
<iframe src="Pages/multiforms.aspx" name="embeddedFrame"
width="100%" height="100%" />
```

At this point, the target attribute set on the multiforms.aspx page is detected and properly handled, as shown in Figure 4-5.

```
<form runat="server" target="embeddedFrame">
    ⋮
</form>
```

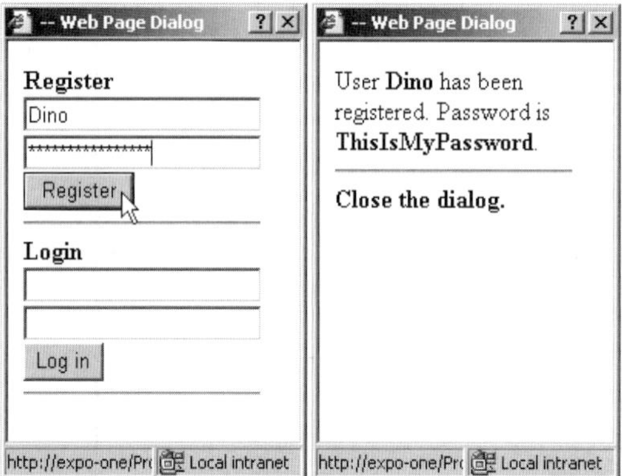


**Figure 4-5** Navigable modal dialogs based on ASP.NET pages.

## Using Embedded Forms

As mentioned earlier, by toggling on and off the visibility of blocks of related controls you can implement sort of pop-up forms as well. In the page, you define a logical form—that is, a block of controls acting as a real form—and hide and show it as needed. Basically, such a logical form would work with the rest of the page in a mutually exclusive way. The following code snippet shows a form with two logical subforms: one with a button and one with the typical login fields. Both are wrapped by a server-side *<div>* panel.

```
<form runat="server">
    <div runat="server" id="RunDlg">
        <asp:button runat="server" text="Login" onclick="OnShowLogin" />
    </div>

    <div runat="server" id="Login" visible="false">
        <hr>
        <b>Login</b><br>
        <asp:textbox runat="server" id="UserName" /><br>
        <asp:textbox runat="server" id="Pswd" textmode="password" /><br>
        <asp:button runat="server" text="Log in" onclick="OnLogIn" />
        <hr>
    </div>
</form>
```

When the button is clicked, the *RunDlg* block is hidden and *Login* is displayed. Note that when the *Visible* attribute is set to *false*, no code will be generated for any control.

```
<script runat="server">
void OnShowLogin(object sender, EventArgs e) {
    RunDlg.Visible = false;
    login.Visible = true;
}
```

```
void OnLogIn(object sender, EventArgs e) {
    RunDlg.Visible = true;
    login.Visible = false;
}
</script>
```

Using this approach, the form expected to work as a modal dialog is the only piece of the page's UI being displayed at a time. Note that for a better implementation of the solution, you can take advantage of user controls to wrap the contents of a server-side *<div>* block. We'll cover user controls in Chapter 10.

## Working with Script Code

When you have input forms that need to be displayed only in certain situations (for example, when the user is not registered), a commonly used approach entails that you keep hidden the optional form and show the user a link to click. (See Figure 4-6.)

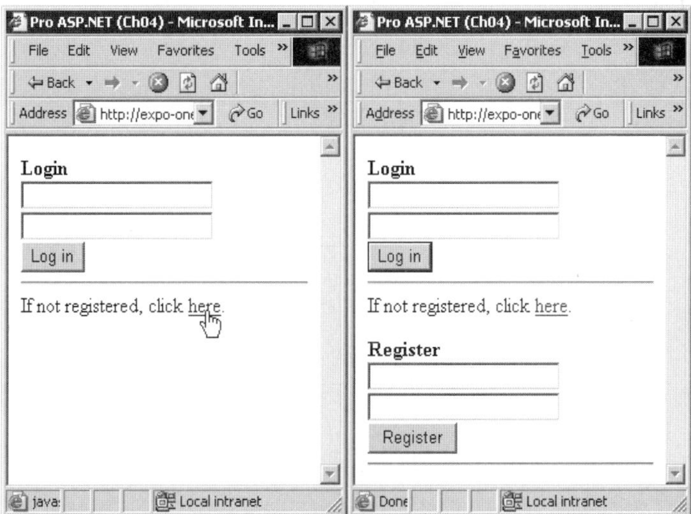


**Figure 4-6** The optional dialog shows up only if the user explicitly requests it.

The overall user interface of the page is cleaner, and only information that's strictly needed is displayed. The downside of this approach is that you need an extra roundtrip to display the optional input form. In some cases, typically when an up-level browser is used, resorting to some client-side script code can be as much as twice effective, giving you a clean user interface and avoiding the extra roundtrip.

## Supporting Multiple Browsers

Browser information is packed in the *HttpBrowserCapabilities* object returned by the *Request.Browser* property. Table 4-3 lists all the available properties.

**Table 4-3 Browser Capabilities**

| Property | Description |
|---|---|
| *ActiveXControls* | Gets whether the browser supports ActiveX controls. |
| *AOL* | Gets whether the client is an America Online browser. |
| *BackgroundSounds* | Gets whether the browser supports background sounds. |
| *Beta* | Gets whether the browser is a beta release. |
| *Browser* | Gets the user agent string transmitted in the HTTP User-Agent header. |
| *CDF* | Gets whether the browser supports Channel Definition Format (CDF) for webcasting. |
| *ClrVersion* | Gets the *Version* object containing version information for the .NET common language runtime installed on the client. |
| *Cookies* | Gets whether the browser supports cookies. |
| *Crawler* | Gets whether the browser is a Web crawler search engine. |
| *EcmaScriptVersion* | Gets the version number of ECMA script supported by the browser. |
| *Frames* | Gets whether the browser supports HTML frames. |
| *Item* | Indexer property, gets the value of the specified browser capability. |
| *JavaApplets* | Gets whether the client browser supports Java applets. |
| *JavaScript* | Gets whether the browser supports JavaScript. |
| *MajorVersion* | Gets the integer number denoting the major version number of the browser. |
| *MinorVersion* | Gets the decimal number denoting the minor version number of the browser. |
| *MSDomVersion* | Gets the version of the Microsoft HTML (MSHTML) document object model that the browser supports. |
| *Platform* | Gets the name of the platform that the client uses. |
| *Tables* | Gets whether the client browser supports HTML tables. |
| *Type* | Gets a string made of the name and the major version number of the browser (for example, Internet Explorer 6 or Netscape 7). |
| *VBScript* | Gets whether the browser supports VBScript. |
| *Version* | Gets a string representing the full (integer and decimal) version number of the browser. |

**Table 4-3 Browser Capabilities**

| Property | Description |
|---|---|
| *W3CDomVersion* | Gets the version of the W3C XML Document Object Model (DOM) supported by the browser. |
| *Win16* | Gets whether the client is a Win16-based computer. |
| *Win32* | Gets whether the client is a Win32-based computer. |

As a margin note, consider that if you're writing a mobile application, you must cast the *Request.Browser* return value to the *MobileCapabilities* object and work with that. The mobile capabilities object is supported only by version 1.1 of the .NET Framework. However, a separate download is available to enable mobile controls support for version 1.0 of the .NET Framework.

The *Browser* property returns the full string contained in the User-Agent header, and using it is probably the most flexible way to make sure the browser has just the characteristics you need to check. However, *Type* is another useful property for verifying the identity of the client browser. The following code shows how to make sure that the browser is Internet Explorer version 4.0 or newer:

```
bool upLevelBrowser = false;
HttpBrowserCapabilities caps = Request.Browser;
if (caps.Browser.ToUpper().IndexOf("IE") > -1) {
    // This is IE. Is version >3?
    upLevelBrowser = (caps.MajorVersion >3);
}
```

By putting this code in the *Page_Load* event, you enable yourself to modify the structure of the page according to the capabilities of the browser.

**Note** The *ClrVersion* property does not include build information, which means you can't track which service pack is installed on the client, if any. For the local machine, you can get full version information about the installed CLR using the following code:

```
Version v = Environment.Version;
Console.WriteLine("{0},{1},{2},{3}", v.Major, v.Minor,
v.Build, v.Revision);
```

If the *Revision* property is *0*, no service pack is installed. If the revision number is *209*, service pack 1 is installed. The revision number for service pack 2 is *288*.

Now that we know a way to distinguish between browsers, let's use this technique to make up-level browsers show optional input forms via script. In the context of this example, an up-level browser is Internet Explorer 4.0 or a newer version.

## Adding Client-Side Scripts

The idea is to obtain the effect shown in Figure 4-6 using client-side DHTML script code on up-level browsers and the classic postback event elsewhere. When the user clicks the hyperlink, what happens depends on the type of the browser. Although clear in the overall design, the solution is trickier to implement than one might think at first. The hidden difficulty revolves around the type of object the user really clicks on. Whatever the browser, the user always clicks a hyperlink with some client script code attached. Because we're talking about ASP.NET pages, any script code is associated with the hyperlink on the server. And this is exactly the issue.

If the browser is up-level, you need to render the clickable hyperlink by using a client-side HTML element—that is, an element without the *runat="server"* attribute.

```
Click <a href="javascript:YourFunc()">here</a>
```

If the browser is down-level, you need to use the ASP.NET *LinkButton* control as shown in the following code:

```
Click <asp:linkbutton runat="server" text="here" onclick="Clicked" />
```

How should you design the page layout to meet this requirement? Let's review a few possibilities, starting with ASP-style code blocks:

```
If not registered, click
<% if (upLevelBrowser) {%>
<a href="javascript:ShowRegisterDlg">here</a>.
<% } else {%>
<asp:linkbutton runat="server" text="here" onclick="ShowRegisterDlg" />.
<% } %>
<hr>
```

Although effective, the solution shown generates messy and rather unreadable code when used on a large scale. It also requires you to declare the *upLevelBrowser* variable as global. Finally, ASP-style code-blocks are deprecated, although ASP.NET fully supports them.

A second possibility entails the use of ASP.NET custom controls smart enough to detect the browser and produce appropriate HTML output. The key advantage of this approach is that you use a single tag and bury all necessary logic in the folds of its implementation. However, because we'll not cover custom controls until Chapter 18, we'll go for a third alternative that falls somewhere in the middle of the previous two.

You use a placeholder control to mark the place in which the hyperlink should appear in one form or the other. Next, in the *Page_Load* event handler, you populate the *Controls* collection of the *PlaceHolder* control with either plain text or a dynamically created instance of the *LinkButton* control. You use plain text—more exactly, a *LiteralControl* instance—if the client is up-level and client script code can be used. You use the *LinkButton* otherwise. The following code snippet shows the page layout:

```
<b>Login</b><br>
<asp:textbox runat="server" id="LogUserName" /><br>
<asp:textbox runat="server" id="LogPassword" textmode="password" /><br>
<asp:button runat="server" text="Log in" onclick="OnLogIn" />
<hr>
If not registered, click <asp:placeholder runat="server" id="theLink" />.
<hr>
```

In the *Page_Load* event handler, you first learn about the browser's capabilities and then configure the placeholder to host an HTML hyperlink or a server-side link button.

```
void Page_Load()
{
    // Check browser capabilities
    bool upLevelBrowser = false;
    HttpBrowserCapabilities caps = Request.Browser;
    if (caps.Browser.ToUpper().IndexOf("IE") > -1) {
        // This is IE. Is version >3?
        upLevelBrowser = (caps.MajorVersion >3);
    }

    // if downlevel (considering only IE4+ uplevel)
    if (upLevelBrowser) {
        AddDhtmlScriptCode(theLink);
        RegPanel.Visible = true;
        RegPanel.Style["display"] = "none";
    }
    else
        AddPostBackCode(theLink);
}
```

If the browser is up-level, the registration panel should be included as HTML but not displayed to the user. For this reason, you must set the *Visible* property to *true*—ensuring that the HTML code for the panel will be generated—and, at the same time, you need to hide the controls from view by resorting to CSS-style properties.

If the browser proves to be down-level—whatever this means to your application—you simply create and configure the link button control to receive the user's clicking and post back.

```
void AddDhtmlScriptCode(PlaceHolder ctl)
{
    // Name of the Javascript function
    string scriptFuncName = "ShowRegisterDlg";

    // Token used to register the Javascript procedure
    // with the instance of the Page object
    string scriptName = "__ShowRegisterDlg";

    // Create the hyperlink HTML code and add it to the placeholder
    string html = "<a href='javascript:{0}()'>{1}</a>";
    html = String.Format(html, scriptFuncName, "here");
    LiteralControl lit = new LiteralControl(html);
    ctl.Controls.Add(lit);

    // Create the Javascript function (must include <script>)
    StringBuilder sb = new StringBuilder("<script language=Javascript>\n");
    sb.Append("function ");
    sb.Append(scriptFuncName);
    sb.Append("() {\n");
    sb.Append("RegPanel.style['display'] = '';");
    sb.Append("\n}\n<");
    sb.Append("/");
    sb.Append("script>");

    // Register the Javascript function with the page so that it can be
    // flushed when the page is rendered
    if (!IsClientScriptBlockRegistered(scriptName))
            this.RegisterClientScriptBlock(scriptName, sb.ToString());
}

void AddPostBackCode(PlaceHolder ctl)
{
    LinkButton link = new LinkButton();
    link.ID = "showRegPanel";
    link.Text = "here";
    link.Click += new EventHandler(this.ShowRegisterDlg);
    ctl.Controls.Add(link);
}
```

There's no need for you to explicitly set the script for postback; adding a server-side control to the page fits the bill. The page will then call back the control to make it render its user interface as HTML.

In Figure 4-7, you can see how the sample page looks in Internet Explorer 6.0 and Netscape 4.7. To see the difference, look at the status bar of the browser windows when the mouse hovers over the hyperlink. Internet Explorer points to a local JavaScript procedure whereas Netscape points to the typical *__doPostBack* JavaScript function that implements the postback in ASP.NET.

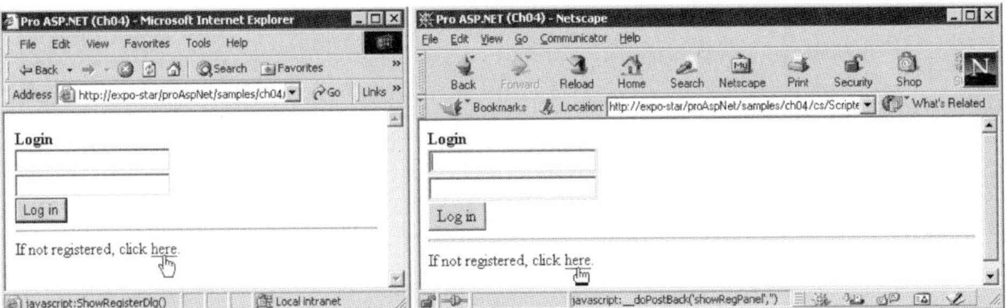

**Figure 4-7** Internet Explorer 6.0 displays the input form using client script code, while Netscape 4.7 resorts to an event postback.

## Registering Script Blocks

As discussed in Chapter 2, the *Page* object provides a couple of methods to inject client-side scripts in the body of the HTML page being generated. The methods are *RegisterClientScriptBlock* and *RegisterStartupScript*.

```
RegisterClientScriptBlock(scriptName, code);
RegisterStartupScript(scriptName, code);
```

Calling either method does not physically insert the JavaScript or the VBScript script code in the page's source code. The code injection takes place only as the final step in the ASP.NET page building process. So what happens to the scripts once either method is called? Look at the signature of both methods.

The latter argument is the string that contains the script code. The former, on the other hand, just names the script. The script code can be registered for output at any time in the page lifetime. Calling either registering method temporarily parks the script code into dedicated and case-sensitive name/value collections. The *scriptName* argument is used as the key to identify and track the script in the collection. The *code* argument, on the other hand, is just the content of the script stored as the value in the collection. Note that each registering method runs its own collection, so script names must be unique only within the scope of the method.

The content of script collections is flushed into the page output when the HTML code for the page is actually created, namely after the *PreRender* event. Each piece of script code must be wrapped by opening and closing *<script>* tags. However, more script functions can be declared in the same *<script>* block, but they will only count for a single entry in the collection.

The script collections are private fields of the *Page* class and are not programmatically accessible. You cannot walk your way through the collections, but you can check whether a script with a given name already exists. Each registering method also features a query counterpart that returns a Boolean value.

Checking the existence of a given named script is critical because duplicates are not allowed and any further attempt to add a script with an existing name will just be ignored. To check the script before registering, use the following code:

```
if (!IsClientScriptBlockRegistered(scriptName))
    RegisterClientScriptBlock(scriptName, code);
if (!IsStartupScriptRegistered(startupScriptName))
    RegisterStartupScript(startupScriptName, startupCode);
```

> **Tip** For your comfort, you might decide to keep the function declaration and the actual function call in different script blocks. You can use *RegisterClientScriptBlock* to declare the function and *RegisterStartupScript* to register the call. This approach perhaps results in more elegant code, but it requires the *Page* object to handle two nonempty collections instead of just one. This isn't really a big concern, but when you have to squeeze out every little bit of performance even that could help. Script collections are initialized only when the first item gets added.

It's also interesting to note that the actual collections classes used are of a special type—*HybridDictionary*. The class implements the methods of the *IDictionary* interface in a very flexible way. It utilizes a *ListDictionary* object as long as the number of items in the collection is relatively small (less than 10). When the size of the dictionary grows beyond the threshold, the class automatically switches to a *Hashtable* object, which manages large collections more efficiently.

## Registering Startup Script Blocks

Where is a script block injected exactly? That mostly depends on which method you use to register the script with the page. If you use *RegisterClientScriptBlock*, the script block is placed right after the opening *<form>* tag. When the script executes, the content of the form has not been initialized. So if the script attempts to access any of the elements in the form, an exception is raised.

In contrast, *RegisterStartupScript* places its script code just before the closing *</form>* tag. In this way, the code runs after the form has been initialized and provides safe access to all constituent controls. In this sense, it is a startup script.

### Registering Hidden Fields

As mentioned, hidden fields shouldn't be used to make context-specific information survive across different requests of the same page. ASP.NET provides more powerful and flexible tools to accomplish that and there's no need for you to resort to hidden fields.

Hidden fields, though, are still a viable tool to pass information to HTML elements defined on the client. You can either define them statically in the page layout or have the ASP.NET runtime create them at render time, in much the same way as the runtime does with script blocks. The method to use is *RegisterHiddenField*.

```
RegisterHiddenField("BookTitle", "Programming ASP.NET");
```

The method takes a couple of arguments: the name of the field and its content. When the method executes, ASP.NET tracks whether an extra hidden field should be created at render time. The previous line of code generates the following HTML code:

```
<input type="hidden" name="BookTitle" value="Programming ASP.NET" />
```

## Page Localization

In the real world, several companies have different Web sites, one per each country in which they have subsidiaries or operate. In many cases, the localized Web site is only a branch of the main Web site located in a subdirectory; more often than not, the Web site is also accessible using the same domain but a local extension. For example, let's say that the Contoso, Ltd is on the Web at *http://www.contoso.com*. Its Italian subsidiary, if any, is normally reachable either at *http://www.contoso.com/italy* or, through a more direct local domain, at *http://www.contoso.it*. In all cases, the localization is achieved by replicating, translating, and adapting existing pages. Is this what ASP.NET page localization is all about? Not exactly.

Actually, ASP.NET page localization and, more generally, the .NET world-ready initiative is aimed at a different result: enabling the *same* application to morph user-interface (UI) and locale-sensitive resources into localized versions. Page localization simply provides a deeply automated mechanism to translate and localize a group of UI-related resources. In no way does page localization provide for overriding and customizing functions. In summary, if your subsidiaries need to create their own Web sites with localized content and structure, page localization is not the right tool. On the other hand, if you're just looking for an effective way to publish some locale-sensitive data in a way that reflects the current culture and sentiment, ASP.NET page localization is just right.

## Culture and Locales

Localization—that is the application's ability to load resources specific to a culture—is only the final step of a more systemic process. To start out, you should be predisposing the application to use a localized user interface and strive to have it grow up independent from cultures and regional settings. In doing so, as the second step of the design process, you should ensure that all localizable resources are clearly isolated from the rest of the code. The idea is that locale-specific resources can be plugged in dynamically without affecting the overall functionality. The page localization finalizes the work and, by dynamically reading resources data, gives international users an interface they feel comfortable with.

### Programming Cultures

In the .NET Framework, a culture is a logical container of information about a specific country culture. Typical culture information includes the writing system, the calendar used, formatting dates, currency, and sorting strings. Technically speaking, a culture is represented by the *CultureInfo* class. The .NET Framework provides a list of predefined cultures in the *System.Globalization* namespace. Cultures are given a name and an identifier and are classified by language and country. To enumerate all the available cultures, you can use the following code:

```
CultureInfo [] cults;
cults = CultureInfo.GetCultures(CultureTypes.AllCultures);
foreach (CultureInfo ci in cults) {
    Console.WriteLine(ci);
}
```

The *CultureInfo* class exposes its information through ad hoc classes such as *DateTimeFormatInfo*, *NumberFormatInfo*, *CompareInfo*, and *TextInfo*. Other .NET Framework classes use *CultureInfo* to accomplish locale-specific operations. For example, the *String* class and the *DataTable* classes use culture information to compare text and column values.

The culture names follow an international standard ratified in RFC 1766. A name is a dash-separated string made of two tokens: the language code and the region code. The language code is a lowercase two-letter code derived from ISO 639-1. The region code is an uppercase two-letter code derived from ISO 3166. A typical culture name is *en-US*, meaning that English is the language and US is the country. The same language can be accompanied with different regions or countries—for example, *en-GB* (United Kingdom) and *en-ZA* (South Africa). Likewise, the same country can have multiple languages—for example, *it-CH* and *fr-CH* identify the culture for Swiss people speaking Italian and French, respectively.

### Invariant and Neutral Cultures

Along with specific cultures in which both the language and region information is known, the .NET Framework supports two other types of cultures. They are the invariant culture and neutral cultures. The invariant culture is represented by the *InvariantCulture* class and has the empty string as the name. This type of culture should be used by applications that have no locale-sensitive data to display or process. The invariant culture is associated with the English language but not with a particular country or region.

On the other hand, a neutral culture is a culture that is associated with a language but not with a country. Note that some classes don't accept neutral culture information. For example, in Chapter 1 we pointed out that the *Culture* attribute on the *@Page* directive must be set to a fully qualified culture name and neutral names are not accepted.

> **Note** A code page is a list of selected character codes ordered in a certain way. Code pages exist to support languages that share common writing systems. By convention, in most code pages the codes 0 through 127 represent the same characters, thus allowing for continuity. Normally, the characters corresponding to codes 128 through 255 differ significantly between code pages. In the .NET Framework, the widespread use of Unicode simplifies the development of globalized applications, eliminating the need to reference a code page. However, code pages are supported through the *Encoding* class.
>
> ```
> Encoding enc = Encoding.GetEncoding(1252);
> ```
>
> The preceding code shows how to get the specified code page. After that, you can use the newly created object wherever encoding information is accepted.

## The ASP.NET Resource Manager

Just like other applications, an ASP.NET application can, and often should, use resources. Resources are an effective way to isolate localizable portions of the application's user interface. In general, a resource is a nonexecutable text associated with the program. Typical resources are images, icons, and internal-use files, but any serializable object can be considered a resource. Application resources are stored outside the application so that they can be recompiled and replaced without affecting and recompiling the application itself.

An ASP.NET application needs to have a primary assembly to contain the default or neutral resources for the application. In addition, you create a number of satellite assemblies each containing localized resources for a particular culture you want to support. The primary resource assembly is installed into the application's Bin directory; the satellite assemblies go in their respective locale-specific subdirectory, as shown in Figure 4-8.

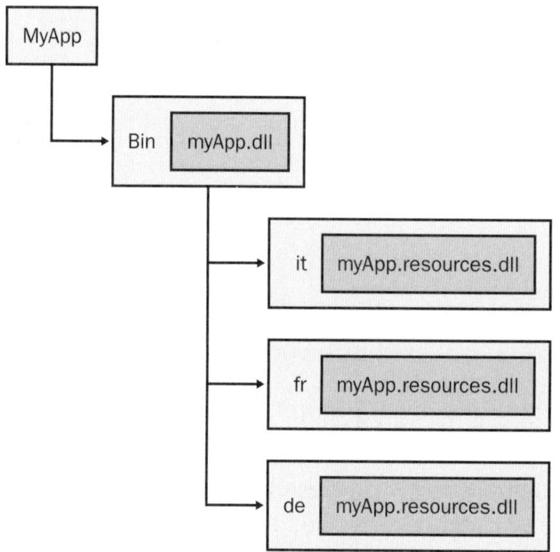


**Figure 4-8** Satellite resource assemblies for an ASP.NET application.

## Creating Satellite Assemblies

The resource file can take various forms, including that of a simple text file or the XML file created by Microsoft Visual Studio and saved with the *.resx* extension. However, only .resources files can be embedded in a .NET executable or compiled into satellite assemblies. You use the Resource File Generator (*resgen.exe*) utility to convert text and XML-based resource files into .resources. The resource file names follow the naming convention *baseName.cultureName.resources*. Typically, the base name is the name of the application.

```
resgen.exe myapp.resx myapp.it.resources
```

Once created, the .resources file should be embedded into an assembly or can even be used as-is as a resource container. To embed the resource file into a satellite assembly, you use the Assembly Linker tool (*al.exe*). On the command line, you indicate the culture (*it* in the next example) and the name of the assembly.

```
al /out:myapp.resources.dll /c:it /embed:myapp.it.resources
```

After you have compiled your satellite assemblies, they all have the same name. The default resource file should be named after the base name and have the .resources extension. The culture-specific files are packaged in satellite assemblies, one for each culture. The default resource file is commonly embedded in your main assembly.

> **Note** You should avoid deploying ASP.NET applications using individual .resources files. While this can be acceptable for other types of applications, it can break XCOPY deployment in ASP.NET. The files, in fact, will be locked until the application shuts down, thus causing locking issues and invalidating the XCOPY deployment. To avoid that, deploy ASP.NET resources in satellite assemblies.

If you develop your application using Visual Studio .NET, resources are managed automatically and compiled within the assembly if the Build Action property in the Properties window is set to Embedded Resource.

### Retrieving Localized Information

The *ResourceManager* class provides access to culture resources at run time. You configure a new instance of the class to look up the resources stored in the satellite assemblies derived from the specified base name.

```
ResourceManager rm;
rm = new ResourceManager("myApp", this.GetType().Assembly);
```

The constructor also requires a second argument because it is the main assembly that contains the default resources. Each resource item is identified by a name, and that name is used to retrieve the value from the currently selected culture. The following code snippet shows how to retrieve the string named "welcome":

```
rm.GetString("welcome");
```

The value will be retrieved from the resource assembly that complies with the current UI culture. A fallback process is started to individuate the resource to use should the requested locale not be available.

The *CurrentUICulture* for the page, or for the current thread, determined what resource assembly the Resource Manager should check.

**Note** A best-practice for ASP.NET applications is setting the *CurrentUICulture* property in the code of the page to ensure that the culture used to process the page matches that of the requesting user. The following code shows how to set the *CurrentUICulture* property to the culture associated with the browser's current settings:

```
Culture c = new CultureInfo(Request.UserLanguages[0]);
Thread.CurrentThread.CurrentUICulture = c;
```

# Page Errors and Tracing

Just like other .NET applications, ASP.NET applications can take advantage of exceptions to catch and handle run-time errors that occur in the code. Exceptions, though, should be just what their name suggests—that is, exceptional events in the life of the application.

As a matter of fact, exceptions seriously affect the average performance of any application, and because ASP.NET applications are very critical and sensitive, you should handle exceptions with extreme care and limit their use as much as possible. A typical bad programming practice is to rely on exceptions to catch any possible error resulting from an operation. Admittedly, wrapping a piece of code with a *try/catch* block makes programming much simpler while offering a single point of control for errors. However, employing this technique on a large scale might result in a dramatic loss of performance. Exceptions are meant to target exceptional events that aren't predictable in other ways. Exceptions should not be used to control the normal flow of the program. If there is a way to detect possible inconsistent situations, by all means use that other method and keep exceptions as the last resort.

Note that a *try/catch* block in the code always causes extra code to be generated and executed. The impact on performance is minimal if the *try* branch executes. The performance hit is relevant if the *catch* block executes instead. For this reason, you should use exceptions only to handle exceptional events in your code.

> **Note** The *debug* attribute on the *@Page* directive forces the ASP.NET runtime to add debug information to the dynamically generated assembly for the page. That information is then used by Visual Studio .NET to debug the application. Outside the development and testing phase, though, debug information makes the assembly unnecessarily heavy and poorly responsive. Make sure you have no *debug=true* attribute left in .aspx when you actually deploy the site.

## Defining Custom Error Pages

Although the concept of an error is nearly identical in all types of applications and platforms, the way in which errors manifest themselves to the users varies quite a bit in terms of context and application. When an unrecoverable error occurs in an ASP.NET page, the user always receives a page that, more or less nicely, informs that something went wrong at a certain point. ASP.NET catches any unhandled exception wandering around the page and transforms it into a page for the user, as shown in Figure 4-9.

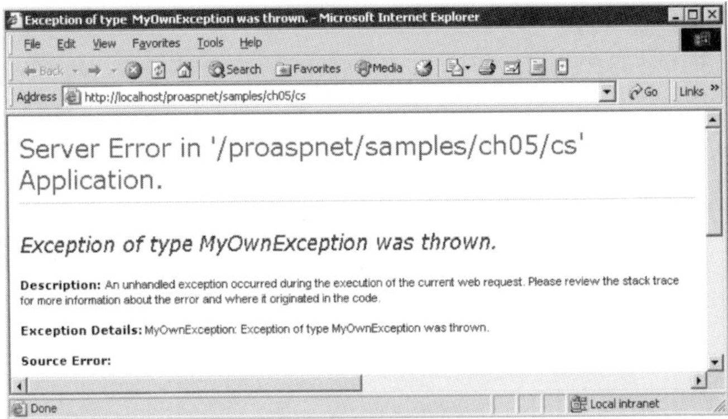


**Figure 4-9** The error page generated by an unhandled exception.

The way in which ASP.NET displays error pages is controlled by the *<customErrors>* section in the configuration file. As we'll see in greater detail in Chapter 12, the section can be defined in the web.config file located in the root folder as well as in a child directory. The following code presents an excerpt from the web.config file created by Visual Studio .NET:

```
<configuration>
  <system.web>
    ⋮
```

```
    <customErrors mode="RemoteOnly" />
  </system.web>
</configuration>
```

When the *mode* property is set to *RemoteOnly* and an error occurs, users receive a generic error page that informs them that something went wrong on the server. The page is not like that in Figure 4-9 in that it doesn't contain stack trace and error details, but I wouldn't say it's really comfortable and user-friendly, as Figure 4-10 demonstrates.

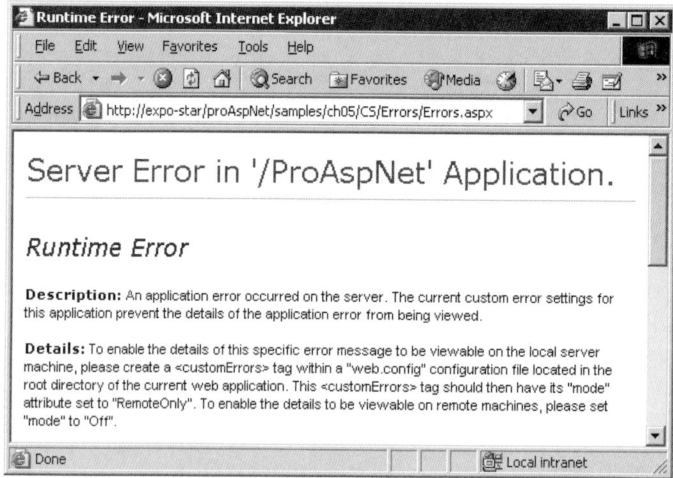


**Figure 4-10** A runtime error occurred on the server. The page does not provide information about the error, but it still can't be said to be a user-friendly page!

The error page of Figure 4-9 is reserved only for the user working on the Web server machine—probably, just the developer whose code caused the error.

## Using Custom Error Pages

The error-handling policy can be changed at will. In particular, ASP.NET can be instructed to always display custom pages to all users—local and remote. To obtain this, you change the *mode* attribute of the *<customErrors>* section to *On*. This is only half the task, though. All users now get a rather inexpressive and uninformative page. To display a more friendly and apologetic page (as shown in Figure 4-11), set web.config as follows:

```
<configuration>
  <system.web>
    <customErrors mode="On" defaultRedirect="GenericError.aspx" />
  </system.web>
</configuration>
```

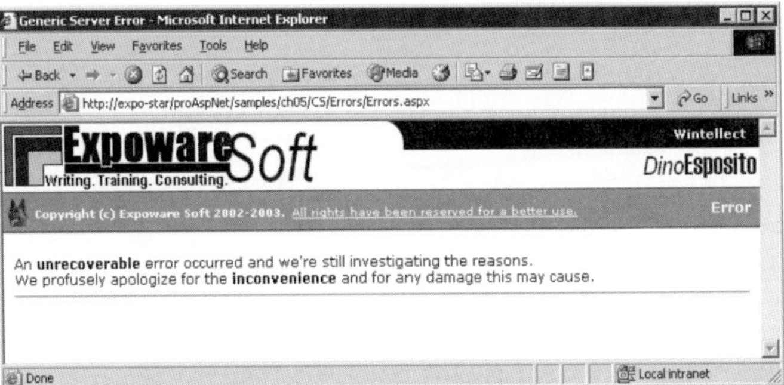


**Figure 4-11** A nice and friendly error page.

In most cases, the error page is made of plain HTML so that no error could recursively be raised. However, should the error page, in turn, originate another error, the default generic page of ASP.NET will be shown. (See Figure 4-10.)

Keeping the mode set to *On* is not a recommended practice. *RemoteOnly* is preferable because it contributes to the Web site security by not showing application details to remote clients. The following code snippet shows the ideal combination that all Web sites should implement: remote users receive a nice message, while the Web master gets detailed information from the ASP.NET runtime.

```
<configuration>
  <system.web>
    <customErrors mode="RemoteOnly"
      defaultRedirect="GenericError.aspx" />
  </system.web>
</configuration>
```

Setting the mode *Off* is useful and recommended only during the development phase when the application runs internally and can help developers to figure out errors and problems more quickly and even remotely. Do not use it in production environments.

> **Caution** If you have plans to change the value of the *mode* attribute in the *<customErrors>* section, pay attention to the fact that the attribute is case sensitive and accepts only the following values spelled as shown: *On*, *Off*, and *RemoteOnly*.

### HTTP Errors

In addition to the customization of application errors, ASP.NET enables you to customize pages to show when HTTP errors occurs. For example, the following web.config file provides a customized error page whenever the user types in the name of a nonexisting resource.

```
<configuration>
  <system.web>
    <customErrors mode="RemoteOnly" defaultRedirect="GenericError.aspx">
        <error statusCode="404" redirect="GenericError.aspx?errID=404" />
        <error statusCode="500" redirect="GenericError.aspx?errID=500" />
    </customErrors>
  </system.web>
</configuration>
```

The *<error>* element indicates the page to redirect the user to when the specified HTTP error occurs. The attribute *statusCode* denotes the HTTP error. Figure 4-12 shows what happens when the user mistypes the name of the URL and the error HTTP 404 (resource not found) is generated. Note that not all HTTP errors can be trapped in this way. Some HTTP errors are handled directly by IIS and never processed by ASP.NET.

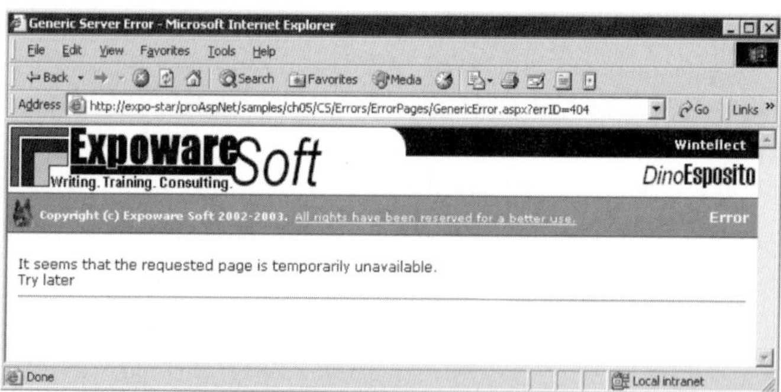


**Figure 4-12** A custom page for the popular HTTP 404 error.

## Tracing the Execution Flow in .NET

The .NET Framework comes with a rather feature-rich set of tools for debugging and tracing applications. In particular, the *Systems.Diagnostics* namespace defines two classes, named *Trace* and *Debug*, whose methods can be used to output messages commenting the execution of the code. This feature is extremely useful to track data inconsistencies, monitor the flow, assert conditions, and even to gather profiling information. The *Trace* and *Debug* classes are essentially identical and work on top of more specialized modules known as *listeners*.

The ASP.NET support for tracing is different and fairly disjointed. We'll first briefly overview the .NET Framework support for tracing and then move on to consider the peculiarity of ASP.NET.

## The Listener Object

The listener acts like a driver and collects and stores tracing messages into a particular medium such as the Windows event log, an application window, or a text file. Each application can have its own set of listeners, which will receive all emitted messages. The application configuration file has a *<trace>* section under *<system.diagnostics>* to add and remove listeners. The .NET Framework provides three predefined listeners:

- ***DefaultTraceListener*** The listener emits messages to the Win32 *OutputDebugString* API function and to the *Debugger.Log* method. When the application runs within Visual Studio .NET, any message shows in the Output window. The *DefaultTraceListener* class is the only listener automatically included in every listeners collection.
- ***TextWriterTraceListener*** The listener redirects output to a *Stream* object, including the console or a file. If the target is a file, the name can be indicated in the configuration file via the *initializeData* attribute. (We'll discuss this more in a moment.) Otherwise, the listener is configured and attached programmatically. In this case, you set the target storage medium using the *Writer* property.
- ***EventLogTraceListener*** The listener redirects all its output to the Windows event log. The class provides the *EventLog* property to get and set the name of the event log. The event log can also be set at configuration time using the *initializeData* attribute.

## Registering and Configuring Listeners

Listeners can be added to an application in two ways: programmatically through the *Listeners* collection of either the *Trace* or *Debug* class, and declaratively using the *<listeners>* subsection in the *<trace>* section of the configuration file. The following code snippet shows how to replace the default listener with the event log listener. In addition, the snippet sets the *autoflush* property to *true*, which means the listener is expected to flush the internal buffer after each write.

```
<system.diagnostics>
   <trace autoflush="true">
     <listeners>
        <add name="eventListener"
          type="EventLogTraceListener"
```

```
            initializeData="MyAppEventLog" />
          <remove type="DefaultTraceListener"/>
       </listeners>
    </trace>
</system.diagnostics>
```

Note that you can use a non–fully qualified name for the listener class as long as the calling application imports the *System.Diagnostics* namespace. To configure the event log tracer to work alone codewise, do as follows:

```
Trace.Listeners.Clear();
EventLogTraceListener evWriter;
evWriter = new EventLogTraceListener(MyAppEventLog);
Trace.Listeners.Add(evWriter);
```

As mentioned, *Debug* and *Trace* classes share the same collection of listeners. Neither of the two classes really owns the listener collection. The collection, instead, is maintained by an assemblywide internal class and accessed by both *Debug* and *Trace*. So if your application adds a listener object to the *Debug.Listeners*, it automatically becomes visible to the *Trace* class as well.

> **Note** Custom listeners can be defined by inheriting from the *TraceListener* base class and overriding methods. At a minimum, a new class would implement the *Write* and *WriteLine* methods. Additional overridable methods are *Fail*, *Close*, and *Flush*.

## ASP.NET Tracing

The ASP.NET subsystem provides a specific and made-to-measure tracing mechanism. Regardless of whether you write messages to the page trace log, a trace-enabled page always contains a series of tables containing performance information about the request and the controls tree.

Although a *<trace>* configuration section does exist in the web.config file to let you configure tracing at the application level, you typically want to control tracing on a per-page basis. However, for large projects you can toggle on and off the trace attribute by using the following code in the application's web.config file:

```
<configuration>
  <system.web>
     <trace enabled="true" pageOutput="true" />
  </system.web>
</configuration>
```

The *enabled* attribute enables tracing on the application, while the *pageOutput* attribute permits output to appear in the page. If *pageOutput* is set to *false* (the default setting), the tracing output is automatically routed to the ASP.NET tracer tool—*trace.axd*. At the end of the project, you simply drop the *<trace>* element from the web.config file or set both attributes to *false*. In this way, you eliminate at the root the risk of inadvertently leaving tracing enabled on one of the application pages.

## Enabling Page Tracing

The *trace* attribute in the *@Page* directive defaults to *false*; if set to *true*, it enables tracing information to appear at the bottom of the page, as shown in Figure 4-13.

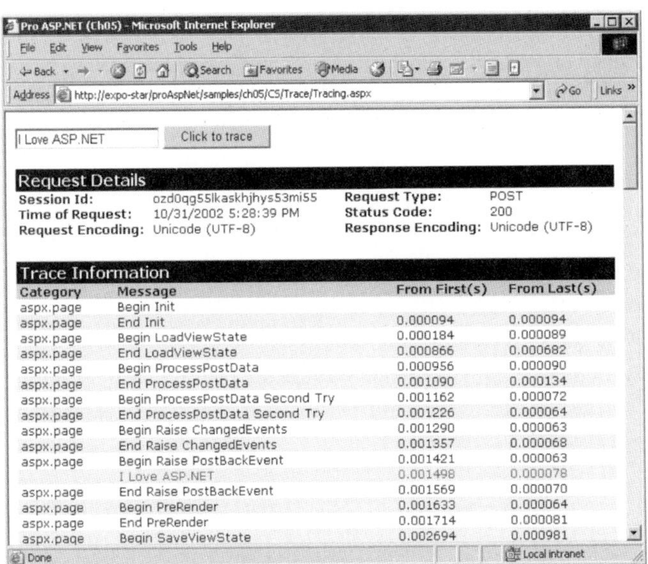


**Figure 4-13** ASP.NET tracing in action.

The trace information is part of the page and, as such, displays through any type of browser that accesses the page. As you can see in the figure, several tables of information show up along with the trace information generated by the page. Additional tables display request details, the control tree, and some useful collections such as cookies, headers, form values, and server variables. If the session and the application state are not empty, the contents of the *Session*- and *Application*-intrinsic properties are also included in the view. In no case are the contents of the *Cache* object flushed to the trace log. (We'll return to this topic in Chapter 14.)

The *@Page* directive also supplies the *TraceMode* attribute to let you choose the order in which the information should be displayed. Feasible values are *SortByCategory* and *SortByTime*. By default, the trace messages appear in the order in which they are emitted. If you set the *TraceMode* attribute to the *SortByCategory* value, the rows appearing in the Trace Information section are sorted by category name. The category to which each row belongs is determined by the method used to emit the message.

### Emitting Trace Messages

An ASP.NET page populates its trace log using methods on the *TraceContext* class. An instance of this class is created when the HTTP request is set up for execution. The trace object is then exposed through the *Trace* property of the *HttpContext* class and is also mirrored by the *Trace* property on the *Page* class.

The *TraceContext* class has a simple interface and features a couple of properties and as many methods. The properties are *IsEnabled* and *TraceMode*. The *IsEnabled* property is a read-only Boolean property that indicates whether tracing is enabled or not. The value that this property returns is affected by the *trace* attribute on the *@Page* directive as well as the *enabled* attribute in the *<trace>* section of the web.config file. The *TraceMode* property gets and sets the order in which the traced rows will be displayed in the page. The property is of type *TraceMode*—an enumeration that includes values such as *SortByCategory* and *SortByTime*.

To emit messages, you can use either of the two methods *Write* and *Warn*. Both methods have three overloads, which all behave in the same way. *Write* and *Warn* are nearly identical methods—the only visible difference is that *Warn* always outputs messages in red.

```
public void Write(string);
public void Write(string, string);
public void Write(string, string, Exception);
```

The simplest overload just emits the specified text in the Message column. (See Figure 4-13.) In the second overload, the first string argument represents the name of the category you want to use for the message—the second argument. The category name can be used to sort trace information and is any name that makes sense to the application to better qualify the message. Finally, the third overload adds an extra *Exception* object in case the message is tracing an error. In this case, the text in the Message column is the concatenation of the specified text and the exception's message.

**Note** Although the text being passed to both *Write* and *Warn* methods is meant to be displayed in HTML pages, no HTML formatting tag is ever processed. The text is written as plain text, so if you attempt to use boldface characters your only result is having a trace message with *<b>* and *</b>* substrings.

## Tracing from External Classes

The ASP.NET *Trace* object is accessible without a fully qualified name from the source code of the .aspx page or from the code-behind class. Custom controls embedded in the page, and their code-behind classes, can also access the tracing subsystem directly. Other classes don't have the same possibility, though.

Suppose your code-behind class delegates an external class to accomplish some tasks. How can the worker class trace in the ASP.NET page? In the context of the worker class, the *Trace* object is unavailable, or at least not in its unqualified form. External classes that want to emit text in the trace log of the current HTTP request can do that using the following expression:

```
System.Web.HttpContext.Current.Trace.Write(category, msg);
```

By writing and registering a custom listener, you could also have the worker class write to the .NET tracing subsystem with the listener routing the text back to ASP.NET. This is probably a more elegant solution, but it's a bit twisted and less efficient. However, a custom listener is as easy to write as shown in the following code:

```
public class AspNetTraceListener : TraceListener
{
    public override void Write(string msg)
    {
        System.Web.HttpContext.Current.Trace.Write(msg);
    }
    public override void WriteLine(string msg)
    {
        System.Web.HttpContext.Current.Trace.Write(msg);
    }
}
```

The newly created listener must now be added to the collection of .NET listeners for the application. In the web.config file, add the following entry:

```
<system.diagnostics>
  <trace>
    <listeners>
      <add name="aspNetListener" type="AspNetListener, YourAssembly" />
```

```
    </listeners>
  </trace>
</system.diagnostics>
```

At this point, make sure the worker class traces text using either the *Debug* or *Trace* class in the *System.Diagnostics* namespace. The just-added ASP.NET listener will route the text to the ASP.NET tracing system.

> **Note** The ASP.NET tracing system does not support its own set of listeners, nor does it support those registered through the diagnostic's *<trace>* section. In addition, there's no known way to modify the output of the trace to show only a few of the standard tables of data.

## The Trace Viewer

ASP.NET also supports application-level tracing through the trace viewer tool. Once tracing has been enabled for the application, each page request routes all the page-specific trace information to the viewer. You can view the trace viewer by requesting *trace.axd* from the root application directory. The trace viewer is shown in Figure 4-14.

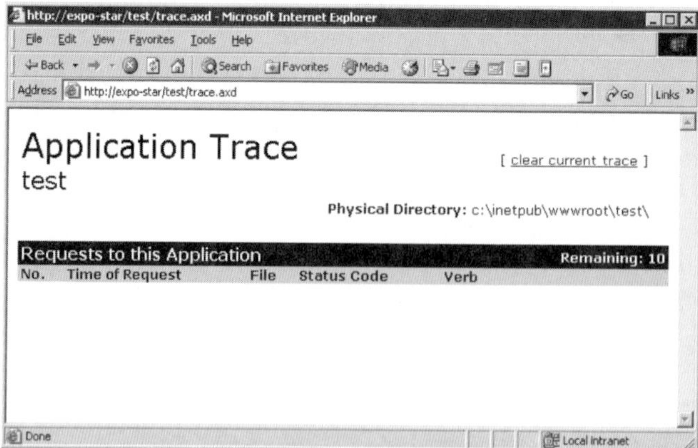


**Figure 4-14** The trace viewer ready for action.

To enable the viewer, you need to have a *<trace>* section in your application web.config file—that is, the configuration file deployed in the root folder.

```
<configuration>
  <system.web>
     <trace enabled="true" />
  </system.web>
</configuration>
```

Actually, most of the settings we will discuss in Chapter 12 about the ASP.NET *<trace>* section apply to the trace viewer. The *pageOutput* attribute, for example, indicates whether the trace output should be visible to the individual pages too or only accessible through the viewer. By default, *pageOutput* is *false* and only the viewer receives trace information. However, each page can individually override this setting by using the trace attribute on the *@Page* directive. The trace viewer caches no more than the number of requests specified by the *requestLimit* attribute (10 by default).

In brief, the ASP.NET trace viewer acts as a centralized console and gathers all the trace information generated by the pages in a certain application. Each request, up to the maximum number fixed by *requestLimit*, is identified by a row in the viewer's interface and can be consulted until the viewer's cache is cleared, as shown in Figure 4-15.

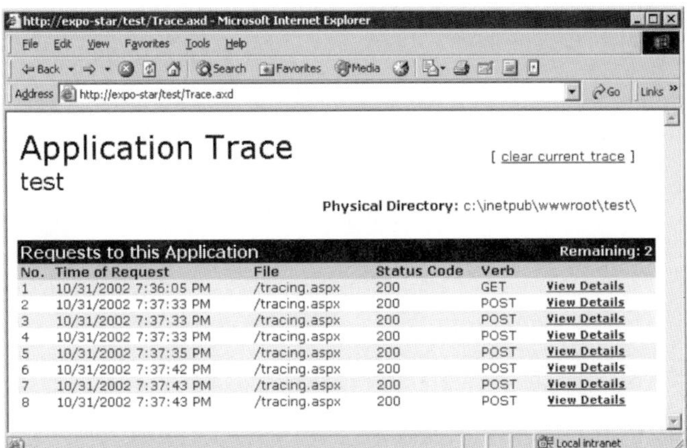


**Figure 4-15** The trace viewer in action.

You activate the viewer by requesting the *trace.axd* URL on the root of the application. AXD is a special resource type that is resolved through the page shown in Figure 4-14. After that, the viewer automatically tracks all requests and caches the full trace for each. When the request limit is reached, no other request will be cached until the log is manually cleared.

**Important** Although you should pay careful attention not to deploy pages with the *trace* attribute turned on, tracing calls can be left in the code for further use. Both the *Write* and *Warn* methods, in fact, return immediately if tracing is not enabled. Although not null, the impact this might have on the performance is negligible. It is especially minor when considering that, in case of need, the tracing mechanism can be turned on declaratively and without touching the code. By simply changing the *<trace>*'s *enabled* attribute in the web.config file, you enable tracing through the viewer. In this way, you can monitor the application—for example, after some user feedback—without stopping it. For the viewer to work, though, trace information must be emitted.

# Conclusion

In this chapter, we examined issues you might face when building pages and interacting with them. Form-based programming is fundamental in ASP.NET because it's the only way to have users and applications interact. ASP.NET pages can have only one server-side form with view-state and control support. To add more forms, you can either resort to old-style and stateless HTML programming or create some sort of logical form controls hosted by the single-server form, basically redirecting the user to the specified page.

Making different pages work together in exchanging data and arguments is the ultimate goal of the *@Reference* directive that allows pages to reference other pages as external libraries.

Often good programs do bad things and raise errors. In the Web world, handling errors is a task architecturally left to the run-time environment running the application. The ASP.NET runtime is capable of providing two types of error pages, both of which are simply impracticable for serious and professional applications. When a user who is locally connected to the application does something that originates an error, by default ASP.NET returns a "geek" page with the stack trace and the full transcript of the exception that occurred. The remote user, on the other hand, receives a less compromising page but certainly not a user-friendly one. Fortunately, though, the ASP.NET framework is flexible enough to let you change the error pages, even to the point of distinguishing between HTTP errors.

Localization is another aspect of page and user interaction that we covered, along with tracing. Unlike localization, tracing is not a feature directly aimed at end users, but when properly used it can make users' experiences much easier and enjoyable while giving programmers solid information to profile and track the application's behavior.

In the next chapter, we'll introduce how to add data to your ASP.NET pages. We'll start with a discussion of ADO.NET object model.

## Resources

- Post Multiple Forms from a Single Page (*http://www.aspnetpro.com/features/2003/04/asp200304pw_f/asp200304pw_f.asp*)
- Build Generic Error Handlers (*http://www.aspnetpro.com/features/2003/05/asp200305dk_f/asp200305dk_f.asp*)
- Internationalize Your ASP.NET Applications (*http://www.devx.com/dotnet/Article/7000*)
- MyTracer Monitors and Traces ASP.NET Apps (*http://msdn.microsoft.com/msdnmag/issues/03/04/CuttingEdge/default.aspx*)
- Customize '404' Errors (*http://www.aspnetpro.com/features/2002/10/asp200210fj_f/asp200210fj_f.asp*)

# Part II

# Adding Data in an ASP.NET Site

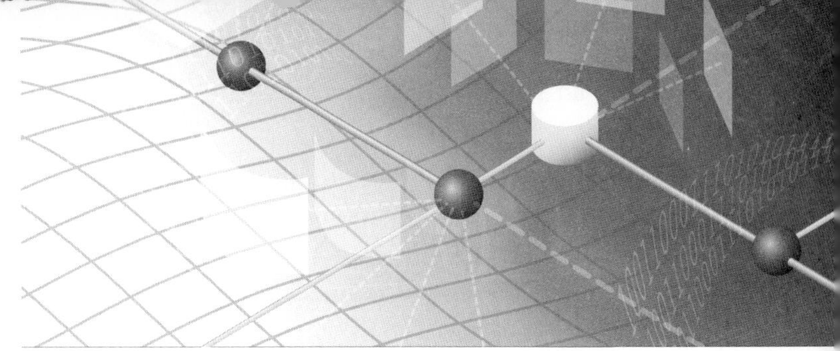

# 5

# The ADO.NET Object Model

*As a general rule, the most successful man in life is the man who has the best information.*

*—Benjamin Disraeli*

ADO.NET is the latest in a long line of database-access technologies that began with the Open DataBase Connectivity (ODBC) API several years ago. Written as a C-style library, ODBC was designed to provide a uniform API to issue SQL calls to various database servers. In the ODBC model, database-specific drivers hide any difference and discrepancy between the SQL language used at the application level and the internal query engine. Next, COM landed in the database territory and started a colonization process that culminated with OLE DB.

OLE DB has evolved from ODBC and, in fact, the open database connectivity principle emerges somewhat intact in it. OLE DB is a COM-based API aimed at building a common layer of code for applications to access any data source that can be exposed as a tabular rowset of data. The OLE DB architecture is composed of two elements—a consumer and a provider. The consumer is incorporated in the client and is responsible for setting up COM-based communication with the data provider. The OLE DB data provider, in turn, receives calls from the consumer and executes commands on the data source. Whatever the data format and storage medium are, an OLE DB provider returns data formatted in a tabular layout—that is, with rows and columns.

Because it isn't especially easy to use and is primarily designed for coding from within C++ applications, OLE DB never captured the heart of programmers, even though it could guarantee a remarkable mix of performance and flexibility. ActiveX Data Objects (ADO)—roughly, a COM automation version of

OLE DB—came a little later just to make the OLE DB technology accessible from Microsoft Visual Basic and ASP applications. When used, ADO acts as the real OLE DB consumer embedded in the host applications. ADO was invented in the age of connected, two-tier applications, and the object model design reflects that. ADO makes a point of programming redundancy: it usually provides more than just one way of accomplishing key tasks, and it contains a lot of housekeeping code. For all these reasons, although it's incredibly easy to use, an ADO-based application doesn't perform as efficiently as a pure OLE DB application.

ADO.NET is a data-access layer tailor-made for the .NET Framework. It was heavily inspired by ADO, which has emerged over the past few years as a very successful object model for writing data-aware applications. The key design criteria for ADO.NET are simplicity and performance. Those criteria typically work against each other, but with ADO.NET you get the power and performance of a low-level interface combined with the simplicity of a modern object model. Unlike ADO, though, ADO.NET has been purposely designed to observe general, rather than database-oriented, guidelines.

Several syntactical differences exist between the object models of ADO and ADO.NET. In spite of this, the functionalities of ADO and ADO.NET look much the same. This is because Microsoft put a lot of effort in aligning some programming aspects of the ADO.NET object model with ADO. In this way, data developers don't need to become familiar with too many new concepts to use ADO.NET and can work with a relatively short learning curve. With ADO.NET, you probably won't be able to reuse much of your existing code. You'll certainly be able, though, to reuse all your skills.

## The .NET Data Access Layer

The key improvements in ADO.NET are the rather powerful disconnected model exposed through the *DataSet* object, the strong integration with XML, and the seamless integration with the rest of the .NET Framework, including ASP.NET applications and Web services. Additionally, the performance of ADO.NET is very good, and the integration with Microsoft Visual Studio .NET is unprecedented. If you're writing a new application in the .NET Framework, deciding whether to use ADO.NET is a no-brainer.

> **Note** Using ADO in .NET applications is still possible, but for performance and consistency reasons its use should be limited to a very few and special cases. For example, ADO is the only way you have to work with server cursors, and ADOX is the variation of ADO that provides you with an object model for managing table structure and schema information. On the other hand, ADO recordsets can't be directly bound to ASP.NET or Microsoft Windows Forms databound controls. We'll cover data binding in Chapter 6 and Chapter 7.

A key architectural element in the ADO.NET infrastructure is the *managed provider*, which can be considered as the .NET counterpart of the OLE DB provider. A managed data provider enables you to connect to a data source and retrieve and modify data. Compared to the OLE DB provider, a .NET managed provider has a simplified data-access architecture made of a smaller set of interfaces and based on .NET Framework data types. Figure 5-1 illustrates the internal structure of a .NET data provider.

A COM-based OLE DB provider is a monolithic component. In contrast, a managed provider is made of a suite of classes, each of which represents a particular step in the connection model that a data-aware application implements. A managed provider is composed of classes used to connect to a particular data source, manage transactions, execute commands, and access result sets. For each of these steps, the managed provider supplies a particular class with its own set of properties, methods, and events. The union of these classes form the logical entity known as the managed provider for that data source.

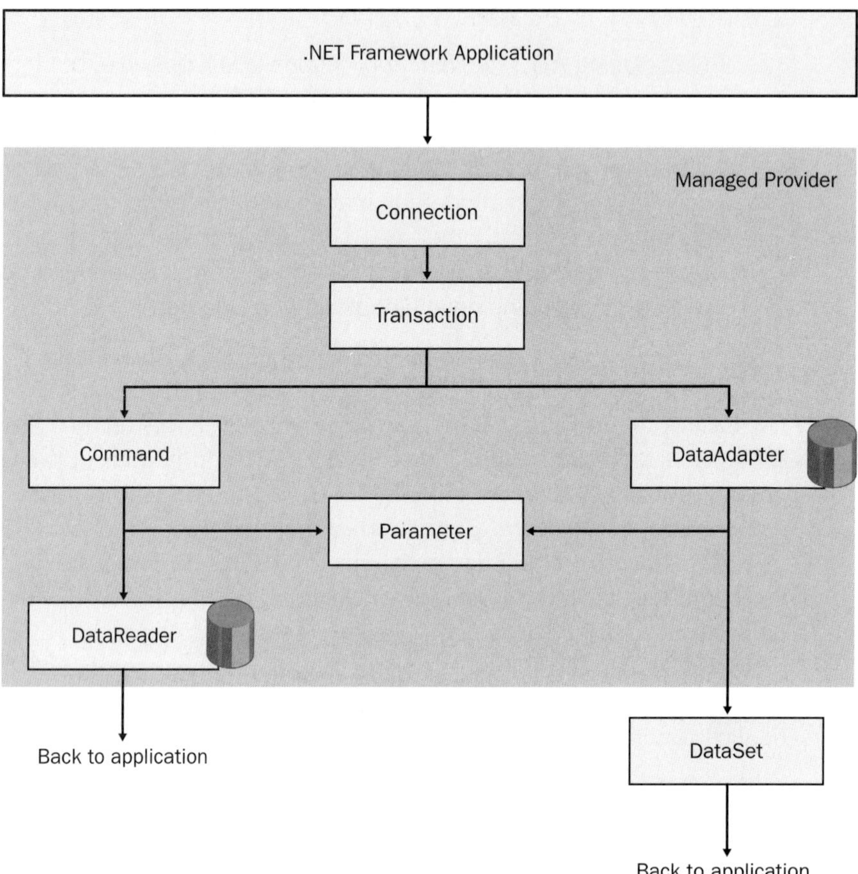


**Figure 5-1** The connections between the .NET Framework classes that form a typical managed provider.

> **Note** In the .NET Framework, each managed provider is characterized by a prefix that qualifies the various classes of the same type. For example, the class that manages connections to Microsoft SQL Server is named *SqlConnection*, while the class that opens a connection to an Oracle database is *OracleConnection*. In the former case, the prefix *Sql* is used; in the latter case, the prefix used is *Oracle*.

## Architecture of a .NET Managed Provider

The classes in the managed provider interact with the specific data source and return data to the application using the data types defined in the .NET Framework. The logical components implemented in a managed provider are those graphically featured in Figure 5-1 and detailed in Table 5-1.

**Table 5-1 Logical Components of a .NET Data Provider**

| Component | Description |
|---|---|
| *Command* | Represents a command that hits the underlying database server |
| *Connection* | Creates a connection with the specified data source, including SQL Server, Oracle, and any data source for which you can indicate either an OLE DB provider or an ODBC driver |
| *DataAdapter* | Represents a database command that executes on the specified database server and returns a disconnected set of records |
| *DataReader* | Represents a read-only, forward-only cursor created on the underlying database server |
| *Parameter* | Represents a parameter you can pass to the command object |
| *Transaction* | Represents a transaction to be made in the source database server |

The functionalities supplied by a .NET data provider fall into a couple of categories:

- Support for disconnected data—that is, the capability of populating the ADO.NET *DataSet* class with fresh data
- Support for connected data access, which includes the capability of setting up a connection and executing a command

Each managed provider that wraps a real-world database server implements all the objects in Table 5-1 in a way that is specific to the data source. The components listed in Table 5-1 are implemented based on methods and properties defined by the interface. Table 5-2 lists possible interfaces for data providers.

**Table 5-2 Interfaces of .NET Data Providers**

| Interface | Description |
|---|---|
| *IDataAdapter* | Populates a *DataSet* object, and resolves changes in the *DataSet* object back to the data source |
| *IDataParameter* | Allows implementation of a parameter to a command |
| *IDataReader* | Reads a forward-only, read-only stream of data created after the execution of a command |
| *IDbCommand* | Represents a command that executes when connected to a data source |
| *IDbConnection* | Represents a unique session with a data source |
| *IDbDataAdapter* | Supplies methods to execute typical operations on relational databases (such as insert, update, select, and delete) |
| *IDbTransaction* | Represents a local, nondistributed transaction |

Note that all these interfaces except *IDataAdapter* are officially considered to be optional. However, any realistic data provider that manages a database server would implement them all. Managed providers that implement only the *IDataAdapter* interface are said to be *simple managed providers*.

## Managed Providers vs. OLE DB Providers

OLE DB providers and managed data providers are radically different types of components that share a common goal—to provide a unique and uniform programming interface for data access. The differences between OLE DB providers and .NET data providers can be summarized in the following points:

- **Component Technology** OLE DB providers are in-process COM servers that expose a suite of COM interfaces to consumer modules. The dialog between consumers and providers takes place through COM and involves a number of interfaces. More roughly, the dialog is fairly formal and based on a rigid etiquette. The OLE DB specification stems from the Universal Data Access (UDA) vision, a Microsoft white paper in which data was perceived as being made of building blocks that ad hoc tools normalized to a common tabular format—the rowset. For this reason, the specification for OLE DB components were rather formal and even a bit quirky. A few years of real-world experience showed the specification to be much too complex, quirky, and error-prone for being ported as is to a new framework—specifically, the .NET Framework.

A .NET data provider contains the gist of OLE DB providers, just as OLE DB providers were based on the battle-tested characteristics of ODBC drivers. A managed data provider is not a monolithic component, but a suite of managed classes whose overall design looks into one *particular* data source rather than blinking at an abstract and universal data source.

- **Internal Implementation** Both types of providers end up making calls into the data-source programming API. In doing so, though, they provide a dense layer of code that separates the data source from the calling application. Learning from the OLE DB experience, Microsoft designed .NET data providers to be more agile and simple. Fewer interfaces are involved, and the conversation between the caller and the callee is more direct and as informal as possible. In OLE DB, data-access components are designed to provide a database-independent layer for accessing generic databases. The value of such a generic layer is that it provides nearly universal access. Its major drawback is the difficulty to deliver database-specific optimizations. In .NET, data access components are simpler and less general, but they're also more practical and effective.
- **Application Integration** Another aspect in .NET that makes the conversation between caller and callee more informal is the fact that managed providers return data using the same data structures that the application would use to store it. In OLE DB, the data-retrieval process is more flexible but also more complex because the provider packs data in flat memory buffers and leaves the consumer responsible for mapping that data into usable data structures, such as the ADO *Recordset* or a user-defined class. In .NET, the integration with the application is total and the managed provider packs return data in a ready-to-use format using types from the .NET Framework.

Calling into an OLE DB provider from within a .NET application is even more expensive because of the type and data conversion necessary to make the transition from the managed environment of the common language runtime (CLR) to the COM world. Calling a COM object from within a .NET application is possible through the COM interop layer, but doing so comes at a cost. In general, to access a data source from within a .NET application, you should always use a managed provider instead of OLE DB providers or ODBC drivers. You should be doing this primarily because of the transition costs, but also because managed providers are normally more modern tools based on an optimized architecture.

Not all data sources, though, have a managed provider available. In these cases, resorting to old-fashioned OLE DB providers or ODBC drivers is a pure necessity. For this reason, the .NET Framework encapsulates in managed wrapper classes the logic needed to call into a COM-style OLE DB provider or a C-style ODBC driver.

> **Note** Data-driven .NET applications are in no way limited to managed providers. They can access virtually any data source for which any of the following data-access components exists: a managed provider, OLE DB provider, or ODBC driver. In terms of raw performance, a managed provider is the fastest approach, but functionally speaking, others are effective as well. Note that in general you'll have a choice of multiple providers from various vendors. They'll certainly supply a common subset of functionality, but they won't necessarily supply the same set of features or the same implementation.

### Data Providers Available in the .NET Framework

The .NET Framework 1.0 supports only two managed providers—those for SQL Server 7.0 or later and those for the main OLE DB providers. A few months after the release of .NET Framework 1.0, Microsoft released as separate downloads a managed provider for ODBC data sources and for Oracle databases. In the .NET Framework 1.1, these additional data providers have been incorporated in the framework. Table 5-3 details the managed providers available in the .NET Framework 1.1.

**Table 5-3 Managed Providers in .NET**

| Data Source | Namespace | Description |
|---|---|---|
| SQL Server | *System.Data.SqlClient* | Targets SQL Server 7.0 and 2000, including XML extensions. To maximize performance, hooks up the database at the wire level using optimized packets. |
| OLE DB providers | *System.Data.OleDb* | Targets OLE DB providers, including SQLOLEDB, MSDAORA, and the JET engine. |

**Table 5-3 Managed Providers in .NET**

| Data Source | Namespace | Description |
|---|---|---|
| ODBC drivers | *System.Data.Odbc* | Targets several ODBC drivers, including those for SQL Server, Oracle, and the Jet engine. |
| Oracle | *System.Data.OracleClient* | Targets Oracle 9i, and supports all of its data types. |

The OLE DB and ODBC managed providers listed in Table 5-3 are not specific to a physical database server, but rather they serve as a bridge that gives instant access to a large number of existing OLE DB providers and ODBC drivers. When you call into OLE DB providers, your .NET applications jumps out of the managed environment and issues COM calls through the COM interop layer.

The managed providers for SQL Server and Oracle, on the other hand, hook up the database server directly to the wire level and obtain a substantial performance advantage. As of version 1.1 of the .NET Framework, Oracle and SQL Server are the only databases for which Microsoft supplies a direct data provider. Third-party vendors supply managed providers for a few other databases such as MySQL. For other major databases—such as IBM DB2, AS/400, Sybase, and Informix—managed providers have been announced and in some cases are already available in beta versions. Having them available on the market is only a matter of time.

### Alternative Ways of Exposing Data

In .NET, managed providers are only the preferred way of exposing database contents—that is, data in a wire format or data that must be accessed concurrently and through transactions. If you just have generic data to publish (for example, a proprietary text or binary file), you should expose it as XML or by using a simple managed provider. If you have a store to expose, an OLE DB provider still makes sense because you plug into all the existing .NET and Win32 OLE DB consumers, from ADO-driven applications to the data transformation services and from SQL Server replication to the distributed query processor.

## Data Sources You Access Through ADO.NET

The .NET data provider is the managed component of choice for database vendors to expose their data in an effective way. Ideally, each database vendor should provide a .NET-compatible API that is seamlessly callable from within managed applications. Unfortunately, this is not yet the case. At this time, only a few database servers can be accessed through ADO.NET and managed providers, but the situation is expected to improve over the next few months as .NET takes root as a platform in the software community. If you look back at the state of the art for ODBC in the early 90s and for OLE DB in the late 90s, you'll see the same clear signs of a technology that is slowly but steadily gaining widespread acceptance. Let's review the situation for the major database management systems (DBMS).

## Accessing SQL Server

As mentioned, Microsoft supplies a managed provider for SQL Server 7.0 and newer versions. Using the classes contained in this provider is by far the most effective way of accessing SQL Server. Figure 5-2 shows how SQL Server is accessed by .NET and COM clients.

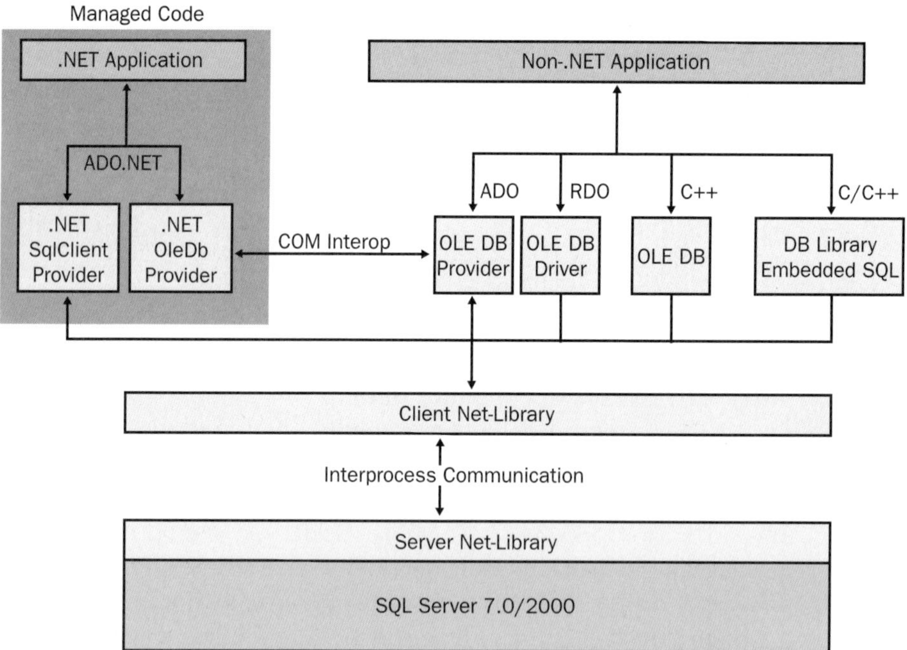


**Figure 5-2** Accessing SQL Server by using the managed provider for OLE DB adds overhead because the objects called must pass through the COM interop layer.

A .NET application can access a SQL Server database by using either the native data provider or the COM OLE DB provider via the managed provider for OLE DB data sources. The rub is that the OLE DB provider—a component named SQLOLEDB—is a COM object that can be used only through the COM interop layer, which seamlessly provides for data and type marshaling. You should always use the native data provider. In general, you should have a good reason to opt for SQLOLEDB. A possible good reason is the need to use ADO rather than ADO.NET as the data-access library. As of version 1.1 of the .NET Framework, ADO.NET doesn't fully cover the same set of features available in ADO. For example, if you need to use server cursors, you must resort to ADO. In this case, you use OLE DB to read from and write to SQL Server.

The SQL Server native provider not only avoids paying the performance tax of going down to COM, it also implements some little optimizations when preparing the command for SQL Server. For example, suppose you need to run the following statement:

```
SELECT * FROM Employees
```

If you run the command using the native managed provider, the SQL code that actually hits the server is slightly different:

```
exec sp_executesql N'SELECT * FROM Employees'
```

The *sp_executesql* system stored procedure brings advantages when a Transact-SQL statement that has parameter values as the only variation is repeatedly executed. Because the statement itself remains constant, the SQL Server query optimizer is likely to reuse the execution plan it has generated for the first execution. Note, though, that for this feature to work better you should use fully qualified object names in the statement string.

In addition, a statement that goes through the managed provider executes as a remote procedure call (RPC). A statement processed by the OLE DB provider runs as a Transact-SQL batch. The RPC protocol increases performance by eliminating much of the parameter processing and statement parsing done on the server.

> **Note** SQL Server can also be accessed using the Microsoft ODBC driver and the classes in the .NET data provider for ODBC. The classes are located in the *System.Data.Odbc* namespace in the .NET Framework 1.1.

## Accessing Oracle Databases

The .NET Framework 1.1 includes a managed provider for Oracle databases. The classes are located in the *System.Data.OracleClient* namespace in the System.Data.OracleClient assembly. Instead of using the managed provider, you can resort to the COM-based OLE DB provider (named MSDAORA) or the ODBC driver. Note, though, that the Microsoft OLE DB provider for Oracle does not support Oracle 9i and its specific data types. In contrast, Oracle 9i data types are fully supported by the .NET managed provider. So by using the .NET component to connect to Oracle you not only get a performance boost, but also increased programming power.

> **Note** The .NET data provider for Oracle requires that Oracle client software (version 8.1.7 or later) be installed on the system before you can use it to connect to an Oracle data source.

Microsoft is not the only company to develop a .NET data provider for Oracle databases. A few months ago, Core Lab was probably the first vendor to ship such a provider—named OraDirect—whose details can be discovered by stepping through the appropriate links at *http://www.crlab.com/oranet.* Oracle also couldn't resist jumping in and developing its own .NET data provider immediately after the official release of the .NET Framework 1.0. The latest updates for this component, named Oracle Data Provider for .NET (ODP.NET), can be found at *http://otn.oracle.com/tech/windows/odpnet.* ODP.NET features high performance access to the Oracle database while providing access to advanced Oracle functionality not otherwise available in .NET through OLE DB and ODBC layers. ODP.NET is part of the Oracle 9i Release 2 Client, but it can be used with any Oracle 8, Oracle 8i, or Oracle 9i database server. Unlike OLE DB and ODBC access layers, ODP.NET has many optimizations for retrieving and manipulating Oracle native types, such as any flavor of large objects (LOBs) and REF cursors. ODP.NET can participate in transactional applications with the Oracle database acting as the resource manager and the Microsoft Distributed Transaction Coordinator (DTC) coordinating transactions.

## Using OLE DB Providers

The .NET data provider for OLE DB providers is a data-access bridge that allows .NET applications to call into data sources for which a COM OLE DB provider exists. While this approach is architecturally less effective than using native providers, it represents the only way to access those data sources when no managed providers are available.

The classes in the *System.Data.OleDb* namespace, though, don't support all types of OLE DB providers and have been optimized to work with only a few of them, as listed in Table 5-4.

**Table 5-4 OLE DB Providers Tested**

| Name | Description |
|---|---|
| Microsoft.Jet.OLEDB.4.0 | The OLE DB provider for the JET engine implemented in Microsoft Access |
| MSDAORA | The Microsoft OLE DB provider for Oracle 7 that partially supports some features in Oracle 8 |
| SQLOLEDB | The OLE DB provider for SQL Server 6.5 and newer |

The preceding list does not include all the OLE DB providers that really work through the OLE DB .NET data provider. However, only the components in Table 5-4 are guaranteed to work well in .NET. In particular, the classes in the *System.Data.OleDb* namespace don't support OLE DB providers that implement any of the OLE DB 2.5 interfaces for semistructured and hierarchical rowsets. This includes the OLE DB providers for Microsoft Exchange (EXOLEDB) and for Internet Publishing (MSDAIPP).

> **Caution** The OLE DB .NET data provider does not work with the OLE DB provider for ODBC (MSDASQL). To access an ODBC data source using ADO.NET, you should use the .NET data provider for ODBC. If you try to set the *Provider* attribute of the connection string to MSDASQL, a runtime error is thrown and no connection is ever attempted.

In general, what really prevents existing OLE DB providers from working properly within the .NET data provider for OLE DB is the set of interfaces they really implement. Some OLE DB providers—for example, those written using the Active Template Library (ATL) or with Visual Basic and the OLE DB Simple Provider Toolkit—are likely to miss one or more COM interfaces that the .NET wrapper requires.

As of version 1.1 of the .NET Framework, there's no native managed data provider for the Jet engine and Microsoft Access databases. As a result, you should use the OLE DB provider.

### Using ODBC Drivers

The .NET data provider for ODBC lets you access ODBC drivers from managed, ADO.NET-driven applications. Although the ODBC .NET data provider is intended to work with all compliant ODBC drivers, it is guaranteed to work well only with the drivers for SQL Server, Oracle, and Jet. Although ODBC might appear to now be an obsolete technology, it's still used in several production environments and for some vendors still represents the only way to connect to their products.

As mentioned earlier, you can't access an ODBC driver through an OLE DB provider. There's no technical reason behind this limitation—it's just a matter of common sense. In fact, calling the MSDASQL OLE DB provider from within a .NET application would drive your client through a double data-access bridge—one going from .NET to the OLE DB provider and one going one level down to the actual ODBC driver.

### Accessing Other Data Sources

The list of databases for which a native managed provider exists is not limited to SQL Server and Oracle. The list, in fact, also includes MySQL, the most popular open-source database server. For more information about MySQL, visit the *http://www.mysql.com* Web site. Recently, a third-party vendor—Core Lab—shipped MySqlDirect .NET, which is a managed provider that uses the native MySQL programming interface to access MySQL databases. The component is targeted to version 3.2 of MySQL and provides only a thin layer of code between ADO.NET and the database server. For more information about the product, go to *http://www.crlab.com/mysqlnet.*

The availability of managed providers is rapidly and constantly evolving, and almost every day we read press releases from database vendors and third-party tool vendors announcing beta versions or plans for supporting the .NET data provider architecture. At the time of this writing, it is amazing to see that in the list of the released .NET data providers we find an open-source database like MySQL but not yet more traditional database servers such as Sybase, Informix, AS/400, and IBM DB2. You can still access those database management systems from within your .NET application by using either the corresponding OLE DB provider or an ODBC driver. However, note that IBM is working on a native DB2 .NET data provider. (For more information, see *http://www7b.software.ibm.com/dmdd/downloads/dotnetbeta/index.html.*) In addition, DataDirect is expected to provide Sybase support soon. You should note that the key advantage of native .NET solutions is that no third-party drivers or bridge solutions are needed, which results in great performance.

## Connecting to Data Sources

The beauty of the ADO.NET object model and managed data providers is that programmers always write their data-access code in the same way, regardless of whether the underlying data source is SQL Server, Oracle, or even MySQL. The programming model is based on a relatively standard sequence of steps that first creates a connection, then prepares and executes a command, and finally processes the data retrieved. In the rest of the chapter, we'll mostly discuss how data classes work with SQL Server 2000. However, we'll promptly point out any aspect that is significantly different than other .NET data providers. To start out, let's see how connections take place.

## The *SqlConnection* Class

The first step in working with an ADO.NET-based application is setting up the connection with the data source. The class that represents a physical connection to SQL Server 2000 is *SqlConnection*, and it's located in the *System.Data.SqlClient* namespace. The class is sealed (that is, not inheritable), cloneable, and implements the *IDbConnection* interface. The class features two constructors, one of which is the default parameterless constructor. The second class constructor, on the other hand, takes a string containing the connection string:

```
public SqlConnection();
public SqlConnection(string);
```

The following code snippet shows the typical way to set up and open a SQL Server connection:

```
string nwind_string = "SERVER=localhost;DATABASE=northwind;UID=...;PWD=...";
SqlConnection nwind_conn = new SqlConnection(nwind_string);
nwind_conn.Open();
⋮
nwind_conn.Close();
```

Table 5-5 details the public properties defined on the *SqlConnection* class. The table also checks the properties the class provides through the *IDbConnection* interface. These properties are important because they form the subset of properties common to all connection classes in the .NET Framework.

**Table 5-5 Properties of the *SqlConnection* Class**

| Property | *IDbConnection* Interface | Description |
|---|---|---|
| *ConnectionString* | Yes | Gets or sets the string used to open the database. |
| *ConnectionTimeout* | Yes | Gets the seconds to wait while trying to establish a connection. |
| *Database* | Yes | Gets the name of the database to be used. |

*(continued)*

**Table 5-5 Properties of the *SqlConnection* Class** *(continued)*

| Property | *IDbConnection* Interface | Description |
|---|---|---|
| *DataSource* | | Gets the name of the instance of SQL Server to connect to. Normally corresponds to the *Server* connection string attribute. |
| *PacketSize* | | Gets the size in bytes of network packets used to communicate with SQL Server. Set to 8192, it can be any value in the range from 512 to 32767. |
| *ServerVersion* | | Gets a string containing the version of the current instance of SQL Server. The version string is in the form of *major.minor.release*. |
| *State* | Yes | Gets the current state of the connection: open or closed. Closed is the default. |
| *WorkstationId* | | Gets the network name of the client, which normally corresponds to the *Workstation ID* connection string attribute. |

The *SqlConnection* class is expected to signal any change of the internal state using the values in the *ConnectionState* enumeration. Many of the acceptable values, though, are reserved for future versions of the .NET Framework. The only state transitions that take place are from Closed to Open when the *Open* method is called, and from Open to Closed when *Close* is called.

An important characteristic to note about the properties of the connection classes is that they are all read-only except *ConnectionString*. In other words, you can configure the connection only through the tokens of the connection string, but you can read attributes back through handy properties. This characteristic of connection class properties in ADO.NET is significantly different than what you find in ADO, where many of the connection properties—for example, *ConnectionTimeout* and *Database*—were read/write.

Table 5-6 shows the methods available in the *SqlConnection* class.

**Table 5-6 Methods of the *SqlConnection* Class**

| Method | *IDbConnection* Interface | Description |
|---|---|---|
| *BeginTransaction* | Yes | Begins a database transaction. Allows you to specify a name and an isolation level. |
| *ChangeDatabase* | Yes | Changes the current database on the connection. Requires a valid database name. |
| *Close* | Yes | Closes the connection to the database. Use this method to close an open connection. |
| *CreateCommand* | Yes | Creates and returns a *SqlCommand* object associated with the connection. |
| *Dispose* | | Calls *Close*. |
| *EnlistDistributed-Transaction* | | If auto-enlistment is disabled, the method enlists the connection in the specified transaction. *Supported only in version 1.1 of the .NET Framework.* |
| *Open* | Yes | Opens a database connection with the property settings specified by the *ConnectionString*. |

Note that if the connection goes out of scope, it is not automatically closed. Later on, but not especially soon, the garbage collector picks up the object instance, but the connection won't be closed because the garbage collector can't recognize the peculiarity of the object and handle it properly. Therefore, you must explicitly close the connection by calling *Close* or *Dispose* before the object goes out of scope.

The *SqlConnection* class fires three events: *Disposed*, *InfoMessage*, and *StateChange*. The event *Disposed* fires when the connection object is being disposed of by the garbage collector. The event *InfoMessage* reaches the client whenever SQL Server has a warning or nonblocking error. Finally, *StateChange* accompanies any valid state transition.

## Configuring Connection Properties

The *ConnectionString* property is the configuration string used to open a SQL Server database. Made of semicolon-separated pairs of names and values, a connection string specifies settings for the SQL Server runtime. Typical information contained in a connection string includes the name of the database, location of the server, and user credentials. Other more operational information, such as connection timeout and connection pooling settings, can be specified too.

> **Note** Although some particular connection strings for the SQL Server .NET data provider might be nearly identical to OLE DB connection strings, in general the list of acceptable properties in the two cases is different.

The *ConnectionString* property can be set only when the connection is closed. Many connection-string values have corresponding read-only properties in the connection class. These properties are updated when the connection string is set. The contents of the connection string are checked and parsed immediately after the *ConnectionString* property is set. Attribute names in a connection string are not case sensitive, and if a given name appears multiple times, the value of the last occurrence is used. Table 5-7 lists the keywords that are supported.

**Table 5-7 Connection-String Keywords**

| Keyword | Description |
|---|---|
| *Application Name* | Name of the client application as it appears in the SQL Profiler. Defaults to *.Net SqlClient Data Provider*. |
| *AttachDBFileName* or *Initial File Name* | The full path name of the file (.mdf) to use as an attachable database file. |
| *Connection Timeout* | The number of seconds to wait for the connection to take place. Default is 15 seconds. |
| *Current Language* | The SQL Server language name. |
| *Database* or *Initial Catalog* | The name of the database to connect to. |
| *Encrypt* | Indicates whether SSL encryption should be used for all data sent between the client and server. Needs a certificate installed on the server. Default is *false*. |
| *Integrated Security* or *Trusted_Connection* | Indicates whether current Windows account credentials are used for authentication. When set to *false*, an explicit user ID and password need to be provided. The special value *sspi* equals *true*. Default is *false*. |
| *Network Library* or *net* | Indicates the network library used to establish a connection to SQL Server. Default is *dbmssocn*, which is based on TCP/IP. |

**Table 5-7 Connection-String Keywords**

| Keyword | Description |
|---|---|
| *Packet Size* | Bytes that indicate the size of the packet being exchanged. Default is 8192. |
| *Password* or *pwd* | Password for the account logging on. |
| *Persist Security Info* | Indicates whether the managed provider should include password information in the string returned as the connection string. Default is *false*. |
| *Server* or *Data Source* | Name or network address of the instance of SQL Server to connect to. |
| *User ID* or *uid* | User name for the account logging on. |
| *Workstation ID* | Name of the machine connecting to SQL Server. |

The network DLL specified by the *Network Library* keyword must be installed on the system to which you connect. If you use a local server, the default library is *dbmslpcn*, which uses shared memory. For a list of options, consult the MSDN documentation.

Any attempt to connect to an instance of SQL Server should not exceed a given time. The *Connection Timeout* keyword controls just this. Note that a connection timeout of 0 causes the connection attempt to wait indefinitely rather than meaning no wait time.

You normally shouldn't change the default packet size, which has been determined based on average operations and workload. However, if you're going to perform bulk operations in which large objects are involved, increasing the packet size can be of help because it decreases the number of reads and writes.

### Secure Connections

Depending on how you configure your instance of SQL Server, you can exploit trusted connections. When working with trusted connections, SQL Server ignores any explicit user ID and password set in the connection string. In this case, the current Windows account credentials are used to authenticate the request. Of course, you must have a login corresponding to those credentials. As we'll see in Chapter 15, for ASP.NET applications this means you must first add the ASPNET login for the databases you want to access programmatically.

When applications read the *ConnectionString* property, the *get* accessor of the property—that is, the piece of code that determines the value being returned—normally strips off any password information for security reasons. The *Persist Security Info* keyword allows you to change this setting. If you set it to *true* (which is strongly discouraged), the connection string is returned as-is and includes password information, if any.

## Connection Pooling

Connection pooling is a fundamental aspect of high-performance, scalable applications. All .NET data providers support connection pooling as Table 5-8 illustrates.

**Table 5-8 Connection Pooling in .NET Data Providers**

| Provider | Connection Pooling Managed By |
|---|---|
| SQL Server | Internal class |
| Oracle | Internal class |
| OLE DB | OLE DB Service component |
| ODBC | ODBC Driver Manager |

The .NET data providers for SQL Server and Oracle manage connection pooling internally using ad hoc classes. Both support local and distributed transactions. For distributed transactions, they automatically enlist in a transaction and obtain transaction details from Windows 2000 Component Services. If automatic enlistment is disabled through the connection string, the method *EnlistDistributedTransaction* allows you to accomplish that manually.

For the OLE DB data provider, connection pooling is implemented through the OLE DB service infrastructure for session pooling. Connection-string arguments (for example, *OLE DB Service)* can be used to enable or disable various OLE DB services including pooling. A similar situation occurs with ODBC, in which pooling is controlled by the ODBC driver manager.

### Configuring Pooling

Some settings in the connection string directly affect the pooling mechanism. The parameters you can control to configure the environment are listed in Table 5-9.

**Table 5-9 Connection-Pooling Keywords**

| Keyword | Description |
|---|---|
| *Connection Lifetime* | Sets the maximum duration in seconds of the connection object in the pool. This value is used when the object is returned to the pool. If the creation time plus the lifetime is earlier than the current time, the object is destroyed. |
| *Connection Reset* | Determines whether the database connection is reset when being drawn from the pool. Default is *true*. |
| *Enlist* | Indicates that the pooler automatically enlists the connection in the creation thread's current transaction context. Default is *true*. |

**Table 5-9 Connection-Pooling Keywords**

| Keyword | Description |
|---|---|
| *Max Pool Size* | Maximum number of connections allowed in the pool. Default is 100. |
| *Min Pool Size* | Minimum number of connections allowed in the pool. Default is 0. |
| *Pooling* | Indicates that the connection object is drawn from the appropriate pool, or if necessary, is created and added to the appropriate pool. Default is *true*. |

To disable connection pooling, you set *Pooling* to *false*. When changing connection-string keywords—including connection-pooling keywords—Boolean values can also be set by using *yes* or *no* instead of *true* or *false*.

### Getting and Releasing Objects

Each connection pool is associated with a distinct connection string and the transaction context. When a new connection is opened, if the connection string does not exactly match an existing pool, a new pool is created. Once created, connection pools are not destroyed until the process ends. This behavior does not affect the system performance because maintenance of inactive or empty pools requires only minimal overhead.

When a pool is created, multiple connection objects are created and added so that the minimum size is reached. Next, connections are added to the pool on demand, up to the maximum pool size. When a connection object is requested, it is drawn from the pool as long as a usable connection is available. A usable connection must currently be unused, have a matching or null transaction context, and have a valid link to the server. If no usable connection is available, the pooler attempts to create a new connection object. When the maximum pool size is reached, the request is queued and served as soon as an existing connection object is released to the pool. Connections are released when you call methods such as *Close* or *Dispose*. Connections that are not explicitly closed might not be returned to the pool unless the maximum pool size has been reached and the connection is still valid.

A connection object is removed from the pool if the lifetime has expired or if a severe error occurred. In this case, the connection is marked as invalid. The pooler periodically scavenges the various pools and permanently removes invalid connection objects.

> **Caution** Pay careful attention not to create a connection string programmatically by concatenating input data together. If you do, you should first validate the data you're putting in the connection string. This little precaution could save you from sneaky attacks through code injection. We'll say more about this in Chapter 15.

## Generic Database Programming

In ADO.NET, data access is strongly typed, in the sense that you must know at all times what data source you're targeting. In ADO, you could write data-access code that worked in a generic way, regardless of the actual database server. For example, the ADO object model provides unique connection and command objects that hide the characteristics of the underlying DBMS. Once you've set the *Provider* property on the *Connection* object, you're pretty much done. At that point, in fact, creating a *Command* object for SQL Server or Oracle requires the same code.

In ADO.NET, you can retain the same behavior only if you choose to use the .NET data provider for OLE DB. In this case, the programming model is exactly that which you might have experienced with ADO. But what if you want to use the native .NET data providers?

In ADO.NET, the connection object must be data-source specific, and there's no way for you to create a connection in an indirect way. However, once you hold a connection object, you can create and execute a command in a generic way regardless of the actual data source in use. Let's take a look at the following code snippet:

```
IDbConnection conn;
if (useOracle)
    conn = (IDbConnection) new OracleConnection(oracle_conn_string);
else    // use SQL Server
    conn = (IDbConnection) new SqlConnection(sqlserver_conn_string);

// Create the command
IDbCommand cmd = conn.CreateCommand(cmd_text);
```

Based on a user setting, the code decides whether a connection to Oracle or SQL Server is to be used. Once created, the connection object is referenced through an interface type—the *IDbConnection* interface—which is common to all ADO.NET connection objects. To create a command—either an *OracleCommand* or *SqlCommand* object—you use the *CreateCommand* method and reference the command by using the *IDbCommand* interface.

After that, you can use the *ExecuteReader* or *ExecuteNonQuery* methods on the *IDbCommand* interface to execute the command. If you use *ExecuteReader*, you get back a sort of managed cursor—the data reader—and can access it generically using the *IDataReader* interface.

> **Note** You cannot fill a *DataSet* object by using a generic database programming pattern. In fact, you can't create the data adapter object in an indirect way as you can with a command. The reason is that, unlike the command object, in some cases the data adapter can create a connection internally and implicitly. To do so, though, it needs to work in a strongly typed way and know what the underlying database server is.

## Other Connection Objects

So far we've discussed the features of the ADO.NET connection objects mostly from a SQL Server perspective. The programming interface of ADO.NET connection objects is similar but not identical. So let's review what the main differences are in the various cases.

### Oracle Connections

The class that represents a physical connection to an Oracle 8.x database is *OracleConnection*, which is located in the *System.Data.OracleClient* namespace. As mentioned earlier, bear in mind that the Oracle managed provider is implemented in the System.Data.OracleClient assembly. All the others, on the other hand, live in the System.Data assembly.

The *OracleConnection* class differs from other connection classes in the .NET Framework because it does not support the *ConnectionTimeout* and *Database* properties. If you set a timeout in the connection string, the value is simply ignored. Likewise, the class doesn't support a *ChangeDatabase* method.

> **Note** The *PacketSize* and *WorkstationId* properties are specific to the SQL Server data provider and aren't available on any other connection class, including *OracleConnection*.

### OLE DB Connections

The .NET data provider for OLE DB communicates to an OLE DB data source through both the OLE DB Service component, which provides connection pooling and transaction services, and the OLE DB provider for the data source. For this reason, the programming interface of the *OleDbConnection* class is slightly different and includes an extra property that just doesn't make sense for a DBMS-specific component. The property is read-only and named *Provider*. It returns the content of the *Provider* keyword in the connection string. The content of *Provider* is normally the program identifier (progID) of the OLE DB provider to use.

In addition, the *OleDbConnection* class features an OLE DB–specific method—*GetOleDbSchemaTable*—that returns a *DataTable* filled with schema information from a data source.

The data provider for OLE DB also provides a static method to release object pools that are in the process of being destroyed. The *ReleaseObjectPool* method gets into the game only after all active connections have been closed and the garbage collector has been invoked. At this time, the connection objects are released, but the resources reserved for the pools are not.

### ODBC Connections

An *OdbcConnection* object represents a unique connection to a data source that is typically identified through an ODBC data source name (DSN) or a plain connection string. The class works by using resources such as ODBC environment and connection handles.

Unlike other connection classes, the *OdbcConnection* class features the *Driver* property to indicate the name of the driver in use and the *ReleaseObjectPool* static method to release the ODBC environment handle. After an environment handle is released, a request for a new connection creates a new environment.

## Executing Commands

Once you have a physical channel set up between your client and the database, you can start preparing and executing commands. The ADO.NET object model provides two types of command objects—the traditional one-off command and the data adapter. The one-off command executes a statement (that is, a Transact-SQL command) or a stored procedure and returns a sort of cursor. Using that, you then scroll through the rows and read data. While the cursor is in use, the connection is busy and open. The data adapter, on the other hand, is a more powerful object that internally uses a command and a cursor. It retrieves and loads the data into a data container class—the *DataSet*. The client application can then process the data while disconnected from the source. The adapter can also be used to set up a batch update mechanism in which all the records changed in memory are submitted to the DBMS in a loop with autogenerated, but modifiable, commands.

## The *SqlCommand* Class

The *SqlCommand* class represents a SQL Server statement or stored procedure. It is a cloneable and sealed class that implements the *IDbCommand* interface. A command executes in the context of a connection and, optionally, a transaction. This situation is reflected by the constructors available in the *SqlCommand* class:

```
public SqlCommand();
public SqlCommand(string);
public SqlCommand(string, SqlConnection);
public SqlCommand(string, SqlConnection, SqlTransaction);
```

The string argument denotes the text of the command to execute, whereas the *SqlConnection* parameter is the connection object to use. Finally, if specified, the *SqlTransaction* parameter represents the transactional context in which the command has to run. Unlike ADO command objects, ADO.NET command objects can never implicitly open a connection. The connection must be explicitly assigned to the command by the programmer and opened and closed with direct operations. The same holds true for the transaction.

Table 5-10 shows the attributes that comprise a command in the.NET data provider for SQL Server. The values in the *IDbCommand* Interface column indicate whether the property is part of the *IDbCommand* interface.

**Table 5-10 Properties of the *SqlCommand* Class**

| Property | *IDbCommand* Interface | Description |
|---|---|---|
| *CommandText* | Yes | Gets or sets the statement or the stored procedure name to execute. |
| *CommandTimeout* | Yes | Gets or sets the seconds to wait while trying to execute the command. Default is 30. |
| *CommandType* | Yes | Gets or sets how the *CommandText* property is to be interpreted. Set to *Text* by default, which means the *CommandText* property contains the text of the command. |
| *Connection* | Yes | Gets or sets the connection object used by the command. Null by default. |

*(continued)*

**Table 5-10 Properties of the *SqlCommand* Class** *(continued)*

| Property | *IDbCommand* Interface | Description |
|---|---|---|
| *Parameters* | Yes | Gets the collection of parameters associated with the command. The actual type of the collection is *SqlParameterCollection*. Empty by default. |
| *Transaction* | Yes | Gets or sets the transaction within which the command executes. The transaction must be connected to the same connection as the command. |
| *UpdatedRowSource* | Yes | Gets or sets how query command results are applied to the row being updated. The value of this property is used only when the command runs within the *Update* method of the data adapter. Acceptable values are in the *UpdateRowSource* enumeration. |

Commands can be associated with parameters, and each parameter is rendered using a provider-specific object. For the SQL Server managed provider, the parameter class is *SqlParameter*. The command type determines the role of the *CommandText* property. The possible values for *CommandType* are:

- ***Text*** The default setting, which indicates the property contains Transact-SQL text to execute directly.
- ***StoredProcedure*** Indicates that the content of the property is intended to be the name of a stored procedure contained in the current database.
- ***TableDirect*** Indicates the property contains a comma-separated list containing the names of the tables to access. All rows and columns of the tables will be returned. Note that *TableDirect* is supported only by the data provider for OLE DB.

Table 5-11 details the methods available on the *SqlCommand* class.

**Table 5-11 Methods of the *SqlCommand* Class**

| Property | *IDbCommand* Interface | Description |
|---|---|---|
| *Cancel* | Yes | Attempts to cancel the execution of the command. No exception is generated if the attempt fails. |
| *CreateParameter* | Yes | Creates a new instance of a *SqlParameter* object. |
| *ExecuteNonQuery* | Yes | Executes a nonquery command, and returns the number of rows affected. |
| *ExecuteReader* | Yes | Executes a query, and returns a read-only cursor—the data reader—to the data. |
| *ExecuteScalar* | Yes | Executes a query, and returns the value in the 0,0 position (first column of first row) in the result set. Extra data is ignored. |
| *ExecuteXmlReader* | | Executes a query that returns XML data and builds an *XmlReader* object. |
| *Prepare* | Yes | Creates a prepared version of the command in an instance of SQL Server. |
| *ResetCommandTimeout* | | Resets the command timeout to the default. |

If the *CommandType* property is set to *TableDirect*, the *Prepare* method does nothing. A *SqlCommand* object executes Transact-SQL code statements wrapping the user-specified text with the system *sp_executesql* stored procedure. The command is sent to SQL Server using tabular data stream (TDS) packets and the RPC protocol.

## Using Parameters

Parameterized commands define their own arguments by using instances of the *SqlParameter* class. Parameters have a name, value, type, direction, and size. In some cases, parameters can also be associated with a source column. A parameter is associated with a command by using the *Parameters* collection.

```
SqlParameter parm = new SqlParameter();
parm.ParameterName = "@employeeid";
parm.DbType = DbType.Int32;
parm.Direction = ParameterDirection.Input;
cmd.Parameters.Add(parm);
```

The following SQL statement uses a parameter:

```
SELECT * FROM employees WHERE employeeid=@employeeid
```

The .NET data provider for SQL Server identifies parameters by name, using the @ symbol to prefix them. In this way, the order in which parameters are associated with the command is not determinant.

> **Note** Named parameters are supported by the managed provider for Oracle but not by the providers for OLE DB and ODBC data sources. The OLE DB and ODBC data sources use positional parameters identified with the question mark (?) placeholder. The order of parameters is important.

### Ways to Execute

As Table 5-11 shows, a *SqlCommand* object can be executed in four different ways: *ExecuteNonQuery*, *ExecuteReader*, *ExecuteScalar*, and *ExecuteXmlReader*. The various executors work in much the same way, but they differ in the return values. Typically, you use the *ExecuteNonQuery* method to perform update operations such as those associated with statements like UPDATE, INSERT, and DELETE. In these cases, the return value is the number of rows affected by the command. For other types of statements, such as SET or CREATE, the return value is -1.

The *ExecuteReader* method is expected to work with query commands, and returns a data reader object—an instance of the *SqlDataReader* class. The data reader is a sort of read-only, forward-only cursor that client code scrolls and reads from. If you execute an UPDATE statement through *ExecuteReader*, the command is successfully executed but no affected rows are returned.

The *ExecuteScalar* method helps considerably when you have to retrieve a single value. It works great with SELECT COUNT statements or for commands that retrieve aggregate values. If you call the method on a regular query statement, only the value in the first column of the first row is read and all the rest are discarded. Using *ExecuteScalar* results in more compact code than you'd get by executing the command and manually retrieving the value in the top-left corner of the rowset.

These three executor methods are common to all command objects. The *SqlCommand* class also features the *ExecuteXmlReader* method. It executes a command that returns XML data, and it builds an XML reader so that the client application can easily navigate through the XML tree. The *ExecuteXmlReader* method is ideal to use with query commands that end with the FOR XML clause or with commands that query for text fields filled with XML data. Note that while the *XmlReader* object is in use, the underlying connection is busy.

### Setting Up Transactions

A SQL Server native transaction is fully represented by an instance of the *SqlTransaction* class. The transaction object is obtained through the *BeginTransaction* method and can be given a name and an isolation level.

```
SqlTransaction tran;
tran = conn.BeginTransaction();
cmd.Connection = conn;
cmd.Transaction = tran;
:
tran.Commit();
```

You terminate a transaction explicitly by using the *Commit* or *Rollback* method. The *SqlTransaction* class supports named savepoints in the transaction that can be used to roll back a portion of the transaction. Named savepoints exploit a specific SQL Server feature—the SAVE TRANSACTION statement.

## Other Command Objects

Let's look at the characteristics of other command objects that, for one reason or another, have not been covered so far.

### Oracle Commands

Oracle commands don't support a timeout, and in fact, the *OracleCommand* object doesn't expose the *CommandTimeout* property. In addition, the class features two extra executor methods—*ExecuteOracleNonQuery* and *ExecuteOracleScalar*. *ExecuteOracleScalar* differs from *ExecuteScalar* only because it returns an Oracle-specific data type. The difference between *ExecuteNonQuery* and *ExecuteOracleNonQuery* is more subtle.

```
public int ExecuteOracleNonQuery(out OracleString rowid);
```

If you're executing an UPDATE statement that affects exactly one row, the *ExecuteOracleNonQuery* method returns a Base64 string as an output parameter. This value identifies the modified row in the database and allows you to write subsequent, related queries in a more powerful way.

### OLE DB Commands

The *OleDbCommand* class does not support the *ExecuteXmlReader* method and limits its support to the three basic executor methods in the *IDbCommand* interface. In addition, it recognizes *TableDirect* as a valid command type. As mentioned earlier, the OLE DB .NET provider does not support named parameters for statements and stored procedures. If parameters are to be used, you should use the question mark (?) placeholder, as shown in the following command:

```
SELECT * FROM Customers WHERE CustomerID = ?
```

As a result, the order in which *OleDbParameter* objects are added to the collection of parameters must correspond to the position of the question mark placeholder for the parameter.

### ODBC Commands

Just like *OleDbCommand*, the *OdbcCommand* class doesn't support named parameters and resorts to the question-mark placeholder and position-based arguments. To execute a stored procedure, the *OdbcCommand* class requires the *CommandText* property to be set using standard ODBC escape sequences for stored procedures. Note that simply setting the property to the name of the stored procedure does not work. Use the following escape sequence for ODBC stored procedures:

```
{call sp_name(?, ?, ?)}
```

In this example, *sp_name* is the name of the stored procedure while the ? placeholder represents an argument to the procedure.

## ADO.NET Data Readers

In the .NET Framework, a reader is a generic type of object used to read data in a variety of formats. A reader is used to read bytes out of a binary stream, lines of text from a text writer, nodes from an XML document, and records from a database-provided stream of data. The data reader class is specific to a DBMS and works like a firehose-style cursor. It allows you to scroll through and read one or more result sets generated by a command. The data reader operates in a connected way and moves in a forward-only direction.

A data reader is instantiated during the execution of the *ExecuteReader* method. The results are stored in a buffer located on the client and are made available to the reader. The reader moves through the result set by using the *Read* method. By using the data reader object, you access data one record at a time as soon as it becomes available. An approach based on the data reader is effective both in terms of minimizing system overhead and improving performance. Only one record is cached at any time, and there's no wait time to have the entire result set loaded in memory. You should note that by default the cached record is accessible only after it has been completely loaded in memory. This might take a while and consume too much memory, if the query includes large binary large object (BLOB) fields. (More on this later in this chapter and also in Chapter 22.)

A data reader object is made of two interfaces—*IDataReader* and *IDataRecord*. *IDataReader* includes general-purpose properties and methods to read data. For example, it includes the methods *Read* and *Close*. *IDataRecord* supplies methods to extract values out of the current record. Table 5-12 shows the properties of the *SqlDataReader* class—that is, the data reader class for SQL Server.

### Table 5-12 Properties of the *SqlDataReader* Class

| Property | Description |
|---|---|
| *Depth* | Returns 0. |
| *FieldCount* | Gets the number of columns in the current row. |
| *HasRows* | Gets a value that indicates whether the data reader contains one or more rows. *This property is not supported in version 1.0 of the .NET Framework.* |
| *IsClosed* | Gets a value that indicates whether the data reader is closed. |
| *Item* | Indexer property. Gets the value of a column in the original format. |
| *RecordsAffected* | Gets the number of rows modified by the execution of a batch command. |

The *Depth* property—a member of the *IDataReader* interface—is meant to indicate the level of nesting for the current row. The depth of the outermost table is always 0; the depth of inner tables grows by one. Most data readers, including the *SqlDataReader* and *OracleDataReader* classes, do not support multiple levels of nesting so that the *Depth* property always returns 0.

The *RecordsAffected* property cumulatively refers to the rows affected by any update statement executed in the command—typically, a batch or a stored procedure. The property, though, is not set until all rows are read and the data reader is closed. The default value of *RecordsAffected* is 1. Note that *IsClosed* and *RecordsAffected* are the only properties you can invoke on a closed data reader.

Table 5-13 lists the methods of the data reader.

### Table 5-13 Methods of the Data Reader Class

| Methods | Description |
|---|---|
| *Close* | Closes the reader object. Note that closing the reader does not automatically close the underlying connection. |
| *GetBoolean* | Gets the value of the specified column as a Boolean. |
| *GetByte* | Gets the value of the specified column as a byte. |
| *GetBytes* | Reads a stream of bytes from the specified column into a buffer. You can specify an offset both for reading and writing. |
| *GetChar* | Gets the value of the specified column as a single character. |

*(continued)*

**Table 5-13 Methods of the Data Reader Class** *(continued)*

| Methods | Description |
|---|---|
| *GetChars* | Reads a stream of characters from the specified column into a buffer. You can specify an offset both for reading and writing. |
| *GetDataTypeName* | Gets the name of the back-end data type in the specified column. |
| *GetDateTime* | Gets the value of the specified column as a *DateTime* object. |
| *GetDecimal* | Gets the value of the specified column as a decimal. |
| *GetDouble* | Gets the value of the specified column as a double-precision floating-point number. |
| *GetFieldType* | Gets the *Type* object for the data in the specified column. |
| *GetFloat* | Gets the value of the specified column as a single-precision floatingpoint number. |
| *GetGuid* | Gets the value of the specified column as a globally unique identifier (GUID). |
| *GetInt16* | Gets the value of the specified column as a 16-bit signed integer. |
| *GetInt32* | Gets the value of the specified column as a 32-bit signed integer. |
| *GetInt64* | Gets the value of the specified column as a 64-bit signed integer. |
| *GetName* | Gets the name of the specified column. |
| *GetOrdinal* | Given the name of the column, returns its ordinal number. |
| *GetSchemaTable* | Returns a *DataTable* object that describes the metadata for the columns managed by the reader. |
| *GetString* | Gets the value of the specified column as a string. |
| *GetValue* | Gets the value of the specified column in its original format. |
| *GetValues* | Copies the values of all columns in the supplied array of objects. |
| *IsDBNull* | Indicates whether the column contains null values. The type for a null column is *System.DBNull.* |
| *NextResult* | Moves the data reader pointer to the beginning of the next result set, if any. |
| *Read* | Moves the data reader pointer to the next record, if any. |

The SQL Server data reader also features a variety of other DBMS-specific get methods. They include methods such as *GetSqlDouble*, *GetSqlMoney*, *GetSqlDecimal*, and so on. The difference between the *GetXXX* and *GetSqlXXX* methods is in the return type. With the *GetXXX* methods, a base .NET Framework type is returned; with the *GetSqlXXX* methods, a .NET Framework wrapper for a SQL Server type is returned—such as *SqlDouble*, *SqlMoney*, or *SqlDecimal.* The SQL Server types belong to the *SqlDbType* enumeration.

All the *GetXXX* methods that return a value from a column identify the column through a 0-based index. Note that the methods don't even attempt a conversion; they simply return data as is and just make a cast to the specified type. If the actual value and the type are not compatible, an exception is thrown.

The *GetBytes* method is useful to read large fields one step at a time. However, the method can also be used to obtain the length in bytes of the data in the column. To get this information, pass a buffer that is a null reference and the return value of the method will contain the length.

## Reading Data with the Data Reader

The key thing to remember when using a data reader is that you're working while connected. The data reader represents the fastest way to read data out of a source, but you should read your data as soon as possible and release the connection. One row is available at a time, and you must move through the result set by using the *Read* method. The following code snippet illustrates the typical loop you implement to read all the records of a query:

```
while (reader.Read()) {
    // process record
}
```

You have no need to explicitly move the pointer ahead and no need to check for the end of the file. The *Read* method returns *false* if there are no more records to read. Unlike the ADO firehose-style cursor, the data reader features no bookmarks, no scrolling, and no bulk-reading methods such as ADO *GetString* and *GetRows*. In contrast, it provides a *GetValues* method to get all the column values in an array of objects.

**Tip** Null values in the returned stream of data can be checked using a handful of methods on the data reader object and row object itself. For example, you can check a column value against null as shown in the following code snippet:

```
if (reader.IsDBNull(colIndex)) {...}
```

To set a null value, use the *System.DBNull.Value* expression, as in the following code snippet:

```
param.Value = System.DBNull.Value;
```

## Command Behaviors

When calling the *ExecuteReader* method on a command object—on any command object regardless of the underlying DBMS—you can require a particular working mode known as a command behavior. *ExecuteReader* has a second overload that takes an argument of type *CommandBehavior*:

```
cmd.ExecuteReader(CommandBehavior.CloseConnection);
```

*CommandBehavior* is an enumeration. Its values are listed in Table 5-14.

**Table 5-14 Command Behaviors for the Data Reader**

| Behavior | Description |
|---|---|
| *CloseConnection* | Automatically closes the connection when the data reader is closed. |
| *Default* | No special behavior is required. Setting this option is functionally equivalent to calling *ExecuteReader* without parameters. |
| *KeyInfo* | The query returns only column metadata and primary key information. The query is executed without any locking on the selected rows. |
| *SchemaOnly* | The query returns only column metadata and does not put any lock on the database rows. |
| *SequentialAccess* | Enables the reader to load data as a sequential stream. This behavior works in conjunction with methods such as *GetBytes* and *GetChars*, which can be used to read bytes or characters having a limited buffer size for the data being returned. When this behavior is set, the record is not automatically and entirely cached in memory, but physical reading occurs as you access the various fields. |
| *SingleResult* | Only the first result set is returned. |
| *SingleRow* | The query is expected to return a single row. |

The sequential-access mode applies to all columns in the returned result set. This means you can access columns only in the order in which they appear in the result set. For example, you cannot read column #2 before column #1. More exactly, if you read or move past a given location you can no longer read or move back. This happens because when the *SequentialAccess* behavior is selected, record contents aren't cached by the reader object. Caching the contents of the records is what enables, for most behaviors, random access to the fields. Combined with the *GetBytes* method, sequential access can be helpful when you must read binary large objects with a limited buffer.

> **Note** You can specify *SingleRow* also when executing queries that are expected to return multiple result sets. In this case, all the generated result sets are correctly returned, but each result set has a single row.

### Closing the Reader

The data reader is not a publicly creatable object. It does have a constructor, but not one that is callable from within user applications. The data-reader constructor is marked as internal and can be invoked only from classes defined in the same assembly—System.Data. The data reader is implicitly instantiated when the *ExecuteReader* method is called. Opening and closing the reader are operations distinct from instantiation and must be explicitly invoked by the application. The *Read* method advances the internal pointer to the next readable record in the current result set. The *Read* method returns a Boolean value indicating whether or not more records can be read. While records are being read, the connection is busy and no operation, other than closing, can be performed on the connection object.

The data reader and the connection are distinct objects and should be managed and closed independently. Both objects provide a *Close* method that should be called twice—once on the data reader (first) and once on the connection. When the *CloseConnection* behavior is required, closing the data reader also closes the underlying connection. In addition, the data reader's *Close* method fills in the values for any command output parameters and sets the *RecordsAffected* property.

> **Tip** Because of the extra work *Close* always performs, closing a reader with success can sometimes be expensive, especially in cases of large and complicated queries. In situations in which you need to squeeze out every little bit of performance, and where the return values and the number of records affected are not significant, you can invoke the *Cancel* method of the associated *SqlCommand* object instead of *Close*. *Cancel* aborts the operation; however, if you call it after reading all rows, you can clean up the reader with less effort.

## Accessing Multiple Result Sets

Depending on the syntax of the query, multiple result sets can be returned. By default, the data reader is positioned on the first of them. You use the *Read* method to scroll through the various records in the current result set. When the last record is found, the *Read* method returns *false* and does not advance further. To move to the next result set, you should use the *NextResult* method. The method returns *false* if there are no more result sets to read. The following code shows how to access all records in all returned result sets:

```
SqlDataReader reader;
reader = cmd.ExecuteReader();
do {
    // Move through the first result set
    while (reader.Read())
    {
        // access the row
    }
}
while (reader.NextResult())
reader.Close();
cmd.Connection.Close();
```

When reading the contents of a row, you can identify the column by either index or name. Using an index results in significantly faster code because the provider can go directly to the buffer. If the column name is specified, the provider uses the *GetOrdinal* method to translate the name into the corresponding index and then performs an index-based access. Note that for the SQL Server data reader, all the *GetXXX* methods actually call into the corresponding *GetSqlXXX* methods. A similar situation occurs for the Oracle data reader, in which the native data is always marshaled to the .NET Framework types. The OLE DB and ODBC readers have only a single set of *get* methods.

> **Note** The .NET Framework version 1.1 extends the programming interface of data readers by adding the *HasRows* method, which returns a Boolean value indicating whether or not there are more rows to read. However, the method doesn't tell anything about the number of rows available. Similarly, there is no method or trick to know in advance how many result sets have been returned.

## Obtaining Schema Information

All data reader classes supply a *GetSchemaTable* method that retrieves metadata information about the columns the query is going to read. *GetSchemaTable* returns a *DataTable* object—that is, a table with one row for each retrieved column and a fixed number of informative columns.

The metadata available can be catalogued in three categories: column metadata, database characteristics, and column attributes. Table 5-15 details the columns. Note that the column metadata is listed in alphabetical order, which is not the order in which they appear in the result set.

**Table 5-15 Metadata Column for a SQL Server Data Reader**

| Metadata Column | Description |
|---|---|
| *AllowDBNull* | Indicates whether the column allows null values. |
| *BaseCatalogName* | Set to null by default. Returns the name of the database that contains the table accessed by the query. |
| *BaseColumnName* | Set to null by default. Returns the original name of the column if an alias is used. |
| *BaseSchemaName* | Set to null by default. Returns the name of the owner (for example, *dbo*) of the database from which the column is retrieved. |
| *BaseServerName* | Set to null by default. Returns the name of the instance of DBMS used by the data reader. |
| *BaseTableName* | Returns the name of the table. |
| *ColumnName* | Name of the column as it appears in the query. If an alias has been used, the aliased name is returned. |
| *ColumnOrdinal* | 0-based position of the column in the result set. |
| *ColumnSize* | Maximum size in bytes of the data allowed in the column. |
| *DataType* | Returns the .NET Framework type the column maps to. |
| *IsAliased* | Indicates whether the column is aliased in the result set. A column is aliased if renamed using the *AS* clause. The original name of aliased columns is stored in the *BaseColumnName* column. |
| *IsAutoIncrement* | Indicates whether the column is marked as auto-increment. |
| *IsExpression* | Indicates whether the content of the column is based on an expression. |
| *IsHidden* | Indicates whether the column is marked as hidden. |
| *IsIdentity* | Indicates whether the column is an identity column. |
| *IsLong* | Indicates whether the column contains BLOB data. Note, though, that the definition of a BLOB is provider-specific. |
| *IsKey* | Indicates whether the column is a key or part of a set of columns that together represent a key. |
| *IsReadOnly* | Indicates whether the column is read-only. |

*(continued)*

**Table 5-15 Metadata Column for a SQL Server Data Reader** *(continued)*

| Metadata Column | Description |
|---|---|
| *IsRowVersion* | Indicates whether the column has a unique identifier value—that is, a row GUID. |
| *IsUnique* | Indicates whether the column can contain duplicates. |
| *NumericPrecision* | Set to null by default. Indicates the maximum precision of the column data. |
| *NumericScale* | Set to null by default. Indicates the number of digits to the right of the decimal point if the column type allows. |
| *ProviderType* | Indicates the type of the column data. The type is expressed as a numeric value corresponding to the type in the database-specific enumeration. For example, an integer column in a SQL Server table returns the value of *SqlDbType.Int*. |

Catalog and owner (schema) information can be retrieved only if explicitly mentioned in the command text. Writing the same query in the following ways affects the contents of the *BaseXXX* columns:

```
SELECT * FROM northwind.dbo.employees
SELECT * FROM employees
```

In the first query, *BaseCatalogName* would be set to *northwind* and *BaseSchemaName* to *dbo*. In the second query, the same information wouldn't be retrieved. Note that this is true only if you're also using the *KeyInfo* command behavior.

**Tip** The *GetSchemaTable* method for SQL Server returns more accurate data if you require the *KeyInfo* command behavior when calling *ExecuteReader*. The *KeyInfo* behavior can be combined with the default behavior so that you can execute a single command and obtain both schema and data:

```
reader = cmd.ExecuteReader(CommandBehavior.KeyInfo |
                           CommandBehavior.CloseConnection)
```

The fields whose values are correctly returned only if the *KeyInfo* behavior is required are: *IsKey*, *BaseTableName*, *IsAliased*, *IsExpression*, and *IsHidden*. Note also that if *KeyInfo* is required, the key columns (if any) are always added at the bottom of the result set but no data is returned for them.

## Special Features of Data Readers

The characteristics of the various provider-specific data readers are nearly identical, with only some differences that are more architectural than functional. We've examined the *SqlDataReader* class, now let's examine the differences with other reader classes supported by the .NET Framework 1.1 data providers.

### Oracle Data Readers

The *OracleDataReader* class provides a personal set of *GetXXX* methods for its own internal types. Some of its methods are *GetOracleBFile*, *GetOracleBinary*, and *GetOracleDateTime*. In Oracle database programming, multiple result sets returned by a query or stored procedure are handled through multiple REF CURSOR objects. For the *NextResult* method to work properly with Oracle databases, you must associate as many output parameters to the command as there are expected result sets. An ADO.NET result set coincides with an Oracle REF CURSOR in the command text. The output parameter names must match the name of the cursors, while their type must be *OracleType.Cursor*. The following code shows how to run a stored procedure (or the command text) that references a couple of cursors named Employees and Orders:

```
// cmd is an OracleCommand object that points to a command or a
// stored procedure. It executes code that creates two REF CURSORs
// called Employees and Orders. Names must match.
OracleParameter p1 = cmd.Parameters.Add("Employees", OracleType.Cursor);
p1.Direction = ParameterDirection.Output;
OracleParameter p2 = cmd.Parameters.Add("Orders", OracleType.Cursor);
p2.Direction = ParameterDirection.Output;
```

### OLE DB Data Readers

The *OleDbDataReader* is the only data reader that fully supports the *Depth* property. It is the only provider that admits hierarchical rowsets (or OLE DB chapters). An example of a hierarchical result set is what you obtain by putting the *MSDataShape* OLE DB provider to work on a SHAPE query. A hierarchical query includes one or more columns that are in effect embedded result sets. Each of these columns is exposed as an *OleDbDataReader* object within the main *OleDbDataReader* object. Of course, rows in the child readers have a higher depth level.

Another little difference between *OleDbDataReader* and other reader classes is that when using the *OleDbDataReader* class in sequential access mode, you can reread the current column value until reading past it. This is not possible with other readers, in which you can read a column value only once.

Finally, when the reader works in *SingleRow* mode, the .NET data provider for OLE DB uses this information to bind data using the OLE DB *IRow* interface if it is available. Using *IRow* instead of the default *IRowset* interface results in faster code.

# ADO.NET Data Adapters

In ADO.NET, the data adapter object acts as a two-way bridge between a data source and the *DataSet* object. The *DataSet* is a sort of disconnected, feature-rich container of data, and the adapter takes care of filling it and submitting its data back to the data source. Viewed from a higher level of abstraction, a data adapter is just a command. It differs from the data reader because it returns a disconnected set of records. In a certain way, the data reader and data adapter are the results of the ADO *Recordset* split into two. Born to be a simple COM wrapper around an SQL result set, the ADO *Recordset* soon became a rather bloated object incorporating three types of cursors—read-only, disconnected, and server.

Compared to ADO, the ADO.NET object model is simpler overall and, more importantly, made of simpler objects. Instead of providing a big monolithic object like the *Recordset*, ADO.NET supplies two smaller and highly specialized objects—the data reader and the *DataSet*. The data reader is generated by a direct query command; the *DataSet* is generated by a data adapter.

The big difference between commands and data adapters is mostly in the way each one returns the retrieved data. A query command returns a read-only cursor—the data reader. The data adapter performs its data access, grabs all the data, and packs it into an in-memory container—the *DataSet*. Under the hood, the data adapter is just an extra layer of abstraction built on top of the command/data reader pair. Internally, in fact, the data adapter just uses a command to query and a data reader to walk its way through the records and fill a user-provided *DataSet*.

## The *SqlDataAdapter* Class

By definition, a data adapter is a class that implements the *IDataAdapter* interface. However, looking at the actual implementation of the adapters in the supported providers, you can see that multiple layers of code are used. In particular, all data adapter classes inherit from a base class named *DbDataAdapter* and implement the *IDbDataAdapter* interface. The relationship is shown in Figure 5-3.

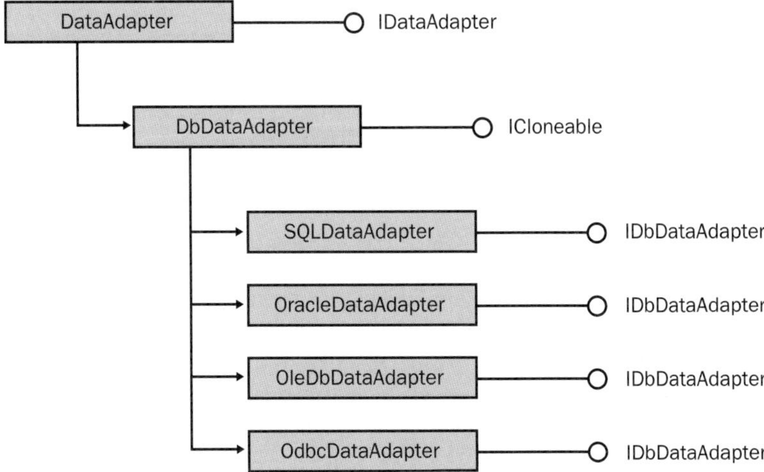


**Figure 5-3** The hierarchy of data adapters and implemented interfaces.

The *DbDataAdapter* class provides the basic implementation of the members defined in the *IDataAdapter* interface. All data adapters implemented in the .NET Framework 1.1 inherit from *DbDataAdapter*.

## Programming the SQL Server Data Adapter

Table 5-16 shows the properties of the *SqlDataAdapter* class—that is, the data adapter class for SQL Server.

**Table 5-16 Properties of the *SqlDataAdapter* Class**

| Property | Description |
|---|---|
| *AcceptChangesDuringFill* | Gets or sets a value that indicates whether or not during the population of the in-memory row insertions must be committed. *True* by default. |
| *ContinueUpdateOnError* | Gets or sets a value that indicates whether in case of row conflicts the update continues or an exception is generated. Used during batch update. |
| *DeleteCommand* | Gets or sets a statement or stored procedure to delete records from the database. Used during batch update. Is a member of the *IDbDataAdapter* interface. |
| *InsertCommand* | Gets or sets a statement or stored procedure to insert new records in the database. Used during batch update. Is a member of the *IDbDataAdapter* interface. |

*(continued)*

**Table 5-16 Properties of the *SqlDataAdapter* Class** *(continued)*

| Property | Description |
|---|---|
| *MissingMappingAction* | Gets or sets a value that determines the action to take when a table or column in the source data is not mapped to a corresponding element in the in-memory structure. Is a member of the *IDataAdapter* interface. |
| *MissingSchemaAction* | Gets or sets a value that determines the action to take when source data does not have a matching table or column in the corresponding in-memory structure. Is a member of the *IDataAdapter* interface. |
| *SelectCommand* | Gets or sets a statement or stored procedure to select records from the database. During batch update, the method is used to download metadata; it is used to select records in a query statement. Is a member of the *IDbDataAdapter* interface. |
| *TableMappings* | Gets a collection that provides the mappings between a source table and an in-memory table. Is a member of the *IDataAdapter* interface. |
| *UpdateCommand* | Gets or sets a statement or stored procedure to update records in the database. Used during batch update. Is a member of the *IDbDataAdapter* interface. |

A data adapter is a two-way channel used to read data from the data source into a memory table and to write in-memory data back to the data source. These two operations can be clearly identified in the list of properties. The four *xxxCommand* members of the *IDbDataAdapter* interface are used to control how in-memory data is written to the database. This is not really true of *SelectCommand*; although *SelectCommand* plays a role in the batch update process. The two *MissingXXX* properties and the *TableMappings* collection—the members of the *IDataAdapter* interface—represent how data read out of the data source is mapped onto client memory.

Once loaded in memory, the (disconnected) data is available for client-side updates. Batch update is the data-provider procedure that posts all the in-memory changes back to the data source. In doing so, a bunch of DBMS-specific commands are required to carry out the three basic operations—insert, update, and delete. The *InsertCommand*, *UpdateCommand*, and *DeleteCommand* properties are *SqlCommand* objects that do just this.

During the population step—that is, when the data adapter is used to load data into an ADO.NET container class—the state of the in-memory table (for example, a *DataTable* object) changes in response to the insertions. As we'll see in more detail in the "ADO.NET Container Objects" section, container objects implement a commit model and assign in-memory rows a state. The row state can be reset to *unchanged* by accepting the change. At least during the filling step, this setting can be controlled through the *AcceptChangesDuringFill* property. Table 5-17 lists the methods on the data adapter objects.

**Table 5-17 Methods of the *SqlDataAdapter* Class**

| Method | Description |
|---|---|
| *Fill* | Populates an in-memory table with rows read from the source. |
| *FillSchema* | Configures an in-memory table so that the schema matches the schema in the data source. |
| *GetFillParameters* | Returns the parameters the user set on the query statement. |
| *Update* | Updates the data source based on the current content of the specified in-memory table. It works by calling the respective INSERT, UPDATE, or DELETE statements for each inserted, updated, or deleted row, respectively, in the table. |

The data adapter uses the *SelectCommand* property to retrieve schema and data from the data source. The connection object associated with the *SelectCommand* does not need to be open. If the connection is closed before the reading occurs, it is opened to retrieve data and then closed. If the connection is open when the adapter works, it remains open.

## Filling a *DataSet* Using a Data Adapter

A data adapter object uses the *Fill* method to populate an in-memory object with data retrieved through a query. The in-memory structure is a *DataSet* or *DataTable* object. As we'll see more clearly in a moment, the *DataSet* is the in-memory counterpart of a DBMS database. It might contain multiple tables (that is, multiple *DataTable* objects) and set up relationships and constraints between tables. Each table, in turn, is made of a number of columns and rows.

Filling a *DataSet* object ultimately means filling one of its tables. The data adapter can create a new table for each result set generated by the query. The table mapping code decides how. Mapping a result set to a *DataSet* is a process articulated in two phases: table mapping and column mapping. During the first step, the data adapter determines the name of the *DataTable* that will contain the rows in the current result set. By default, each *DataTable* is given a default name you can change at will. The default name of the *DataTable* depends on the signature of the *Fill* method that was used for the call. For example, let's consider the following two *Fill* calls:

```
DataSet ds = new DataSet();
adapter.Fill(ds);
adapter.Fill(ds, "MyTable");
```

In the first call, the name of the first result set generated by the query defaults to Table. If the query produces multiple result sets, additional tables will be named Table1, Table2, and so on, appending a progressive index to the default name. In the second call, the first result set is named MyTable and the others are named after it: MyTable1, MyTable2, and so forth. The procedure is identical; what really changes in the two cases is the base name.

The names of the tables can be changed at two different moments. You can change them after the *DataSet* has been populated or, when using table mapping, you can define settings that will be used to name the tables upon creation. You define a table mapping on a data adapter object using the *TableMappings* property.

> **Note** You can also use the *Fill* method to populate a single *DataTable*. In this case, only the first result set is taken into account and only one mapping phase occurs—column mapping.
>
> ```
> DataTable dt = new DataTable();
> adapter.Fill(dt);
> ```
>
> The preceding code shows how to use the *Fill* method to populate a *DataTable*.

## The Table-Mapping Mechanism

The .NET data provider assigns a default name to each result set generated by the query. The default name is Table or any name specified by the programmer in the call to *Fill*. The adapter looks up its *TableMappings* collection for an entry that matches the default name of the result set being read. If a match is found, the data adapter reads the mapped name. Next, it attempts to locate in the *DataSet* a *DataTable* object with the name specified in the mapping, as shown in Figure 5-4.

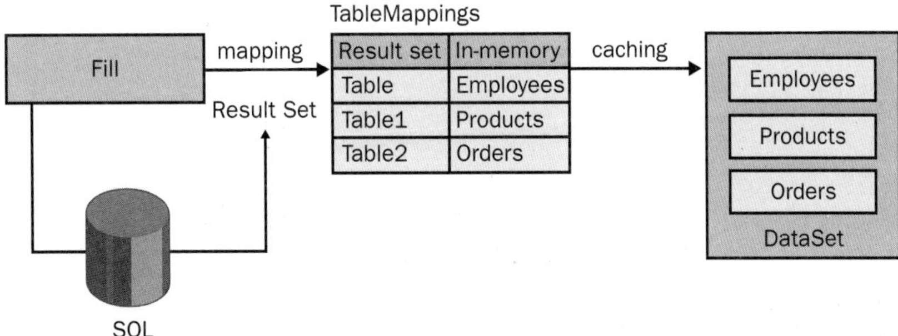


**Figure 5-4** Mapping a result set onto a *DataSet* object.

If the result set named Table has been mapped to Employees, a table named Employees is searched in the *DataSet*. If no such *DataTable* object exists, it gets created and filled. If such a *DataTable* exists in the *DataSet*, its content is merged with the contents of the result set.

The *TableMappings* property represents a collection object of type *DataTableMappingCollection*. Each contained *DataTableMapping* object defines a pair of names: a source table name and an in-memory table name. Here's how to configure a few table mappings:

```
DataSet ds = new DataSet();
DataTableMapping dtm1, dtm2, dtm3;
dtm1 = adapter.TableMappings.Add("Table", "Employees");
dtm2 = adapter.TableMappings.Add("Table1", "Products");
dtm3 = adapter.TableMappings.Add("Table2", "Orders");
adapter.Fill(ds);
```

It goes without saying that the default names you map onto your own names must coincide with the default names originated by the call to the *Fill* method. In other words, suppose you change the last line of the previous code snippet with the following one:

```
adapter.Fill(ds, "MyTable");
```

In this case, the code won't work any longer because the default names will now be MyTable, MyTable1, and MyTable2. For these names, the *TableMappings* collection would have no entries defined. Finally, bear in mind you can have any number of table mappings. The overall number of mappings doesn't necessarily have to be related to the expected number of result sets.

## The Column-Mapping Mechanism

If table mapping ended here, it wouldn't be such a big deal for us. In fact, if your goal is simply to give a mnemonic name to your *DataSet* tables, use the following code. The final effect is exactly the same.

```
DataSet ds = new DataSet();
adapter.Fill(ds);
ds.Tables["Table"].TableName = "Employees";
ds.Tables["Table1"].TableName = "Products";
```

The mapping mechanism, though, has another, rather interesting, facet: column mapping. Column mapping establishes a link between a column in the result set and a column in the mapped *DataTable* object. Column mappings are stored in the *ColumnMappings* collection property defined in the *DataTableMapping* class. The following code shows how to create a column mapping:

```
DataSet ds = new DataSet();
DataTableMapping dtm1;
dtm1 = adapter.TableMappings.Add("Table", "Employees");
dtm1.ColumnMappings.Add("employeeid", "ID");
dtm1.ColumnMappings.Add("firstname", "Name");
dtm1.ColumnMappings.Add("lastname", "FamilyName");
adapter.Fill(ds);
```

Figure 5-5 extends the previous diagram (Figure 5-4) and includes details of the column-mapping mechanism.

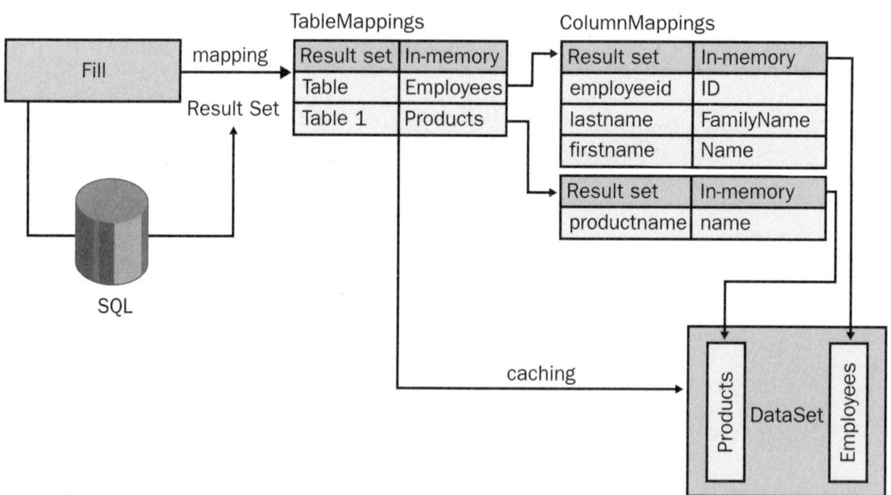


**Figure 5-5** How the table and column mappings control the population of the *DataSet.*

In the preceding code, the source column *employeeid* is renamed to *ID* and placed in a *DataTable* named *Employees.* The name of the column is the only argument you can change at this level. Bear in mind that all this mapping takes place automatically within the body of the *Fill* method. When *Fill* terminates, each column in the source result set has been transformed into a *DataTable* column object—an instance of the *DataColumn* class.

## Missing Mapping Action

The *Fill* method accomplishes two main operations. First, it maps the source result sets onto in-memory tables. Second, it fills the tables with the data fetched from the physical data source. While accomplishing either of these tasks, the *Fill* method could raise some special exceptions. An exception is an anomalous situation that needs to be specifically addressed codewise. When the adapter can't find a table or column mapping, or when a required *DataTable* or *DataColumn* can't be found, the data adapter throws a kind of lightweight exception.

Unlike real exceptions that must be resolved in code, this special breed of data adapter exceptions have to be resolved declaratively by choosing an action from a small set of allowable options. Data adapters raise two types of lightweight exceptions: missing mapping actions and missing schema actions.

A missing mapping action is required in two circumstances that can occur when the data adapter is collecting data to fill the *DataSet*. You need it if a default name is not found in the *TableMappings* collection, or if a column name is not available in the table's *ColumnMappings* collection. The data adapter's *MissingMappingAction* property is the tool you have for customizing the behavior of the data adapter in face of such an exception. Allowable values for the property, which are listed in Table 5-18, come from the *MissingMappingAction* enumeration.

**Table 5-18 The *MissingMappingAction* Enumeration**

| Value | Description |
|---|---|
| *Error* | An exception is generated if a missing column or table is detected. |
| *Ignore* | The unmapped column or table is ignored. |
| *Passthrough* | Default option, add the missing table or column to the structure. |

Unless you explicitly set the *MissingMappingAction* property prior to filling the data adapter, the property assumes a default value of *Passthrough*. As a result, missing tables and columns are added using the default name. If you set the *MissingMappingAction* property to *Ignore*, any unmapped table or column is simply ignored. No error is detected, but there will be no content for the incriminating result set (or one of its columns) in the target *DataSet*. If the *MissingMappingAction* property is set to *Error*, the adapter is limited to throwing a *SystemException* exception whenever a missing mapping is detected.

Once the data adapter is done with the mapping phase, it takes care of actually populating the target *DataSet* with the content of the selected result sets. Any required *DataTable* or *DataColumn* object that is not available in the target *DataSet* triggers another lightweight exception and requires another declarative action: the missing schema action.

## Missing Schema Action

A missing schema action is required if the *DataSet* does not contain a table with the name that has been determined during the table-mapping step. Similarly, the same action is required if the *DataSet* table does not contain a column with the expected mapping name. *MissingSchemaAction* is the property you set to indicate the action you want to be taken in case of an insufficient table schema. Allowable values for the property come from the *MissingSchemaAction* enumeration and are listed in Table 5-19.

**Table 5-19 The *MissingSchemaAction* Enumeration**

| Value | Description |
|---|---|
| *Error* | An exception is generated if a missing column or table is detected. |
| *Ignore* | The unmapped column or table is ignored. |
| *Add* | The default option. Completes the schema by adding any missing item. |
| *AddWithKey* | Also adds primary key and constraints. |

By default, the *MissingSchemaAction* property is set to *Add*. As a result, the *DataSet* is completed by adding any constituent item that is missing—*DataTable* or *DataColumn*. Bear in mind, though, that the schema information added in this way for each column is very limited. It simply includes name and type. If you want extra information—such as the primary key, autoincrement, read-only, and allow-null settings—use the *AddWithKey* option instead.

Note that even if you use the *AddWithKey* option, not all available information about the column is really loaded into the *DataColumn*. For example, *AddWithKey* marks a column as autoincrement, but it doesn't set the related seed and step properties. Also the default value for the source column, if any, is not automatically copied. Only the primary key is imported; any additional indexes you might have set in the database are not. As for the other two options, *Ignore* and *Error*, they work exactly as they do with the *MissingMappingAction* property.

## Prefilling the Schema

*MissingMappingAction* and *MissingSchemaAction* are not as expensive as real exceptions, but they still affect your code. Put another way, filling a *DataSet* that already contains all the needed schema information results in faster code. The advantage of this approach is more evident if your code happens to repeatedly fill an empty *DataSet* with a fixed schema. In this case, using a global *DataSet* object pre-filled with schema information helps to prevent all those requests for recovery actions. The *FillSchema* method just ensures that all the required objects are created beforehand.

```
DataTable[] FillSchema(DataSet ds, SchemaType mappingMode);
```

*FillSchema* takes a *DataSet* and adds as many tables to it as needed by the query command associated with the data adapter. The method returns an array with all the *DataTable* objects created (only schema, no data). The mapping-mode parameter can be one of the values defined in the *SchemaType* enumeration. The *SchemaType* enumeration values are listed in Table 5-20.

**Table 5-20 The *SchemaType* Enumeration**

| Value | Description |
|---|---|
| *Mapped* | Apply any existing table mappings to the incoming schema. Configure the *DataSet* with the transformed schema. Recommended option. |
| *Source* | Ignore any table mappings on the data adapter. Configure the *DataSet* using the incoming schema without applying any transformations. |

The *Mapped* option describes what happens when mappings are defined. *Source*, on the other hand, deliberately ignores any mappings you might have set. In this case, the tables in the *DataSet* retain their default name and all the columns maintain the original name they were given in the source tables.

## How Batch Update Works

Batch update consists of the submission of an entire set of changes to the database. The batch update basically repeats the user actions that produced the changes but has the database—rather than the *DataSet*—as the target. Batch update assumes that the application enters its changes to the data set in an offline manner. In a multiuser environment, this might pose design problems if users concurrently access on the server the same data you're editing offline. When you post your changes on a record that another person has modified in the meantime, whose changes win out?

### Data Conflicts and Optimistic Lock

The possibility of data conflicts represents a design issue, but it isn't necessarily a problem for the application. Batch update in a multiuser environment creates conflict only if the changes you enter are somewhat implied by the original values you have read. In such a case, if in the time elapsed between your fetch and the batch update someone else has changed the rows, you might want to reconsider or reject your most recent updates. Conflicts detected at update time might introduce significant overhead that could make the batch update solution much less exciting. In environments with a low degree of data contention, batch update can be effective because it allows for disconnected architectures, higher scalability, and considerably simpler coding.

To submit client changes to the server, use the data adapter's *Update* method. Data can be submitted only on a per-table basis. If you call *Update* without specifying any table name, a default name of Table is assumed. If no table exists with that name, an exception is raised.

```
adapter.Update(ds, "MyTable");
```

The *Update* method prepares and executes a tailor-made INSERT, UPDATE, or DELETE statement for each inserted, updated, or deleted row in the specified table. Rows are processed according to their natural order, and the row state determines the operation to accomplish. The *Update* method has several overloads and returns an integer, which represents the number of rows successfully updated.

When a row being updated returns an error, an exception is raised and the batch update process is stopped. You can prevent this from happening by setting the *ContinueUpdateOnError* property to *true*. In this case, the batch update terminates only when all the rows have been processed. Rows for which the update completed successfully are committed and marked as unchanged in the *DataSet*. For other rows, the application must decide what to do and restart the update if needed.

> **Note** The batch update is a loop that executes one user-defined database command for each inserted, modified, or deleted row in a *DataSet* table. In no way does the batch update process send the whole *DataSet* to the database for server-side processing.

## Command Builders

The data adapter provides a bunch of command properties—*InsertCommand*, *DeleteCommand*, and *UpdateCommand*—to let the programmer control and customize the way in which in-memory updates are submitted to the database server. These properties represent a quantum leap from ADO, in which update commands were SQL commands silently generated by the library. If you don't quite see the importance of this change, consider that with ADO.NET you can use stored procedures to perform batch updates and even work with non-SQL data providers.

The commands can also be generated automatically and exposed directly to the data-adapter engine. Command-builder objects do that for you. A command-builder object—for example, the *SqlCommandBuilder* class—cannot be used in all cases. The automatic generation of commands can take place only under certain circumstances. In particular, command builders do not generate anything if the table is obtained by joining columns from more than one table and if calculated—or aggregate—columns are detected. Command builders are extremely helpful and code-saving only when they are called to deal with single-table updates. How can a command builder generate update statements for a generic table? This is where the fourth command property—the *SelectCommand* property—fits in.

A command builder employs *SelectCommand* to obtain all the metadata necessary to build the update commands. To use command builders, you must set *SelectCommand* with a query string that contains a primary key and a few column names. Only those fields will be used for the update, and the insertion and key fields will be used to uniquely identify rows to update or delete. Note that the command text of *SelectCommand* runs in the provider-specific way that makes it return only metadata and no rows.

The association between the data adapter and the command builder is established through the builder's constructor, as shown in the following code:

```
SqlCommand cmd = new SqlCommand();
cmd.CommandText = "SELECT employeeid, lastname FROM Employees";
cmd.Connection = conn;
adapter.SelectCommand = cmd;
SqlCommandBuilder builder = new SqlCommandBuilder(adapter);
```

The builder requests metadata and generates the commands the first time they are required and then caches them. Each command is also exposed through a particular method—*GetInsertCommand*, *GetUpdateCommand*, and *GetDeleteCommand*. Note that these methods return temporary command objects but *not* the real command objects that will be used to carry the batch update on. For this reason, any changes made to the command objects obtained in this way are lost. If you want to use the autogenerated commands as a base for your own further changes, you should first assign them to the corresponding *XXXCommand* properties of the data adapter and then enter changes. The command builder won't overwrite any command property that is not null.

**Note** The behavior of data adapters and command builders for other managed providers does not differ in a relevant way from what we described here for the SQL Server .NET data provider.

### The Case of Server Cursors

As of version 1.1 of the .NET Framework, ADO.NET does not support server cursors, such as the ADO *adOpenKeyset* and *adOpenDynamic* cursors. If you absolutely need that functionality in your application, there's probably no better choice than sticking to ADO. In a future version of the .NET Framework, the architecture of the .NET managed provider is expected to be enhanced to allow for server cursors. You should not expect it to be a general implementation of server cursors, though. Rather, it will be a database-specific implementation.

Server cursors will be exposed to applications through a new executor method in the provider's command class and return an instance of a new data-oriented class. For SQL Server, this class is tentatively named *SqlResultSet*.

## ADO.NET Container Objects

The *System.Data* namespace contains several collection-like objects that, combined, provide an in-memory representation of the DBMS relational programming model. The *DataSet* class looks like a catalog, whereas the *DataTable* maps to an individual table. The *DataRelation* class represents a relationship between tables, and the *DataView* creates a filtered view of a table's data. In addition, the *System.Data* namespace also supports constraints and a relatively simple model of indexing.

The facilities of the memory-resident database model tout a programming model in which disconnection is a key feature rather than a precise requirement. Using the *DataSet* model, for example, you can filter and sort the data on the client before it gets to the middle tier. Having such facilities available within the *DataSet* means that once the data is there, you don't need to go back to the database to get a different view on the data. The data stored in the *DataSet* is self-sufficient, which makes the whole model inherently disconnected.

The *DataSet* is great for storing state that survives across page requests—for example, cached catalog information, a shopping cart, or similar kinds of data. Storing a *DataSet* in ASP.NET global objects such as *Session* or *Application* doesn't have the same scalability implications that it had in ASP. ADO.NET objects are thread safe for read operations, but they need to be explicitly synchronized for write operations. The *DataSet*, though—and more generally, the disconnected model—is not appropriate for just any sort of Web application.

> **Note** It can be argued that in a Web application, using the *DataSet* as the data container attached to a command object might be a solution. This solution, though, is problematic if you consider Windows Forms applications in which you can leverage the power of the client. Generally, an interesting use of the *DataSet* that makes sense both for Web and desktop scenarios is in moving data around between components and tiers. The *DataSet* is great at encapsulating tables of data and relationships. It can also be passed around between tiers as a monolithic object. Finally, it can be serialized into and out of XML, meaning that data and related schema can be moved between tiers in a loosely coupled manner.

The *DataSet* class is the principal component in the ADO.NET object model, but several others are satellite classes that play a fundamental role. ADO.NET container classes are listed Table 5-21.

**Table 5-21 ADO.NET Container Classes**

| Class | Description |
|---|---|
| *DataSet* | An in-memory cache of data made of tables, relations, and constraints. Serializable and remotable, it can be filled from a variety of data sources and works regardless of which one is used. |
| *DataTable* | Logically equivalent to a disconnected ADO *Recordset*. Represents a relational table of data with a collection of columns and rows. |
| *DataColumn* | Represents a column in a *DataTable* object. |
| *DataRow* | Represents a row in a *DataTable* object. |
| *DataView* | Defined on top of a particular table. Creates a filtered view of data. Can be configured to support editing and sorting. The data view is not a copy of the data—just a mask. |
| *DataRelation* | Represents a relationship between two tables in the same *DataSet*. The relationship is set on a common column. |
| *UniqueConstraint* | Represents a restriction on a set of table columns in which all values must be unique. |
| *ForeignKeyConstraint* | Represents an action enforced on a set of table columns when a value or row is either deleted or updated. The columns must be in a primary key/foreign key relationship. |

A key point to remember about ADO.NET container classes is that they work regardless of the data source used. You can populate the tables in a *DataSet* by using the results of a SQL Server query as well as file system information or data read out of a real-time device. Even more importantly, none of the ADO.NET container classes retains information about the source. Like array or collection objects, they just contain data. Unlike array or collection objects, though, they provide facilities to relate and manage data in a database-like fashion.

> **Note** Of all the ADO.NET container classes, only *DataSet* and *DataTable* can be serialized using the .NET Framework formatters—the *BinaryFormatter* and *SoapFormatter* classes. Only the *DataSet* can be serialized to XML. The *DataSet* class supports two flavors of XML serialization—through the *WriteXml* method and through the XML serializer.

## The *DataSet* Object

The *DataSet* class inherits from the *MarshalByValueComponent* class and implements interfaces as shown in Figure 5-6.

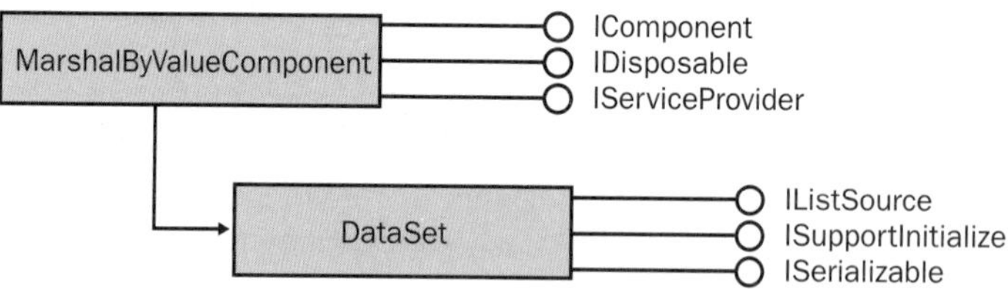


**Figure 5-6** The structure of the *DataSet* class.

The parent class provides the *DataSet* with the capability of being marshaled by value, meaning that a copy of the serialized object is passed down to remote callers. Other base behaviors are provided by the implemented interfaces. The *IListSource* interface makes it possible to return a data-bound list of elements, while the *ISupportInitialize* interface allows for a *BeginInit* and *EndInit* pair of methods to bracket initialization of properties. Finally, *ISerializable* makes the class capable of controlling how its data is serialized to a .NET formatter. Table 5-22 lists the properties of the *DataSet* class.

**Table 5-22 Properties of the *DataSet* Class**

| Property | Description |
|---|---|
| *CaseSensitive* | Gets or sets a value that indicates whether string comparisons within *DataTable* objects are case sensitive. |
| *DataSetName* | Gets or sets the name of the *DataSet*. |
| *DefaultViewManager* | Gets the default view manager object—an instance of the *DataViewManager* class—that contains settings for each table in the *DataSet*. |
| *EnforceConstraints* | Gets or sets a value that indicates whether constraint rules are enforced when attempting any update operation. |
| *ExtendedProperties* | Gets the collection of customized user information associated with the *DataSet*. |
| *HasErrors* | Gets errors in any of the child *DataTable* objects. |
| *Locale* | Gets or sets the locale information used to compare strings within the tables. |
| *Namespace* | Gets or sets the namespace of the *DataSet*. |
| *Prefix* | Gets or sets the prefix that aliases the namespace of the *DataSet*. |
| *Relations* | Gets the collection of the relations set between pairs of child tables. |
| *Tables* | Gets the collection of contained tables. |

The *Namespace* and *Prefix* properties affect the way in which the *DataSet* serializes itself to XML. The name of the *DataSet* is also used to set the root node of the XML representation. If the *DataSetName* is empty, the *NewDataSet* string is used. The methods of the class are listed in Table 5-23.

**Table 5-23 Methods of the *DataSet* Class**

| Method | Description |
|---|---|
| *AcceptChanges* | Commits all the changes made to all the tables in the *DataSet* since it was loaded or since the last time the method was called. |
| *Clear* | Removes all rows in all tables. |
| *Clone* | Copies the structure of the *DataSet*, including all table schemas, relations, and constraints. No data is copied. |

*(continued)*

**Table 5-23 Methods of the *DataSet* Class** *(continued)*

| Method | Description |
|---|---|
| *Copy* | Makes a deep copy of the object, including schema and data. |
| *GetChanges* | Returns a copy of the *DataSet* containing only the changes made to it since it was last loaded or since *AcceptChanges* was called. |
| *GetXml* | Returns the XML representation of the data stored. |
| *GetXmlSchema* | Returns the XSD schema for the XML string representing the data stored in the *DataSet*. |
| *HasChanges* | Indicates whether there are new, deleted, or modified rows in any of the contained tables. |
| *InferXmlSchema* | Replicates into the *DataSet* the table structure inferred from the specified XML document. |
| *Merge* | Merges the specified ADO.NET object (*DataSet*, *DataTable*, or an array of *DataRow* objects) into the current *DataSet*. |
| *ReadXml* | Populates the *DataSet* reading schema and data from the specified XML document. |
| *ReadXmlSchema* | Replicates into the *DataSet* the table structure read from the specified XML schema. |
| *RejectChanges* | Rolls back all the changes made to all the tables since it was created or since the last time *AcceptChanges* was called. |
| *Reset* | Empties tables, relations, and constraints, resetting the *DataSet* to its default state. |
| *WriteXml* | Serializes the *DataSet* contents to XML. |
| *WriteXmlSchema* | Writes the *DataSet* structure as an XML schema. |

To make a full, deep copy of the *DataSet*, you must resort to the *Copy* method. Only in this case, you duplicate the object. The following code does not duplicate the object:

```
DataSet tmp = ds;
```

If you simply assign the current *DataSet* reference to another variable, you duplicate the reference but not the object. Use the following code to duplicate the object:

```
DataSet tmp = ds.Copy();
```

The *Copy* method creates and returns a new instance of the *DataSet* object and ensures that all the tables, relations, and constraints are duplicated. The *Clone* method is limited to returning a new *DataSet* object in which all the properties have been replicated but no data in the tables is copied.

## Merging *DataSet* Objects

A merge operation is typically accomplished by a client application to update an existing *DataSet* object with the latest changes read from the data source. The *Merge* method should be used to fuse together two *DataSet* objects that have nearly identical schemas. The two schemas, though, are not strictly required to be identical.

The first step in the merge operation compares the schemas of the involved *DataSet* objects to see whether they match. If the *DataSet* to be imported contains new columns or a new table source, what happens depends on the missing schema action specified. By default, any missing schema element is added to the target *DataSet*, but you can change the behavior by choosing the *Merge* overload that allows for a *MissingSchemaAction* parameter.

As the second step, the *Merge* method attempts to merge the data by looking at the changed rows in the *DataSet* to be imported. Any modified or deleted row is matched to the corresponding row in the existing *DataSet* by using the primary key value. Added rows are simply added to the existing *DataSet* and retain their primary key value.

The merge operation is an atomic operation that must guarantee integrity and consistency only at its end. For this reason, constraints are disabled during a merge operation. However, if at the end of the merge the original constraints can't be restored—for example, a unique constraint is violated—an exception is thrown, but no uploaded data gets lost. In this case, the *Merge* method completely disables constraints in the *DataSet*. It sets the *EnforceConstraints* property to *false* and marks all invalid rows in error. To restore constraints, you must first resolve errors.

## The *DataSet* Commit Model

When the *DataSet* is first loaded, all the rows in all tables are marked as unchanged. The state of a table row is stored in a property named *RowState*. Allowable values for the row state are in the *DataRowState* enumeration listed in Table 5-24.

**Table 5-24 States of a Table Row**

| Value | Description |
|---|---|
| *Added* | The row has been added to the table. |
| *Deleted* | The row is marked for deletion from the parent table. |
| *Detached* | Either the row has been created but not yet added to the table or the row has been removed from the rows collection. |
| *Modified* | Some columns within the row have been changed. |
| *Unchanged* | No changes have been made since the last call to *AcceptChanges*. This is also the state of all rows when the table is first created. |

The *AcceptChanges* method has the power to commit all the changes and accept the current values as the new original values of the table. After *AcceptChanges* is called, all changes are cleared. The *RejectChanges* method, on the other hand, rolls back all the pending changes and restores the original values. Note that the *DataSet* retains original values until changes are committed or rejected.

The commit model is applicable at various levels. In particular, by calling *AcceptChanges* or *RejectChanges* on the *DataSet* object, you commit or roll back changes for all the rows in all the contained tables. If you call the same methods on a *DataTable* object, the effect is for all the rows in the specified table. Finally, you can also accept or reject changes for an individual row in a particular table.

## Serializing Contents to XML

The contents of a *DataSet* object can be serialized as XML in two ways, which I'll call *stateless* and *stateful*. Although these expressions are not common throughout the ADO.NET documentation, I feel that they perfectly describe the gist of the two possible approaches. A stateless representation takes a snapshot of the current instance of the data and renders it according to a particular XML schema—the ADO.NET normal form—as shown in the following code:

```
<MyDataSet>
    <Employees>
        <ID>...</ID>
        <Name>...</Name>
    </Employees>
    ⋮
    <Orders>
        <OrderID>...</OrderID>
        <OrderDate>...</OrderDate>
        <Amount>...</Amount>
    </Orders>
</MyDataSet>
```

The root node appears after the *DataSetName* property. Nodes one level deeper represent rows of all tables and are named as the table. Each row node contains as many children as there are columns in the row. This code snippet refers to a *DataSet* with two tables—Employees and Orders—with two and three columns, respectively. That kind of string is what the *GetXml* method returns and what the *WriteXml* method writes out when the default write mode is chosen.

```
dataSet.WriteXml(fileName);
dataSet.WriteXml(fileName, mode);
```

A stateful representation, on the other hand, contains the history of the data in the object and includes information about changes as well as pending errors. Table 5-25 summarizes the writing options available for use with *WriteXml* through the *XmlWriteMode* enumeration.

**Table 5-25 The *XmlWriteMode* Enumeration**

| Write Mode | Description |
|---|---|
| *IgnoreSchema* | Writes the contents of the *DataSet* as XML data without schema. |
| *WriteSchema* | Writes the contents of the *DataSet*, including an inline XSD schema. The schema cannot be inserted as XDR, nor can it be added as a reference. |
| *DiffGram* | Writes the contents of the *DataSet* as a DiffGram, including original and current values. |

*IgnoreSchema* is the default option. The following code demonstrates the typical way to serialize a *DataSet* to an XML file:

```
StreamWriter sw = new StreamWriter(fileName);
dataset.WriteXml(sw);    // defaults to XmlWriteMode.IgnoreSchema
sw.Close();
```

A DiffGram is an XML serialization format that includes both the original values and current values of each row in each table. In particular, a DiffGram contains the current instance of rows with the up-to-date values plus a section where all the original values for changed rows are grouped. Each row is given a unique identifier that is used to track changes between the two sections of the DiffGram. This relationship looks a lot like a foreign-key relationship. The following listing outlines the structure of a DiffGram:

```
<diffgr:diffgram
    xmlns:msdata="urn:schemas-microsoft-com:xml-msdata"
    xmlns:diffgr="urn:schemas-microsoft-com:xml-diffgram-v1">
    <DataSet>
    ⋮
    </DataSet>

    <diffgr:before>
    ⋮
    </diffgr:before>

    <diffgr:errors>
    ⋮
    </diffgr:errors>
</diffgr:diffgram>
```

The *<diffgr:diffgram>* root node can have up to three children. The first is the *DataSet* object with its current contents, including newly added rows and modified rows (but not deleted rows). The actual name of this subtree depends on the *DataSetName* property of the source *DataSet* object. If the *DataSet* has no name, the subtree's root is *NewDataSet*. The subtree rooted in the *<diffgr:before>* node contains enough information to restore the original state of all modified rows. For example, it still contains any row that has been deleted as well as the original content of any modified row. All columns affected by any change are tracked in the *<diffgr:before>* subtree. The last subtree is *<diffgr:errors>*, and it contains information about any errors that might have occurred on a particular row.

> **Note** The XML serialization of the *DataSet* object is a relatively large topic that deserves much more space than this section allows. The topic is covered in detail in Chapters 9 and 10 of my book, *Applied XML Programming for Microsoft .NET* (Microsoft Press, 2002).

## The *DataTable* Object

The *DataTable* object represents one table of in-memory data. Mostly used as a container of data within a *DataSet*, the *DataTable* is also valid as a stand-alone object that contains tabular data. The internal structure of the class is identical to that depicted in Figure 5-6 for the *DataSet*. The *DataTable* and *DataSet* are the only ADO.NET objects that can be remoted and serialized.

Just as with a *DataSet*, a *DataTable* can be created programmatically. In this case, you first define its schema and then add new rows. The following code snippet shows how to create a new table within a *DataSet*:

```
DataSet ds = new DataSet();
DataTable tableEmp = new DataTable("Employees");
tableEmp.Columns.Add("ID", typeof(int));
tableEmp.Columns.Add("Name", typeof(string));
ds.Tables.Add(tableEmp);
```

The table is named Employees and features two columns—ID and Name. The table is empty because no rows have been added yet. To add rows, you first create a new row object by using the *NewRow* method:

```
DataRow row = tableEmp.NewRow();
row["ID"] = 1;
row["Name"] = "Joe Users";
tableEmp.Rows.Add(row);
```

The *DataTable* contains a collection of constraint objects that can be used to ensure the integrity of the data and signals changes to its data-firing events.

Let's have a closer look at the programming interface of the *DataTable*, beginning with properties. Table 5-26 lists the properties of the *DataTable* class.

**Table 5-26 Properties of the *DataTable* Class**

| Property | Description |
|---|---|
| *CaseSensitive* | Gets or sets whether string comparisons are case-sensitive. |
| *ChildRelations* | Gets the collection of child relations for this table. |
| *Columns* | Gets the collection of columns that belong to this table. |
| *Constraints* | Gets the collection of constraints maintained by this table. |
| *DataSet* | Gets the *DataSet* this table belongs to. |
| *DefaultView* | Gets the default *DataView* object for this table. |
| *DisplayExpression* | Gets or sets a display string for the table. Used in the *ToString* method together with *TableName*. |
| *ExtendedProperties* | Gets the collection of customized user information. |
| *HasErrors* | Gets a value that indicates whether there are errors in any of the rows. |
| *Locale* | Gets or sets locale information used to compare strings. |
| *MinimumCapacity* | Gets or sets the initial starting size for the table. |
| *Namespace* | Gets or sets the namespace for the XML representation of the table. |
| *ParentRelations* | Gets the collection of parent relations for this table. |
| *Prefix* | Gets or sets the prefix that aliases the table namespace. |
| *PrimaryKey* | Gets or sets an array of columns that function as the primary key for the table. |
| *Rows* | Gets the collection of rows that belong to this table. |
| *TableName* | Gets or sets the name of the *DataTable* object. |

The *ExtendedProperties* property is a collection shared by several ADO.NET objects, including *DataSet* and *DataColumn*. It manages name/value pairs and accepts values of object type. You can use this collection as a generic cargo variable in which to store any user information. Although the *ExtendedProperties* collection can accept any object, you should always store strings. If you use something other than strings, you might run into troubles if the *DataTable* gets serialized at some time. When the table is serialized, any item in the *ExtendedProperties* collection is serialized as a string using the output of the *ToString* method. This fact doesn't ensure that the object will be correctly restored during the deserialization step. The methods of the *DataTable* class are listed in Table 5-27.

**Table 5-27 Methods of the *DataTable* Class**

| Method | Description |
|---|---|
| *AcceptChanges* | Commits all the pending changes made to the table. |
| *BeginInit* | Begins the initialization of the table. Used when the table is used on a form or by another component. |
| *BeginLoadData* | Turns off notifications, index maintenance, and constraints while loading data. |
| *Clear* | Removes all the data from the table. |
| *Clone* | Clones the structure of the table. Copies constraints and schema, but doesn't copy data. |
| *Compute* | Computes the given expression on the rows that meet the specified filter criteria. Returns the result of the computation as an object. |
| *Copy* | Copies both the structure and data for the table. |
| *EndInit* | Ends the initialization of the table. Closes the operation started with *BeginInit*. |
| *EndLoadData* | Turns on notifications, index maintenance, and constraints after loading data. |
| *GetChanges* | Gets a copy of the table containing all changes made to it since it was last loaded or since *AcceptChanges* was called. |
| *GetErrors* | Gets an array of all the *DataRow* objects that contain errors. |
| *ImportRow* | Performs a deep copy of a *DataRow*, and loads it into the table. Settings, including original and current values, are preserved. |
| *LoadDataRow* | Finds and updates a specific row. If no matching row is found, a new row is created using the given values. Uses the primary keys to locate the row. |
| *NewRow* | Creates a new *DataRow* object with the schema as the table. |
| *RejectChanges* | Rolls back all changes that have been made to the table since it was loaded or since the last time *AcceptChanges* was called. |
| *Reset* | Resets the *DataTable* object to its default state. |
| *Select* | Gets the array of *DataRow* objects that match the criteria. |

Any row in the *DataTable* is represented by a *DataRow* object, whereas the *DataColumn* object represents a column. The *Select* method implements a simple but effective query engine for the rows of the table. The result set is an array of *DataRow* objects. The filter string is expressed in an internal language that looks like that used to build WHERE clauses in a SQL SELECT statement. The following line of code is a valid expression that selects all records in which the ID is greater than 5 and the name begins with A:

```
tableEmp.Select("ID >5 AND Name LIKE 'A%'");
```

Refer to the .NET Framework documentation for the full syntax supported by the *Select* method. Note that it's the same language you can use to define expression-based *DataTable* columns.

## Performing Computations

The *Compute* method of the *DataTable* class calculates a value by applying a given expression to the table rows that match a specified filter. Expressions can include any sort of Boolean and arithmetic operators, but they can also include more interesting aggregate functions such as *Min*, *Max*, *Count*, and *Sum*, plus a few more statistical operators such as average, standard deviation, and variance. The following code counts the rows in which the Name column begins with A:

```
int numRecs = (int) tableEmp.Compute("Count(ID)", " Name LIKE 'A%'");
```

The *Compute* method has two possible overloads—one that takes only the expression to compute and one that also adds a filter string, as shown in the preceding code. Note that all aggregate functions can operate on a single column. This means you can directly compute the sum on two columns, as in the following pseudo-code:

```
Sum(quantity * price)
```

To compute functions on multiple columns, you can leverage the capabilities of the *DataColumn* object and, in particular, its support for dynamic expressions. For example, you can define an in-memory column named *order_item_price* as follows:

```
tableEmp.Columns.Add("order_item_price", typeof(double), "quantity*price");
```

At this point, you can compute the sum of that column using the following expression:

```
Sum(order_item_price)
```

## Columns of a Table

A *DataColumn* object represents the schema of a column in a *DataTable* object. It provides properties that describe the characteristics and capabilities of the column. The *DataColumn* properties include *AllowDBNull*, *Unique*, *ReadOnly*, *DefaultValue*, and *Expression*. As discussed earlier, some of these properties are automatically set with the corresponding information read from the data source—at least when the data source is a database.

A *DataColumn* object has a name and type; sometimes it can also have an associated expression. The content of an expression-based column is a function of one or more columns combined with operators and aggregates to form a full expression. When an expression-based column is created, ADO.NET precalculates and caches all the values for the column as if they were native data. At the same time, ADO.NET tracks the columns involved and monitors them for changes. It does so by registering an internal handler for the *DataTable*'s *RowChanged* event. When a row changes in one of the columns involved in the expression, the computed column is automatically refreshed.

Expression-based columns are extremely powerful for setting up more effective and practical forms of data binding, as we'll see in the next chapter. In addition, expression-based columns work side by side with table relations and, using both, you can implement really powerful features. We'll demonstrate this later in the "Data Relations" section.

## Rows of a Table

The data in a table is represented with a collection of *DataRow* objects. A row has a state, an array of values, and possibly error information. The *DataTable* maintains various versions of the row. You can query for a particular version at any time using the *Item* accessor property. The following code snippet shows how to read the original value of a column in a particular *DataRow* object. By default, you are returned the current value.

```
Response.Write(row["Name", DataRowVersion.Original].ToString());
```

All the values in a row can be accessed either individually or as a whole. When accessing all the values in a row, you use the *ItemArray* property, which passes you an array of objects, one for each column. The *ItemArray* property is a quick way to read values from a row and to set all the columns on a row in a single shot.

The *DataRow* class doesn't have a public constructor. As a result, a data row can be created only implicitly using the *NewRow* method on a base table. The *NewRow* method populates the *DataRow* object with as many entries as there are columns in the *DataTable*. In this case, the table provides the schema for the row, but the row is in no way a child of the table. To add a row to a *DataTable*, you must explicitly add it to the *Rows* collection.

```
tableEmp.Rows.Add(row);
```

Note that a *DataRow* object cannot be associated with more than one table at a time. To load a row into another table, you can use the *ImportRow* method, which basically duplicates the *DataRow* object and loads it into the specified table. A row can be detached from its parent table using the *Remove* method. If you use the *Delete* method, on the other hand, the row will be marked for deletion but still remain part of the table.

> **Note** Objects removed from a parent collection are not automatically destroyed or, at least, not until they go out of scope and become fodder for the garbage collector. This consideration holds true for several ADO.NET objects including, but not limited to, the *DataRow*. A *DataTable*, for example, can be detached from the *DataSet* by simply removing it from the *Tables* collection. However, this doesn't mean that the *DataTable* is automatically deleted as an object.

## Table Constraints

A constraint is a logical rule set on a table to preserve the integrity of the data. For example, a constraint determines what happens when you delete a record in a table that is related to another one. The .NET Framework supports two types of constraints—*ForeignKeyConstraint* and *UniqueConstraint*.

In particular, the *ForeignKeyConstraint* class sets the rules that govern how the table propagates changes to related tables. For example, suppose you have two related tables, one with employees and one with orders. What happens when an employee is deleted? Should you delete all the related records too? The *ForeignKeyConstraint* object associated with the Employees table will determine what is related to it in the Orders table. You create a *ForeignKeyConstraint* object as shown below:

```
DataColumn c1 = tableEmp.Columns("empID");
DataColumn c2 = tableOrd.Columns("empID");
ForeignKeyConstraint fk = new ForeignKeyConstraint("EmpOrders", c1, c2);
// configure the constraint object
tableOrd.Constraints.Add(fk);
```

The *ForeignKeyConstraint* constructor takes the name of the object plus two *DataColumn* objects. The first *DataColumn* object represents the column (or the columns) on the parent table; the second *DataColumn* object represents the column (or the columns) in the child table. The constraint is added to the child table and is configured using the *UpdateRule*, *DeleteRule*, and *AcceptRejectRule* properties. While setting the *UpdateRule* and *DeleteRule* properties, you use values taken from the *Rule* enumeration. *AcceptRejectRule* is the enumeration used to look for the *AcceptRejectRule* property of the same name. For updates and deletions, the child table can cascade the change or set the involved rows to null or default values. Alternately, the child table can simply ignore the changes. The *AcceptRejectRule* property is processed when the *AcceptChanges* method is called on the parent row to commit changes. The choices for the constraint are limited to either cascading or ignoring changes.

The *UniqueConstraint* class ensures that a single column (or an array of columns) have unique, nonduplicated values. There are several ways to set a unique constraint. You can create one explicitly using the class constructor and adding the resulting object to the *Constraints* collection of the *DataTable*.

```
UniqueConstraint uc;
uc = new UniqueConstraint(tableEmp.Columns("empID"));
tableEmp.Constraints.Add(uc);
```

A unique constraint can also be created implicitly by setting the *Unique* property of the column to *true*. In contrast, setting the *Unique* property to *false* resets the constraint. In addition, adding a column to the in-memory primary key for a table would automatically create a unique constraint for the column. Note that a primary key on a *DataTable* object is an array of *DataColumn* objects that is used to index and sort the rows. The *Select* method on the *DataTable* exploits the index as well as other methods on the *DataView* class do.

> **Note** When you define a *DataColumn* as the primary key for a *DataTable* object, the table automatically sets the *AllowDBNull* property of the column to *false* and the *Unique* property to *true*. If the primary key is made of multiple columns, only the *AllowDBNull* property is automatically set to *false*.

## Data Relations

A data relation represents a parent/child relationship between two *DataTable* objects in the same *DataSet*. In the .NET Framework, a data relation is represented by a *DataRelation* object. You set a relation between two tables based on matching columns in the parent and child tables. The matching columns in the two related tables can have different names, but they must have the same type. All the relations for the tables in a *DataSet* are stored in the *Relations* collection. Table 5-28 lists the properties of the *DataRelation* class.

**Table 5-28 Properties of the *DataRelation* Class**

| Property | Description |
|---|---|
| *ChildColumns* | Gets the child *DataColumn* objects for the relation. |
| *ChildKeyConstraint* | Gets the *ForeignKeyConstraint* object for the relation. |
| *ChildTable* | Gets the child *DataTable* object for the relation. |

**Table 5-28 Properties of the *DataRelation* Class**

| Property | Description |
|---|---|
| *DataSet* | Gets the *DataSet* to which the relation belongs. |
| *ExtendedProperties* | Gets the collection that stores user information. |
| *Nested* | Gets or sets a value that indicates whether the relation should render its data as nested subtrees when the *DataSet* is rendered to XML. (More on this later in the "Serializing a Data Relation" section.) |
| *ParentColumns* | Gets the parent *DataColumn* objects for the relation. |
| *ParentKeyConstraint* | Gets the *UniqueConstraint* object that ensures unique values on the parent column of the relation. |
| *ParentTable* | Gets the parent *DataTable* object for the relation. |
| *RelationName* | Gets or sets the name of the *DataRelation* object. The name is used to identify the relation in the *Relations* collection of the parent *DataSet* object. |

When a *DataRelation* is created, two constraints are silently created. A foreign-key constraint is set on the child table using the two columns that form the relation as arguments. In addition, the parent table is given a unique constraint that prevents it from containing duplicates. The constraints are created by default, but by using a different constructor you can instruct the *DataRelation* to skip that step. The *DataRelation* class has no significant methods.

## Creating a Data Relation

The *DataRelation* class can be seen as the memory counterpart of a database table relationship. However, when a *DataSet* is loaded from a database, DBMS-specific relationships are not processed and loaded. As a result, data relations are exclusively in-memory objects that must be created explicitly with code. The following snippet shows how:

```
DataColumn c1 = tableEmp.Columns("empID");
DataColumn c2 = tableOrd.Columns("empID");
DataRelation rel = new DataRelation("Emp2Orders", c1, c2);
DataSet.Relations.Add(rel);
```

Given two tables, Employees and Orders, the preceding code sets up a relationship between the two based on the values of the common column *empID*. What are the practical advantages of such a relation? After the relation is set, the parent *DataTable* knows that each row might have a bunch of child related rows. In particular, each employee in the Employees table has an array of related rows in the Orders table. The child rows are exactly those where the value of the *Orders.empID* column matches empID column on the current Employees row.

ADO.NET provides an automatic mechanism to facilitate the retrieval of these related rows. The method is *GetChildRows*, and it's exposed by the *DataRow* class. *GetChildRows* takes a relation and returns an array filled with all the *DataRow* objects that match.

```
foreach(DataRow childRow in parentRow.GetChildRows("Emp2Orders"))
{
    // Process the child row
}
```

Another important facility ADO.NET provides for data relations has to do with table calculations and expression-based columns.

## Performing Calculations on Relations

A common task in many real-world applications entails that you manage two related tables and process, given a parent row, the subset of child records. In many situations, processing the child rows just means performing some aggregate computations on them. This is just one of facilities that ADO.NET and relations provide for free. Let's suppose that, given the previous employees-to-orders relation, you need to compute the total of orders issued by a given employee. You could simply add a dynamically computed column to the parent table and bind it to the data in the relation:

```
tableEmp.Columns.Add("Total", typeof(int),
    "Sum(child(Emp2Orders).Amount)");
```

> **Caution** Although powerful and easy to use, ADO.NET disconnected features are not all extremely useful in ASP.NET applications. To exploit a relation to its fullest, you need to have full tables in memory or, at least, all the records in both tables that you need to display. As you surely understand, although this is possible, it makes the SQL code significantly more complex. But there's a subtler point to consider. A relation implies multiple tables, which implies multiple SELECT statements. In highly concurrent environments, this requires a rather heavy serializable transaction. Should you resort to an old-fashioned query using INNER JOIN in spite of the redundant data it returns? Not necessarily; returning multiple result sets in a single call would require less bandwidth and the same transactional penalty.

The new column Total contains, for each employee, a value that represents the sum of all the values in the Amount column for the child rows of the relation. In other words, now you have a column that automatically computes the total of orders issued by each employee. The keyword *child* is a special syntax element of the language that ADO.NET expressions support. Basically, the *child* keyword takes a relation name and returns an array of *DataRow* objects that is the child of that relation.

### Serializing a Data Relation

The *Nested* property on the *DataRelation* object affects the way in which the parent *DataSet* is rendered to XML. By default, the presence of a relation doesn't change the XML schema used to serialize a *DataSet*. All the tables are therefore rendered sequentially under the root node. A nested relation changes this default schema. In particular, a nested relation is rendered hierarchically with child rows nested under the parent row.

A *DataSet* with Employees and Orders tables is rendered according to the following pattern:

```
<MyDataSet>
    <Employees empid="1" name="Joe Users" />
    ⋮
    <Orders empid="1" amount="6897" … />
    <Orders empid="1" amount="19713" … />
    ⋮
</MyDataSet>
```

If a relation exists between the tables and is set as nested, the XML schema changes as follows:

```
<MyDataSet>
    <Employees empid="1" name="Joe Users">
        <Orders empid="1" amount="6897" … />
        <Orders empid="1" amount="19713" … />
    </Employees>
    ⋮
</MyDataSet>
```

The child rows are taken out of their natural place and placed within the subtree that represents the parent row.

## The *DataView* Object

The *DataView* class represents a customized view of a *DataTable*. The relationship between *DataTable* and *DataView* objects is governed by the rules of a well-known design pattern: the document/view model. The *DataTable* object acts as the document, whereas the *DataView* behaves as the view. At any moment, you can have multiple, different views of the same underlying data.

More importantly, you can manage each view as an independent object with its own set of properties, methods, and events.

The view is implemented by maintaining a separate array with the indexes of the original rows that match the criteria set on the view. By default, the table view is unfiltered and contains all the records included in the table. By using the *RowFilter* and *RowStateFilter* properties, you can narrow the set of rows that fit into a particular view. Using the *Sort* property, you can apply a sort expression to the rows in the view. Table 5-29 lists the properties of the *DataView* class.

**Table 5-29 Properties of the *DataView* Class**

| Property | Description |
|---|---|
| *AllowDelete* | Gets or sets a value that indicates whether deletes are allowed in the view. |
| *AllowEdit* | Gets or sets a value that indicates whether edits are allowed in the view. |
| *AllowNew* | Gets or sets a value that indicates whether new rows can be added through the view. |
| *ApplyDefaultSort* | Gets or sets a value that indicates whether to use the default sort. |
| *Count* | Gets the number of rows in the view after the filter has been applied. |
| *DataViewManager* | Gets the *DataViewManager* object associated with this view. |
| *Item* | An indexer property. Gets a row of data from the underlying table. |
| *RowFilter* | Gets or sets the expression used to filter out rows in the view. |
| *RowStateFilter* | Gets or sets the row state filter used in the view. |
| *Sort* | Gets or sets the sorting of the view in terms of columns and order. |
| *Table* | Gets or sets the source *DataTable* for the view. |

The filter can be an expression, the state of the rows, or both. The *RowStateFilter* property, in particular, takes its acceptable values from the *DataViewRowState* enumeration and allows you to filter based on the original or current values of the row, or on modified, added, or deleted rows. The *RowFilter* property supports the same syntax as the *DataTable*'s *Select* method.

A *DataView* does not contain copies of the table's rows. It is limited to storing an array of indexes that is updated whenever any of the filter properties is set. The *DataView* object is already connected to the underlying *DataTable*, of which it represents a possibly filtered and/or sorted view. The *AllowXXX* properties only let you control whether the view is editable or not. By default, the view is fully editable. Table 5-30 lists the methods of the *DataView* class.

**Table 5-30 Methods of the *DataView* Class**

| Method | Description |
|---|---|
| *AddNew* | Adds a new row to the view and the underlying table. |
| *BeginInit* | Begins the initialization of the view. |
| *CopyTo* | Copies items from the view into an array. |
| *Delete* | Deletes the row at the specified index in the view. The row is deleted from the table too. |
| *EndInit* | Ends the initialization of the view. |
| *Find* | Finds a row in the view by the specified key value. |
| *FindRows* | Returns an array of row objects that match the specified key value. |
| *GetEnumerator* | Returns an enumerator object for the *DataView*. |

Both the *AddNew* and *Delete* methods affect the underlying *DataTable* object. Multiple changes can be grouped using the pair *BeginInit*/*EndInit*.

## Navigating the View

The contents of a *DataView* object can be scrolled through a variety of programming interfaces, including collections, lists, and enumerators. The *GetEnumerator* method, in particular, ensures that you can walk your way through the records in the view using the familiar *for...each* statement. The following code shows how to access all the rows that fit into the view:

```
DataView myView = new DataView(table);
foreach(DataRowView rowview in myView)
{
    // dereferences the DataRow object
    DataRow row = rowview.Row;
    ⋮
}
```

When client applications access a particular row in the view, the *DataView* class expects to find it in an internal cache of rows. If the cache is not empty, the specified row is returned to the caller via an intermediate *DataRowView* object. The *DataRowView* object is a kind of wrapper for the *DataRow* object that contains the actual data. You access row data through the *Row* property. If the row cache is empty, the *DataView* class fills it up with an array of *DataRowView* objects, each of which references an original *DataRow* object. The row cache is refreshed whenever the sort expression or the filter string are updated. The row cache can be empty either because it has never been used or because the sort expression or the filter string have been changed in the meantime. Figure 5-7 illustrates the internal architecture of a *DataView* object.

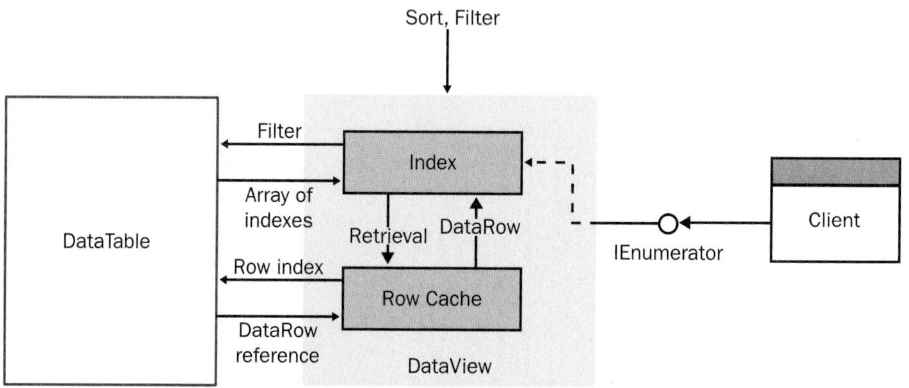


**Figure 5-7** The internal structure of a *DataView* object.

## Finding Rows

The link between the *DataTable* and the *DataView* is typically established at creation time through the constructor:

```
public DataView(DataTable table);
```

However, you could also create a new view and associate it with a table at a later time using the *DataView*'s *Table* property. For example:

```
DataView dv = new DataView();
dv.Table = dataSet.Tables["Employees"];
```

You can also obtain a *DataView* object from any table. In fact, the *DefaultView* property of a *DataTable* object just returns a *DataView* object initialized to work on that table.

```
DataView dv = dt.DefaultView;
```

Originally, the view is unfiltered and the index array contains as many elements as the rows in the table. To quickly find a row, you can either use the *Find* or *FindRows* method. The *Find* method takes one or more values and returns an array with the indexes of the rows that match. The *FindRows* method works in much the same way, but it returns an array of *DataRowView* objects rather than indexes. Both methods accept a sort key value to identify the rows to return.

> **Note** The contents of a *DataView* can be sorted by multiple fields by using the *Sort* property. You can assign to *Sort* a comma-separated list of column names, and even append them with *DESC* or *ASC* to indicate the direction.

## Conclusion

The ADO.NET object model is made of two main subtrees—the managed providers and the database-agnostic container classes. Managed providers are the new type of data source connectors and replace the COM-based OLE DB providers of ADO and ASP. As of today, very few managed providers exist to connect to commercial DBMS. The .NET Framework version 1.1 includes two native providers—one for SQL Server and one for Oracle—and support for all OLE DB providers and ODBC drivers. Third-party vendors also support MySQL and provide alternative providers for Oracle. (Providers for other popular DBMS systems are in the works.)

A managed provider is faster and more apt than any other database technology for data access tasks. Especially effective with SQL Server, it hooks up at the wire level and removes any sort of abstraction layer. In this way, a managed provider makes it possible for ADO.NET to return to callers the same data types they would use to refresh the user interface. Functionally speaking, managed providers don't provide the same set of features as ADO. In particular, server cursors and the schema object model are not supported in this version of ADO.NET but are expected for the next major release.

A managed provider supplies objects to connect to a data source, execute a command, and then grab or set some data. The ADO.NET object model provides a special type of command—the data adapter—which is different because it returns a disconnected container object—the *DataSet*. Central to the ADO.NET infrastructure, the *DataSet* can be considered the in-memory counterpart of a DBMS catalog. Disconnected programming is useful and powerful but not always suited for simple and not too heavily layered Web applications.

In the next chapter, we'll see practical examples of how to bind data to user interface controls and we'll start seeing why disconnected data containers are not always the most effective tools to use over the Web to manage large quantities of data.

## Resources

- *Microsoft ADO.NET*, by David Sceppa (Microsoft Press, 2002)
- *Pragmatic ADO.NET*, by Shawn Wildermuth (Addison-Wesley, 2002)
- *Applied XML Programming for Microsoft .NET*, by Dino Esposito (Microsoft Press, 2002)

# 6

# Creating Bindable Grids of Data

*Imagination is more important than knowledge.*

—*Albert Einstein*

Data-bound controls play a key role in the development of ASP.NET applications. Data-driven controls allow you to associate the whole interface, or individual properties, with one or more columns read out of a .NET-compliant data source. We already mentioned data-bound controls in Chapter 3 and reviewed their basics. In this chapter, we'll delve into the details of an extremely versatile data-bound control that is a fixed presence in any real-world ASP.NET application—the *DataGrid* control.

The *DataGrid* control renders a multicolumn, fully templated grid and provides a highly customizable, Microsoft Excel–like user interface. In spite of the rather advanced programming interface and the extremely rich set of attributes, the *DataGrid* simply generates an HTML table with interspersed hyperlinks to provide interactive functionalities such as sorting, paging, selection, and in-place editing.

According to the naming convention set in Chapter 3, the *DataGrid* control is said to be an iterative control and displays a list of records according to a given graphical template. Unlike other iterative controls, such as the *Repeater* and *DataList* controls that we'll dig out in Chapter 9, the *DataGrid* features a relatively rigid and inflexible graphical model. The data bound to a *DataGrid* is always rendered like a table, therefore, in terms of rows and columns. As we'll see later in the chapter, though, the contents of the cells in a column can be customizable to some extent using system-provided as well as user-defined templates.

## The *DataGrid* Control

The *DataGrid* is a column-based control that supports various types of data-bound columns, including text columns, templated columns, and command columns. You associate the control with a data source by using the *DataSource* property. Just as for other data-bound controls, no data will be physically loaded and bound until the *DataBind* method is called. The simplest way of displaying a table of data using the ASP.NET grid is as follows:

```
<asp:DataGrid runat="server" id="grid" />
```

Once the control has been placed into the page, you bind it to the data source and display the resulting HTML code.

```
string connString = "SERVER=localhost;DATABASE=northwind;UID=sa;";
string cmdText = "SELECT firstname, lastname, title FROM employees";

void Page_Load(object sender, EventArgs e)
{
    // Run the query and get some data to display
    DataTable data = ExecuteQuery(cmdText, connString);

    // Bind the data to the grid
    grid.DataSource = data;
    grid.DataBind();
}

DataTable ExecuteQuery(string cmdText, string connString)
{
    SqlDataAdapter adapter = new SqlDataAdapter(cmdText, connString);
    DataTable data = new DataTable();
    adapter.Fill(data);
    return data;
}
```

Although it's effective in terms of retrieval and display, the preceding code is hardly usable in real applications because it's too minimal. Figure 6-1 shows the output.

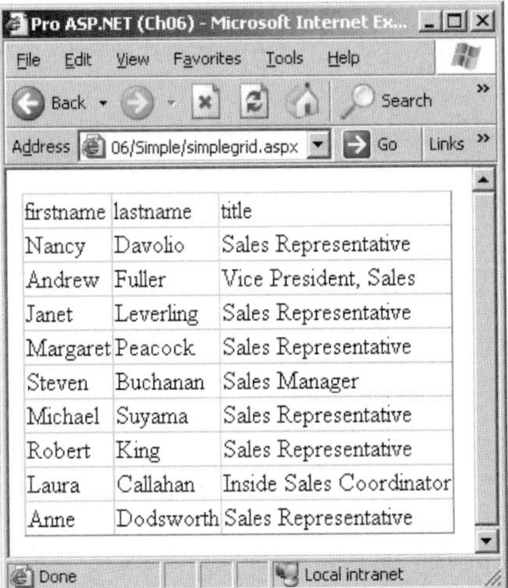


**Figure 6-1** A too simple and minimal *DataGrid* control in action.

This simple *DataGrid* sample has the following drawbacks:

- **Poor user interface** A grid of data rows is aimed at the end user to make as seamless as possible her interaction with the application. For this reason, a clear and graceful combination of colors, styles, and fonts is an absolute must.
- **Data binding and caching** Performance-wise, the simple application just shown runs the query whenever the page is invoked. By design, the *DataGrid* control needs to be re-bound to its data at each request. Getting data repeatedly from the database is a necessity when the data gets stale frequently, but it's relatively ineffective in other situations. In this case, server-side caching techniques can make the difference.
- **Column mapping** In this sample, all the columns in the query are mapped to the grid and all have the same settings. A real-world grid, on the other hand, would bind each column independently using different settings and an individual user-interface pattern.
- **Scrolling and navigation** All the rows in the query resultset are included in the view regardless of the total number. In a more realistic scenario, only a relatively small number of rows are retrieved or just displayed. An effective support for data paging is essential for real-world grids.

- **Sorting and page interaction** Rarely is a grid of data read-only and completely static. More likely, you'll need to implement row selection and then drill-down and sort the records in various ways. None of these functionalities are supported in the sample code we've considered so far.

The *DataGrid* is a powerful and versatile control. Frankly, I admit that I have yet to find anything that can't be accomplished with an appropriate mix of methods and event handlers. Let's review the programming interface of the control.

## Properties of the *DataGrid* Control

The *DataGrid* control inherits from the *BaseDataList* class and implements the *INamingContainer* interface. The *BaseDataList* abstract class provides a common set of functionality for all data listing controls, including *DataList* and *DataGrid*. As we saw in Chapter 2, the *INamingContainer* interface is a marker interface that doesn't require the implementation of any methods but only indicates that the class has some features. In particular, the interface marks the class as a naming container.

Table 6-1 lists the properties of the *DataGrid* class, but it doesn't include properties the control inherits from *Control* and *WebControl*.

**Table 6-1 Properties of the *DataGrid* Class**

| Property | Description |
|---|---|
| *AllowCustomPaging* | Sets custom paging, or indicates whether it is enabled. *AllowPaging* must be set to *true* for this setting to work. |
| *AllowPaging* | Sets paging, or indicates whether paging is enabled. |
| *AllowSorting* | Sets sorting, or indicates whether sorting is enabled. |
| *AlternatingItemStyle* | Gets the style properties for alternating rows. |
| *AutoGenerateColumns* | Sets column objects to be automatically created and displayed for each field in the data source, or indicates whether this option is enabled. *True* by default. |
| *BackImageUrl* | Gets or sets the URL of the image to display as the background of the control. |
| *CellPadding* | Sets the space (in pixels) to remain between the cell's border and the embedded text, or indicates how much space remains. |

**Table 6-1 Properties of the *DataGrid* Class**

| Property | Description |
|---|---|
| *CellSpacing* | Sets the space (in pixels) to remain, both horizontally and vertically, between two consecutive cells, or indicates how much space remains. |
| *Columns* | Gets a collection of *DataGridColumn* objects that represent the columns in the *DataGrid* control. |
| *Controls* | Gets a collection of all the child controls in the grid. |
| *CurrentPageIndex* | Gets or sets the index of the currently displayed page. |
| *DataKeyField* | Gets or sets the key field in the bound data source. |
| *DataKeys* | Gets a collection that stores the key values of all records displayed as a row in the grid. The column used as the key is defined by the *DataKeyField* property. |
| *DataMember* | Gets or sets a string that indicates the specific table in a multimember data source to bind to the grid. The property works in conjunction with *DataSource*. If *DataSource* is a *DataSet* object, *DataMember* contains the name of the particular table to bind. |
| *DataSource* | Gets or sets the data source object that contains the values to populate the control. |
| *EditItemIndex* | Gets or sets the index of the grid's item to edit. |
| *EditItemStyle* | Gets the style properties for the item being edited. |
| *FooterStyle* | Gets the style properties for the footer section of the grid. |
| *GridLines* | Sets whether all cells must have the border drawn. |
| *HeaderStyle* | Gets the style properties for the heading section of the grid. |
| *HorizontalAlign* | Gets or sets the horizontal alignment of the text in the grid. |
| *Items* | Gets the collection of the currently displayed items. |
| *ItemStyle* | Gets the style properties for the items in the grid. |
| *PageCount* | Gets the number of pages required to display all bound items. |
| *PagerStyle* | Gets the style properties for the paging section of the grid. |
| *PageSize* | Gets or sets the number of items to display on a single page. |
| *SelectedIndex* | Gets or sets the index of the currently selected item. |
| *SelectedItem* | Gets a *DataGridItem* object that represents the selected item. |
| *SelectedItemStyle* | Gets the style properties for the currently selected item. |
| *ShowFooter* | Sets whether the footer is displayed. *False* by default. |
| *ShowHeader* | Sets whether the header is displayed. |
| *VirtualItemCount* | Gets or sets the virtual number of items in the *DataGrid* control when custom paging is used. |

The characteristic traits of the *DataGrid* control are the *Columns* and *Items* collections, the *xxxStyle* properties, and the data-binding properties. All columns in the grid are represented by an object with its own set of properties and methods. Several types of columns are available to implement the most common tasks. In general, not all rows in the bound data source are included in the HTML code for the client. The *Items* collection returns only the displayed rows.

The *DataGrid* properties allow you to improve the grid's look and feel. You can set properties both declaratively through attributes set in the ASP.NET page layout and programmatically through properties set on the *DataGrid* control. When setting attributes, you can either set the property individually at the *<asp:datagrid>* level or group related properties on a per-item basis. For example, suppose you want to set the background color of the column headers to a particular color. You can do that through the headerstyle-backcolor attribute at the root level, as shown here:

```
<asp:DataGrid runat="server" id="grid"
    headerstyle-backcolor="brown">
```

However, you can also define the *<HeaderStyle>* child node within the *<asp:DataGrid>* declaration and set its *BackColor* attribute:

```
<asp:DataGrid runat="server" id="grid" ...>
    <HeaderStyle BackColor="brown">
    ⋮
</asp:DataGrid>
```

The effect is the same, but the second option looks more elegant and is easier to maintain. This is also the type of code that Microsoft Visual Studio .NET generates when you drop a *DataGrid* control on a Web form. The following schema illustrates the ASP.NET layout of the control:

```
<asp:DataGrid runat="server" ... >
    <AlternatingItemStyle ... />
    <EditItemStyle ... />
    <FooterStyle ... />
    <HeaderStyle ... />
    <ItemStyle ... />
    <PagerStyle ... />
    <SelectedItemStyle ... />
    <Columns>
    ⋮
    </Columns>
</asp:DataGrid>
```

## Constituent Elements of a *DataGrid*

The output of a *DataGrid* control is made of several constituent elements grouped in the *ListItemType* enumeration. Each element plays a clear role and has a precise location in the user interface of the control, as Figure 6-2 shows.

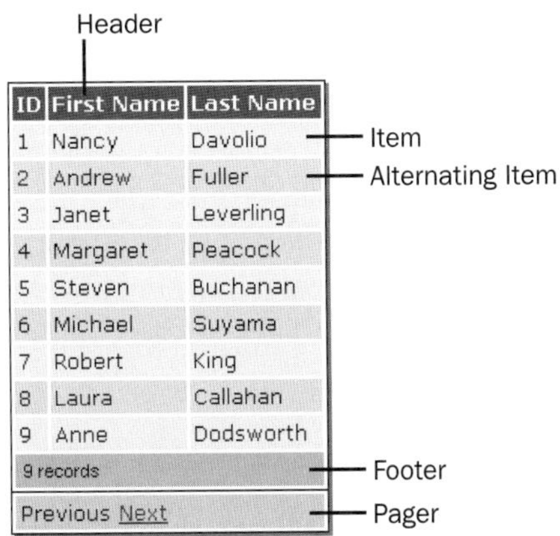


**Figure 6-2** The layout of a *DataGrid* control.

The *DataGrid* user interface comprises the logical elements listed in Table 6-2. Each element has its own style property—that is, the set of graphical settings that are automatically applied by the control.

**Table 6-2 Graphical Elements that Form a Data Grid**

| Item Type | Description |
|---|---|
| AlternatingItem | Represents a data-bound row placed in an odd position. Useful if you want to use different styles for alternating rows. *AlternatingItemStyle* is the property that lets you control the look and feel of the element. |
| EditItem | Represents the item, or alternating item, currently displayed in edit mode. *EditItemStyle* lets you control the look and feel of the element. |
| Footer | Represents the grid's footer. The element can't be bound to a data source and is styled using the settings in the *FooterStyle* property. |
| Header | Represents the grid's header. The element can't be bound to a data source and is styled using the settings in the *HeaderStyle* property. |
| Item | Represents a data-bound row placed in an even position. Styled through the *ItemStyle* property. |

*(continued)*

**Table 6-2 Graphical Elements that Form a Data Grid** *(continued)*

| Item Type | Description |
|---|---|
| Pager | Represents the pager element you use to scroll between pages. The element can't be bound to a data source and is styled using the settings in the *PagerStyle* property. The pager can be placed at the top or bottom of the grid's table and even in both places. |
| SelectedItem | Represents the item, or alternating item, currently selected. The property that defines its look and feel is *SelectedItemStyle*. |

Each time one of the constituent elements is about to be created, the grid fires an *ItemCreated* event for you to perform some application-specific tasks. We'll examine the use of the *ItemCreated* event later in the chapter.

## Data Source Rows and Displayed Rows

By design, the *DataGrid* control displays the data stored in a data source object. Each row in the data source is potentially a row in the grid. However, this one-to-one mapping doesn't always correspond to reality. The *DataSource* property contains the *ICollection*-based binding object; the *Items* property contains a collection of objects representing the rows of the grid. The *Items* collection is automatically filled when the *DataBind* method is called. Each element in the *Items* collection supplies a *DataItem* property that is set with the object that corresponds to the row in the data source. An item object is an instance of the *DataGridItem* class that inherits from *TableRow*.

The *Items* collection doesn't provide methods to add or remove items to the collection. However, the *ItemCreated* event provides a way for you to control when an item is added and determine its contents and configuration. Note that only bindable items are contained in the *Items* collection. The header, footer, and pager are not included in the collection.

The index properties of the *DataGrid* refer to the rows displayed rather than to the underlying data source. When the item with an index of 1 is selected, the second displayed item is selected, but this piece of information says nothing about the position of the corresponding source record. The data-source index for the item object is stored in the *DataSetIndex* property on the *DataGridItem* class. *DataSetIndex* returns the absolute position in the overall data source of the record represented by the current item. Although functional, this method isn't especially handy in some common scenarios, such as when you want to select a row and retrieve a bunch of associated records. In such a case, you need to know the value of the key field in the underlying data source row.

The *DataKeys* collection and the *DataKeyField* property provide an effective shortcut designed specifically to work in similar situations. When you configure a *DataGrid* control, you can store the name of a key field in the *DataKeyField* property. During the data-binding phase, the control extracts from the data source the values for the specified key field that correspond to the rows being displayed. As a result, the index of the selected row in the *Items* collection can be used with *DataKeys* to get the key value for the underlying data-source row. Let's consider the following declaration, which refers to a grid that displays information about the employees of a company:

```
<asp:DataGrid runat="server" id="grid" DataKeyField="employeeid" ... >
```

To get the ID of the selected employee—to be used to implement, say, a drill-down view—you simply use the following code:

```
int empID = grid.DataKeys[grid.SelectedIndex];
```

The *DataKeys* collection is automatically filled by the control based on the value of the *DataKeyField* property and the bound data source.

## Events of the *DataGrid* Control

The *DataGrid* control has no specific methods worth mentioning. The control programming interface features a variety of methods, but all of them are inherited from various base classes—*Control*, *WebControl*, and *BaseDataList*. Table 6-3 lists the events that the control fires during its lifecycle.

**Table 6-3 Events of the *DataGrid* Class**

| Event | Description |
|---|---|
| *CancelCommand* | The user clicked to cancel any updates made on the current item being edited. |
| *DeleteCommand* | The user clicked to start a delete operation on the current item. |
| *EditCommand* | The user clicked to put the current item in edit mode. |
| *ItemCommand* | The user clicked any command button within the grid control. |
| *ItemCreated* | The *DataGrid* control has created a new item during its initialization process. |
| *ItemDataBound* | This occurs after a grid item is bound to data. |
| *PageIndexChanged* | The user clicked to see a new page of data. |
| *SelectedIndexChanged* | The user clicked to select a different item. |
| *SortCommand* | The user clicked to start a sort operation on a column. |
| *UpdateCommand* | The user clicked to save any updates made on the item currently being edited. |

The *CancelCommand* and *UpdateCommand* events are fired under special circumstances—that is, when an item is being edited. (We'll cover the *DataGrid* in-place editing capability later in the chapter.) The *CancelCommand* event signals that the user clicked the Cancel button to cancel all pending changes. The *UpdateCommand* event denotes the user's intention to persist all the changes. Note that any code necessary to update the underlying data source must be manually written by the programmer.

The other command events—*EditCommand*, *DeleteCommand*, and *SortCommand*—indicate that the user required a particular action by clicking on command buttons within the user interface of the grid. Typically, the user will click a link in the heading section to sort by a particular column and a row-specific button to delete or edit that row. If the grid contains multiple pages, *PageIndexChanged* signals when the user selects a new page. Note that all these events describe situations that the ASP.NET code is called to handle after a postback. For example, the *PageIndexChanged* event occurs when the user clicks and the page posts back to the server.

> **Note** In addition to the events just listed, the *DataGrid* control fires all the standard events of Web controls including *Load*, *Init*, *PreRender*, and *DataBinding*. In particular, you might want to write a handler for *PreRender* if you need to modify the HTML code generated for the grid. The *DataBinding* event, on the other hand, is the entry point in the grid's binding process. The event, in fact, is fired from within the *DataBind* method as the first step before the whole binding process begins.

## The *DataGridItem* Object

A *DataGridItem* object represents a table row within a *DataGrid* control. A data grid item can be a data row, but it can also be the heading section, footer, or pager. All the data-bound items of a *DataGrid* control are grouped in a *DataGridItemCollection* and are programmatically accessed via the *Items* property. The programming interface of a data grid data item is the *DataGridItem* class. The class is characterized by the properties listed in Table 6-4.

**Table 6-4 Properties of the *DataGridItem* Class**

| Property | Description |
|---|---|
| *DataItem* | Gets or sets the data item behind the row within the *DataGrid* control. |
| *DataSetIndex* | Gets the index number that characterized the object stored in the *DataItem* property in the bound data source. |
| *ItemIndex* | Gets the index of the item represented by the *DataGridItem* object in the *Items* collection of the *DataGrid* control. |
| *ItemType* | Gets the type of the item represented by the *DataGridItem* object in the *DataGrid* control. |

Note that the table includes only the properties specific to the class. All properties inherited from parent classes haven't been listed.

## The Data-Binding Process for the *DataGrid* Control

The data-binding process for a *DataGrid* control begins when the *DataBind* method is called. The *DataGrid* class doesn't really override the method but exploits the method as supplied by the *BaseDataList* class. This implementation is pretty simple and doesn't do more than raise the *DataBinding* event for the class. The internal handler of the *BaseDataList* class first clears all the child controls and the view state and then calls a protected method named *CreateControlHierarchy*, as in the following pseudo-code:

```
protected virtual void OnDataBinding(EventArgs e)
{
    // call the parent's event handler
    base.OnDataBinding(e);

    // Clear the collection of child controls
    Controls.Clear();

    // Clear the view state container
    ClearChildViewState();

    // Build the grid
    CreateControlHierarchy();

    // Monitor the view state for changes
    TrackViewState();
}
```

The *CreateControlHierarchy* method is responsible for setting up the hierarchy of controls and HTML code that actually makes up the final grid. The most important thing that happens within the body of *CreateControlHierarchy* is the creation of the various grid items. For each created item, a pair of correlated events are raised—*ItemCreated* and *ItemDataBound*.

### *ItemCreated* and *ItemDataBound* Events

Whenever a new *DataGrid* item is created, an *ItemCreated* event is sent to applications. The event is fired immediately after the *DataGridItem* object is created and before it is added to the resulting HTML table. (The output of a *DataGrid* control is always a plain old HTML table.) The following delegate illustrates the prototype of the event handlers:

```
public delegate void DataGridItemEventHandler(
    object sender,
    DataGridItemEventArgs e
);
```

The event handler receives an argument of type *DataGridItemEventArgs*, which contains data related to the involved item. The *DataGridItemEventArgs* class features an extra *Item* property initialized with the freshly created *DataGridItem* object. When the *ItemCreated* event is raised, the binding between the underlying data row and the grid's row has not yet been set. The data binding takes place only when the *ItemDataBound* event reaches the application. The initialization step occurs in the following order:

- ***DataGridItem* creation** The new grid item object is created and initialized. At this point, it is a stand-alone object not bound yet to the grid and data.
- ***ItemCreated* event** The *ItemCreated* event is fired to let applications know that a new item has been created. The event data includes information about the new item. Once the event handler terminates, the item is added to the HTML table being generated.
- **Data binding** If the *DataGrid* item supports data binding, the underlying row is associated with the table row. The *DataItem* property on the new grid item object is set correctly.
- ***ItemDataBound* event** The *ItemDataBound* event is fired, and applications can read the actual values bound to normal and alternating rows.

Note that if you define a handler for the *ItemDataBound* event, it will also be called for the creation of nonbindable items, such as the header or footer. In this case, the *DataItem* property on the *DataGridItem* object is null, as expected.

### Why Is *ItemCreated* Raised Twice?

When a page that includes a *DataGrid* control posts back, the *ItemCreated* event is raised twice. The event is first raised during the restoration of the page view state. The *DataGrid* control, in fact, stores its data row objects in the view state. When the view state is re-created, all items are instantiated and reinitialized.

Note that in this case, *ItemCreated* is raised for all the items stored in the view state, and therefore, for all the items displayed in the previous page. For example, suppose that the grid displays ten rows and you click to view another page. Suppose also that the new page would display, say, three rows. While processing the page request, the *DataGrid* control first fires *ItemCreated* ten times, one for each item cached in the view state that is restored. Next, while generating the output for the new page, the *DataGrid* fires the pair *ItemCreated* and *ItemDataBound* for each item to be displayed in the new page—three times only.

The second notification arrives when the page is being built and the *DataGrid* output code is ready to be generated. In this case only, *ItemCreated* is followed by an *ItemDataBound* event. Figure 6-3 shows the two moments in which the event is fired.

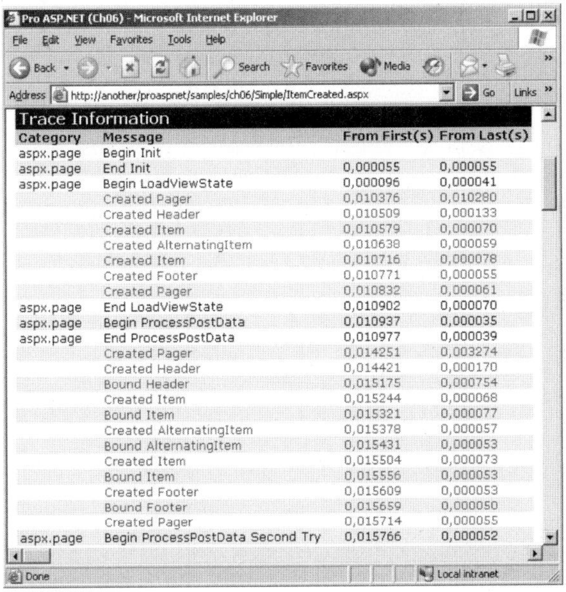

| Category | Message | From First(s) | From Last(s) |
|---|---|---|---|
| aspx.page | Begin Init | | |
| aspx.page | End Init | 0,000055 | 0,000055 |
| aspx.page | Begin LoadViewState | 0,000096 | 0,000041 |
| | Created Pager | 0,010376 | 0,010280 |
| | Created Header | 0,010509 | 0,000133 |
| | Created Item | 0,010579 | 0,000070 |
| | Created AlternatingItem | 0,010638 | 0,000059 |
| | Created Item | 0,010716 | 0,000078 |
| | Created Footer | 0,010771 | 0,000055 |
| | Created Pager | 0,010832 | 0,000061 |
| aspx.page | End LoadViewState | 0,010902 | 0,000070 |
| aspx.page | Begin ProcessPostData | 0,010937 | 0,000035 |
| aspx.page | End ProcessPostData | 0,010977 | 0,000039 |
| | Created Pager | 0,014251 | 0,003274 |
| | Created Header | 0,014421 | 0,000170 |
| | Bound Header | 0,015175 | 0,000754 |
| | Created Item | 0,015244 | 0,000068 |
| | Bound Item | 0,015321 | 0,000077 |
| | Created AlternatingItem | 0,015378 | 0,000057 |
| | Bound AlternatingItem | 0,015431 | 0,000053 |
| | Created Item | 0,015504 | 0,000073 |
| | Bound Item | 0,015556 | 0,000053 |
| | Created Footer | 0,015609 | 0,000053 |
| | Bound Footer | 0,015659 | 0,000050 |
| | Created Pager | 0,015714 | 0,000055 |
| aspx.page | Begin ProcessPostData Second Try | 0,015766 | 0,000052 |



**Figure 6-3** Tracing the events raised during the binding process of the *DataGrid*.

How can you avoid having your event handler called during the view-state restoration phase? The rub is that there's no specific information available with the event data structure that allows you to detect this situation. A possible trick is using a global state variable—a Boolean flag—to track whether the code is entered in the data-binding phase or not. If the *ItemCreated* is called when this flag is set to *false*, the call is because of view-state restoration. The beginning of the data-binding phase is signaled by the *DataBinding* event.

```
<asp:datagrid runat="server" id="grid"
    onitemcreated="ItemCreated"
    onitemdatabound="ItemDataBound"
    ondatabinding="TraceDataBinding" />
```

The handler of the *DataBinding* event has a simple structure, as shown below:

```
void TraceDataBinding(object sender, EventArgs e) {
    m_isBindingData =  true;
    Trace.Warn("Data binding...");
}
void ItemCreated(object sender, DataGridItemEventArgs e) {
    if (m_isBindingData)
        Trace.Warn("Created " + e.Item.ItemType.ToString());
}
```

Finally, note that the footer and header items are always created regardless of the setting of the *ShowFooter* and *ShowHeader* properties. The pager object, on the other hand, is created only if the *AllowPaging* property is set to *true*. It is interesting to note that the grid is composed of two pager objects—one on the first row and one on the last row. Using the *PagerStyle* property, you can decide how many pagers, or which one, are actually displayed. If needed, a *DataGrid* can also have two pager objects that work in synchronization. In any case, bear in mind that two *ItemCreated* events are fired for pagers.

## Binding Data to the Grid

A *DataGrid* control is formed by data-bindable columns. By default, the control includes all the data-source columns in the view. You can change this behavior by setting the *AutoGenerateColumns* property to *false*. In this case, only the columns explicitly listed in the *Columns* collection are displayed. The *DataGrid* control supports a variety of column types, which differ from one another mostly in how each represents the data. You are required to indicate the type of the column if you add it to the *Columns* collection; otherwise, if automatic generation is used, all columns are of the simplest type—the *BoundColumn* column type. As Table 6-5 shows, a *BoundColumn* object displays the contents of the corresponding data source field by using labels.

**Table 6-5 Types of Columns**

| Column Type | Description |
|---|---|
| *BoundColumn* | The contents of the column are bound to a field in a data source. Each cell displays as plain text. |
| *ButtonColumn* | This type displays a command button for each item in the column. The text of the button can be data-bound. The command name of the button must be common to all the items in the column. You can control the graphical style of the button—push button or link button. |
| *EditColumn* | This is a particular type of button column associated with a command named *Edit*. When in edit mode, the whole row is drawn using text boxes rather than literals. |
| *HyperLinkColumn* | This type displays the contents of each item in the column as a hyperlink. The text of the hyperlink can be bound to a column in the data source or it can be static text. The target URL can be data-bound too. Clicking a hyperlink column causes the browser to jump to the specified URL. Supports target frames. |
| *TemplateColumn* | This type displays each cell of the column following a specified ASP.NET template. It also allows you to provide custom behaviors. |

Note that the *AutoGenerateColumns* property and the *Columns* collection are not mutually exclusive. If both properties are set to *true* and the collection is not empty, the *DataGrid* will first show the user-defined columns and then all the ones that autogeneration would produce.

You normally bind columns using the *<columns>* tag in the body of the *<asp:datagrid>* server control, as the following code demonstrates:

```
<asp:datagrid runat="server" id="grid" ... >
⋮
  <columns>
    <asp:BoundColumn runat="server" DataField="employeeid"
        HeaderText="ID" />
    <asp:BoundColumn runat="server" DataField="firstname"
        HeaderText="First Name" />
    <asp:BoundColumn runat="server" DataField="lastname"
        HeaderText="Last Name" />
  </columns>
</asp:datagrid>
```

Alternatively, you can create a new column of the desired class, fill its member properly, and then add the class instance to the *Columns* collection. Here is some code to add a *BoundColumn* object to a grid:

```
BoundColumn bc = new BoundColumn();
bc.DataField = "firstname";
bc.HeaderText = "First Name";
grid.Columns.Add(bc);
```

The order of the columns in the collection determines the order in which the columns are displayed in the *DataGrid* control.

## Data-Bound Columns

All grid column types inherit from the *DataGridColumn* class and have a few common properties such as the header text, footer and item style, and visibility flag. Table 6-6 details the properties shared by all types of columns.

**Table 6-6 Properties of the *DataGridColumn* Class**

| Property | Description |
|---|---|
| *FooterStyle* | Gets the style properties for the footer of the column. |
| *FooterText* | Gets or sets the static text displayed in the footer of the column. |
| *HeaderImageUrl* | Gets or sets the URL of an image to display in the header. |
| *HeaderStyle* | Gets the style properties for the header of the column. |
| *HeaderText* | Gets or sets the static text displayed in the header of the column. |
| *ItemStyle* | Gets the style properties for the item cells of the column. |
| *SortExpression* | Gets or sets the expression to pass to the *OnSortCommand* method when a column is selected for sorting. |
| *Visible* | Sets whether the column is visible in the *DataGrid* control. |

The *BoundColumn* class represents a *DataGrid* column type that is bound to a data field. The specific properties available on the class are listed in Table 6-7.

**Table 6-7 Properties of the *BoundColumn* Class**

| Property | Description |
|---|---|
| *DataField* | Gets or sets the data-source column to bind to. |
| *DataFormatString* | Gets or sets the string that specifies the display format for the cells in the column. |
| *ReadOnly* | Sets whether the items in the column can be edited. *False* by default. |

The key properties to set up a grid column are *DataField*, which represents the name of the column to bind, and *DataFormatString*, which allows you to format the displayed text to some extent. The *ReadOnly* property has effect only if an edit command column is added to the grid. In this case, the cells in the column are switched to edit mode according to the value of the property.

The following code snippet adds two columns and specifies for each the header text and the source column. In addition, the second column is given a format string to make it look like a currency value with right alignment.

```
<asp:boundcolumn runat="server" datafield="quantityperunit"
    headertext="Packaging" />
<asp:boundcolumn runat="server" datafield="unitprice"
    headertext="Price" DataFormatString="{0:c}">
    <itemstyle width="80px" horizontalalign="right" />
</asp:boundcolumn>
```

Note that graphical settings for a column must be specified using a child style tag.

## Configuring the Column Footer

As mentioned, the footer in a *DataGrid* control is hidden by default. To turn it on, you must set the *ShowFooter* property to *true*. As usual, you can do that either declaratively or programmatically. The footer style can be fully modified through the *FooterStyle* property at the grid level or on a per-column basis.

The footer, though, is not a bindable element and doesn't supply system-provided aggregate functions (for example, Count, Sum). The footer also doesn't provide a predefined way to modify its structure. The footer is rendered through an empty row, so it maintains the same column structure as other rows. If this suits you, use the column's *FooterText* property to assign it HTML content. If you want a footer with a different number of columns, write a handler for *ItemCreated* and hook up the moment in which the footer is created. The following code snippet shows how to make the footer display a single cell that spans the entire grid width:

```
void ItemCreated(Object sender, DataGridItemEventArgs e) {
    ListItemType elemType = e.Item.ItemType;
    if (elemType == ListItemType.Footer)
    {
        // Remove all the cells but one
        TableCellCollection tcc = e.Item.Cells;
        int nTotalCols = tcc.Count;
        for (int i=0; i<nTotalCols-1; i++)
            e.Item.Cells.RemoveAt(0);

        // Only 1 cell left at this time ...
        TableCell c = e.Item.Cells[0];
        c.ColumnSpan = nTotalCols;

        // Set any text to be displayed
        c.Text = "...";
    }
}
```

The footer is a *DataGridItem* object and, as such, a special type of table row. The *Cells* collection provides access to all the row cells you can modify at will as a *TableCell* object.

### Using Cascading Style Sheets Styles

When creating a *DataGrid* control, you inevitably need to tune up some of its visual settings for a more user-friendly result. This normally means that you change the font family, font size, and width and color of the text and borders. The code necessary to obtain the desired graphical effect might be replicated for several other pages in the same application. Because many visual settings of a Web control are actually rendered as cascading style sheets (CSS)–style properties, you can group all of them into a CSS class. Next, you reference the style from the control (including *DataGrid* controls) by using the *CssClass* property.

Another, slightly more elegant, way to solve the issue is by deriving from the *DataGrid* a new control that simply uses the specified settings as the new default settings.

## HyperLink Columns

The *HyperLinkColumn* class is a column type that contains a hyperlink for each cell. The programmer can control the text of the hyperlink and the URL to navigate. In particular, both fields can be bound to a column in the data source. Table 6-8 details the properties specific to the class.

**Table 6-8 Properties of the *HyperLinkColumn* Class**

| Property | Description |
|---|---|
| *DataNavigateUrlField* | Gets or sets the data source column to bind to the URL of the hyperlinks in the column. |
| *DataNavigateUrlFormatString* | Gets or sets a parametric structure for the URL. |
| *DataTextField* | Gets or sets the data source column to bind to the text caption of the hyperlinks. |
| *DataTextFormatString* | Gets or sets the display format for the hyperlinks text. |
| *NavigateUrl* | Gets or sets the static URL to link to when a hyperlink in the column is clicked. |
| *Target* | Gets or sets the name of the target window or frame in which the linked page will be displayed. |
| *Text* | Gets or sets the static text caption to display for the hyperlinks in the column. |

Note that if you set the *Text* property, the *NavigateUrl* property, or both, all hyperlinks in the column will share the same caption and URL. Use the *DataTextField* and *DataNavigateUrlField* properties to associate the text and URL of the hyperlink with columns in the database. Finally, note that if *DataNavigateUrlField* and *NavigateUrl* are both set at the same time, the *DataNavigateUrlField* takes precedence.

The following code snippet demonstrates how to create a column of product names that, if clicked, displays a product information page in a frame. The *DataTextField* property indicates the source column for the hyperlink caption. The *DataNavigateUrlFormatString* property defines the format of the URL to use. The final URL is the productinfo.aspx page with a query string in which the ID argument is automatically set with the information read from the *DataNavigateUrlField* property—that is, *productid* in the following code:

```
<asp:hyperlinkcolumn runat="server" datatextfield="productname"
    headertext="Product"
    datanavigateurlfield="productid"
    datanavigateurlformatstring="productinfo.aspx?id={0}"
    target="ProductView">
    <itemstyle width="200px" />
</asp:hyperlinkcolumn>
```

The color of the hyperlinks can be controlled using CSS styles. In particular, you can set up a hover color with the following style block:

```
<style>a:hover {color:red;}</style>
```

## Formatting URLs and Column Names

There are some limitations in the use of column and URL names in *DataGrid* programming. In particular, the *DataField* and *DataTextField* properties don't allow you to combine more field names. Because of this restriction, you can have a single column displaying first and last name only if such a column is included in the underlying data source.

Even though the *DataField* and *DataTextField* properties don't support expressions, you can resort to dynamically created expression-based columns to work around the issue. In Chapter 5, we saw how to create such columns. The following code adds a *FullName* column to a *DataTable* object:

```
table.Columns.Add("FullName", typeof(string),
    "lastname + ', ' + firstname");
```

The newly created *FullName* column is then bound to the desired *DataGrid* column as you would do with any other column. This solution might be more effective than having the database management system (DBMS) return a calculated column. Later in the chapter, we'll examine an even more effective trick based on templated columns.

By using the *DataTextField* and *DataNavigateUrlField* properties together, you can make the URL of the hyperlink parametric. However, by default you are limited to just one parameter—the value bound to the *DataNavigateUrlField* field. To use a hyperlink bound to any number of arguments, you should resort to templated columns, as we'll see later in the section "Templated Columns."

## Using Frames

When the cell of a hyperlink column is clicked, the browser jumps to the specified URL and displays the linked contents in the window specified by the *Target* property. Allowable values for the *Target* property are a few special names like *_self*, *_blank*, *_top*, *_parent*, and any name that individuates a frame window both inline and located in a frameset. If no target has been set, the current page is refreshed.

The following code shows how to display in an Internet Explorer inline frame window the output of a hyperlink column:

```
<iframe name="ProductView" frameborder="no"
    height="100%" style="border:solid 1px;" />
```

The various code snippets considered so far are all excerpts from the sample application shown in Figure 6-4.

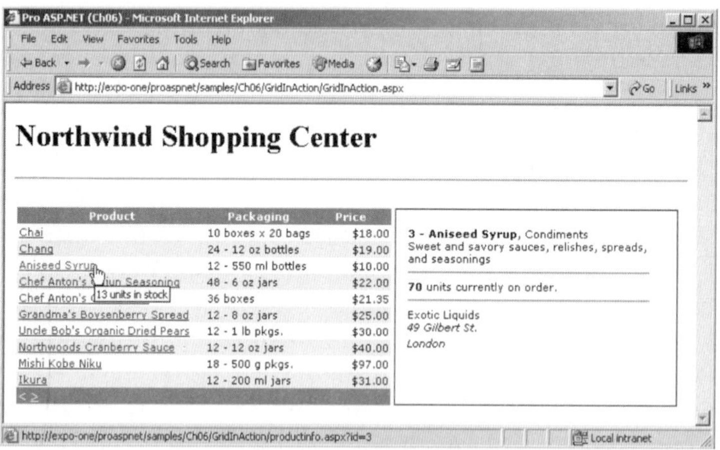


**Figure 6-4** A realistic *DataGrid* control in action.

The white box on the right of the grid is an inline frame with a modified border named *ProductView*. Note that the name of the frame must begin with a letter and is case insensitive. The frame is refreshed whenever a hyperlink is clicked in the column.

**Note** The *<iframe>* tag is part of the HTML 4.0 specification and is supported by Internet Explorer 4.0 and later. Downlevel Netscape browsers don't support it. Netscape 4.x browsers support a similar tag instead. The name of this browser-specific tag is *<layer>*.

## Bindable ToolTips

As you can see in Figure 6-4, a ToolTip appears when the mouse hovers over the hyperlink. The ToolTip is not a bindable element in any type of column. However, with a relatively simple piece of code, you can make it bindable and use it to display extra fields on demand. In Figure 6-4, in fact, the ToolTip displays information about the number of items in stock for a given product.

To bind a data-source column to the *ToolTip* property of a Web control, you need a handler for the *ItemDataBound* event:

```
void ItemDataBound(object sender, DataGridItemEventArgs e) {
    ListItemType itemType = e.Item.ItemType;
    if (itemType == ListItemType.Item ||
        itemType == ListItemType.AlternatingItem)
    {
        DataRowView drv = (DataRowView) e.Item.DataItem;

        // Extract the first control in the first cell of the row
        WebControl webCtl = (WebControl) e.Item.Cells[0].Controls[0];
        WebCtl.ToolTip = drv["unitsinstock"] + " units in stock" ;
    }
}
```

In the handler, you first verify the type of the item being bound and then access the *DataItem* property. The test on the *ItemType* property serves to filter out the cases in which a selected or edited item is being bound to data. The *DataItem* property refers to the data object behind the particular row the grid is processing. As long as you use ADO.NET objects as the data source, the *DataItem* can be successfully cast to a *DataRowView* object.

**Note** The *DataItem* property is set to a non-null object only during the *ItemDataBound* event. The same code won't work if attached to the *ItemCreated* event because at that time the *DataItem* property would be uninitialized.

You use the contents of the *DataItem* property to prepare a row-specific string and bind it to the *ToolTip* property of a particular control located anywhere in the row. In particular, the previous code snippet associates the ToolTip with the first control in the first cell—the <*a*> tag representing the hyperlink.

## Command Columns

The *ButtonColumn* class represents a command column and contains a user-defined button for each cell in the column. Functionally similar to hyperlink columns, button columns are different because they generate a postback event on the same URL. To handle the click on a button, you write the *ItemCommand* event handler and check the *CommandName* property of the column button. Although the caption of each button can be bound to a data-source column, more often than not a button column has static text displayed through all the cells. Table 6-9 shows the properties that characterize the *ButtonColumn* class.

**Table 6-9 Properties of the *ButtonColumn* Class**

| Property | Description |
|---|---|
| *ButtonType* | Gets or sets the type of button to display in the column—a link button or push button. |
| *CommandName* | Gets or sets a string that represents the command to perform during the postback after a button in the column is clicked. |
| *DataTextField* | Gets or sets a source column to bind to the caption of the button. |
| *DataTextFormatString* | Gets or sets the string that specifies the display format for the caption in each command button. |
| *Text* | Gets or sets the caption displayed in the buttons of the column. |

The idea behind the button column is that you execute a particular action after the user clicks on a row. All buttons in the column are associated with some script code that posts the page back and executes the *ItemCommand* server-side procedure. Within that procedure, you use the command name to distinguish between multiple button columns and you use the *ItemIndex* property of the *DataGridItem* class to know about the particular row that was clicked.

**Caution** Unlike what happens with other actions related to button controls in ASP.NET pages, validation is not performed when buttons in a *ButtonColumn* are clicked. To perform validation in a *ButtonColumn*, use a templated column and add a *Button* or *LinkButton* control to it.

## Handling a User's Clicking

To handle the user's clicking on the buttons in a *ButtonColumn*, you write a handler for the *DataGrid*'s *ItemCommand* event. The handler requires the following prototype:

```
void ItemCommandHandler(
    object sender,
    DataGridCommandEventArgs e);
```

The *DataGridCommandEventArgs* structure makes available three key properties: *Item*, which represents the grid item where the click occurred, plus *CommandName* and *CommandSource*. The *CommandName* property is the name of the command associated with the clicked button, whereas *CommandSource* is the button object that raised the click event. A fourth property is mentioned in the documentation—*CommandArgument*, which represents an argument for the command. This property, though, is not defined in the programming interface of the *ButtonColumn* class and subsequently is not used in the *ItemCommand* event handler.

The following code illustrates the typical structure of the *ItemCommand* handler:

```
void ItemCommand(object sender, DataGridCommandEventArgs e) {
    switch(e.CommandName)
    {
        case "AddToCart":
            AddToCart(e.Item.ItemIndex);
            break;
        ⋮
    }
}
```

In this sample, the *AddToCart* method is passed the ordinal position of the clicked item. In other cases, you might want to use that information to retrieve the key associated with the clicked row. As mentioned earlier, the *DataKeys* collection on the *DataGrid* does just that for you.

You can use a picture to define the caption of the button. The following code shows how to accomplish this by simply using an HTML string that includes a static *<img>* tag. This trick can be used, and works, with any type of column. However, it does not work if you change the button type from the default *linkbutton* to *pushbutton*.

```
<asp:buttoncolumn runat="server" headertext=""
    buttontype="linkbutton" commandname="AddToCart"
    Text="<img title='Add to cart...' border='no' src='images/cart.gif' />">
    <itemstyle width="30px" horizontalalign="right" />
</asp:buttoncolumn>
```

Figure 6-5 shows a grid with a button column that represents the user interface of a simple shopping cart.

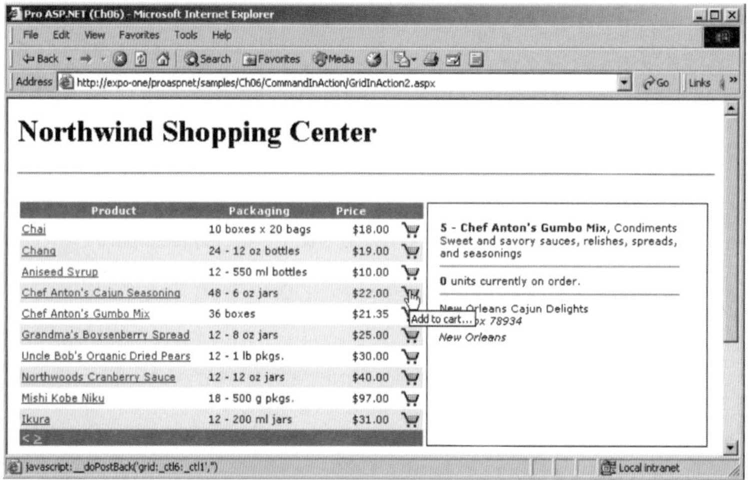


**Figure 6-5** A *DataGrid* with a button column.

## Implementing a Simple Shopping Cart

When the user clicks on the shopping cart button, the page posts back and requests the execution of the method, if any, associated with the *DataGrid*'s *ItemCommand* event. In the previous code snippet, this method is *AddToCart*. It takes the index of the clicked row, retrieves some information from the underlying data item, and then adds a new row to a memory-resident *DataTable* object. This data table is the effective shopping cart and is stored in *Session* to survive across page requests.

The shopping cart is set up the first time the page is accessed—that is, when *IsPostBack* returns *false*—and is retrieved from *Session* for successive requests. The underlying *DataTable* object contains three fields—*ProductName*, *Quantity*, and *Price*—and is bound to a second grid to let users view the current list of orders. As you can see in Figure 6-6, the shopping cart *DataGrid* shows a footer section in which the number of ordered items and the total price are computed and displayed. To make such calculations, we use the *Compute* method on the *DataTable* object.

```
// m_cart is the DataTable that contains the shopping cart
int totalItems = Convert.ToInt32(m_cart.Compute("Count(quantity)", ""));
int totalPrice = Convert.ToInt32(m_cart.Compute("Sum(price)", ""));

// Write the total number of items in the cart
e.Item.Cells[0].Text = totalItems.ToString();

// Write the total amount for the items in the cart
e.Item.Cells[2].HorizontalAlign = HorizontalAlign.Right;
e.Item.Cells[2].Text = String.Format("{0:c}", totalPrice);
```

The shopping cart grid also features a button column to remove an item from the cart. The associated code removes the clicked row from the *DataTable* that represents the shopping cart.

**Figure 6-6** A simple shopping cart in action implemented using *DataGrid* controls.

### The *Select* Button Column

A special type of button column is the select column. It is a normal *ButtonColumn* with a command name of *select*. When you click on such a column, the *DataGrid* automatically redraws the selected row using a different class of settings—those defined under the *<selecteditemstyle>* node. There is no need for you to write an *ItemCommand* handler; the described behavior is built in.

```
<asp:ButtonColumn runat="server" text="Select" CommandName="Select" />
```

The style of the selected row—at most one at a time—is set using the *SelectedItemStyle* property. It can be as easy as the following code:

```
<selecteditemstyle backcolor="cyan" />
```

The text of the button column can be replaced with a picture, as discussed earlier for the shopping cart. The change of the selected item is signaled with the *SelectedIndexChanged* event. However, before this event is fired, the application can handle the related *ItemCommand*. Note that the value of the *DataGrid*'s *SelectedIndex* property has not been changed yet when *ItemCommand* arrives. It is set to the new index when *SelectedIndexChanged* reaches the application.

This characteristic alone allows you to implement a nice feature—deselecting the item after two consecutive clicks. In this case, you first cache the old selected item in the *ItemCommand* event handler; then you compare this index with the new selected index within the *SelectedIndexChanged* event. If the two match, you're clicking on a selected item, which will then be unselected. To unselect a selected item, you set the *SelectedIndex* property to -1.

```
void ItemCommand(object sender, DataGridCommandEventArgs e) {
    // Command names ARE case-sensitive
    switch(e.CommandName) {
        case "select":
            m_currentSelectedIndex = grid.SelectedIndex;
            break;
        ⋮
    }
}
void SelectedIndexChanged(object sender, EventArgs e) {
    if (m_currentSelectedIndex == grid.SelectedIndex) {
        grid.SelectedIndex = -1;
        return;
    }
    ⋮
}
```

> **Note** The comparison of command names made within a *switch* statement is case-sensitive and must perfectly match the name of the command as specified in the column declaration. This said, the *select* command in the column declaration can be specified with any case and is understood by the *DataGrid* engine in a case-insensitive way.

If you want the clicked item to appear with the selected style while displaying the product information in a separate frame, you should switch to a button column instead of the hyperlink column.

```
<asp:buttoncolumn runat="server" DataTextField="productname"
    headertext="Product" commandname="select">
    <itemstyle width="200px" />
</asp:buttoncolumn>
```

When the *SelectedIndexChanged* fires, you change the *Src* attribute of the frame component and make it point to the given URL. You retrieve the key value associated with the selected row by using the *DataKeys* collection:

```
void SelectIndexChanged(object sender, EventArgs e)
{
    int productID = (int) grid.DataKeys[grid.SelectedIndex];
    string url = String.Format("productinfo.aspx?id={0}", productID);
    ProductView.Attributes["Src"] = url;
}
```

Note, though, that to programmatically configure the frame you must mark it as *runat=<;$QD>server<;$QD>*, as in the following code:

```
<iframe runat="server" id="ProductView" frameborder="no"
    height="100%" style="border:solid 1px;"></iframe>
```

Figure 6-7 shows the final result.

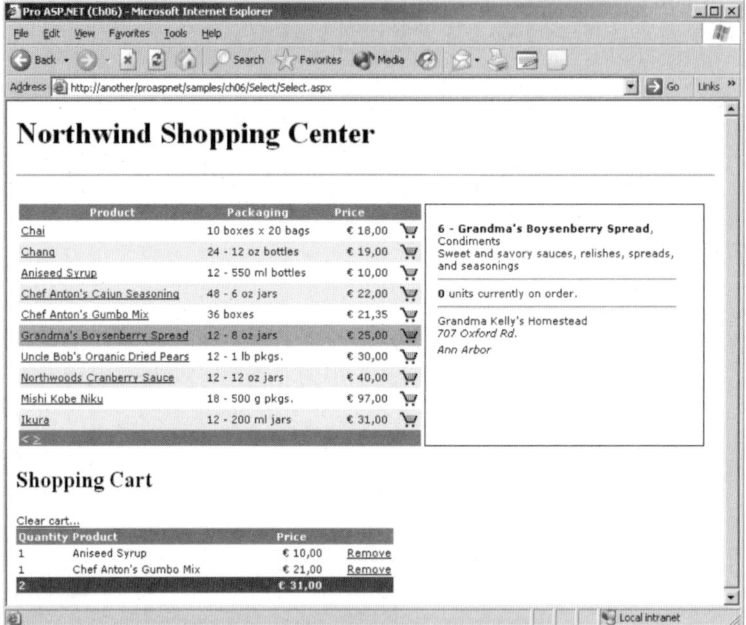


**Figure 6-7** A shopping cart application in which the item being added or viewed is displayed with a selected style.

> **Caution** The selected item can be changed programmatically by setting the *SelectedIndex* property of the *DataGrid* control. Note, though, that if you select a new item through code, the *SelectedIndex-Changed* code is not automatically executed. As long as that code is important, you should add an explicit call in the method.

# Enhancing the *DataGrid*

So far, we assumed that the *DataGrid* control was large enough to contain and display all the items in the data source. In a real-world scenario, though, a couple of additional functions are often needed—paging and sorting. The *DataGrid* control provides good built-in support for both functions. Also, the code you are required to write to implement these functions is limited and, more importantly, can be easily embedded in derived controls.

In this section, I'll focus the discussion on how to page and sort data through the grid. However, I'll do that paying particular attention to the programming interface of the control and blissfully skip over important aspects of data-driven applications, such as scalability and performance. Chapter 7 will be entirely devoted to rewriting the same application discussed here, but with more realistic considerations and optimization in mind. The content of this section focuses on the set of methods and events you can leverage on the *DataGrid* control.

## Paging the Grid Content

In real-world scenarios, the size of a data source easily exceeds the real estate of the page. Data paging is the contrivance that many applications adopt to both gain in scalability and present a more helpful page to the user. Especially on the Web, displaying only a few rows at a time is a more effective approach than downloading hundreds of records that stay hidden most of the time. Setting up a data-paging mechanism requires a certain amount of work from both the control and the page side.

The *DataGrid* control provides some built-in facilities to let the programmer easily switch to a new page according to the user's clicking. The control needs to know how many items should be displayed per page, what type of functionality is required for the pager, and the data source to page through. In return for this, the control tracks the current page index, extracts the rows that fit into the particular page, and refreshes the user interface. Whenever the page index changes, an event is fired to the application—the *PageIndexChanged* event.

### Caching the Data Source

The *DataGrid* control supports two types of paged data sources—built-in paging and custom paging. The standard way of paging is based on the assumption that all the records to scroll through are memory resident. The *DataGrid* is bound to the source all the time and extracts only the rows to display in each particular page. Note that the data source is not saved with the page's view state, so you are responsible for rebinding the data source at each postback.

Because the data source is lost at each response, caching is vital for effective standard paging. You download all the data the first time the page is accessed, store the data set into the application's *Cache* object or the session memory, and rebind until the application is closed or the session is over. In real-world applications, data caching is a double-edged sword. On one hand, it significantly speeds up data retrieval; on the other hand, it taxes the Web server's memory and potentially affects the overall scalability of the application. The scope of the data is another factor to consider carefully. If the data is shared by all sessions and doesn't get stale often, you can store it once in a global object. If you need to store a distinct copy of the data for each session, standard paging is probably not the smartest approach you can take, as it requires a lot of memory and, even worse, pushes an application architecture that doesn't scale really well. We'll delve much deeper into this topic in Chapter 7 when we'll introduce and discuss the second paging mechanism available—custom paging. For now, let's assume all the data is downloaded once and stored in the application's *Cache* object.

```
void Page_Load(object sender, EventArgs e) {
    if (!IsPostBack) {
        LoadDataFromDatabase();
        ⋮
    }
    ⋮
    BindData();
}
void LoadDataFromDatabase() {
    DataTable data = ExecuteQuery(cmdText, connString);
    Cache["AppData"] = data;
}
void BindData() {
    DataTable data = (DataTable) Cache["AppData"];
    ⋮
    grid.DataSource = data;
    grid.DataBind();
}
```

As this code demonstrates, the data is loaded only once and cached in memory. Whenever the page posts back, data is retrieved from the cache and bound to the *DataGrid* control.

## Built-In Paging Support

To enable paging in a *DataGrid* control, you must set the *AllowPaging* property to *true*. When the property is turned on, the control user interface automatically acquires an extra component—the grid pager. The pager is a built-in toolbar with links to move from one page to the next or the previous. You normally configure the pager declaratively by specifying the working mode and a few visual settings. The maintenance of the component is in the care of the *DataGrid* control. The *PageSize* property lets you control the number of rows each page should contain. By default, this value is set to 10.

After turning the pager on, you're only halfway done. The pager is displayed and updated, but it's not functional until you write and register a handler for the *DataGrid*'s *PageIndexChanged* event.

```
<asp:datagrid runat="server" id="grid"
    ⋮
    allowpaging="true"
    onpageindexchanged="PageIndexChanged">
```

The delegate for the *PageIndexChanged* event is shown below. It passes down to the handler a data structure of type *DataGridPageChangedEventArgs*.

```
public delegate void DataGridPageChangedEventHandler(
    object source,
    DataGridPageChangedEventArgs e
);
```

The class inherits from *EventArgs* and features two extra properties—*CommandSource* and *NewPageIndex*. The former represents the source of the event. Because the event is fired only when a button in the pager is clicked, the event source is nothing more than the pager itself—a *DataGridItem* object. The *NewPageIndex* property contains the updated index of the page to show. The *DataGrid* internal engine calculates the correct index of the new page based on the button the user actually clicked.

The following code shows the typical (and minimal) page-changed handler for a *DataGrid* control. It sets the grid's *CurrentPageIndex* property with the new page index and rebinds to the data.

```
void PageIndexChanged(object sender, DataGridPageChangedEventArgs e) {
    grid.CurrentPageIndex = e.NewPageIndex;
    BindData();
}
```

When the *DataGrid*'s *DataBind* method executes, the control extracts from the data source the subset of rows that fits into the current page. Those records are loaded into the *Items* collection and are used to generate the HTML output for the control.

Just as with row selection, you can programmatically change the page by updating the value of the *CurrentPageIndex* property. However, also in this case no related event is ever fired to the application. Another little gotcha you might want to be aware of occurs when you page a grid with a selected row or a row that is currently being edited. Changing the page doesn't reset the value of *SelectedIndex* and *EditItemIndex* properties. As a result, if you have selected, say, the third item on a page and move to the next page, the third item will also be selected on the new page. To avoid this, you can reset the *SelectedIndex* property to -1 in the *PageIndexChanged* event handler.

```
void PageIndexChanged(object sender, DataGridPageChangedEventArgs e) {
    // Cancels the selection
    grid.SelectedIndex = -1;
    ProductView.Attributes["Src"] = "about:blank";

    grid.CurrentPageIndex = e.NewPageIndex;
    BindData();
}
```

The preceding code clears the selection index and frame upon page changes.

## Customizing the Pager Component

The pager component is a table row made of a single cell that spans the whole width of the grid. You can obtain a reference to the pager in two ways—either through the *CommandSource* member of the *DataGridPageChangedEventArgs* data structure during the *PageIndexChanged* event or through the event data available within the *ItemCreated* event. In particular, the *ItemCreated* event is useful because it allows you to customize the pager structure beyond imagination. For example, you could add ToolTips to existing links, insert new link buttons, and even embed a completely user-defined pager. I'll demonstrate this in Chapter 7.

The *DataGrid* control provides some built-in properties to also let you declaratively customize the pager bar. In particular, you can choose between two display modes—numeric pages and next-prev mode. By default, the pager is made of two link buttons: one pointing to the previous page and one pointing to the next page. The default text that is associated with these links is < for the previous button and > for the next button. You can change the text for each link using the *PrevPageText* and *NextPageText* properties. The text replacement can occur both declaratively and programmatically. In the latter case, you do it through the *PagerStyle* property of the *DataGrid* control. The following code, on the other hand, shows how to proceed declaratively:

```
<pagerstyle backcolor="gray" forecolor="white" font-name="webdings"
    font-size="12pt" prevpagetext="3" nextpagetext="4" />
```

The font of the pager is set to *Webdings*, in which the strings 3 and 4 are equivalent to the characters ◀ and ▶.

The display mode of the pager is controlled by the *Mode* property, whose acceptable values are *NumericPages* and *NextPrev*. The *Mode* property takes its values from the *PagerMode* enumeration. The default setting is *NextPrev* and results in two buttons, one to move to the previous page and one to jump to the next page. The *DataGrid* control automatically enables and disables the links according to the current page.

When working in numeric pages mode, the pager displays as many links as there are pages in the data source. The *PageCount* read-only property informs you about the total number of available pages. Figure 6-8 shows the two pager modes.

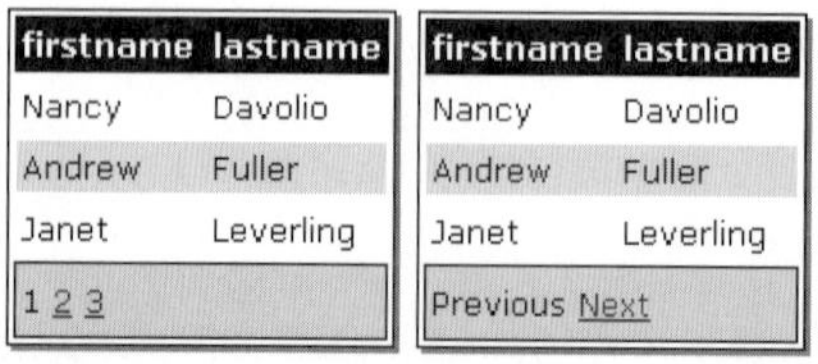

| firstname | lastname |
|---|---|
| Nancy | Davolio |
| Andrew | Fuller |
| Janet | Leverling |
| 1 2 3 | |

| firstname | lastname |
|---|---|
| Nancy | Davolio |
| Andrew | Fuller |
| Janet | Leverling |
| Previous Next | |

**Figure 6-8** The two pager modes, face to face.

In numeric pages mode, the pager shows the index of the current page as plain, nonclickable text. On the other hand, there's no explicit information about the current page index in the default mode. This information can be added manually using the advanced customization mechanism supplied by the *ItemCreated* event. The following code inserts a new label control with page information between the page links:

```
if (e.Item.ItemType == ListItemType.Pager) {
    if (cartGrid.PagerStyle.Mode == PagerMode.NextPrev) {
        TableCell pager = e.Item.Cells[0];
        Label ctl = new Label();
        ctl.Font.Name = "verdana";
        ctl.Font.Size = FontUnit.Point(8);
        ctl.Text = String.Format(" <b>Page {0}</b> ",
            1 + cartGrid.CurrentPageIndex);
        pager.Controls.AddAt(1, ctl);
    }
}
```

The final results are shown in Figure 6-9.

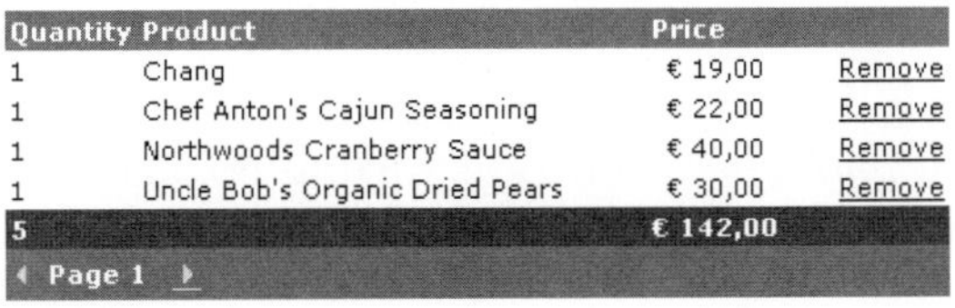

| Quantity | Product | Price | |
|---|---|---|---|
| 1 | Chang | € 19,00 | Remove |
| 1 | Chef Anton's Cajun Seasoning | € 22,00 | Remove |
| 1 | Northwoods Cranberry Sauce | € 40,00 | Remove |
| 1 | Uncle Bob's Organic Dried Pears | € 30,00 | Remove |
| 5 | | € 142,00 | |
| ◂ Page 1 ▸ | | | |

**Figure 6-9** Page information dynamically inserted between the links of a pager.

## Sorting the Data

To enable the *DataGrid*'s sorting capabilities, you set the *AllowSorting* property to *true*. When sorting is enabled, the *DataGrid* gains the ability of rendering the header text of columns as links. You can associate each column with a sorting expression by using the *SortExpression* property. A sorting expression is any comma-separated sequence of column names. Each column name can be enriched with an order qualifier such as DESC or ASC. DESC indicates a descending order, while ASC denotes the ascending order. The ASC qualifier is the default; if omitted, the column is sorted ascendingly. The following code sets up the *DataGrid* column for sorting on the *productname* data source column:

```
<columns>
    <asp:buttoncolumn runat="server"
        DataTextField="productname"
        HeaderText="Product"
```

```
        SortExpression="productname" />
    ⋮
</columns>
```

As Figure 6-10 shows, the header of the column is rendered as a link.

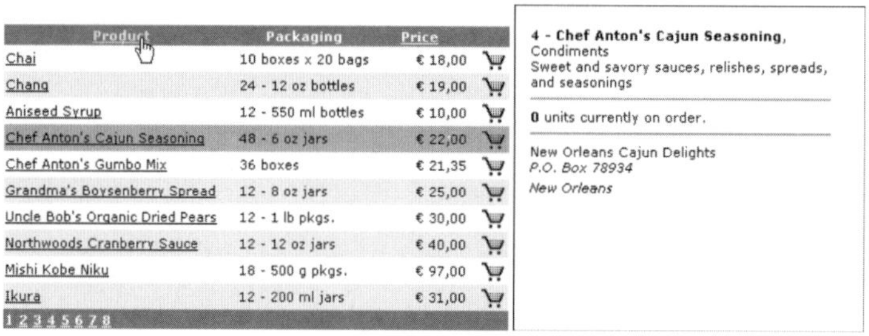

**Figure 6-10** A *DataGrid* with a couple of sortable columns.

When you click the header of the column, the page posts back and runs the code associated with the *SortCommand* event.

```
<asp:datagrid runat="server"
    ⋮
    onsortcommand="SortCommand" />
```

The *DataGridSortCommandEventArgs* structure contains an extra property named *SortExpression*, which contains the sort expression of the column.

```
void SortCommand(object sender, DataGridSortCommandEventArgs e)
{
    // sort the data source
    // bind the data source
}
```

The event handler must accomplish two tasks—sorting the source and binding the data back to the grid. The sorting can take place in any way that is suitable to your application. Typically, if you're working with cached data (as we're doing now), you use the sorting capabilities of the ADO.NET objects. Otherwise, you can run another query against the DBMS and obtain a properly sorted recordset.

Let's modify the *BindData* method to make it capable of supporting sorted views of data. The code first retrieves the data from the *Cache* object and then sorts it using a *DataView* object. (See Chapter 5.)

```
void SortCommand(object sender, DataGridSortCommandEventArgs e) {
    ViewState["DataSortExpression"] = e.SortExpression;
    BindData();
}
void BindData() {
    DataTable data = (DataTable) Cache["AppData"];
```

```
    DataView dv = data.DefaultView;
    dv.Sort = (string) ViewState["DataSortExpression"];
    grid.DataSource = dv;
    grid.DataBind();
}
```

We need to pass the sort expression from the *SortCommand* method to the *BindData* method, which will actually prepare and bind the sorted view of data to the grid. Judging from the preceding code, there would be no need to use the view state. (As we'll discuss in more detail in Chapter 14, minimizing the use of the view state is a key factor in ASP.NET optimization.) You could actually pass the sort expression as an argument to the *BindData* method, but that would work only to sort data after a user click. If you don't save the sort expression in some sort of persistent location (*Session* is fine as well), that information would get lost with the next postback. In particular, you lose the sort as soon as you move to the next page.

> **Caution** Caching a *DataView* to feed the *DataGrid*'s built-in paging engine will not work because the *DataView* class does not store any data. Storing a *DataView* would simply cache the indexes of an underlying *DataTable* object. Unfortunately, though, there will be no track of that table across postbacks if you don't cache it too!

## Auto-Reverse Sorting

Although functional, the sorting mechanism discussed so far is too simplistic and unusable for real-world applications. First, the user has no feedback about the column the data is sorted by. Second, users might want to reverse the order of the data while maintaining the same sort expression. Auto-reverse sorting is a feature that automatically switches from ascending to descending order, and vice versa, when you click a column that is already sorted.

The *ViewState*-based sorting mechanism we discussed earlier already provides a firm infrastructure to build auto-reverse sorting.

```
void SortCommand(object sender, DataGridSortCommandEventArgs e)
{
    // Cache the column sort expression
    string newExpr = e.SortExpression;

    // Compare the new and the cached sort expression. If the two
    // match, then a DESC qualifier is silently appended.
    string oldExpr = (string) ViewState["DataSortExpression"];
    if (oldExpr == newExpr)
```

```
        ViewState["DataSortExpression"] = newExpr + " DESC";
    else
        ViewState["DataSortExpression"] = newExpr;

    // Bind the data
    BindData();
}
```

Any information stored in the page's *ViewState* persists across two successive requests for the same page. In light of this, the current sort expression is available while processing the next request along with the expression associated with the clicked column. If the two expressions match, you're clicking on an already sorted column. This behavior is normally a prelude to reversing the order of the sort.

The code just shown does exactly that, at least in a good number of circumstances. There's an implicit assumption in the preceding listing. It tacitly assumes no sort expression in any columns would ever use the (redundant) keyword ASC to denote an ascending order; it also assumes no descending order is requested. As long as any sort expression is made of a single column name with no order qualifier, the code would work perfectly in providing auto-reverse sorting.

> **Caution** The sorting infrastructure described here needs some improvement to work in all cases regardless of the sort expressions used. In particular, it has a couple of shortcomings. It doesn't work well if multicolumn sorting is used and if a column must be sorted in a descending way by default. A more general approach entails writing a function to parse all the columns in the expression and invert the order for each of them. This approach is described in detail in my book *Building Web Solutions with ASP.NET and ADO.NET* (Microsoft Press, 2002).

## Providing Feedback About Sorting

To give some feedback to the user about the sorted column, you need to programmatically modify the header of the column. You hook up the creation of the header by writing an *ItemCreated* event handler.

```
void ItemCreated(object sender, DataGridItemEventArgs e)
{
    switch(e.Item.ItemType){
        case ListItemType.Header:
            SetupHeader(e);
            break;
```

```
    }
}
void SetupHeader(DataGridItemEventArgs e)
{
    // Is the current sort expression descending?
    string sortExpr = (string) ViewState["DataSortExpression"];
    bool isDesc = sortExpr.EndsWith(m_DESC);

    // Remove the DESC keyword from the sort expression
    string pureSortExpr = sortExpr.Replace(m_DESC, "");

    // Loop through columns to find a matching expression
    for (int i=0; i<grid.Columns.Count; i++)
    {
        // Draw the glyph to reflect sorting direction. The
        // glyph is rendered through an extra label
        string colSortExpr = grid.Columns[i].SortExpression;
        if (pureSortExpr == colSortExpr && colSortExpr != "")
        {
            TableCell cell = e.Item.Cells[i];
            Label lblSorted = new Label();
            lblSorted.Font.Name = "webdings";
            lblSorted.Font.Size = FontUnit.XSmall;
            lblSorted.Text = (isDesc ? " 6" :" 5");
            cell.Controls.Add(lblSorted);
        }
    }
}
```

The label added alongside the header text is a webding glyph that represents a triangle pointed up (as in Figure 6-11) or down.

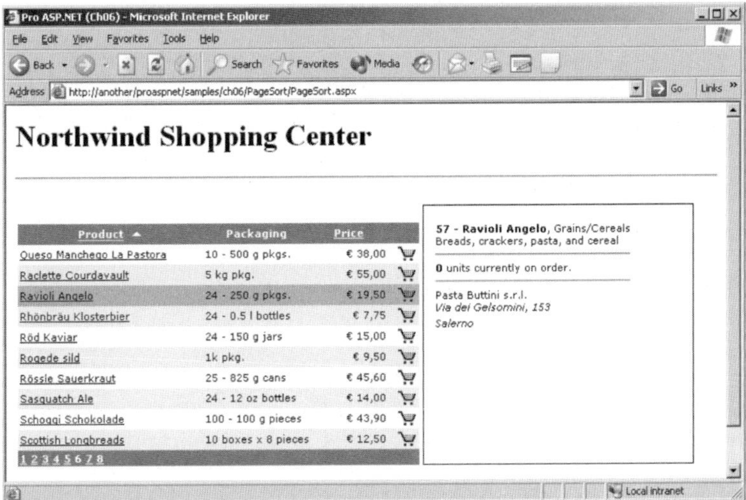


**Figure 6-11** An auto-reverse *DataGrid* providing feedback about the current sort.

> **Note** How can you return to the original sort once you sorted the data source by clicking on column headers? To restore the original sort, you simply clear the current expression and refresh the data.

## Templated Columns

Templated columns allow you to create combinations of HTML text and server controls to design a custom layout for any column. The controls within a templated column can be bound to any combination of fields in the data source. In particular, you can group more fields in a single expression and even embellish the expression with HTML attributes such as boldface or italic style. Templates are column-specific and cannot be applied to autogenerated columns. If you want more columns to share the same template, you can duplicate the code only in the ASP.NET page for each column.

A templated column is recognized by the *<TemplateColumn>* tag and rendered by the *TemplateColumn* class. The body of the tag can contain up to four different templates: *ItemTemplate*, *EditItemTemplate*, *HeaderTemplate*, and *FooterTemplate*. Just as any other column type, a templated column can have a header text and a sort expression. Templated columns, though, do not have an explicit data source field to bind. To bind a template column to one or more data fields, you use a data-binding expression and the *DataBinder* class. The *DataBinder* class provides a simpler syntax than data-binding expressions, but it doesn't let you obtain more than single-value data binding. In particular, you use the *DataBinder*'s *Eval* method to evaluate data-bound expressions at run time and return the value properly cast. For example, the following code snippet shows a templated column that mimics the behavior of a *BoundColumn* object associated with the *lastname* column:

```
<asp:templatecolumn runat="server" headertext="Last Name">
    <itemtemplate>
        <asp:label runat="server" Text='<%#
             DataBinder.Eval(Container.DataItem, "lastname") %>' />
    </itemtemplate>
</asp:templatecolumn>
```

By using *DataBinder.Eval*, you can access any number of fields in the currently bound data source. In addition, you can combine them in any order to obtain any sort of expression, which is otherwise impossible using a simpler bound or button column.

## Available Templates

*ItemTemplate* is the property that lets you define the layout and content of each cell in the column. Other available templates would let you define the structure of the column header (*HeaderTemplate*) and footer (*FooterTemplate*). Furthermore, you can decide the behavior and appearance of the column when a cell is being edited through the *EditItemTemplate* template. I'll have more to say about column in-place editing in the later section "DataGrid In-Place Editing." Table 6-10 summarizes the available column templates and gives a hint about their usage.

**Table 6-10 Supported Column Templates**

| Template Name | Usage |
|---|---|
| ItemTemplate | Contains the template for the items in a *DataGrid* column.<br>`<ItemTemplate>`<br>`  <asp:label runat="server" text= '<%# ... %>'`<br>`</ItemTemplate>`<br>You can use any combination of HTML text and ASP.NET controls to populate the column. |
| EditItemTemplate | Controls the contents of the item selected for editing in the column of the *DataGrid* control. Places the controls you need for editing the cell between the opening and closing *<EditItemTemplate>* tags.<br>`<EditItemTemplate>`<br>`  <asp:textbox runat="server" text= '<%# ... %>'`<br>`</EditItemTemplate>` |
| HeaderTemplate | Contains the template for the heading section.<br>`<HeaderTemplate>`<br>`  <asp:label runat="server" text= "Header">`<br>`</HeaderTemplate>`<br>If you omit this template, the column header is rendered with a label, or with a hyperlink if sorting is enabled. By specifying a custom template, you make yourself responsible to provide the user interface needed to enable sorting on the column. |
| FooterTemplate | Contains the template for the footer section of the column. The default value is a null reference.<br>`<FooterTemplate>`<br>`  <asp:label runat="server" text= "...">`<br>`</FooterTemplate>`<br>The footer is displayed only if the *ShowFooter* property of the *DataGrid* is set to *true*. |

The template properties in the table are exposed by the *TemplateColumn* class as data members of a type that inherits from the *ITemplate* interface. Template-based properties are declaratively set with plain text in the layout of ASP.NET pages. You can programmatically define a template property by writing and instantiating a class that implements the *ITemplate* interface.

In addition to templates, the *TemplateColumn* class provides a few style properties—*ItemStyle*, *HeaderStyle*, and *FooterStyle*—that you use to customize the appearance of items on a per-column basis. The usage of these properties is nearly identical to the same properties seen for other types of columns.

## Combining Multiple-Source Columns

A template column is typically used to combine multiple data-source columns into a single *DataGrid* column. A template column allows you to bind, say, the last and first name of an employee to the same column using some HTML styles to make it even more compelling. The following code snippet demonstrates how to concatenate the first and last name:

```
<itemtemplate>
    <%# "<b>" + DataBinder.Eval(Container.DataItem, "lastname") +
        "</b>, " + DataBinder.Eval(Container.DataItem, "firstname") %>
</itemtemplate>
```

The *DataBinder.Eval* method takes two arguments, the second of which is the name of the data-source column. The first argument is the data object bound to the particular row being processed. The *Container.DataItem* expression returns the *DataItem* property on the underlying *DataGrid* item.

The item template can be described in terms of plain ASP.NET text as well as resorting to some ASP.NET layout code. The following code snippet rewrites the same code discussed a moment ago, but it uses a *Label* control and sets the *ToolTip* property:

```
<itemtemplate>
    <asp:label runat="server"
        text='<%# "<b>" + DataBinder.Eval(Container.DataItem, "lastname") +
        "</b>, " + DataBinder.Eval(Container.DataItem, "firstname") %>'
        tooltip='<%# "Born on " +
        DataBinder.Eval(Container.DataItem, "birthdate", "{0:d}") %>' />
</itemtemplate>
```

As you can see, the *DataBinder.Eval* method features a third argument, which is the format string for the bound value. The output generated by the code is shown in Figure 6-12.

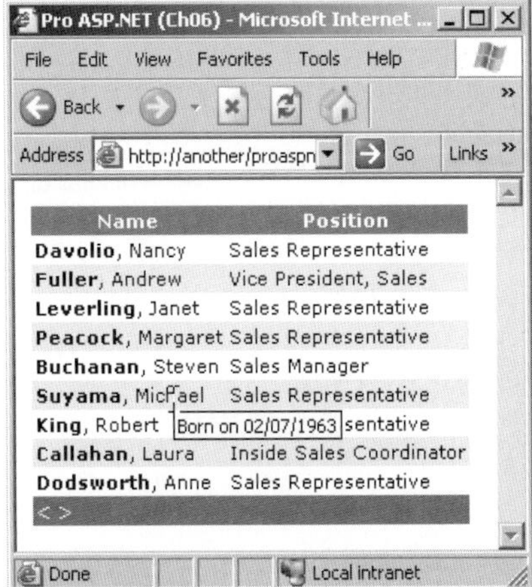


**Figure 6-12** A templated column employs custom styles and bound ToolTips.

## Using Multiple Arguments with HyperLink Columns

As we saw earlier, the *HyperLinkColumn* class can navigate to parametric and data-bound URLs. The column expands arguments automatically but doesn't let you specify more than one argument per URL. More often than not, you'll find this limitation too restrictive. Is there a way to have a hyperlink column with a URL that embeds multiple arguments? Templated columns make this possible. The HTML output of a *HyperLinkColumn* cell is an *<a>* tag. If you create a templated column and make it output an anchor element, you can closely control the structure of the resultant hyperlink and specify as many data-bound arguments as needed.

The following code defines a *DataGrid* templated column that provides the same functionality as a hyperlink column but supports up to four URL arguments:

```
<asp:TemplateColumn runat="server">
<itemtemplate>
    <a runat="server"
        target="frInfo"
        href='<%# "moreinfo.aspx" +
        "?id=" + DataBinder.Eval(Container.DataItem, "employeeid") +
        "&first=" + DataBinder.Eval(Container.DataItem, "firstname") +
        "&last=" + DataBinder.Eval(Container.DataItem, "lastname") +
        "&position=" + DataBinder.Eval(Container.DataItem, "title")
        %>'>More...
    </a>
</itemtemplate>
</asp:TemplateColumn>
```

The structure of the template is extremely simple and just builds up an anchor tag in which the *href* attribute and the text are data bound to as many fields as needed. Figure 6-13 shows the final results.

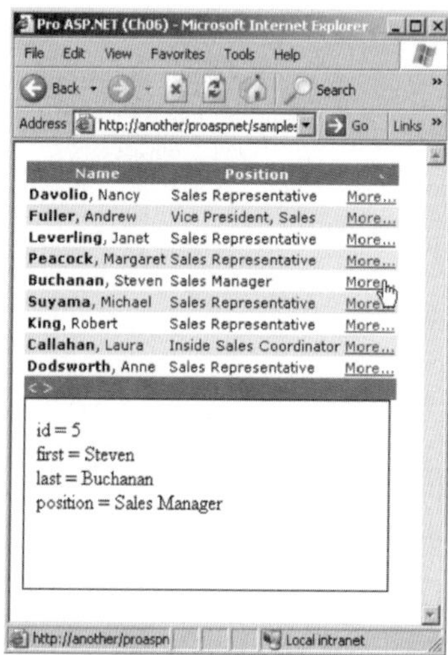

**Figure 6-13** A templated column that acts as a multiparameter hyperlink column.

> **Note** To some extent, templated columns are functionally similar to hooking up the *ItemCreated* event and can modify the *DataGrid* items on the fly. Templates are extremely flexible, but with them you pay parsing costs that make them less efficient overall than hooking an event. Although the difference is not always relevant, you should avoid templates if you have another way to accomplish the same task.

## Enhancing the Shopping Cart Application

A templated column allows you to enhance the shopping cart by adding the possibility of specifying how many items of a given product will be purchased. The idea is to replace the button column used for adding items to the shopping cart with a template column in which the button is preceded by a text box, as in Figure 6-14.

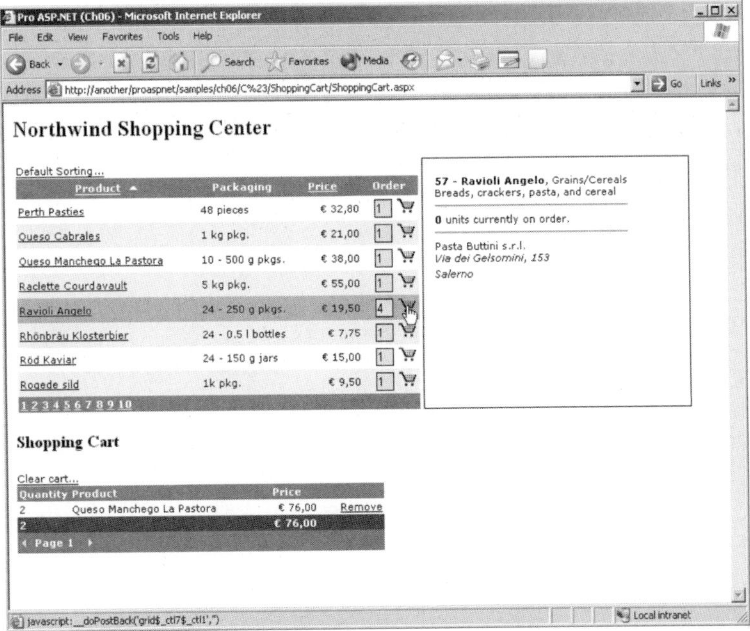

**Figure 6-14** Using a templated column to enhance the shopping cart application.

The source code of the template looks like the following:

```
<asp:templatecolumn runat="server" headertext="Order">
    <itemstyle width="60px" horizontalalign="right" />
    <itemtemplate>
        <asp:textbox runat="server" id="qty" text="1"
            width="20px" maxlength="1"
            font-size="x-small" backcolor="yellow"
            style="border:solid 1px;" />
        <asp:linkbutton runat="server"
            commandname="AddToCart"
            text="<img title='Add to cart...' border='no'
                src='images/cart.gif' />" />
    </itemtemplate>
</asp:templatecolumn>
```

The template is composed of a text box and link button whose text is a static *<img>* tag. The procedure to handle the click doesn't need to change. Reading the value entered in the text box when the page posts back to add to the shopping cart is a bit more tricky. You must retrieve the text-box control in the subtree of controls rooted in the templated cell. You can do that either by index or by name. To find a control by name in its proper naming container, you use the *FindControl* method. Be sure the *FindControl* method is called on the *DataGrid* item object, not on the page or anywhere else. The following code shows how to rewrite the *AddToCart* method to add the specified number of items:

```
void AddToCart(DataGridItem item, int rowIndex)
{
    ⋮
    int defaultQuantity = 1;
    TextBox ctl = (TextBox) item.FindControl("qty");
    if (ctl != null)
        defaultQuantity = Convert.ToInt32(ctl.Text);

    row["quantity"]= defaultQuantity;
    row["productname"] = tableRow["productname"];
    row["price"] = (decimal) (defaultQuantity *
        Convert.ToDecimal(tableRow["unitprice"]));
    m_cart.Rows.Add(row);
    ⋮
}
```

The *DataGridItem* object that gets passed to *AddToCart* is the *e.Item* object taken from the event data:

```
void ItemCommand(object sender, DataGridCommandEventArgs e)
{
    // Command names ARE case-sensitive
    switch(e.CommandName)
    {
        case "AddToCart":
            AddToCart(e.Item, e.Item.ItemIndex);
            break;
        ⋮
    }
}
```

## DataGrid In-Place Editing

A *DataGrid* control displays mostly read-only data. If editing is needed, you select the row to update and post a request for another page. The new page contains an edit form with input fields and links to persist or reject the changes. This is probably the most effective pattern for editing data over the Web and certainly the pattern that provides the highest level of flexibility. With *DataGrid* controls, though, another simpler, but just as effective, model of data editing is possible. The new model is known as in-place editing and mimics the behavior of an Excel worksheet. When you trigger the event that begins the editing phase, the visible part of the grid is redrawn and—like cells in Excel—the row selected for editing is rendered in a different way, using text-box controls instead of literals and labels. At the same time, the *DataGrid* control completes its own user interface with a couple of button links to allow you to commit or rollback changes.

In-place editing doesn't require much work to be completely set up but, at the same time, is not appropriate for all types of applications and not functional in all operating contexts. All in all, if you have to edit the content of single and relatively small tables that have no special validation or business logic to apply, in-place editing is extremely handy and powerful.

## Configuring the Built-In Edit Engine

The key object for in-place editing is the *EditCommandColumn* class. The column adds a link button to all rows of the grid. When the link is clicked, the page posts back and the cells of the row are drawn in edit mode. How a column behaves in edit mode depends on the column type. For example, button and hyperlink columns are completely ignored in edit mode. Bound and templated columns, on the other hand, change their rendering when the row is being edited. In particular, bound columns are rendered using text boxes in place of literals, whereas templated columns display the contents of the *<EditItemTemplate>* section, if any. Here is a typical declaration for an edit column:

```
<asp:editcommandcolumn runat="server"
    EditText="Edit" UpdateText="OK" CancelText="Cancel">
    <itemstyle width="30px" horizontalalign="center" backcolor="yellow" />
</asp:editcommandcolumn>
```

The properties specific to the *EditCommandColumn* class are listed in Table 6-11.

**Table 6-11 Properties of the *EditCommandColumn* Class**

| Property | Description |
|---|---|
| *ButtonType* | Gets or sets the button type for the column. Acceptable values are defined in the *ButtonType* enumeration. Default is *LinkButton*. |
| *CancelText* | Gets or sets the text to display for the Cancel command button when the row is being edited. |
| *EditText* | Gets or sets the button text to display to let the user click and edit the contents of the row. |
| *UpdateText* | Gets or sets the text to display for the Update command button when the row is being edited. |

The edit column initially displays a link (or a push) button to click to enter in the edit mode. The text displayed in each cell of the column is not data-bound but can only be a literal string (for example, Edit) or anything else you can define through HTML tags (for example, an image). The text to use is read through the *EditText* property. When the row enters in edit mode, the *EditItemIndex* property is automatically set to the 0-based index of the row, the cells are rendered using text boxes, and the Edit button is replaced with two new buttons—one to save the changes and one to cancel. The text for these two buttons can be controlled using the *UpdateText* and *CancelText* properties.

Clicking any edit buttons fires an ad hoc event—*EditCommand*, *UpdateCommand*, or *CancelCommand*—for which programmers should provide handlers.

```
<asp:datagrid runat="server" id="grid"
    ⋮
    oneditcommand="EditCommand"
    oncancelcommand="CancelCommand"
    onupdatecommand="UpdateCommand">
    ⋮
</asp:datagrid>
```

The *DataGrid* control provides a built-in mechanism for editing rows, but the programmer is still responsible for supplying the actual code that updates the underlying data source. Likewise, the programmer is responsible for any start-up or clean-up operation that needs to be accomplished when the editing begins or is canceled. The following code snippet shows typical event handlers for in-place editing:

```
void EditCommand(object sender, DataGridCommandEventArgs e) {
    // Set the current item to edit mode
    grid.EditItemIndex = e.Item.ItemIndex;

    // Refresh the grid
    BindData();
}

void CancelCommand(object sender, DataGridCommandEventArgs e) {
    // Cancel edit mode for the row
    grid.EditItemIndex = -1;

    // Refresh the grid
    BindData();
}

void UpdateCommand(object sender, DataGridCommandEventArgs e) {
    // Cancel edit mode for the row
    grid.EditItemIndex = -1;

    // Update the data source
    // *** do something here

    // Refresh the grid
    BindData();
}
```

Figure 6-15 shows the two phases of the row-editing process.

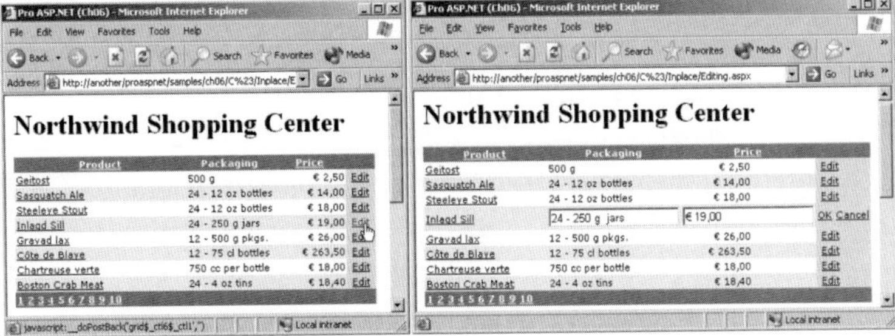

**Figure 6-15** The in-place editing process in action.

## Setting Up the Template of the Row

As you can see in Figure 6-15, there's a significant difference in the style of the row before and during the editing. Any visual setting you apply to the row in read mode is lost when the row enters the edit mode. To obtain a consistent user interface, there's no other way than intervening when the row is created—that is, when the *ItemCreated* event fires for an item of type *EditItem*.

```
void ItemCreated(object sender, DataGridItemEventArgs e) {
    ListItemType itemType = e.Item.ItemType;
    switch(itemType)
    {
        case ListItemType.EditItem:
            SetupEditItem(e);
            break;
        ⋮
    }
}
```

In this case, the *DataGridItem* is the table row that contains the row to edit. You can walk your way through the various cells and modify font and styles at your convenience. For example, the following code changes the style of the all text boxes:

```
void SetupEditItem(DataGridItemEventArgs e) {
    foreach(TableCell cell in e.Item.Cells)
    {
        // Skip if a readonly cell is found
        if (cell.Controls.Count <=0)
            continue;

        Control ctl = cell.Controls[0];
        if (ctl is TextBox)
        {
            TextBox t = (TextBox) ctl;
            t.BackColor = Color.Yellow;
            t.BorderStyle = BorderStyle.Outset;
            t.BorderColor = Color.BlueViolet;
            t.BorderWidth = Unit.Point(1);
            t.Width = Unit.Percentage(100);
```

```
            t.Font.Name = "verdana";
            t.Font.Size = FontUnit.Point(8);
        }
    }
}
```

The text that characterizes the link buttons can be made of HTML-rich text and include formatting and images as well. For example, the following code uses a GIF file for the edit text:

```
EditText="<img src='edit.gif' border='no' align='absmiddle' alt='Edit'>"
```

The final results are shown in Figure 6-16.

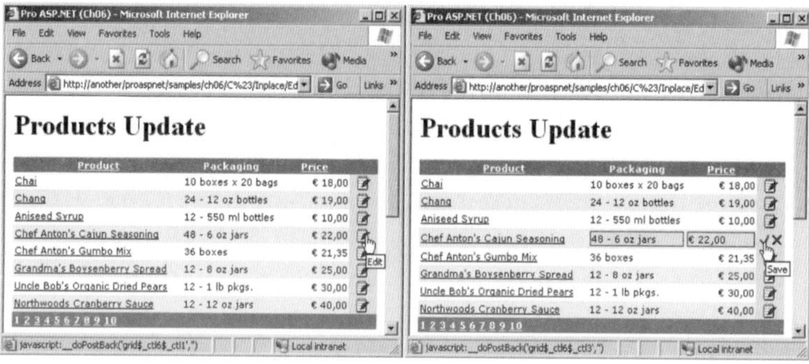

**Figure 6-16** The in-place editing process in action after applying cosmetic changes.

Not all cells in a row are actually editable. As mentioned, cells belonging to hyperlink and button columns cannot be edited and cells of bound columns are editable by default. The *BoundColumn* class has a *Readonly* attribute that if set to *true* (*false* is the default) would make the cell read-only and leave it unaffected by the editing mode. By contrast, cells of templated columns are read-only by default and enter into edit mode only if you explicitly define an edit template.

> **Note** Just as for the row selection, the row editing mode is persisted across page changes. For example, suppose you are editing the third row on a page. If you jump to another page, the third row would automatically display in edit mode too. This happens because the *EditItemIndex* property—the property that determines which row is being edited—is never reset during the page changed postback. To avoid this behavior, reset the *EditItemIndex* property to -1 in your own *PageIndexChanged* event handler.

### Validation and Edit Templates

The in-place editing, as we've built it so far, is simple and easy but comes with quite a long list of shortcomings. In particular, only the visible fields are updateable and the initial text of the text boxes defaults to the display text of the cell. As you can see in Figure 6-16, this is a bit impractical if you have formatting rules applied or computed columns. In addition, the use of automatically generated edit controls forces you to use indexes to retrieve the new values from text boxes and no validation or special input policies are possible. For example, you can't check whether a date or a ZIP code is really entered or figure out a way to force users to pick up values from a closed list.

All these issues are solved at the root if you don't use *DataGrid* in-place editing and resort to a more traditional approach based on ad hoc pages or user controls. However, by also using edit templates, the *DataGrid* in-place editing can be enhanced to some extent. Let's see how to edit the price of a product without formatting text and making sure that a valid price is entered.

The first step in accomplishing this is turning the unit price column into a templated column. The following code would do the job:

```
<asp:templatecolumn runat="server" headertext="Price">
    <itemstyle width="80px" horizontalalign="right" />
    <itemtemplate>
        <%# DataBinder.Eval(Container.DataItem, "unitprice", "{0:c}")%>
    </itemtemplate>
</asp:templatecolumn>
```

Replacing the original bound column with this one doesn't change the appearance of the page but produces one relevant effect—the Price column is no longer editable. Templated columns, in fact, are read-only by default. To make the price editable, we need to add an edit template, as shown here:

```
<asp:templatecolumn runat="server" headertext="Price">
⋮
<edititemtemplate>
    <asp:textbox runat="server" id="priceBox" backcolor="yellow"
        font-name="verdana" font-size="8pt" style="border:solid 1px;"
        text='<%#
          DataBinder.Eval(Container.DataItem, "unitprice", "{0:N}")%>'
    />
</edititemtemplate>
</asp:templatecolumn>
```

The column's edit template includes a text-box server control that we can configure as needed for fonts and styles. Not a minor point is the fact that we can now also explicitly set the ID of the control. The default text of the text box is set using the *DataBinder.Eval* method, for which we can choose the formatting rules that best apply. For example, *{0:N}* indicates that the price is displayed as a standard number with thousand separators and two decimal digits. Note that with templated columns, the *ItemCreated* trick we set up earlier for customizing the look and feel of the text box doesn't work any longer. If you want to control the visual settings of the text box, you can work on the control declaration in the template.

If validation is required, you simply add the validation control that best suits your needs. For example, you add a *RangeValidator* if you want to make sure the new value falls in a specified range:

```
<asp:RangeValidator runat="server" id="priceValidator"
    ControlToValidate="priceBox"
    Display="Dynamic"
    Text="<span title='Must be a price from 2,00 to 400,00.'>*</span>"
    MinimumValue="2,00" MaximumValue="400,00"
    Type="Currency" />
```

The type of the data in the control is set to *Currency* to allow for currency characters to be entered if needed. The *MinimumValue* and *MaximumValue* properties define the range of allowed values. As we saw in Chapter 3, the *Text* property indicates the short text to display alongside the text-box control should the validation not be successful. You normally set the *Text* property to an asterisk, an exclamation mark, or any expression that might serve to capture the user's attention. You might also set it to descriptive text, but this is sometimes impractical for space constraints. In this case, you store a short alert expression into *Text* and set the *ErrorMessage* property to a full description. *ErrorMessage* would be displayed only in the validation summary of the page, if any.

A smart trick to get the best of both solutions is associating an HTML ToolTip with the short alert text in the *Text* property. To obtain that, you can wrap the text in a *<span>* tag and set the *title* attribute as needed. When using a validation control in a *DataGrid* cell, you should always set the *Display* property to *Dynamic* to ensure that the label with the error message is created in the page only if strictly needed. This contrivance normally produces a better graphical result. Figure 6-17 shows the validation control in action.

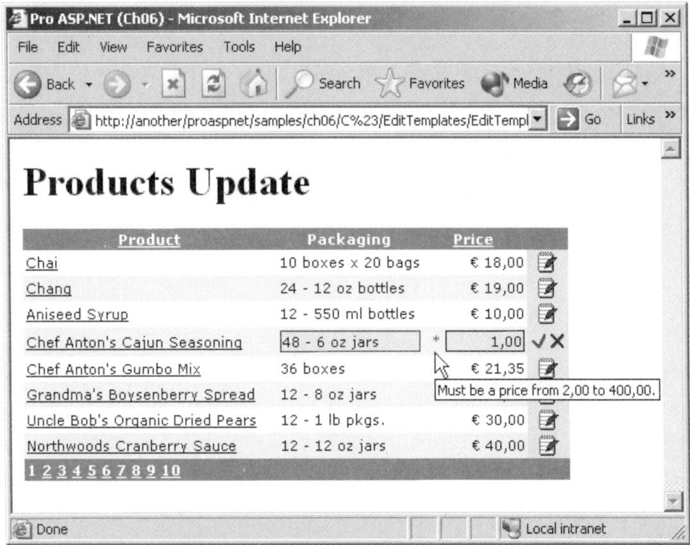


**Figure 6-17** Validating the input values in a *DataGrid* control.

Note that validation on the page is performed only when the update command button is clicked.

## Persisting Changes

The final step of in-place editing is persisting the changes to the underlying data source. Before performing the physical update, though, you must first retrieve the new values from the text boxes or drop-down lists in the editing cells. The code you use to retrieve values differs depending on whether the default or a custom edit template is used. When the user clicks to save the changes, the page posts back and executes any code associated with the *UpdateCommand* event.

To start out, the event handler resets to -1 the index of the row being edited and cancels the editing mode. Next, it retrieves the new values and prepares the commands needed to update the underlying data source. For Web applications, direct SQL commands are probably the fastest way to persist changes, at least when data conflicts are not critical events. On the other hand, when the logic of the application requires that the code update the *same* record read (that is, a record that has not been modified in the time between your reading and writing), then resorting to ADO.NET batch update allows you to exploit the framework facilities for data conflicts. (We covered batch updates in Chapter 5.)

## Retrieving Input Values

To read the input values, you retrieve the instances of the corresponding controls and extract their contents. When the in-place editing feature is implemented in the default way—that is, without edit templates—the preferred way to retrieve the involved text boxes is by position.

```
// Retrieve the second column of the row
// (e is the event data (DataGridCommandEventArgs class))
Control = e.Item.Cells[1].Controls[0];
if (ctl == null)
    return;
string packaging = ((TextBox) ctl).Text;
```

The preceding code shows how to retrieve the value of the text box in the second column of the row. The index of the *Cells* collection is the 0-based position of the edited column. The index is absolute and doesn't consider any read-only column in the middle. Of the specified cell, you then take the first control, which is a *TextBox* control by design. Note that the value read out of the text box must be converted to the destination type—that is, the type of the corresponding source column. This feature alone makes it significantly more complex than using the default editing template with formatted columns. In fact, you must be able to read the column's value free of all formatting text (for example, the currency symbol).

You must identify input controls by position also because the text boxes are created by the *DataGrid* control and are given a predefined ID that you can only guess or determine empirically. All text boxes are created by the time the *ItemCreated* event fires, however. So by writing such an event handler, you could change the text-box ID on the fly and use a custom but unambiguous name. The following code snippet slightly enhances the code we discussed earlier to customize the style of the editing text boxes:

```
foreach(TableCell cell in e.Item.Cells)
{
    // Skip if a readonly cell is found
    if (cell.Controls.Count <=0)
        continue;

    Control ctl = cell.Controls[0];
    if (ctl is TextBox) {
        TextBox t = (TextBox) ctl;
        t.ID = "MyTextBox";
        ⋮
    }
}
```

The name of the underlying database column is a good (and unique) replacement for the system-provided ID.

If you use edit templates, things are easier because you use your own text boxes and give them your own IDs, which are fixed and unique. In this case, retrieving the input values is as easy as the following code:

```
// priceBox is the ID of the textbox in the edit template
ctl = item.FindControl("priceBox");
if (ctl == null)
    return;
double price = Convert.ToDouble(((TextBox) ctl).Text);
```

Using *FindControl* is easier to code and more readable, but slower than just using indexes and position-based access.

## Updating the Data Source

Once you hold all the new data, updating the underlying data source is simply a matter of preparing and executing a SQL command. Using parameters makes code more clear and also constitutes an extra line of defense against malicious SQL attacks. Command parameters, in fact, are strongly typed and match exactly the database type. If you set up the command using parameters, a string would never be passed in place of a number, which is one of the typical ways SQL injections occur. (More on this in Chapter 15.)

```
// Prepare the command
string updText = "UPDATE products " +
                 "SET quantityperunit=@packaging, " +
                 "unitprice=@price WHERE productid=@productid";
SqlConnection cnn = new SqlConnection(connString);
SqlCommand cmd = new SqlCommand(updText, cnn);
cmd.Parameters.Add("@productID", SqlDbType.Int).Value = productID;
cmd.Parameters.Add("@packaging", SqlDbType.NVarChar).Value = packaging;
cmd.Parameters.Add("@price", SqlDbType.Money).Value = price;

// Execute the command
cnn.Open();
cmd.ExecuteNonQuery();
cnn.Close();
```

The command executes during the postback event that originates from the user's clicking of the Update link. After that, the data source must be re-bound to the *DataGrid* control for display purposes. However, an extra step might be needed this time. If you configured the grid to use cached data (as we did in this chapter), for the changes to show up you must invalidate and refresh the current cache. As a result, the complete code for the *UpdateCommand* event looks like the following:

```
void UpdateCommand(object sender, DataGridCommandEventArgs e)
{
    // Cancel edit mode for the row
    grid.EditItemIndex = -1;
```

```
    // Update the data source
    UpdateDataSource((int) grid.DataKeys[e.Item.ItemIndex], e.Item);

    // Reload the data and refresh the grid
    LoadDataFromDatabase();
    BindData();
}
```

The *DataGrid* in-place editing is quick and effective, but it also has the drawback of allowing for only one row at a time to be edited. If you want a full-page edit grid control, you must define all template columns and configure them to use data-bound text boxes rather than literals. If you do so, though, the update mechanism is entirely your own, but it doesn't require code different from the solutions we examined in this chapter.

## Conclusion

In this chapter, we examined the *DataGrid* ASP.NET control, which is a type of component that all Web applications need to employ in one shape or another. All Web applications, in fact, at a certain point in their life cycle are called to display data. More often than not, this data is in tabular format.

As long as the data to display can be articulated in rows and columns, the *DataGrid* control is ideal to display it. The control provides facilities to select and edit single rows, page through a bound data source, and sort and filter views. In addition, you can customize all the cells in a column by using any data-bound template made of any combination of HTML and ASP.NET text. To top it off, a fair number of events signal to user applications the key events in the control's lifecycle. Good examples of such events are *ItemCreated* and *ItemDataBound*, just to name those that provide for the deepest types of customization. Other events such as *SelectedIndexChanged*, *ItemCommand*, and *PageIndexChanged* are more specific but equally useful.

The in-place editing feature is a piece of cake, as it is easy to configure and powerful to exploit. We could discuss the fact that this type of editing—designed to resemble Excel worksheets—is not appropriate for all applications and pages. However, as long as you can functionally afford the feature, in-place editing can save you a lot of coding and increase productivity by at least one order of magnitude.

So what should your opinion be about the *DataGrid* control after this chapter? The control is definitely the richest and most powerful of all ASP.NET Web controls. However, if you look at the amount of code we've put in all the pages we've built in this chapter, you can't help but have doubts. If the *DataGrid* is so powerful and feature-rich, why do we need to write all that code? The answer is not simple and probably touches Microsoft policies for public controls. Although incredibly rich with functions and settings, the *DataGrid* is only a small portion of a real-world control. For paging, editing, and sorting, it provides only an easily extensible infrastructure for which you have to write the missing, application-specific code.

Although the *DataGrid* control could be even richer than it is today in ASP.NET 1.1, no general-purpose control would ever be so perfect as to need virtually no customization code. The reason is that all applications have a grid of data to display, but all applications need their own grid. As a result, applications either use a generic grid to configure and customize programmatically or employ a tailor-made control in which extensions have been hard-coded once and for all. Fortunately, though, the *DataGrid* is part of an object-oriented framework, so deriving new classes is easier than ever before. Finally, note that we've used inline code for all the samples we developed in this chapter. Given the amount of code we had to write, a page code-behind class wouldn't have been a bad idea.

While introducing the chapter, we mentioned that the *DataGrid* is not the most flexible of all iterative data-bound controls. After that, we didn't do anything else but emphasize the flexibility of the control. What's up with that? The *DataGrid* is an extremely flexible control, but it can only display tables of data. Other components—the *DataList* and the *Repeater*—let you gain more precise control over the binding process and even produce a nontabular output. We'll examine other iterative controls in Chapter 9.

In the next chapter, we'll discuss ways to paginate and navigate through large amounts of data in a Web application. In particular, we'll focus on the importance of writing ad hoc SQL code to balance various contrasting requirements, such as minimizing the data to transfer, maximizing performance, and improving scalability.

## Resources

- Building Web Solutions with ASP.NET and ADO.NET (Microsoft Press, 2002)
- Alternate by value (*http://www.aspnetpro.com/features/2003/02/asp200302de_f/asp200302de_f.asp*)
- Sort Data on the Fly (*http://www.aspnetpro.com/features/2002/12/asp200212wf_f/asp200212wf_f.asp*)
- Keep Your DataGrid Position (*http://www.aspnetpro.com/features/2002/12/asp200212ht_f/asp200212ht_f.asp*)
- Summary Rows in DataGrid Controls (*http://msdn.microsoft.com/library/en-us/dndive/html/data01102002.asp*)

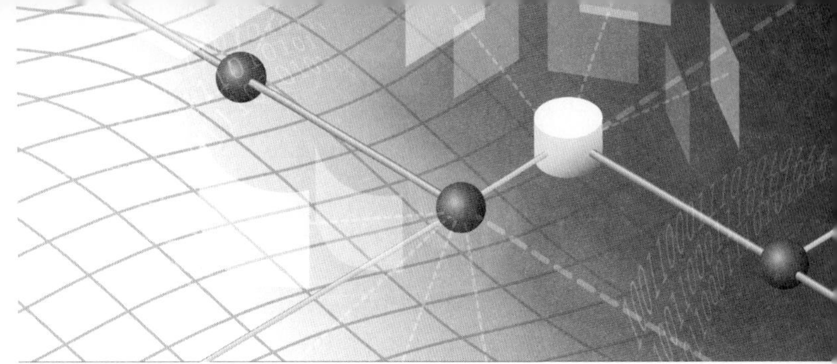

# 7

# Paging Through Data Sources

*Men acquire a particular quality by constantly acting a particular way.... You become just by performing just actions, temperate by performing temperate actions, brave by performing brave actions.*

*—Aristotle*

In real-world scenarios, pagination is an important issue when you have a lot of records to display. To preserve a good level of scalability and performance on the server, you might decide to show the records that form the key view of your application in equally sized pages. You would then want to create a pager bar that has a bunch of ad hoc buttons that allow users to navigate between pages. So with a data source, a sized view, and a pager bar, you are pretty much done; the *DataGrid* itself would do the job of paging the records.

As we saw in the previous chapter, setting up the *DataGrid* control to work in paging mode is easy and effective. First you enable data paging by setting the *AllowPaging* property to *true*. Next you decide the style for user-interface elements related to pagination. Internally, the *DataGrid* control takes care of extracting from the bound data source the records that fall in the range of the current page. When you work with large-sized data sources, the risk of taxing the Web server's memory too much is high. For mostly read-only data globally shared by all sessions, caching for pagination can be a feasible solution. However, the accuracy of this statement depends on the effective size of the data source. Caching a few dozen, or even hundreds, of records is much different than caching a few thousand!

If session-specific data is to be paged, binding and caching the entire data source should be avoided because the data would be loaded for each user, potentially degrading overall scalability. However, if you're determined to exploit the *DataGrid*'s built-in paging capabilities without caching data somewhere and somehow, you inevitably experience the paradox of pagination. The *DataGrid* control requires you to load and bind the data source at each request. If caching is not used, you execute a query at each request. You could end up querying for 1000 records (if that is the size of the entire data source) to display only the 20 that fit in the requested page.

## Custom Paging with *DataGrid* Controls

In situations in which you have to display session-specific or highly volatile data, you can exploit another feature of the *DataGrid* control—custom pagination. When custom pagination is enabled, the control does not implement any algorithm to page over a bound data source. The *DataGrid* still supplies the built-in infrastructure for paging (the pager bar, informational properties, and events), but it expects the programmer to set the *DataSource* property with only the records to be displayed for a given page.

When working in custom-paging mode, the *DataGrid* control does not locate and extract the records that fall into the given page. It simply assumes all the records currently associated with the *DataSource* property form the page. The advantage is that only the records that fit into the page are held in memory, resulting in a significant savings in the amount of system resources used. Because the records are obtained by querying the database, you always display up-to-date data, which is a strict requirement for databases that get stale relatively quickly. A less pleasant side effect of this approach is that, depending on the database management system (DBMS) you're using and the style of the pager you expect to provide, coming up with a page-based query command might not be easy. In this chapter, though, we'll focus on providing basic strategies for custom paging.

The layout of the code you need to write is not significantly different whether you use default or custom pagination. You have to provide the content of the page in both cases—the whole source for built-in pagination, and only the current page if custom paging is turned on. There are clear differences in how the two approaches work in terms of overall performance and scalability. Factors that determine which method to use are (in order of priority):

1. How often your data gets stale and needs to be updated
2. The scope of the data, be it session or application
3. The size of the overall data source to page through

The more static your data is, the more you can exploit caching, both data and page-output caching. (We'll cover page-output caching in Chapter 14.) The more dynamic your data is, the more you should try to minimize the amount of data being read and stored. In systems that need to be highly–scalable, support a variable, and have a normally high number of concurrent users (not all Web systems are like this), you should also have a middle tier that can be scaled out to mitigate the impact that data retrieval has on performance.

Let's see how to turn custom pagination on for ASP.NET applications and examine the complications raised in real-world implementations.

## Enabling Custom Pagination

To enable custom pagination for ASP.NET *DataGrid* controls, you must ensure that both *AllowPaging* and *AllowCustomPaging* properties are set to *true*. This can be done declaratively through the ASP.NET page layout using the following code:

```
<asp:datagrid runat="server" id="grid"
    ⋮
    AllowPaging="true"
    AllowCustomPaging="true"
    OnPageIndexChanged="PageIndexChanged">
```

Alternatively, you can programmatically set these properties to *true* during page loading or whenever it makes sense to your application:

```
void Page_Load(object sender, EventArgs e) {
    grid.AllowPaging = true;
    grid.AllowCustomPaging = true;
    PageIndexChanged += new DataGridPageChangedEventHandler(
        this.PageIndexChanged);
}
```

Setting the *AllowPaging* property to *true* tells the *DataGrid* control that the support for paging must be initialized (that is, the pager must be displayed). Setting the *AllowCustomPaging* property to *true* instructs the control not to page through the data source but to just read and display all the data items bound to the *DataSource* property.

In addition to enabling pagination, you must provide settings for the pager and the page size. This is the same as for normal pagination. The pager and the page size take default values, so it's not necessary to explicitly set them in your code—although you can if you don't like the standard settings. However, you must supply a valid handler for the *PageIndexChanged* event. This event is fired whenever the user clicks on a page button or in any way causes, even programmatically, the current page to change. The event handler to write is based on the *DataGridPageChangedEventHandler* delegate type. (For more information on default paging, see Chapter 6.)

### Setting the Virtual Item Count

During the execution of the *DataBind* method, the *DataGrid* control extracts all the items from *DataSource* and copies them into the *Items* collection. This behavior is common to both paging scenarios. What differs in the two cases is the subset of data items extracted from *DataSource*. The *DataGrid* control determines the page count, dividing the total number of items by the page size. In the case of default pagination, the total number of items is given by the record count in the data source.

With custom pagination, on the other hand, the data source contains only the records that fit in the page being displayed. The total number of items to page through can't be inferred from any available data. For this reason, you must provide that number by using an ad hoc property—the *VirtualItemCount* property. The following code shows the typical way to retrieve a value to set the property. This sample procedure simply executes a SELECT COUNT query on the Northwind Products table.

```
public void SetVirtualItemCount()
{
    // Set up the connection
    string strConn = "...";
    SqlConnection conn = new SqlConnection(strConn);

    // Set up the command
    string strCmd = "SELECT COUNT(*) FROM products";
    SqlCommand cmd = new SqlCommand(strCmd, conn);

    // Execute the command
    conn.Open();
    int nItemCount = (int) cmd.ExecuteScalar();
    conn.Close();

    // Set the grid's virtual item count
    grid.VirtualItemCount = nItemCount;
    return;
}
```

Note the use of the command's *ExecuteScalar* method to retrieve a single, scalar value from a query. The *DataGrid* control uses the virtual item count information to properly set up the pager bar. Setting the *AllowCustomPaging* and *VirtualItemCount* properties are two requirements for the *DataGrid* custom pagination.

## Paging Using Key Values

With custom pagination, the trick is to figure out a (customized) way to page through records using SQL commands. Because the contents of each page are retrieved with an individual query, the command text must be designed to return a precise subset of the records that match certain criteria. Data paging means that you have a base query command but need to scroll through its resultset one page at a time. How can you force the DBMS to return only a particular portion of the selected records? Unfortunately, there's no official answer to this question, but a few best practices have been identified over the years. More important, these best practices—usually, smart SQL tricks—are database specific.

> **Important** Generally, we could say the difficulty of getting pages of records out of a query can be traced back to the nature and design of the SQL language. Within SQL, there's no explicit notion of the record position. Any record can be identified through the value of any of its fields by using the WHERE clause or server cursors and the FETCH statement. Specific DBMS systems, then, might add custom features to support position-based row identification. Oracle, for example, does that through the ROWNUM keyword; Microsoft SQL Server uses different tools, which aren't, functionally speaking, completely equivalent.

To start experimenting with custom paging, let's consider a simple, maybe even simplistic, case. The assumption we make here is not unrealistic, but it's too strong a requirement for most real-world cases. In addition, it has a few shortcomings that make it suitable only for read-only tables. Let's suppose the table to page through has a column (not necessarily a key column) with numeric values unfolded in regular succession. By *regular succession*, we mean that given an index, the corresponding value can be determined algorithmically, just like a mathematical succession.

Figure 7-1 shows the rows that form the Products table in the Northwind database. Focus on the productid column and its sequence of values.

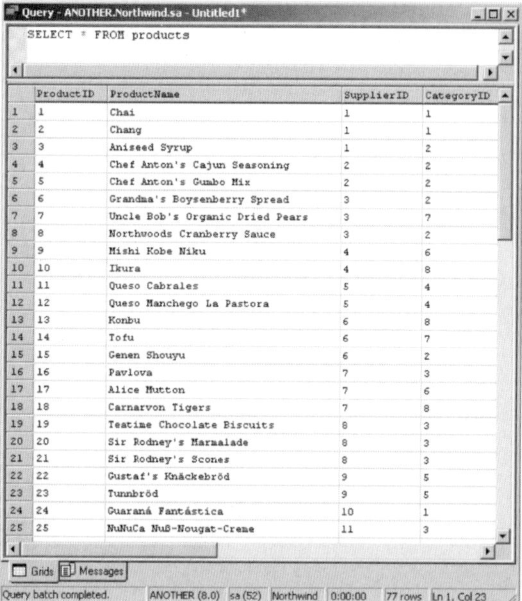

| | ProductID | ProductName | SupplierID | CategoryID |
|---|---|---|---|---|
| 1 | 1 | Chai | 1 | 1 |
| 2 | 2 | Chang | 1 | 1 |
| 3 | 3 | Aniseed Syrup | 1 | 2 |
| 4 | 4 | Chef Anton's Cajun Seasoning | 2 | 2 |
| 5 | 5 | Chef Anton's Gumbo Mix | 2 | 2 |
| 6 | 6 | Grandma's Boysenberry Spread | 3 | 2 |
| 7 | 7 | Uncle Bob's Organic Dried Pears | 3 | 7 |
| 8 | 8 | Northwoods Cranberry Sauce | 3 | 2 |
| 9 | 9 | Mishi Kobe Niku | 4 | 6 |
| 10 | 10 | Ikura | 4 | 8 |
| 11 | 11 | Queso Cabrales | 5 | 4 |
| 12 | 12 | Queso Manchego La Pastora | 5 | 4 |
| 13 | 13 | Konbu | 6 | 8 |
| 14 | 14 | Tofu | 6 | 7 |
| 15 | 15 | Genen Shouyu | 6 | 2 |
| 16 | 16 | Pavlova | 7 | 3 |
| 17 | 17 | Alice Mutton | 7 | 6 |
| 18 | 18 | Carnarvon Tigers | 7 | 8 |
| 19 | 19 | Teatime Chocolate Biscuits | 8 | 3 |
| 20 | 20 | Sir Rodney's Marmalade | 8 | 3 |
| 21 | 21 | Sir Rodney's Scones | 8 | 3 |
| 22 | 22 | Gustaf's Knäckebröd | 9 | 5 |
| 23 | 23 | Tunnbröd | 9 | 5 |
| 24 | 24 | Guaraná Fantástica | 10 | 1 |
| 25 | 25 | NuNuCa Nuß-Nougat-Creme | 11 | 3 |

**Figure 7-1** A screen shot with some of the rows in the Northwind.Products table.

The productid column is made of integer, progressive values that start from 1. The regularity of the succession extends over the whole column and is never broken. In light of this, the value at row *n* is a function of a certain expression *F*:

```
value = F(n)
```

In particular, for the productid column the function is extremely simple and summarized by the following succession:

```
F(0) = 1
F(n+1) = F(n)+1
```

When the table provides a column with a regular succession of values, the following SQL code allows you to extract in a very flexible and generic way the rows that form a given page:

```
SELECT * FROM products WHERE
productid >= F(PageSize*(PageIndex-1)+1) AND
productid <= F(PageSize*PageIndex)
```

Because the size of the page is a fixed setting, the only variable parameter in the expression is the index of the page. The following listing shows a full application that pages through a list of products:

```
private SqlDataReader m_dataReader;
private string m_connString =
    "DATABASE=Northwind;SERVER=localhost;UID=sa;";
private string m_cmdCount = "SELECT COUNT(*) FROM products";
private string m_cmdQuery = "SELECT productid AS 'ID', " +
    "productname AS 'Product', quantityperunit AS 'Packaging' " +
    "FROM products " +
    "WHERE productid >=@minProductID AND productid <=@maxProductID";

void Page_Load(object sender, EventArgs e) {
    if (!Page.IsPostBack)
        SetVirtualItemCount();
    BindData();
}

SqlDataReader CreateDataSource(int nPageIndex) {
    // page index is assumed to be 0-based
    int pageSize = grid.PageSize;
    int minProductID = pageSize * nPageIndex + 1;
    int maxProductID = pageSize * (nPageIndex + 1);

    // Set up the command
    SqlConnection conn = new SqlConnection(m_connString);
    SqlCommand cmd = new SqlCommand(m_cmdQuery, conn);
    cmd.Parameters.Add("@minProductID", SqlDbType.Int).Value = minProductID;
    cmd.Parameters.Add("@maxProductID", SqlDbType.Int).Value = maxProductID;

    // Execute the command through a global data reader
    conn.Open();
    m_dataReader = cmd.ExecuteReader(CommandBehavior.CloseConnection);
    return m_dataReader;
}

void PageIndexChanged(object sender, DataGridPageChangedEventArgs e) {
    grid.CurrentPageIndex = e.NewPageIndex;
    BindData();
}

void BindData() {
    m_dataReader = CreateDataSource(grid.CurrentPageIndex);
    grid.DataSource = m_dataReader;
    grid.DataBind();
    m_dataReader.Close();
}

void SetVirtualItemCount() {
    SqlConnection conn = new SqlConnection(m_connString);
    SqlCommand cmd = new SqlCommand(m_cmdCount, conn);
```

```
        // Execute the command
        conn.Open();
        int nItemCount = (int) cmd.ExecuteScalar();
        conn.Close();

        grid.VirtualItemCount = nItemCount;
        return;
}
```

Figure 7-2 shows the custom paging application in action.

Notice a couple of things in Figure 7-2. The pager bar is displayed on top of the grid, and the check box allows you to switch between the pager styles. The code discussed so far works regardless of the paging mode you opt for.

## Fixed-Size *DataGrid* Controls

The *DataGrid* control is rendered as an HTML table, so the actual size of the HTML table depends on a number of factors, including the font, length of the text, and number of items displayed. Especially when you're paging through a data source using a grid control, it can be annoying to have the body of the page move up or down a few pixels each time the height of the grid changes. Setting the *Width* property to a specified maximum number of pixels allows you to maintain a fixed width for the grid. The same trick doesn't work for the height. In this case, the drawback is that the final page of the grid (which normally contains a smaller number of items) is stretched to occupy the fixed height. A possible workaround is padding the data source with empty rows prior to binding to the grid. An even better approach, one that doesn't require any programmatic work, is to wrap the *DataGrid* in a fixed-height HTML table with an empty row at the bottom:

```
<table style="..." bgcolor="...">
    <tr><td><asp:datagrid .../></td></tr>
    <tr><td height="100%"></td></tr>
</table>
```

The unique cell of the bottom row must have a 100 percent height so that it will automatically occupy any space left by the topmost grid. Combine this structure with some ad hoc visual settings and you'll have the grid paging always within the boundaries of the parent table. In particular, you might want to use a borderless *DataGrid* and define border settings on the table. Also, you should use the same background color for the table and the grid.

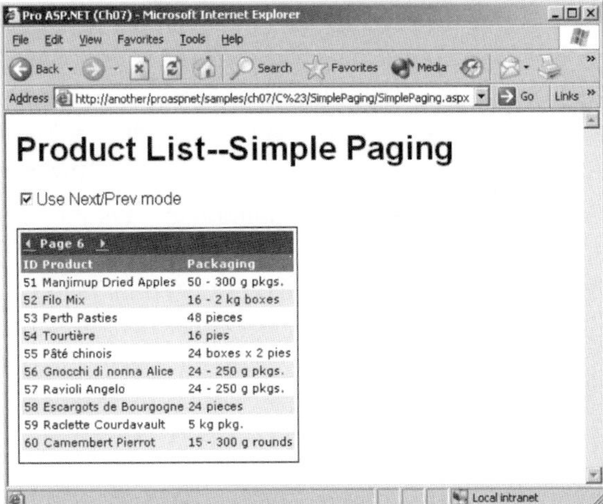


**Figure 7-2** The grid exploits the characteristics of the productid column to page through records.

## Shortcomings of the Key-Based Approach

There are pros and cons with this column-based approach. It is simple to code and effective in returning a compact resultset that is immediately bindable and requires no further preparation work. Column updates do not affect the functionality, and row insertion is a nonissue too, as long as you guarantee and preserve the regularity of the succession. On the downside, though, I should mention that this technique works only with primarily read-only, look-up tables.

Deletions are one type of operation that can really nullify the functionality of this technique. The deletion of a row creates a hole in the succession, which then breaks the arithmetic rule set up to identify the first record in the page. You can try to work around the issue by resorting to nonidentity, custom-made columns that can be programmatically updated. In other words, you must perform the deletion through a stored procedure that first executes the deletion and then reorders the index column. To make this approach more complex, though, consider that in some cases the stored procedure (or, in general, the sequence of statements involved) needs to be embedded in a transaction.

In the remainder of the chapter, we'll analyze more powerful approaches that work in a larger number of cases. We'll discuss the solutions based on the paging mode you want to support—for example, next/previous navigation and random access to pages. However, no matter which approach you choose to control paging, don't forget to set the virtual item count.

> **Note** The *DataGrid* is the only ASP.NET control that provides a built-in infrastructure for pagination. The *DataList* is the control that most closely resembles the *DataGrid* in terms of functionality. The key difference between the two is just pagination. However, if you use custom paging and don't mind using external link buttons to navigate, obtaining a pageable *DataList* is not a hard task at all. We'll examine the *DataList* in Chapter 9 and review how to extend it to support pagination.

# Next/Previous Navigation

When we want to move to the next or previous page, a more general query command can be used to leverage any column that has unique values but which might not form a regular succession. The idea is that you cache the first and last key values in the currently displayed page and select the previous (or next) page based on that. If the page size is set to 10, moving to the previous page entails selecting the first 10 records whose key value is less than the cached value. If you move to the next page, the first 10 records with a key greater than the cached last key are selected.

## Defining the SQL Code

With the *NextPrev* pager mode, you can view only pages close to the currently displayed one—that is, pages immediately previous to or following the page you are viewing. This constraint enables us to set up ad hoc SQL code that works regardless of the values in the key column. To sum it up, the pivot column doesn't have to be the key column—it only has to contain unique values. For the SQL code to work, you need to cache the value on this key column for the first and last items in the page. The values require persistent storage that survives across page requests. These key values can be stored in the view state:

```
ViewState["FirstKey"] = grid.DataKeys[0];
ViewState["LastKey"] = grid.DataKeys[grid.Items.Count-1];
```

This code stores in the view state the minimum and maximum key values in the page. The key values are retrieved from the *DataKeys* collection, and the name of the key column is set using the *DataKeyField* property. Prior to executing the query command, the value of the key is read back from the view state, as shown here:

```
// going to page back
int productID = Convert.ToInt32(ViewState["FirstKey"]);
// going to page ahead
int productID = Convert.ToInt32(ViewState["LastKey"]);
```

Let's have a look at the SQL code to move to the previous record and to move to the next record. Later in the "Adding First and Last Buttons" section, we'll discuss how to move to the first record and move to the last record.

## Moving to the Previous Record

When the user clicks to view the previous page of a data source, the grid has cached the key values for the first and last records displayed in the current page. Assuming a default page size of 10, the records that fit in the previous page are the last 10 whose key value is less than the first key of the current page.

In SQL Server, the TOP *n* clause allows you to select the first *n* records that match. Unfortunately, though, there's no equivalent clause that lets you select the last *n* matching records. To obtain the same result, you must resort to a little trick and use a virtual table. You use the following Transact-SQL (T-SQL) code. The key column is productid.

```
SELECT * FROM
(SELECT TOP 10 productid, productname, quantityperunit
    FROM products WHERE productid <@productID ORDER BY productid DESC) AS t
ORDER BY productid
```

Before we discuss the query any further, a few general points need to be addressed. The code here is not standard SQL but is written in the SQL dialect that SQL Server supports—the Transact-SQL language. It can't be considered a general solution, as it exploits features of recent versions of SQL Server and might not be supported by other DBMS. Unlike the SQL code we considered for the application in Figure 7-2, the code shown here can't be used with just any database server. The features that make it to some extent unique and SQL Server–specific are the TOP *n* clause and the use of subqueries.

The T-SQL code used to query for the previous page is based on two nested queries. The innermost query selects the first 10 records that have a key value less than the first key displayed in the current page. Because the table is queried in descending order, the top 10 records are actually the last 10 but are listed from the highest to the lowest key. We name this in-memory table *AS t* and, through the outermost query, select all the records in it ordered by the key column. This final operation returns the last 10 records sorted in the natural ascending order.

> **Important** Very few databases support the TOP *n* clause in the SELECT statement. The TOP clause was originally introduced in Microsoft Access and then imported into SQL Server beginning with version 7. It has no counterpart in SQL Server version 6.5 nor in any version of Oracle. Oracle, though, has an alternative mechanism that is in some aspects even more powerful. (We'll discuss this feature more in the "Selecting Records in Oracle" section later in the chapter.) Informix SQL does provide a TOP-like behavior through the FIRST clause. Generally, the SET ROWCOUNT statement, although a bit less flexible, can be used as a rougher counterpart when the TOP clause is not supported. The main difference is that the TOP clause is command specific, whereas the SET ROWCOUNT statement is a global environment setting.

> **Note** Many T-SQL statements that include subqueries can sometimes be formulated as joins. Other statements, like ours here, can be posed only with subqueries. In T-SQL, there is usually no relevant performance difference between a statement that includes a subquery and a functionally equivalent command that does not. In some cases, though, a join gets slightly better performance. What's important to note for our purposes, though, is that subqueries can be significantly faster than server cursors and temporary tables. Server cursors, in particular, should always be your last resort.

## Moving to the Next Record

Extracting the records to display in the next page is a bit easier and faster once you know the last key in the current page. In this case, the TOP *n* clause works just fine and without the need of other tricks. The following T-SQL code simply selects the top 10 records with a key value greater than the last key (the productid column) in the page.

```
SELECT TOP 10 productid, productname, quantityperunit
FROM products WHERE productid >@productID
```

Both the commands we've examined so far, for moving to the previous and next records, use a parameter named *@productID*. This parameter is set with the value retrieved from the view state for the first or last key according to the previous or next command to execute.

### Setting Up the Next/Previous Navigation

The following code shows the initialization step of the sample application that demonstrates next/previous pagination:

```
void Page_Load(object sender, EventArgs e) {
    if (!Page.IsPostBack)
    {
        SetVirtualItemCount();
        ViewState["LastKey"] = 0;
        ViewState["FirstKey"] = 0;
        m_cmdText = m_cmdQueryNext;
        BindData();
    }
}
```

The default value of the view-state entries is 0, and the records that fit in the first page are retrieved as a next-page command with a *LastKey* value of 0.

The command to execute is decided by looking at which link the user clicked to page back or forth. The ASP.NET page is fired by the *PageIndex-Changed* event when the user clicks to page back or forth. The event doesn't provide explicit information about the direction of the paging. However, you can easily figure it out by comparing the values of the *CurrentPageIndex* property and the *NewPageIndex* event data member.

```
if (grid.CurrentPageIndex > e.NewPageIndex)
    // moving forward
else
    // moving back
```

At the time the *PageIndexChanged* fires, the new page index has not yet been set. Moreover, you have to explicitly set it in the event handler.

Knowing whether you're moving to the next or previous record is important in this case because, based on it, we decide which query command to run. Another way to obtain that information is by exploiting the services of the *Item-Command* event. The sample code discussed here implements this technique because it's more general and will work even with future extensions.

When the user clicks to change pages, regardless of whether it is to page back or forth, the *DataGrid* fires an *ItemCommand* event in which the *Com-mandName* member is set to *Page*. The *CommandArgument* member, on the other hand, is accordingly set to *Next* or *Prev*. All these keywords don't have to be addressed as literals—predefined constants should be used instead. The following code shows the *ItemCommand* event handler:

```
void ItemCommand(object sender, DataGridCommandEventArgs e)
{
    switch(e.CommandArgument.ToString())
    {
        case DataGrid.NextPageCommandArgument:
            m_direction = GridNavigation.Next;
            break;
        case DataGrid.PrevPageCommandArgument:
            m_direction = GridNavigation.Previous;
            break;
    }
}
```

The code stores in an application global variable a value that indicates the direction of the paging. The *GridNavigation* values belong to a user-defined type that has been defined mostly for clarity:

```
public enum GridNavigation : int
{
    First = -2,
    Previous = -1,
    Next = 1,
    Last = 2
}
```

Notice that the enumeration also includes command names to access the first and last pages of the data source. I'll discuss this feature in the next section, "Adding First and Last Buttons." The following listing illustrates the mechanism that allows the sample application to fetch records using the SQL commands discussed earlier. Note that the code employs a data reader (instead of a slower *DataTable*) to bind data to the *DataGrid*:

```
void BindData() {
    m_dataReader = CreateDataSource();
    grid.DataSource = m_dataReader;
    grid.DataBind();
    m_dataReader.Close();

    // Configure for the view state
    ViewState["FirstKey"] = grid.DataKeys[0];
    ViewState["LastKey"] = grid.DataKeys[grid.Items.Count-1];
}

SqlDataReader CreateDataSource() {
    // page size is assumed to be 10
    int productID = 0;
    string cmdText = "";
    switch(m_direction)
```

```
    {
        case GridNavigation.Previous:
            productID = Convert.ToInt32(ViewState["FirstKey"]);
            cmdText = m_cmdQueryPrev;
            break;
        case GridNavigation.Next:
            productID = Convert.ToInt32(ViewState["LastKey"]);
            cmdText = m_cmdQueryNext;
            break;
    }
    return ExecuteCommand(cmdText, productID);
}

SqlDataReader ExecuteCommand(string cmdText, int productID) {
    SqlConnection conn = new SqlConnection(m_connString);
    SqlCommand cmd = new SqlCommand(cmdText, conn);
    cmd.Parameters.Add("@productID", SqlDbType.Int).Value = productID;

    // Execute the command through a global data reader
    conn.Open();
    m_dataReader = cmd.ExecuteReader(CommandBehavior.CloseConnection);
    return m_dataReader;
}
```

As mentioned in Chapter 5, you can populate a list-bound control like the *DataGrid* using a data reader object. The data reader works connected to the data source. For this reason, you must close it after calling the control's *DataBind* method. The data reader is marked with the *CloseConnection* flag so that closing the reader would automatically close the underlying connection. The *CreateDataSource* method examines the determined direction and sets the command text to execute and the key value to use as a parameter.

## Selecting Records in Oracle

Speaking of Oracle databases, you should note that named parameters in Oracle must be prefixed with a colon (:). In SQL Server, you precede the name of parameters by using the @ symbol. The SQL language supported by Oracle databases doesn't provide a facility like the TOP *n* clause for SELECT statements. However, particularly for data paging, the Oracle database provides an even more powerful feature than TOP—the ROWNUM operator.

The ROWNUM operator returns the ordinal position of a row in a resultset. In light of this, and given a page size of 10, moving to a page requires the following, surprisingly simple, query:

```
SELECT * FROM table WHERE
ROWNUM > (PageIndex*(PageSize-1)+1 AND ROWNUM > (PageIndex*PageSize)
```

The ROWNUM operator has a drawback that should be discussed. An Oracle database assigns the unique index before sorting the result set. So if you have a query that includes an ORDER BY clause, the sequence of ROWNUM values is not ordered as the clause indicates. To fix things up, you must use an outermost query that does not require sorting.

## Adding First and Last Buttons

A next/previous navigation model can be made even richer by using a pair of extra links for the first and last pages of the data source. In this case, though, you can't count on any support from the *DataGrid* control. You must modify the pager bar on the fly to accommodate for the extra buttons, add a handler for the *Click* event, and update the view.

The following code shows how you can modify the pager bar by adding a text label displaying the number of the current page (as mentioned in Chapter 6) and the links for the first and last pages. The key procedure is the *ItemCreated* event handler:

```
void ItemCreated(object sender, DataGridItemEventArgs e) {
    if (e.Item.ItemType == ListItemType.Pager) {
        if (grid.PagerStyle.Mode == PagerMode.NextPrev) {
            TableCell pager = e.Item.Cells[0];
            AddPageLabel(pager);
            AddLinkFirstPage(pager);
            AddLinkLastPage(pager);
        }
    }
}
```

### Creating Link Buttons Dynamically

The First and Last buttons are to be added as link buttons or labels, depending on the page index. If the link can be clicked to go to the first or last page, you render the button as a link; otherwise, you render it as a label or a disabled link. Because the standard pager renders disabled buttons as labels, we'll use this approach here too. Let's consider adding the First button. No significant changes are expected for the Last button.

The First button must be disabled only if the current page is the first. Put another way, the First button must be rendered as a link button only if the Previous button is a link. The Previous button is the first in the *Controls* collection. You check its type and then create a *LinkButton* or *Label* control accordingly:

```
void AddLinkFirstPage(TableCell pager)
{
    if(pager.Controls[0] is LinkButton) {
        LinkButton btnFirst = new LinkButton();
        btnFirst.Font.Name = grid.PagerStyle.Font.Name;
        btnFirst.Font.Size = grid.PagerStyle.Font.Size;
```

```
        btnFirst.ForeColor = grid.PagerStyle.ForeColor;
        btnFirst.Text = "<<";
        if (btnFirst.Font.Name == "webdings")
            btnFirst.Text = "7";
        btnFirst.Click += new EventHandler(GoToFirstPage);
        pager.Controls.AddAt(0, btnFirst);
    }
    else
    {
        Label btnFirst = new Label();
        btnFirst.Font.Name = grid.PagerStyle.Font.Name;
        btnFirst.Font.Size = grid.PagerStyle.Font.Size;
        btnFirst.ForeColor = grid.PagerStyle.ForeColor;
        btnFirst.Text = "<<";
        if (btnFirst.Font.Name == "webdings")
            btnFirst.Text = "7";
        pager.Controls.AddAt(0, btnFirst);
    }
}
```

You ensure that the font and color used for the First button are identical to those used for other buttons in the pager. You read the default settings from the *DataGrid*'s *PagerStyle* object. A nice feature you can add is setting the caption of the button to a Webdings symbol if Webdings is the current pager font. The value of 7 corresponds to the ◂◂ symbol. For the Last page, you use the value 8, which corresponds to the ▸▸ glyph.

You add the control to the *Controls* collection at a specified position, as shown in Figure 7-3.

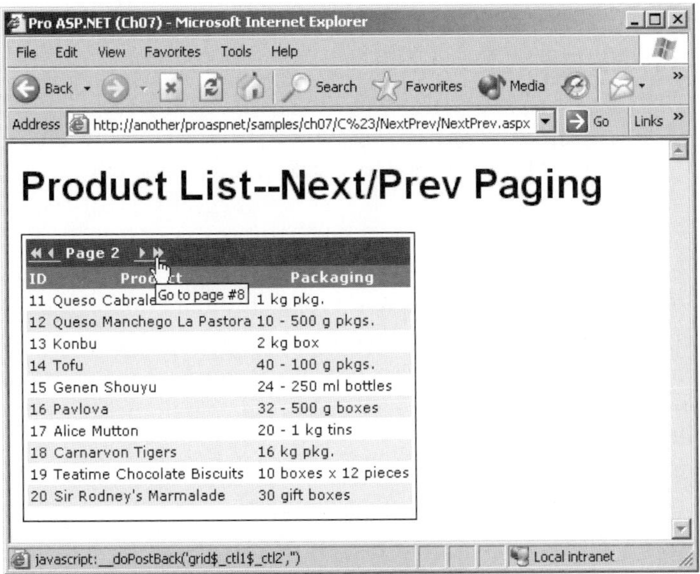


**Figure 7-3** The new pager bar with a pair of First and Last buttons.

The command to select the records of the first page is straightforward and consists of a pretty simple SELECT command:

```
SELECT TOP 10 productid, productname, quantityperunit FROM products
```

Getting the records of the last page is a bit more involved. The problem has two facets. Because users can click on the Last button at any time, we can't assume we know the last key of the last page. Knowing this value would make the query trivial; unfortunately, we do not know it. The second issue to consider is that we don't know exactly how many records would fit in the last page, as that depends on the page size and the size of the data source. The following query would select the last *n* records in the data source with a key value greater than the specified value:

```
SELECT * FROM (
    SELECT TOP {0} productid, productname, quantityperunit
    FROM products
    WHERE productid >@productID ORDER BY productid DESC)
    AS t ORDER BY productid
```

The key value we use does not determine the resultset, but the higher value we use the smaller subset of records the query would process. The *{0}* placeholder in the query is dynamically replaced with the computed number of records in the last page. Here's the necessary code:

```
SqlDataReader CreateDataSource() {
    switch(m_direction) {
        ⋮
        case GridNavigation.Last:
            productID = Convert.ToInt32(ViewState["LastKey"]);
            int nRem = grid.VirtualItemCount % grid.PageSize;
            nRem = (nRem == 0 ?grid.PageSize :nRem);

            // Replaces the placeholder to include the effective
            // number of records in the last page
            cmdText = String.Format(m_cmdQueryLast, nRem);
            break;
    }
}
```

The nonzero modulus obtained by dividing the data source size by the page size is the number of rows to retrieve for the last page. If the modulus is zero, the last page is full and the number of rows to retrieve matches the page size.

### Setting the Click Handler

What happens when the user clicks on the First or Last button? The action taken depends on the registered *Click* event handler:

```
btnFirst.Click += new EventHandler(GoToFirstPage);
btnLast.Click += new EventHandler(GoToLastPage);
```

In Microsoft Visual Basic .NET, you register handlers using the *AddHandler* keyword. The structure of both handlers is similar and refers to the code built in the *PageIndexChanged* event handler.

```
void GoToFirstPage(object sender, EventArgs e) {
    m_direction = GridNavigation.First;
    GoToPage(sender, 0);
}
void GoToLastPage(object sender, EventArgs e) {
    m_direction = GridNavigation.Last;
    GoToPage(sender, grid.PageCount-1);
}
void GoToPage(object sender, int nPageIndex) {
    // page number is 0-based
    DataGridPageChangedEventArgs evPage;
    evPage = new DataGridPageChangedEventArgs(sender, nPageIndex);
    PageIndexChanged(sender, evPage);
}
```

As the code illustrates, going to the first or last page is resolved in terms of a page transition accomplished through the standard pager buttons. The *GoToPage* method invokes the user's defined code for the *PageIndexChanged* event. The code assumes that such an event handler is defined—a reasonable assumption as we're speaking of code for paging.

Figure 7-4 shows the final page of the grid. Note that the height of the grid *seems* to be constant. As we explained in the sidebar "Fixed-Size *DataGrid* Controls," this is only a trick performed using a wrapper HTML table element.

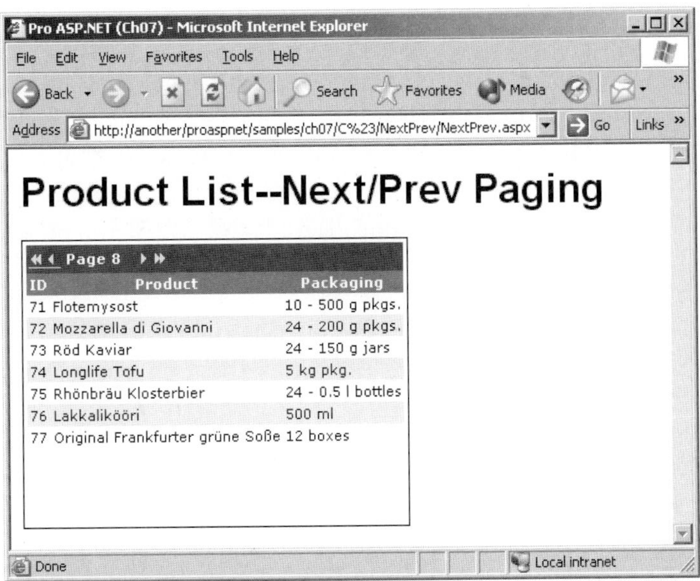


**Figure 7-4** The final page of the grid.

### Adding ToolTips to the Pager

As shown in Figure 7-3, the pager buttons include ToolTips. Each ToolTip indicates the number of the page the button would move you to. The index of the next or previous page is a fundamental piece of information if no other feedback is provided about the current page. With next/previous navigation, users don't know what page they're currently viewing, so ToolTips help considerably. In the sample code discussed here, the current page index is displayed through a label, so ToolTips aren't really necessary.

You can add ToolTips on the fly to pager buttons as well as header cells. In both cases, all you need to do is write a handler for the *ItemCreated* event. The following code shows how to proceed with the Previous button—the second button in the pager:

```
if (e.Item.ItemType == ListItemType.Pager) {
    if (grid.PagerStyle.Mode == PagerMode.NextPrev) {
        TableCell pager = e.Item.Cells[0];
        WebControl ctl = (WebControl) pager.Controls[1]);
        ctl.ToolTip = String.Format("Go to page #{0}",
        grid.CurrentPageIndex);
    }
```

Note that the *CurrentPageIndex* property returns 0-based values, whereas the displayed page indexes are 1-based. For this reason, the 1-based index of the previous page coincides with the *CurrentPageIndex* property. Similarly, the index of the next page is *CurrentPageIndex* plus 2.

## Random Page Navigation

Let's examine the tricks of data pagination when the *NumericPages* pager mode is used. In this case, we can't rely on any features and values in the previously viewed page. Data access must be independent from external parameters and only a function of the page index and page size. The ROWNUM statement of Oracle databases is ideal for setting up a random-access paging mechanism. Unfortunately, other databases, including SQL Server, don't provide for that. In this section, we'll discuss and put to work an alternative trick based entirely on the SQL language.

A page that uses a grid in *NumericPages* pager mode has a much simpler layout (and involves less code) than a page based on the *NextPrev* pager mode. For one thing, a unique SQL command is needed and used regardless of the page to be accessed. Second, the direction of the navigation is unimportant and doesn't require ad hoc handling. Let's have a closer look at the necessary SQL statement.

## Selecting a Specified Page of Records

To select from a SQL Server database only the records that fit into the specified page (identified by an index), a rather complex and nested query is necessary. The resultset is selected in three steps. First you get the smallest resultset that includes the desired records. Next you get rid of the additional records, and then you sort the remaining rows properly.

Suppose that, given a page size of 10, you want to obtain the records of page 3 according to a particular order. The last 10 rows of the first 30 are the rows you are looking for. How can you get them? Let's see what happens with the Products table in the Northwind database:

```
SELECT TOP 10 * FROM
    (SELECT TOP 30 * FROM products ORDER BY productid) AS t1
ORDER BY productid DESC
```

This nested query selects the correct subset of records but in the reverse order. It takes the first 10 rows out of the first 30 in descending order. A third query must be placed to wrap this code with the sole goal of sorting the previous resultset:

```
SELECT * FROM
    (SELECT TOP 10 * FROM
        (SELECT TOP 30 * FROM products ORDER BY productid) AS t1
    ORDER BY productid DESC) AS t2
ORDER BY productid
```

The following listing shows how this statement is turned into .NET executable code. Replace the numeric values with a pair of *{n}* placeholders, and run the following code:

```
string cmdText = String.Format(m_cmdQuery,
    grid.PageSize, grid.PageSize*pageIndex);
SqlConnection conn = new SqlConnection(m_connString);
SqlCommand cmd = new SqlCommand(cmdText, conn);
conn.Open();
m_dataReader = cmd.ExecuteReader(CommandBehavior.CloseConnection);
conn.Close();
```

One problem raised with this code is that the last page always shows up with 10 records—the regular records plus the last in the previous page. The culprit of this is the SELECT TOP 10 outer query. A simple way to work around this issue is by associating the TOP clause with the actual number of rows in the final page:

```
int recsInLastPage = grid.VirtualItemCount % grid.PageSize;
if (recsInLastPage == 0)
    recsInLastPage = grid.PageSize;
```

```
int sizeOfPage = grid.PageSize;
if (pageIndex == grid.PageCount)
    sizeOfPage = recsInLastPage;
string cmdText = String.Format(m_cmdQuery,
    sizeOfPage, grid.PageSize*pageIndex);
```

The code discussed so far includes two sorting operations that are not lightweight ones. However, indexes are just the right tool to leverage to make the query run faster. Using a clustered index on the ORDER BY field (productid, in the preceding example) speeds the query up immensely; using a clustered primary key index would speed things up even more—an order of magnitude faster.

For completeness, you might also want to consider the following, functionally equivalent, version of the query:

```
SELECT * FROM
    (SELECT TOP 30 * FROM products ORDER BY productid) AS t1
WHERE productid NOT IN
    (SELECT TOP 20 productid FROM products ORDER BY productid)
```

The idea is that you first select the minimum number of records that will contain the desired subset, and then you run an outer query in which you filter out the records that don't belong to the page. For example, if page #3 is to be retrieved, you discard the records of the first two pages. This second query also doesn't suffer from the last-page drawback we had to fix earlier. In terms of raw performance, the second query runs statistically slower than the first except in one circumstance—when you have additional criteria set on the table. If the main query, which was *SELECT * FROM products* in the previous example, contains a WHERE clause, especially for larger tables, the second query tends to run about 15 percent faster. The break-up point seems to be around 150,000 records. As a disclaimer, I want to recommend that you don't take this statistical analysis for pure gold but instead roll your own before you make a decision.

> **Note** The TOP clause doesn't accept parameters, so it's hard with this trick to use code from within a stored procedure. However, the SQL Server query engine can still do a good job reusing the execution plans of the subqueries.

## Customizing the Structure of the Pager

When working in *NumericPages* pager mode, the pager bar is made of a single table cell populated with an alternate sequence of links and blank literals. One link is actually a nonclickable label control. By default, the links and the label have simple numeric captions, which makes the pager bar difficult to read.

Unfortunately, the *DataGrid* control doesn't support a format string for the links in the numeric pager bar. To customize the text of the buttons, you can only write the usual *ItemCreated* handler:

```
void ItemCreated(object sender, DataGridItemEventArgs e) {
    if (e.Item.ItemType == ListItemType.Pager) {
        if (grid.PagerStyle.Mode != PagerMode.NumericPages)
            return;

        TableCell pager = (TableCell) e.Item.Cells[0];
        for (int i=0; i<pager.Controls.Count; i+=2)
        {
            object o = pager.Controls[i];
            if (o is LinkButton) {
                LinkButton h = (LinkButton) o;
                h.Text = "[" + h.Text + "]";
            } else {
                Label l = (Label) o;
                l.Font.Bold = true;
                l.Text = "Page " + l.Text;
            }
        }
    }
}
```

The modified grid is shown in Figure 7-5.

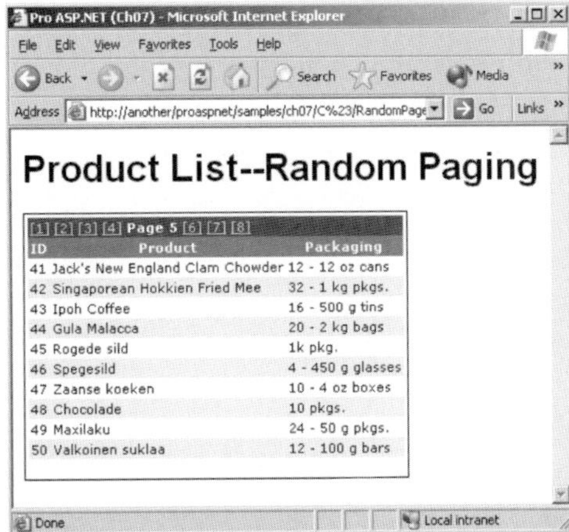


**Figure 7-5** A *DataGrid* control with a customized numeric pager bar.

In some cases, a particularly large data source might lead to a too-long list of links for the real estate of the pager bar. The pager's *PageButtonCount* property lets you control how many links are to be displayed. By default, *PageButtonCount* is set to 10. If extra buttons are required, the *DataGrid* adjusts for extra pagination buttons, as shown in Figure 7-6.

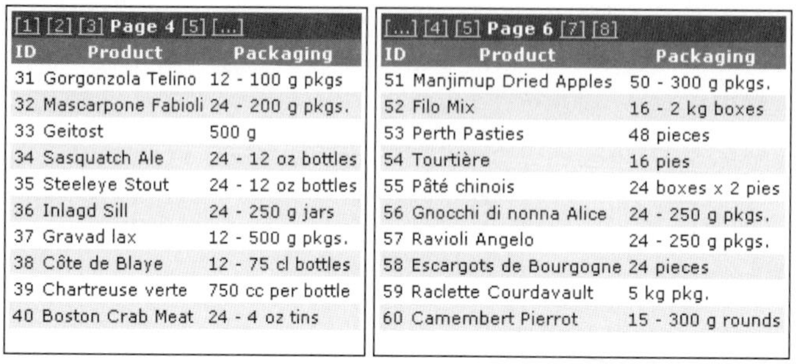

[1] [2] [3] **Page 4** [5] [...]

| ID | Product | Packaging |
|---|---|---|
| 31 | Gorgonzola Telino | 12 - 100 g pkgs |
| 32 | Mascarpone Fabioli | 24 - 200 g pkgs. |
| 33 | Geitost | 500 g |
| 34 | Sasquatch Ale | 24 - 12 oz bottles |
| 35 | Steeleye Stout | 24 - 12 oz bottles |
| 36 | Inlagd Sill | 24 - 250 g jars |
| 37 | Gravad lax | 12 - 500 g pkgs. |
| 38 | Côte de Blaye | 12 - 75 cl bottles |
| 39 | Chartreuse verte | 750 cc per bottle |
| 40 | Boston Crab Meat | 24 - 4 oz tins |

[...] [4] [5] **Page 6** [7] [8]

| ID | Product | Packaging |
|---|---|---|
| 51 | Manjimup Dried Apples | 50 - 300 g pkgs. |
| 52 | Filo Mix | 16 - 2 kg boxes |
| 53 | Perth Pasties | 48 pieces |
| 54 | Tourtière | 16 pies |
| 55 | Pâté chinois | 24 boxes x 2 pies |
| 56 | Gnocchi di nonna Alice | 24 - 250 g pkgs. |
| 57 | Ravioli Angelo | 24 - 250 g pkgs. |
| 58 | Escargots de Bourgogne | 24 pieces |
| 59 | Raclette Courdavault | 5 kg pkg. |
| 60 | Camembert Pierrot | 15 - 300 g rounds |

**Figure 7-6** A pager bar with ellipsis buttons when too many links are required.

## Building a Completely Customized Personal Pager

Although the *DataGrid* doesn't provide a built-in mechanism to plug in a custom pager, you can always replace the standard pager with your own. You can hide the pager by turning off its *Visible* attribute. However, nothing really prevents you from displaying both the ordinary pager and a personal pager:

```
<pagerstyle visible="false" />
```

The personal pager is any custom toolbar appended at the bottom of the grid. The *DataGrid* and your personal pager are two rows of the same table, as in the following schema:

```
<table>
<tr><td>
    <asp:datagrid ...> ... </asp:datagrid>
</td></tr>
<tr><td>
    personal pager goes here
</td></tr>
</table>
```

The following code shows how to transform the pager in a numeric text box with a button to jump to the specified page:

```
<asp:panel runat="server">
    <asp:label runat="server" text="Page" />
    <asp:textbox runat="server" id="txtGoto" width="20px" height="20px"
        text="1" style="border:solid 1px;" />
    <asp:button runat="server" Text="Go" height="20px" font-size="8pt"
        onclick="GoToPage" />
</asp:panel>
```

The code that actually moves to the specified page is as follows:

```
void GoToPage(object sender, EventArgs e) {
    int pageIndex = Convert.ToInt32(txtGoto.Text)-1;
    if (pageIndex >=0) {
        grid.CurrentPageIndex = pageIndex;
        BindData();
    }
}
```

The *GoToPage* method doesn't include any validation logic. You can either validate the content of the text box programmatically or resort to a range validator control. (See Chapter 3.)

```
<asp:rangevalidator runat="server" id="gotoValidator"
    ControlToValidate="txtGoto"
    ForeColor="white"
    Font-Size="8pt"
    Display="Dynamic"
    ErrorMessage="Page not found"
    MinimumValue="1"
    Type="Integer" />
```

The lower bound of the range can be set declaratively to 1. As for the upper bound, you have to set it dynamically—for example, in the *BindData* method.

```
gotoValidator.MaximumValue = grid.PageCount.ToString();
```

Figure 7-7 shows a grid control with a personal pager bar.

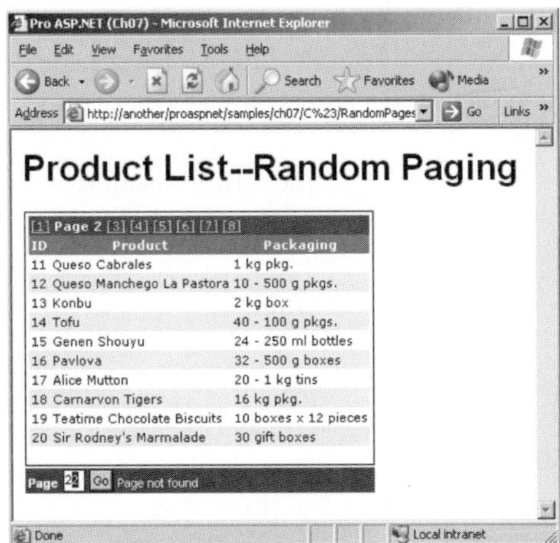


**Figure 7-7** A *DataGrid* control with a personal pager along with the standard pager. The two work side by side without any conflicts.

# Logical Navigation

So the *DataGrid* control—unique among the ASP.NET data-bound controls—provides two basic types of paging, which differ in the way in which the page content is retrieved. With default paging, you bind the control to the whole data set and then make it responsible for selecting the subset of records that fits in each displayed page. Custom paging, on the other hand, is based on the assumption that the programmer puts into the control's data source only the records that should be displayed in the current page. Does this cover all the possible needs you might have when it comes to planning navigation through a data set? The answer is debatable.

The types of paging you get for free from the *DataGrid* control certainly do not cover all the possible real-world scenarios you might be facing. On the other hand, by exploiting the *DataGrid* custom-paging infrastructure, you can easily build new paging engines that fit into your application's architecture.

To top off this chapter, we'll demonstrate how to use the *DataGrid* custom-paging mechanism to set up a sort of logical data navigation—that is, a navigation engine that displays variable-length pages that are selected based on a logical condition rather than a physical position.

## Changing the Pager's Perspective

In the *DataGrid* control, all the pages except the last one are the same size, as specified through the *PageSize* property. You select each page to display from the links of the variable-length pager bar. The pager bar contains as many links as there are pages to display. With the help of a practical example, let's see how this model deals with a scenario in which you have a fixed number of pages, each with a variable length.

Suppose you have a query to select all the orders issued by customers in a given year. Using the paging approach discussed so far, you would have a long list of (possibly numbered) pages displayed to the users. Are you really sure that your users would love to scroll through a year's worth of orders by page? How could they orientate themselves in the results once you show them a menu of, say, 40 meaningless page indexes? Wouldn't it be much better if you grouped orders, say, by month or by company? In the traditional way of paging, you keep the page size constant but provide a variable-length pager bar. Logical navigation does just the opposite—it keeps the pager bar size constant but accepts pages of any length (almost any length, actually).

We'll discuss the underpinnings of logical navigation by grouping data by months. However, the mechanism we'll use here is rather general and applies to a number of everyday scenarios: grouping customers or contacts by initials, sales by year or quarters, and bills by weeks or days.

## Is the *DataGrid* Appropriate for the Task?

Although we can successfully employ the *DataGrid* control for this type of navigation—a special case of custom paging—there's an upper bound we must set for the control to work. The limitation is in the maximum number of rows that can be displayed per page. This number can be any value—yet we have to set it and configure other parameters of the grid accordingly. (We'll discuss this further in the next section.)

Is there another control we can use instead? The *DataList* control is one of the few alternatives we can rely on. As we'll more clearly see in Chapter 9, the *DataList* is a data-bound list of rows, each sequentially displayed according to an ASP.NET template. The *DataList* doesn't pose any limitation on the number of items you can display in a page, but, on the other hand, this happens only because the *DataList* doesn't have the notion of paging and doesn't provide any built-in facilities.

In summary, you can use both the *DataGrid* and the *DataList* for the task, but neither of them is the perfect tool for a logical navigation of data. Both would work, but both require some adjustments.

## Configuring the *DataGrid*

A *DataGrid* used to implement a logical navigation of data requires some ad hoc settings. First you might want to use a topmost pager bar because the list of items can be long and a topmost pager can simplify movements. For the same reason, a double pager bar would also be more useful. Next you should opt for a *NumericPages* pager mode and then write an *ItemCreated* handler to customize the text displayed. For example, you can turn 1 into January, 5 into May, and so forth.

Finally you should carefully choose the values for the *DataGrid*'s *PageSize* and *VirtualItemCount* properties and for the *PagerStyle*'s *PageButtonCount* property. These properties are key to forcing the *DataGrid* to support logical data navigation. By design, the control can't show more items than the number of *PageSize* states. You can set *PageSize* with any value. Let's assume we don't need to display more than 100 rows per page. The *PageButtonCount* property determines how many buttons are displayed in the pager bar. By default, this value is set to 10. Because we plan to have month names on the pager bar, we must raise this value to 12. Subsequently, the virtual item count is a computed value—1200 (that is, *PageSize* * *PageButtonCount*).

In this way, the grid will always display through 12 pages, each of which can have no more than 100 rows.

## Binding the Data Source

As mentioned, logical navigation is a special case of custom paging. Whenever the user clicks to view a new page, an ad hoc data source is created based on the page index. You can use the page index directly to obtain the data source or, more generally, use it to reference another data structure (for example, a collection or an array) with more specific information. In the sample scenario we're considering now, the page index would suffice, as it directly represents the index of a month. Let's see how to modify the pager bar to reflect months rather than indexes.

### Modifying the Pager Bar

To modify the pager bar of a *DataGrid*, you write an *ItemCreated* handler. The handler will process all nonliteral controls in the pager bar and transform the default text—a 1-based number—into a month name. To increase flexibility, the name of the month is generated through an intermediate *DateTime* object corresponding to the first day of that month in the current year. This date is then formatted into the month name. The *ItemCreated* handler is shown here:

```
void ItemCreated(object sender, DataGridItemEventArgs e) {
    if (e.Item.ItemType == ListItemType.Pager &&
        grid.PagerStyle.Mode == PagerMode.NumericPages)
    {
        TableCell pager = (TableCell) e.Item.Controls[0];
        for(int i=0; i<pager.Controls.Count; i+=2) {
            object o = pager.Controls[i];
            if (o is LinkButton) {
                // Text is the 1-based number of the month
                LinkButton lb = (LinkButton) o;
                DateTime dt = new DateTime(2003,
                    Convert.ToInt32(lb.Text), 1);
                lb.Text = " " + dt.ToString("MMM") + " ";
            }
            else
            if (o is Label) {
                Label l = (Label) o;
                DateTime dt = new DateTime(2003,
                    Convert.ToInt32(l.Text), 1);
                l.Text = " " + dt.ToString("MMMM") + " ";
                l.BackColor = grid.HeaderStyle.BackColor;
                l.ForeColor = grid.HeaderStyle.ForeColor;
            }
        }
    }
}
```

As mentioned earlier, a pager bar built in *NumericPages* pager mode is made of a sequence of link buttons and a single label, all interspersed with blank literal controls. To skip over literals, we use a step of 2 in the *for* loop. When the *i*-th control in the pager is a Label control, its value represents the currently selected month. To differentiate it even further, we use a distinct group of visual settings. In particular, we use the same font and colors of the grid's header and draw the month name in its full extension instead of abbreviating it. The final effect is shown in Figure 7-8, and the tab-style look is free!

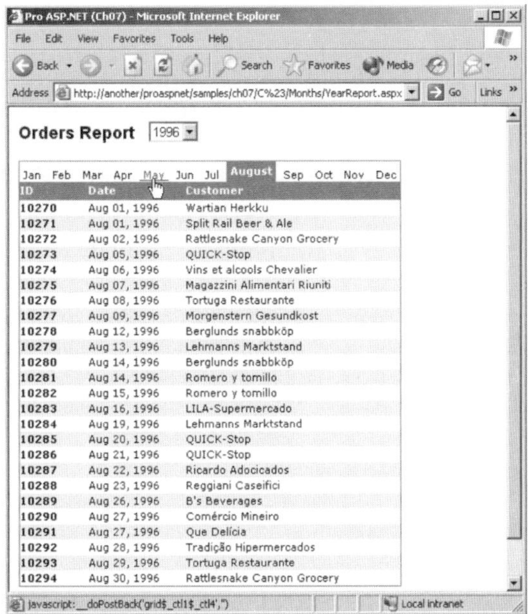


**Figure 7-8** A customized grid that displays data grouped by months rather than by pages.

## Selecting the Page's Rows

Each page in the grid displays the resultset generated by the following query with two parameters:

```
SELECT o.orderid, o.orderdate, c.companyname
FROM orders AS o
INNER JOIN customers AS c ON o.customerid=c.customerid
WHERE Year(orderdate)=@TheYear AND Month(orderdate)=@TheMonth
```

The year is selected only once per page through the drop-down list. The month is determined from the page index. The method that creates the data source is shown here:

```
DataTable CreateDataSource(int nYear, int nMonth) {
    SqlConnection conn;
    conn = new SqlConnection(m_connString);
    SqlCommand cmd = new SqlCommand(m_cmdQuery, conn);
    cmd.Parameters.Add("@TheYear", SqlDbType.Int).Value = nYear;
    cmd.Parameters.Add("@TheMonth", SqlDbType.Int).Value = nMonth;

    SqlDataAdapter da = new SqlDataAdapter(cmd);
    DataTable dt = new DataTable();
    da.Fill(dt);
    return dt;
}
```

In this case, the data source is fully identified by the page index. Generally, the page index is only the starting point to get any information useful for obtaining the final data source. For example, suppose you're paging through the customers of your company. In this case, a user interface in which pages are rendered as groups of initials (for example, A-D, E-H, and so forth) produces much more user-friendly results. To obtain that, only minimal changes to the discussed infrastructure are needed.

To start out, you define an array of information that will be accessed through the page index. In this case, you define each page with a string of initials and store the resulting array in the view state. (You can use any structure as long as it is serializable.)

```
void Page_Load(object sender, EventArgs e) {
    if (!IsPostBack) {
        ArrayList a = new ArrayList();
        a.Add("a-b-c-d");
        a.Add("e-f-g-h");
        a.Add("i-j-k-l");
        a.Add("m-n-o");
        a.Add("p-q-r");
        a.Add("s-t-u");
        a.Add("v-w-x-y-z");
        ViewState["PageMap"] = a;
        grid.VirtualItemCount = a.Count*100; //100 is max page size
        LoadData();
    }
}
```

The query that creates the data source adds a LIKE criterion to the WHERE clause for each letter in the selected string of initials:

```
private DataTable CreateDataSource() {
    // Retrieve the paging info
    ArrayList info = (ArrayList) ViewState["PageMap"];
    string strInitials = info[grid.CurrentPageIndex].ToString();
```

```
    // Prepare the SQL command to execute
    StringBuilder sb = new StringBuilder("");
    sb.Append(m_cmdQuery);

    // Append a WHERE clause for each initial in the comma-separated string
    string[] a = strInitials.Split('-');
    for(int i=0; i<a.Length; i++) {
        sb.Append("customerid LIKE '");
        sb.Append(a[i].ToUpper());
        sb.Append("%'");
        if (i < a.Length-1)
            sb.Append(" OR ");
    }
    string strCmd = sb.ToString();
    SqlDataAdapter da = new SqlDataAdapter(strCmd, m_connString);
    DataTable dt = new DataTable();
    da.Fill(dt);
    return dt;
}
```

Figure 7-9 shows the final results.

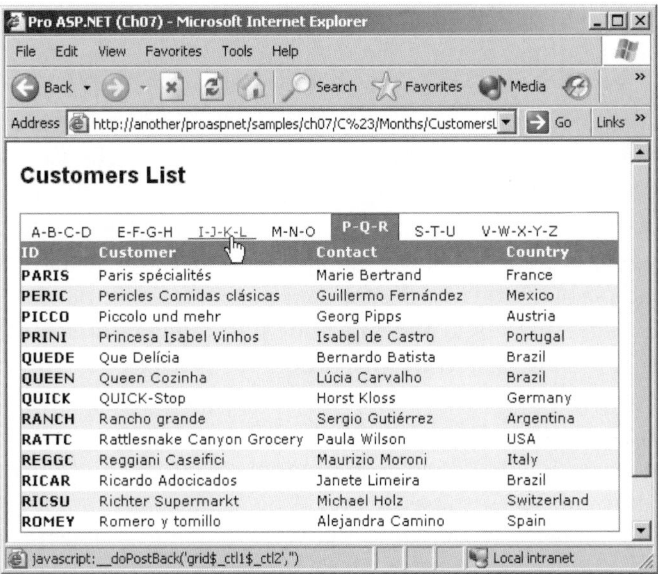


**Figure 7-9** A customized grid that displays logically grouped data.

## Conclusion

No matter what type of application you are building—whether it's a Web application, Microsoft Windows application, or Web service—you can rarely afford downloading and caching the whole data source you're expected to display. Sometimes, test environments might lead you to believe such a solution works great and is the preferable one. Even more often, test environments lie and mislead you. The size of the data source does matter, and the more the application must be scaled the more size does matter.

The *DataGrid* control has two ways of paging. In one case, you bind the control to the whole data source and let it go. For Web applications, this approach is twice as risky. For one thing, you must be sure you tested the application with sample databases of the proper order of magnitude. Also, a Web application loses its state across two successive requests and the *DataGrid* control doesn't employ countermeasures to avoid that. As a result, each time the page is requested, the data source must be restored. In summary, either you can afford caching the whole data source or opt for the second type of paging—custom paging. In addition, while computing the size of the data source, don't forget to multiply it by a factor if the data to cache is session specific!

Custom paging is a memory-effective technique. Only the data needed at a particular time is loaded into memory. If this approach sounds familiar—perhaps familiar even to the point of déjà vu—you're more than right. Custom paging is a common best practice for paging—integrated here with an ASP.NET server control and exposed by the framework. You should consider using custom paging for everything except small and global data with a low level of volatility.

A second problem to consider for data paging is the structure and the content of each page. What's a page in your particular context? Is it simply a sequence of data rows listed in any order? Or is a page a group of related records that respond to some criteria? In this chapter, we showed how to customize paging to make a *DataGrid* display rows grouped by months or name. SQL commands are key elements to setting up functional and effective pagination. Paging through the resultset returned by a query is not a feature the SQL language supports natively as part of the SQL-92 standard. For this reason, you should look carefully at the features of the SQL language for the particular DBMS you're using.

In the next chapter, we'll look at how to make the data-access layer more effective and data-driven applications more user-friendly. We'll consider compound queries and scalability, but also reporting and master/detail views.

## Resources

- Data Paging: Display Your Data One Page at a Time (*http://www.aspnetpro.com/features/2002/05/asp200205wf_f/asp200205wf_f.asp*)
- Customizing Pagination (*http://www.aspnetpro.com/features/2002/03/asp200203de_f/asp200203de_f.asp*)
- Paging Results with ASP.NET's PagedDataSource (*http://www.sitepoint.com/article/921*)
- Paging with Repeater control in ASP.NET (*http://www.charon.co.uk/content.asp?CategoryID=4&ArticleID=21*)
- Design a Custom Paging Solution *(http://www.fawcette.com/dotnetmag/2002_10/magazine/columns/architecting)*

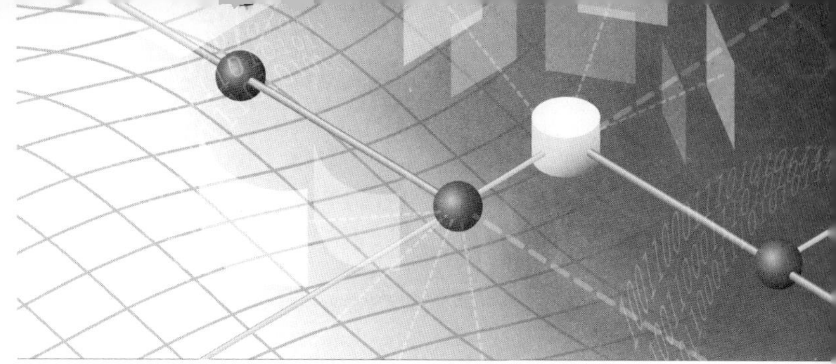

# 8

# Real-World Data Access

*Adults should put in their work the same seriousness that children put in their games.*

*—Friedrich Nietzsche*

Almost all data-driven applications look alike. They need to fetch data across different tables, join columns, and filter data based on some user-specific criteria. Data-driven applications must also format data in such a way that it can be easily (and pleasantly) consumed by end-users. In this context, the organization of the output, pagination, and editing models are key issues. More often than not, data is made of cross-related tables in which parent/child relationships are necessary to define the data model and to extract a specific subset of information (for example, detail views and subtotals) quickly and easily.

All distributed applications must be scalable to some extent. In general, Web applications are more sensitive to the issue of scalability than desktop, client/server applications. If a Web application is deployed over the Internet and made open to anonymous users—for example, a shopping Web site—providing a good, if not optimal, level of scalability is a sort of survival test. Scalability is related to performance, but it can't be identified exclusively with that. Likewise, performance affects scalability. However, they're not synonymous. For example, an application with a long response time will often have an overall software architecture that scales well, either up or out, to avoid performance degradation as the number of users grows. On the other hand, you will often run across extremely fast and super-optimized applications whose designs are not very scalable. A general law of performance tuning states that you must know the underpinnings of a system to devise tricks to increase the throughput.

In summary, optimizing performance involves making assumptions and choosing average values as indicators of the typical workload. In contrast, scalability just refers to the system's ability of maintaining the same level of performance as the number of concurrent users and the workload grows.

In general, caching data does not seem to be an optimal choice for all Web applications because it consumes valuable resources on a per-user or per-application basis. As a result, having less memory available to the Web server might lead to performance degradation. An application that needs to be *only* fast should be as stateless as possible and, subsequently, avoid caching state information. On the other hand, if you're developing an application that needs to be both fast *and* scalable, you should carefully consider caching data at some level to reduce the workload on middle-tier processing components. In addition, the more tiered your system is, the more options you have to scale it out as long as disconnected caches of data can be moved across the tiers. In the area of speed and scalability, ADO.NET helps considerably. ADO.NET doesn't perform magic or provide a ready-to-use solution for every scenario. The true power of ADO.NET is the set of tools it supplies for you to build highly scalable and reasonably fast Web applications that are suited to your needs.

The *DataSet* and its satellite classes (*DataRelation* in particular) are efficient and effective tools that primarily offer options to accomplish common tasks in real-world, data-driven Web applications. After evaluating the characteristics and expectations of your particular application, you should choose the right combination of old-style and new-style programming. Do not trust those who depict ADO.NET as a magic wand that makes Web applications fast and scalable with nothing more than a simple touch. And also don't trust those who completely disregard ADO.NET. At a minimum, ADO.NET provides you with new and powerful tools. It's up to you, then, to decide in any given situation whether they can help or not.

This chapter is divided in three parts, the first of which is about the ADO.NET best practices for executing cross-table commands—the typical commands of a real Web application. The other parts tackle two specific issues—subtotaling and master/detail views—whose effective implementation depends to some extent on the execution of compound queries.

## Compound Commands

Even the simplest Web application has a rather complex and interrelated structure of databases. While a database with dozens of related tables, views, constraints, and triggers is not that common, I have yet to see a (nontoy) Web application with less than a handful of related tables. As a result, the need for Web applications to execute commands against a multitude of tables is more concrete than ever and, therefore, must be properly addressed.

The problem with more complicated databases has to do with both queries and updates. Users should be able to access and filter related rows, such as all orders generated within a given period by a particular customer. They also must be able to update or delete rows in a way that does not violate the consistency and integrity of the database. Some databases resort to server-side constraints to block undesired changes. The fact that most database administrators use this strategy to stay on the safe side is not a good reason to avoid code that could potentially corrupt the database. Ideally, client applications should submit changes that respect the database structure and its internal update rules (for example, relationships and constraints).

## Conducting Multiple Queries

In light of the ADO.NET capabilities, we can recognize two ways of conducting multiple queries that span across multiple tables—an old way and a new way. The old-fashioned way is typical of ADO and any former data-access technology. Based on the SQL JOIN command, this well-known programming technique returns a single data structure that is quite easy to filter but hard to update and is populated with redundant data.

The alternative approach, touted by the ADO.NET disconnected model, exploits the capabilities of the *DataSet* object—that is, a multitable cache of data. The idea is that you split the original query into two or more distinct queries and gather the results in separate tables within the same *DataSet* object. The queries can be run individually or grouped in a stored procedure or in a batch. Using split queries results in a much more compact data set that can be easily managed via the programming interface of the *DataSet* and *DataRelation* objects. Separate queries managed through ADO.NET support cascading changes and batch updates, and they don't require synchronization code to be written on your end to retrieve the children of a parent row. On the downside, filtering records over a relation is not particularly easy.

### Using Joined Queries

Suppose you need to obtain, grouped by customer, all orders issued in a given year. You don't want all the orders, though, only those with at least 30 items. In addition, you want the name of the employee who processed the order and the name of the company that issued it. The query can be written like this:

```
SELECT o.CustomerID, od.OrderID, o.OrderDate, o.ShippedDate,
       SUM(od.Quantity * od.UnitPrice) AS price,
       c.CompanyName, e.LastName
FROM Orders o INNER JOIN
     Customers c ON c.CustomerID=o.CustomerID INNER JOIN
     Employees e ON e.EmployeeID=o.EmployeeID INNER JOIN
     [Order Details] od ON o.OrderID=od.OrderID AND o.OrderID=od.OrderID
```

```
WHERE (YEAR(o.OrderDate) = 1997)
GROUP BY o.CustomerID, c.CompanyName, od.OrderID, o.OrderDate,
         o.ShippedDate, e.LastName
HAVING (SUM(od.Quantity) > 30)
ORDER BY o.CustomerID, od.orderid
```

The query spans the Northwind tables—Orders, Order Details, Customers, and Employees. It retrieves all orders with more than 30 items and is grouped by customer and filtered by year. Viewed through Microsoft SQL Server Query Analyzer, the result set looks like Figure 8-1.

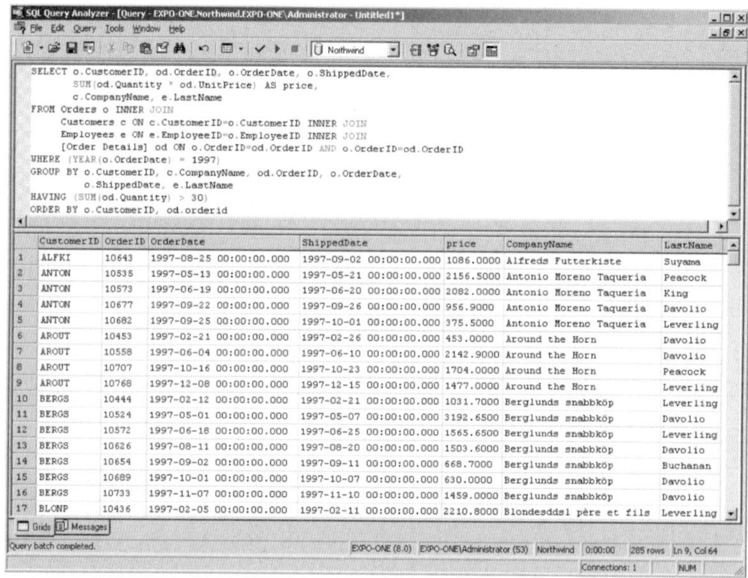


| | CustomerID | OrderID | OrderDate | ShippedDate | price | CompanyName | LastName |
|---|---|---|---|---|---|---|---|
| 1 | ALFKI | 10643 | 1997-08-25 00:00:00.000 | 1997-09-02 00:00:00.000 | 1086.0000 | Alfreds Futterkiste | Suyama |
| 2 | ANTON | 10535 | 1997-05-13 00:00:00.000 | 1997-05-21 00:00:00.000 | 2156.5000 | Antonio Moreno Taquería | Peacock |
| 3 | ANTON | 10573 | 1997-06-19 00:00:00.000 | 1997-06-20 00:00:00.000 | 2082.0000 | Antonio Moreno Taquería | King |
| 4 | ANTON | 10677 | 1997-09-22 00:00:00.000 | 1997-09-26 00:00:00.000 | 956.9000 | Antonio Moreno Taquería | Davolio |
| 5 | ANTON | 10682 | 1997-09-25 00:00:00.000 | 1997-10-01 00:00:00.000 | 375.5000 | Antonio Moreno Taquería | Leverling |
| 6 | AROUT | 10453 | 1997-02-21 00:00:00.000 | 1997-02-26 00:00:00.000 | 453.0000 | Around the Horn | Davolio |
| 7 | AROUT | 10558 | 1997-06-04 00:00:00.000 | 1997-06-10 00:00:00.000 | 2142.9000 | Around the Horn | Davolio |
| 8 | AROUT | 10707 | 1997-10-16 00:00:00.000 | 1997-10-23 00:00:00.000 | 1704.0000 | Around the Horn | Peacock |
| 9 | AROUT | 10768 | 1997-12-08 00:00:00.000 | 1997-12-15 00:00:00.000 | 1477.0000 | Around the Horn | Leverling |
| 10 | BERGS | 10444 | 1997-02-12 00:00:00.000 | 1997-02-21 00:00:00.000 | 1031.7000 | Berglunds snabbköp | Leverling |
| 11 | BERGS | 10524 | 1997-05-01 00:00:00.000 | 1997-05-07 00:00:00.000 | 3192.6500 | Berglunds snabbköp | Davolio |
| 12 | BERGS | 10572 | 1997-06-18 00:00:00.000 | 1997-06-25 00:00:00.000 | 1565.6500 | Berglunds snabbköp | Leverling |
| 13 | BERGS | 10626 | 1997-08-11 00:00:00.000 | 1997-08-20 00:00:00.000 | 1503.6000 | Berglunds snabbköp | Davolio |
| 14 | BERGS | 10654 | 1997-09-02 00:00:00.000 | 1997-09-11 00:00:00.000 | 668.7000 | Berglunds snabbköp | Buchanan |
| 15 | BERGS | 10689 | 1997-10-01 00:00:00.000 | 1997-10-07 00:00:00.000 | 630.0000 | Berglunds snabbköp | Davolio |
| 16 | BERGS | 10733 | 1997-11-07 00:00:00.000 | 1997-11-10 00:00:00.000 | 1459.0000 | Berglunds snabbköp | Davolio |
| 17 | BLONP | 10436 | 1997-02-05 00:00:00.000 | 1997-02-11 00:00:00.000 | 2210.8000 | Blondesddsl père et fils | Leverling |

**Figure 8-1** The result of a query that makes intensive use of JOIN statements.

You can immediately see how much redundant data the result set contains. The query counts about 300 records, and each of them has a high likelihood of containing a duplicate customer or employee name. The main characteristic of a join query is that it returns data as a monolithic block. As mentioned, this is good news and bad news at the same time. The good news is the data is held in the same block of memory, works great for presentation purposes, and can be further filtered by simply adding some criteria to the object that represents it—either an ADO *Recordset* or an ADO.NET *DataTable*. The bad news is, the result set does not make good use of memory and might raise scalability issues. Also, keeping changes synchronized with the database is not trivial. Finding a match between an element in the result set and a table record is challenging, and this makes it hard to keep the data synchronized and even to apply changes.

ADO hierarchical recordsets have been an attempt to better sort things out. They gave developers a chance to design a hierarchical query through a made-to-measure (and, frankly, horrible) syntax. As a result, a tree of parent and child *Recordset* objects reduced the redundancy of data and made synchronization simpler. The main drawbacks of ADO hierarchical recordsets are the inability to access more than one data source and the overly simple update model. To this list, we should then add the annoyance of working with the notorious SHAPE language, which is needed to build such recordsets.

Another subtle point in favor of joined queries is the inherent transaction support that SQL Server (and in general any database management system) guarantees to individual commands. A complex query, especially if it includes subqueries or views, is made of different low-level operations that run in the context of the same implicit transaction. This guarantees that no concurrency issue would ever be raised, even for highly volatile databases. We'll return to this point later in the chapter in the "Respecting Data Integrity" section.

## Paging Through the Results of *Any* Query

In Chapter 7, "Paging Through Data Sources," we discussed various ways of paging through the results of a query. In particular, we focused on building queries that return a page of data. However, we used very simple commands to query just a single table. The paging techniques we discussed can be applied to any query, even though they might sometimes require adjustments. In general, the pattern used to retrieve a page is as follows:

```
SELECT * FROM
    (SELECT TOP PageSize * FROM
        (SELECT TOP PageSize*PageIndex * FROM (query) AS t1
    ORDER BY KeyColumn DESC) AS t2
ORDER BY KeyColumn
```

Note that if you're going to sort by multiple columns you must add the DESC qualifier to all column names. If the *query* placeholder is a subquery, it can contain an inner ORDER BY clause only if a TOP clause is present. If you don't actually need a TOP clause, use TOP 100 PERCENT.

To greatly simplify coding, you could also define a view. Adapting the random paging sample we saw in Chapter 7 to work on the aforementioned orders query requires only minor changes. (See joins.aspx in the book samples.)

## Using Distinct Queries

An alternative approach made particularly attractive by ADO.NET is separating an otherwise nested and complex query into multiple simpler queries. There's a double advantage to doing so. First, the amount of data returned to the client is significantly smaller. Second, the functionality of the ADO.NET *DataSet* object makes managing multiple tables straightforward.

Next, I'll show you a way to split the preceding query into smaller and relatively independent pieces. The query consists of three subqueries: getting a filtered view of orders and details, plus getting a view of related employees and customers, respectively.

The first query (shown below) selects all orders containing at least 30 items. In this slightly revised version, the query doesn't join with the Customers and Employees tables to get *foreign* information about the customer and employee who participated in the order.

```
SELECT o.CustomerID, od.OrderID, o.OrderDate, o.ShippedDate,
       SUM(od.Quantity * od.UnitPrice) AS price
FROM Orders o INNER JOIN
     Customers c ON c.CustomerID=o.CustomerID INNER JOIN
     Employees e ON e.EmployeeID=o.EmployeeID INNER JOIN
     [Order Details] od ON o.OrderID=od.OrderID AND o.OrderID=od.OrderID
WHERE (YEAR(o.OrderDate) = 1997)
GROUP BY o.CustomerID, od.OrderID, o.OrderDate, o.ShippedDate
HAVING (SUM(od.Quantity) > 30)
ORDER BY o.CustomerID, od.orderid
```

The other two queries serve only the purpose of providing extra information about the involved employees and customers. In their simplest form, the queries are written as follows:

```
SELECT employeeid, lastname FROM employees
SELECT customerid, companyname FROM customers
```

Of course, in this case all employees and customers will be selected, which is not exactly what a joined query would return. However, depending on the structure and goals of the application, this shortcut might be acceptable. In general, employees and customers represent data that has low volatility and, as such, is ideal for caching. The issue here is the size of the tables. If your company has thousands of employees and customers, caching entire tables might not be the best approach.

A query that returns only the employees and the customers referenced by the first query might be much more complex to write, however. It mostly depends on the complexity of the search criteria. The more sophisticated the criteria is, the more complex the child queries are, and subsequently, the higher the price is for the query. As usual, fine-tuning the query subsystem of an application is a delicate art.

Let's continue with the example and analyze what's needed to obtain only the employees and customers involved with the orders selected by the first query. The criteria set for these queries require you to group the information by orders and compute the quantity of orders (at least 180 in the following sample). Given this subset of orders, you can then extract distinct employees or customers:

```
SELECT DISTINCT * FROM
    (SELECT c.customerid, c.companyname FROM Customers c INNER JOIN
            Orders o ON o.customerid=c.customerid INNER JOIN
            [Order Details] od ON o.OrderID=od.OrderID
    WHERE (YEAR(o.OrderDate) = 1997)
    GROUP BY o.orderid, c.customerid, c.companyname
    HAVING (SUM(od.Quantity) > 180)
    ) AS t1
```

Similarly, for employees you use the following third query:

```
SELECT DISTINCT * FROM
    (SELECT e.employeeid, e.lastname, e.title FROM employees e INNER JOIN
        Orders o ON o.employeeid=e.employeeid INNER JOIN
        [Order Details] od ON o.OrderID=od.OrderID
    WHERE (YEAR(o.OrderDate) = 1997)
    GROUP BY o.orderid, e.employeeid, e.lastname, e.title
    HAVING (SUM(od.Quantity) > 180)
    ) AS t1
```

As you can see, in this case we're going to run three complex queries rather than just one. In other circumstances, filtering the satellite tables is considerably easier and faster. As we'll also see throughout this chapter, ADO.NET is not a magic solution and effective SQL commands are now, more than ever, essential for creating effective applications.

> **Note** Many Web applications cache global data in global objects such as *Cache*, *Application*, or *Session*. (We'll review these objects in detail in Chapter 14, "ASP.NET State Management.") A warning, though, must be raised here. Suppose you decide to split a complex query into separate queries and also decide to keep child queries simple by creating look-up tables with employee and customer information. Where do you cache that data? If you store data in *Session* or *Cache*—it depends on the required scope—be aware that both objects might be subject to unexpected clean-up because of process recycling (see Chapter 2), low memory conditions, or both. You should always check whether the cache is still there and reload it if necessary. In summary, consider that look-up tables might need to be frequently refreshed.

All the queries you obtained can be grouped in a SQL batch or stored procedure and handed off to a data adapter for actual population. You get back a *DataSet* with as many tables as there are queries in the statement. You can access and index tables individually and create in-memory relations between tables. Note that relationships must be set up manually because no feature in ADO.NET provides for automatic reading and processing of database relationship objects and constraints. For more information about ADO.NET relations, see Chapter 5, "The ADO.NET Object Model."

**Tip** Relations also offer a quick way to simulate in-memory JOINs. Suppose you have two tables (named Orders and Employees) filled with information on orders and employees, respectively. To create a relation between the two tables based on the common field employeeid, you would use the following code:

```
DataRelation rel = new DataRelation("Emp2Ord",
    employees.Columns["employeeid"],
    orders.Columns["employeeid"]);
data.Relations.Add(rel);
```

Finally, to add a new column to the Orders table that points to the lastname column in the parent table according to the relation, you would use the following code:

```
orders.Columns.Add("EmployeeName",
    typeof(string), "Parent(Emp2Ord).lastname");
```

To read the last name of the employee, you would simply refer to the newly created EmployeeName column on the in-memory Orders table.

## Respecting Data Integrity

Another issue to consider is data consistency. A complex query that runs as a single SELECT statement works in the context of an implicit transaction and looks like an atomic piece of code. When you split that into separate queries, you should also consider the impact that concurrency might have on the state of the database. What if a customer is concurrently deleted or an order is modified between the subqueries? It might or might not be a problem for the application. In case it is, though, you must consider protecting the subqueries in a transaction so that other users are prevented from updating or inserting rows while the queries are executing.

Transactions are a unit of work that execute according to four principles—atomicity, consistency, isolation, and durability—often cumulatively known as ACID. For our purposes, the key element is isolation. The isolation property refers to the database's ability to shield each running transaction from the effects of other concurrently running transactions. If a transacted query is running at the same time someone else is updating the database, the final results can vary depending on the level of isolation set. Normally each transacted operation can have the level of isolation it needs. If the application needs absolute data consistency and cannot afford phantom rows, the only appropriate isolation level is *serializable*. A serializable transaction unlocks the tables only upon completion. With this level of isolation, reading uncommitted data (a process known as *dirty reads*) and getting phantom rows is not possible. Phantom rows refer to any situation in which transactions work on misaligned sets of data. A phantom row is a row that one transaction added but is unknown to the other concurrent transaction. Likewise, a row visible in one transaction but physically deleted by another is an example of phantom rows. Serializable transactions should be the last resource in database programming because they seriously affect the overall concurrency of the system.

If you need the power of serializable transactions without its burden, you can opt for a sort of compromise between joined and distinct queries. You first run the query by using nested JOINs as needed. Next, once the result set has been downloaded in an ADO.NET environment, you process the original *DataTable* and split its contents into smaller tables. On the server, the query works as a monolithic piece of code; the application, though, sees it as the union of distinct but related tables.

```
SELECT o.customerid, c.companyname, e.employeeid, e.lastname,
       od.orderid, o.orderdate, o.shippeddate,
       SUM(od.quantity*od.unitprice) AS price
FROM Orders AS o
INNER JOIN Customers AS c ON c.customerid=o.customerid
INNER JOIN Employees AS e ON e.employeeid=o.employeeid
INNER JOIN [Order Details] AS od ON o.orderid=od.orderid
    WHERE Year(o.orderdate) = @TheYear AND od.orderid=o.orderid
    GROUP BY o.customerid, c.companyname, od.orderid,
        o.orderdate, o.shippeddate, e.employeeid, e.lastname
    HAVING SUM(od.quantity) >@TheAmount
ORDER BY o.customerid
```

The next listing shows the structure of the code that works on the preceding query:

```
DataSet SplitData(DataSet ds)
{
    // Assumes that the DataSet has one table named Orders. The 2nd
```

```
    // column is CompanyName; the 4th column is LastName
    DataSet _dataset = new DataSet();

    // Make a full worker copy of the DataSet
    _dataset = ds.Copy();

    // Extract tables
    CreateCustomers(_dataset, ds);
    CreateEmployees(_dataset, ds);

    // Remove columns from Orders(companyname [2] and lastname [4])
    // so that the original table doesn't contain any longer data
    // moved into distinct tables
    _dataset.Tables["Orders"].Columns.RemoveAt(1);
    _dataset.Tables["Orders"].Columns.RemoveAt(3);

    return _dataset;
}
```

The code makes a full deep copy of the source *DataSet*, which will be used as the Orders table in the resulting new *DataSet*. This new *DataSet* then adds dynamically created tables for customers and employees. Finally, the columns now included in child tables are removed from the Orders table. The following code shows how the satellite Customers table is created:

```
// Create Customers
static void CreateCustomers(DataSet _dataset, DataSet orig)
{
    DataTable _customers = orig.Tables["Orders"].Clone();
    _customers.TableName = "Customers";

    // Remove unneeded columns (no data is involved)
    // Only the first two columns (CustomerID and CompanyName) are kept
    for(int i=2; i<_customers.Columns.Count - 1; i++)
        _customers.Columns.RemoveAt(2);

    // Fill with data
    string customerKey = "";
    foreach(DataRow row in _dataset.Tables["Orders"].Rows)
    {
        // Already sorted by CustomerID
        if(customerKey != row["customerid"].ToString())
        {
            // select distinct
            _customers.ImportRow(row);
            customerKey = row["customerid"].ToString();
        }
    }
```

```
    // Add to the DataSet
    _dataset.Tables.Add(_customers);
}
```

> **Note** A similar approach can also be used if you have an existing stored procedure to retrieve the data and want to manage its return data through distinct in-memory tables. If you can't modify the existing stored procedure, this approach is a viable solution.

## Conducting Cross-Table Updates

When it comes to updating cross-related tables, the order in which each constituent statement executes is critical. For example, you can't delete an order without also deleting all its details. Likewise, you aren't normally allowed to add an invoice detail row without first adding its parent row. When related tables are involved, changes flow from the parent to the children in different ways, depending on the type of change—update, delete, or insert.

In general, there are two ways of conducting table updates—through a direct connection or batch update. In the direct connection case, you typically open a connection and execute the stored procedure or the SQL batch with all the logic and data you need to apply. In the batch update case, you typically yield to a middle-tier component, which takes care of submitting data to the database, possibly in an asynchronous way. This approach in a Web scenario requires you to serialize the data to be submitted from the Web server layer down to an internal tier, which holds a physical connection to the database. The availability of an easy-to-serialize object such as the *DataSet* and the powerful batch update mechanism of data adapters give you the tools to build highly scalable applications. But how can you effectively use these tools?

### Cascading Changes

As mentioned in Chapter 5, a foreign key constraint set on a *DataTable* restricts the action performed when a value in a column is either deleted or updated. In a parent/child relationship between two tables, deleting a value from the parent table can affect the child rows in various ways. Typically, the child rows are also deleted. However, in some cases, the cascading action sets the child rows to null or default values. The action that works best for you can be programmatically selected using the programming interface of the *ForeignKeyConstraint* class.

What really matters, though, is that ADO.NET provides the tools to configure the runtime environment to automatically cascade changes from parent to child rows. Such a mechanism is important because it allows you to work on a *DataSet* object, enter changes, and if needed, have them propagated through the tree. When you have gone through all the changes, ADO.NET guarantees that all the tables in the *DataSet* have been properly updated. In addition, the *DataSet* is a disconnected and serializable object and is ideal for delivering the new image of the data to the middle-tier component for physical updates.

## The Batch Update

Data submission is the process in which all in-memory changes are passed on to the back-end system for permanent storage. In ADO.NET, submission does not consist of a block of data being sent to the database—Microsoft SQL Server 2000 or any other—in a single shot. An ADO.NET batch update just executes individual statements on the target system, one for each change that needs to be submitted. For the most part, statements will be SQL statements.

The *DataSet* object can submit data to the database in batch mode by using the data adapter's *Update* method. Data can be submitted only on a per-table basis. The *Update* method prepares and calls a tailor-made statement for each inserted, updated, or deleted row in the specified *DataTable* object.

```
adapter.Update(dataSet, tableName);
```

The cascading changes feature guarantees that all the tables in the *DataSet* are in sync and consistent. The batch update is its natural complement, as it allows you to submit changes, one table at a time, to the database.

Rows are scanned and processed according to their natural order (their position in the table's *Rows* collection). If you need to process rows in a particular order, you must split the overall update process into various subprocesses, each working on the selected bunch of rows you need. For example, if you have parent/child related tables, you might want to start by modifying rows in both tables. Next, you delete rows in the child table, and after that, you delete rows in the parent table. Finally, you insert new rows in the parent table and finish with insertions into the child table. The following code snippet shows how to select and submit only the rows that have been added to a table:

```
// Submit all the rows that have been added to a given table
DataRow[] arrayOfRows = table.Select("", "", DataViewRowState.Added);
adapter.Update(arrayOfRows);
```

This solution is made possible by the fact that one of the *Update* overloads takes an array of *DataRow* objects, an overload that provides for the greatest flexibility.

> **Important** When serializing a *DataSet* object across the tiers of a system for update purposes, you're much better off using the subset of the *DataSet* that contains the changed rows. You get this smaller version by using the *GetChanges* method. If you're batch-updating from within the same AppDomain, though, this technique won't result in a significant improvement in performance.

## Detecting and Resolving Update Conflicts

Data updates are based on a decidedly optimistic vision of concurrency. What happens if, by the time you attempt to apply your changes to the back-end system, someone else has modified the same records? Technically speaking, in this case you have a *data conflict*. How to handle conflicts is strictly application-specific, but the reasonable options can be easily summarized in three points: the first-win, last-win, and ask-the-user options:

- **First-win** The conflict is resolved by silently and automatically dropping the latest change—that is, the one you were trying to submit. To implement a first-win approach, you simply set the *ContinueUpdateOnError* property on the data adapter to *true*. If *ContinueUpdateOnError* is set to *true*, no exception is thrown when an error occurs during the update of a row. The error information is stored in the *RowError* property of the corresponding row. The batch-update process continues with subsequent rows.
- **Last-win** Your changes are applied regardless of the current status of the row. To implement this approach, you have to ensure only that the SQL command used to carry the update is not too restrictive to generate a data conflict. A data conflict, in fact, is raised when the SQL command finds no row to affect. If you build the SQL command so that it updates or deletes rows that match a primary key field, no data conflict will ever be raised. Conflict-aware SQL code is code generated by ADO.NET command-builders in which the WHERE clause ensures that the current and original status of the row match prior to proceeding with the statement. In the last-win approach, a special case is represented by the situation in which another user deleted the row you are trying to update. In this case, you should drop your change.

- **Ask-the-user** You should choose this route when the other two options don't work in all cases you can foresee. By default, a data conflict raises a *DBConcurrencyException* exception. Note that the exception is not raised if you set the *ContinueUpdateOnError* property to *true*. The *Row* property on the exception class returns a reference to the row in error. By reading the properties of such a *DataRow* object, you have access to both proposed and original values. You have no access to the underlying value, but you can obtain that by issuing another query against the database. At the end of the day, resolving the conflict means opting either for a first-win or last-win approach. In this case, you let the user decide, but you must provide him or her with enough information.

For Web applications, you normally choose one of the first two options and try to ensure that the update always ends without going back to the user for further interaction.

> **Important** Conflicts are not detected automatically by some special feature built into the ADO.NET runtime. Conflicts are caught only if the commands used to carry the batch update have certain characteristics. In particular, conflict-aware commands have quite a long WHERE clause, one in which the primary key is first checked to verify the identity of the row and then a number of other columns are checked against the values they had when the *DataSet* was originally built. You control the columns in the WHERE clause in two ways: either by writing your own commands (as shown in the upcoming text) or by setting the *SelectCommand* property of the data adapter. (See Chapter 5.)
>
> An alternative way of detecting conflicts is by using a timestamp column. You add a timestamp column to a table and set it with the current time whenever you update the table. This trick greatly simplifies both the operations needed to check whether a conflict is going to happen (forward checking) and the command itself. Checking a single field is much easier than checking multiple columns!

## Stored Procedures in Batch Updates

One of the biggest drawbacks of the ADO batch update was that it was impossible for the user to intervene and modify the commands being used for the update. As discussed in Chapter 5, ADO.NET allows you to configure the command—insert, update, or delete—to use for any event and gives you a chance to link it to source columns. The following code shows how to use a stored procedure for all the updated rows of the table:

```
adapter.UpdateCommand = new SqlCommand();
adapter.UpdateCommand.CommandText = "sp_myUpdate";
adapter.UpdateCommand.CommandType = CommandType.StoredProcedure;
adapter.UpdateCommand.Connection = conn;

p1 = new SqlParameter("@empID", SqlDbType.Int);
p1.SourceVersion = DataRowVersion.Original;
p1.SourceColumn = "employeeid";
adapter.UpdateCommand.Parameters.Add(p1);

p2 = new SqlParameter("@firstName", SqlDbType.NVarChar, 10);
p2.SourceVersion = DataRowVersion.Current;
p2.SourceColumn = "firstname";
adapter.UpdateCommand.Parameters.Add(p2);

p3 = new SqlParameter("@lastName", SqlDbType.NVarChar, 20);
p3.SourceVersion = DataRowVersion.Current;
p3.SourceColumn = "lastname";
adapter.UpdateCommand.Parameters.Add(p3);
```

Notice the pair of properties, *SourceColumn* and *SourceVersion*, that allows you to define what column and what version of the column should be bound to the parameter. The possibility of using a stored procedure adds an unprecedented level of flexibility to the batch update, especially when cross-referenced tables are involved.

## Using Transactions in Batch Updates

To execute transacted commands, you can either use the transaction-related statements of the database management system (DBMS) you're working with or rely on the .NET data provider's abstraction of a transaction. There's virtually no difference between the two approaches, as the .NET abstraction of a transaction simply exists in a managed wrapper that triggers a call to the underlying transactional infrastructure. When you call the *BeginTransaction* method on the connection object of a .NET data provider, a new transaction command executes over the connection. Let's consider the following snippet:

```
conn.Open();
SqlTransaction tran = conn.BeginTransaction();
⋮
tran.Commit();
conn.Close();
```

If you spy on the process by using a profiler tool, you'll see the following sequence of commands hitting the database:

```
SET TRANSACTION ISOLATION LEVEL READ COMMITTED;BEGIN TRANSACTION
⋮
COMMIT TRANSACTION
```

So the ADO.NET transaction object is useful because it makes the code you're writing less dependent on the physical structure of the database, but no significant difference occurs under the hood.

Once created, the transaction must be associated with the command or the commands you are about to run. For batch updates, this means the *UpdateCommand*, *InsertCommand*, and *DeleteCommand* must share the same transactional context.

## Retrieving Server-Generated Values

A frequent problem of cross-table updates is that you have to use some values generated by the database for further statements within the same stored procedure or SQL batch. A typical situation in which this problem arises is when triggers are involved as well as identity columns. If you're using direct commands or stored procedures, there's not much that ADO.NET does for you. You must address the issue using the tools the database provides you with. Typically, using a subsequent query that reads critical values back fits the bill. The values can be exposed through output parameters or additional result sets. If identity columns are involved, you use the identity functions of the DBMS to retrieve them. For example, with SQL Server 2000, you use the SCOPE_IDENTITY function.

If you're using batch updates, ADO.NET provides a couple of built-in mechanisms that enable you to know the values actually stored in the database as a result of the update. The first mechanism is based on the *UpdatedRowSource* property of the command object. The other mechanism leverages the *RowUpdated* event on the data adapter object. Let's examine how to use each to retrieve the value of an identity column when a new record is added.

The *UpdatedRowSource* property tells the command object to look for values returned by the INSERT and UPDATE statements and to assign them to the *DataRow* object being updated in the batch. The net effect of this property is that, at the end of the batch, each inserted or updated row in the *DataTable* contains exactly the values of its counterpart in the database. If identity columns or triggers are around, the original, in-memory values of the row are automatically updated with the actual values stored in the database. Sounds great? It is, indeed, but for it to happen, a bit of work is required on your side. In particular, you have to define the insert and the update commands as stored procedures or SQL batches so that they execute the appropriate query to read values back. In other words, the ADO.NET batch update provides some handy facilities but there's only way to get server-generated—by reading them back with a batch query.

The *UpdatedRowSource* property is designed to look for output parameters, the first row of the next query, both, or neither. By default, the option to look for both is selected. The following batch inserts a new row into the Employees database whose employeeid column is the identity. Next, it retrieves the last identity value generated in the scope.

```
INSERT INTO employees (lastname, firstname) VALUES (@LName, @FName)
SELECT SCOPE_IDENTITY() AS employeeid
```

If you assign the previous statements to the *InsertCommand* property of a data adapter, the *UpdatedRowSource* property will catch the newly generated identity value and pass it along to the *DataRow* object being updated. By setting the *UpdatedRowSource* property to *Both* (the default) or *FirstReturnedRecord*, each inserted row processed through the batch update will have its employeeid column updated. You don't have to write any additional code.

**Caution** It's highly recommended that you *don't* use this technique if commands are to be autogenerated using a command builder. The statements generated by a command builder don't include the required additional query and are generated when the data adapter's *Update* method is called. At this time, it is too late for editing the command text to add the extra query. You should not use the *UpdatedRowSource* property if you are using command builders.

The SCOPE_IDENTITY function returns the last identity value inserted into an identity column in the same stored procedure, trigger, function, or batch. If you're using SQL Server 7.0 or earlier, use @@IDENTITY instead. SCOPE_IDENTITY, IDENT_CURRENT, and @@IDENTITY are similar functions in that they return values inserted into identity columns. For more information on the difference between these features, see the SQL Server Books Online.

Whenever the data adapter is going to update a row within a batch update, it fires a couple of events—*RowUpdating* and *RowUpdated*. *RowUpdating* fires before the update takes place and *RowUpdated* fires immediately after. The following code shows how to specify an event handler for the *RowUpdated* event.

```
adapter.RowUpdated += new SqlRowUpdatedEventHandler(RowUpdated);
```

The event passes back a data structure of type *SqlRowUpdatedEventArgs* in which the *Row* property returns an updated row. (We're using SQL Server as the data provider; the code would have to be adapted for other providers.) The *RowUpdated* event is provided mostly for databases that don't support stored procedures, multiple queries, and output parameters. Want an example? Microsoft Access.

> **Important** Bear in mind that the automatic update of the *DataRow* occurs only during batch updates and only if you add output parameters to the command (for example, a stored procedure) or additional queries to retrieve particular fields. Also note that the name of the retrieved column must match the name of the *DataTable* column. That's why we aliased SCOPE_IDENTITY in the earlier sample (on page 403).

## Data Reporting and Subtotals

In ASP.NET, the *DataGrid* is the ideal tool for building feature-rich data reports. As we've seen in Chapter 6, "Creating Bindable Grids of Data," and Chapter 7, it provides for paging, sorting, and advanced customization of the data displayed. Despite its adeptness at building feature-rich reports, the *DataGrid* does not have an ad hoc feature to automatically compute functions on the values listed in a given column. In Chapter 6, we demonstrated how to add a footer to a table built with the *DataGrid* and how to modify the structure of the footer to display totals. In computing totals for a column, though, we exploited the programming interface of the *DataTable* and *DataRelation* objects.

Keep in mind that a total is a scalar value you display only in a single place—typically, a cell in the footer bar. Displaying a total doesn't in any way affect the rows you display in the grid. Unfortunately, the same can't be said for displaying column subtotals—they do affect rows you display in the grid.

A subtotal is a non–data-bound row that is interspersed with the data rows of the grid. Like a footer bar, it can have any structure and normally displays summary information that relates to the records found after the beginning of the table or the last subtotal. For example, if your grid displays orders grouped by customers, a subtotal row could count the number and total amount of all orders issued by each customer. The *DataGrid* control doesn't provide any built-in facility that works in this scenario, but with an appropriate combination of SQL and ASP.NET coding you can make it happen.

## Summarizing or Aggregating Values

The key point to understand about *DataGrid* controls is that they don't distinguish between rows in the bound data source. All the bound rows are displayed and any attempt to insert fake rows programmatically is destined to fail or, even worse, to violate the consistency of the output. On the other hand, bound rows can be displayed with different styles, even radically different styles.

As a result, any subtotaling rows you want to display must be part of the data source you associate with the grid. These rows must be easily recognizable so that the *ItemDataBound* and *ItemCreated* event handlers can apply any necessary styling. How can you add summary rows to the data source? There are two possibilities. You can either ask the database to compute subtotal rows, or you can add blank rows and populate them with ad hoc data. In many cases, the database subtotaling capabilities will match your expectations. If you need to control the whole process of aggregation, or if the database you're targeting doesn't provide subtotaling support, you should opt for a pure ADO.NET approach.

### The WITH ROLLUP Operator

Subtotaling makes particular sense if you're also grouping data. SQL Server provides the WITH ROLLUP operator as an extension to the GROUP BY clause of a SELECT statement. The operator works by adding summary rows to the result set according to a specified template. The summary row will have the same layout as all other columns, but you can customize the content of each column to some extent. Let's consider a sample query: getting all orders issued in a given year (say, 1997) grouped by customers. The SQL query to start with is the following:

```
SELECT o.customerid, od.orderid, SUM(od.quantity*od.unitprice) AS price
FROM Orders o, [Order Details] od
WHERE YEAR(o.orderdate)=1997 AND od.orderid=o.orderid
GROUP BY o.customerid, od.orderid
ORDER BY o.customerid, od.orderid
```

Figure 8-2 shows the results as they appear in SQL Query Analyzer. The arrows indicate where we would like to have subtotal rows.

Let's rewrite the query to use the WITH ROLLUP operator and compute order subtotals per customer:

```
SELECT
    o.customerid AS MyCustomerID,
    CASE GROUPING(od.orderid) WHEN 0 THEN od.orderid ELSE 99999 END
        AS MyOrderID,
    SUM(od.quantity*od.unitprice) AS OrderAmount
FROM Orders o, [Order Details] od
```

```
WHERE Year(orderdate) = 1997 AND od.orderid=o.orderid
GROUP BY o.customerid, od.orderid WITH ROLLUP
ORDER BY o.customerid, MyOrderID
```

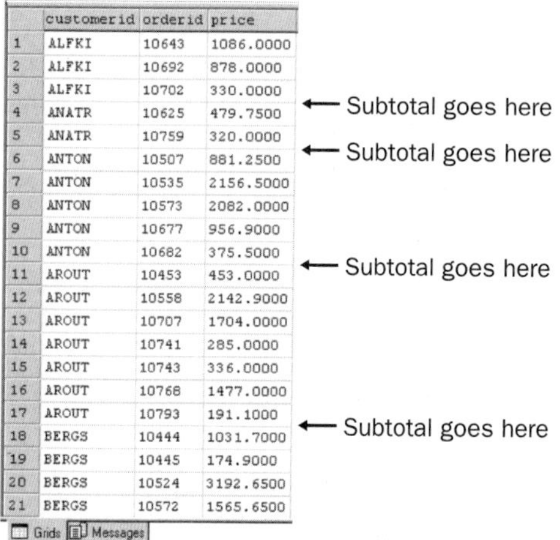

| | customerid | orderid | price |
|---|---|---|---|
| 1 | ALFKI | 10643 | 1086.0000 |
| 2 | ALFKI | 10692 | 878.0000 |
| 3 | ALFKI | 10702 | 330.0000 |
| 4 | ANATR | 10625 | 479.7500 |
| 5 | ANATR | 10759 | 320.0000 |
| 6 | ANTON | 10507 | 881.2500 |
| 7 | ANTON | 10535 | 2156.5000 |
| 8 | ANTON | 10573 | 2082.0000 |
| 9 | ANTON | 10677 | 956.9000 |
| 10 | ANTON | 10682 | 375.5000 |
| 11 | AROUT | 10453 | 453.0000 |
| 12 | AROUT | 10558 | 2142.9000 |
| 13 | AROUT | 10707 | 1704.0000 |
| 14 | AROUT | 10741 | 285.0000 |
| 15 | AROUT | 10743 | 336.0000 |
| 16 | AROUT | 10768 | 1477.0000 |
| 17 | AROUT | 10793 | 191.1000 |
| 18 | BERGS | 10444 | 1031.7000 |
| 19 | BERGS | 10445 | 174.9000 |
| 20 | BERGS | 10524 | 3192.6500 |
| 21 | BERGS | 10572 | 1565.6500 |



**Figure 8-2** A result set that groups order information by customer.

The first thing to notice is that the GROUP BY clause has been extended to include the WITH ROLLUP operator. The second column—originally od.orderid—has been replaced with a more complex CASE...WHEN construct. The CASE...WHEN statement is a simple flow controller, however. The resulting column contains the corresponding od.orderid value if the guarded value is 0; otherwise, it contains 99999. This brings us to the role of the GROUPING function.

GROUPING is an aggregate function that takes the name of a column in the GROUP BY clause and returns an additional column with 0/1 values. A value of 0 means the row has been generated by the query; a value of 1 indicates the row is a summary row added by the ROLLUP operator. The following code snippet shows how to add an extra column to the query. The *IsSummary* column indicates whether the row is a subtotal.

```
SELECT GROUPING(od.orderid) IsSummary,
⋮
```

In the preceding statement, no extra column is actually returned to the user, but the orderid column in the regular query is assigned a special value (99999 or whatever value you decide to use) if the row contains summary values.

The result set of the WITH ROLLUP query contains summary rows characterized by the 99999 value in the MyOrderID field. (If you can't figure out a neutral value for a column, just add an additional 0/1 column based on the output of the GROUPING function.) An appropriate order in the query makes any summary rows appear as the last row of each group. Displaying subtotals is now a simple matter of styling the grid.

| | MyCustomerID | MyOrderID | OrderAmount |
|---|---|---|---|
| 1 | NULL | 99999 | 658388.7500 |
| 2 | ALFKI | 10643 | 1086.0000 |
| 3 | ALFKI | 10692 | 878.0000 |
| 4 | ALFKI | 10702 | 330.0000 |
| 5 | ALFKI | 99999 | 2294.0000 |
| 6 | ANATR | 10625 | 479.7500 |
| 7 | ANATR | 10759 | 320.0000 |
| 8 | ANATR | 99999 | 799.7500 |
| 9 | ANTON | 10507 | 881.2500 |
| 10 | ANTON | 10535 | 2156.5000 |
| 11 | ANTON | 10573 | 2082.0000 |
| 12 | ANTON | 10677 | 956.9000 |
| 13 | ANTON | 10682 | 375.5000 |
| 14 | ANTON | 99999 | 6452.1500 |
| 15 | AROUT | 10453 | 453.0000 |

Grids Messages

**Figure 8-3** Rollup information in a grouped query.

> **Note** The ROLLUP operator is not the only aggregator available in SQL Server 2000. SQL Server 2000 also supports COMPUTE BY, although it is used only for backward compatibility. Contentwise, the result set generated by a ROLLUP operation is identical to that returned by a COMPUTE BY statement. Other differences, though, tip the scales in favor of ROLLUP. For example, ROLLUP returns a single result set. In contrast, COMPUTE BY returns multiple result sets that increase the complexity of code necessary to handle the data. In addition, only ROLLUP can be used in a server cursor, and the query optimizer can sometimes generate more efficient execution plans for it.
>
> The CUBE operator, on the other hand, has programmatic characteristics that assimilate it with ROLLUP. The result set generated, though, is quite different because CUBE explodes data and produces a superset of groups with cross-tabulation of every column to the value of other columns.

## A Pure ADO.NET Approach

If the database doesn't support any aggregate operator that groups data, you can calculate the needed values yourself and insert the summary rows manually with a bit of ADO.NET coding. A possible way of doing that entails the steps shown in the following paragraphs.

Fetch any needed data. You do this by executing a couple of queries against the database. The first retrieves all orders to be displayed but is limited to returning the customer ID, order ID, and total amount of the order.

```
SELECT customerid, od.orderid, SUM(od.quantity*od.unitprice) AS price
    FROM Orders o, [Order Details] od
    WHERE Year(orderdate) = @nYear AND od.orderid=o.orderid
GROUP BY od.orderid, o.customerid ORDER BY o.customerid
```

The second query selects all distinct customers and for each of them counts the orders and computes the total:

```
SELECT c.customerid, c.CompanyName,
    Total=SUM(od.quantity*od.unitprice),
    TotalOrders=COUNT(DISTINCT od.OrderID)
FROM Customers c, [Order Details] od, Orders o
WHERE Year(orderdate)=@nYear AND
      c.CustomerID=o.CustomerID AND
      o.OrderID=od.OrderID
GROUP BY c.CompanyName, c.CustomerID ORDER BY c.customerid
```

Once the two tables are in memory, you programmatically add empty rows to the orders table and create a sorted view of the table so that the empty rows show up as the last row of each customer group. Next, you can customize a little bit of the text shown by the additional rows so that the final output looks like Figure 8-4. The full source code for the Subtotal sample is available in the book samples.

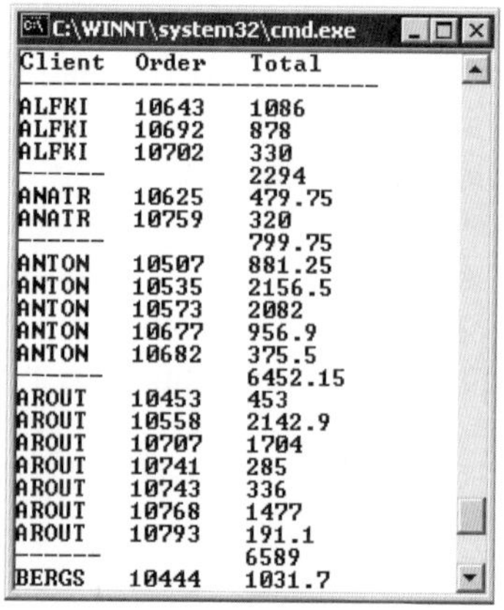

```
C:\WINNT\system32\cmd.exe
Client  Order   Total
--------------------------
ALFKI   10643   1086
ALFKI   10692   878
ALFKI   10702   330
-----           2294
ANATR   10625   479.75
ANATR   10759   320
-----           799.75
ANTON   10507   881.25
ANTON   10535   2156.5
ANTON   10573   2082
ANTON   10677   956.9
ANTON   10682   375.5
-----           6452.15
AROUT   10453   453
AROUT   10558   2142.9
AROUT   10707   1704
AROUT   10741   285
AROUT   10743   336
AROUT   10768   1477
AROUT   10793   191.1
-----           6589
BERGS   10444   1031.7
```

**Figure 8-4** A console application that adds summary rows to the tables of a *DataSet*.

## Setting Up the *DataGrid*

Let's take the result set shown in Figure 8-3 and display it through a *DataGrid* control. The output looks like Figure 8-5. The rows with a black background are the summary rows added by the ROLLUP operator. Notice, though, that the highlighted background in the figure is only a graphical effect on the picture. The *DataGrid* control has no built-in logic to detect a summary row. Adding such logic is exactly the goal of this section.

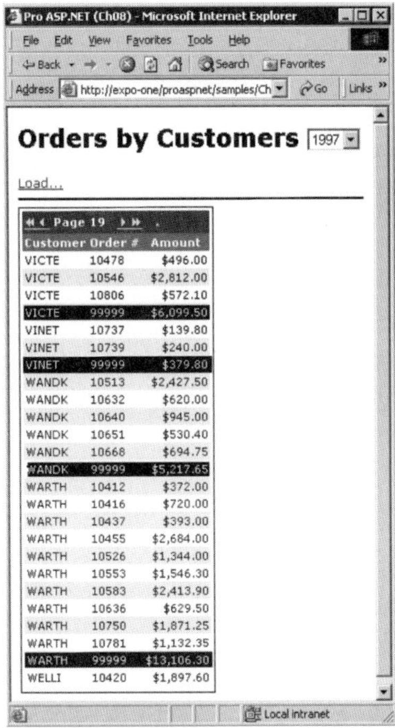


**Figure 8-5** Displaying the output of a *ROLLUP* query using a *DataGrid* control.

Having summary rows in the data source is not enough. We must be able to distinguish summary rows from ordinary bound rows and render the summary rows with different visual styles.

When the *DataGrid* is rendered in HTML, it fires a couple of events to the page—*ItemCreated* and *ItemDataBound*. As we saw in Chapter 6, by hooking those events you can analyze the data object being drawn and set its styles. In doing so, you test the value of the MyOrderID column against the well-known value of 99999 and decide whether that row is to be rendered as a summary row.

## Formatting the Summary Row

When the *ItemCreated* event fires, no data has yet been bound to the *DataGrid* item. You can apply visual styles only from within the *ItemCreated* event. However, before creating the appearance of a summary row, we first need to verify that it is a summary row. To verify that the current row is just a summary row, we need to access the underlying data object and check its MyOrderID column. *ItemCreated* is not the ideal place to check for this condition, so let's hook *ItemDataBound* instead. The following code shows the *ItemDataBound* event handler for the sample page shown in Figure 8-6.

```
void ItemDataBound(object sender, DataGridItemEventArgs e)
{
    CustomizeItem(e);
}

void CustomizeItem(DataGridItemEventArgs e)
{
    DataRowView drv = (DataRowView) e.Item.DataItem;
    if (drv != null)
    {
        // Current row is a summary row
        if ((int) drv["MyOrderID"] == 99999)
        {
            // Yellow background and bold font
            e.Item.BackColor = Color.Yellow;
            e.Item.Font.Bold = true;

            // Remove the cell with the Order ID
            e.Item.Cells.RemoveAt(1);

            // Span the Customer ID cell to cover two cells
            e.Item.Cells[0].ColumnSpan = 2;
            e.Item.Cells[1].HorizontalAlign = HorizontalAlign.Right;
        }
    }
}
```

Summary rows are given a different background color and a boldface font. In addition, we also modify the structure of the row by removing the second cell (the one containing the order ID) and enlarging the first to span over two logical cells. The last column, which contains the total amount of the order, is then right-aligned. Note that after a cell is removed, you must reassign any properties (for example, horizontal alignment) to all the cells.

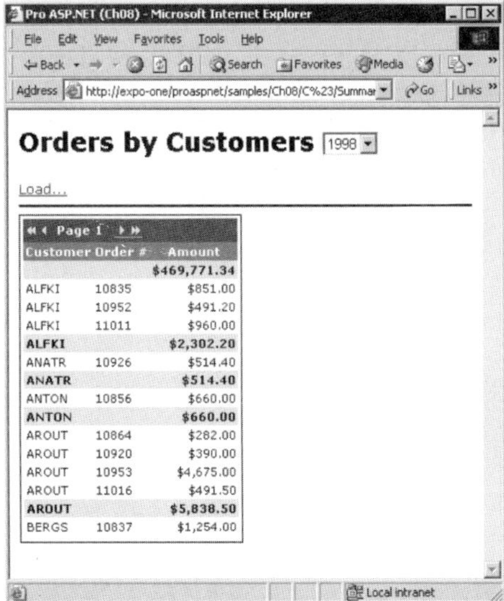


**Figure 8-6** Summary rows display with different styles and a different layout.

## Setting Up the Footer

As you can see in Figure 8-6, the first row in the result set contains the total of all orders selected by the query. If you're going to display a list of orders, keep in mind that information simply doesn't belong on the page. You can remove the first row of the *DataTable* at any time before you bind it to the *DataGrid*.

```
// Fill the DataSet
DataSet ds = new DataSet();
da.Fill(ds, "Orders");

// Remove the first row but cache the total of orders
decimal total = (decimal) ds.Tables["Orders"].Rows[0]["total"];
ds.Tables["Orders"].Rows.RemoveAt(0);
ViewState["TotalAmountOfOrders"] = total;
```

To remove a row within a table, you call the *RemoveAt* method on the *Rows* collection. The *RemoveAt* method can take either a *DataRow* object or the 0-based index of the row to remove. The row is physically detached from the table, but it's not destroyed as an object until it goes out of scope.

The Total column on the first row contains the total amount of all the orders issued by all customers in the specified year. That information might be valuable as well, but it's better to display it in the footer. To have it available for each request, we cache it in the page view state or in any other global repository:

```
void CustomizeFooter(DataGridItemEventArgs e)
{
    e.Item.Cells[2].HorizontalAlign = HorizontalAlign.Right;
    e.Item.Cells[2].Text = String.Format("{0:c}",
        ViewState["TotalAmountOfOrders"]);
}
```

Figure 8-7 shows the total of all orders displayed in the footer.

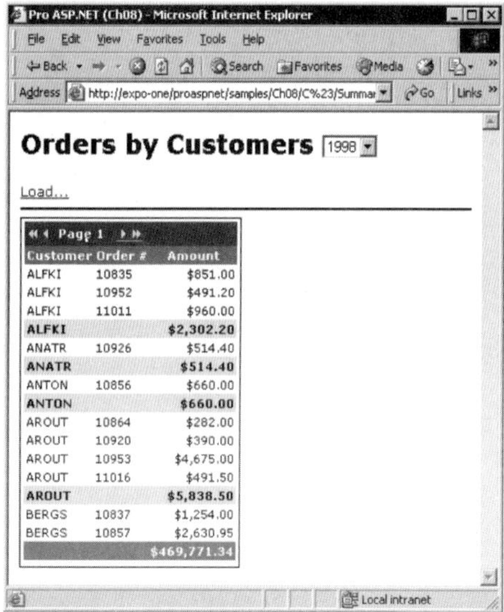


**Figure 8-7** The footer shows the total of all orders.

## Adding Statistical Information

So far we've used a summary row in which the customerid column dumbly repeated the ID of the above customer. While this is a possibility, more useful information can be provided. For example, you could count the orders that a given customer has issued in the year, and spice it up with some statistics, such as a calculation of the orders as a percentage of the total volume for the year:

```
void CustomizeItem(DataGridItemEventArgs e)
{
    DataRowView drv = (DataRowView) e.Item.DataItem;
    if (drv != null)
    {
        // current row is a summary row
        if ((int) drv["MyOrderID"] == 99999)
```

```
        {
            // Yellow background and bold font
            e.Item.BackColor = Color.Yellow;
            e.Item.Font.Bold = true;

            // Remove the cell with the Order ID
            e.Item.Cells.RemoveAt(1);

            // Set up the alignment for the last column
            e.Item.Cells[1].HorizontalAlign = HorizontalAlign.Right;

            // Count the orders for the customer
            DataTable dtOrders = drv.Row.Table;
            int orderCount = (int) dtOrders.Compute(
                "Count(customerid)",
                "customerid='"+drv["customerid"]+"'") -1;

            // Calculate the percentage of the total volume
            decimal amount = (decimal) drv["price"];
            decimal total = (decimal) ViewState["TotalAmountOfOrders"];
            decimal percent = 100 * amount / total;

            // Set up the first cell
            e.Item.Cells[0].ColumnSpan = 2;
            e.Item.Cells[0].Style["font-weight"] = "400";
            e.Item.Cells[0].Style["font-size"] = "80%";
            string msg = String.Format("{0} order(s) [{1:n}%]",
                orderCount, percent);
            e.Item.Cells[0].Text = msg
        }
    }
}
```

There are many ways to count the orders for each customer. Probably the most effective way consists of calculating them once and caching the few bytes somewhere in the view state or session state. In the following sample code, we count them each time using the *Compute* method of the *DataTable* object. (This is definitely not a smart choice for a real application, but it gives us a chance to show an interesting use of the ADO.NET model.)

```
int count = dtOrders.Compute("Count(customerid)",
    "customerid='" + drv["customerid"] + "'") -1;
```

Of course, you must subtract one from the total because it also includes the summary row.

Finally, as the code shows, you can use custom visual settings for each cell in the row. The first cell, in fact, is displayed without boldface type and with a font size 80 percent smaller than the default, as shown in Figure 8-8.

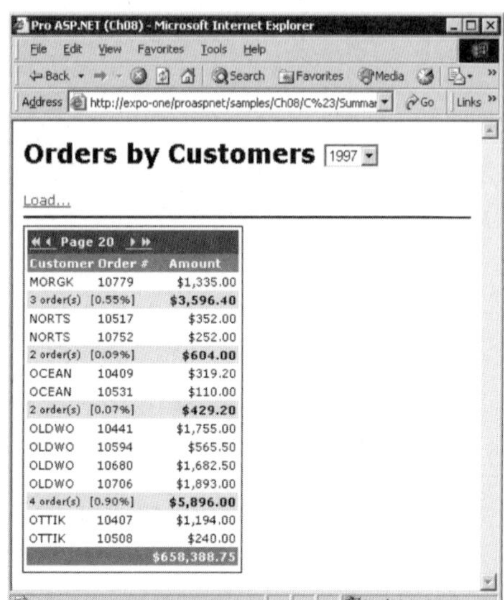


**Figure 8-8** Statistical information shown in the summary row.

The summary information can take up any number of rows in the grid. However, if multiple rows are necessary, you should insert additional rows yourself using the approach discussed earlier.

## Master/Detail Views

Applications based on interrelated tables often need to provide a hierarchical navigation mechanism to enable users to sort through various parent/child table relationships. For example, a user can pick a customer from a menu and then see all the orders the selected customer has issued. Next, the user can click on a particular order and have all its details displayed. When such parent/child relationships exist, a child table is always associated with a particular element on the parent table. What, then, would be an effective way of retrieving and displaying parent/child information in an ASP.NET application?

ADO.NET provides a rich in-memory, database-like infrastructure that makes it particularly easy to define relationships between tables and extract child rows from parent rows. The downside is that a roundtrip occurs whenever a user clicks on a row to go one level down or up. As a result, the page posts back and is completely rebuilt from scratch. The hierarchical data that is necessary to fill the page is either cached on the Web server or downloaded over and over again from the database. As discussed in Chapter 6 and Chapter 7, caching is an excellent choice if you can afford it. Otherwise, retrieving small pieces of data, and retrieving them only when you need them, is an alternative technique that consumes a minimum amount of server resources. If you're caching data across page requests, do it using the *DataSet* object and create as many relationships as needed. Doing this will allow you to retrieve the related rows quickly and effectively.

In the rest of this chapter, we'll build a master/detail application that addresses issues you'll encounter in the real world. The application contains three related grids that display customers, orders for a customer, and the details of an order. We'll use the *SelectedIndexChanged* event to command a more specific query and drill down into the data. We'll also use different techniques for paging and sorting the data. The different views of the data are implemented using inline frames.

## Listing the Customers

The sample page we'll consider is made of a master grid that pages through a set of customers. We'll use custom paging and also add sorting capabilities to the *DataGrid*. Figure 8-9 shows the grid in action with an applied filter that selects only the customers based either in Italy or Spain.

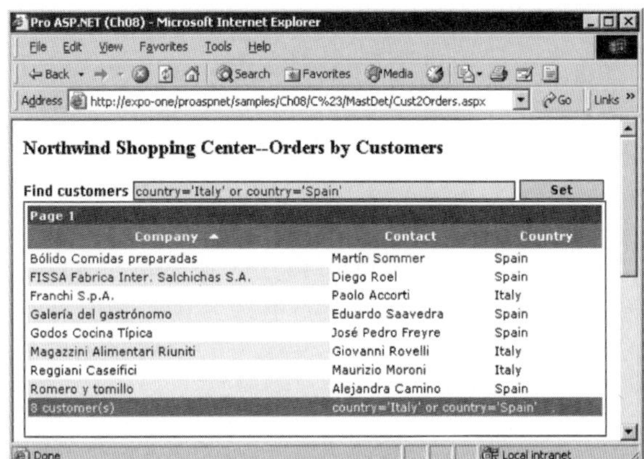


**Figure 8-9** A sortable and pageable grid that lets you select a customer. By clicking on the customer name, you can see the orders the customer has issued.

The grid retrieves only the records that fit in the current page based on the sort expression. This is a combination of styles we didn't fully cover in Chapter 6 and Chapter 7 when we explored the paging and sorting mechanism of the grid. If you plan to use custom paging and sorting together, you can't use a client-side mechanism (for example, a *DataView*) to sort records. The *DataView* in fact has limited visibility over the set of records and would actually sort only records in the current page. Sometimes this feature is acceptable, sometimes not. If you want full sorting—that is, if you want to page through customers in a given order—the query command used to retrieve a page of records must be slightly enhanced.

## Custom Paging and Sorting

To get a page of records, we use a query made of three nested SELECT statements that select the right subset and then re-order it. (See Chapter 7.) It's useful to recall the scheme we discussed earlier in this chapter in the "Paging Through the Results of Any Query" sidebar. The placeholders in boldface are elements you must configure properly.

```
SELECT * FROM
    (SELECT TOP size * FROM
        (SELECT TOP size*index *
            FROM (query ORDER BY KeyCol ASC) AS t0) AS t1
    ORDER BY KeyCol DESC) AS t2
ORDER BY KeyCol ASC
```

The *query* element is any SELECT statement that defines the set of records to be displayed. It can be as complex as needed and can include any clauses that make sense with a SELECT statement. In its simplest form, the *query* placeholder is the name of the table. As you can see, the *KeyCol* placeholder indicates the column (or the columns) to sort by. Each occurrence of the *KeyCol* placeholder is associated with a sort direction. If you request a default ascending order, only the second occurrence must be set to DESC. We fully explained the reason for this in Chapter 6. Of course, if you want to invert the direction, all direction placeholders must be reversed too. Note that if multiple columns are used, you must reverse the direction of each of them.

In this way, what you get from SQL Server is a properly sorted result set that can be bound to the grid without further manipulations. The following listing shows the new version of the *BindData* method:

```
void BindData() {
    string sortby = (string) ViewState["DataSortExpression"];
    DataTable _data = CreateDataSource(1 + grid.CurrentPageIndex, sortby);
    grid.DataSource = _data;
    grid.DataBind();
}
```

As we mentioned in Chapter 6, sorting is a subtle and complex operation that can add unnoticed overhead to your Web application. Going down to the database only for sorting is probably a bad hit to overhead, but if we're already using the database to page through a data set, asking it to return sorted data is a minor addition and probably the most effective approach.

> **Note** The Oracle ROWNUM operator numbers the rows in the result set before the sort is applied. So if you want rows sorted in some way, you must nest queries so that the innermost retrieves and sorts data and the outermost just ensures rows are correctly numbered. While I'm speaking of Oracle ROWNUM, I should mention that the next version of SQL Server is expected to support a similar feature but, at the time of this writing, the form, implementation, and syntax have not been decided upon.

### The Selection Mechanism

When the user selects a row in the master grid, the *SelectedIndexChanged* event fires and updates the *SelectedIndex* property with the 0-based index of the row. As mentioned in Chapter 6, when the user clicks on a *DataGrid* column with a command name of *select*, two events are raised: *ItemCommand* and then *SelectedIndexChanged*. This sequence of events simplifies the implementation of the item deselection. While processing *ItemCommand*, the *SelectedIndex* property has not yet been updated. So you store the selected index in a global variable and compare it with the new selected index. If the two match, the user clicked two consecutive times on the same item. At this point, you deselect the item.

```
void ItemCommand(object sender, DataGridCommandEventArgs e) {
    switch(e.CommandName) {
        case "select":
            m_currentSelectedIndex = grid.SelectedIndex;
            break;
    }
}
void SelectedIndexChanged(object sender, EventArgs e) {
    if (m_currentSelectedIndex == grid.SelectedIndex) {
        UnselectItem();
        return;
    }
    SelectItem();
}
void SelectItem() {
    string custID = (string) grid.DataKeys[grid.SelectedIndex];
    string url = String.Format("orderslist.aspx?custid={0}", custID);
    ordersView.Attributes["Src"] = url;
}
```

When a customer is selected, the page refreshes the orders frame that points to a second page named orderslist.aspx. The page receives the ID of the customer as a query parameter, performs a query against the orders, and finally lists all the orders associated with that customer.

Note that if you can afford caching all the data, including customers and orders, you can easily retrieve the orders for a customer using a relation between the tables.

### Using Inline Frames

Inline frames are browser windows that can be placed anywhere in the HTML code by using the *<iframe>* tag. The *<iframe>* tag is part of the HTML 4.0 standard. Note, though, that not all browsers support this element, which has been part of the Internet Explorer arsenal since version 4.0. Old Netscape Navigator 4.x browsers support a similar element, named *<layer>*, with a nearly identical overall goal and syntax.

There are no ASP.NET server controls to map the functionality of the *<iframe>* tag. If you mark it with the *runat* attribute, the ASP.NET runtime will render it using an instance of the *HtmlGenericControl* class. The following code declares a frame with a solid, single-line, flat border and no scrolling capabilities:

```
<iframe runat="server" id="ordersView"
    frameborder="no"
    scrolling="no"
    style="border:solid 1px;"
    width="100%"
    height="270px" />
```

To set the URL that the frame will display, you use the *Src* attribute. Note, though, that you can't set the *Src* attribute through a property because the *HtmlGenericControl* class doesn't provide for that. You must set it as an explicit HTML attribute using the *Attributes* collection.

```
ordersView.Attributes["Src"] = url;
```

To unselect a customer and clear the page with its orders displayed, you simply make the frame point to the *about:blank* URL. The *about* protocol is supported by most browsers, including old versions of Netscape browsers.

## Listing the Orders

The orderslist.aspx page has a structure that is nearly identical to its parent page (cust2orders.aspx). It gets the customer ID from the query string and uses that to perform an ad hoc query against the database. The orders are then displayed through a pageable *DataGrid* control. One of the columns of the grid is a *But-*

*tonColumn* with a command name of *select*, which makes the items displayed truly selectable.

Normally the text of a *ButtonColumn* is a hyperlink element rendered with the default styles—that is, underlining and visited-link or active-link colors. To make it look like normal yet selectable text, you can resort to the following style declaration:

```
<style>
    a:hover {color:red;text-decoration:underline;}
    a       {text-decoration:none;}
</style>
```

The text will be underlined in red only when the mouse hovers over the text, as shown in Figure 8-10.

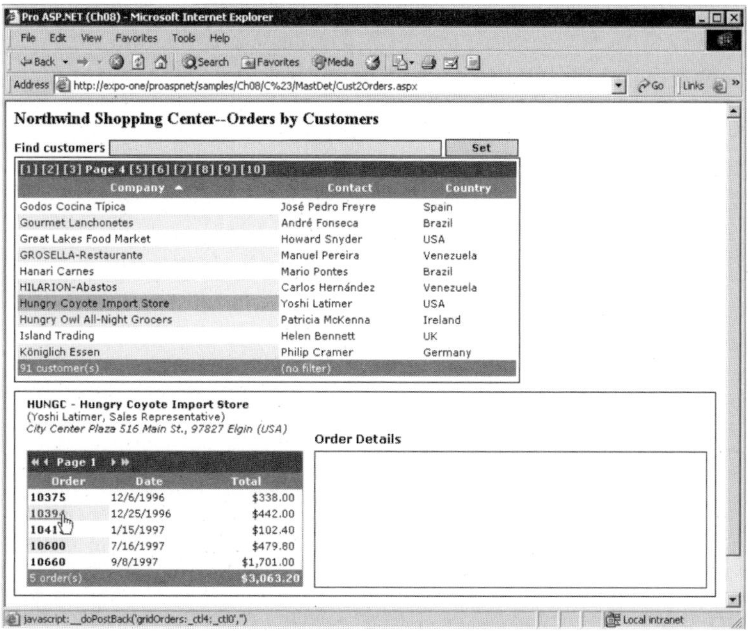


**Figure 8-10** A pageable grid that shows the orders for a customer. By clicking on the order ID, you can see the details of that order.

## Smart Caching

The orders *DataGrid* is pageable but does not use custom paging. It also does not cache all orders. It caches only the orders the grid needs to display—that is, the orders that relate to a given customer. The pagination takes place automatically within the *DataGrid* and is completely handled by the control.

Because the role of the grid is to display an unfiltered list of orders for a customer, chances are that concurrent users working in different sessions might be accessing the same set of records. For this reason, the population of the orders *DataGrid* occurs in two steps. First the code attempts to locate a slot in the ASP.NET global *Cache* object that contains the orders for the customers. If found, no database access is performed and the records are retrieved from memory. Otherwise, a query is run and the results are copied in to the *Cache* for further access by the same, or other, users.

```
void Page_Init(object sender, EventArgs e)
{
    // Store the current customer ID
    string tmp = (string) Request.QueryString["CustID"];
    m_currentCustomerID = tmp.Substring(0, 5);

    // Store the name of the DataSet as used within Cache
    m_dataSetName = String.Format(m_dataSetName, m_currentCustomerID);
}
```

The *Init* event fires at the beginning of the page request lifecycle. All the global data you set here is visible to all the other methods that are called as the request processing proceeds. In particular, we need to retrieve data from *Cache* to set up the footer. The footer is configured during the *DataGrid*'s *ItemCreated* event, which occurs before the page's *Load* event. For this reason, we need to store the name of the cache slot and the customer ID into global variables at the very beginning of the request processing.

> **Note** Each processing of a request results in a sequence of methods—event handlers, actually—being called one after the next. Any global variables you set at any point in this cycle work as expected. You can't, on the other hand, set global variables and expect that they will survive the request. If you need this to happen, use the *ViewState* object or any other global data container such as *Session* or *Cache*.

The naming convention used to recognize the slot within *Cache* that contains the orders of a particular customer is illustrated in the following line:

```
private string m_dataSetName = "Orders [{0}]";
```

The code in *Page_Init* replaces the placeholder with the actual customer ID read out of the query string. Also note that only the first five characters are taken into account—the known maximum length of a customer ID. As we'll see in Chapter 15, "ASP.NET Security," this simple trick can save you from a lot of trouble with malicious code and SQL injection attacks. The following code is used to populate the orders grid:

```
void DataFromSourceToMemory() {
    // Attempt to locate the orders from the cache in case other users
    // already retrieved them. Otherwise, read from the database
    DataSet ds;
    ds = (DataSet) Cache[m_dataSetName];
    if (ds == null)
        ds = PhysicalDataRead();

    // Stores orders in the cache
    Cache[m_dataSetName] = ds;
}
```

The *DataSet* we're caching for each accessed customer is made of two tables—the orders table and further customer information table. The second table holds only one record with registration data about the customer. Note that the *DataSet* is obtained using a SQL batch—that is, a couple of concatenated SQL statements. Both statements require the use of a parameter—the customer ID. Because the parameter is the same in both cases—and thanks to the SQL Server .NET provider's named parameters—you specify it only once. This wouldn't have been possible with position-based parameters.

## Adding Templated Columns

In the Northwind database, orders are registered with a required date and a ship date. Users, though, might appreciate a simple flag positioned beside an order to denote whether the order shipped on time or not. Later, if needed, they could drill down and find date-related details. If you don't plan to show more than a Boolean flag to signify the delay of an order, you can modify the query to make SQL Server return a computed Boolean column. Otherwise, you query for both the *shippeddate* and *requireddate* columns and create an in-memory computed column to store the Boolean flag.

```
// Get the data
DataSet _data = new DataSet();
adapter.Fill(_data);
_data.Tables["Table"].TableName = "Orders";

// Add a custom column comparing ShippedDate and RequiredDate
_data.Tables["Orders"].Columns.Add("Delayed", typeof(bool),
    "shippeddate > requireddate");
```

How can you display this information? Although effective, a True or False string might not be a particularly friendly solution. In addition, rows with the most common value (say False, meaning that the order shipped on time) shouldn't be displayed. A better solution would be to display a new column that indicates when an order was delayed. What about templated columns? The following code shows the declaration of a templated column in which the contents of each cell is an elaboration of the newly added *Delayed* column:

```
<asp:TemplateColumn runat="server" HeaderText="Delay"
    ItemStyle-HorizontalAlign="center"
    ItemStyle-Font-Name="wingdings 2">
    <ItemTemplate>
        <%# ((bool)DataBinder.Eval(Container.DataItem,
            "Delayed") ?"P" :"") %>
    </ItemTemplate>
</asp:TemplateColumn>
```

In particular, the template displays a Wingdings symbol (the checkmark) or the empty string based on the Boolean value in the source column. Of course, for this to happen you must have the Wingdings 2 font installed.

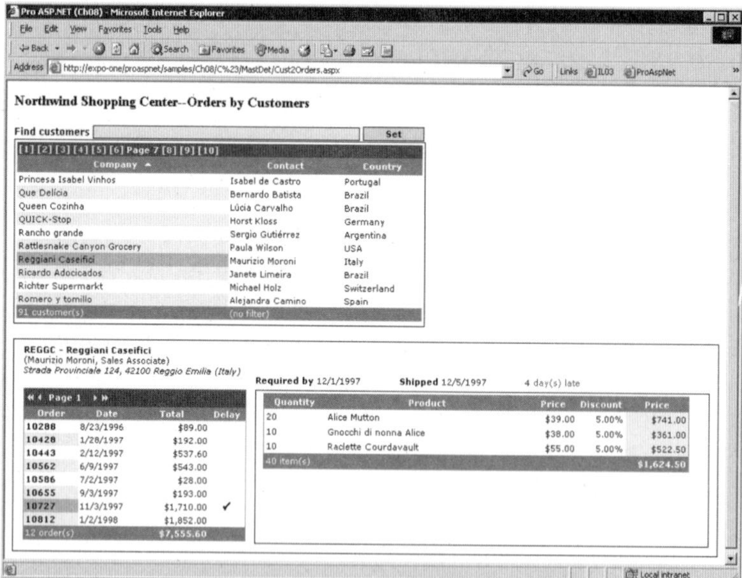

**Figure 8-11** The last column shows a check symbol to indicate the corresponding order shipped after being delayed.

## Listing the Order Details

The orderslist.aspx page contains a child frame that points to the orderdetails.aspx page. This page is aimed at showing the details of a particular order. The page receives the order ID through the query string, downloads the few records that describe the items in the order, and populates a nonpageable *DataGrid* control.

The orderdetails.aspx page is fired when the user clicks to select an order. When this happens, a label is also updated with further information about the ship date and the required date of shipment for the order. The difference between the two dates is expressed in terms of days.

The various totals you see on the footer of the grids are calculated using the *Compute* method on the *DataTable* object.

# Conclusion

The complexity of the code we examined in this chapter is really close to the physical threshold beyond which one normally starts looking at ways to implement reusability and encapsulation. The master/detail views and subtotaling applications we've built so far make intensive use of certain features of the *DataGrid* control that I simply cut and pasted from one source file to the next. There has to be a better way of reusing code in ASP.NET! Actually, a (much) better way does exist, and we'll start looking at it in Chapter 10 and get into more detail in Chapter 18 and Chapter 19.

Real-world programming is a powerful mix of best practices, design patterns, and those finer touches that always marks the difference between good and not-quite-as-good applications. However, a deep knowledge and understanding of the platform is a must. Speaking of ASP.NET in particular, the required knowledge spans the world of .NET and touches on the land of SQL.

Many real-world applications are based on a web of interrelated and interconnected databases. Designing effective queries and update strategies is critical. Keeping an eye on the overall scalability is a must. Providing awesome, user-friendly features is just what you live (and work) for. Right? SQL is the glue that holds databases and data-driven applications together, but SQL—in the real world—is not a complete standard. Yes, there was once the SQL 92 platform, but since then each vendor has added feature upon feature to provide better functionality. So you should know the SQL engine you're using to write effective code. And in ASP.NET, you also must know the client-side engine that interacts with the back end. This engine is ADO.NET.

ADO.NET doesn't add magic to your arsenal of tricks and techniques. It doesn't reduce database programming to mere declarative programming, in which you build working code by simply pointing and clicking. Several times in this chapter (and even more often in ADO.NET books such as David Sceppa's *Microsoft ADO.NET* [Microsoft Press, 2002]), you find described tools and classes that kindly and generously do most of the work for you. In the same sources, you normally find notes that warn you against using those tools and classes in real-world applications. The command-builder object or even the batch update, for example, greatly simplify the update process, but you must know what they do and how they do it. Chances are that to fix your application you just need to work around their standard behavior. ADO.NET can do a lot of things for you, but it can do even more if you know how to instruct it.

This chapter discussed a few general points typical of all Web applications of some complexity. In the next chapter, we'll move away from the rather ubiquitous *DataGrid* control to consider more flexible alternatives, such as the *Repeater* and *DataList* controls. The next chapter opens Part III of the book, which is entirely devoted to system-provided ASP.NET rich controls.

## Resources


- *Microsoft ADO.NET Core Reference*, by David Sceppa (Microsoft Press, 2002)
- *Programming Visual Basic .NET*, by Francesco Balena (Microsoft Press, 2002)—see the ADO.NET section
- Tackle Data Concurrency Exceptions Using the DataSet Object (*http://msdn.microsoft.com/msdnmag/issues/03/04/DataConcurrency/default.aspx*)
- Implement a Data Access Layer for Your App with ADO.NET (*http://msdn.microsoft.com/msdnmag/issues/03/04/DataAccessLayer/default.aspx*)

# Part III

# ASP.NET Controls

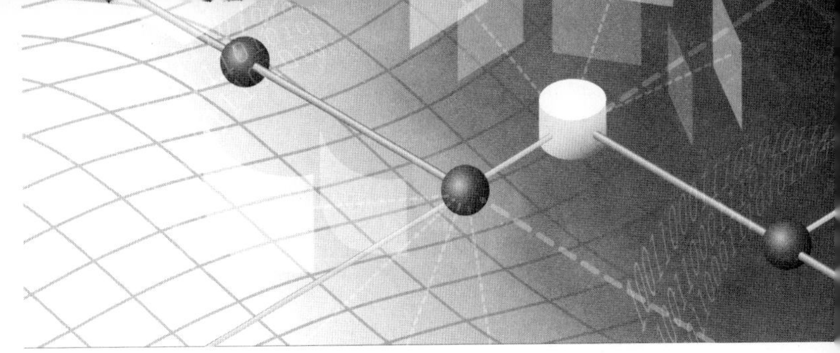

# 9

# ASP.NET Iterative Controls

*Be sincere; be brief; be seated.*

—*Franklin D. Roosevelt*

Iterative controls are a special type of data-bound controls that combine two key capabilities. They support ADO.NET-compliant data sources and supply a template-based mechanism to create free-form user interfaces.

In Part II of the book, while covering database programming and techniques, we covered the *DataGrid* control in great detail. Technically speaking, the *DataGrid* control is certainly an iterative control in the sense that it iterates over a bound data source to generate its user interface, one row after the next. Although the *DataGrid* is highly customizable, it can't go beyond the boundaries of a column-based representation of the data. For example, the *DataGrid* supports templates, but only within the cells of a column. Other tasks are only for the bravest—for example, redesigning the layout of an individual row, or altering the default template of the control's output to employ multiple rows per record or multiple columns per data source. In some cases, by resorting to dirty and smart tricks you can customize the *DataGrid*, such as displaying subtotals as we did in Chapter 8, "Real-World Data Access." Generally, though, the *DataGrid* is not the ideal tool to use when you need a more free-form display of data. For this purpose, the *Repeater* and *DataList* controls, each with its own set of pros and cons, seem to be more appropriate.

# What's an Iterative Control, Anyway?

Before looking under the hood of the *Repeater* and *DataList* controls, let's discuss in general terms the expected features of iterative and templated controls. A control is said to be *iterative* if it provides the ability to loop over a set of data items in order to apply some layout elements to each of them. In addition, an iterative control works by applying an ASP.NET template to each data item. It exposes the individual data item as a customizable and configurable stand-alone object that holds its own set of properties, methods, and events.

According to this definition, what is the role of all controls that show a list of data rows? Are the *DropDownList* and *CheckBoxList* controls, just to name a few, iterative controls? Is the *DataGrid* iterative as well?

## Iterative Controls vs. List Controls

The big difference between, say, a *DropDownList* control and what we recognize here as iterative controls—that is, the *Repeater* and *DataList*—is all in how each control shows its contents. The *DropDownList* control uses a drop-down list and doesn't provide relevant facilities for you to change the user interface of each displayed item.

Similarly, the *CheckBoxList* control displays a list of selectable options whose value and displayed text can be bound to a data source. With this list control, you can apply some relatively simple HTML formatting to each item. However, you can't do that with a stand-alone object that represents the list item. More specifically, you have no object that is equivalent to the *DataGridItem* class of the *DataGrid* control. If you want to render, say, some items of the check-box list in boldface type, you can only modify the text of the single item being displayed and wrap it in a *<b>* element. Although this is (much) better than nothing, it's still too little for complex applications that need more advanced display features.

In summary, iterative controls differ from list controls because of their greater rendering flexibility. An iterative control lets you apply an ASP.NET template to each row in the bound data source. A list control, on the other hand, provides a fixed and built-in template for each data item. List controls are customizable to some extent, but you can't change anything other than the text displayed. No changes to layout are supported.

On the other hand, using a list control is considerably easier than setting up an iterative control, as we'll see in a moment. Defining templates requires quite a bit of declarative code, and if accomplished programmatically, it requires that you write a class that implements the *ITemplate* interface. A list control needs only data binding.

## Iterative Controls vs. the *DataGrid* Control

The *DataGrid* is an iterative control because it displays the contents of a data source by using customizable templates in which the programmer can easily access and configure each constituent element—from the data rows to the header and from the footer to the pager. However, the *DataGrid* can also be considered a list control because the customization facilities it provides don't allow you to break the rigid scheme of a tabular, multicolumn representation of data.

The *DataGrid* has more advanced features than the *Repeater* and *DataList*—particularly, paging. On the other hand, it doesn't offer the same level of flexibility as iterative controls. In a certain sense, it's a sort of highly specialized, off-the-shelf version of an iterative control.

Using a *Repeater* control, and even more easily using a *DataList*, you can build a grid of data. Note also that you can't always use a *DataGrid* control to reproduce the same output you can with either a *Repeater* or *DataList*. Table 9-1 summarizes the differences among the *DataGrid*, iterative controls, and list controls.

**Table 9-1 Outlining Iterative and List Controls**

| | **Rendering** | **Usage** |
|---|---|---|
| *DataGrid* Control | Loop over data, and create a tabular representation of data allowing for column-specific templates. | Use when you have tabular data to display. If the data is not naturally tabular but can be rendered as such, consider iterative controls too. |
| Iterative Controls | Loop over data-bound items, and apply a user-defined template. | Use when you have data to render as a monolithic structure in a free-form way. |
| List Controls | Loop over data-bound items, and apply an immutable, control-specific template. | Use when you don't need item-specific customization and you like the standard user interface. |

## The *Repeater* Control

The *Repeater* is a data-bound control that displays data using a custom layout. It works by repeating a specified ASP.NET template for each item displayed in the list. The *Repeater* is a rather basic templated data-bound control. It has no built-in layout or styling capabilities. All formatting and layout information must be explicitly declared and coded using HTML tags and ASP.NET classes.

## Programming Interface of the *Repeater* Control

The *Repeater* class inherits from *Control* and acts as a naming container by implementing the marker interface *INamingContainer*. Table 9-2 lists the properties exposed by the control, not counting those inherited from the base class *Control*.

**Table 9-2 Properties of the *Repeater* Control**

| Property | Description |
|---|---|
| *AlternatingItemTemplate* | Gets or sets the template that defines how every other item is to be rendered. |
| *DataMember* | Gets or sets the specific table in the *DataSource* that is to be bound to the control. |
| *DataSource* | Gets or sets the data source that provides any data for populating the list. |
| *FooterTemplate* | Gets or sets the template that defines how the footer is rendered. |
| *HeaderTemplate* | Gets or sets the template that defines how the header is rendered. |
| *Items* | Gets a *RepeaterItemCollection* object—that is, a collection of *RepeaterItem* objects. Each element of the collection represents a displayed data row in the *Repeater*. |
| *ItemTemplate* | Gets or sets the template that defines how items are rendered. |
| *SeparatorTemplate* | Gets or sets the template that defines how separators between items are rendered. |

For the most part, properties are the template elements that form the control's user interface. Aside from that, the *Items* property contains the list of child items that are associated with each displayed data row. The *RepeaterItem* object is the *Repeater*'s counterpart of the *DataGridItem* object we discussed in earlier chapters. The *Repeater* populates the *Items* collection by enumerating all the data objects in its bound data source. In no way does the control filter the contents of the *Items* collection. All the rows contained in the data source are mapped onto a *RepeaterItem* object and inserted in the collection. The *RepeaterItemCollection* class is a plain collection class with no special or peculiar behavior.

Just as in the *DataGridItem* class, the *RepeaterItem* class is used to represent any type of constituent item and is not limited to data items. You distinguish between types using the familiar *ListItemType* enumeration. A few properties characterize the programming interface of the *RepeaterItem* class. The *RepeaterItem* class is self-explanatory once you know about the *DataGridItem* class and have a look at its properties—*ItemIndex*, *ItemType*, and *DataItem*.

## Binding a *Repeater* to Data

Just like any other data-bound ASP.NET control, the *Repeater* generates its user interface only when a call to its *DataBind* method is made. *DataBind* is the only method in the control's interface aside from those directly inherited from parent classes. A call to *DataBind* causes the control to rebuild its control hierarchy and related view state. Before the whole process starts, the *DataBinding* event fires.

The call to *DataBind* is necessary to have the HTML code for the control be generated and added to the output stream. In addition to the events defined on the *Control* class, the *Repeater* exposes three additional events—*ItemCreated*, *ItemCommand*, and *ItemDataBound*. (See Table 9-3.) Their overall behavior is nearly identical to that of the analogous events in the *DataGrid*.

**Table 9-3 Events of the *Repeater* Control**

| Event | Description |
|---|---|
| *ItemCommand* | Fires when a button is clicked within the *Repeater* control. |
| *ItemCreated* | Fires when a repeater item is being created. |
| *ItemDataBound* | Fires after an item in the *Repeater* has been bound to underlying data. The event occurs before the data item is added to the *Items* collection. (Note that only items and alternating items are bindable.) |

The *DataBinding* event fires before all the events listed in Table 9-3. The sequence of data-binding events is triggered by the call to *DataBind*. As the very first step, the *Repeater* fires the *DataBinding* event and then begins building the control's hierarchy. Events in Table 9-3 occur only at this time, in the order we're going to discuss in the next section.

## How the *Repeater* Builds the Output

An internal, protected method of the *Control* class named *CreateControlHierarchy* is responsible for the generation of the HTML code sent to the browser. This method connects to the data source and then runs a loop over the items in the bound collection. (See the "Resolving the Data Source" sidebar later in the chapter for more information on how the *Repeater* resolves the reference to the run-time data-bound object.)

The following pseudocode illustrates the process that leads to the creation of the *Repeater* output.

```
if (headerTemplate != null)
    CreateItem(ListItemType.Header);

int _counter = 0;
RepeaterItem _repItem;
```

```
foreach(object _dataItem in DataSource) {
    if (useSeparator && _counter > 0)
        CreateItem(ListItemType.Separator);
    if (_counter % 2)
        _repItem = CreateItem(_counter, ListItemType.Item, _dataItem);
    else
        _repItem = CreateItem(_counter, ListItemType.AlternatingItem,
            _dataItem);
    Items.Add(_repItem);

    _counter ++;
}

if (footerTemplate != null)
    CreateItem(ListItemType.Footer);
```

The *Repeater* first applies the header's template, if any. Next, it walks its way through the collection of bound objects and applies the *ItemTemplate* or the *AlternatingItemTemplate* as appropriate. Each item template might be interspersed with a separator template, if any has been provided. Finally, at the end of the loop, the footer's template is applied only once.

Within the *CreateItem* placeholder, a new *RepeaterItem* object is created and initialized to default values. Next, the *ItemCreated* event fires and then the object is added to the *Items* collection. As explained for *DataGrid* controls in Chapter 6, "Creating Bindable Grids of Data," the *ItemCreated* event occurs twice, the first time of which is before the whole data binding process begins. This just means that the *CreateItem* placeholder is invoked twice. The second time, the *DataBind* method is invoked on the newly created *RepeaterItem* object and then *ItemDataBound* fires. The following listing shows the pseudocode for the *CreateItem* placeholder.

```
RepeaterItem CreateItem(int index, ListItemType itemType,
    bool dataBind, object dataItem)
{
    RepeaterItem _repItem;
    RepeaterItemEventArgs e;

    _repItem = new RepeaterItem(itemIndex, itemType);
    e = new RepeaterItemEventArgs(_repItem);
    ApplyItemTemplate(_repItem);
    if (dataBind)
        _repItem.DataItem = dataItem;
    OnItemCreated(e);
    Controls.Add(_repItem);
    if (dataBind)
    {
```

```
            _repItem.DataBind();
            OnItemDataBound(e);
        }

        return _repItem;
    }
```

The *ApplyItemTemplate* placeholder renders a piece of code that instantiates all the controls and the literals contained in a bound template. This point leads us straight to the question: what's a template, anyway?

## Templates of the *Repeater* Control

We've already met ASP.NET templates in Chapter 6 while examining the templated columns of *DataGrid* controls. Speaking abstractly, a template is a block of server controls, literals, and HTML text that is used as a monolithic output element. To some extent, you can think of a template as a dynamically defined ASP.NET control with a composite interface that can be defined either declaratively using client and server tags or programmatically via ad hoc classes.

At a minimum, the *Repeater* must provide the *ItemTemplate* template. Unspecified templates are simply ignored; however, if you also omit the *ItemTemplate* template, the *Repeater* will have blank output.

In most cases, you define a template using declarative code. For example, the following code shows how to generate output that looks like that of a *DataGrid*:

```
<asp:Repeater runat="server" id="Repeater1">
<HeaderTemplate>
    <table>
        <thead>
            <td> <b>ID</b> </td>
            <td> <b>First Name</b> </td>
            <td> <b>Last Name</b> </td>
        </thead>
</HeaderTemplate>

<ItemTemplate>
    <tr>
        <td bgcolor="white">
            <%# ((DataRowView)Container.DataItem)["EmployeeID"] %></td>
        <td bgcolor="white">
            <%# ((DataRowView)Container.DataItem)["FirstName"] %></td>
        <td bgcolor="white">
            <%# ((DataRowView)Container.DataItem)["LastName"] %></td>
    </tr>
</ItemTemplate>

<AlternatingItemTemplate>
    <tr>
```

```
        <td bgcolor="#eeeeee">
            <%# ((DataRowView)Container.DataItem)["EmployeeID"] %></td>
        <td bgcolor="#eeeeee">
            <%# ((DataRowView)Container.DataItem)["FirstName"] %></td>
        <td bgcolor="#eeeeee">
            <%# ((DataRowView)Container.DataItem)["LastName"] %></td>
    </tr>
</AlternatingItemTemplate>

<FooterTemplate>
    <tfoot style="color:white">
        <td bgcolor="gray" colspan="3">
            <%# "<b>" + ((DataView)Repeater1.DataSource).Count +
                "</b> employees found."%></td>
    </tfoot>
    </table>
</FooterTemplate>
</asp:Repeater>
```

Figure 9-1 shows what this *Repeater* control looks like.

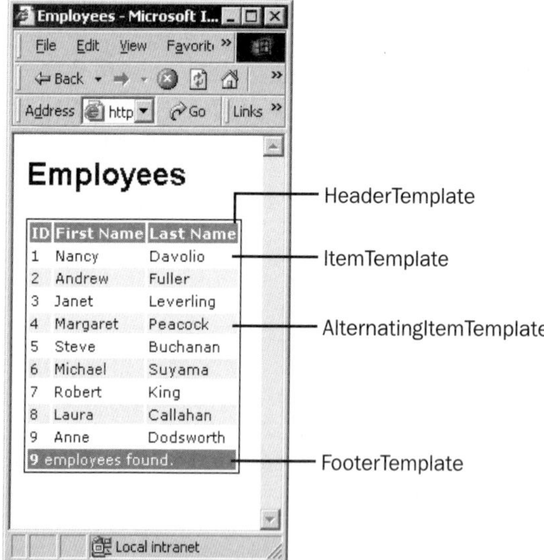


**Figure 9-1** The *Repeater* control can do whatever a *DataGrid* can do, even though it might require a lot of coding. The opposite is not true.

In this case, the data source of the *Repeater* control is a *DataView* object.

```
DataSet _data = new DataSet();
string _conn = "SERVER=localhost;DATABASE=Northwind;UID=sa;";
string _query = "SELECT employeeid, firstname, lastname FROM employees";
SqlDataAdapter _adapter = new SqlDataAdapter( _query, _conn);
_adapter.Fill(_data);
```

```
Repeater1.DataSource = _data.Tables[0].DefaultView;
Repeater1.DataBind();
```

As you can see, a lot of casting is needed to keep the compiler quiet and avoid errors. Many of those explicit casts can be avoided if you resort to the *DataBinder* object and its late-binding *Eval* method.

The final output of the *Repeater* is simply the summation of the HTML generated by each involved template. As illustrated in the aforementioned example, the *Repeater* control allows you to split HTML tags across the various templates.

## The *ITemplate* Interface

The *Repeater* class references a template through the *ITemplate* interface, meaning that a template is always treated as an instance of any class that implements the *ITemplate* interface. In spite of this, you are allowed to specify a template by using server-side tags and HTML tags. What's up?

When the page is compiled, all the fragments defined within a template block are compiled into an internal object that implements the *ITemplate* interface. Set the *debug* attribute of the *@Page* directive to *true*, and look into the actual code being generated for the page shown in Figure 9-1. (See Chapter 2, "Web Forms Internals," for instructions on how to do this and retrieve the correct source file.) The *Repeater* is built using the following code. Note that the code shown here is the same code generated by the ASP.NET compiler—it's just made more readable.

```
// Instantiate the Repeater object
Repeater __ctrl = new Repeater();
Repeater1 = __ctrl;
__ctrl.ID = "Repeater1";

// Build the template for the header
BuildTemplateMethod _builder;
_builder = new BuildTemplateMethod(__BuildControl__control3);
CompiledTemplateBuilder _template = new CompiledTemplateBuilder(_builder);
__ctrl.HeaderTemplate = _template;

// Build other templates
⋮
```

The *CompiledTemplateBuilder* class is listed in the ASP.NET documentation, but it's not documented. The same holds true for the *BuildTemplateMethod* delegate.

```
public delegate void BuildTemplateMethod(Control control);
```

The constructor of the *CompiledTemplateBuilder* class takes an instance of the delegate and calls it back to build a template class based on the source of the specified control. What's the *_control3* in the source code? It's simply the literal control that contains all the source code of the *<HeaderTemplate>* tag.

```
void __BuildControl__control3(Control __ctrl)
{
    IParserAccessor __parser = (IParserAccessor) __ctrl;
    LiteralControl _header = new LiteralControl("text of <headertemplate>");
    __parser.AddParsedSubObject(_header);
}
```

When a template is instantiated, all the child controls are instantiated and then rendered to HTML. This is what happens in the preceding procedure using the methods on the *IParserAccessor* interface. If you want to create templates programmatically, there are simpler ways, and we'll look at a couple of them in a moment. In the meantime, let's review the definition of the *ITemplate* interface.

The *ITemplate* interface consists of a single method, named *InstantiateIn*.

```
void InstantiateIn(Control container);
```

The expected behavior of *InstantiateIn* is intuitive: it programmatically creates all the child controls to be used in the template. All the controls are added to the container's *Controls* collection. If needed, the newly created controls can be bound to the data source by adding a handler for the *DataBinding* event.

## Creating Templates Programmatically

There are basically two ways to set template properties programmatically. The simplest way is by using the *LoadTemplate* method of the *Page* class. *LoadTemplate* takes only one argument, that being the name of the .ascx file that describes the template. The file name must have an *.ascx* extension. .ascx is the typical extension of Web user control files. (We'll cover Web user controls in the Chapter 10, "Web Forms User Controls.") You create a file-based template using the following code:

```
Repeater1.ItemTemplate = Page.LoadTemplate("item_template.ascx");
```

The template file can be written in any .NET language and doesn't necessarily have to be written in the language of the page. The *LoadTemplate* method can be used to load the layout code for any template property, including *HeaderTemplate* and *FooterTemplate*. The following code shows how to write an .ascx control to emulate the behavior of the page shown in Figure 9-1:

```
<%@ Control Language="C#" %>
<tr>
    <td bgcolor="white">
    <%# DataBinder.Eval(((RepeaterItem)Container).DataItem,
"EmployeeID")%>
    </td>
    <td bgcolor="white">
    <%# DataBinder.Eval(((RepeaterItem)Container).DataItem, "FirstName")
 %>
```

```
    </td>
    <td bgcolor="white">
    <%# DataBinder.Eval(((RepeaterItem)Container).DataItem, "LastName") %>
    </td>
</tr>
```

The use of *DataBinder* in this case contributes significantly to clarifying the code. Without it, you would have to cast *Container* to *RepeaterItem* (unnecessary within the page) and then *DataItem* to *DataRowView*.

The second way to set template properties programmatically is by using a class that implements the *ITemplate* interface. Using a class that implements *ITemplate* achieves the same effect as using *LoadTemplate* and an .ascx file. Here is an example the class:

```
public class MyItemTemplate : ITemplate
{
    public void InstantiateIn(Control container)
    {
        // Create the <tr> element
        TableRow _row = new TableRow();

        // Add the employeeID <td>
        TableCell _empID = new TableCell();
        _empID.DataBinding += new EventHandler(BindEmpID);
        _row.Cells.Add(_empID);

        // Add the lastname <td>
        TableCell _lname = new TableCell();
        _lname.DataBinding += new EventHandler(BindLName);
        _row.Cells.Add(_lname);

        // Add the firstname <td>
        TableCell _fname = new TableCell();
        _fname.DataBinding += new EventHandler(BindFName);
        _row.Cells.Add(_fname);

        // Add the row to the container
        container.Controls.Add(_row);
    }

    public void BindEmpID(object sender, EventArgs e)
    {
        TableCell cell = (TableCell) sender;
        RepeaterItem container = (RepeaterItem) cell.NamingContainer;
        DataRowView _row = (DataRowView) container.DataItem;

        cell.Text = _row["EmployeeID"].ToString();
    }
```

```
    public void BindLName(object sender, EventArgs e)
    {
        TableCell cell = (TableCell) sender;
        RepeaterItem container = (RepeaterItem) cell.NamingContainer;
        DataRowView _row = (DataRowView) container.DataItem;

        cell.Text = _row["LastName"].ToString();
    }

    public void BindFName(object sender, EventArgs e)
    {
        TableCell cell = (TableCell) sender;
        RepeaterItem container = (RepeaterItem) cell.NamingContainer;
        DataRowView _row = (DataRowView) container.DataItem;

        cell.Text = _row["FirstName"].ToString();
    }
}
```

## Resolving the Data Source

You should note that the *DataGrid* control, as well as the *Repeater* and the *DataList*, manage the data source through the generic interface of the *object* class. However, underneath this common and somewhat too simple interface, quite different objects can be used. How can iterative controls distinguish between *DataTable*, *DataSet*, *DataView*, and even custom collections?

Iterative controls use an internal class named *DataSourceHelper* to resolve any issues related to the actual data source to bind to. In a certain way, the helper class straightens differences out and normalizes all possible sources to the root collection interface *IEnumerable*. (*ICollection* descends from *IEnumerable*, and *IList*, in turn, inherits from *ICollection*.)

*DataSet* and *DataTable*, for example, don't implement *IList* directly. They implement *IListSource*, from which the helper class extracts an *IList*-compliant array. A similar pattern can be observed with the *DataView*, *DataViewManager*, and *PagedDataSource* classes. All these classes act as proxies between the control and an embedded object—for example, a *DataTable*. Although they implement *IList*, an intermediate interface is needed to bind and publish the schema of the underlying data source. The *ITypedList* interface provides the tools to extract a valid enumerable list from these objects too.

In summary, iterative controls access and manipulate their data items through the *IEnumerable* interface. However, an extra step is necessary to normalize all possible data sources to *IEnumerable*. This is a subtle problem that arises if you're going to write a list-bound control yourself. We'll tackle this problem in Chapter 20, "Data-Bound and Templated Controls."

Note that the type of the data item depends on the data source that has been bound to the *Repeater*. The *sender* argument refers to the control that is being bound to the data—the *TableCell*. The *NamingContainer* property is only a shortcut to obtain a reference to the parent *Repeater*. In this case, the *Repeater* is the naming container of the cell; however, this technique should be used with a grain of salt. If the bound control or its parent is a naming container itself, the technique will fail.

## Working with the *Repeater* Control

The output that a *Repeater* control can generate for you is any HTML code that can be obtained by repeating ASP.NET templates for all rows in a data source. The overall output can be bound within a table as well as flow as plain HTML text. The *Repeater* control doesn't provide any facility for formatting or styling the output, so whatever effect you need must be manually coded. Note also that you don't necessarily have to bind an ADO.NET object such as *DataTable* or *DataView*. Arrays of custom classes, hash tables, and, in general, any objects that implement the *IEnumerable* interface (or any of its derivates) are acceptable. Of course, you are responsible for casting the *Container.DataItem* expression to the right type.

Let's build a page that lists some information about the customers stored in the Microsoft SQL Server Northwind database. We did this several times in past chapters, but we did it by using a *DataGrid* control or a list control. In those cases, though, we were limited by the fixed template of the controls and could show only text. The greater flexibility of the *Repeater* control allows us to create a sort of Web form for each customer. In particular, our goal is to list minimal information about customers along with a check box. When the page is refreshed, all checked items will display with different colors and more information.

## Designing the Templates

For a realistic *Repeater* control, the item template is a fundamental tool for showing the actual data. The *Repeater* also needs to have the header template, which is normally used to introduce the user to the information displayed below. The separator template is effective to graphically separate one item from the next. It's especially needed if you use the alternating item template. In this example, we provide a simple implementation of the separator, making it include only a thin horizontal ruler—an *<hr>* element. However, the separator template might be the ideal tool to use when you need to display summary rows or subtotals.

### Building the Page

The following listing illustrates the underpinnings of the page shown in Figure 9-2. It contains a few templates for the header, data items, and separator.

```
<asp:repeater runat="server" id="Repeater1">
    <HeaderTemplate>
        <div style="background-color:yellow;">Customers</div>
        <small>Check to see more information</small><br><br>
    </HeaderTemplate>

    <ItemTemplate>
        <span style="display:none;">
            <%# m_checkBox = (CheckBox) FindCheckBox(Container) %>
    </span>

        <asp:checkbox runat="server" id="ExpandButton" />
        <%# ShowHeader(Container.DataItem) %><br>
        <%# ShowInfoBar(Container.DataItem) %>
        <%# ShowAddressBar(Container.DataItem) %>
    </ItemTemplate>

    <SeparatorTemplate>
        <hr style="border:solid 1px black;height:1px;" />
    </SeparatorTemplate>
</asp:repeater>
```

The header template is applied only once, whereas the separator is applied before every displayed item except the first. We modified the default style of the *<hr>* element to make it one-pixel thin. The core of the page is in the *<ItemTemplate>* section. Let's examine its constituent pieces.

You see that the item's template begins with a rather odd hidden *<span>* tag. Next, it includes a check box and three additional functions, each run within a data-bound code block, *<%# ... %>*. As clearly visible in Figure 9-2, address information is displayed for checked customers and all information appears in blue, even though this last effect is not perceivable from a grayscale picture.

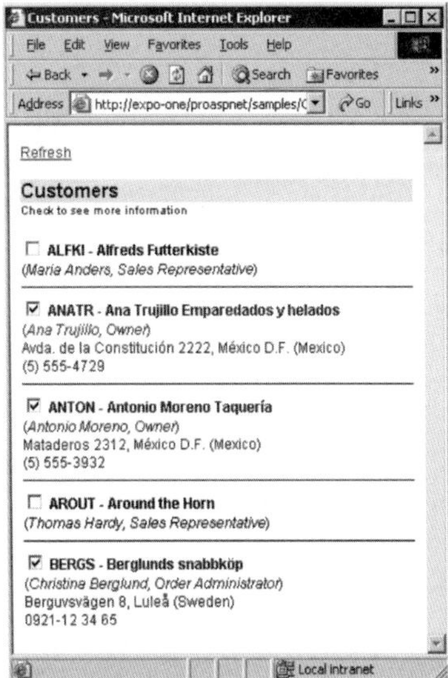


**Figure 9-2** The *Repeater* in action, showing information about customers.

The *ShowHeader*, *ShowInfoBar*, and *ShowAddressBar* output the various blocks of information that make up the customer's form. *ShowHeader* outputs the boldface line with the customer code and name. *ShowInfoBar* generates the italicized line with contact details. Finally, *ShowAddressBar* shows the address of the customer and other personal information such as the phone number. All these functions take the data item and return the HTML-formatted string to add to the page's output stream.

```
private string ShowHeader(object dataItem)
{
    // Determine the color to use
    string color = (m_checkBox.Checked ?"blue" :"black");

    // Set up the pattern of the final HTML string
    string _output = "<b style='color:{0};'>{1} - {2}</b>";

    // Fill in the placeholders
    DataRowView _row = (DataRowView) dataItem;
    _output = String.Format(_output,
        color, _row["customerid"], _row["companyname"]);

    // Return the output string
    return _output;
}
```

The other helper routines have a similar structure. (See this book's sample code.) The key thing going on here is the how the function determines the color to use. Aside from that, it simply casts the *Container.DataItem* expression to the actual type—*DataRowView* in this case. Let's see the initialization code of the page.

```
CheckBox m_checkBox;

public void Page_Load(object sender, EventArgs e) {
    if (!IsPostBack)
        BindData();
}

private void BindData() {
    DataSet _data = new DataSet();

    string _conn = "SERVER=localhost;DATABASE=Northwind;UID=sa;";
    string _query = "SELECT TOP 5 * FROM customers";
    SqlDataAdapter _adapter = new SqlDataAdapter(_query, _conn);
    _adapter.Fill(_data);

    // Bind to a DataView
    // The type of the data item will be DataRowView
    Repeater1.DataSource = _data.Tables[0].DefaultView;
    Repeater1.DataBind();
}
```

The *m_checkBox* global variable is reinitialized whenever the item template is processed. As a global variable, it is visible and accessible from within any methods on the page. The check-box variable is initialized when the data item is created.

## The Initialization Step

While the repeater's output is being generated, the check-box control is instantiated, but it has yet to be updated with the user's information. If you need to do something when an item is created, you could write either an *ItemCreated* or *ItemDataBound* handler. You can also resort to the following trick, in which we run initialization code at the beginning of the template.

```
<ItemTemplate>
    <span style="display:none;">
        <%# m_checkBox = (CheckBox) FindCheckBox(Container) %>
    </span>
    ⋮
</ItemTemplate>
```

The solutions are not completely equivalent because the various events occur at different times. During the initialization step, the first event that hits the page is *ItemCreated*. At this point, all controls in the templates have been created and initialized. However, they have yet to be bound to the data.

A detail that often goes unnoticed is that when *ItemCreated* fires, the ID of each child control has not yet been associated with the correct naming container—the *RepeaterItem*. If you watch the *UniqueID* property of, say, the check-box control during the *ItemCreated* event, you'll see that it equals *ExpandButton*. Later, when the *DataBind* method has been called on the *RepeaterItem* object, each child control is mapped to the actual container. The *UniqueID* property becomes *Repeater1:_ctlX:ExpandButton*, where *_ctlX* indicates the particular item. This is the situation observed from within the *FindCheckBox* helper function we used in the preceding code. Depending on what you really need to do during the initialization of data items, using *ItemCreated* or the tricks discussed might lead to significantly different results. On the other hand, the *ItemDataBound* event occurs as the final step in the initialization process and hits the application at the end of the template data binding.

## Retrieving Child Controls

We need to know whether each item's *CheckBox* is checked, because this affects the way in which the item itself is rendered. At the time we need that information, the most reliable way to get it is by reading the value directly from *Request.Form*. To do this, we should know the unique ID of the check box.

The ID of the check box is not yet known when *ItemCreated* fires, and *ItemDataBound* occurs when the HTML output of the template has already been generated. (Look back at the "How the *Repeater* Builds the Output" section earlier, and you'll see that *OnItemBound* fires immediately after the call to *DataBind* for each repeater's item.) That's why a piece of code placed at the beginning of the item template is an effective trick. There might be other ways of accomplishing the same task, but I find this approach both easy to understand and functional.

The global variable *m_checkBox* is not strictly needed. However, if it's used, it optimizes your code because there's no need to call *FindControl* each time you need to access the item-specific instance of the *ExpandButton* check box.

## Handling Postbacks

To retrieve the item-specific instance of a child control, you use the *FindControl* method from within the actual container—the *RepeaterItem* object.

```
CheckBox ctl = (CheckBox) container.FindControl("ExpandButton");
```

Note that calling the *FindControl* method exposed by the *Page* wouldn't work because *FindControl* explores only the subtree rooted in the naming container. You pass the identifier for the control to be found. Note that the identifier doesn't have to be the client-side and unique ID that is used within the page. The contents of the ASP.NET *ID* property is just fine. The following listing illustrates how we retrieve the item-specific instance of the *CheckBox* control and update its properties reading from the request's *Form* collection.

```
private CheckBox FindCheckBox(Control container)
{
    // Retrieve the item-specific instance of the checkbox
    CheckBox ctl = (CheckBox) container.FindControl("ExpandButton");
    if (ctl == null)
        return null;

    // Update the state of the control
    ctl.Checked = (Page.Request.Form[ctl.UniqueID]=="on");

    // Return the instance of the control
    return ctl;
}
```

Although at this time the state of the child controls has not been restored, the correct value is held in the *Request.Form* collection. The *FindCheckBox* method anticipates the restoration of the current logical state of the check-box field. In addition, it contributes to making the instance globally available within the template. Accessing the check box directly through the *m_checkBox* variable is faster than running *FindControl* each time.

## A Scrollable List of Data Items

In Chapter 6 and Chapter 7 ("Paging Through Data Sources"), we discussed how to page through the records bound to a *DataGrid* control. Both the *Repeater* and *DataList* have no built-in support for pagination. However, the template-based nature of such controls lends itself well to implementing a scrolling mechanism. Bear in mind that any scrolling capabilities rely on the capabilities of the underlying browser and in particular are tied to the level of support the browser provides for version 2 of cascading style sheets (CSS2).

The page shown in Figure 9-3 employs two *Repeater* controls. The first one displays a push button for each customer initial; the other one populates the page with information about all the customers whose company name starts with the selected letter. The second *Repeater* is nearly identical to the one we discussed in the previous section. The only significant change has to do with the layout of the HTML output, which now supports text overflow.

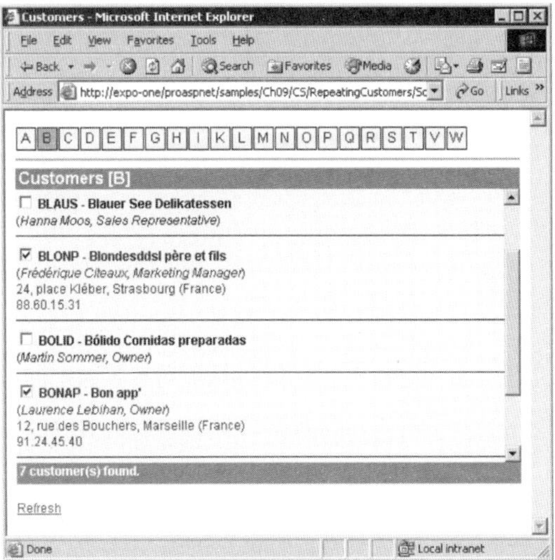


**Figure 9-3** A page that features two *Repeater* controls; one to pick the initial and one to display the related customers in a scrollable area.

## Handling the Click Event

As mentioned earlier, the *Repeater* control doesn't have any built-in mechanisms to render its contents according to special formatting rules. The resulting text, therefore, flows as you write it—either horizontally or vertically. In the previous example, we built a vertical list of data items. Let's see how to create a horizontal strip of data items. We display a push button for each distinct initial found in the companyname column of the Customers table.

```
SELECT DISTINCT substring(companyname, 1, 1) AS Initial FROM customers
```

To display items horizontally, the *Repeater* must build an HTML table with one row and as many cells as there are items in the query's result set.

```
<asp:repeater runat="server" id="Picker" OnItemCommand="ItemCommand">
<HeaderTemplate>
    <table border="0" cellspacing="1" cellpadding="0"><tr>
</HeaderTemplate>

<ItemTemplate>
    <td>
    <asp:button runat="server" style="border:solid 1px;width=20px;"
        BackColor='<%# GetBackColor(Container.DataItem) %>'
        Text='<%# DataBinder.Eval(Container.DataItem, "Initial")%>'
        CommandName='<%# DataBinder.Eval(Container.DataItem, "Initial")%>'
    />
    </td>
</ItemTemplate>
```

```
<FooterTemplate>
    </tr></table><hr>
</FooterTemplate>
</asp:repeater>
```

Each data item is rendered as a push button with a few parametric properties—*BackColor*, *Text*, and *CommandName*. *Text* and *CommandName*, in particular, are bound to the same value—the contents of the Initial column in the data set. The *CommandName* property represents the keyword associated with a command object within an iterative control.

Whenever the user clicks any of the letter buttons, the *ItemCommand* event fires. The sample page handles the *ItemCommand* event as follows:

```
private void ItemCommand(object sender, RepeaterCommandEventArgs e)
{
    BindData(e.CommandName);
}

private void BindData(string initial)
{
    // Store the current initial
    ViewState["Initial"] = initial;

    // Get the necessary data with a single SQL batch
    string _cmdText = m_cmdInitial + ";";
    _cmdText += String.Format(m_cmdCustmrs, initial);
    SqlDataAdapter _adapter = new SqlDataAdapter(_cmdText, m_connString);
    DataSet _data = new DataSet();
    _adapter.Fill(_data);

    // Rename tables
    _data.Tables[0].TableName = "Initials";
    _data.Tables[1].TableName = "Customers";

    // Bind data
    Picker.DataSource = _data.Tables["Initials"].DefaultView;
    Picker.DataBind();
    Customers.DataSource = _data.Tables["Customers"].DefaultView;
    Customers.DataBind();
}
```

The current initial letter is cached in the *ViewState* and persists across successive requests of the same page. Note that the result set with all the initials could have effectively been cached in *Cache* or *Application* because of its relatively low level of volatility.

## Making the Control Scroll

The trick to making a portion of an HTML page scroll vertically and horizontally is the *overflow* CSS style. Most popular browsers recognize about a hundred style-sheet properties, most of which are CSS1 recommendations. The *overflow* attribute is specific to CSS2 and supported by Microsoft Internet Explorer 5.0 and later. The *overflow* attribute controls how a container element (for example, a *<div>*) displays its content if it's not the same size as the container.

```
<HeaderTemplate>
    <div style="background-color:gray;color:white;height:20px;">
        <%# SetHeader() %>
    </div>
    <div style="background-color:lightcyan;height:260px;overflow:auto;">
</HeaderTemplate>
```

Possible values for the *overflow* attribute are listed in Table 9-4.

**Table 9-4 Possible Values for the *overflow* CSS Attribute**

| Value | Description |
|---|---|
| *auto* | Uses scrollbars only if needed. |
| *hidden* | Clips any text that exceeds the fixed container's size. |
| *visible* | Default value, ignores any difference between the fixed size of the container and the contained text. |
| *scroll* | Uses both horizontal and vertical scrollbars. A scrollbar that isn't really needed is disabled. |

The header template defines two *<div>* tags, the latter of which is given a fixed height and will contain the output generated by the items. Nothing is to be changed in the *<ItemTemplate>* section. A *<FooterTemplate>* section, conversely, is needed to close the pending *<div>* tag and provide a footer for summary information.

```
<FooterTemplate>
    </div>
    <div style="background-color:gray;color:white;height:20px;">
        <%# SetFooter() %>
    </div>
</FooterTemplate>
```

The following code is used to show the count of customers displayed in the table:

```
private string SetFooter() {
    string _text = "{0} customer(s) found.";
    ICollection _coll = (ICollection) Customers.DataSource;
    return String.Format(_text, _coll.Count);
}
```

## Repeating with Custom Classes

As mentioned earlier, you don't necessarily bind an ADO.NET object to an iterative control. If you use your own classes to store data, those classes can also be used to populate a *Repeater* as well as a *DataList* control. The data source must be an array of class instances. To access individual properties, you then use *DataBinder.Eval* as you would with a *DataTable*.

```
private void BindData()
{
    string _conn = "SERVER=localhost;DATABASE=Northwind;UID=sa;";
    string _query = "SELECT firstname, lastname FROM employees";
    SqlDataAdapter _adapter = new SqlDataAdapter(_query, _conn);
    DataTable _data = new DataTable();
    _adapter.Fill(_data);

    ArrayList values = new ArrayList();
    foreach(DataRow _row in _data.Rows)
        values.Add(new Employee(
            _row["LastName"].ToString(),
            _row["FirstName"].ToString()));

    Repeater1.DataSource = values;
    Repeater1.DataBind();
}
public class Employee
{
    private string _lastname;
    private string _firstname;

    public Employee(string lname, string fname) {
        _lastname = lname;
        _firstname = fname;
    }

    public string LastName {
        get {return _lastname;}
    }

    public string FirstName {
        get {return _firstname;}
    }
}
```

As you can guess, with the *DataBinder.Eval* method you can access only public properties on your class.

```
<ItemTemplate>
<tr>
```

```
    <td><%# DataBinder.Eval(Container.DataItem, "LastName") %></td>
    <td><%# DataBinder.Eval(Container.DataItem, "FirstName") %></td>
</tr>
</ItemTemplate>
```

If you bind an iterative control to an array of classes, you can't rely on any ready-made tool to sort data. You must sort the array yourself using the *IComparer* interface to define your own rules. (See the MSDN documentation for the *IComparer* interface.)

# The *DataList* Control

Functionally speaking, the *DataList* is a data-bound control that falls somewhere in between the *Repeater* and the *DataGrid*. It begins where the *Repeater* ends and terminates a little before the starting point of the *DataGrid* control. In some unrealistically simple cases, you can even take some code that uses a *Repeater*, replace the control, and not even notice any difference. Looking at the programming interface, though, the *DataList* is much more similar to the *DataGrid*.

In spite of such deep similarities, the *DataList* is a control with its own personality and a set of features that make it unique and ideal in a number of situations. Compared to the *Repeater*, the *DataList* control comes with a full bag of goodies and new features, mostly in the area of graphical layout. The control overtakes the *Repeater* in several respects. For example, it supports directional rendering, meaning that items can flow horizontally or vertically to match a specified number of columns. Furthermore, just as with the *DataGrid*, it provides facilities to retrieve a key value associated with the current data row and has built-in support for selection and in-place editing. In addition, the *DataList* control supports more templates and can fire some extra events beyond those of the *Repeater*. Data binding and the overall behavior are nearly identical for the *Repeater* and *DataList* controls.

## Programming Interface of the *DataList* Control

The *DataList* is smarter than the *Repeater* and works by making some assumptions about the expected results. This is good news and bad news for you as a programmer. It means that in some cases much less code is needed to accomplish the same effect; on the other hand, it also indicates that you should know the behavior of the control very well to govern it. For example, the *DataList* assumes that no HTML tag is split across templates. This fact isn't a problem per se, but it can result in badly formed or totally unexpected HTML output. In addition, by default the *DataList* renders its entire output as an HTML table, meaning that if this is exactly what you want, there's no need for you to comply with *<table>* or *<td>* elements.

Before we look in detail at the programming interface of the *DataList* control, let's see what we should do to make the previous example (the scrolling page) work with a *DataList*. Once you have replaced *<asp:repeater>* with *<asp:datalist>*, set the *RepeatDirection* property to *Horizontal* on the Picker control.

```
<asp:datalist runat="server" id="Picker"
    RepeatDirection="Horizontal"
    RepeatLayout="Flow"
    OnItemCommand="ItemCommand">
```

Both the Picker and Customers control also need to have the *RepeatLayout* property set to the value of *Flow*.

```
<asp:datalist runat="server" id="Customers"
    RepeatLayout="Flow">
```

Finally, modify the item template of the Picker control by removing any text other than the *<asp:button>* declaration. Likewise, remove the header and the footer template—the *DataList* will automatically provide the formatting features that you have to code yourself when the *Repeater* is used. The final result is shown in Figure 9-4.

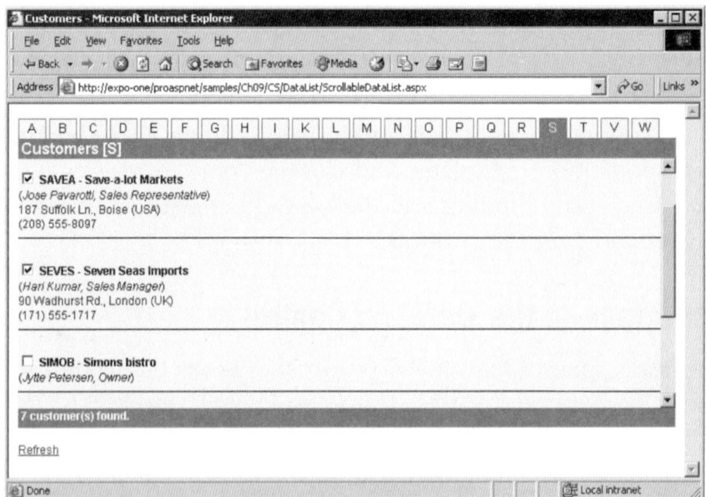


**Figure 9-4** The previously discussed scrollable list implemented with *DataList* controls.

The *DataList* has no methods aside from those provided by parent controls. It features a lot of properties and fires quite a few events. The *DataList* control is declared as follows:

```
public class DataList : BaseDataList, INamingContainer, IRepeatInfoUser
```

Like the *DataGrid* control, it inherits from *BaseDataList* and implements the *INamingContainer* interface. In addition, the *DataList* class implements the *IRepeatInfoUser* interface. The *IRepeatInfoUser* interface defines the properties and methods that must be implemented by any list control that repeats a list of items. This interface is also supported by the *CheckBoxList* and *RadioButtonList* controls. However, all of its properties and methods are marked as private and, as such, are inaccessible from within the user code.

### Properties of the *DataList* Control

Table 9-5 lists the properties of the *DataList* control. The table doesn't include properties inherited from *Control* and *WebControl*.

**Table 9-5 Properties of the *DataList***

| Property | Description |
|---|---|
| *AlternatingItemStyle* | Gets the style properties for alternating rows. |
| *AlternatingItemTemplate* | Gets or sets the template for alternating items. |
| *CellPadding* | Gets or sets the space (in pixels) between the cell's border and the embedded text. |
| *CellSpacing* | Gets or sets the space (in pixels) between two consecutive cells, both horizontally and vertically. |
| *Controls* | Gets the collection of all the child controls in the list. |
| *DataKeyField* | Gets or sets the key field in the bound data source. |
| *DataKeys* | Gets a collection that stores the key values of all the records displayed in the list. The column used as the key is the one stored in the *DataKeyField* property. |
| *DataMember* | Gets or sets a string that indicates the specific table in a multimember data source to bind. The property works in conjunction with *DataSource*. If *DataSource* is a *DataSet* object, then *DataMember* contains the name of a child table to bind. |
| *DataSource* | Gets or sets the data source object that contains the values to populate the control. |
| *EditItemIndex* | Gets or sets the 0-based index of the item to edit. |
| *EditItemStyle* | Gets the style properties for the item being edited. |

*(continued)*

**Table 9-5 Properties of the *DataList*** *(continued)*

| Property | Description |
|---|---|
| *EditItemTemplate* | Gets or sets the template for the item selected for editing. |
| *ExtractTemplateRows* | Gets or sets a value that instructs the *DataList* to extract the constituent rows from any HTML table in the templates. The extracted rows are then combined to create a single, all-encompassing HTML table. Set to *false* by default. |
| *FooterStyle* | Gets the style properties for the footer section. |
| *FooterTemplate* | Gets or sets the template for the footer section. |
| *GridLines* | Gets or sets a value that indicates whether all cells must have the border drawn. The property is ignored if the *RepeatLayout* property is set to *RepeatLayout.Flow*. |
| *HeaderStyle* | Gets the style properties for the heading section. |
| *HeaderTemplate* | Gets or sets the template for the heading section. |
| *HorizontalAlign* | Gets or sets the horizontal alignment of the text in the list. |
| *Items* | Gets the collection of the currently displayed items. |
| *ItemStyle* | Gets the style properties for the items in the list. |
| *ItemTemplate* | Gets or sets the template for the items in the *DataList*. |
| *RepeatColumns* | Gets or sets the number of columns to display. |
| *RepeatDirection* | Gets or sets a value that indicates whether the *DataList* control displays its items vertically or horizontally. |
| *RepeatLayout* | Gets or sets a value that indicates whether the output of the control is displayed within an automatically created table or by using a flow layout. In a flow layout, text is output in free form. |
| *SelectedIndex* | Gets or sets the index of the currently selected item. |
| *SelectedItem* | Gets the *DataListItem* object that represents the currently selected item. |
| *SelectedItemStyle* | Gets the style properties for the selected item. |
| *SelectedItemTemplate* | Gets or sets the template for the currently selected item. |
| *SeparatorStyle* | Gets the style properties of the separator used to break text between consecutive items. |
| *SeparatorTemplate* | Gets or sets the template for the separator. |
| *ShowFooter* | Gets or sets a value that indicates whether the footer section is to be displayed. |
| *ShowHeader* | Gets or sets a value that indicates whether the heading section is to be displayed. |

The *ShowFooter* and *ShowHeader* properties are both set to *true* by default, but they're considered only if the *FooterTemplate* and *HeaderTemplate* properties, respectively, are non-null.

The data binding process of the *DataList* control is nearly identical to that of the *Repeater*, and the generation of the output also takes place according to the same rules. However, the *DataList* control has a richer programming interface that lets you handle two additional states—selected and editing. The currently selected item is tracked through the *SelectedIndex* and *SelectedItem* properties. The same occurs for the item being edited. In this case, the property is *EditItemIndex*. The in-place editing mechanism of a *DataList* is identical to that of a *DataGrid* control. (See Chapter 6.)

### Events of the *DataList* Control

Table 9-6 lists the events that, under various circumstances, the *DataList* control can fire. The list doesn't include the base events (for example, *Load* and *DataBinding*) the class inherits from *Control* and *WebControl*.

**Table 9-6 Events Fired by the *DataList***

| Event | Description |
|---|---|
| *CancelCommand* | Fires when a button with a command name of *Cancel* is clicked for a displayed item. |
| *DeleteCommand* | Fires when a button with a command name of *Delete* is clicked for a displayed item. |
| *EditCommand* | Fires when a button with a command name of *Edit* is clicked for a displayed item. |
| *ItemCommand* | Fires when a button is clicked within the *DataList* control. |
| *ItemCreated* | Fires when a *DataList* item is being created. |
| *ItemDataBound* | Fires after an item in the *DataList* has been bound to its underlying data. The event occurs before the data item is added to the *Items* collection. (Note that only items and alternating items are bindable.) |
| *SelectedIndexChanged* | Fires when a new item is selected in the *DataList*. |
| *UpdateCommand* | Fires when a button with a command name of *Update* is clicked for a displayed item. |

With the exception of *ItemCreated* and *ItemDataBound*, all the events relate to the execution of some sort of command. *ItemCommand* is the base command event and always fires before the more specific event, such as *EditCommand* or *DeleteCommand*. Regardless of the name, *SelectedIndexChanged* also is a command event that fires when a button with the command name of *Select* is clicked.

> **Note** Command buttons don't necessarily have to be item specific. Any button within the user interface of the *DataList* control can be given a special command name, such as Edit or Delete. The effect is always that of firing the related event. Of course, if the button is not item specific, the logic of the application must determine the affected item and decide the proper action.

The Update and Cancel command buttons are normally generated by the *DataList* itself when a particular item enters into edit mode. Finally, note that the *DataList* class provides constants to identify special command names in a parametric way. The constants are *CancelCommandName*, *DeleteCommandName*, *EditCommandName*, *SelectCommandName*, and *UpdateCommandName*. They are implemented as static properties (*shared properties* according to Microsoft Visual Basic .NET jargon).

## Formatting Capabilities

As mentioned earlier, the *Repeater* control is a general-purpose iterator and is limited to generating templated text without applying any extra formatting rules. The *DataList* control, on the other hand, provides additional features specifically for controlling the layout of the list. In particular, the *DataList* can render surrounding table rows and cells around its template-defined elements. This capability allows you to build more advanced and user-friendly layouts with less code. Key elements for taking advantage of this enhanced set of capabilities are the *RepeatColumns*, *RepeatDirection*, and *RepeatLayout* properties. They let you specify the number of columns the output will span and the direction (vertical or horizontal) in which to render the data items.

### Table and Flow Layout

The *RepeatLayout* property takes its values from the *RepeatLayout* enumeration, which consists of two possibilities—*Table* and *Flow*. The default is *Table*. If the layout is set to *Flow*, the *DataList* wraps any template element within a *<span>* tag. Next, it automatically adds a *<br>* element if the rendering direction is vertical. You should note that vertical is the default direction. If the direction is horizontal, the output text simply flows in a concatenated HTML string. The following *DataList* output is for a vertical *Flow* layout:

```
<span id="DataList1">
    <span> header template </span>
    <br>
```

```
    <span> item template </span>
    <br>
    <span> separator template </span>
    ⋮
    <span> footer template </span>
</span>
```

The *Table* mode saves you from a lot of HTML coding if you're just going to build an HTML table. The following *DataList* output is for a vertical *Table* layout:

```
<table id="DataList1">
    <tr>
        <td> header template </td>
    </tr>
    <tr>
        <td> item template </td>
    </tr>
    <tr>
        <td> separator template </td>
    </tr>
        ⋮
    <tr>
        <td> footer template </td>
    </tr>
</table>
```

If the direction is horizontal, the layout of the table is slightly different and is composed of only three table rows—the header, one row for all the items, and the footer.

```
<table id="DataList1">
    <tr>
        <td> header template </td>
    </tr>
    <tr>
        <td> item template </td>
        <td> separator template </td>
        ⋮
    </tr>
    <tr>
        <td> footer template </td>
    </tr>
</table>
```

When the *ExtractTemplateRows* property is set to *true*, the *DataList* control extracts table rows out of all declared templates and merges them into an all-encompassing table. The *ExtractTemplateRows* property allows you to create a single table from other smaller tables defined for each *DataList* template. The use of the property is subject to a few restrictions. In particular, you must provide a well-formed *Table* control (the *<asp:table>* tag) for each template you want to include in the output. An exception would be thrown if you specify the table using the HTML *<table>* element or the ASP.NET *HtmlTable* control—the *<table runat="server">* element. Note also that *all* templates must be expressed using the *Table* control and that only the rows of the tables will be displayed. All other content in the templates will be ignored. The following code shows how to define a table in an item template:

```
<ItemTemplate>
    <asp:table runat="server">
        <asp:tablerow runat="server">
            <asp:tablecell runat="server">
                <%# DataBinder.Eval(Container.DataItem, "Name") %>
            </asp:tablecell>
        </asp:tablerow>
    </asp:table>
</ItemTemplate>
```

The *ExtractTemplateRows* property is really helpful only when you're going to create quite a complex structure in which tables with different templates are to be merged together. You can use the *ColumnSpan* and *RowSpan* properties of the *TableCell* object to control the number of columns and rows the cell spans.

> **Note** When the *ExtractTemplateRows* property is set to *true*, the *RepeatColumns*, *RepeatDirection*, and *RepeatLayout* properties are ignored and do not affect the appearance of the *DataList* control.

## Extracting Template Rows

Let's drill down into a common scenario in which *ExtractTemplateRows* proves extremely useful. Suppose that you need to create a report in which multiple rows for each data item should be displayed. Assuming that you want it to work with a table of customers, let's say that you want to display the customer ID and name on the first row and the address on the second.

With a *Repeater*, you could accomplish this by defining a table in the header template and then defining a couple of rows for each item. If you don't mind using a *Repeater*, this is just fine. However, the *DataList* control has styling and formatting capabilities that one wouldn't easily sacrifice. The *DataList*, though, doesn't let you break HTML elements across templates. In other words, this means that you cannot place the opening tag of a table in the header and close it in the footer.

The *DataList* control requires that you express the layout of each template using stand-alone tables. You can use, for instance, a table for the header and a table for the item template. However, if you set the *ExtractTemplateRows* property to *true*, all the rows of the various tables will automatically converge into a unique, all-encompassing table.

```
<asp:datalist runat="server" id="list" extracttemplaterows="true">
    <AlternatingItemStyle backcolor="palegoldenrod" />
    <headerstyle backcolor="brown" forecolor="white"
        font-size="larger" font-bold="true" horizontalalign="center" />

    <HeaderTemplate>
    <asp:table runat="server">
        <asp:tablerow runat="server">
            <asp:tablecell runat="server">Customer</asp:TableCell>
            <asp:tablecell runat="server">Contact</asp:TableCell>
        </asp:tablerow>
    </asp:table>
    </HeaderTemplate>

    <ItemTemplate>
    <asp:table runat="server">
        <asp:tablerow runat="server" font-bold="true">
            <asp:tablecell runat="server">
            <%# DataBinder.Eval(Container.DataItem, "CustomerID") %>
            </asp:tablecell>
            <asp:tablecell runat="server">
            <%# DataBinder.Eval(Container.DataItem, "ContactName") %>
            </asp:tablecell>
        </asp:tablerow>
        <asp:tablerow runat="server">
            <asp:tablecell runat="server" columnspan="2">
            <%# DataBinder.Eval(Container.DataItem, "Address") + " - " +
                DataBinder.Eval(Container.DataItem, "City")   %>
            </asp:tablecell>
        </asp:tablerow>
    </asp:table>
    </ItemTemplate>
</asp:datalist>
```

At display time, the *DataList* merges the two *Table* objects and removes any table element that is not an instance of the *TableRow* class. The final table contains two columns, and each record displays on two different rows, the second of which contains a single cell spanning two columns. The *DataList* control is smart enough to consistently manage visual settings (for example, the alternating item styles) for all table rows that actually participate in a data item row. The results are shown in Figure 9-5.

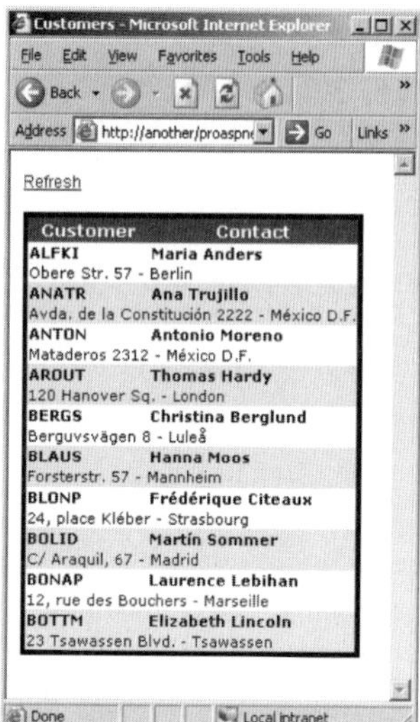


**Figure 9-5** The *DataList* shows a data table in which all records display in two table rows.

> **Note** The need to merge multiple tables explains the strict requirement set on the use of the *<asp:table>* tag, which corresponds to the *Table* object. The *DataList* builds the resulting table object in memory. If you use a *<table>*, whether it's with or without the *runat* attribute, other objects are involved and the trick won't work.

## Multicolumn Rendering

The output of a *DataList* control can be rendered over multiple columns whose number you specify by using the *RepeatColumns* property. By default, the text displays in one column. You can create multicolumn output by using either a flow or a table layout. However, the ideal way of repeating items over multiple columns is within a fixed table layout. Figure 9-6 shows the effect of the *RepeatColumns* property along with some possible shortcomings.

```
<asp:datalist runat="server" id="list" RepeatColumns="3">
    ⋮
</asp:datalist>
```

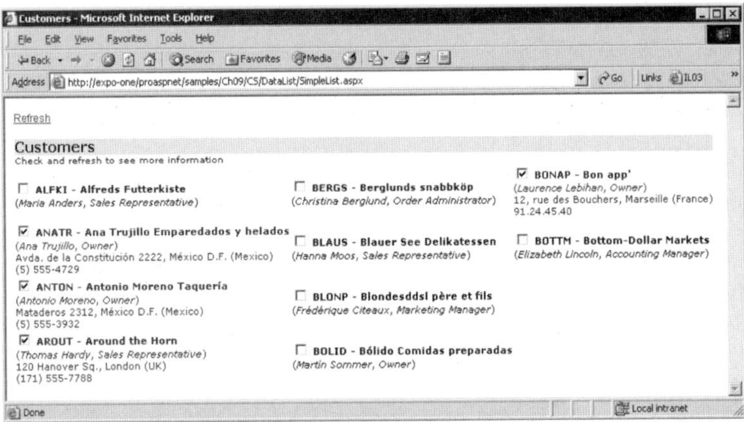


**Figure 9-6** A *DataList* control that renders its output over three columns.

As you can see, the vertical alignment of the cells is the default and no properties are allowed to modify it programmatically.

## Templates of the *DataList* Control

In addition to all the templates supported by the *Repeater* control, the *DataList* control supports two new templates—*SelectedItemTemplate* and *EditItemTemplate*. The *SelectedItemTemplate* template lets you control the contents and functionality of the selected item. The *EditItemTemplate* template takes care of in-place editing in much the same way as with *DataGrid* controls.

### The *SelectedItemTemplate* Template

The appearance of the selected item is controlled by the *SelectedItemStyle* property. The following code changes the background color of the selected item to the specified color:

```
<SelectedItemStyle backcolor="cyan" />
```

As for the *DataGrid* control, you must trigger the selection process using a command button labeled with the *Select* command name. If you want to do more, such as adding information or controls to the currently selected item, you can even replace the default template with a new one. You specify a template for the selected item through the *<SelectedItemTemplate>* tag. A similar mechanism greatly simplifies the building of master/detail views. Once the row has been selected, in fact, you display an ad hoc template that includes any child tables that are needed.

If you need to programmatically access the currently selected item, you use the *SelectedItem* property. It returns the instance of the *DataListItem* object that corresponds to the specified index. For each displayed row, the *DataKeys* collection contains the source values stored in the column that the *DataKeyField* column specifies.

```
// Get the key of the currently selected record and
// drills down into the available data
int key = (int) list.DataKeys[list.SelectedIndex];
GetChildData(key);
```

Items can be selected programmatically by setting the *SelectedIndex* property to a 0-based value. A value of –1 means that no item is currently selected. Note that the value stored in the *SelectedIndex* property is persisted in the view state and survives across consecutive page requests. For this reason, you should reset it whenever a new page of data is displayed.

### The *EditItemTemplate* Template

You use the *EditItemTemplate* property to control the contents of the item selected for editing in a *DataList* control. The look and feel of the item selected for editing is controlled by the *EditItemStyle* property. The *EditItemIndex* property contains the 0-based index of the item being edited. Also, this value is cached in the view state, so you should reset it whenever your data set is bound to the control changes.

The in-place editing feature of the *DataList* control is nearly identical to *DataGrid* in-place editing when all columns are based on templates. The *DataList* fires the *EditCommand* event when the user clicks a button associated with the *Edit* command. However, the control enters into edit mode only if the event handler sets the *EditItemIndex* to a 0-based value. When the user clicks to commit the changes, the *UpdateCommand* event fires. You retrieve the current values from input fields using the *FindControl* method and then proceed to persist those changes. The overall procedure is identical to what we saw in Chapter 6 regarding *DataGrid* controls.

## Working with the *DataList* Control

Let's add item selection to the page shown in Figure 9-4. The idea is to transform the scrollable area of the *DataList* into something that closely resembles a custom list box. The *DataList* renders its contents vertically using the *Flow* layout. To start, let's remove the *<hr>* element from the separator template so that we save a few pixels of space.

```
<SeparatorTemplate>
</SeparatorTemplate>
```

Note that an empty *SeparatorTemplate* is not ignored but is rendered with an extra *<br>* element. To set up a functional and effective selection mechanism, we need to handle the *SelectedIndexChanged* event and define the *SelectedItemStyle*. In this case, we don't need to change the template of the item. That feature would be needed to make the component support drill-down functionality, however.

If you've played a little bit with the page shown in Figure 9-4, you should have noticed that whenever you refresh the view (for example, you checked a few items), the scrollbar is reset to its topmost position. This is boring, especially if you have a relatively long list of items; you scroll the view to locate the item to expand and then when the page is refreshed, the item of interest is out of view. This is another problem we'll address in a moment.

## Adding Support for Selection

The first point to consider is, how can we make a displayed item selectable? We need to add a command button labeled with the special keyword *Select*. If, for some reason, you need more control over the whole process of selection, you could give the clickable element any command name. Next, when *ItemCommand* fires, you recognize the command and activate the selection yourself by setting the *SelectedIndex* property to a correct index. Note that the default process—applying a particular style and template—begins at this point. The trigger for the process is buried in the code that sets the *SelectedIndex* property.

### Making an Item Selectable

The header of each item—that is, the customer's ID and company name—is a good candidate to become the trigger for the selection. Instead of rendering it as plain text, we surround it with a link button.

```
<asp:linkbutton runat="server"
    CommandName="Select"
    Text='<%# SetCustomerName(Container.DataItem) %>' />
```

The text of the link is defined by the following function that simply concatenates a couple of source columns:

```
private string SetCustomerName(object dataItem)
{
    DataRowView _row = (DataRowView) dataItem;
    string _output = "<b>{0} - {1}</b>";
    _output = String.Format(_output,
        _row["customerid"], _row["companyname"]);

    return _output;
}
```

The appearance of the link button is controlled by a couple of page-wide styles that we also used in previous chapters.

```
<style>
    a:hover {color:red;text-decoration:underline;}
    a       {text-decoration:none;}
</style>
<body vlink="black" link="black" ... />
```

The combined effect of these settings is that the link displays as normal text until the mouse moves over it. When that happens, the color switches to red and an underline appears to restore the typical look and feel of HTML clickable elements, as shown in Figure 9-7.

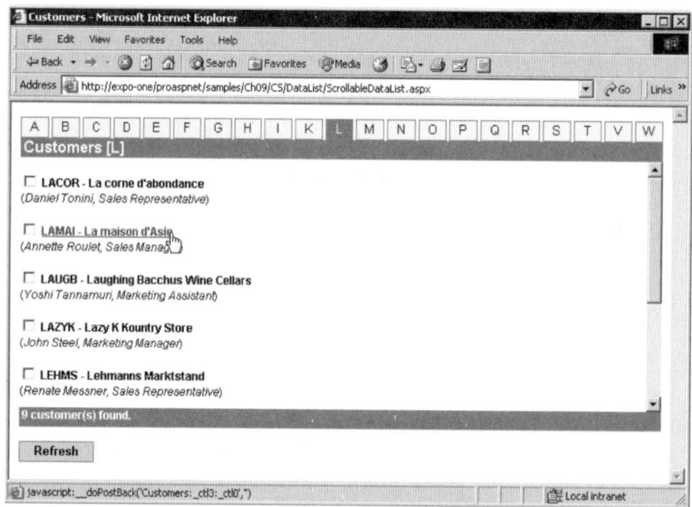


**Figure 9-7** A selectable element in the output of a *DataList* control.

With *DataGrid* controls, the following tag would suffice to set the background color when a row is selected:

```
<SelectedItemStyle backcolor="cyan" />
```

If you use that tag with a *DataList* control, though, the graphical aspect of the selected row is not what you would expect. As Figure 9-8 shows, with a *Flow* layout only the individual controls have the background color changed.

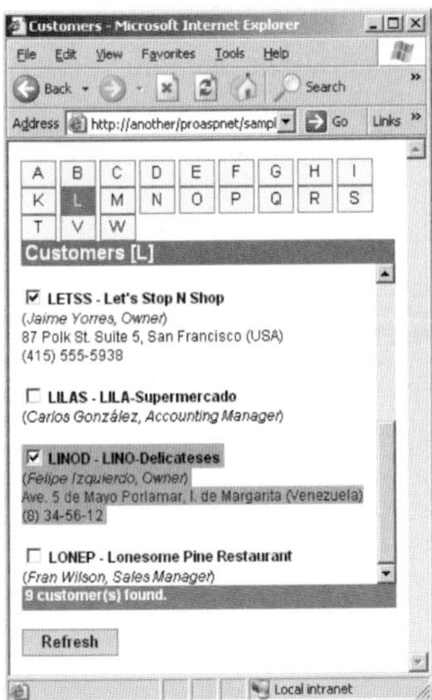


**Figure 9-8** A selectable element in the output of a *DataList* control.

To extend the new background color to the whole row, use the following style declaration, which adds an explicit width. The result is shown in Figure 9-9.

```
<SelectedItemStyle backcolor="cyan" width="100%" />
```

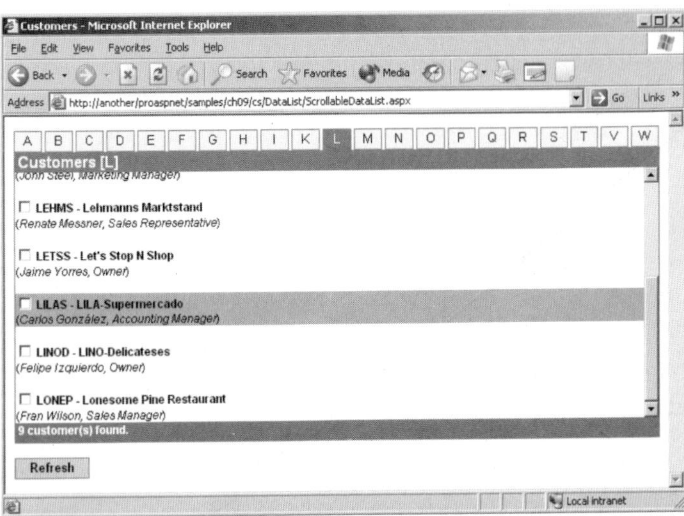


**Figure 9-9** A listbox-like selection in a *DataList* control.

At this point, we have a fully functional infrastructure for handling the item selection event. To take a particular action on the selected item, register a handler for the *SelectedIndexChanged* event and update the user interface.

## Keeping the Selected Item in View

The second problem—ensuring that the portion of the *DataList* output that contains the selected item is included in the current view—requires a more subtle solution. In this example, we made the *DataList* output scrollable by surrounding the data items with a *<div>* element and setting the *<div> overflow* style property to the value of *auto*.

However, when the page posts back, the scrollbar that lets you move back and forth over the *DataList* output is not automatically restored to the position occupied beforehand. Suppose that you scroll down and select one of the last customers in the list. When the page is re-created after the selection, the scrollbar is reset and the selected item is not in the default view. As a result, you have to scroll down again to see its updated content. Is there an automatic way to scroll a particular item into view?

The Dynamic HTML (DHTML) object model provides a large number of HTML elements with a method named *scrollIntoView*. The following JavaScript function illustrates the working of the *scrollIntoView* DHTML method:

```
<SCRIPT>
function ScrollToElem(ctlName)
{
    var elem = document.all(ctlName);
    if (elem == null)
        return;
    elem.scrollIntoView(true);
}
</SCRIPT>
```

The function takes the ID of an HTML element as its sole argument. Next, it attempts to locate the element in the page object model. If successful, it calls the *scrollIntoView* method to ensure the specified element is visible within its container. The container can be the page as well as a container tag such as *<div>*. The Boolean argument you pass to the method indicates whether the element must be shown at the top or the bottom of the view. Although this trick is not acceptable with all browsers, it represents the only possibility we have to scroll an HTML element into view. Let's see how to integrate this piece of code with the existing *DataList*.

To call the *scrollIntoView* method, we need to assign a unique HTML name to all the data items displayed by the *DataList*. Furthermore, the ID we assign to each item must be easily accessible from within the *SelectedIndex-Changed* event handler. Whenever a new item is selected, we execute some

ASP.NET code that configures the HTML page's *onload* method. In particular, we link the page's *onload* method to the JavaScript function just shown. The function is passed as an argument the name of the DHTML object that represents the currently selected *DataList* item.

In the following code snippet, we surround the contents of an item with a *<span>* tag whose ID matches the value of the *customerid* column for the item being rendered:

```
<ItemTemplate>
    <span ID='<%# DataBinder.Eval(Container.DataItem, "customerid") %>'>
    ⋮
    </span>
</ItemTemplate>
```

In addition, we set the *DataKeyField* property of the *DataList* with the name of the *customerid* column and add a handler for the *SelectedIndexChanged* event.

```
<asp:datalist runat="server" id="Customers"
    RepeatLayout="Flow"
    DataKeyField="customerid"
    OnSelectedIndexChanged="SelectedIndexChanged">
⋮
```

When the user selects a new item, we retrieve the value of key field—the *customerid* column—and prepare the JavaScript call to link with the *onload* event on the HTML page.

```
public void SelectedIndexChanged(object sender, EventArgs e)
{
    // Get the customerid of the currently selected item
    string custID = (string) Customers.DataKeys[Customers.SelectedIndex];

    // Prepare the Javascript call.
    // For example, if the current item has an ID of ALFKI, the
    // Javascript call will be ScrollToElem('ALFKI')
    string js = "ScrollToElem('{0}')";
    js = String.Format(js, custID);

    // Register the Javascript call with the onload event
    TheBody.Attributes["onload"] = js;
}
```

The final step entails that we bind the JavaScript call to the *onload* event of the HTML page. There are two ways of accomplishing this from within ASP.NET code. You can either use the *Page RegisterStartupScript* method or set the *onload* attribute on the *<body>* tag. I have chosen the second option because it's clearer and more intuitive. As we saw in Chapter 1, "The Web

Forms Model," to programmatically assign a property on the body of the page, you must first give it an ID and mark it as *runat="server"*.

```
<body runat="server" id="TheBody" ...>
```

The net effect of these changes is that whenever the user selects a new item, the page posts back and executes the *SelectedIndexChanged* method. The method updates the JavaScript function call associated with the page's *onload* event to reflect the current item. Next, the page is rendered and sent back to the browser. On the client, the *onload* event scrolls into view the piece of HTML code that corresponds to the currently selected item of the server-side *DataList* control.

## Adding Support for Paging

The *DataList* control has a more free-form user interface than the *DataGrid* control. This consideration alone makes the *DataList* control particularly compelling to many developers who have the need to create interactive reports outside the relatively standard visualization pattern employed by grids. For example, no matter how powerful and customizable a grid can be, you can hardly force it to display a data-source column in more columns or rows of data. By contrast, you can easily obtain that flexibility using *DataList* controls. However, the *DataList* control doesn't support pagination.

Pagination is the control's ability to display equally sized blocks of data according to an internal index the user can modify through links. The *DataGrid* user interface incorporates a pager bar element, which is nothing more than a table row with links to internal pieces of code that handle the page movements. The *DataList* user interface doesn't provide any predefined link bar for pagination, meaning that the host page can define anywhere in the body a couple of links to move the data source back and forth.

### Rendering Pages of Data

The following code snippets illustrate the page-level code that controls the current index and the contents of the current page:

```
private void OnPreviousPage(object sender, EventArgs e)
{
    CurrentPageIndex -= 1;
    RefreshPage();
}

private void OnNextPage(object sender, EventArgs e)
{
    CurrentPageIndex += 1;
    RefreshPage();
}
```

The code adjusts the page index—a global variable named *CurrentPageIndex*—and binds the data to the *DataList* control. *RefreshPage* is a page-level helper routine that extracts the data to bind from the database or, more logically, from a server-side cache.

```
private void RefreshPage()
{
    DataTable _data = GetData();
    AdjustPageIndex(_data.Rows.Count);

    CurrentPage.Text = (CurrentPageIndex +1).ToString();
    list.DataSource = GetPage(_data, CurrentPageIndex);
    list.DataBind();
}
private DataTable GetData()
{
    // Try to get the data from the session cache
    DataTable _data = (DataTable) Session["MyData"];

    // If no data is available, read from the database
    if (_data == null)
        _data = LoadData();

    return _data;
}
```

The *GetPage* method is responsible for extracting the right subset of rows that fit into the current page. The page of data is returned as a *DataTable* object and is bound to the *DataList*.

```
private DataTable GetPage(DataTable dt, int pageIndex)
{
    if (dt==null)
        dt = LoadData();

    int firstIndexInPage = (CurrentPageIndex*PageSize);
    DataRowCollection rows = dt.Rows;

    DataTable target = dt.Clone();
    for (int i=0; i<PageSize; i++)
    {
        int index = i+firstIndexInPage;
        if (index < rows.Count)
            target.ImportRow(rows[i+firstIndexInPage]);
        else
            break;
    }

    return target;
}
```

The function clones the original table of data and creates a new, smaller table with only the rows that fit into the specified page index. The *Clone* method creates a new empty object with the same structure as the sample. The *ImportRow* method duplicates and copies a new row from one *DataTable* object to another. Note that a deep copy of the row is necessary because ADO.NET objects can't be contained in more than one parent object.

> **Note** As we saw in Chapter 6 and Chapter 7, the *DataGrid* control supports two flavors of pagination—automatic and custom. In automatic paging, you bind the control to a data source for the lifetime of the control and, while you page, the control itself takes care of extracting all the records that need to be displayed. Custom paging, on the other hand, loads in memory all the records to display. Implementing a form of custom paging for a *DataList* control is straightforward and, in a certain way, this is exactly what we did when we created a list of buttons with the initials of the available customers. The preceding code completes the demonstration showing how to extract records from a cache of rows. However, note that the *DataGrid* control relies on an ad hoc class to perform paging related tasks—the *PagedDataSource* class. You could rewrite this code using an instance of the *PagedDataSource* class for the actual pagination.

### Tracking the Page Index

For effective pagination, at least a couple of properties are needed: *CurrentPageIndex* and *PageSize*. The sample page in Figure 9-10 defines them as global properties on the page. If you plan to incorporate the code discussed here in a self-contained control, *CurrentPageIndex* and *PageSize* have to be public properties on the new class.

The *CurrentPageIndex* property contains the 0-based index relative to the current page. The *PageSize* property defines the maximum number of rows permitted per page.

```
public int PageSize = 12;
public int CurrentPageIndex
{
    get {
        if (ViewState["CurrentPageIndex"] == null)
            return 0;
        int _tmp = (int) ViewState["CurrentPageIndex"];
```

```
        return _tmp;
    }
    set {ViewState["CurrentPageIndex"] = value;}
}
```

It's interesting to note that unlike *PageSize*, *CurrentPageIndex* must necessarily be persisted across multiple page requests. This can easily be done using the *ViewState* collection. As the preceding code clearly shows, the value of the property is not stored in a class member but in the page *ViewState* bag. This ensures that its value will always be up to date.

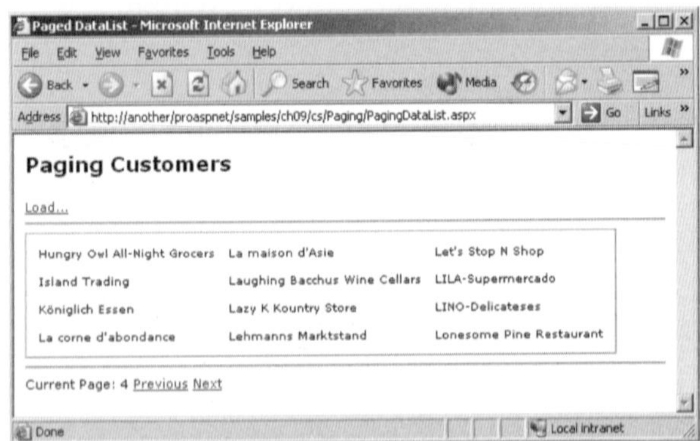


**Figure 9-10** All the customers are displayed one page at a time in three columns of data. The link buttons provide for page movements and cause the *DataList* to refresh its contents.

# Conclusion

In this chapter, we examined the characteristics of two iterative controls available with the ASP.NET programming platform. The two controls are the *Repeater* and *DataList* controls. A third iterative control—the *DataGrid*—has been widely covered in previous chapters. Iterative controls differ from list controls because of their native support for templates and their extremely flexible rendering engine. Iterative and list controls have some points in common too. Both can be bound to a data source and display a list of items. The key point is in the algorithm and the templates that each control, and category of controls, employs.

In an ideal scale, the *Repeater* is the simplest of all controls, but also the most flexible; the *DataGrid* has the richest set of features but is also the one that ties the developer to a multicolumn, tabular view. The *DataList* control falls somewhere in the middle, but it's logically closer to the *DataGrid* control. Just like the *Repeater*, the *DataList* displays the contents of a data-bound list through ASP.NET templates. But just like the *DataGrid*, it supports selecting and in-place editing and can have its look and feel customized using style properties.

Compared to the *Repeater* control, the *DataList* also shows off predefined layouts and more advanced formatting capabilities. Compared to the *DataGrid*, on the other hand, it lacks a key functionality: the ability to page through bound data. In this chapter, we've exploited the features of iterative controls, along with some HTML and JavaScript tricks, to build more effective and powerful components, and we discussed how to work around the lack of paging support in the *DataList* control.

In particular, we've seen how to build a sort of custom list box in which each item is free and based on a template. We wrote a lot of code in each page, both C# (or Visual Basic .NET) and ASP.NET layout code. It's about time we start practicing with more compact software elements that provide some level of code reusability. In Chapter 10, in fact, we'll cover Web user controls.

# Resources

- Paging in DataList (*http://www.aspalliance.com/das/datalistpaging.aspx*)
- Creating Master-Detail Listings using ASP.NET controls (*http://www.dotnetbips.com/displayarticle.aspx?id=184*)
- Paging Results with ASP.NET's PagedDataSource (*http://www.sitepoint.com/article/921*)

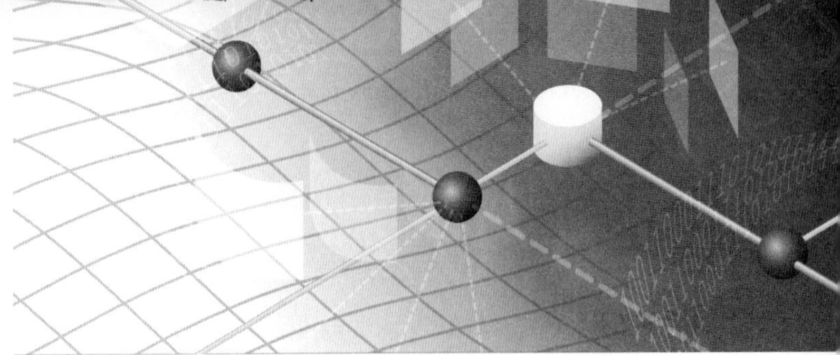

# 10

# Web Forms User Controls

*Divide and rule, a sound motto. Unite and lead, a better one.*
—*Wolfgang Goethe*

While designing the new version of ASP, Microsoft spent a considerable amount of time developing a powerful and effective extensibility model. As a result, the old ASP was completely redesigned and made fully component-based. In doing this, Microsoft killed two birds with a single stone. For one thing, they could easily integrate the new Web platform—ASP.NET—with the surrounding and emerging .NET Framework. In addition, they came up with a stable and consolidated extensibility model based on inheritance and other object-oriented programming techniques. Enter ASP.NET and its families of controls.

At the highest level of abstraction, ASP.NET provides two types of component-based extensibility—custom controls and user controls. With custom controls, you create a new control inheriting from a base class (for example, *WebControl* or *Control*) or extend an existing class. A custom control is primarily a class built to behave like a control and provide a given set of functionalities—for example, a text box or a drop-down list. The user interface is a secondary aspect and is often created programmatically and rendered by concatenating HTML text. (We'll devote the entire Part V of the book to custom controls.) With user controls, you group a few controls together in a sort of embeddable child Web form. Although user controls can appear to be not particularly object-oriented at first, the class you come up with is built on top of a base class—the *UserControl* class.

# What's a User Control, Anyway?

A user control is primarily a Web form made of any combination of server and client controls sewn together with server and client script code. A user control has a rich user interface, even though you can also program it as if it were an encapsulated component. As with Microsoft Visual Basic ActiveX controls, all constituent controls are protected and inaccessible if not made available through a public programming interface.

My favorite definition to describe a user control is that it's an embeddable Web form. The similarity between user controls and pages is not coincidental. (By the way, one of the first names assigned to this technology was *pagelets*.) You create a user control in much the same way you create a Web form. When you're done with code and layout, you give the resulting file a mandatory .ascx extension and then you can use the control with any ASP.NET page. Pages see the new control as a monolithic component and work with it as with any other built-in Web control. If you're familiar with Dynamic HTML (DHTML) scriptlets, look at user controls just as you look at their ASP.NET counterpart. Creating a Web user control is simpler and faster than creating a custom control.

## The *UserControl* Class

User controls are server files with an .ascx extension that are referenced from within ASP.NET pages. They offer Web developers an easy way to capture and reuse common pieces of the user interface. Web user controls are compiled when first requested and cached in ways similar to *Page* objects. As with a page, you can develop them using code-behind or inline code. Unlike pages, though, user controls cannot be called independently. Internet Information Services (IIS), in fact, is configured to block and deny any requests directed at .ascx URLs. As a result, user controls can be called only from .aspx pages or other user controls that contain them.

> **Note** In their simplest form, user controls can be seen as a more flexible alternative to server-side includes (SSI). However, thinking of user controls only as a smarter form of SSI is highly reductive. User controls can expose their own object model instead of copying a piece of static HTML text. They're live objects and can be used just like any other ASP.NET server control.

*UserControl* is the .NET Framework class that represents an .ascx file when called from within an .aspx file. It inherits from *TemplateControl*, which is the base abstract class that provides a base set of functionality to both *Page* and *UserControl*. (This set of relationships is another element that marks the structural affinity between Web pages and user controls.)

```
public class UserControl : TemplateControl, IAttributeAccessor
```

The *TemplateControl* class implements the *INamingContainer* interface and adds to the programming interface of the *Control* class a few methods such as *LoadControl*, *LoadTemplate*, and *ParseControl*. The first two methods load a user control and a template from an external .ascx file. The *ParseControl* method parses an input string into an instance of a control or user control as appropriate.

## Base Properties of User Controls

Table 10-1 lists the properties of the *UserControl* class, but it doesn't include those inherited from *TemplateControl*.

**Table 10-1 Properties of the *UserControl* Class**

| Property | Description |
|---|---|
| *Application* | Gets the *HttpApplicationState* object for the current request. |
| *Attributes* | Gets the collection of all attributes declared in the user control tag. |
| *Cache* | Gets the *Cache* object associated with the current application. |
| *IsPostBack* | Gets whether the user control is being loaded for the first time or in response to a postback event. |
| *Request* | Gets the *HttpRequest* object for the current request. |
| *Response* | Gets the *HttpResponse* object for the current request. |
| *Server* | Gets the *HttpServerUtility* object for the current request. |
| *Session* | Gets the *HttpSessionState* object for the current request. |
| *Trace* | Gets the *TraceContext* object for the current request. |

As you can see, the class provides properties to access all the intrinsic objects of an ASP.NET application plus the *IsPostBack* value, which is critical information to all ASP.NET components. A user control features all the various flavors of ID properties (*ID*, *ClientID*, and *UniqueID*) and acts as a naming container for all its child controls. As usual, the list of child controls is accessible via the *Controls* collection.

## Base Methods of User Controls

The *UserControl* class features only a few methods in addition to those inherited from base classes. Inherited methods include commonly used functions such as *DataBind*, *FindControl*, and *LoadTemplate*. The methods of the *UserControl* class appear in Table 10-2.

**Table 10-2 Methods of the *UserControl* Class**

| Property | Description |
|---|---|
| *DesignerInitialize* | Performs any initialization steps on the user control that are required by RAD designers. |
| *InitializeAsUserControl* | Completes the initialization of the *UserControl* object that has been created declaratively. |
| *MapPath* | Returns the physical file path that corresponds to the given virtual path. Note that the method maps the path from the .ascx file's location, not the page's location. |

The *DesignerInitialize* and *InitializeAsUserControl* methods are rarely used in normal pages and are there mostly for internal use by the .NET Framework. In particular, the *InitializeAsUserControl* method makes sure the user control is initialized properly. The most important thing it does is hook up automatic event handlers. In other words, this method ensures methods named *Page_Load* or *Page_Init*, if present, are invoked during the control's *Load* and *Init* events. Table 10-3 shows the list of automatic event handlers that are supported.

**Table 10-3 Automatic Event Handlers Hooked by the *UserControl* Class**

| Event Handler | Description |
|---|---|
| *OnTransactionAbort*, *Page_AbortTransaction* | Event *AbortTransaction*, occurs when a user aborts a transaction. |
| *OnTransactionCommit*, *Page_CommitTransaction* | Event *CommitTransaction*, occurs when a user commits a transaction in a transacted page. (See Chapter 1.) |
| *Page_DataBind* | Event *DataBind*, occurs when the control binds to a data source. |
| *Page_Error* | Event *Error*, occurs when an unhandled exception is thrown. |
| *Page_Init* | Event *Init*, occurs when the control is initialized. |

**Table 10-3 Automatic Event Handlers Hooked by the *UserControl* Class**

| Event Handler | Description |
|---|---|
| *Page_Load* | Event *Load*, occurs when the control is loaded into the page. |
| *Page_PreRender* | Event *PreRender*, occurs when the control is about to render its contents. |
| *Page_Unload* | Event *Unload*, occurs when the control is going to be unloaded from memory. |

The events listed in this table are also the events supported by all user controls.

## Converting Pages into User Controls

User controls and pages have so much in common that transforming one into the other is no big deal. However, in most cases you need to convert a page into a user control. As we'll see in a moment, it's a simple operation that takes only a few steps.

To start, make sure the user control does not contain any of the following tags: *<html>*, *<body>*, or *<form>*. Eliminating such tags will help to avoid conflicts, because the layout of the control will be merged with the layout of the hosting page and tags like *<html>* and *<body>* must be unique in the final page. As for the *<form>* tag, you can have as many form elements as needed, but only one can be marked with the *runat* attribute. So remove from the original page any reference you might have to a *<form runat="server">* element. If you have HTML forms, on the other hand, leave them on. (An HTML form is the *<form>* tag without the *runat* attribute.)

Once any offending HTML tags have been removed, rename the file with an .ascx extension. This is the key that will enable special treatment on the file. Furthermore, if the page you're converting contains an *@Page* directive, change it to an *@Control* directive.

### The *@Control* Directive

The *@Control* and *@Page* directives share several attributes. The list of attributes supported by user controls is shown in Table 10-4.

**Table 10-4 Attributes of the *@Control* Directive**

| Attribute | Description |
|---|---|
| *AutoEventWireup* | Indicates whether the control's events are automatically bound to methods with a particular name. The default is *true*. |
| *ClassName* | Indicates an alias for the name of the class that will be created to render the user control. This value can be any valid class name, but it should not include a namespace. |
| *CompilerOptions* | A sequence of compiler command-line switches used to compile the control's class. |
| *Debug* | Indicates whether the control should be compiled with debug symbols. If *true*, the source code of the class is not deleted and can be retrieved as discussed in Chapter 2. |
| *Description* | Provides a text description of the control. |
| *EnableViewState* | Indicates whether view state for the user control is maintained across page requests. The default is *true*. |
| *Explicit* | Determines whether the page is compiled using the Visual Basic *Option Explicit* mode. Ignored by languages other than Visual Basic .NET. *False* by default. |
| *Inherits* | Defines a code-behind class for the user control to inherit. Can be any class derived from *UserControl*. |
| *Language* | Specifies the language used throughout the control. |
| *Strict* | Determines whether the page is compiled using the Visual Basic *Option Strict* mode. Ignored by languages other than Visual Basic .NET. *False* by default. |
| *Src* | Specifies the source file name of the code-behind class to dynamically compile when the user control is requested. |
| *WarningLevel* | Indicates the compiler warning level at which you want the compiler to abort compilation for the user control. |

From within a control, you cannot set any property that affects the overall behavior of the page. For example, you cannot enable or disable tracing, nor can you enable or disable session-state management.

You use the *Src* attribute of the *@Control* directive to develop the control using a code-behind schema. The *Src* attribute points to the C# or Visual Basic .NET class that contains the logic of the component. You should note, though, that the *Src* attribute is not recognized and supported by RAD designers such as Microsoft Visual Studio .NET. If you develop the control with Visual Studio .NET, in fact, the code-behind class is bound to the source file in a different way. The code of the class is compiled in the project assembly and made available to the ASP.NET runtime through the *Inherits* attribute. For editing purposes only, Visual Studio .NET tracks the name of the code-behind file using the custom attribute *CodeBehind*. If you use another editor, say Web Matrix, the *Src* attribute can be used to let the ASP.NET runtime know where the code of the component should be read from and dynamically compiled.

> **Note** The *@Control* directive makes it possible to use different languages for the user control and the page. For example, you can use Visual Basic .NET in the user control and C# in the calling page. The interaction between the two occurs at the level of compiled classes and therefore uses the common intermediate language (IL).

Finally, note that giving a user control an alias by using the *ClassName* attribute is not strictly necessary but is highly recommended. The *ClassName* attribute allows the user control to be strongly typed when it is added to a container programmatically.

## Fragment Output Caching

User controls also provide an optimized version of a performance-related feature specific to Web Forms pages—output caching. We'll cover page output caching in great detail in Chapter 14, "ASP.NET State Management." Output caching is an ASP.NET system feature that caches the response of a page so that subsequent requests to the same URL can be satisfied without executing the page but simply by returning the cached output. (By the way, note that IIS 6.0 supports this feature at the Web-server level, thus supporting all types of Web applications.)

Output caching can take place at two levels—for the entire page or for a portion of a page. User controls are the smallest unit of a page whose output is cacheable. To make the entire page cacheable, you place an *@OutputCache* directive within the .aspx file. As a result, the whole output of the page will be cached according to the parameters you specify. To cache only a portion of the page, you first isolate that portion in a user control and then declare the *@OutputCache* directive in the .ascx file.

When caching the output of a user control, you must set at least a couple of attributes—*Duration* and *VaryByParam*. The following code snippet caches the output of the user control for 60 seconds:

```
<% @OutputCache Duration="60" VaryByParam="None" %>
```

Page and control output caching is smart enough to let you save distinct output, even output based on the parameters in a GET query string. See Chapter 14 for more details.

> **Important** Custom controls and user controls are two different and distinct ways to create user-defined controls for ASP.NET applications. Both have pros and cons, and each have advantages in particular scenarios. User controls are ideal if you have to encapsulate a rich and complex user interface and keep it separate from the page. A user control can also be separated into two files—the .ascx file representing the layout, and the file with the code (either a source file or an assembly).
>
> Custom controls are implemented in an assembly and expose both the user interface and the object model programmatically. Unlike user controls, custom controls better leverage the power of object-oriented programming (OOP) in the sense that they can be built from existing classes and new classes can be derived from them. Although user controls could technically be derived from existing controls, the presence of a distinct layout file makes inheritance a bit more problematic.

## Developing User Controls

The structure of a user control is not much different than that of a regular Web page. It is composed of a directive section, inline code, and the graphical layout of the control. The inline code—that is, the *<script runat="server">* block—can be omitted if you use a code-behind file. Although nothing prevents you from writing user-interface-less user controls, the user interface (UI) is the most important part of the control and typically the most compelling reason for writing one. The typical structure of an .ascx file is shown as follows:

```
<%@ Control Language="C#" %>
<script runat="server">

    // Insert user control code here
    //

</script>
<!-- Insert content here -->
```

Many Web sites have pieces of the user interface that must be repeated in a large number of pages. Typical examples are: headers and footers, login and search forms, menus and panels. A login form doesn't need a complex object model and often doesn't need one at all. In other situations, you need to add a layer of logic on top of the control and make it programmable from within the host page. To start with user controls, let's see how to build a tab-strip control with a relatively simple object model.

## Building a *TabStrip* User Control

A typical tab-strip control is made of a series of buttons laid out in a single row. When users click on a tab, the control selects the particular tab and fires an event to the host page. The page will in turn update and refresh its own user interface. Figure 10-1 shows the final form.

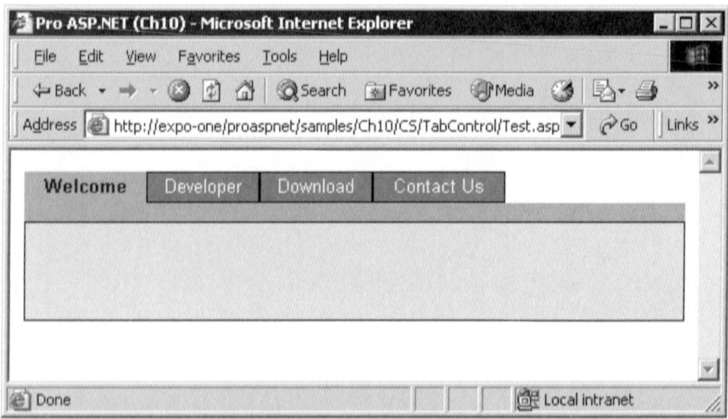


**Figure 10-1** The *TabStrip* control in action within a sample page.

The user interface of the control is generated using a *Repeater* control and consists of a single-row HTML table in which each cell contains a button. Just below the table, an empty, tiny panel separates the tab strip from the rest of the page. The control acts as a simple selector and doesn't include any smart code to process the click event. Whenever the user clicks any of the tabs, a postback event is generated back to the page. The page is also responsible for creating the tabs to display. In this example, we represent a tab with a simple string. In more real-world scenarios, you might want to use an ad hoc class to describe a tab and include a key value, a ToolTip, a Boolean state (enabled/disabled), or maybe a URL.

```
<%@ Control Language="C#" ClassName="TabStrip" %>
<%@ Import Namespace="System.Drawing" %>

<script runat="server">
// Tabs to display
public ArrayList Tabs;
```

```
private void Page_Init(object sender, EventArgs e) {
    Tabs = new ArrayList();
}

private void Page_Load(object sender, EventArgs e) {
    if (!IsPostBack) {
        BindData();
    }
}

private void BindData() {
    __theTabStrip.DataSource = Tabs;
    __theTabStrip.DataBind();
}
</script>

<asp:Repeater runat="server" id="__theTabStrip">
    <headertemplate>
        <table cellpadding="0" cellspacing="0" border="0" ><tr>
    </headertemplate>

    <itemtemplate>
        <td>
            <asp:button runat="server" id="__theTab"
                style="border:solid 1px black"
            text='<%# Container.DataItem %>' />
        </td>
    </itemtemplate>

    <footertemplate>
        </tr></table>
    </footertemplate>
</asp:Repeater>
<asp:panel runat="server" id="__theSep" width="100%" backcolor="gray" />
```

The *Tabs* array contains the string to display as the caption of each tab. The object is initialized in the control's *Page_Init* event and consumed during the rendering phase of the control. The caller page typically populates the *Tabs* collection in its *Page_Load* event.

Before taking the *TabStrip* user control to the next level, let's see what's needed to include a user control in a Web page.

## Including a User Control in a Page

A user control is inserted in a Web page by using a custom tag marked with the *runat* attribute. The control instance has an ID and can be programmed using that name. The server tag is divided in two parts—a tag prefix and a tag name. In the following code snippet, the tag prefix is *mspo* and the tag name is *tabstrip*.

```
<mspo:tabstrip runat="server" id="menu" />
```

If you give the control the asp prefix, or no prefix at all, the ASP.NET runtime will look for the needed class only in the *System.Web* assembly. Because the user control is not implemented there, an exception is thrown. How do you register a tag name and prefix for a user control? And how do you bind both with an .ascx file?

## The *@Register* Directive

The *@Register* directive associates aliases with namespaces and class names to provide a concise notation to reference custom and user controls within Web pages. Table 10-5 details the attributes of the directive.

**Table 10-5 Attributes of the *@Register* Directive**

| Attribute | Description |
|---|---|
| *Assembly* | The assembly in which the namespace associated with the tag prefix resides. The assembly name does not include a file extension. |
| *Namespace* | The namespace to associate with the tag prefix. |
| *Src* | The relative or absolute location of the user control file to associate with the tag prefix and name. The file name must include the .ascx extension. |
| *TagName* | A tag name to alias the custom or user control. (It is *tabstrip* in the code snippet shown previously.) |
| *TagPrefix* | A tag prefix to alias the namespace of the control, if any. (It is *mspo* in the code snippet shown previously.) |

You use the *@Register* directive in one of two ways. The first way is to register a custom control—that is, a server control that you write as a class—and you use the following syntax:

```
<%@ Register tagprefix="..." namespace="..." assembly="..." %>
```

The second way is to register a user control. To do this, you use the following syntax:

```
<%@ Register tagprefix="..." tagname="..." src="..." %>
```

A server control is represented by two parts—a prefix and a tag name. The prefix identifies a namespace and subsequently the assembly in which the code for the user control is located. For user controls, the namespace defaults to *ASP* and the class name is the value of the control's *ClassName* attribute. For example, it is *ASP.TabStrip* for the sample code we just discussed. The assembly is dynamically created the first time the ASP.NET runtime accesses the resource. The tag name is any unique name you use to refer to the user control within a client page. Different pages can use different tag names for the same user control.

For a custom control, you indicate the namespace and assembly and specify any namespace prefix you like better. The tag name, on the other hand, is fixed and must match the custom control class name.

### Setting Up a User Control

Although absolute path names can be used to register a user control, you should always use relative names. However, you should be aware that any code within a user control is always executed taking the URL of the control as the base URL. This means that if the user control needs to access an image in the application's Images folder, you can't just use a relative path like the following one:

```
<img src="images/logo.gif" />
```

To address the right location, you could either move one or more folders back or, better yet, indicate a relative path that begins from the root. In the former case, you use .. to move one level up in the virtual Web space; in the latter case, you use the tilde (~) character to indirectly refer the root directory of the application.

```
<img src="~/images/logo.gif" />
```

To register the *TabStrip* control, you use the following registration directive:

```
<%@ Register TagPrefix="mspo" TagName="TabStrip" Src="tabstrip.ascx" %>
```

An instance of the user control is created upon page loading. Just as for Web pages, a class that represents the control is created on the fly and cached in the ASP.NET temporary folders. Any updates to the source code of the .ascx file (or the code-behind class) are immediately detected and invalidate the existing assembly. In no case do you need to compile the user control to make it available to the page. (To sum it up, there's just one case in which you need to compile it first—when the control is included in code-behind pages. I'll say more about this in the "Getting Serious About User Controls" section later in this chapter.)

## Building a User-Control Object Model

When running, a user control is an instance of a dynamically created class. The class derives from *UserControl* and belongs to the *ASP* namespace. The actual name of the user control class depends on whether or not you set the *ClassName* attribute in the *@Control* directive. If a class name was not specified, the ASP.NET runtime generates a default name based on the .ascx file name. For example, a user control defined in a sample .ascx file generates a class named *ASP.sample_ascx*.

For a user control, as well as for Web pages, every property or method that is marked as public is externally callable and, as such, part of the control's object model. The following code snippet declares a couple of read/write properties that represent the background and foreground color of the unselected tabs:

```
<script runat="server">
    public Color BackColor
    {
        get {return (Color) ViewState["BackColor"];}
        set {ViewState["BackColor"] = value;}
    }
    public Color ForeColor
    {
        get {return (Color) ViewState["ForeColor"];}
        set {ViewState["ForeColor"] = value;}
    }
    ⋮
</script>
```

The qualifier *public* is essential to make the property (or the method) externally visible and callable.

> **Note** To make sure the contents of a property are retrieved when the page posts back, you should store it in the control's *ViewState* collection. Basically, you use a slot in the *ViewState* as the storage medium of the property. However, note that if you're simply exposing at the user-control level the property of an embedded control, you don't need to resort to the view state. In that case, in fact, the embedded control takes care of the variable persistence.

## Adding Properties

At a minimum, the *TabStrip* control should expose properties to let you add tabs, track the current index, and set background and foreground colors for selected and unselected tabs.

```
<script runat="server">
// Tabs to display
public ArrayList Tabs = new ArrayList();

// Current Tab (read-only)
```

```
public int CurrentTabIndex
{
    get {return (int) ViewState["CurrentTabIndex"];}
}

// Background color
public Color BackColor
{
    get {return (Color) ViewState["BackColor"];}
    set {ViewState["BackColor"] = value;}
}

// Selected background color
public Color SelectedBackColor
{
    get {return (Color) ViewState["SelectedBackColor"];}
    set {ViewState["SelectedBackColor"] = value;}
}

// Foreground color
public Color ForeColor
{
    get {return (Color) ViewState["ForeColor"];}
    set {ViewState["ForeColor"] = value;}
}

// Selected foreground color
public Color SelectedForeColor
{
    get {return (Color) ViewState["SelectedForeColor"];}
    set {ViewState["SelectedForeColor"] = value;}
}
⋮
</script>
```

A property on a user control is any publicly accessible variable. If you need to perform special tasks when reading or writing the value of the property, you can define *get* and *set* accessors. A *get* accessor is a special procedure that returns the value of the property. Likewise, the *set* accessor is a method that sets the value of the property. The lack of an accessor automatically disables the corresponding function, thus making the property read-only or write-only. In the preceding code, the *CurrentTabIndex* property is read-only.

All the properties except *Tabs* use accessors and persist their value to the control's view state. The contents of the *Tabs* collection are lost and must be rebuilt whenever the page posts back. As we'll see in more detail in Chapter 14, the view state might affect the download time of the page. All the information you store in the *ViewState* collection, in fact, is encoded as Base64 and transmitted back and forth between the Web server and the browser. Information that is not strictly tied to choices made by the user should not be stored in the view state. Following this guideline will keep Web pages lean and mean.

> **Note** According to the aforementioned guideline, color properties should not be stored in the view state because the page author is the only one responsible for their values. As such, you can explicitly hard-code the colors to use in the control's declaration within the host page. The same can't be said for the *CurrentTabIndex* property, whose value depends on what the user does.

User control properties can be set both declaratively and programmatically. If you opt for a declarative approach, the name of the property is used as a tag attribute.

```
<mspo:tabstrip runat="server" id="menu"
    selectedbackcolor="cyan" />
```

In this case, you can use strings only to specify the value. To set the background color, you use a string that represents the desired color. ASP.NET will attempt to convert the assigned string into a valid value of the expected type. On the other hand, if you set a property programmatically, you must pass values of the correct type.

```
void Page_Load(object sender, EventArgs e)
{
    // Since the Tabs collection is not stored in the view state,
    // you must populate it each time the page posts back. This code
    // must be placed outside the IsPostBack branch.
    menu.Tabs.Add("Welcome");
    menu.Tabs.Add("Developer");
    menu.Tabs.Add("Download");
    menu.Tabs.Add("Contact Us");

    if (!IsPostBack)
    {
        // Do here all the things that need to be done only the
        // first time the control is loaded in the page.
        // For example, select here the page to be displayed
        // by default.
        ⋮
    }

    // Set colors programmatically
```

```
    menu.SelectedBackColor = Color.Green;
    menu.SelectedForeColor = Color.White;
    menu.BackColor = Color.LightGray;
    menu.ForeColor = Color.Black;
}
```

The instance of the user control is identified using the ID of the control. If you're handling properties that do not rely on the view state, you should configure them each time the page posts back, without distinguishing between the first load and postbacks.

The selected tab is rendered with different colors, which are applied through data-bound expressions, as shown here:

```
<itemtemplate>
    <td>
        <asp:button runat="server" id="__theTab"
            BorderWidth="1px"
            BorderStyle="solid"
            BorderColor='<%# SetBorderColor(Container) %>'
            text='<%# Container.DataItem %>'
            font-bold='<%# (Container.ItemIndex == CurrentTabIndex) %>'
            backcolor='<%# SetBackColor(Container) %>'
            forecolor='<%# SetForeColor(Container) %>' />
    </td>
</itemtemplate>
```

The *SetXXX* functions are internal members that compare the current tab index with the index of the item being created and decide which color to apply.

```
private Color SetBackColor(object elem)
{
    RepeaterItem item = (RepeaterItem) elem;
    if (item.ItemIndex == CurrentTabIndex)
        return SelectedBackColor;
    return BackColor;
}
```

## Initializing the User Control

When you create a user control with inline code—as we're doing here—you can't write code that executes in the user control class constructor. If you just add some code for the default constructor, you get a compile error because the ASP.NET runtime has already defined a constructor with the same parameter types.

```
public TabStrip()
{
    ⋮
}
```

Any constructor overloads you define will be ignored by the ASP.NET runtime. However, you can use such overloads if you create the user control dynamically. (We'll discuss this later in the section "Loading Controls Dynamically".) If the user control is developed with a code-behind, the constructor can be successfully managed. So what's the issue if you can't execute your own code in the default constructor?

Suppose you have a few properties that should take default values. Normally, you would initialize these values in the class constructor and set them to default values. In the case we're considering, we need to instantiate the *ArrayList* object that implements the *Tabs* collection and set the default page index and colors. If the properties do not make use of accessors, you simply assign a default value when declaring them.

```
public ArrayList Tabs = new ArrayList();
```

This is not possible, though, if you need accessors.

The *Page_Init* event is the first piece of the control's code in which you can insert your own instructions.

```
private void Page_Init(object sender, EventArgs e)
{
    // Check to see if defined declaratively or in
    // the page's Init event
    if (ViewState["SelectedBackColor"] == null)
        SelectedBackColor = Color.White;
    if (ViewState["SelectedForeColor"] == null)
        SelectedForeColor = Color.Blue;
    if (ViewState["BackColor"] == null)
        BackColor = Color.Gray;
    if (ViewState["ForeColor"] == null)
        ForeColor = Color.White;
    if (ViewState["CurrentTabIndex"] == null)
        ViewState["CurrentTabIndex"] = 0;
}
```

Note, though, that the control's *Page_Init* event fires when the ASP.NET runtime already did a lot of work constructing the page. In particular, it comes after the user control has been instantiated and configured with the properties declaratively set in the page layout. The *Init* event of the control precedes the page *Init* event. In contrast, the page *Load* event comes earlier than the *Load* event on child controls.

In short, you can't simply treat the *Page_Init* event of the control as a replacement for the constructor. If you do so, you'll overwrite any settings defined in the control's tag. So how can you assign default values to all properties without overwriting any values that might have been set declaratively?

You should set the default value only if the property is unassigned. The way in which you detect that the property is unassigned is application specific. For example, if the property is part of the view state, you can check the *ViewState* collection against null.

## Adding Methods

The next step in the process of building a functional and reusable tab-strip control is adding a method to programmatically select a particular tab. So far, in fact, the selection can only be triggered by the user when she clicks a button. The *Select* method will do that programmatically. Here is the prototype of the *Select* method:

```
public void Select(int index)
```

The method takes an integer argument, which is the 0-based index of the tab to select. Internally, it sets the current tab index and rebinds the data.

```
public void Select(int index) {
    // Ensure the index is a valid value, otherwise select the first
    if (index <0 || index >Tabs.Count)
        index = 0;

    // Updates the current index. Must write to the view state
    // because the CurrentTabIndex property is read-only
    ViewState["CurrentTabIndex"] = index;

    // Ensure the bottom panel is of the selected color
    __theSep.BackColor = SelectedBackColor;

    // Refresh the user interface
    BindData();
}
```

A method on a user control is simply a public method defined either as inline code or in the code-behind class. Note that the *Select* method can't set the current tab index by using the public property. The reason is that the property is read-only (that is, it lacks a *set* accessor), and subsequently no code within the class can set it explicitly. The workaround is to directly access the *ViewState*, where the values of the property are actually stored.

The sample page can now offer some user-interface elements to let users select tabs programmatically. The following code snippet shows a text box in which you can type the index of the tab to select and a link button to execute the code:

```
<asp:textbox runat="server" id="tabIndex" width="30px" />
<asp:linkbutton runat="server" text="Select tab" onclick="OnSelectTab" />
```

The *OnSelectTab* event handler simply calls the *Select* method on the user control, as Figure 10-2 demonstrates.

```
void OnSelectTab(object sender, EventArgs e) {
    menu.Select(Convert.ToInt32(tabIndex.Text));
}
```

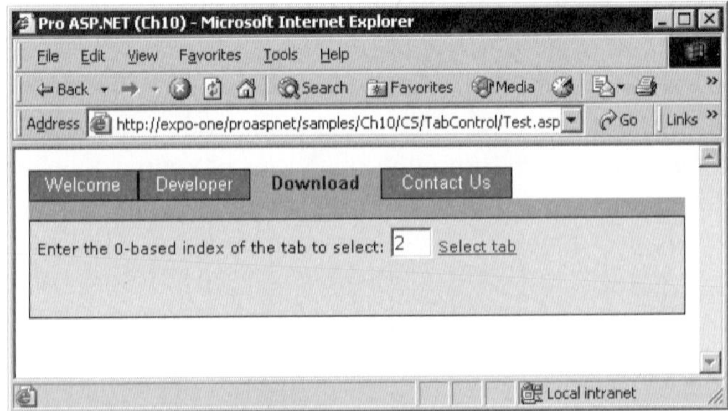


**Figure 10-2** A new link button commands the selection of a particular tab.

The *Select* method acts as the *set* accessor of the *CurrentTabIndex* property. If you want to read the index of the current tab, you use the property; if you want to programmatically set a particular tab, you use the method.

## Handling User-Control Events

So far we've built a user control that displays its own user interface and allows users to select tabs. For a control such as the *TabStrip*, though, the key feature has not been implemented yet. How can a page that hosts the control be notified of a user's clickings? A tab strip makes sense if the page can detect the selection changed event and properly refresh. For example, the page could generate different content according to the selected tab; alternatively, it can redirect the user to a child page within a frame or simply jump to a new URL. To let the page know about the selection, we must add an event to the user control.

### Adding the *SelectionChanged* Event

Within the *TabStrip* control, the selection changes whenever the user clicks the buttons or when the page calls the *Select* method. Let's define an event named *SelectionChanged*.

```
public event SelectionChangedEventHandler SelectionChanged;
```

An event is a special property bound to a delegate. A delegate is a reference to a method signature. An instance of a delegate is actually a pointer to a function with a well-known signature. The .NET Framework provides a general-purpose delegate for event handlers—the *EventHandler* class. Here is the prototype of such event handlers:

```
public delegate void EventHandler(object sender, EventArgs e);
```

The *EventHandler* delegate represents all methods that take an *object* and an *EventArgs* argument and return *void*. This predefined delegate is good as long as you don't need to pass custom data back to the caller. You should use it only for events that work as simple notifications of some server-side event. In this case, we need to pass at least the index of the selected tab. So let's define a custom delegate and a custom event data structure.

```
public delegate void SelectionChangedEventHandler(
    object sender, SelectionChangedEventArgs e);
```

A custom delegate for the event differs from *EventHandler* for the custom data structure used to carry event arguments. The common naming convention for events entails using the name of the event (*SelectionChanged* in this case) to prefix both the delegate and the data structure name.

```
public class SelectionChangedEventArgs : EventArgs
{
    public int Position;     // 0-based index of the selected tab
}
```

The *SelectionChangedEventArgs* structure inherits from *EventArgs* and adds an integer property that represents the 0-based index of the selected tab. An instance of this data structure will be created and initialized when the event occurs within the user control.

## Firing a Custom Event

To better handle custom events, you might want to define a helper routine like the one shown at the end of this paragraph. The name you choose for this routine is unimportant. Likewise, the method qualifiers (*protected*, *virtual*) are subject to your personal preferences. Let's say that declaring such a helper routine as protected and overridable is considered a best programming practice that is widely employed in the .NET Framework itself. My suggestion is that either you declare it as protected and virtual or don't declare it at all.

```
// Helper function that fires the event by executing user-defined code
protected virtual void OnSelectionChanged(SelectionChangedEventArgs e)
{
    // SelectionChanged is the event property. Check if the user defined it
```

```
    if (SelectionChanged != null)
        SelectionChanged(this, e);
}
```

The routine doesn't do much—it just ensures the event property is not null and makes the call. However, it adds an extra layer of code that, if made overridable, can help derived classes to customize the behavior more easily and effectively.

At this point, firing the event becomes simply a matter of initializing the data structure and calling the helper function. The event is fired by the *Select* method.

```
public void Select(int index) {
    // Ensure the index is a valid value
    if (index <0 || index >Tabs.Count)
        index = 0;

    // Updates the current index. Must write to the view state
    // because the CurrentTabIndex property is read-only
    ViewState["CurrentTabIndex"] = index;

    // Ensure the bottom panel is of the selected color
    __theSep.BackColor = SelectedBackColor;

    // Refresh the UI
    BindData();

    // Fire the event to the client
    SelectionChangedEventArgs ev = new SelectionChangedEventArgs();
    ev.Position = CurrentTabIndex;
    OnSelectionChanged(ev);
}
```

When the user clicks on the tabs, the underlying *Repeater* control we used to create the control's user interface fires an *ItemCommand* event. The embedded handler for the *ItemCommand* event just calls into *Select*.

```
private void ItemCommand(object sender, RepeaterCommandEventArgs e)
{
    // Select the tab that corresponds to the clicked button
    Select(e.Item.ItemIndex);
}
```

Now that the user control fires an event, let's see what's needed on the caller page to detect and handle it.

## Handling a Custom Event

A .NET component that wants to sink events emitted by controls must write a handler whose prototype matches that of the event delegate. How you bind the handler with the event on a particular instance of the component is language specific. For example, in C#, you create a new instance of the event handler class and add it to the component's event property.

```
// YourHandler is the actual name of the handler in your code
menu.SelectionChanged += new SelectionChangedEventHandler(YourHandler);
```

In Visual Basic .NET, you can use the *AddHandler* keyword, as shown here:

```
' YourHandler is the actual name of the handler in your code
AddHandler menu.SelectionChanged, AddressOf YourHandler
```

This technique is not always necessary in ASP.NET applications. In ASP.NET, in fact, you can also register event handlers declaratively using the *OnXXX* attribute, where *XXX* stands for the actual name of the event property.

```
<mspo:menu runat="server" id="menu"
    SelectedBackColor="cyan"
    OnSelectionChanged="SelectionChanged" />
```

Here is the *SelectionChanged* event handler:

```
void SelectionChanged(object sender, TabStrip.SelectionChangedEventArgs e)
{
    msg.Text = "Selected tab #" + e.Position.ToString();
}
```

Note that the name of the custom event data class must be prefixed with the name of the user control class. The reason for this requirement is that the event data class is defined within the user control class. Figure 10-3 shows the *TabStrip* user control, which includes a *SelectionChanged* event handler.

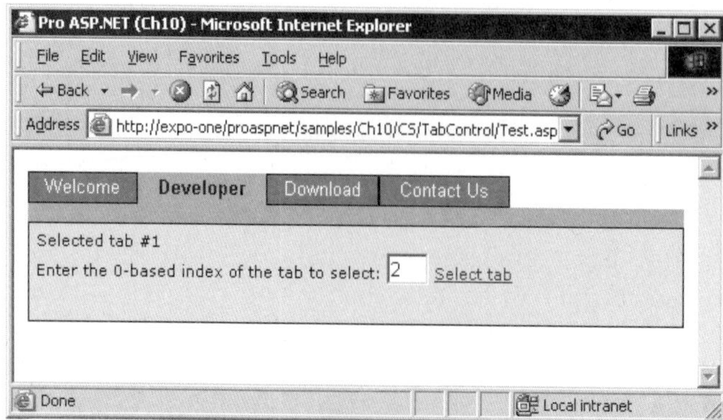


**Figure 10-3** The user selects the second tab, and the application detects the change and properly refreshes.

# Getting Serious About User Controls

In Chapter 9, "ASP.NET Iterative Controls," we created quite complex user interfaces by combining iterative controls and HTML advanced features such as text overflow. That code addresses common needs and, therefore, might be employed in other pages or applications. Unfortunately, as we wrote it, it's hardly reusable. To work around this issue, let's try to rewrite as a user control some of the *Repeater*-based code we discussed in Chapter 9. In doing so, we'll also address an interesting and real-world aspect of control development—data binding. Incidentally, data binding is also a reasonable next step for the user control we have just built. A data-bound version of the *TabStrip* user control would use the results of a SQL query to automatically generate the tabs.

Earlier in this chapter, we mentioned that user controls can be developed using inline code as well as a code-behind. For the sake of completeness, in the next sample, we'll use and examine the code-behind approach.

# Building Data-Bound User Controls

In most cases, a data-bound user control is not really different than a data-free control. The only relevant difference is that a data-bound control features a few properties that bind it to an *ICollection*-based data source object—mostly, but not necessarily, an ADO.NET object. In Chapter 9, we used a *Repeater* control to build a list of buttons, each with a letter name. Such neat and handy functionality clashes with all the boilerplate code that is needed to set it up. With their powerful mix of user-interface and back-end code, user controls seem to be the right tool to leverage for reaching a satisfactory solution.

## The *ButtonList* User Control

The *ButtonList* control is made of an .ascx file and a code-behind file. Its link is set in the *@Control* directive. The layout of the .ascx file is fairly simple and contains a *Repeater* control to enumerate all the bound items and create a push button for each. In addition, a thin one-row table is placed below the *Repeater* for a better graphical effect.

```
<%@ Control Language="C#" ClassName="ButtonList"
    Inherits="ProAspNet.CS.Ch10.ButtonList"
    Src="ButtonList.ascx.cs" %>

<asp:repeater runat="server" id="__theMenu">
    <HeaderTemplate>
        <table border="0" cellspacing="0" cellpadding="0"><tr>
    </HeaderTemplate>
```

```
    <ItemTemplate>
        <td valign="bottom">
            <asp:button runat="server" id="TheButton"
                style="border:solid 1px gray" />
        </td>
    </ItemTemplate>

    <FooterTemplate>
        </tr></table>
    </FooterTemplate>
</asp:repeater>
<asp:panel runat="server" id="__theSep" width="100%" />
```

Because the control is developed using a code-behind, you must use the *Inherits* attribute on the *@Control* directive. It tells the ASP.NET runtime what the base class is from which the dynamic control class is to be derived. You set *Inherits* with the fully qualified name of the code-behind class. If you use Visual Studio .NET, this happens by default; if you use Web Matrix, on the other hand, remember to set it yourself. If you omit the *Inherits* attribute, the ASP.NET runtime would ignore your code-behind class and use *UserControl* instead. In addition to using *Inherits*, you can specify *Src* to let ASP.NET know about the location of the source code to compile. If *Src* is omitted, ASP.NET assumes that the needed assembly is already available in one of the common paths and complains if the needed assembly isn't found.

The .ascx file contains only the skeleton of the control's user interface. As you can see, there's no data-binding expression and no event handlers. When you work with code-behind classes, isolating all executable code in the source file is considered a best practice because it guarantees full separation between code and layout.

### The Programming Interface of the *ButtonList* Control

The *ButtonList* control exposes a few properties, as listed in Table 10-6. These properties are primarily related to the data-binding mechanism, which leverages the data binding of the underlying *Repeater* control.

**Table 10-6 Properties of the *ButtonList* Control**

| Property | Description |
|---|---|
| *ButtonWidth* | Integer that indicates the width in pixels of the buttons |
| *CurrentButtonCommand* | Gets the command name of the currently selected button |
| *CurrentButtonIndex* | Gets the 0-based index of the currently selected button |
| *DataSource* | Indicates the data source used to populate the control |

**Table 10-6 Properties of the *ButtonList* Control**

| Property | Description |
|---|---|
| *DataTextField* | Indicates the name of the data source column used to render the caption of the buttons |
| *DataValueField* | Indicates the name of the data-source column used to express the command associated with the buttons |

The *DataSource* property plays the same role as in other data-bound controls. It provides a collection of data items the control will use to populate its own user interface. A couple of columns from this data source are used to render the caption and the command name of each button. The command name of a *Button* object is a string that uniquely identifies that button and is used to detect events. When binding data to this control, you should set *DataValueField* to a column with unique values. Note that the value will be converted into a string, so be sure you choose a column that maintains unique values after being converted into a string. All the properties except *DataSource* are cached in the view state.

The contents of the *DataSource* are cached internally in the ASP.NET *Cache* object. This shouldn't be a big issue because the number of records bound to the *ButtonList* control is not expected to be high.

```
public object DataSource {
    get {return Cache[DataSourceName];}
    set {Cache[DataSourceName] = value;}
}
```

The data source is cached in a slot with a unique name. The name is determined using the ID of the control. This guarantees that multiple controls in the same page work correctly and without conflicts. As mentioned, all the other properties are cached in the control's view state, which, in turn, is flushed in the page's view state.

```
public string DataTextField {
    get {return (string) ViewState["DataTextField"];}
    set {ViewState["DataTextField"] = value;}
}
```

The view state is specific to the individual control, so there's no need to figure out a scheme for unique names. When writing a *get* accessor for a property, you should always make sure the value you read is not null. This is especially true if you deal with objects such as *Cache*, *Session* or *ViewState*.

The overall data-binding mechanism of the *ButtonList* control mirrors the data-binding engine of the *Repeater* control. In particular, the *DataBind* method is nothing more than a wrapper.

```
private void DataBind() {
    __theMenu.DataSource = DataSource;
    __theMenu.DataBind();
}
```

The *ButtonClicked* event completes the programming interface of the control. The event fires whenever the user clicks a button. The client page receives a custom structure containing the index and the command of the button. We'll return to this in the next section, "Generating the Output." The implementation of the event is identical to the event we discussed for the *TabStrip* user control earlier in this chapter.

> **Note** The slots in the *Cache* object are subject to be emptied if the system runs low on memory. It's a good practice to make sure you always check against null all the properties that depend on *Cache*. If the slot is null, your code should be smart enough to restore the correct value.

## Generating the Output

When the control is initialized—that is, after the constructor is called—it hooks up its own set of events. In this case, we need to register handlers for some events fired by the embedded *Repeater* control.

```
private void HookUpEvents() {
    __theMenu.ItemCommand += new RepeaterCommandEventHandler(ItemCommand);
    __theMenu.ItemCreated += new RepeaterItemEventHandler(ItemCreated);
    __theMenu.ItemDataBound += new RepeaterItemEventHandler(ItemBound);
}
```

During the *ItemCreated* event, we take care of the appearance of each button and decide about colors, borders, and size. In particular, the selected button is larger than others and highlighted.

```
protected void ItemCreated(object sender, RepeaterItemEventArgs e)
{
    if (e.Item.ItemType != ListItemType.Item &&
        e.Item.ItemType != ListItemType.AlternatingItem)
        return;
```

```
    // Retrieve the item being created
    RepeaterItem item = e.Item;
    bool isSelected = IsSelectedItem(item);
    Button btn = (Button) item.FindControl("TheButton");

    // Customize the appearance
    if (isSelected) {
        btn.BackColor = SelectedBackColor;
        btn.ForeColor = SelectedForeColor;
        btn.Height = Unit.Pixel(23);
        btn.Width = Unit.Pixel(ButtonWidth*150/100);
    }
    else
    {
        btn.BackColor = BackColor;
        btn.ForeColor = ForeColor;
        btn.Height = Unit.Pixel(20);
        btn.Width = Unit.Pixel(ButtonWidth);
    }
}
```

Note that although the colors are not exposed as public properties, they are used as if they were. (If you want to enhance the *ButtonList* control, this feature shouldn't be too hard to add, especially in light of your previous experience with the *TabStrip* control.) Pay attention to the type of the item being created, and exit the *ItemCreated* event handler if the *Repeater* is not creating an item of type *Item* or *AlternatingItem*.

When *ItemCreated* fires, the item has not yet been bound to data. So, to adjust the caption and the command name for the button, we need to wait for the *ItemDataBound* event.

```
protected void ItemBound(object sender, RepeaterItemEventArgs e)
{
    if (e.Item.ItemType != ListItemType.Item &&
        e.Item.ItemType != ListItemType.AlternatingItem)
        return;

    // Retrieve the item being bound to data
    RepeaterItem item = e.Item;
    Button btn = (Button) item.FindControl("TheButton");

    // Bind to data
    btn.Text = DataBinder.Eval(item.DataItem,
        DataTextField).ToString();
    btn.CommandName = DataBinder.Eval(item.DataItem,
        DataValueField).ToString();
}
```

The *DataBinder* class is used to bind properties with data. Note that the code-behind class (from which all this code is excerpted) doesn't know anything about ADO.NET and doesn't even import the *System.Data* namespace.

Finally, when the user clicks one of the buttons, the *Repeater* fires the *ItemCommand* event.

```
protected void ItemCommand(object sender, RepeaterCommandEventArgs e)
{
    // Update the internal state
    CurrentButtonCommand = e.CommandName;
    CurrentButtonIndex = e.Item.ItemIndex;

    // Refresh the UI
    DataBind();

    // Fire the ButtonClicked event to the client
    ButtonClickedEventArgs ev = new ButtonClickedEventArgs();
    ev.ButtonCommand = CurrentButtonCommand;
    ev.ButtonIndex = CurrentButtonIndex;
    OnButtonClicked(ev);
}
```

The *RepeaterCommandEventArgs* class contains both the index of the clicked item and its command name. These two pieces of information are packed into a *ButtonClickedEventArgs* structure and passed to the client's handler, if any.

### Setting Up a Client Page

So much for the *ButtonList* control, let's see how to set up a client page that intends to use the control. The following directive registers the control for use within the page:

```
<%@ Register TagPrefix="mspo"
TagName="ButtonList" Src="buttonlist.ascx" %>
```

Once more, note that you can change at will the content of the *TagName* and *TagPrefix* attributes. If the control has been developed using code-behind, chances are you have to also import the namespace of the control. This namespace might be needed to access any public element that is included in the package, such as enumeration and related classes. If you use code-behind, you can control the location of each public element in the namespace. If inline code is used, everything is the child of the user control class. Let's consider the following code snippet, which reflects the structure of the code-behind class:

```
namespace ProAspNet.CS.Ch10
{
    public class ButtonClickedEventArgs : EventArgs
    {
```

```
        public string ButtonCommand;
        public int ButtonIndex;
    }

    public class ButtonList : UserControl
    {
        ⋮
    }
}
```

In this case, the *ButtonClickedEventArgs* class is not a child of *ButtonList*. With inline code, the overall structure of the code would have been slightly different.

```
namespace ASP
{
    public class ButtonList : UserControl
    {
        ⋮

        public class ButtonClickedEventArgs : EventArgs
        {
            ⋮
        }
    }
}
```

Defining the *ButtonClickedEventArgs* class outside the user control class is just a matter of preference. If you want, you can certainly move that code as a subclass within the *ButtonList* definition. If you do this, there's no need to import the *ProAspNet.CS.Ch10* namespace, but you should prefix the class name with *ButtonList*. The following code declares a couple of *ButtonList* controls sharing the same handler for the *ButtonClicked* event:

```
<mspo:buttonlist runat="server" id="initialStrip"
    onbuttonclicked="ButtonClicked" />
<mspo:buttonlist runat="server" id="yearStrip"
    buttonwidth="50"
    onbuttonclicked="ButtonClicked" />
```

The page is responsible for downloading data from a data source and binding it to the controls.

```
void Page_Load(object sender, EventArgs e) {
    if (!IsPostBack) {
        BindInitials();
        BindYears();
    }
}
```

In the sample code we're considering, *BindInitials* and *BindYears* execute the following queries:

```
-- Get the first letter of all customer names
SELECT DISTINCT substring(companyname, 1, 1) AS Initial FROM customers
-- Get the years for which at least an order exists
SELECT DISTINCT year(orderdate) AS year FROM orders
```

The *ButtonList* controls are initialized with the following code:

```
initialStrip.DataSource = _data.Tables["Initials"];
initialStrip.DataTextField = "Initial";
initialStrip.DataValueField = "Initial";
initialStrip.DataBind();
```

Figure 10-4 shows the final results.

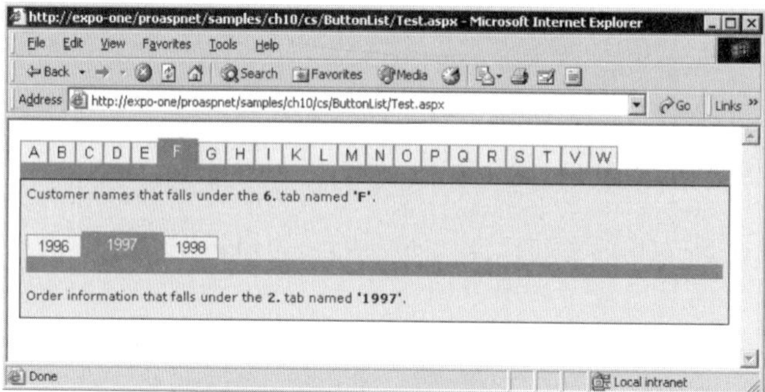


**Figure 10-4** Two *ButtonList* controls in action within the same page.

The code that handles the *ButtonClicked* event for both controls is as follows:

```
// Namespace "ProAspNet.CS.Ch10" imported
void ButtonClicked(object sender, ButtonClickedEventArgs e)
{
    string t1 = "Customer names that falls under the <b>{0}.</b> " +
                "tab named <b>'{1}'</b>.";
    string t2 = "Order information that falls under the <b>{0}.</b> " +
                "tab named <b>'{1}'</b>."

    // Recognize the sender and update a label control
    if (sender.Equals(initialStrip))
        msg1.Text = String.Format(t1, 1 + e.ButtonIndex, e.ButtonCommand);
    else
        msg2.Text = String.Format(t2, 1 + e.ButtonIndex, e.ButtonCommand);
}
```

## Loading Controls Dynamically

Just like any other ASP.NET server controls, user controls can be created programmatically. Unlike server controls, though, you normally don't use the *new* operator to instantiate user controls but resort to the *LoadControl* method on the containing page.

```
Control ctl = LoadControl("ButtonList.ascx");
```

*LoadControl* returns a generic reference to a *Control* object, so you need to cast the reference to the appropriate strong type to be able to set individual properties and use the control at its fullest. The *ClassName* attribute in the *@Control* directive represents the only means you have to name the user control class in a way that is both easy to remember and consistent with the expected behavior.

To cast an object to a user-control strong type, you need to have a reference to the assembly that contains the compiled code of the control. Doing this is precisely the role of the *@Reference* directive.

### The *@Reference* Directive

When you create the user control programmatically, the strong type for the user control is available to the page only after you have created a reference to it. The following code creates a reference to the *ButtonList* user control created in the buttonlist.ascx file:

```
<%@ Reference Control="buttonlist.ascx" %>
```

The net effect of this directive is to make available in the context of the Web Forms page a reference to a type that represents the specified control. The type is named *ASP.buttonlist_ascx* if the user control doesn't contain a *ClassName* attribute; otherwise, it is named *ASP.XXX*, in which *XXX* is the content of the *ClassName* attribute.

The *@Reference* directive declaratively indicates that another user control or page should be dynamically compiled and linked against the current page or control. The directive supports only two, mutually exclusive, attributes—*Page* and *Control*. Both point to a URL and identify the Web element to bind to the current page or control. Once you hold a reference to the .ascx file, you can create instances of the user control programmatically.

```
ButtonList btn = (ButtonList) LoadControl("buttonlist.ascx");
```

In general, you use the *@Register* directive to register user controls that are declared in the page layout and instantiated by the system. You use the *@Reference* directive if you create the controls programmatically.

> **Note** If the user control has been developed using inline code, you need *@Reference* to reference to its strong type. However, if the user control has been authored using a code-behind class, *@Register* would also suffice. If both the caller page and the user control apply the code-behind model, yet another change is needed. We'll discuss this change later in the "Referencing User Controls from Code-Behind Pages" section.

## Adding Dynamically Created Controls to the Page

Creating and casting the user control is only the first step. After setting all the individual properties you need to customize, you have the problem of adding the control to the container page. Doing this is as easy as adding the control to the *Controls* collection of the page.

```
ButtonList btn = (ButtonList) LoadControl("buttonlist.ascx");
// customize the ButtonList control
Page.Controls.Add(btn);
```

However, there's a more reliable approach to ensure the dynamically created control is placed exactly where you decided. You put a *PlaceHolder* marker control where you want the user control to display and then add the dynamic instance to the *Controls* collection of the *PlaceHolder*.

```
<asp:placeholder runat="server" id="YearStripPlaceHolder" />
```

At the beginning of the section, we mentioned that you normally don't use the *new* operator to instantiate user controls. This is only a common practice; no technical limitation forces you to do so. The following code demonstrates how to create a *ButtonList* control and bind it to a placeholder:

```
// Global variable
ButtonList yearStrip;

// Execute after the constructor when all declared controls
// have been initialized
public void Page_Init(object sender, EventArgs e)
{
    // Instantiate the user control. Might use a more
    // specialized constructor, if any
    yearStrip = new ButtonList();

    // Complete the initialization by adding default handlers
    yearStrip.InitializeAsUserControl(Page);
```

```
    // Set the ID of the control
    yearStrip.ID = "yearstrip";

    // Set some custom properties
    yearStrip.ButtonWidth = 70;

    // Add a handler for the user control's ButtonClicked event
    yearStrip.ButtonClicked += new ButtonClickedEventHandler(BtnClicked);

    // Must use a placeholder to make sure the control is added
    // within a runat=server area
    YearStripPlace.Controls.Add(yearStrip);
}
```

The *AddHandler* operator in Visual Basic .NET and the += operator in C# provide a way for you to add event handlers to control instances dynamically.

### Referencing User Controls from Code-Behind Pages

To include a user control in a Web page, you must first register it so that the ASP.NET runtime can locate and dynamically bind the needed assembly to the page. In doing so, you also obtain a strong reference to the user control class that allows for programmatic creation of controls. However, so far we've been making decisions based on creating simple Web pages—that is, Web pages that don't have a code-behind class.

Examining things from a pure ASP.NET perspective, the situation in which both the page and the user control are written in code-behind mode is a special one and requires a little more care. Amazingly enough, though, if you always develop your ASP.NET applications with Visual Studio .NET, you'll probably never run into this gotcha.

The *@Register* and *@Reference* directives configure the runtime environment so that all the needed assemblies are linked to the ASP.NET page that contains a user control. As a result, any reference to the user control, even a strong-typed one, can be successfully resolved. Can we say the same for a C# class or a Visual Basic .NET class? When the caller is a code-behind page, you write all its code in, say, a C# class. How can you reference the *ButtonList* type from here? The C# language has no special construct that emulates the behavior of the ASP.NET directives. As a result, any reference to *ButtonList* in the class is destined to raise a compiler error.

To work around this obstacle, you must also write the user control in code-behind mode. When you're done, compile the class that represents the user control into an assembly. In practice, instead of relying on the ASP.NET runtime for a dynamic compilation, you deploy the control as a precompiled unit that C# classes can easily locate.

```
<%@ Control Language="C#"
    Classname="ButtonList"
    Inherits="ProAspNet.CS.Ch10.ButtonList" %>
```

Be aware that in this case the *Src* attribute in the *@Control* directive is redundant and even harmful and must be removed. As the declaration just shown indicates, the code of the *ButtonList* control is contained in the specified class implemented in one of the available assemblies. If you leave the *Src* attribute, the compiler raises an error because it finds two assemblies with the same set of public symbols—the one you created and the one ASP.NET creates on the fly while processing the *Src* attribute. In general, the *Inherits* and *Src* attributes can work together, but not if both represent the same class.

> **Note** Because Visual Studio .NET always uses the code-behind model for whatever ASP.NET component it creates, this issue passes unnoticed because it doesn't cause problems and doesn't require special care. There's a caveat though. If you, being unaware of the internal structure of the Visual Studio user controls, copy the source files of a running application into another virtual directory, it doesn't work until you also copy the binaries.

## Conclusion

User controls are a type of ASP.NET server control you can easily create by using the same techniques you've learned for common Web pages. Little code is normally required for building a user control, but in some cases Web Forms user controls can also be codeless. However, there's no technical limitation to what a user control can do, and the amount and complexity of the embedded code depends only on the functionality you want to obtain.

User controls offer an easy way to partition and reuse common user-interface elements across applications. They are ideal whenever the reuse of layout and graphical functionality is critical. You can top off this component with some code that gets compiled on the fly like a Web page; however, quick and effective reuse of user-interface functionality is the primary objective of Web Forms user controls. Like pages, user controls can be developed with inline code as well as code-behind classes. User controls are not the ideal tool to leverage if you need to build a hierarchy of controls according to a pure object-oriented model. Although not impossible to obtain, inheritance is not the goal of user controls. Just the presence of a fair quantity of layout code makes user-control inheritance harder. You can stuff the code of a user control into a class and reuse it; but the associated layout information remains a separate entity that's a bit harder to manage programmatically. If you're going to build a control others can inherit from, you should drop user controls in favor of more flexible custom controls. We'll cover custom controls in Part V.

We started this chapter by building an interactive control just to emphasize how the user control technology can help you to reuse common pieces of a Web site. Next, we built an object model on top of it. The summation of an advanced user interface with a layer of business logic constitutes a powerful model that can be helpful in any scenario in which you need rich and reusable components.

In Chapter 11, "ASP.NET Mobile Controls," we'll complete our overview of ASP.NET controls by taking a look at mobile controls. The ASP.NET mobile controls are a set of ASP.NET server controls that can generate Wireless Markup Language (WML), compact HTML, and HTML content for a variety of devices. Note that the ASP.NET mobile controls have been integrated with the .NET Framework only since version 1.1.

# Resources


- KB 316370—Visual Studio .NET Does Not Generate a Code-Behind Declaration for Web User Controls
- KB 308378—Perform Fragment Caching in ASP.NET by Using Visual C# .NET
- Creating a File-Upload User Control with ASP.NET (*http://www.15seconds.com/issue/010504.htm*)
- Create Localizable Web User Controls (*http://www.fawcette.com/vsm/2002_09/online/villeda*)
- Event Handling between Custom User Controls that are loaded at Run Time (*http://www.asptoday.com/catalogue/aspcontent/20021211_01.html*)

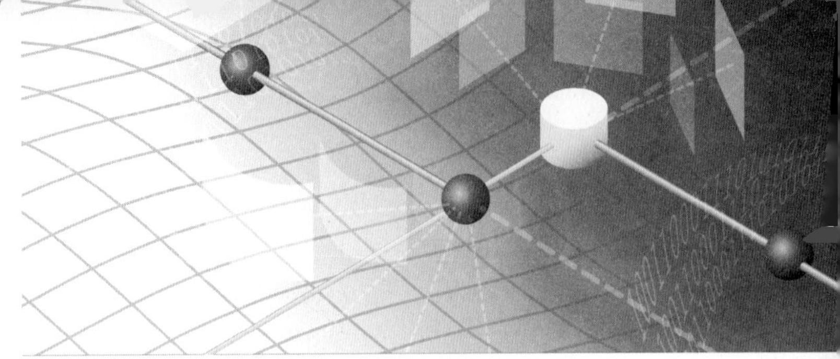

# 11

# ASP.NET Mobile Controls

*HTML and WML are similar markup languages, more or less like Italian and Spanish. As an Italian, you could grab the sense of what Spanish speaking people are saying, but if you need to write correct Spanish, then that's a totally different story.*

*—Luca Passani, Openwave*

Years ago, one of the factors for the rapid adoption of ASP was the level of programmability it added on top of HTML. Not only could you apply some business logic to generate appropriate HTML tags, you could also straighten out the differences between the browsers. The overall architecture has been redesigned and empowered with ASP.NET, which provides a thicker abstraction layer and a richer object model fully integrated with the .NET Framework. In addition, ASP.NET 1.1 incorporates mobile controls. Mobile controls provide an abstracted programming model to build wireless Web applications. ASP.NET mobile controls are a revised version of the Microsoft Mobile Internet Toolkit (MMIT)—the SDK for mobile wireless devices. An integral part of the .NET Framework 1.1, the MMIT is available as a separate download for the .NET Framework version 1.0.

ASP.NET mobile controls enable you to build Web applications for wireless devices using the same rich application model that characterizes development for desktop browsers. Mobile controls target a variety of devices such as cell phones, pagers, the Pocket PC, and other personal digital assistants (PDA) such as Palm and BlackBerry devices. ASP.NET mobile controls extend the Web Forms model of ASP.NET in two ways—devices and ad hoc controls. All supported devices are listed in a new section of the machine.config file (discussed in Chapter 12, "Configuration and Deployment"). It's an extensible list open to the contribution of third parties, who can register new devices as well as new controls.

Registering a new device mostly means providing a list of characteristics (for example, screen size or markup language), and then one of the built-in adapters can be used by the .NET Framework to generate device-specific output. Less frequently, you need to write a new adapter too. You don't need to call into the adapter or manually write device-specific code; instead, you simply write mobile applications using the ASP.NET mobile controls and the ASP.NET object model. Based on the configuration information, Mobile Web Forms detect the underlying device and adaptively renders the output of controls by using the specific markup language and logic. ASP.NET mobile controls abstract a subset of ASP.NET server controls and intelligently render your application on the target device. In addition, several mobile-specific controls are provided, such as the *PhoneCall* control. The .NET Framework 1.1 provides a handful of built-in controls but remains open to third-party contributions.

Mobile Web applications can be developed using the Mobile Designer in Microsoft Visual Studio .NET as well as any other editor, such as Web Matrix or Notepad. Because ASP.NET mobile applications are .NET applications, you can develop them using any common language runtime (CLR)–compliant programming language.

In this chapter, we'll provide an overview of the ASP.NET mobile controls, discuss the basics of the mobile technology, and take a quick tour of the Visual Studio .NET mobile features.

## Architecture of Mobile Controls

ASP.NET mobile controls are an extension of ASP.NET desktop server controls. Another way of characterizing mobile controls is to say they are the twin brother of desktop controls. Mobile controls add the capability of adapting to the device that is making the request. Automatic browser detection is a key aspect of mobile applications and controls and is probably a bit more important for them than for desktop controls.

Desktop controls are rendered in different modes to accommodate a few client targets (for example, Internet Explorer 5.0, HTML 3.2, and HTML 4.0). Although the final output can vary a lot from one target to the next, the area of markup most affected is style. Validation controls are controls whose output varies significantly from one target browser to another. Desktop server controls always generate HTML code. Although differences exist between the HTML 3.2 and HTML 4.0 standards, and between standards and the implementations of individual browsers, we're still far from the untangled mess of dialects and syntaxes that characterize the markup in the mobile world. For this reason, browser detection is implemented at a lower level than user code. Basically, the ASP.NET mobile runtime evaluates the browser's user agent and selects the appropriate device adapter object to use for any task that involves the request. (A user agent is a request header that contains information about the capabilities of the browser.) As a result, any mobile controls conform to the capabilities of the particular device it is running on.

The set of supported wireless devices is rather heterogeneous and ranges from full-featured browsers found on PDAs to small cell phone displays featuring WML browsers. As a result, not just the markup output but also the design of the application might significantly change from one device to the next. In general, a multiauthoring tool for mobile controls must abstract a number of aspects: different markup languages, vendor-specific implementations of the same markup, and different form factors (such as display size and programmable buttons). ASP.NET mobile controls internally handle much of the boring device-specific rendering and let you focus on the Web-application logic.

## Multiple Markup Languages

ASP.NET mobile controls support a few types of markup languages, which are listed in Table 11-1. Acceptable values don't include all possible wireless markup languages, but they certainly include the most popular ones.

**Table 11-1 Markup Languages in ASP.NET Mobile Controls**

| Markup | Description |
|---|---|
| Compact HTML 1.0 | Subset of HTML 3.2, has been specifically designed for mobile phones and in general for battery-powered, low-memory devices. Abbreviated as cHTML. The language is widely used in Japanese I-Mode devices. |
| HTML 3.2 | Relatively old version of HTML, is supported by high-end PDAs such as Pocket PC 2002, Palm, and BlackBerry devices. |
| WML 1.1, WML 1.2 | The Wireless Markup Language (WML) is probably the most popular wireless language. It has been developed as a part of a larger initiative aimed at defining an application protocol for wireless devices—the Wireless Application Protocol (WAP). WML lets you program the keys of a mobile phone, such as softkeys and the numeric pad. |
| XHTML | XHTML is the XML reformulation of HTML and a key element of the WAP 2.0 standard. There are several flavors of XHTML out there. The Device Update 2.0 of ASP.NET Mobile Controls supports XHTML Mobile Profile. It is available for download at *http://msdn.microsoft.com/vstudio/device/mobilecontrols*. |

The list has a couple of noticeable omissions—the Handheld Device Markup Language (HDML) and the newest version 1.3 of the Wireless Markup Language (WML). However, be aware that new devices—and possibly even new markup languages—can be added to the list of supported devices at any time.

The required markup language that the controls should generate is set through a read-only string property in the *MobileCapabilities* class—*PreferredRenderingType*.

## Compact HTML

As the name implies, Compact HTML (cHTML) is a simplified version of HTML developed for less powerful browsers embedded in cell phones and other small-screen devices. The cHTML language consists of a mix of HTML 2.0 and HTML 3.2 tags optimized for navigation and text display.

The cHTML language supports hyperlinks, text scrolling, forms, and data submission. It doesn't provide much layout and formatting capabilities because of the rather spartan user interface (UI) of such devices. So tables, frames, cascading style sheets (CSS), fonts, and scripting are not supported. Just the lack of scripting support in cHTML provides a prime example of the great job done by ASP.NET device adapters. Adapters force the exclusive generation of server-side code for data validation, and they always implement postback events through a form's data submission. For more information on cHTML, take a look at *http://www.w3.org/TR/1998/NOTE-compactHTML-19980209*.

> **Note** The cHTML markup language is mostly used in Japan by I-Mode devices, although some experiments have been made in Europe, particularly in the Netherlands. Some browsers—specifically the newest Openwave XHTML browser—support cHTML internally to access I-Mode sites.

## HTML 3.2

HTML 3.2 is a more basic version of HTML, whose latest version is numbered 4.0. HTML 3.2 is the markup language for most down-level browsers, such as Netscape Navigator 3.x. HTML 3.2 is also supported in Pocket Internet Explorer. Key differences between HTML 4.0 and 3.2 include the addition of cascading style sheets and the Dynamic HTML (DHTML) object model. In general, targeting HTML 3.2 is fair for many ASP.NET applications and doesn't constitute a restriction in the overall functionality. The HTML 3.2 specification is available at *http://www.w3.org/TR/REC-html32*.

### Wireless Markup Language

Historically speaking, the WML language was the standard markup language that emerged as the result of joint efforts to standardize one proprietary language—the HDML. Created through an initiative of the WAP Forum (now renamed to Open Mobile Alliance, and which can be found at *http://www.openmobilealliance.org*), the WML language is founded on a strict XML syntax and shares only a few tags with HTML. Some examples of the shared tags are *<input>*, *<select>*, *<a>*, *<p>*, and *<img>*. However, even in the context of the same tag (for example, *<input>*), the intended behavior might be different. WML tags are case-sensitive, while HTML tags are not.

On a more technical note, WML pushes the idea of cards, which represent the various states of the application. A card is like a wizard page, and most of the application's life is spent navigating between cards. In addition, WML supports a form of exception handling to catch errors that occur in a card.

## The Wireless Application Protocol

A key point with the mobile controls is that you don't need to worry about the markup language or transport mechanism used for the request. However, learning a little more about the WAP protocol is helpful anyway. The WML language was developed as part of a wider initiative aimed at ruling the world of wireless development. The WAP Forum was started in 1997 with the declared goal of defining the technologies that would unify the world of wireless applications. WAP is a suite of wireless-specific specifications adapted from open Web standards such as HTML and TCP/IP.

To access a Web site using a mobile device, you type the URL in the mobile browser and have the browser create an HTTP-like request (which can optionally be encrypted) that travels toward the back-end Web server over the Wireless Session Protocol (WSP). The WSP protocol uses packets whose overall semantics are similar to HTTP packets. Unlike HTTP, though, WSP transfers binary packets to save bandwidth. WSP packets are physically transported by the Wireless Transaction Protocol (WTP), the wireless counterpart of TCP, as shown in Figure 11-1.

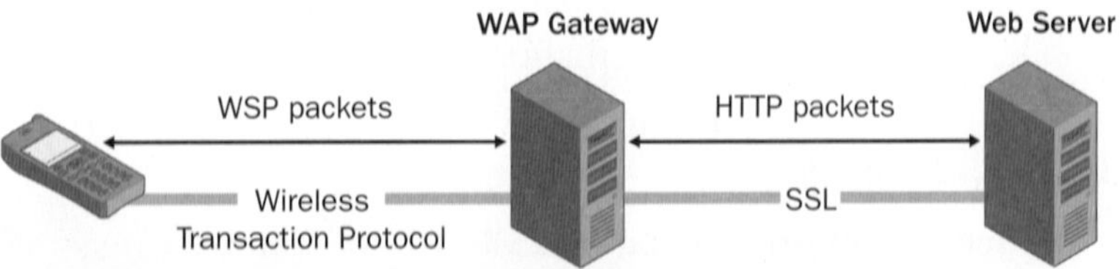


**Figure 11-1** Architecture of wireless Web applications.

The connection between the mobile device and the WAP gateway can be secured using the Wireless Transport Layer Security (WTLS) protocol. The WAP gateway is a server that translates the WSP request into conventional HTTP and forwards it to the back-end Web server.

> **Note** The Open Mobile Alliance released the WAP 2.0 standard in September 2001. Although 100 percent backward compatibility is guaranteed, the new standard is geared toward a full convergence between the wireless Web and the conventional HTTP-based Web. The WAP 2.0 standard is heavily based on XHTML and brings the power of CSS to the wireless world by introducing WCSS, which is an abridged version of Web CSS for wireless devices.

The Web server receives the request and performs any needed operations. The returned output is an HTTP response that contains a WML document. After receiving the WML stream, the gateway removes any unneeded headers and translates it into binary packets. The response is then forwarded back to the device and displayed. (Actually, the WML-to-binary translation consists of a simple tokenization in which each tag and attribute is mapped to a single byte.)

## Overview of Mobile Controls

ASP.NET mobile controls are server controls and thus require their *runat* attribute to be set to *server*. They execute on the server and for this reason can exploit the potential of the .NET Framework in spite of the modest amount of memory typically available on wireless devices. All mobile controls inherit from the *MobileControl* base class, which in turn inherits from *Control*. In this relationship, both server and mobile controls share a common set of properties, methods, and events. Mobile Web forms, on the other hand, inherit from the *MobilePage* class. Later in the chapter, we'll write a sample mobile application using Visual Studio .NET. In the meantime, let's learn more about the hierarchy of mobile controls and their internal plumbing.

### Mobile Controls Hierarchy

ASP.NET mobile controls can be logically grouped in five categories: container, text, validation, list, and miscellaneous controls. Table 11-2 lists them all in alphabetical order. Some of these controls work in much the same way as ASP.NET Web Forms controls do. However, mobile controls also provide adaptive rendering for mobile devices. We'll discuss adaptive rendering more later in the "Adaptive Rendering" section.

**Table 11-2 ASP.NET Mobile Controls**

| Mobile Control | Description |
|---|---|
| *AdRotator* | Provides advertisement rotation in the same way that the ASP.NET *AdRotator* control does. |
| *Calendar* | Provides date-picking functionality mimicking the behavior of the ASP.NET *Calendar* control. |
| *Command* | Similar to the ASP.NET *Button* control, causes a postback event after users click. |
| *CompareValidator* | Identical to the ASP.NET *CompareValidator* control. |
| *CustomValidator* | Identical to the ASP.NET *CustomValidator* control. |
| *Form* | The control is similar to the *HtmlForm* control of ASP.NET pages. However, multiple form controls are admitted on mobile pages. |
| *Image* | Identical to the ASP.NET *Image* control. |
| *Label* | Identical to the ASP.NET *Label* control. |
| *Link* | Represents a hyperlink to another form on a mobile page or an arbitrary URL. Similar to the ASP.NET *HyperLink* control. |
| *List* | Similar to the ASP.NET *Repeater* and *DataList* controls, applies templates to bound data. Supports device-specific templates. |
| *ObjectList* | Similar to the ASP.NET *DataGrid* control, displays multiple fields for each data item and supports multiple commands. |
| *Panel* | Provides grouping mechanism for organizing controls in much the way the ASP.NET *Panel* control does. |
| *PhoneCall* | For devices that support phone calls, the control represents a link to a phone number to call. Similar to the *mailto* tag of HTML hyperlinks. |
| *RangeValidator* | Identical to the ASP.NET *RangeValidator* control. |
| *RegularExpression-Validator* | Identical to the ASP.NET *RegularExpressionValidator* control. |
| *RequiredFieldValidator* | Identical to the ASP.NET *RequiredFieldValidator* control. |
| *SelectionList* | Displays a list of data-bound items with different styles. It can be configured to behave like a drop-down or check-box list. Selection, however, does not automatically cause the control to post back. The change of selection, though, will fire a server event with the next postback. |
| *StyleSheet* | Invisible control, can be used to organize styles to apply to other controls. Can contain multiple style definitions. |

*(continued)*

**Table 11-2 ASP.NET Mobile Controls** *(continued)*

| Mobile Control | Description |
|---|---|
| *TextBox* | Represents a single-line text-box control. Does not support read-only and multiline. |
| *TextView* | Used to display large blocks of text, supports basic text formatting and pagination. |
| *ValidationSummary* | Similar to the *ValidationSummary* control of ASP.NET, displays the results of the validation in a separate form. |

Almost all mobile controls have a counterpart in the family of ASP.NET server controls or, at a minimum, a control that looks alike. *PhoneCall* and *TextView* are the only two without an equivalent control. Other controls, such as *SelectionList* and *Command*, group the functionality of multiple ASP.NET controls. The programming interface of validation controls, on the other hand, is nearly identical to ASP.NET; a key difference here is that not all devices support client-side validation. Figure 11-2 shows graphically the relationships between controls. Controls with a white background are abstract classes.

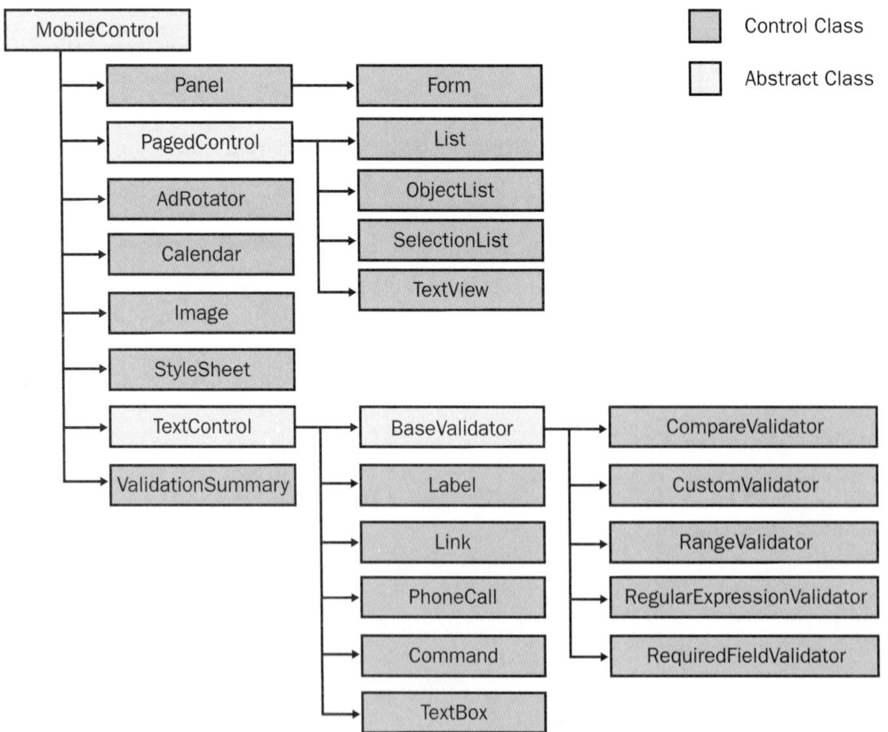


**Figure 11-2** The ASP.NET mobile control class hierarchy.

Before taking a closer look at the characteristics of each group of controls, let's learn more about the structure of an ASP.NET mobile page.

## ASP.NET Mobile Pages

The *MobilePage* class is the base class for all ASP.NET mobile Web pages and inherits from the ASP.NET *Page* class. In other words, a mobile page is in no way different from a user-defined page class such as a code-behind class. An .aspx page that intends to use ASP.NET mobile controls must declare its base class by using the *Inherits* attribute on the *@Page* directive.

```
<%@ Page Inherits="System.Web.UI.MobileControls.MobilePage" %>
```

In addition, all mobile controls are perceived as custom controls and must be explicitly registered in all pages. As we saw in the previous chapter, this can be done using the *@Register* directive.

```
<%@ Register TagPrefix="mobile"
    Namespace="System.Web.UI.MobileControls"
    Assembly="System.Web.Mobile" %>
```

> **Note** The prefix *mobile*, although extremely intuitive, is totally arbitrary and can be replaced with any other string. You should note, though, that the whole documentation of ASP.NET mobile controls uses the prefix *mobile*. If you're authoring the page using Visual Studio .NET, using the prefix *mobile* is mandatory. In fact, once a mobile project has been set up, Visual Studio .NET defaults to *mobile* and doesn't recognize any new prefix. As a result, either you manually update the prefix each time you drop a new control on the designer or the page won't compile!

The following listing shows a simple page that displays the name of the wireless language being used by the device:

```
<%@ Page Language="C#"
    Inherits="System.Web.UI.MobileControls.MobilePage" %>
<%@ Register TagPrefix="mobile"
    Namespace="System.Web.UI.MobileControls"
    Assembly="System.Web.Mobile" %>
<%@ Import Namespace="System.Web.Mobile" %>
```

```
<script runat="server">
void Page_Load(object sender, EventArgs e) {
    MobileCapabilities mobCaps = (MobileCapabilities) Request.Browser;
    theBrowser.Text = mobCaps.PreferredRenderingType;
}
</script>

<mobile:Form runat="server">
    Language is
    <mobile:Label runat="server" font-bold="true" id="theBrowser" />
</mobile:Form>
```

The page contains a *Label* control that renders with boldface type and some literal text. During the page *OnLoad* event, the code retrieves the preferred rendering type from the requesting device, reads related settings from the configuration file, and displays it. The *MobileCapabilities* class is defined in the *System.Web.Mobile* namespace; the controls, on the other hand, are all defined in the *System.Web.UI.MobileControls* namespace. When viewed through a device that incorporates the Openwave browser, the page looks like the one shown in Figure 11-3.

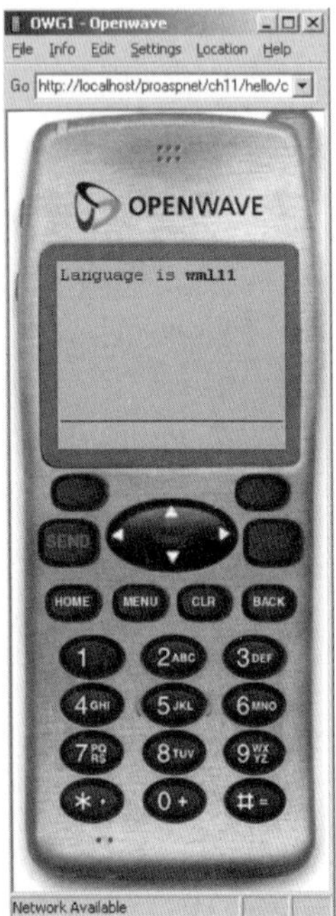


**Figure 11-3** The first mobile application in action as seen through the Openwave emulator.

> **Note** The mobile samples in this chapter were tested with the Openwave emulator included with the Openwave SDK version 4.1.1. This SDK is free of charge and can be downloaded from Openwave (*http://developer.openwave.com/download*). Not all emulators are supported by the ASP.NET mobile controls. For a list of emulators to test your mobile applications, check out *http://www.asp.net/mobile/DeviceSimulators.aspx*. For a list of tested devices and emulators, check out *http://www.asp.net/mobile/testeddevices.aspx*.

The mobile page detected the device capabilities and generated the following WML 1.1 output:

```
<html>
  <head>
    <meta http-equiv="Cache-Control" content="max-age=0"/>
  </head>
  <p:card>
    <p:do type="accept">
      <p:noop/>
    </p:do>
    <p>Language is
      <b>wml11</b>
    </p>
  </p:card>
</html>
```

Interestingly, the same page is also viewable through Internet Explorer. In this case, the target language is HTML 3.2. Figure 11-4 shows the Internet Explorer version of the page.

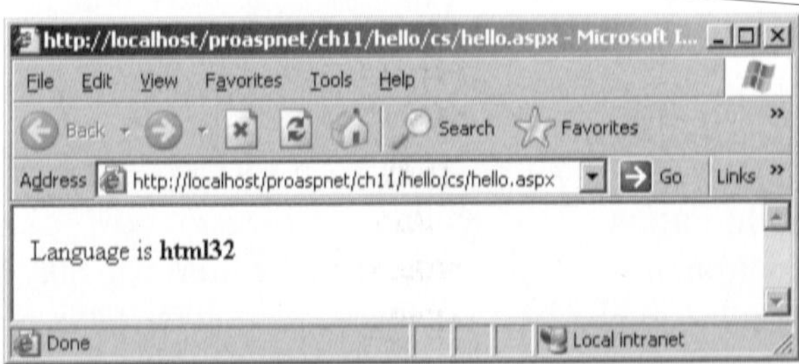


**Figure 11-4** The same mobile application rendered by Internet Explorer.

In this case, the output sent to the device is completely different.

```
<html><body>
<form id="_ctl0" name="_ctl0" method="post"
    action="hello.aspx?__ufps=261294">
<input type="hidden" name="__VIEWSTATE" value="...">
<input type="hidden" name="__EVENTTARGET" value="">
<input type="hidden" name="__EVENTARGUMENT" value="">
<script language=javascript><!--
function __doPostBack(target, argument){
  var theform = document._ctl0
  theform.__EVENTTARGET.value = target
  theform.__EVENTARGUMENT.value = argument
  theform.submit()
}
// -->
</script>
Language is <b>html32</b></form></body></html>
```

> **Note** A variety of emulators exist to test the interface of a mobile application at development time. Although you should never ship a wireless application without first seriously testing it on real devices, emulators are indeed extremely helpful to prototype the user interface. Visual Studio .NET lets you register browsers for mobile applications by selecting Browse With from the File menu.

A *MobilePage* object can contain only a *Form* or *StyleSheet* control. Literal text placed outside a form is ignored. If other controls are used outside the boundaries of a form, a compiler error is raised. All needed text and controls must always be placed within a form. A mobile page must contain at least one form; multiple forms are supported, but only one is visible at a time. A style sheet is not required for a mobile page. However, you can't indicate more than one style sheet per page.

## Pagination in Mobile Pages

ASP.NET mobile controls provide a mechanism for automatically partitioning the form's contents into smaller portions of markup code. This mechanism is known as *pagination*. When you use pagination, these segments of content are automatically formatted to fit the target device. The final output is also completed with common user-interface elements that you can use to browse to other pages.

By default, pagination is not activated for a form. To activate pagination, you must set the *Paginate* property of the *Form* to *true*. You should note that although pagination can be enabled on individual controls, the setting has no effect if the *Paginate* property of the containing form is set to *false*. The *Form* control also provides other properties—such as *PageCount*, *CurrentPage*, and *PagerStyle*—that allow you to control pagination behavior. You can also specify pagination for a particular control on a form by using the *ControlToPaginate* property of the form with the ID of the control.

The main motivation for pagination is to not exceed the memory capabilities of the device with a too large page. Pagination is particularly effective for controls that display large amounts of data; it's often redundant for forms that display interactive and input controls. The pagination is implemented by sectioning the structure of the form or the control into pieces. Some controls (for example, the *List* control) handle pagination internally and decide themselves how to break their output. Other controls are managed by the container controls; to be effectively pageable, they must contain child controls or fit entirely in a single page.

## The Life Cycle of a Mobile Page

The life cycle of an ASP.NET mobile page is nearly identical to the life cycle of a conventional Web Forms page. The events are the same, even though the system's behaviors before and after the various events are different. The phases in the cycle are summarized as follows:

- **Page initialization** At this phase, the page determines the device adapter to use and sets the *Adapter* property on the *MobilePage* class. The device adapter is an instance of one of the classes listed in the *<mobileControls>* section of the configuration files. Default adapters are registered in machine.config; in web.config, you could add application-specific adapters. The search for the adapter begins with the machine.config file and then proceeds to the root web.config and any innermost web.config that might have been defined. The adapter is picked up based on the detected characteristics of the underlying device. Note that the adapter is cached for performance so that the search is conducted only once per user agent. The event you can hook up at this time is the *Init* event both on the page and the adapter.
- **Loading the view state** During this phase, any saved state for the page is restored. There is no event associated with this phase. Gaining more control over this phase requires the override of the *LoadViewState* method of the page.

- **Loading postback data** The page loads all incoming *<form>* data cached in *Request* and updates the page properties accordingly. No user event is associated with this phase. Gaining more control over this phase requires the override of the *LoadPostData* method of the page.
- **Loading the user code** The page is ready to execute any initialization code related to the logic and behavior of the page. The page fires the *Load* event and performs device adapter–specific loading of information. To control this phase, you can handle the *Load* event both on the page and the adapter.
- **Send postback change notifications** Controls in the page raise change events in response to state changes between the current and previous postbacks. Any further change entered by the *Load* event handler is also taken into account to determine any difference. A control must implement the *IPostBackDataHandler* interface to get a chance from the page to fire a state change event during this phase. No user event is provided.
- **Handle postback events** The page executes the .aspx code associated with the client-side event that caused the postback. It's the heart of the ASP.NET Web Forms model.
- **Pre-rendering** The code can perform its last updates before the output is rendered. The event developers can hook up from a mobile page or the device adapter at this phase is *PreRender*. Pagination occurs at this time. During this phase, the output of the page is determined based on the pagination settings.
- **Saving the view state** During this phase, the page serializes its state to a string, which will then be persisted—typically, through a hidden field. No user event is associated with this phase.
- **Page rendering** The page generates the output to be rendered to the client. The adapter is responsible for accessing and rendering child controls in the appropriate order. The event is *Render* and is available on both the page object and the device adapter.
- **Page unload** This phase performs the device adapter–specific cleanup and unloading. The event is *Unload* and is available on both the page object and the device adapter.

In summary, mobile pages differ from conventional ASP.NET pages in particular because of the initialization step. At that phase, in fact, mobile pages and controls have to determine the device adapter to use from the list of registered objects. The adapter is exposed through the *Adapter* property, and pages and controls refer to it for rendering.

## Device Adapters

Although the programmer writes ASP.NET mobile applications in a device-independent fashion, a set of device adapters take care of translating the high-level description of a user interface into the device-specific presentation layer. Interesting analogies exist between device drivers in Microsoft Windows and device adapters in ASP.NET mobile controls. Both control a device by generating device-specific command text; device adapters just generate that in the form of markup languages. Device adapters are the bridge between individual mobile controls and target devices. For any given device, each mobile control can have a unique adapter and each instance of a control is bound to a corresponding instance of an adapter. The availability of an adapter is critical for the appropriate rendering of mobile controls. In general, for each supported device, the following classes can be defined:

- **Page adapter** Associated with the page, this class provides view-state and postback functionality, as well as methods that save and load device-specific control-state information, such as pagination information and the currently active form. The page adapter is also responsible for preparing the response to the client and for rendering the skeleton of the page. The page adapter class implements the *IPageAdapter* interface.
- **Form adapter** Associated with the form control, this adapter provides methods that handle device-specific form-based interactivity. In addition, it should supply methods that adapt a generic form to the particular device. For example, the fields of the forms could be paginated or grouped into a menu. Finally, the form adapter must be able to render the skeleton of the form.
- **Control adapter** This is the base class for control adapters and is also the base class for page and form adapters. It provides methods for rendering control postback events and style properties.
- **Text writer** The text writer class is not an adapter class, but it works in conjunction with adapters. The text writer class inherits from the *HtmlTextWriter* class and performs all rendering for a control. An instance of the text writer class is created and passed through every adapter for rendering purposes. The text writer usually contains helper methods to perform tasks such as encoding data.

The ASP.NET Mobile Controls toolkit contains a few device adapters, one for each supported markup language—cHTML, XHTML, HTML, and WML. As mentioned, XHTML has been added to the list in the Device Update 2.0.

## Container Controls

ASP.NET mobile controls include a couple of controls—*Panel* and *Form*—that act as containers of other controls. The *Form* control differs from *Panel* in that it supports posting of data, whereas the *Panel* represents a simple static group of related controls. Multiple panels can be nested and included in forms; forms, on the other hand, cannot be nested.

### The *Panel* Control

The following code demonstrates a couple of panels containing plain text with minimal formatting. Note that not all attributes are supported on all devices. For example, background and foreground colors are ignored by cell phones.

```
<mobile:Form runat="server">
    <mobile:Panel runat="server" Font-Bold="true" Alignment="Right">
        <mobile:Label runat="server">Programming ASP.NET</mobile:Label>
    </mobile:Panel>
    <mobile:Panel runat="server" BackColor="yellow">
        <mobile:Label runat="server">Dino Esposito</mobile:Label>
    </mobile:Panel>
</mobile:Form>
```

A panel can contain any ASP.NET mobile control other than *MobilePage*, *Form*, or *StyleSheet* controls. Panel controls do not have a visual representation and cascade any style properties down to the individual controls. Both the layout and style of the child controls are mediated by the device adapter.

Note that the *Panel* control could be used to define pagination segments. In addition, a *Panel* control can also work as a sort of placeholder to contain dynamically generated child controls.

### The *Form* Control

The *Form* control represents the outermost container of controls within a mobile page. The *Form* control features common-use properties such as *Action* and *Method*. In particular, *Action* defaults to the empty string, which causes a postback to the same URL. A form fires events when activated and deactivated.

A page can contain multiple forms, but only one form is rendered to the browser at a time. The currently active form can be set and retrieved through the *ActiveForm* property. When multiple forms are active on the same page, you can move from one to the other by using a *Link* control.